D1602175

TEACHINGS AND COMMENTARIES
on the
DOCTRINE *and* COVENANTS

ALSO BY ED J. PINEGAR
Latter-day Commentary on the Old Testament
(with Richard J. Allen)
Teachings and Commentaries on the Book of Mormon
(with Richard J. Allen)
The Ultimate Missionary Companion
Latter-day Commentary on the New Testament
Lengthen Your Shuffle

ALSO BY RICHARD J. ALLEN
Latter-day Commentary on the Old Testament
(with Ed J. Pinegar)
Teachings and Commentaries on the Book of Mormon
(with Ed J. Pinegar)

TEACHINGS AND COMMENTARIES
on the
DOCTRINE and COVENANTS

ED J. PINEGAR, RICHARD J. ALLEN,
and KARL R. ANDERSON

Covenant Communications, Inc.

Published by Covenant Communications, Inc.
American Fork, Utah

Copyright © 2004 by Ed J. Pinegar, Richard J. Allen, and Karl R. Anderson

Cover painting *Brother Joseph* © David Lindsley

Cover and book design © 2004 by Covenant Communications, Inc.

All rights reserved. No part of this work may be reproduced by any means without the express written permission of Covenant Communications, Inc., P.O. Box 416, American Fork, UT 84003. This work is not an official publication of The Church of Jesus Christ of Latter-day Saints. The views expressed within this work are the sole responsibility of the author and do not necessarily reflect the position of The Church of Jesus Christ of Latter-day Saints, Covenant Communications, Inc., or any other entity.

Printed in Canada
First Printing: October 2004

10 09 08 07 06 05 04   10 9 8 7 6 5 4 3 2 1

ISBN 1-59156-632-0

PREFACE

The study of the Doctrine and Covenants is the study of light, life, the divine restoration of covenant principles and keys, and the unfolding of the dispensation of the fulness of times through modern-day prophets. It is truly a book about miracles.

The wonder of life is all around us, working its daily miracles of sprouting and growing, blossoming and producing. Every man, woman, and child who has ever lived has been witness to the refreshing partnership of rain, sun, earth, and seed—all generating, year in and year out, the verdure of nature and the bounties of the harvest.

There is a spiritual side to this everyday wonder. The prophet Jeremiah captured the essence of it in moving metaphorical language: "Blessed is the man that trusteth in the Lord, and whose hope the Lord is. For he shall be as a tree planted by the waters, and that spreadeth out her roots by the river, and shall not see when heat cometh, but her leaf shall be green; and shall not be careful in the year of drought, neither shall cease from yielding fruit" (Jer. 17:7–8). Alma cultivated with inspired skill similar symbolism in his masterful discourse wherein he likened faith to a seed that unfolds, when nourished with diligence and patience, as "a tree springing up unto everlasting life" (Alma 32:41).

When viewed from the heavenly perspective—with an eye that encompasses all of mankind—this process of nurtured growth becomes the framework for understanding God's design for the salvation of His children. Days become generations; seasons become dispensations; the light of the sun becomes the light of the Son. The Apostle Peter looked forward to a time when spiritual growth would surge, expanding beneath the canopy of modern revelation: "Repent ye therefore, and be converted, that your sins may be blotted out, when the times of refreshing shall come from the presence of the Lord; and he shall send Jesus Christ, which before was preached unto you: Whom the heaven must receive until the times of restitution of all things, which God hath spoken by the mouth of all his holy prophets since the world began" (Acts 3:19–21).

These predicted times of refreshing dawned during the spring of 1820 when the young Joseph Smith experienced, amidst effulgent rays of glory, the vision of the Father and the Son, declaring once again the word of truth to a world hungering for pure light. As the Restoration of the gospel unfolded through divine intervention in modern times, blessing after blessing emerged to grace the lives of all those willing to respond with faith and humility to the call to become "fellowcitizens with the saints, and of the household of God" (Eph. 2:19). The Book of Mormon whispered from the dust—this "marvelous work and a wonder" foretold by Isaiah (Isa. 29:14)—to restore the fulness of the gospel in the form of another witness for Jesus Christ. Line upon line, precept upon precept, the pages of the Doctrine and Covenants brought forth the essence of covenant wisdom and priesthood power, allowing the church and kingdom of God to arise "out of obscurity and out of darkness, the only true and living church upon the face of the whole earth, with which I, the Lord, am well pleased" (D&C 1:30).

From the squalor of his confinement in Liberty Jail, the Prophet Joseph Smith was buoyed up on the wings of inspiration to celebrate the triumph of the spirit of faith and virtue within the hearts and souls of the obedient of Zion: "Let thy bowels also be full of charity towards all men, and to the household of faith, and let virtue garnish thy thoughts unceasingly; then shall thy confidence wax strong in the presence of God; and the doctrine of the priesthood shall distil upon thy soul as the dews from heaven. The Holy Ghost shall be thy constant companion, and thy scepter an unchanging scepter of righteousness and truth; and thy dominion shall be an everlasting dominion, and without compulsory means it shall flow unto thee forever and ever" (D&C 121:45–46).

It is through such passages that the vitality of the gospel of Jesus Christ is confirmed to the honest-at-heart in our time, resonating with hope and faith, edifying those who seek to embrace the principles and ordinances of salvation and learn to cultivate the "godly walk and conversation" ordained for adoption by the Saints of God (see D&C 20:69).

The study of the Doctrine and Covenants is a study of God's love for His children, for in these pages are laid down with clarity the principles and procedures for building Zion—as both a pattern of righteous living and a place where God can dwell with His people. By far the most important edition of the Doctrine and Covenants is the "edition" that resides in the heart and soul of each sincere and willing reader as a living testament of devotion to the Lord and His covenant plan of redemption. Alma taught: "He that will not harden his heart, to him is given the greater portion of the word, until it is given unto him to know the mysteries of God until he know them in full" (Alma 12:10). How much of the word is found "in us," as Alma put it (Alma 12:13), is a measure of the quality of our hearts as receptacles of truth and our willingness to seek the confirmation of the Holy Spirit.

The Lord spoke of the scriptures as residing in His own bosom: "And a commandment I give unto thee [Sidney Rigdon]—that thou shalt write for him [the Prophet Joseph Smith]; and the scriptures shall be given, even as they are in mine own bosom, to the salvation of mine own elect" (D&C 35:20). It is our sacred commission to accept the word of God, "line upon line, precept upon precept" (2 Ne. 28:30; D&C 98:12) and write it within our bosom, just as it comes from the bosom of Christ. Paul spoke of the Saints of God in terms of living epistles: "Ye are our epistle written in our hearts, known and read of all men: Forasmuch as ye are manifestly declared to be the epistle of Christ ministered by us, written not with ink, but with the Spirit of the living God; not in tables of stone, but in fleshy tables of the heart" (2 Cor. 3:2–3). In writing the word of truth upon our own hearts through the prayerful study of the scriptures, we emulate the Father, in whose image we are created, and by whom we shall be judged through His Son: "And behold, all things are written by the Father; therefore out of the books which shall be written shall the world be judged" (3 Ne. 27:26).

The authors offer this volume as an adjunct to the systematic process of acquiring more and more of the word of God—especially as it pertains to the Doctrine and Covenants and Church history. The approach used is thematic, each major theme in the reading selection being addressed in a consistent pattern of study that includes relevant scriptural passages; a "moment of truth" giving the historical context of pertinent sections from the Doctrine and Covenants; selected statements from the Lord's modern-day prophets; one or more illustrations and applications for our time; and a concluding summary. The readers are encouraged to "liken the scriptures" unto themselves, as Nephi counseled, "that ye may have hope" (1 Ne. 19: 23, 24).

The authors wish to express appreciation for the undeviating support of the staff members of Covenant Communications and their devoted interest in this project. Special thanks go to managing editor Shauna Humphreys and to Annalisa Wiggins for their extraordinary commitment to the refinement and polishing of the text.

Special thanks go to Pat Pinegar, wife of Ed Pinegar; Carol Lynn Allen, wife of Richard Allen; and Joyce Anderson, wife of Karl Ricks Anderson, for their support and encouragement as this work progressed to its completion.

ABBREVIATIONS

AGQ   Joseph Fielding Smith. *Answers to Gospel Questions.* 5 vols. Salt Lake City: Deseret Book, 1957–66.

CHMR   Joseph Fielding Smith. *Church History and Modern Revelation.* 4 vols. Salt Lake City: The Church of Jesus Christ of Latter-day Saints, 1946–49.

CR   Conference Report. Salt Lake City: The Church of Jesus Christ of Latter-day Saints.

DCE   Hoyt W. Brewster Jr. *Doctrine and Covenants Encyclopedia.* Salt Lake City: Bookcraft, 1988.

DS   Joseph Fielding Smith. *Doctrines of Salvation.* Ed. Bruce R. McConkie. 3 vols. Salt Lake City: Bookcraft, 1954–56.

HC   Joseph Smith. *History of The Church of Jesus Christ of Latter-day Saints.* Ed. B. H. Roberts. 7 vols. Salt Lake City: The Church of Jesus Christ of Latter-day Saints, 1932–51.

JD   Brigham Young and others. *Journal of Discourses.* 26 vols. Liverpool: George Q. Cannon, 1855–86.

MD   Bruce R. McConkie. *Mormon Doctrine.* 2nd ed. Salt Lake City: Bookcraft, 1966.

RPJS   Lyndon W. Cook. *The Revelations of the Prophet Joseph Smith: A Historical and Biographical Commentary of the Doctrine and Covenants.* Salt Lake City: Deseret Book, 1985.

TETB   Ezra Taft Benson. *The Teachings of Ezra Taft Benson.* Salt Lake City: Bookcraft, 1988.

TGBH   Gordon B Hinckley. *Teachings of Gordon B. Hinckley.* Salt Lake City: Deseret Book, 1997.

THWH   Howard W. Hunter. *The Teachings of Howard W. Hunter.* Ed. Clyde J. Williams. Salt Lake City: Bookcraft, 1997.

TPJS   Joseph Smith. *Teachings of the Prophet Joseph Smith.* Comp. Joseph Fielding Smith. Salt Lake City: Deseret Book, 1976.

TSWK   Spencer W. Kimball. *The Teachings of Spencer W. Kimball.* Ed. Edward L. Kimball. Salt Lake City: Bookcraft, 1982.

TABLE OF CONTENTS

CHAPTER ONE

THE GIFT *of* MODERN REVELATION: INTRODUCTION *to the* DOCTRINE *and* COVENANTS

Reading Assignment: Explanatory Introduction to the Doctrine and Covenants; Doctrine and Covenants 1; Introduction to *Our Heritage*.

Additional Reading: Doctrine and Covenants 18:33–36; 84:60; 88:66.

The Doctrine and Covenants becomes an essential part of our spiritual life. The Prophet Joseph Smith said, "In these infant days of the Church, there was great anxiety to obtain the word of the Lord upon every subject that in any way concerned our salvation" (HC, 1:207). Thus, the Doctrine and Covenants is a glorious book of scripture given directly to our generation. It contains the will of the Lord for us in these last days that precede the second coming of Christ. It contains many truths and doctrines not fully revealed in other scripture. Like the Book of Mormon, it will strengthen those who carefully and prayerfully study from its pages.

Do we, as Saints of the Most High God, treasure the word He has preserved for us at so great a cost? Are we using these books of latter-day revelation to bless our lives and resist the powers of the evil one? This is the purpose for which they were given. How can we not stand condemned before the Lord if we treat them lightly by letting them do no more than gather dust on our shelves? (Ezra Taft Benson, Ensign, *November 1986, 80)*

THEMES *for* LIVING

1. The Lord's Ultimate Warning
2. Remembering and Honoring the Covenants
3. The Certainty of the Word of God

INTRODUCTION

With the dawning of the latter-day Restoration, mankind was once again favored with the blessings of constant divine revelation. The Book of Mormon arose from the dust of antiquity through prophetic inspiration to restore the "fulness of the gospel of Jesus Christ to the Gentiles and to the Jews also" (D&C 20:9; see also D&C 27:5; 42:12). Moreover, essential doctrines and commandments were revealed, line upon line, through the Prophet Joseph Smith as the Lord ushered in the dispensation of the fulness of times and cast "greater views" (D&C 10:45) upon the plan of salvation prepared from before the foundation of the world. A powerful record of the Lord's ongoing endowment of truth for the building up of His kingdom in the latter days is contained in the book of Doctrine and Covenants.

In many ways, this book is the audible proclamation of God as a warning and a blessing for life during the final phase of the earth's existence leading up to the Second Coming. Elder Neal A. Maxwell articulates this observation:

> If asked which book of scripture provides the most frequent chance to "listen" to the Lord talking, most individuals would at first think of the New Testament. The New Testament *is* a marvelous collection of the deeds and many of the doctrines of the Messiah. But in the Doctrine and Covenants we receive the voice as well as the word of the Lord. We can almost "hear" him talking. Words like these sink into one's marrow as well as into one's mind, for the majesty and power of the Lord are so evident: "Thus saith the Lord your God, even Jesus Christ, the Great I Am, Alpha and Omega, the beginning and the end, the same which looked upon the wide expanse of eternity, and all the seraphic hosts of heaven, before the world was made" (D&C 38:1). . . . In many ways the Doctrine and Covenants is the modern equivalent of the thundering directness of Sinai, when the finger of the Lord wrote on the two tablets of stone (Ex. 31:18)—portions of the Doctrine and Covenants with the "thou shalt nots" (D&C 42) and the "Alpha and Omegas" are given by the voice of the Lord. Indeed, the repeated interlacing of truths in the Doctrine and Covenants with those of other books of scripture shows a precision too great to have been managed by something as clumsy as a computer. Only divine direction could achieve this grand consistency. (*Ensign,* December 1978, 4–6)

If the Doctrine and Covenants is a scriptural overture of the heavenly campaign to prepare God's children for the Second Coming, then section 1 strikes beautiful opening notes to this magnificent opus. President Ezra Taft Benson pointed out: "The Doctrine and Covenants is the only book in the world that has a preface written by the Lord Himself. In that preface He declares to the world that His voice is unto all men (see D&C 1:2), that the coming of the Lord is nigh (see verse 12), and that the truths found in the Doctrine and Covenants will all be fulfilled (see verses 37–38)" (*Ensign,* November 1986, 79). Just as section 1 is the gateway to the Lord's modern-day canon of counsel and wisdom, so is the book itself the overarching framework for action by God's chosen servants to honor and preserve covenant valor among "the children of the prophets" (3 Ne. 20:25) and build up the kingdom of God, which is the stone "cut out without hands" that "became a great mountain, and filled the whole earth" (Dan. 2:35). The destiny of this unfolding divine saga is clear, for the prophet declared, with utter certainty, that "it shall stand for ever" (Dan. 2:44).

MOMENT OF TRUTH

Section 1: Given through the Prophet Joseph Smith on November 1, 1831, in Hiram, Portage County, Ohio, a town located some thirty miles southeast of Kirtland. The occasion was a special conference of the priesthood held on November 1 and 2, at which the following were received: section 1, section 67, section 68 (verses 1–13), section 133, and the testimony of the Doctrine and Covenants included in the explanatory introduction to the work. Known as the "Lord's Preface" (see D&C 1:6), this revelation was "received by inspiration" (*HC,* 1:222). It was such a moving experience to the ten men present (Joseph Smith, Oliver Cowdery, David Whitmer, John Whitmer, Peter Whitmer Jr., Sidney Rigdon, William E. McLellin, Orson Hyde, Luke S. Johnson, and Lyman E. Johnson) that a statement was prepared, testifying to the world that they knew that the revelations were of the Lord (see Enrichment section below). It was intended that this testimony be published at the front of the book.

During this conference, "The Literary Firm" (predecessor to Deseret News Press) was organized to print the revelations. They voted to print ten thousand copies but subsequently reduced the number of copies to three thousand. In July 1833, a mob in Independence, Missouri, destroyed the printing press and all but a few unbound sheets of the Book of Commandments.

After receiving section 1, the Prophet Joseph Smith wrote in his journal that "the conference voted that they prize the revelations to be worth to the Church the riches of the whole earth, speaking temporally. The great benefits to the world which result from the Book of Mormon and the revelations which the Lord has seen fit in His infinite wisdom to grant unto us for our salvation, and for the salvation of all that will believe, were duly appreciated" (*HC,* 1:235–36).

1. THE LORD'S ULTIMATE WARNING

THEME: The dispensation of the fulness of times is the final episode in mortal history prior to the Second Coming. "Wherefore, the Lord God will proceed to make bare his arm in the eyes of all the nations, in bringing about his covenants and his gospel unto those who are of the house of Israel" (1 Ne. 22:11). The Lord's voice of warning is proclaimed to all the world through the mouthpiece of His prophets, as recorded in holy writ in the form of commandments and revelations. "Therefore, tarry ye, and labor diligently, that you may be perfected in your ministry to go forth among the Gentiles for the last time, as many as the mouth of the Lord shall name, to bind up the law and seal up the testimony, and to prepare the saints for the hour of judgment which is to come" (D&C 88:84). The Lord's prefatory voice of warning is a sober and compelling reminder that this latter-day work is the ultimate directive for all mankind to repent and come unto the Lord Jesus Christ. If they will do so, He will heal their wounds and teach them how to abide the day of His coming.

MODERN PROPHETS SPEAK

Bruce R. McConkie:

> In the dispensation of the fulness of times, the members of the true Church are directed by the Lord to warn the world of the desolation and destruction that is to be poured out without measure upon the wicked and ungodly (D&C 1:4; 63:37, 57–58; 84:114; 109:41; 112:5; 124:106; 134:12). "For this is a day of warning, and not a day of many words. For I, the Lord, am not to be mocked in the last days" (D&C 63:58). "It becometh every man who hath been warned to warn his neighbor" (D&C 88:81). (*MD,* 828–29)

Spencer W. Kimball:

> Few men have ever knowingly and deliberately chosen to reject God and his blessings. Rather, we learn from the scriptures that because the exercise of faith has always appeared to be more difficult than relying on things more immediately at hand, carnal man has tended to transfer his trust in God to material things. Therefore, in all ages when men have fallen under the power of Satan and lost the faith, they have put in its place a hope in the "arm of the flesh" and in "gods of silver, and gold, of brass, iron, wood, and stone, which see not, nor hear, nor know" (Dan. 5:23)—that is, in idols. . . . Whatever thing a man sets his heart and his trust in most is his god;

and if his god doesn't also happen to be the true and living God of Israel, that man is laboring in idolatry. (*Ensign,* June 1976, 4)

LIKENING THE SCRIPTURES TO OUR LIVES

Doctrine and Covenants 1:4 The Lord's preface to the Doctrine & Covenants sounds "a voice of warning" to all the people.

Application: The word of the Lord is to help people do that which is right in preparation for His judgments. The Doctrine and Covenants is that voice from the Lord to His disciples in the latter day (see D&C 1:7–10, 12–16, 31–33). If we fail to heed the voice of His servants, we are under condemnation (see 3 Ne. 28:34–35).

2. REMEMBERING AND HONORING THE COVENANTS

THEME: What is the armor of God that will enable us to endure and survive the calamitous tribulations of the final days? The Lord outlines key strategies in His "preface" to the Doctrine and Covenants (section 1): follow the prophets, trust in the Lord, strengthen your faith, remember and honor sacred covenants, promulgate the word of God to all the world, keep the commandments, repent, learn wisdom through the instructions of the Lord, remain humble (and thus strong), and build up the kingdom.

MODERN PROPHETS SPEAK

Melvin J. Ballard:
> I understand from this [D&C 1:17–18, 22–24] that the Lord plainly knew the condition of the world, what it was in 1830, and what it would be today. . . . Knowing the calamities that were coming to his children, unless they changed their course, knowing their disposition that there would be no repentance in their hearts, and yet with a great desire to save them, he called upon his servant, Joseph Smith, to warn men, to call repentance, and others to join in this great proclamation to all men: "Repent, for the kingdom of God is at hand" [33:10; 42:7]. And not only to warn men that there was peril and danger ahead, but to offer the means of escape from the perils that would come. (CR, October 1923, 30–31)

Boyd K. Packer:
> The position that The Church of Jesus Christ of Latter-day Saints is the only true

Church upon the face of the earth is fundamental. . . . Now to those who think us uncharitable, we say that it was not devised by us; it was declared by Him, for he gave commandments to the early brethren, and I quote: 'And also those to whom these commandments were given, might have power to lay the foundation of this church, and to bring it forth out of obscurity and out of darkness, the only true and living church upon the face of the whole earth, with which I, the Lord, am well pleased, speaking unto the church collectively and not individually (D&C 1:30).

Now this is not to say that the churches, all of them, are without some truth. They have some truth—some of them very much of it. They have a form of godliness. Often the clergy and adherents are not without dedication, and many of them practice remarkably well the virtues of Christianity. They are, nonetheless, incomplete. By his declaration, ". . . they teach for doctrines the commandments of men, having a form of godliness, but they deny the power thereof" (JS—H 1:19). (Quoted in Daniel H. Ludlow, *A Companion to Your Study of the Doctrine and Covenants,* 2 vols. [Salt Lake City: Deseret Book, 1978], 1:50)

ILLUSTRATIONS FOR OUR TIMES

Weak Things of the Earth/World

There is a difference between the weak (D&C 84:106) and the weak things of the earth or world (D&C 1:19; 35:13; 133:59). The former are those whose faltering faith needs strengthening, while the latter are they whose spiritual strength confounds the so-called wise and strong of the world. The Prophet Joseph Smith was considered unlearned, unlettered, and weak by the world, but through him the Lord showed forth His wisdom (D&C 124:1; 2 Ne. 3:13). The Lord does not work after the expectations or ways of the world (see 1 Cor. 1:26–31).

Elder Bruce R. McConkie has provided an excellent example to illustrate this point:

"Question: Who is better qualified to preach the gospel, a fifty-year-old college president of world renown who has many scholastic degrees, or a nineteen-year-old high school graduate who has no scholastic stature whatever?

"Answer: The one who has a testimony of the gospel and who is so living as to have the companionship and guidance of the Holy Spirit.

"Question: How is it that the weak things of the earth confound the mighty and strong?

"Answer: True religion is not a matter of intellectuality or of worldly prominence or renown, but of spirituality; and they are not weak but strong in the realm of spiritual things" (*Doctrinal New Testament Commentary,* 3 vols. [Salt Lake City: Bookcraft, 1965–73], 2:316).

Commenting upon those who are called to positions of leadership within the Church, Elder Spencer W. Kimball said: "I would not say that those leaders whom the Lord chooses are necessarily the most brilliant, nor the most highly trained, but they are chosen, and when chosen of the Lord they are his recognized authority, and the people who stay close to them have safety" (CR, April 1951, 104).

"For my thoughts are not your thoughts, neither are your ways my ways, saith the Lord" (Isa. 55:8). ("Weak Things of the Earth/World," *DCE,* 628)

LIKENING THE SCRIPTURES TO OUR LIVES

Doctrine and Covenants 1:31–32 In His mercy, the Lord makes an allowance for the sinner who repents.

Application: The Lord makes clear that He "cannot look upon sin with the least degree of allowance" (D&C 1:31). Nevertheless, He will forgive all who repent and keep the commandments. Sin can have no degree of allowance before God because the law of justice must be fulfilled. Mercy is provided for the repentant through the Atonement of the Lord Jesus Christ and satisfies the law of justice. In order to qualify for mercy, we must repent (see D&C 19:15–19) so that through the grace of God we can be forgiven (see D&C 58:42–43). When we abide in sin and fail to keep the commandments, we lose the light of the Lord (see D&C 60:3) and the Spirit is withdrawn (see Morm. 1:13–14). Notwithstanding our failings, the Lord freely forgives the penitent who come to Him with a broken heart and a contrite spirit.

3. THE CERTAINTY OF THE WORD OF GOD

THEME: The word of God will not pass away but will be fulfilled, "whether by mine own voice or by the voice of my servants, it is the same" (D&C 1:38). Such certainty in uncertain times ought to bring us in humility to feast on the words of Christ. We are invited to search these commandments (D&C 1:37), wherein is the way to eternal life (John 5:39), yet so many refuse this rich offering that would guide all our actions unerringly (see 2 Ne. 32:3, 7).

MODERN PROPHETS SPEAK

Ezra Taft Benson:

The most important prophet, so far as we are concerned is the one who is living in our day and age. This is the prophet who has today's instructions from God to us today. God's revelation to Adam did not instruct Noah how to build the ark. Every generation has need of the ancient scripture plus the current scripture from the living prophet. Therefore, the most crucial reading and pondering which you should do is of the latest inspired words from the Lord's mouthpiece. That is why it is essential that you have access to and carefully read his words in current Church publications. (Korea Area Conference Report, 1975, in *TETB,* 52)

J. Reuben Clark Jr.:

Only the President of the Church, the Presiding High Priest, is sustained as Prophet, Seer, and Revelator for the Church, and he alone has the right to receive revelations for the Church, either new or amendatory, or to give authoritative interpretations of scriptures that shall be binding on the Church, or change in any way the existing doctrines of the Church. . . . Counselors in the First Presidency and the members of the Twelve are also sustained as prophets, seers, and revelators, which gives them a special spiritual endowment in connection with their teaching. (*Church News,* July 31, 1954, 9–10)

Harold B. Lee:

[In general conference we hear] more inspired declarations on most every subject and problem about which [we] have been worrying. If you want to know what the Lord would have the Saints know and to have his guidance and direction for the next six months, get a copy of the proceedings of this conference, and you will have the latest word of the Lord as far as the Saints are concerned. (CR, October 1973, 168)

ILLUSTRATIONS FOR OUR TIMES

Living Prophets

The Lord bore solemn witness to the sanctity of the prophetic commission when He declared, in section 1 of the Doctrine and Covenants, that His word would be fulfilled, "whether by mine own voice or by the voice of my servants, it is the same" (verse 38). The sublime mantle and office of prophet of the Lord is surely an awesome responsibility unlike any other bestowed on mortal beings. To have the opportunity to follow such living prophets of the Lord is the gateway to blessings untold. Elder

Sheldon F. Child remarked of this privilege: "If God loves us enough to send us prophets, then we need to love Him enough to follow them" (*Ensign,* November 2003, 9).

To the world, it is a strange thing that the Lord has once again restored the prophetic office to the earth. How are prophets to be viewed and received in this modern-day culture of relative values and materialistic aspirations? An interesting event in the life of the Prophet Joseph Smith illustrates the self-imposed gulf that modern thinkers tend to erect between themselves and their peers who serve as prophets, conveying the word of the Lord as authorized representatives of Deity. On Friday morning, November 6, 1835, in Kirtland, Joseph Smith was introduced to a man from the eastern part of the country. This man expressed surprise upon meeting the Prophet. "After hearing my name, he remarked that I was nothing but a man, indicating by this expression, that he had supposed that a person to whom the Lord should see fit to reveal His will, must be something more than a man. He seemed to have forgotten the saying that fell from the lips of St. James, that Elias was a man subject to like passions as we are, yet he had such power with God, that He, in answer to his prayers, shut the heavens that they gave no rain for the space of three years and six months; and again, in answer to his prayer, the heavens gave forth rain, and the earth gave forth fruit [James 5:17–18]. Indeed, such is the darkness and ignorance of this generation, that they look upon it as incredible that a man should have any intercourse with his Maker" (*HC,* 2:302).

To the Saints of God, it is no incredible thing that prophets speak again for the Lord. It is the most normal of all procedures to accept and honor the living oracles of the heavens. It is a privilege to ponder the words of such men and savor the wisdom they impart through inspiration—for we know through the Spirit that they reflect the truth of the gospel. As the Lord stated in the final verse of section 1 of the Doctrine and Covenants: "For behold, and lo, the Lord is God, and the Spirit beareth record, and the record is true, and the truth abideth forever and ever. Amen" (D&C 1:39). (Allen)

A Prophet Repeats
President Ezra Taft Benson vividly underscored the importance of the Lord's preface to the Doctrine and Covenants on a windy, frigid, wintry day in 1986. President Spencer W. Kimball had just passed away, and President Benson was preparing to be sustained as his successor in two weeks. He came to Hiram, Ohio, on March 22 to break ground for the Hiram Ward meeting house. Dressed in a heavy coat and warmed by portable heaters, he stood at a makeshift podium. He was sheltered only by a tent which had been erected within sight of the Johnson home, where the revelation was received.

His voice breaking with emotion, he welcomed almost two thousand Saints who gathered to witness this historic event. After greeting the crowd, this newly designated prophet of God said that the most important words that he could speak would be to read aloud the Lord's words as spoken in section 1 of the Doctrine and Covenants. Everyone listened with renewed attention and appreciation as he carefully read those words verbatim. He then closed and sat down. That was his entire message. If a latter-day prophet considered these words so important, perhaps it would behoove each of us to sit down and carefully seek with the Spirit for additional insights as we again read those inspired words. (Anderson)

LIKENING THE SCRIPTURES TO OUR LIVES

Doctrine and Covenants 18:33–36 We are to testify that the voice of the Lord has again spoken from the heavens (see also D&C 84:60; 88:66).

Application: When we study the scriptures, do we envision the Lord actually speaking to us through His servants? Do we hear in our hearts and minds the Spirit of the Lord conveying the messages of truth and wisdom? Do we listen to His chosen servants as if the Lord Himself were uttering the messages of salvation? To do so is to hear the voice of the Lord resonating through our lives and prompting us to follow the pathway of righteousness (on this subject, see also 1 Kgs. 19:14; John 10:2–5; 1 Ne. 17:45; 2 Ne. 1:26; D&C 85:6).

ENRICHMENT

Testimony of the Witnesses
The testimony concerning the verity of the Lord's revelations to that date was given by inspiration at the conference of November 1 and 2, 1831, and appears at the front of the Doctrine and Covenants: "We therefore feel willing to bear testimony to all the world of mankind, to every creature upon the face of all the earth and upon the islands of the sea that the Lord has borne record to our souls, through the Holy Ghost, shed forth upon us, that these commandments were given by inspiration of God, and are profitable for all men, and are verily true. We give this testimony unto the world, the Lord being our helper and it is through the grace of God, the Father, and His Son, Jesus Christ, that we are permitted to have this privilege of bearing this testimony unto the world, that the children of men may be profited thereby" (*HC*, 1:226).

SUMMARY

A careful reading of the Lord's preface, section 1, reveals that it is His "Proclamation to the World" regarding the revelations for the latter days. He bears witness to the world that Joseph Smith is His servant and that the Church is true. This knowledge may only be avoided at great peril (see verses 1–7). The message of the section 1 of the Doctrine and Covenants—and, indeed, of the book as a whole—is the Lord's ultimate warning unto His Church and unto all the world to "hearken" unto His voice, remembering and honoring the covenants with humility and devotion, and with full understanding of the certainty that His word will be fulfilled, either unto our eternal condemnation or unto our eternal joy. It is little wonder that President Ezra Taft Benson characterized the Doctrine and Covenants as the capstone of our religion: "The Book of Mormon is the 'keystone' of our religion, and the Doctrine and Covenants is the capstone, with continuing latter-day revelation. The Lord has placed His stamp of approval on both the keystone and the capstone" (CR, April 1875, 105; *Ensign,* May 1987, 83). Let us commit ourselves to following both sources of divine truth with valor and endurance.

CHAPTER TWO

"BEHOLD, I AM JESUS CHRIST, *the* SAVIOR *of the* WORLD"

Reading Assignment: Doctrine and Covenants 18:10–13; 19:15–19, 23–24; 20; 34:3; 50:41–44; 58:42–43; 76:22–24, 62–70; 88:14–18; 93:33.

Additional Reading: *Attributes of Christ*—Doctrine and Covenants 6:20–21, 32–37; 19:1–3; 29:1–2; 38:1–3; 43:34; 45:3–5; 50:44; 76:5; 93:5–19; 133:42–52; 136:22; *Atonement of Christ*—2 Nephi 9; Alma 7:11–12; 11:42–44; 34. *Additional Resource*—Topical Guide, "Jesus Christ."

As absolute as the certainty that you have in your hearts that tonight will be followed by dawn tomorrow morning, so is my assurance that Jesus Christ is the Savior of mankind, the Light that will dispel the darkness of the world, through the gospel restored by direct revelation to the Prophet Joseph Smith. (David O. McKay, quoted in Gordon B. Hinckley, TGBH, 198)

THEMES *for* LIVING

1. Doctrine and Covenants: A Modern Testament of Jesus Christ
2. The Gift of the Atonement
3. Becoming More Like Christ

INTRODUCTION

Just as the Book of Mormon is "Another Testament of Jesus Christ" (subtitle since 1982), the Doctrine and Covenants is a modern, latter-day testament of Jesus Christ the Redeemer. It is likewise a dynamic chronicle of His dealings with humankind as the chief cornerstone of the kingdom of God and the "author of eternal salvation unto all them that obey him" (Heb. 5:9). In the pages of the Doctrine and Covenants, we see unfolding before our eyes the design of the Lord to sanctify His people through covenant practices and ordinances—line upon line and precept upon precept (Isa. 28:10, 13; 2 Ne. 28:30; D&C 98:12; 128:21)—and endow them with truth and light for the journey back home into His presence. From the pages of this sacred volume, we hear His voice of loving kindness and paternal warning calling us together to follow the prophets in faith, worship in truth and valor, and assist tirelessly in the campaign to gather Israel's remnants from the four quarters of the earth for the inauguration of the millennial reign. Confirmed throughout the Doctrine and Covenants are the godly attributes we are commanded to emulate in order to become "partakers of the divine nature" (2 Pet. 1:4) and rise to our potential as "children of the covenant" (3 Ne. 20:26). The Doctrine and Covenants testifies with consuming power of the life and mission of the Holy One of Israel and illuminates the miracle of the Atonement in a personal and moving manner that brings God's love home to us in personal, moving, and inspiring ways. May we thank the Lord in humility for the gift of the Doctrine and Covenants as yet another pillar of strength in our lives. May we search its pages for counsel in the ongoing quest for "immortality and eternal life" (Moses 1:39).

MOMENT OF TRUTH

The word of the Lord to the Prophet Joseph Smith and the gathering Saints in December of 1833 included this commandment: "And seek the face of the Lord always, that in patience ye may possess your souls, and ye shall have eternal life" (D&C 101:38). The Prophet Joseph was the epitome of one who seeks the face of the Lord with untiring devotion. His exemplary quest to "seek the face of the Lord always" is recorded in unforgettable episodes in the pages of the Doctrine and Covenants. The magnificent visions granted the prophet of the Restoration are ample evidence that the worthy and anointed can seek and find the face of the Lord—whose qualities and mission are reflected in exquisite detail throughout this sacred volume of modern scripture.

Though the passages in the Doctrine and Covenants that testify of the Savior and His atoning sacrifice are myriad, we find especially penetrating insights into His redeeming nature in select verses of sections 19, 76, and 93. Following are brief summaries of the setting and background to these extraordinary sections.

Section 19: Given in March 1830, in Manchester, Ontario County, New York. Martin Harris, who had underwritten the publication of the Book of Mormon at the E. B. Grandin printing establishment in Palmyra, became nervous about his invest- ment and importuned the Prophet Joseph Smith repeatedly to inquire of the Lord for direction. In the revelation, Martin Harris is comforted by the Lord and yet at the same time commanded multiple times to repent and keep the commandments given to him, lest the Lord should have to humble him with His almighty power (verse 20). In the course of the divine communication, the Lord gives a truly unique and power- ful account of the atoning experience of Gethsemane. Joseph Fielding Smith extols the virtues of the revelation: "It is one of the great revelations given in this dispensa- tion; there are few of greater import than this. The doctrine of the atonement of the Lord, as directly applying to the individual, and his exposition of 'Eternal Punishment,' as here set forth, give to the members of the Church light which was not previously known" (*CHMR,* 1:80–81).

Section 76: Given February 16, 1832, in Hiram, Portage County, Ohio. The Prophet reports in his journal: "Upon my return from Amherst conference, I resumed the translation of the Scriptures. From sundry revelations which had been received, it was apparent that many important points touching the salvation of man, had been taken from the Bible, or lost before it was compiled. It appeared self-evident from what truths were left, that if God rewarded every one according to the deeds done in the body the term 'Heaven,' as intended for the Saints' eternal home must include more kingdoms than one. Accordingly, on the 16th of February, 1832, while translating St. John's Gospel, myself and Elder Rigdon saw the following vision" (*HC,* 1:245). This revelation is one of the greatest statements in all of the scriptures about the postmor- tal phase of existence, with its several domains of glory to which all mankind (save only the sons of perdition) will be assigned according to individual obedience and compliance with the Lord's commandments. The revelation is a witness to the divin- ity of the Savior and His sacred mission of redemption.

Section 93: Given on May 6, 1833, in Kirtland, Ohio, at the Newel K. Whitney store (probably in the translating room). At the time, the Prophet Joseph Smith was still engaged in the inspired translation of the Bible and attending to important develop- ments in building the kingdom, as mob violence was raising its ugly head. This choice section of significant doctrine was evidently given in partial fulfillment of Doctrine and Covenants 90:14: "And from time to time, as shall be manifested by the Comforter, receive revelations to unfold the mysteries of the kingdom." Part of this section is apparently the record of John the Baptist (see verses 8–17). The Lord also promised that "if you are faithful you shall receive the fulness of the record of John" (verse 18). He also specified why He gave this instruction (verse 19): "I give unto you these sayings that you may understand and know how to worship, and know what you worship, that you may come unto the Father in my name, and in due time receive of his fulness." Is the Church Christ-centered? Section 93 should answer this question emphatically. No doubt this section and section 76 were strongly behind the answer Joseph Smith gave to the question, "What are the fundamental principles of your religion?" He replied, "The fundamental principles of our religion are the testimony of the Apostles and Prophets, concerning Jesus Christ, that He died, was buried, and rose again the third day, and ascended into heaven; and all other things which pertain to our religion are only appendages to it" (*HC,* 3:30; see D&C 20:21–29).

1. DOCTRINE AND COVENANTS: A MODERN TESTAMENT OF JESUS CHRIST

THEME: The Doctrine and Covenants is a solemn witness of our Savior Jesus Christ and testifies of His divine mission and mercy.

MODERN PROPHETS SPEAK

"The Living Christ: The Testimony of the Apostles, The Church of Jesus Christ of Latter-day Saints":

> As we commemorate the birth of Jesus Christ two millennia ago, we offer our testimony of the reality of His matchless life and the infinite virtue of His great atoning sacrifice. None other has had so profound an influence upon all who have lived and will yet live upon the earth.
>
> He was the Great Jehovah of the Old Testament, the Messiah of the New. Under the direction of His Father, He was the creator of the earth. "All things were made by him; and without him was not any thing made that was made" (John 1:3). Though sinless, He was baptized to fulfill all righteousness. He "went about doing good" (Acts 10:38), yet was despised for it. His gospel was a message of peace and goodwill. He entreated all to follow His example. He walked the roads of Palestine, healing the sick, causing the blind to see, and raising the dead. He taught the truths of eternity, the reality of our premortal existence, the purpose of our life on earth, and the potential for the sons and daughters of God in the life to come.
>
> He instituted the sacrament as a reminder of His great atoning sacrifice. He was arrested and condemned on spurious charges, convicted to satisfy a mob, and sen-

tenced to die on Calvary's cross. He gave His life to atone for the sins of all mankind. His was a great vicarious gift in behalf of all who would ever live upon the earth.

We solemnly testify that His life, which is central to all human history, neither began in Bethlehem nor concluded on Calvary. He was the Firstborn of the Father, the Only Begotten Son in the flesh, the Redeemer of the world.

He rose from the grave to "become the firstfruits of them that slept" (1 Cor.15:20). As Risen Lord, He visited among those He had loved in life. He also ministered among His "other sheep" (John 10:16) in ancient America. In the modern world, He and His Father appeared to the boy Joseph Smith, ushering in the long-promised "dispensation of the fulness of times" (Eph. 1:10).

Of the Living Christ, the Prophet Joseph wrote: "His eyes were as a flame of fire; the hair of his head was white like the pure snow; his countenance shone above the brightness of the sun; and his voice was as the sound of the rushing of great waters, even the voice of Jehovah, saying:

"I am the first and the last; I am he who liveth, I am he who was slain; I am your advocate with the Father" (D&C 110:3–4).

Of Him the Prophet also declared: "And now, after the many testimonies which have been given of him, this is the testimony, last of all, which we give of him: That he lives!

"For we saw him, even on the right hand of God; and we heard the voice bearing record that he is the Only Begotten of the Father—

"That by him, and through him, and of him, the worlds are and were created, and the inhabitants thereof are begotten sons and daughters unto God" (D&C 76:22–24).

We declare in words of solemnity that His priesthood and His Church have been restored upon the earth—"built upon the foundation of . . . apostles and prophets, Jesus Christ himself being the chief corner stone" (Eph. 2:20).

We testify that He will someday return to earth. "And the glory of the Lord shall be revealed, and all flesh shall see it together" (Isa. 40:5). He will rule as King of Kings and reign as Lord of Lords, and every knee shall bend and every tongue shall speak in worship before Him. Each of us will stand to be judged of Him according to our works and the desires of our hearts.

We bear testimony, as His duly ordained Apostles—that Jesus is the Living Christ, the immortal Son of God. He is the great King Immanuel, who stands today on the right hand of His Father. He is the light, the life, and the hope of the world. His way is the path that leads to happiness in this life and eternal life in the world to come. God be thanked for the matchless gift of His divine Son. (The First Presidency and the Quorum of the Twelve, *Ensign,* April 2000, 2)

LIKENING THE SCRIPTURES TO OUR LIVES

Doctrine and Covenants 19:15–19 The Lord has commanded us to repent and enjoy the loving comfort of His Atonement. Those who do not repent will suffer even as the Lord has suffered.

Application: When we understand and appreciate that Jesus is the Christ who suffered and died for us and that through repentance we might be forgiven and live again in the presence of the Father, then we will change. This is the essence of the Atonement—the centerpiece of the plan of happiness: it draws all mankind to Christ through His atoning sacrifice. He shelters the faithful from suffering for sin, if they will turn to Him. Thus the Doctrine and Covenants, like all scripture, testifies of Christ and His divine mission (see also D&C 50:44–45; 76:22–24).

2. THE GIFT OF THE ATONEMENT

THEME: The mission of God the Father and His Son Jesus Christ is to "bring about the immortality and eternal life of man" (Moses 1:39). Such could not transpire except there should be an infinite atonement that opened the way for humankind to be saved by obedience through the "merits, and mercy, and grace of the Holy Messiah" (2 Ne. 2:8). "We believe that through the Atonement of Christ, all mankind may be saved, by obedience to the laws and ordinances of the Gospel" (A of F 1:3).

MODERN PROPHETS SPEAK

Jeffrey R. Holland:

> Even as there are these unrestricted blessings flowing from Christ's sacrifice, . . . other aspects of the Atonement are conditional, requiring such effort as "repentance and faith on the name of the Lord God Omnipotent." The conditional blessings of the gospel, in both time and eternity, are predicated upon the moral agency and personal discipline of the individual before they can be fully efficacious. For example, while all members of the human family are freely and universally given reprieve from Adam's transgression

through no effort of their own, they are not given reprieve from their own sins unless they follow the commandments of Christ. (*Christ and the New Covenant: The Messianic Message of the Book of Mormon* [Salt Lake City: Deseret Book, 1997], 217–18)

ILLUSTRATIONS FOR OUR TIMES

Faith in the Atonement

Faith, beyond the gift, and agency became verbs, not concepts. I resolved: If I have a choice, which I do, then I choose to have faith—faith in the Lord, in the Atonement, in prayer, in repentance, in forgiveness, in service, in my potential, and in the goodness and potential of others for exaltation; faith in the scriptural fact that the Lord does not make status exceptions about who may share in his blessings but all people "are privileged the one like unto the other, and none are forbidden" (2 Ne. 26:28); faith that the Holy Ghost, keeper of all truth, can witness and imprint on my soul my worth, an imprint that with nurturing can withstand all false assessments—and I choose to nurture; faith that as I rely on the Lord through exercised faith, I am capable of overcoming all barriers, self-imposed or otherwise; faith that in my process of perfection, I can eventually attain all the attributes of godliness.

I am a daughter of a *Heavenly* Father. I can "reasonably expect to become like [him]" (Henry B. Eyring, *Excellence* [Salt Lake City: Deseret Book, 1984], 20). I had not realized before how dependent that expectation is upon my exercised faith. Constant nurturing is an essential that I had not previously understood or fully employed. I now recognized it as the practical complement to knowledge and faith.

In the past I had had difficulty letting go of my trespasses, even some minor ones. I somehow felt a sort of humility in their remembrance; I also felt a persistent sort of futility in my righteous reachings. Truly exercising my faith in Christ, I began to see that repentance and forgiveness afforded me a reconciliation with Christ and my Heavenly Father that I had never before allowed. I let go of those trespasses, the misconstrued humility, and the persistent futility. I decided to actually trust in the sacrifice and promise of the Lord.

With new perspective I understood that this life is to prepare me to meet God and become like him. It was understood by all concerned that as I grappled with life I would commit my share of sins. What I have learned about myself is that once I really understand what is right to do, I usually persist in the right. It is to my eternal benefit to forgive myself for sins I have repented of, sins that I committed not because I clearly desired to do evil but because I did not perceive clearly the benefits of righteousness. As I repent, the Lord offers me forgiveness, a forgiveness that is consecrated as I take the sacrament each week. The Lord in his perfection is able to forgive me; I do him honor to complement his forgiveness of me with my own. I also further my progression, aligning myself consistently closer to godhood.

These spiritual insights did not occur in an instant, but there is that moment forever cut out of time when I decided to doubt no longer. And then I decided to exercise faith consistently. That has made all the difference. (Blythe Darlyn Thatcher, "Happily Hereafter," in *LDS Women's Treasury: Insights and Inspiration for Today's Woman,* ed. Jay A. Parry [Salt Lake City: Deseret Book, 1997], 346)

LIKENING THE SCRIPTURES TO OUR LIVES

Doctrine and Covenants 18:10–11 The Lord values the salvation of our souls above all else.

Application: Let us rejoice in the knowledge that every one of us has great worth in the eyes of the Redeemer, so much so that He gave His life for us in a divine mission to reclaim all who would come unto Him with a broken heart and a contrite spirit. Let us be the source of joy for our Savior, just as He is the source of life for us. Remember that the only way to make the Atonement efficacious in our lives is to repent. The effort of genuine repentance is what we do to qualify for the grace of God and our Savior's atoning sacrifice (see 2 Ne. 25:23).

3. BECOMING MORE LIKE CHRIST

THEME: The Doctrine and Covenants helps us to understand Christ—His character, His power, His attributes—so that we can emulate His example and become more like Him. "Therefore, what manner of men ought ye to be? Verily I say unto you, even as I am" (3 Ne. 27:27).

MODERN PROPHETS SPEAK

Neal A. Maxwell:

> Much of the message of the holy scriptures concerns the nature, character, and attributes of God and His Son, Jesus Christ: "I give unto you these sayings that you may understand and know how to worship, and know what you worship, that you may come unto the Father in my name, and in due time receive of his fulness" (D&C 93:19).

> Therefore, it becomes clear both logically and scripturally that the only real *veneration* of Jesus is *emulation* of Him. Indeed, striving to become like Him is a special way of bearing and sharing our testimony of Him.

Jesus has told us that if we truly love Him, we will keep His commandments; and keeping and doing His commandments surely puts and keeps us on the lengthy pathway to perfection. (*Even As I Am* [Salt Lake City: Deseret Book, 1982], 1)

ILLUSTRATIONS FOR OUR TIMES

Becoming Disciples of Christ

As missionaries and missionary leaders, we talk of Christ, we preach of Christ, we testify of Christ. All of us who are serving the Lord in the mission field are disciples, hoping to be pure ambassadors of our Savior, Jesus Christ.

As ambassadors of Christ, we must remember that everything connected with God's plan exists through and by His beloved Son, Jesus Christ. The foundation of the Church is his gospel, and central to the gospel is the Atonement of Christ. When we live the gospel of Jesus Christ, when we believe in the principles and ordinances of faith, repentance, covenant making and the gift of the Holy Ghost, we believe in those things because of Jesus Christ. We are his disciples and ambassadors. The light that we hold (see 3 Ne. 18:24) is the Lord Jesus Christ. As Elder Hans B. Ringger so eloquently explains,

"The foundation and guiding light for all our decisions is the gospel of Jesus Christ and His message to the world. The teachings of Christ must be embedded in our desire to choose the right and in our wish to find happiness. His righteous life must be reflected in our own actions. The Lord not only teaches love, He is love. He not only preached the importance of faith, repentance, baptism, and the gift of the Holy Ghost, He lived accordingly. His life reflected the gospel that He preached. There was and is total harmony between His thoughts and His actions" (*Ensign,* May 1990, 25).

We cannot bear testimony of this Church and this kingdom without knowing Jesus Christ, the Savior of the world. When we know Christ, we can hold up his light; he is the light and the life of the world (see John 8:12). And when we hold up that light, then we truly become his disciples.

In 3 Nephi 15:12, Jesus Christ tells his disciples that "ye are a light unto this people," and he explains that they will bless all of Heavenly Father's children. Earlier, Christ had instructed the Nephites not to put their light under a bushel, but to put it "on a candlestick, and it giveth light to all that are in the house" (3 Ne. 12:15). That same instruction applies to each of us: when we possess the light of Jesus Christ, we must not put it under a bushel. That light must be held up, and then—and only then— will we be true and worthy representatives of our Savior Jesus Christ.

We must not be manipulative salespeople. We must be disciples of Christ. All the knowledge and skills we learn must be magnified by the power of God, by the attributes of Christ, by the Spirit of the Lord, by the mind and will of the Lord. (Ed J. Pinegar, *Especially for Missionaries,* 4 vols. [American Fork, UT: Covenant Communications, 1997], 4:1–2)

An Apostle's Testimony

It should be the goal of every member of the Church not only to gain a testimony of Jesus Christ but to progress beyond that and come to know Him. Each member of the Church can gain the same testimony of Christ that even an Apostle possesses.

President Boyd K. Packer bore personal witness of this progression. He said that, as a young soldier, "I was on Ie Shima, a tiny speck of an island off the northwest coast of Okinawa. . . . One calm, clear, moonlit night I sat alone on a cliff, high above the beach. . . . I had a burning witness of the restored gospel of Jesus Christ. I had some knowledge of the scriptures from hours and days and weeks and months of study. . . . It has been 59 years. . . . I do not know now any more surely that Jesus is the Christ, the Son of God, the only begotten of the Father than I did as a soldier boy, sitting on the cliff. . . . There is one difference. Now, I know the Lord. I bear witness of Him and invoke His blessings upon you" (Boyd K. Packer, CES Annual Evening with a General Authority, February 6, 2004; video copy in possession of Karl Ricks Anderson; see also Lucile C. Tate, *Boyd K. Packer: A Watchman on the Tower* [Salt Lake City: Bookcraft, 1995], 59–60, 279).

LIKENING THE SCRIPTURES TO OUR LIVES

Doctrine and Covenants 19:23 "Learn of me, and listen to my words; walk in the meekness of my Spirit, and you shall have peace in me."

Application: As we learn of and follow Christ, we become like Him, the very Prince of Peace. Trusting our lives to Him by living His gospel can bring us peace.

ENRICHMENT

Christ's Direction of the Church

As I have studied Church history, I have often pondered what it was that caused the early Saints to be willing, literally, to sacrifice everything—even their own lives—to establish the Church. It is obvious that the early Saints sustained Joseph as the Prophet and mouthpiece of the Lord. However, it also quickly became clear as I looked at their lives that they understood the difference between the mouthpiece and the source! Three early leaders—Brigham Young, John Taylor, and Newel K. Whitney—understood this distinction clearly.

Brigham Young loved Joseph Smith. His loyalty to him is legendary. Yet it wasn't Joseph "the man" he followed but, he said, the "man of God" who received and taught "the revelations of Jesus Christ" (*Deseret News Weekly*, 27 February 1856, 403). He said he did not "serve" Joseph Smith, but the doctrine of Christ "the Lord has revealed through him" (*Millennial Star,* September 15, 1850, 275).

John Taylor was converted through the efforts of Parley P. Pratt. He returned the favor in altering Parley's perspective when Parley faltered and became critical of Joseph Smith during Kirtland's period of severe apostasy. John Taylor said that Parley "with many others . . . were passing under a dark cloud." President Taylor told Parley, "I am surprised to hear you speak so, Brother Parley. Before you left Canada you bore a strong testimony to Joseph Smith being a Prophet of God, and to the truth of the work he has inaugurated; and you said you knew these things by revelation, and the gift of the Holy Ghost. You gave to me a strict charge to the effect that though you or an angel from heaven was to declare anything else I was not to believe it. Now Brother Parley, it is not man that I am following, but the Lord. The principles you taught me led me to Him, and I now have the same testimony that you then rejoiced in. If the work was true six months ago, it is true today; if Joseph Smith was then a prophet, he is now a prophet." John concluded by saying, "he soon made all right with the Prophet Joseph, and was restored to full fellowship" (B. H. Roberts, *The Life of John Taylor* [Salt Lake City: Bookcraft, 1963], 40).

Newel K. Whitney hesitated to accept his call as bishop. When Joseph Smith extended the call, Newel replied, "Brother Joseph, I can't see a Bishop in myself." Joseph then explained that the call didn't come from him and told Newel, "Go and ask the Lord about it." Bishop Whitney did just that. As he prayed alone in his room, a voice said to him, "Thy strength is in me" (Orson F. Whitney, CR, June 1919, 47). Recognizing that the Lord not only led the Church but was its very strength, Newel accepted this calling, and his capabilities were multiplied.

Christ often bore a first-person witness of Himself to His early leaders. In addition, He assured them of His caring leadership. Examples follow:

The Savior's First-Person Testimony of Himself
Jesus, speaking through the Prophet Joseph Smith, assured His Saints often of who it was that led them:

> "I am Jesus Christ, the Son of God" (D&C 6:21; 10:57; 11:28; 14:9; 35:2; 36:8; 52:44).

> "I am . . . Christ the Lord" (D&C 19:1).

> "I am . . . the Redeemer of the world" (D&C 19:1).

"I am Jesus Christ" (D&C 19:24; 49:28; 51:20; 63:60; 68:6).

"I am the Son of God" (D&C 45:52).

"I am Christ" (D&C 38:4).

"I am Jesus Christ, the Savior of the world" (D&C 43:34).

"I am the Son of the living God" (D&C 68:6).

"I am God" (D&C 101:16).

The Savior's Assurance of His Leadership

Similarly, the Lord assured His Saints often that He led them, watched over them, spoke to them, and was their Savior:

"Be of good cheer, for I will lead you along" (D&C 78:18).

"I will go before you and be your rearward; and I will be in your midst" (D&C 49:27).

"I am in your midst, and I have not forsaken you" (D&C 61:36).

"My blessings continue with you" (D&C 82:23).

"I will go before your face. I will be on your right hand and on your left, and my Spirit shall be in your hearts, and mine angels round about you, to bear you up" (D&C 84:88).

"I will be with you . . . in whatsoever place ye shall proclaim my name" (D&C 112:19).

"These words are not of man nor of men, but of me, even Jesus Christ, your Redeemer" (D&C 31:13).

"God shall be with you forever and ever" (D&C 122:9).

"There is no weapon that is formed against you shall prosper" (D&C 71:9).

"I will fight your battles" (D&C 105:14).

"I, the Lord, have raised up [my Church] in these last days" (D&C 53:1).

Christ's leadership was made even more evident as He personally appeared to Joseph Smith and the early Saints. During the New York and Kirtland periods, the Savior appeared in vision to Joseph Smith and at least thirty other early leaders on at least fourteen occasions. Probably five hundred witnesses were present on those occasions, and many observed the outward manifestations of these visions.

In 1884, George Q. Cannon, a member of the First Presidency, recognized that there were still "men alive who have beheld the Son of God, who have heard His voice, and who have been ministered unto by Him in this our day and generation." He then acknowledged the power of these latter-day appearances to strengthen our faith, as he asked, "In the face of these testimonies . . . is it any wonder that faith grows in the hearts of the people of God, the Latter-day Saints?" (*JD*, 25:158). Small wonder that in paying Christmas tribute to the Christ, Elder James E. Talmage wrote, "He has manifested Himself in person to His prophets in the present dispensation, and has spoken with them as one man speaks with another" ("Our Lord the Christ," *Improvement Era,* December 1932). This acknowledgment and living testimony continues to the present day, for President Gordon B. Hinckley has stated: "I know that I am not the head of this Church. The Lord Jesus Christ is its head. He is its living head. My mission, my chief responsibility, my greatest honor comes in bearing solemn testimony of His living reality" (*TGBH,* 285–86). (Anderson)

SUMMARY

The Doctrine and Covenants is truly a modern testament of Jesus Christ. It enriches the Book of Mormon's detailed view of the Atonement as God's greatest gift to humankind. Through the pages of the Doctrine and Covenants, we can learn the key steps for becoming more like Christ—in thought, in word, and in deed. This sacred volume of the Restoration, conjoined with the other standard works of the Church, provides a sure road map for achieving our covenant goals and returning one day to the presence of the Lord. Thus we can obediently transcend the limitations of our earthly existence and fulfill the divine decree to "seek the face of the Lord always, that in patience ye may possess your souls, and ye shall have eternal life" (D&C 101:38).

CHAPTER THREE

"I HAD SEEN *a* VISION"

Reading Assignment: Joseph Smith—History 1:1–26; *Our Heritage*, pages 1–4.

Additional Reading: Topical Guide, "Apostasy"; "Restoration."

I thank my Father in Heaven for the testimony I have of the reality of the First Vision. I have stood among the trees where Joseph knelt as a boy, and heard the whisperings of the Spirit that it happened as he said it happened. . . .

I read this morning a part of Joseph Smith's testimony of the First Vision. You are all familiar with it. His going into a grove, pleading with the Lord, a light shining above him, and then the appearance of the Father and the Son. I read that testimony and thought of it. I said to myself, "If every one of us knew in our hearts that that statement is true, then we would know that all else which follows it, which came through the restoration of the gospel, is true also." And we would walk and live with greater faithfulness. (Gordon B. Hinckley, TGBH, 225)

THEMES *for* LIVING

1. The Great Apostasy Required a Restoration of All Things
2. Joseph Smith: The Prophet of the Restoration
3. The First Vision: The Beginning of the Restoration
4. Eternal Verities and Doctrines Manifested in the First Vision

INTRODUCTION

"Oh, how lovely was the morning!" begins the beloved hymn recounting Joseph Smith's first uttered prayer in a shady grove that has become sacred to generations of truth-seekers everywhere. What occurred that spring morning in 1820 changed the course of earth's history. From the foundations of the world, this moment had been planned and anticipated as an essential step in Heavenly Father's design: "That in the dispensation of the fulness of times he might gather together in one all things in Christ, both which are in heaven, and which are on earth; *even* in him" (Eph. 1:10). The First Vision ended generations of spiritual darkness fostered by the great Apostasy—that general falling away from truth foretold by the Savior and His Apostles.

The sequence of events inaugurated by the First Vision resulted in the complete restoration of the gospel, reestablishing the living Church and kingdom of God through the instrumentality of the Prophet Joseph Smith. The process of restoring the gospel unfolded systematically—at great sacrifice—over the ensuing years under divine guidance until the Prophet's mission was complete. He then sealed his work and his testimony through martyrdom on June 27, 1844. In the pages of the Doctrine and Covenants, we see the steps of the Restoration in all of its exciting majesty. Through the Spirit of the Holy Ghost, the sincere student of truth can find confirmation of the mighty work of God in these latter days, even that "marvelous work and a wonder" (Isa. 29:14) which opened the gates of salvation and joy for God's children. We are thereby enabled to look forward with greater hope to the Lord's Second Coming.

MOMENT OF TRUTH

The restoration of the gospel and kingdom of God took place in a sequence of events that is splendidly summarized by the following verses from the Doctrine and Covenants:

> And again, what do we hear? Glad tidings from Cumorah! Moroni, an angel from heaven, declaring the fulfilment of the prophets—the book to be revealed. A voice of the Lord in the wilderness of Fayette, Seneca county, declaring the three witnesses to bear record of the book! The voice of Michael on the banks of the Susquehanna, detecting the devil when he appeared as an angel of light! The voice of Peter, James, and John in the wilderness between Harmony, Susquehanna county, and Colesville, Broome county, on the Susquehanna river, declaring themselves as possessing the keys of the kingdom, and of the dispensation of the fulness of times! And again, the voice of God in the chamber of old Father Whitmer, in Fayette, Seneca county, and at sundry times, and in divers places through all the travels and tribulations of this Church of Jesus Christ of Latter-day Saints! And the voice of Michael, the archangel;

the voice of Gabriel, and of Raphael, and of divers angels, from Michael or Adam down to the present time, all declaring their dispensation, their rights, their keys, their honors, their majesty and glory, and the power of their priesthood; giving line upon line, precept upon precept; here a little, and there a little; giving us consolation by holding forth that which is to come, confirming our hope! (D&C 128:20–21)

1. THE GREAT APOSTASY REQUIRED A RESTORATION OF ALL THINGS

THEME: It is the Lord's will to share truth and light with His children to the extent that they will soften their hearts and accept His gospel principles. Apostasy is a state of existence in which hearts are hardened against divine light and truth. Alma taught the dissenter Zeezrom this key dichotomy between soft and hard, light and darkness: "And therefore, he that will harden his heart, the same receiveth the lesser portion of the word; and he that will not harden his heart, to him is given the greater portion of the word, until it is given unto him to know the mysteries of God until he know them in full" (Alma 12:10). Once humankind has fully rejected the light of God and dwindled in unbelief, a restoration from heaven is needed.

MODERN PROPHETS SPEAK

Boyd K. Packer:

> The Church you belong to, The Church of Jesus Christ of Latter-day Saints, is the restored Church. . . .

> Following the Crucifixion of Christ an apostasy occurred. Leaders began to "teach for doctrines the commandments of men." They lost the keys of authority and closed themselves off from the channels of revelation. That lost authority could not just be repossessed. It had to be restored by those who held the keys of authority.

> The Church of Jesus Christ of Latter-day Saints is not a remodeled version of another church. It is not an adjustment or a correction or a protest against any other church. (*Ensign*, November 2003, 24)

James E. Talmage:

> The restored Church affirms that a general apostasy developed during and after the apostolic period, and that the primitive Church lost its power, authority, and graces as a divine institution, and degenerated into an earthly organization only. The significance and importance of the great apostasy, as a condition precedent to the re-establishment

of the Church in modern times, is obvious. . . . The evidence of the decline and final extinction of the primitive Church among men is found in scriptural record, and in secular history. (*The Great Apostasy* [Salt Lake City: Deseret Book, 1958], iii)

ILLUSTRATIONS FOR OUR TIMES

The Spiritual Orbit

On occasion I have found it useful to turn to astronomy for symbolic help in gaining a fuller understanding of the severe implications of the apostasy. Heavenly bodies (including satellites) move in elliptical orbits, with the controlling center of gravity at one of the locus points of the ellipse—for example, the moon moving about the earth, or the earth moving about the sun. As the earth moves in its orbit, its distance from the sun varies, the furthest point being the *apogee* and the closest the *perigee.* All orbiting bodies follow this same pattern.

The word *apogee* is interesting in its linguistic relationship to the word *apostasy.* The prefix *apo* is common to both words. *Apo* (from the Greek) means "away from." In that sense, apostasy implies moving away from a set of principles or values, thus abandoning one's beliefs, or "standing far away from" the truth. Similarly, *apogee* means away from the earth—implying being at the furthest distance from home base.

When we are on a course that takes us away from our center of gravity, we are moving toward the "apogee of existence," toward that point in our journey that represents the furthest distance away from home base, warmth, truth, and light. The scriptures are replete with references to the Savior as being the source of light and life: "Behold, I am Jesus Christ, the Son of God. I am the life and the light of the world" (D&C 11:28). "I am the light and the life of the world. I am Alpha and Omega, the beginning and the end" (3 Ne. 9:18; see also John 9:5; 12:46; 3 Ne. 11:11; 15:9; Ether 4:12; D&C 12:9; 45:7). Our charge is to stay close to the Savior, to be part of His plan of life and perfection—the plan of salvation. In Lehi's dream, those who did not press forward to the tree of life—the love of God—fell away and were lost in the mists of darkness.

Where there has been an apostasy, or a falling away, there is a vacuum that can be redressed only through a restoration, bringing humankind once again into a closeness with the Lord and His gospel. Such a restoration was launched on a grand scale through Joseph Smith's vision in the spring of 1820. The Prophet Joseph was an instrument in the Lord's hands "unto the bringing of them out of darkness unto light—yea, out of hidden darkness and out of captivity unto freedom" (2 Ne. 3:5).

Heavenly Father has again established His covenant from which humankind had strayed (see D&C 1:15, 17, 22), but the need remains individually for vigilance in order to stay on the pathway that will bring us ever closer to Christ (see D&C 84:54–58). In a sense, we sometimes find ourselves moving in orbits where we are close to the

Lord, and at other times, through our imperfect behavior, doubts, and pride, "far from" Him (see Isa. 29:13; Mosiah 5:13). The process of sincere repentance can help us move back into a relationship of confidence and comfort close to the Lord (see D&C 121:45). The spiritual orbit we seek is the restored gospel of Jesus Christ, which brings us through grace and redeeming love toward the light: "And that which doth not edify is not of God, and is darkness. That which is of God is light; and he that receiveth light, and continueth in God, receiveth more light; and that light groweth brighter and brighter until the perfect day" (D&C 50:23–24). (Allen)

LIKENING THE SCRIPTURES TO OUR LIVES

Doctrine and Covenants 4:1–2 In our day, the Lord has commenced a marvelous work and a wonder, a work that is of more importance to the eternal salvation of man than anything else. We have a major part in this work, and the Lord desires our full heart, strength, and mind to move His cause forward.

Application: We should rejoice in the restoration of gospel truths and ordinances that provide for us a way to return to the presence of our Heavenly Father. Let us guard against apostasy in all of its manifestations by putting on the armor of God (see Eph. 6:11–18; D&C 27:15–18) and strengthening others at all times (see D&C 81:5; 108:7; Alma 31:34–35).

2. JOSEPH SMITH: THE PROPHET OF THE RESTORATION

THEME: As John Taylor taught, "Joseph Smith, the Prophet and Seer of the Lord, has done more, save Jesus only, for the salvation of men in this world, than any other man that ever lived in it" (D&C 135:3). He was the instrument through whom the Lord brought about the restoration of His kingdom in this, the dispensation of the fulness of times: "For I deign to reveal unto my church things which have been kept hid from before the foundation of the world, things that pertain to the dispensation of the fulness of times" (D&C 124:41).

MODERN PROPHETS SPEAK

Gordon B. Hinckley:

> How great indeed is our debt to [Joseph Smith]. . . . It was he who brought us a true knowledge of God the Eternal Father and His Risen Son, the Lord Jesus Christ. During the short time of his great vision he learned more concerning the nature of

Deity than all of those who through centuries had argued that matter in learned councils and scholarly forums. He brought us this marvelous book, the Book of Mormon, as another witness for the living reality of the Son of God. To him, from those who held it anciently, came the priesthood, the power, the gift, the authority, the keys to speak and act in the name of God. He gave us the organization of the Church and its great and sacred mission. Through him were restored the keys of the holy temples, that men and women might enter into eternal covenants with God, and that the great work for the dead might be accomplished to open the way for eternal blessings.

He was the instrument in the hands of the Almighty. He was the servant acting under the direction of the Lord Jesus Christ in bringing to pass this great latter-day work.

We stand in reverence before him. He is the great prophet of this dispensation. He stands at the head of this great and mighty work which is spreading across the earth. He is our prophet, our revelator, our seer, our friend. Let us not forget him. . . . God be thanked for the Prophet Joseph. (*TGBH*, 514)

ILLUSTRATIONS FOR OUR TIMES

Those among the Lord's chosen who labored closely with the Prophet Joseph bore fervent witness of the heavenly commission that he fulfilled. Here are a few examples:

Brigham Young:

I appear before you to bear my testimony to the truth of "Mormonism," that Joseph Smith, jun., was a Prophet called of God, and that he did translate the Book of Mormon by the gift and power of the Holy Ghost. This same testimony all can bear, who have received and continue to retain the Spirit of the Gospel. (*JD*, 4:33)

Parley P. Pratt:

I bear this testimony this day, that Joseph Smith was and is a Prophet, Seer, and Revelator—an Apostle holding the keys of this last dispensation and of the kingdom of God, under Peter, James, and John. And not only that he was a Prophet and Apostle of Jesus Christ, and lived and died one, but that he now lives in the spirit world, and holds those same keys to usward and to this whole generation. (*JD*, 5:196)

John Taylor:

At first I believed it on the testimony of others, and then obtained a knowledge for myself. If there is no other man under the heavens that knows that Joseph Smith is a Prophet of God I do, and I bear testimony of it to God, angels and men. (*JD*, 10:130–31)

Wilford Woodruff:

> Joseph Smith was what he professed to be, a prophet of God, a seer and revelator. He laid the foundation of this church and kingdom, and lived long enough to deliver the keys of the kingdom to the elders of Israel, unto the twelve apostles. (*The Discourses of Wilford Woodruff,* ed. G. Homer Durham [Salt Lake City: Bookcraft, 1946], 35)

Like these prophets, millions of people today testify that Joseph Smith is indeed the prophet of the Restoration. This testimony is the vitality of the Church.

LIKENING THE SCRIPTURES TO OUR LIVES

Doctrine and Covenants 21:4–6 The words of the apostles and prophets are to be received as if directly from the mouth of the Lord. Those who follow these words will be protected from evil and strengthened by the powers of heaven.

Application: We are given the word of God through our prophet-leaders. Let us faithfully heed their words and live by them, lest we stand under condemnation (see 3 Ne. 28:34–35).

3. THE FIRST VISION: THE BEGINNING OF THE RESTORATION

THEME: The Restoration unfolded under divine watchcare in perfectly ordered steps—beginning with the resumption of communication with the heavens (the First Vision), continuing with the bringing forth of the Book of Mormon ("the fulness of the gospel of Jesus Christ"—D&C 20:9) and the establishment of the kingdom of heaven on earth (including the authority of the priesthood and all attendant ordinances), and culminating in the ongoing gathering of the Saints to holy places (stakes and temples) as designated through prophetic leadership. All of this rested upon the foundation of a true knowledge of Deity as established through the First Vision and confirmed by the witness of the Holy Spirit to the Saints.

MODERN PROPHETS SPEAK

Ezra Taft Benson:

> The first vision of the Prophet Joseph Smith is bedrock theology to the Church. The adversary knows this and has attacked Joseph Smith's credibility from the day he announced the visitation of the Father and the Son. You should always bear testimony to the truth of the First Vision. Joseph Smith did see the Father and the Son. They conversed with him as he said they did. . . . If we do not accept this truth—if we have

not received a witness about this great revelation—we cannot inspire faith in those whom we lead. (*TETB,* 101)

ILLUSTRATIONS FOR OUR TIMES

Joseph's Contemporaries Share Their Witness

Latter-day Saints were not the only contemporaries who described the First Vision as related to them by Joseph Smith. A nonmember editor of the *Pittsburg Gazette* interviewed the Prophet in Nauvoo, then published an article on him. The editor discussed the reformation that preceded the First Vision, the young boy's quest to know which church to join, and Joseph's compliance with James's admonition on prayer. Then he described the First Vision as related by Joseph Smith:

"I saw a light," he quoted Joseph Smith as saying, "and then a glorious personage in the light, and then another personage, and the first personage said to the second, Behold my beloved Son, hear him.—I then addressed this second person, saying, O Lord, what Church shall I join? He replied, 'don't join any of them, they are all corrupt.'"

Alexander Neibaur, a convert who gathered with the Saints in Nauvoo, described in his journal what Joseph told him during a dinner conversation. Brother Neibaur wrote that the Prophet said he had been "struck" by a passage on prayer in the Bible and so went into the woods to pray. After his tongue cleaved temporarily to the roof of his mouth, he saw a fire which gradually drew nearer to him. He "saw a personage in the fire, light complexion, blue eyes. . . . [Another] person came to the side of the first. Mr. Smith then asked, must I join the Methodist Church. No, they are not my People, [they] have gone astray. There is none that Doeth good, not one, but this is my Beloved Son harken ye him."

President John Taylor was another contemporary "intimately acquainted" with Joseph who described the First Vision as it was related to him by the Prophet. "I have travelled with him [Joseph Smith]," he wrote. "I have been with him in private and in public; I have associated with him in councils of all kinds; I have listened hundreds of times to his public teachings, and his advice to his friends and associates of a more private nature. I have been at his house and seen his deportment in his family. . . . I was with him . . . when he died, when he was murdered in Carthage. . . . I testify before God, angels, and men that he was a good, honourable, virtuous man . . . that his private and public character was unimpeachable—and that he lived and died as a man of God." . . .

Elder Taylor not only declared that he personally learned from Joseph Smith the basic truths unfolded during the First Vision, but proclaimed that Joseph Smith's

1838 history discussing events preceding the organization of the Church was accurate. (Milton V. Backman Jr., *Ensign,* January 1986, 36–37)

LIKENING THE SCRIPTURES TO OUR LIVES

James 1:5 The conduit of heaven, the source of all knowledge and light, is open to each of us if we will ask in faith, nothing wavering.

Application: This beautiful promise that prompted young Joseph to pray that day in the grove is our promise as well. We too can communicate with God and receive direction and personal revelation. One lesson of the First Vision is the reality of revelation based on the sincerity of faith.

4. ETERNAL VERITIES AND DOCTRINES MANIFESTED IN THE FIRST VISION

THEME: The First Vision opened the floodgates of divine truth with revelation concerning the Father and the Son—Their true nature and character—together with an assessment of the condition of an apostate world. The urgent need for the Restoration was apparent, for the Lord had to build up His kingdom anew.

MODERN PROPHETS SPEAK

B. H. Roberts:

> The very existence of the Church of Jesus Christ of Latter-day Saints presupposes that the world had gone wrong, that the world had corrupted the Gospel of Jesus Christ and hence there was a necessity for the restoration of the Gospel, and a restoration of the Priesthood of God to administer in its ordinances and proclaim it to the world. . . .

> The Lord clearly declares that this Church, which He had given His servants strength to organize, is the "only true and living Church upon the face of this whole earth." (*Collected Discourses,* ed. Brian H. Stuy, 5 vols. [Burbank, CA, and Woodland Hills, UT: B.H.S. Publishing, 1987–1992] 5:135–36)

James E. Faust:

> The First Vision confirms the fact there are three separate Gods: God the Father—Elohim, to whom we address our prayers; Jesus the Christ—Jehovah; and the Holy Ghost—the Comforter, through whose spirit we may know the truth of all things. . . .

What resulted from the First Vision, which opened the prophesied dispensation of the fulness of times?

1. The Book of Mormon, another witness for Christ, was received.

2. The priesthood, or authority to perform saving ordinances, was restored, including the sealing powers of the priesthood.

3. The Church of Jesus Christ was again organized on the earth.

4. Revelations came to the Prophet Joseph Smith for the building of the kingdom of God upon the earth, declaring the universal salvation of mankind.

5. Keys, principles, and powers were restored for the carrying out of the three great missions of the Church—the preaching of the gospel, the means of perfecting the Saints, and temples and ordinances therein for the redemption of the living and the dead. (*Ensign,* May 1984, 67)

Joseph Fielding Smith:

I would like to call your attention to one little thing in the first vision of the Prophet Joseph Smith. It is very significant, and Joseph Smith did not know it. If he had been perpetrating a fraud, he would not have thought of it. You will recall in your reading that the Father and the Son appeared, and the Father introduced the Son and told the Prophet to hear the Son.

Now suppose the Prophet had come back from the woods and had said the Father and the Son appeared to him, and the Father said, "Joseph, what do you want?" and when he asked the question and told him what he wanted, the Father had answered him; then we would know that the story of the Prophet could not be true.

All revelation comes through Jesus Christ. I have not time to go into the scriptures and give references for that, but that is the fact. (*AGQ,* 1:16)

ILLUSTRATIONS FOR OUR TIMES

Teach Doctrine

The successors to the Prophet Joseph Smith—our modern-day prophet-leaders of the Church—confirm at every juncture the necessity of staying the course within the doctrinal bounds the Lord has set in order to preserve, protect, secure, and nurture His kingdom:

Joseph F. Smith:

> I am proud to say that I have accepted and have tried to keep and honor every word that has proceeded from the mouth of God through him. As—"It is written, man shall not live by bread alone, but by every word that proceedeth out of the mouth of God." No one will dare to accuse me of side-tracking from, or of refusing to obey any doctrine taught by or revealed through the Prophet Joseph Smith. (CR, October 1910, 4)

Boyd K. Packer:

> There are doctrines which, if understood, will bring a perspective toward and a composure regarding problems which otherwise have no satisfactory explanation. (*Ensign,* May 1991, 7)

Robert D. Hales:

> With the help of the Lord and His doctrine, all the hurtful effects from challenges a family may meet can be understood and overcome. (*Ensign,* May 1999, 32)

LIKENING THE SCRIPTURES TO OUR LIVES

Joseph Smith—History 1:15–17, 19 Our Father in Heaven and His Son Jesus Christ appeared to the boy Joseph in the grove of trees. This vision was the inauguration of the dispensation of the fulness of times. The fulness of knowledge is available to all those who will, like the boy Joseph, approach the throne of God with a humble heart and unyielding faith.

Application: When we understand the doctrine and appreciate its significance, it has a profound effect upon our feelings and actions. Note the doctrines taught through the First Vision:

1. God does hear and answer our prayers. Therefore, we should make prayer the framework of our daily lives (see Alma 34:17–28; James 1:5–6; 3 Ne. 18:18; 20:1).

2. The devil is real. Beware of his temptations and snares, for he seeks to destroy us (see 2 Ne. 1:18; 9:37; 28:19–29; Mosiah 2:32; Hel. 8:28; D&C 10:12; 29:39). Searching the scriptures should be a daily prescription for spiritual health and welfare (see 1 Ne. 15:24).

3. There is a God in heaven. Jesus Christ is His Beloved Son. They are separate beings with glorified bodies. We are created in Their image and thus possess a divine heritage as the children of God.

4. There was an apostasy. This fact was confirmed by the Lord when He taught the boy Joseph that none of the churches were true but, rather, were an abomination in His sight. There can be but one true church.

5. Hypocrisy is condemned of God. We are to be pure in heart—a Zion people.

6. The heavens are open to those with faith. Personal revelation can be ours as we exercise faith according to the will of God.

SUMMARY

Through a careful and prayerful study of the scriptures and historical accounts relating to the First Vision and the Restoration, we can come to a greater appreciation of the tremendous outpouring of blessings in this, the dispensation of the fulness of time. The great Apostasy required a restoration of all things through a modern-day prophet—Joseph Smith. The First Vision was the beginning of the restorative process that saw the coming forth of the Book of Mormon in 1830 through divine guidance, followed soon thereafter by the establishment of the Lord's Church, with all the priesthood keys and ordinances essential to the salvation of mankind. The eternal verities and doctrines revealed through the First Vision have been supplemented by the Lord over the ensuing years (line by line and precept by precept) so that the work of the Lord has gained that momentum prophesied by Daniel: a stone that was cut from the mountain without hands rolling forth to fill the entire world. Yet the Restoration still continues through modern-day prophets, successors to the Prophet Joseph, who deliver the word of the Lord.

CHAPTER FOUR

"REMEMBER *the* NEW COVENANT, EVEN *the* BOOK *of* MORMON"

Reading Assignment: Joseph Smith—History 1:27–65; Doctrine and Covenants 3; 5; 10; 17; 20:5–15; 84:54–62; *Our Heritage,* pages 5–10.

Additional Reading: Doctrine and Covenants 1:29; 3:1–3, 18–20; 10:14, 43; 17:6; 19:26–27; 20:8–15; 33:16; 42:12; 84:54–58; 1 Nephi 9:5–6; 19:3; Words of Mormon 1:7; Moroni 10:3–5.

I told the brethren that the Book of Mormon was the most correct of any book on earth, and the keystone of our religion, and a man would get nearer to God by abiding by its precepts, than by any other book. (Joseph Smith, HC, 4:461)

THEMES *for* LIVING

1. How the Lord Prepares His Servants: The Schooling of the Prophet Joseph to Bring Forth the Book of Mormon
2. Latter-day Miracle: The Word of God from Ancient America
3. How the Law of Witnesses Blesses Our Lives
4. Our Personal Responsibility to the Book of Mormon

INTRODUCTION

There is no greater introduction to the study of the Book of Mormon than the words of the Lord Himself. In the "Revelation on Church Organization and Government" (section 20) given through the Prophet Joseph Smith in April 1830, the Lord proclaims the following:

> And gave him [Joseph Smith] power from on high, by the means which were before prepared, to translate the Book of Mormon; Which contains a record of a fallen people, and the fulness of the gospel of Jesus Christ to the Gentiles and to the Jews also; Which was given by inspiration, and is confirmed to others by the ministering of angels, and is declared unto the world by them—Proving to the world that the holy scriptures are true, and that God does inspire men and call them to his holy work in this age and generation, as well as in generations of old; Thereby showing that he is the same God yesterday, today, and forever. Amen. Therefore, having so great witnesses, by them shall the world be judged, even as many as shall hereafter come to a knowledge of this work. And those who receive it in faith, and work righteousness, shall receive a crown of eternal life; But those who harden their hearts in unbelief, and reject it, it shall turn to their own condemnation. (D&C 20:8–15)

MOMENT OF TRUTH

The period of time preceding that glorious witness by the Lord in 1830 (D&C 20:8–15) was filled with momentous events that resulted in the coming forth of the Book of Mormon. The extraordinary sequence of visits by the angelic messenger Moroni to Joseph Smith began on Sunday, September 21, 1823, and culminated four years later on September 22, 1827, when Moroni entrusted him with the sacred plates and commissioned him to commence with the inspired translation. That inexorable process was not without its reversals and trials before the world was privileged, after fourteen hundred years, to receive once again the word of God in its fulness as another witness of the divinity and Atonement of Jesus Christ. Doctrine and Covenants 3, 5, 10, and 17 are especially cogent chronicles of how the Lord guided the unfolding of this "marvelous work and a wonder" (Isa. 29:14) that was to become a keystone of the restored gospel. Below is a brief summary of the historical background of these four sections to aid the reader in establishing a framework for pondering and applying the themes of this chapter.

Section 3: Given through the Prophet Joseph during the month of July 1828 at Harmony, Susquehanna County, Pennsylvania, located some 150 miles from Palmyra, New York, where Isaac Hale, Emma Smith's father, lived. Joseph and Emma had moved there around December of 1827 because of intense persecution in Manchester, New York. For a period of time, Martin Harris, a well-to-do Palmyra farmer, had assisted Joseph Smith as scribe in the translation of the Book of Mormon. During the period April 12 to June 14, 1828, the first 116 pages of the manuscript (taken from "the Book of Lehi") were completed and subsequently lost by Martin Harris. The Lord expresses to the Prophet the serious and deleterious nature of this act: "Behold, you have been entrusted with these things, but how strict were your commandments; and remember also the promises which were made to you, if you did not transgress them. And behold, how oft you have transgressed the commandments and the laws of God, and have gone on in the persuasions of men. For, behold, you should not have feared man more than God" (D&C 3:5–7). Soon thereafter, a penitent and chastened prophet again received the gift and means for continuing the translation of the Book of Mormon, this time commencing with the smaller plates of Nephi (see *HC*, 1:21–23).

Section 5: Given through the Prophet Joseph Smith in March 1829 at Harmony, Susquehanna County, Pennsylvania. Though he had worked already as scribe for the prophet a year before, Martin Harris had come to Harmony to seek further confirmation that Joseph indeed possessed the sacred plates. He wanted to see the plates, but the Lord would not show him unless he was humble and acting according to God's will. Martin's first desire to witness the plates was for self-aggrandizement. We learn here that the Lord knows our motives and wants purity of heart. The Lord is clear concerning His design for witnessing the truth to His children (verses 11–18), which led to the eventual calling of the Three Witnesses. This section is also pivotal in its designation of Joseph Smith as the Lord's mouthpiece in these latter days. The Church would not be organized for another year, but the Lord makes it known here that He has again called a prophet on the earth.

Section 10: Given through the Prophet Joseph Smith during the summer of 1828 at Harmony, Susquehanna County, Pennsylvania. In this section, the Lord reveals that He had prepared a way to frustrate the evil designs of those into whose hands the first 116 pages of manuscript had fallen—He would cause Joseph to begin the translation anew from the smaller plates of Nephi to prevent wicked men from altering the lost section to make it seem different from any version that would subsequently be translated. The following explanation was included by the Prophet in the first edition of the Book of Mormon (1830):

> As many false reports have been circulated respecting the following work, and also many unlawful measures taken by evil designing persons to destroy me, and also the work, I would inform you that I translated, by the gift and power of God, and caused to be written, one hundred and sixteen pages, the which I took from the

Book of Lehi, which was an account abridged from the plates of Lehi, by the hand of Mormon; which said account, some person or persons have stolen and kept from me, notwithstanding my utmost exertions to recover it again—and being commanded of the Lord that I should not translate the same over again, for Satan had put it into their hearts to tempt the Lord their God, by altering the words, that they did read contrary from that which I translated and caused to be written; and if I should bring forth the same words again, or, in other words, if I should translate the same over again, they would publish that which they had stolen, and Satan would stir up the hearts of this generation, that they might not receive this work: but behold, the Lord said unto me, I will not suffer that Satan shall accomplish his evil design in this thing: therefore thou shalt translate from the plates of Nephi, until ye come to that which ye have translated, which ye have retained; and behold ye shall publish it as the record of Nephi; and thus I will confound those who have altered my words. I will not suffer that they shall destroy my work; yea, I will shew unto them that my wisdom is greater than the cunning of the Devil. Wherefore, to be obedient unto the commandments of God, I have, through his grace and mercy, accomplished that which he hath commanded me respecting this thing. I would also inform you that the plates of which hath been spoken, were found in the township of Manchester, Ontario county, New-York. (*RPJS*, 18–19; see also *HC*, 1:20–23)

Section 17: Given through the Prophet Joseph Smith during the month of June 1829 in Fayette, Seneca County, New York. Historian Lyndon W. Cook gives the following summary of the background to this revelation:

> In March 1829, before Joseph Smith became acquainted with Oliver Cowdery, the Lord revealed the following promise: "And the testimony of three witnesses will I send forth of my word" (D&C 5:15). During the translation the Prophet and his scribe discovered Moroni's instruction to the modern translator that he would be privileged to "show the plates unto three" [Ether 5:2–4]. The Prophet noted, "Almost immediately after we had made this discovery, it occurred to Oliver Cowdery, David Whitmer, and the aforesaid Martin Harris . . . that they would have me inquire of the Lord to know if they might not obtain of him the privilege to be these three special witnesses" [*HC*, 1:52–53]. Accordingly the Prophet inquired of the Lord and received section 17. (*RPJS*, 27–28)

The official testimony of these witnesses is printed in the introduction of the Book of Mormon. Though each of these witnesses eventually apostatized, none of them ever recanted his testimony of the verity of the Book of Mormon or of Joseph's translation of it from the gold plates. (Two of them, Oliver Cowdery and Martin Harris, did return to the Church years after the Prophet's death and were rebaptized.)

1. HOW THE LORD PREPARES HIS SERVANTS: THE SCHOOLING OF THE PROPHET JOSEPH TO BRING FORTH THE BOOK OF MORMON

THEME: The design of the Lord, from the foundation of the world, was to gather all things in one during the dispensation of the fulness of times—the final dispensation before His Second Coming (see Eph. 1:10; D&C 27:13; 29:8; 84:100). Thus, the prophet of the Restoration, Joseph Smith, was commissioned of the Lord and schooled by heavenly beings for the work of the ministry—step by step, line upon line—until he was ready to commence and complete the magnificent work to which he was called.

MODERN PROPHETS SPEAK

Orson F. Whitney:

> It was no accident, no chance happening—Joseph Smith's going into the grove that spring morning. . . . It was an event predestined, heaven-inspired. I once thought that any good boy who prayed in faith could see just what Joseph saw. But I have put away that childish notion. I have learned that all boys are not Joseph Smiths. God hears and answers the prayers of the humblest of his children; but he answers them as seemeth him best, and not always in the same way. He gives according to the capacity of the one who receives. . . .

> It was no ordinary man that went into the woods that morning to pray. It was a Prophet, a Seer. Joseph Smith was not made a prophet by the people who held up their hands for him on the sixth of April, 1830, when this Church was organized. He was already a prophet, chosen as Abraham had been, before he was born; ordained, like Jeremiah, before he was formed in the flesh. The people merely "sustained" him in that position, manifesting by the uplifted hand that they were willing to follow him as their leader, and to accept of his ministrations in that capacity. He was already a prophet, already a seer; God had made him such in advance. But all men are not Joseph Smiths. He was a man like unto Moses. He was the rarest human being that has walked this earth in the past two thousand years. And why did he go into the grove that morning and pray for wisdom and light? It was because the time had come. *The Hour* had struck, and *The Man* was there—the man whom God had provided. (CR, April 1920, 122–23)

ILLUSTRATIONS FOR OUR TIMES

The Importance and Power of Preparation

We find key counsel—in terms of measuring up—in one succinct phrase: "if ye are prepared ye shall not fear" (D&C 38:30). Elder Adam S. Bennion phrased it thus: "All life bears witness to the fact that ample preparation is the key to success" ("Facing Life," *Improvement Era,* November 1931).

Later in his life, Elder Bennion identified a feature of mortality: "Notice that Jesus lived only thirty-three years, and of the thirty-three years He took thirty for preparation. . . . Ten-elevenths of His life He gave to preparation" (*BYU Speeches of the Year,* February 2, 1954, 5).

This is not to say that preparation means standing still, waiting idly. President Heber J. Grant taught that the Lord develops us through a combination of time and our own effort: "It has been said, 'All things come to him who waits,' but I have no faith in this saying, unless in connection with the instruction contained in the lines: 'Still achieving, still pursuing, Learn to *labor* and wait'" ("Work, and Keep Your Promises," *Improvement Era,* January, 1900).

We should have faith that the Lord accomplishes things "in his own time, and in his own way, and according to his own will" (D&C 88:68). Indeed, one cannot help but wonder at all the labors the Prophet Joseph Smith performed in fourteen short years. This was largely due to the Lord's behind-the-scenes steps in preparing the earth for the Restoration of the gospel. It is in His power to raise up or overthrow nations, and "all things have been done in the wisdom of him who knoweth all things" (2 Ne. 2:24).

The writers of the Book of Mormon frequently felt this guidance (see W of M 1:6 and footnotes). Here is a valuable insight into its careful preparation:

> This ancient preparation of the Book of Mormon was as unique as its latter-day translation. And its divine preparation is the key to its power and importance. The Lord carefully prepared the prophets who wrote this record, especially the three major ones: Nephi, Mormon, and Moroni. Nephi began the record, left us more of his own writings than did any other Book of Mormon prophet, and gave directions concerning future inclusions. Mormon abridged and commented on the record. Moroni concluded the record, abridged the book of Ether, and later delivered the gold plates to Joseph Smith (D&C 27:5). (Bruce A. Van Orden and Brent L. Top, eds., *Doctrines of the Book of Mormon: 1991 Sperry Symposium on the Book of Mormon* [Salt Lake City: Deseret Book, 1992], 71)

Such extensive foreknowledge extends to our own lives, as well as those of the prophets. We can accomplish great things in life if we are sufficiently prepared to play our part.

LIKENING THE SCRIPTURES TO OUR LIVES

Doctrine and Covenants 10:4–5 "Do not run faster or labor more than you have strength and means provided to enable you to translate; but be diligent unto the end. Pray always, that you may come off conqueror; yea, that you may conquer Satan, and that you may escape the hands of the servants of Satan that do uphold his work."

Application: Part of the Lord's schooling of Joseph Smith was teaching him to balance and understand his roles in life and the work he was called to. The Lord emphasizes here that a man or woman does not have enough strength alone to accomplish His work. Joseph had to learn to rely on the Lord's strength and direction of his own ability. So we should be prudent as stewards of the Lord, balancing our efforts in wisdom and pacing our devoted service in keeping with our capacities. Nevertheless, we should pray for victory and remember that the Lord will sustain and support us in our valiant efforts to help build the kingdom of God. "For behold, I do not require at their hands to fight the battles of Zion; for, as I said in a former commandment, even so will I fulfil—I will fight your battles" (D&C 105:14; see 98:37).

2. LATTER-DAY MIRACLE: THE WORD OF GOD FROM ANCIENT AMERICA

THEME: The Lord Himself identified the nature of the miracle by which His word from all branches of Israel would be restored: "And it shall come to pass that my people, which are of the house of Israel, shall be gathered home unto the lands of their possessions; and my word also shall be gathered in one. And I will show unto them that fight against my word and against my people, who are of the house of Israel, that I am God, and that I covenanted with Abraham that I would remember his seed forever" (2 Ne. 29:14).

MODERN PROPHETS SPEAK

Ezra Taft Benson:

> The ancient preparation of the Book of Mormon, its preservation, and its publication verify Nephi's words that "the Lord knoweth all things from the beginning; wherefore, he prepareth a way to accomplish all his works among the children of men; for behold, he hath all power unto the fulfilling of all his words" (1 Ne. 9:6). . . . The origin, preparation, translation, and verification of the truth of the Book of Mormon have all been retained in the hands of the Lord, and the Lord makes no mistakes. You can be assured of that. (*A Witness and a Warning: A Modern-Day Prophet Testifies of the Book of Mormon* [Salt Lake City: Deseret Book, 1988], 31)

ILLUSTRATIONS FOR OUR TIMES

The Lord Preserves His Record—The Book of Mormon

The writers of the ancient record were commanded to keep the record safe (see, for example, Alma's instructions to his son Helaman in Alma 37). Joseph was likewise reminded by the angel Moroni (see JS—H 1:60). He was attacked and had to struggle to his utmost in order to preserve the record. His mother recorded many incidents which required ingenuity and outright exertion. Here is one such time:

> Joseph kept the Urim and Thummim constantly about his person, by the use of which he could in a moment tell whether the plates were in any danger. . . .
>
> The plates were secreted about three miles from home, in the following manner: Finding an old birch log much decayed, excepting the bark, which was in a measure sound, he took his pocketknife and cut the bark with some care, then turned it back and made a hole of sufficient size to receive the plates, and, laying them in the cavity thus formed, he replaced the bark; after which he laid across the log in several places some old stuff that happened to lie near, in order to conceal, as much as possible, the place in which they were deposited.
>
> Joseph took the plates from their place and, wrapping them in his linen frock, placed them under his arm and started for the house After walking a short distance in the road, he thought it would be safer to leave the road and go through the woods. Traveling some distance after he left the road, he came to a large windfall, and as he was jumping over a log, a man sprang up from behind and gave him a heavy blow with a gun. Joseph turned around and knocked him to the ground, and then ran at the top of his speed. About half a mile further, he was attacked again in precisely the same way. He soon brought this one down also and ran on again, but before he got home, he was accosted the third time with a severe stroke with a gun. When he struck the last one, he dislocated his thumb, which, however, he did not notice till he came in sight of the house. He threw himself down in the corner of the fence to recover his breath. As soon as he was able, he rose and finished his race for the house, where he arrived altogether speechless from fright and the exhaustion of running. (Lucy Mack Smith, *The Revised and Enhanced History of Joseph Smith by His Mother*, ed. Scot Facer Proctor and Maurine Jensen Proctor [Salt Lake City: Deseret Book, 1996], 142–44; see also B. H. Roberts, *A Comprehensive History of the Church*, 6 vols. [Salt Lake City: Deseret Book, 1902–32, 1:91–92])

LIKENING THE SCRIPTURES TO OUR LIVES

Doctrine and Covenants 10: 57–70 The Book of Mormon contains a history of the inhabitants of the ancient Americas. It was translated from a record kept by a branch of the house of Jacob, which was led by the hand of the Lord to the promised land. This book lends credence to the Bible and dispels contention concerning the points of the gospel. Those who will accept the gospel as set forth in the Book of Mormon will build their foundation upon the immovable rock of Jesus Christ and will be empowered to withstand the wiles of the devil.

Application: The Book of Mormon is a gift of the Lord's universal, divine love. He states here the reasons for which it is given: to show the works of other branches of Israel, to bring forth light and the true points of His doctrine, to end contention among His children, and to help us all understand the scriptures and the mysteries of heaven. These are the Lord's reasons, and so should be our motivation in studying this sacred record. The Lord is inclusive and universal in His love. His gospel is a gospel of peace, administered freely through His atoning sacrifice. Let us likewise be inclusive, loving, peaceful, and devoted in our service, enduring to the end, as we feast upon the light and fulness of the word of God imparted through the Book of Mormon and the other standard works.

3. HOW THE LAW OF WITNESSES BLESSES OUR LIVES

THEME: "In the mouth of two or three witnesses shall every word be established" (2 Cor. 13:1) is how the Apostle Paul declared the Lord's doctrine of witnessing. With the coming forth of the Book of Mormon, the Lord again provided authentic voices to testify personally of truths straight from heaven. Within the pages of the Book of Mormon, God indicates that entire compilations of written testimonies stand as witnesses, (see 2 Ne. 29:8), and He will use "as many witnesses as seemeth him good" (2 Ne. 27:14), speaking "according to [His] own pleasure" (2 Ne. 29:9). Multiple witnesses confirm vital truth, the final witness being the Holy Spirit. In the final analysis, all things "witness that there is a Supreme Creator" (Alma 30:44).

MODERN PROPHETS SPEAK

Joseph Fielding Smith:
> True to this principle of divine witnesses, the Lord declared that the Book of Mormon would bear witness of itself, to the condemnation of all who should read

and reject it; but this was not all, he would appoint witnesses to bear record of it to the world. Therefore, he chose three special witnesses, who not only beheld the plates from which the Book of Mormon came, but did so in the presence of an angel. The testimony of these three men is printed in each copy of the Book of Mormon. These men have declared that this presentation of the plates also received the testimony of God who spoke to them and commanded them to bear witness of the book to all the world. Each of these three remained true to that testimony to their death, never wavering no matter what else they may have done.

Besides these three were eight others who also testified to seeing the plates, and not one of these ever denied that testimony, though some could not stand the extreme pressure which persecution put upon them.

In this manner the Lord fulfilled the law of divine witnesses. The people in the world are therefore duly warned, and if they fight against the Book of Mormon and condemn its teachings, they shall answer for it before the judgment seat of God. (*AGQ,* 2:198)

ILLUSTRATIONS FOR OUR TIMES

The Witnesses Remained Firm in Their Testimony

Oliver Cowdery:

> What did Oliver Cowdery (one of the three witnesses to the Book of Mormon) say, after he had been away from the Church years and years? He saw and conversed with the angels, who showed him the plates, and he handled them. He left the Church because he lost the love of truth; and after he had traveled alone for years, a gentleman walked into his law office and said to him, "Mr. Cowdery, what do you think of the Book of Mormon now? Do you believe that it is true?" He replied, "No, sir, I do not!" "Well," said the gentleman, "I thought as much; for I concluded that you had seen the folly of your ways and had resolved to renounce what you once declared to be true." "Sir, you mistake me; I do not believe that the Book of Mormon is true; I am past belief on that point, for I *know* that it is true, as well as I know that you now sit before me." "Do you still testify that you saw an angel?" "Yes, as much as I see you now; and I know the Book of Mormon to be true." Yet he forsook it. Every honest person who has fairly heard it knows that "Mormonism" is true, if they have had the testimony of it; but to practice it in our lives is another thing. (Brigham Young, *Discourses of Brigham Young,* sel. John A. Widtsoe [Salt Lake City: Deseret Book, 1954], 110)

Martin Harris:

In 1869, efforts were renewed to bring Martin Harris to Utah. William H. Homer, Edward Stevenson, Brigham Young, and many other Latter-day Saints helped him financially to make the journey. Still active and vigorous at age eighty-seven, Martin Harris, accompanied by Edward Stevenson, arrived by train in Salt Lake City on August 30, 1870. He accepted rebaptism as evidence of his reaffirmation of faith on September 17, 1870, and, at Brigham Young's invitation, publicly testified of the Book of Mormon. He moved to Harrisville, then to Smithfield, Utah, . . . and in 1874 to Clarkston, Utah, where he died on July 10, 1875, after once more bearing testimony of the Book of Mormon.

Martin Harris inspired a folk-hero tradition that has lasted down to the present. In 1983 the Church's musical play *Martin Harris: The Man Who Knew* was produced in Clarkston. The play marked a fourth generation's rehearsal of Martin Harris's witness: "Yes, I did see the plates on which the Book of Mormon was written. I did see the angel, I did hear the voice of God, and I do know that Joseph Smith is a true Prophet of God, holding the keys of the Holy Priesthood" ("The Last Testimony of Martin Harris," recorded by William H. Homer in a statement sworn before J. W. Robinson, April 9, 1927, Church Historical Archives). (Daniel H. Ludlow, ed., *Encyclopedia of Mormonism,* 4 vols. [New York: Macmillan, 1992], 2:576)

David Whitmer:

This testimony was given in 1881, because a certain individual had said that David Whitmer had declared to him that his testimony was not true. David Whitmer calls attention to the fact that this man lied.

"Unto all nations, kindred, tongues and people unto whom these presents shall come—It having been represented by one John Murphy of Polo (Caldwell County) Missouri that I had in a conversation with him last summer, denied my testimony as one of the three witnesses to the *Book of Mormon*—

"To the end therefore, that he may understand me now, if he did not then, and that the world may know the truth, I wish now, standing as it were, in the very sunset of life, and in the fear of God, once for all to make this public statement:

"*That I have never at any time, denied that testimony or any part thereof,* which has so long since been published with that book, as one of the three witnesses.
Those who know me best, will know that I have always adhered to that testimony." (Joseph Fielding Smith, *DS,* 1:223–24)

LIKENING THE SCRIPTURES TO OUR LIVES

Doctrine and Covenants 17:2–3 In order to obtain a view of the spiritual things of the Lord, we must first show forth our faith, even as the prophets of old.

Application: The Three Witnesses exercised faith in order to gain the privilege of witnessing holy things. That experience obligated them to bear testimony to the world confirming the divinity of the work. Similarly, all faithful Saints of God participate in the miracle of knowing through the Spirit that the gospel is true. "No man can say that Jesus is the Lord, but by the Holy Ghost" (1 Cor. 12:3). That blessing obligates us, in turn, to share our sincere testimony with others at all times.

4. OUR PERSONAL RESPONSIBILITY TO THE BOOK OF MORMON

THEME: How favored of the Lord are those who have received, or who will yet receive, this sacred volume of scripture that confirms, alongside the Holy Bible, that Jesus is the Christ, the Redeemer, the Holy One of Israel! How great is our responsibility to study and ponder the message contained in the Book of Mormon and seek the blessing of the Holy Spirit to know that it is true. President Gordon B. Hinckley has pondered: "I cannot understand why the Christian world does not accept this book. I would think they would be looking for anything and everything that would establish without question the reality and the divinity of the Savior of the world" (*Ensign,* November 2002, 81).

MODERN PROPHETS SPEAK

Gordon B. Hinckley:

> Without reservation I promise you that if you will prayerfully read the Book of Mormon, regardless of how many times you previously have read it, there will come into your hearts an added measure of the Spirit of the Lord. There will come a strengthened resolution to walk in obedience to his commandments, and there will come a stronger testimony of the living reality of the Son of God. (*TGBH,* 41)

Ezra Taft Benson:

> The Book of Mormon must be re-enthroned in the minds and hearts of our people. We must honor it by reading it, by studying it, by taking its precepts into our lives and transforming them into lives required of the true followers of Christ. President Joseph Fielding Smith said: "It seems to me that any member of this Church would

never be satisfied until he or she had read the Book of Mormon time and time again, and thoroughly considered it so that he or she could bear witness that it is in very deed a record with the inspiration of the Almighty upon it, and that its history is true. . . . No member of this Church can stand approved in the presence of God who has not seriously and carefully read the Book of Mormon" (CR, October 1961, 18). (*TETB*, 57)

ILLUSTRATIONS FOR OUR TIMES

The Role of the Book of Mormon in Church History and Future

Following President Spencer W. Kimball's death, and two weeks before he would be sustained as President of the Church, President Benson traveled to Kirtland, Ohio, on March 22, 1986. He deeply desired to visit in the Newel K. Whitney store. It was there that section 84 was given. The message and theme of his presidency that he would soon deliver in general conference was centered on Doctrine and Covenants 84:54–57, and he wanted to stand where it was originally revealed. I had the privilege of accompanying him in Kirtland. His mind focused on Joseph sitting in that plain and simple revelation room. We read together these words that the Lord dictated to Joseph Smith, "And your minds in times past have been darkened because of unbelief, and because you have treated lightly the things you have received—Which vanity and unbelief have brought the whole church under condemnation. And this condemnation resteth upon the children of Zion, even all. And they shall remain under this condemnation until they repent and remember the new covenant, even the Book of Mormon and the former commandments which I have given them, not only to say, but to do according to that which I have written" (D&C 84:54–57).

We then went into the School of the Prophets room, where President Benson told a few of us who had gathered, "I hope you will pray for me. I need it. I have five conference addresses to make in two weeks. I love the Latter-day Saints. I am determined to do all I can to further the work and give it direction. The Lord is not well pleased with us in the attention we are giving to the Book of Mormon. We need it in our homes and families. It represents the answers to the problems of today. Flora and I try to read it once every year. She reads better with one eye than I do with two. We have done it for sixty years of glorious life together. I recommend it to any of you." President Benson then bore his testimony and said, "This work will prevail in spite of the adversary. It will fill the earth as these early brethren knew."

President Benson expressed his deep feelings and the inspiration he had received regarding his charge to the Church. Two weeks later he explained it to the Church. His instruction:

> The Lord inspired His servant Lorenzo Snow to reemphasize the principle of tithing to redeem the Church from financial bondage. In those days the General Authorities took

that message to the members of the Church. Now, in our day, the Lord has revealed the need to reemphasize the Book of Mormon to get the Church and all the children of Zion out from under condemnation—the scourge and judgment. . . . This message must be carried to the members of the Church throughout the world. . . . I promise you that from this moment forward, if we will daily sup from its pages and abide by its precepts, God will pour out upon each child of Zion and the Church a blessing hitherto unknown—and we will plead to the Lord that He will begin to lift the condemnation—the scourge and judgment. Of this I bear solemn witness. (*Ensign,* May 1986, 78)

That same special day, in Hiram, Ohio, I watched as a sixteen-year-old young man—recently baptized—approached and said he wanted to ask President Benson how one prepares to become a prophet. As he shook President Benson's hand, President Benson said, "Before you ask your question, let me ask you a question. Are you going on a mission?" The young man hesitatingly replied, "Yes," and then started his question with, "How do you prepare to . . . ?" President Benson interrupted him and replied, "Read the Book of Mormon and then read it again, again, and again. You do that, and you will be one of the best missionaries the Church has ever had." (Anderson)

LIKENING THE SCRIPTURES TO OUR LIVES

Doctrine and Covenants 84:54–57 Church members must repent for treating lightly the revelations they have received and remain under condemnation until they remember and act according to the new covenant of the Book of Mormon and the other commandments given them.

Application: We are taught that the Church as a whole is still under this condemnation. Our responsibility as individuals and as a church is to not just read the Book of Mormon, but study, cherish, apply, and share its teachings. If we do not, the work of so many prophets to preserve and bring it forth would be in vain and the work of the Lord would stop, in our lives and in the world as a whole. Truly, our responsibility to this book is great. We owe so much to those who made its teachings accessible to us.

SUMMARY

The purpose of the Lord in bringing forth the Book of Mormon is elucidated plainly by Moroni in the Title Page: "Which is to show unto the remnant of the house of Israel what great things the Lord hath done for their fathers; and that they may know the covenants of the Lord, that they are not cast off forever—And also to the convincing of the Jew and Gentile that Jesus is the Christ, the Eternal God, manifesting himself unto all nations." Great and inspiring stories from the past, great covenants for the present, great hope for the future—all founded upon the mission and Atonement of Jesus Christ—these are the purposes of the Book of Mormon.

We can deepen our grasp of this monumental work by (1) studying how the Lord prepares His servants for accomplishing all that He asks of them, memorably demonstrated in the consecrated life of the Prophet Joseph Smith; (2) accepting the Book of Mormon as a latter-day miracle that brings to life the word of God revealed through His prophets in ancient America, chosen men who were blessed to view our day and leave a heritage of vital instruction to prepare us for the Second Coming; (3) believing the words of the Lord's witnesses who testify of the truthfulness of the Book of Mormon—especially the witness of the Spirit given to those who seek truth with faith and devotion, nothing doubting; and (4) remaining steadfast in maintaining covenants and principles of the gospel that are taught in the Book of Mormon.

Let us always remember, with equal certainty, the witness of the Almighty Himself: "And he [Joseph Smith] has translated the book, even that part which I have commanded him, and as your Lord and your God liveth it is true" (D&C 17:6).

CHAPTER FIVE

"THIS IS *the* SPIRIT *of* REVELATION"

Reading Assignment: Doctrine and Covenants 6; 8; 9; Joseph Smith—History 1:8–17.

Additional Reading: Doctrine and Covenants 5:24; 25:10; 30:2; 63:23; 88:63–64; 138:1–11.

> *After we experienced our spiritual birth, Heavenly Father counseled and corrected us, and we were instructed, enlightened, and edified in His holy presence. Now that we have experienced our physical birth in mortality, He desires to continue to communicate with us and to give us counsel and direction. He does this through personal revelation, which involves preparation, prayer, and promptings. Personal revelation is one of the greatest gifts and blessings we can receive. (L. Lionel Kendrick,* Ensign, *September 1999, 7)*

THEMES *for* LIVING

1. Personal Revelation Conditioned on Faith and Guidance from the Holy Spirit
2. Preparation and Worthiness: The Keys to Receiving Personal Revelation

INTRODUCTION

The promise of the Lord unto His children is magnificent: "But unto him that keepeth my commandments I will give the mysteries of my kingdom, and the same shall be in him a well of living water, springing up unto everlasting life" (D&C 63:23). This chapter will discuss how to draw living water from the well of inspiration. One of the greatest lessons of the Restoration is the availability of such rivers of revelation from the Almighty to all who will approach Him in faith and humility, nothing doubting. "For he that diligently seeketh shall find; and the mysteries of God shall be unfolded unto them, by the power of the Holy Ghost, as well in these times as in times of old, and as well in times of old as in times to come; wherefore, the course of the Lord is one eternal round" (1 Ne. 10:19; see also D&C 20:11–12). Personal revelation is conditioned on following specific steps that the Lord, in His mercy and love, has taught us through the scriptures and the words of modern-day prophets.

MOMENT OF TRUTH

We perceive in the experiences of Joseph Smith and Oliver Cowdery relative to the translation of the Book of Mormon mighty and unforgettable lessons in the operation of the Spirit. Faith, humility, devotion, focused activation of both mind and heart, and a willingness to subsume one's will to the will of the Father—these are the essential steps for receiving the inspiration of the Almighty. Sections 6, 8, and 9 of the Doctrine and Covenants provide a vital and dynamic syllabus for the themes of this chapter. Here is a brief summary of the setting and background for these passages.

Section 6: Given through the Prophet Joseph Smith in April 1829 at Harmony, Susquehanna County, Pennsylvania. In his journal, the Prophet entered the following:

> On the 5th day of April, 1829, Oliver Cowdery came to my house, until which time I had never seen him. He stated to me that having been teaching school in the neighborhood where my father resided, and my father being one of those who sent to the school, he went to board for a season at his house, and while there the family related to him the circumstance of my having received the plates, and accordingly he had come to make inquiries of me. Two days after the arrival of Mr. Cowdery (being the 7th of April) I commenced to translate the Book of Mormon, and he began to write for me, which having continued for some time, I inquired of the Lord through the Urim and Thummim, and obtained the following [D&C 6]. (*HC,* 1:32–33)

Oliver later commented on his experiences with the Prophet Joseph: "These were days never to be forgotten—to sit under the sound of a voice dictated by the *inspiration* of heaven, awakened the utmost gratitude of this bosom! Day after day I continued, uninterrupted, to write from his mouth, as he translated, with the *Urim* and *Thummim,* or as the Nephites would have said, 'Interpreters,' the history, or record, called 'The Book of Mormon'" (*Messenger and Advocate* 1 [October 1834]: 14).

Section 8: Given through the Prophet Joseph Smith in April 1829 at Harmony, Susquehanna County, Pennsylvania. The Lord had bestowed the opportunity to translate on Oliver Cowdery if he desired it (see D&C 6:25). Oliver did so desire, and the Prophet inquired of the Lord on this subject and received what is now section 8 (see *HC,* 1:36–37).

Section 9: Given through the Prophet Joseph Smith in April 1829, at Harmony, Susquehanna County, Pennsylvania. With the Lord's permission and commission, Oliver Cowdery had proceeded to translate the Book of Mormon, even as Joseph was doing. However, Oliver's faith was insufficient to receive the essential inspiration to accomplish the task, and the Lord here instructs him through the Prophet to be content to serve for the time being as scribe (see *HC,* 1:36–37).

1. PERSONAL REVELATION CONDITIONED ON FAITH AND GUIDANCE FROM THE HOLY SPIRIT

THEME: The early experience of Joseph and Oliver is instructive to us in gaining personal revelation. From their tutorial of receiving revelation, we learn (1) that we must ask for it and (2) that we must act on it. We also learn that this revelation comes by the Spirit (D&C 6:24) and is manifest in our minds and hearts (D&C 8:2).

MODERN PROPHETS SPEAK

Boyd K. Packer:
> The flow of revelation depends on your faith. . . . As you test gospel principles by believing without knowing, the Spirit will begin to teach you. Gradually your faith will be replaced with knowledge. (*Ensign,* November 1994, 60)

John A. Widtsoe:
> How did the Prophet Joseph Smith obtain his first revelation, his first vision? He desired something. In [a grove of trees], away from human confusion, he summoned all the strength of his nature; there he fought the demon of evil, and, at length, because of the strength of his desire and the great effort that he made, the Father and the Son descended out of the heavens and spoke eternal truth to him. (*Utah Genealogical and Historical Magazine* 12 [April 1921]: 63)

ILLUSTRATIONS FOR OUR TIME

The Joy of Teaching by the Spirit

One constant promise regarding the spirit of revelation is, "Ye are to be taught from on high" (D&C 43:16). I have personally witnessed this principle operating in the classroom. I have often observed students receiving promptings unrelated to the subject at hand. From firsthand experience, I also know of spiritual impressions a teacher or speaker receives when under the direction of the Spirit. Elder Marion G. Romney once said, "I always know when I am speaking under the inspiration of the Holy Ghost because I always learn something from what I've said" (Boyd K. Packer, *Teach Ye Diligently,* rev. ed. [Salt Lake City: Deseret Book, 1991], 357). To me, nothing exceeds the joy of teaching when the Spirit is present. The Spirit prompts thoughts and words that may not have been—could not have been—prepared in advance, yet are needed by those who listen. (Anderson)

LIKENING THE SCRIPTURES TO OUR LIVES

Doctrine and Covenants 8:9–10 "And, therefore, whatsoever you shall ask me to tell you by that means, that will I grant unto you, and you shall have knowledge concerning it. Remember that without faith you can do nothing; therefore ask in faith."

Application: The Lord instructs us here that faith is the basis of revelation. It was Joseph's faith that inspired him to approach God in the first place as a young boy (see James 1:5–6; JS—H 1:11–14). So our faith can bring personal revelation and witness.

2. PREPARATION AND WORTHINESS: THE KEYS TO RECEIVING PERSONAL REVELATION

THEME: One of the foremost necessities of preparation to be taught by the Lord is humility—the willingness to be taught, without preconceived notions (see Jacob 4:10).

MODERN PROPHETS SPEAK

Bruce R. McConkie:

> I think our concern is to get personal revelation, to know for ourselves . . . what the mind and the will of the Lord is as pertaining to us in our individual concerns and to receive confirmation of his mind and will as pertaining to his church. . . . My suggestion is that we need to devote an increasingly large portion of our time in the

actual pursuit of knowledge in the spiritual realm. When we deal with spiritual real-ities, we are not talking about gaining something by reason alone, . . . through the senses alone, but we are talking about revelation. We are talking about learning how to come to a knowledge of the things of God by attuning the spirit that we have to the eternal Spirit of God. Such a course, primarily, is the channel and way that rev-elation comes to an individual. . . . Now I say that we are *entitled* to revelation. Every member of the Church . . . is entitled to get revelation from the Holy Ghost; he is entitled to entertain angels; he is entitled to view the visions of eternity; and . . . he is entitled to see God the same way that any prophet in literal and actual reality has seen the face of Deity. (*New Era,* June 1980, 46)

ILLUSTRATIONS FOR OUR TIMES

"Behold, Thou Art . . ."

The scriptures that illustrate the Lord's personal relationship with His sons and daughters have always struck me with great force, given the implication for our spir-itual lives and development. In answer to the Lord's question about who the Apostles said He was, Peter answered: "Thou art the Christ, the Son of the Living God." In response, the Lord confirmed the personal bond with His chief Apostle: "Blessed art thou, Simon Bar-jona: for flesh and blood hath not revealed it unto thee, but my Father which is in heaven. And I say also unto thee, That thou art Peter, and upon this rock I will build my church; and the gates of hell shall not prevail against it" (Matt.16:13–18). This kind of language—"I am Christ/Thou art Peter"—reflects a unique and inspiring kind of relationship between God and man.

Note the extraordinary words the Lord spoke to Moses on the mount: "And God spake unto Moses, saying: Behold, I am the Lord God Almighty, and Endless is my name; for I am without beginning of days or end of years; and is not this endless? And, behold, thou art my son; wherefore look, and I will show thee the workmanship of mine hands; but not all, for my works are without end, and also my words, for they never cease. . . . And I have a work for thee, Moses, my son; and thou art in the simil-itude of mine Only Begotten; and mine Only Begotten is and shall be the Savior, for he is full of grace and truth; but there is no God beside me, and all things are present with me, for I know them all" (Moses 1:3–4, 6). Again: "I am the Lord God/Thou art my son." In bestowing similar trust upon the prophet Nephi, son of Helaman, the Lord said, "Behold, thou art Nephi, and I am God" (Hel. 10:6).

This formula of "Thou art . . ." occurs frequently in the early sections of the Doctrine and Covenants as well. To the prophet of the Restoration, the Lord said, "Behold, thou art Joseph, and thou wast chosen to do the work of the Lord" (D&C 3:9; see 14:2, 9–11). To the Prophet's scribe, the Lord said, "Behold, I am God; give heed unto my word. . . . Behold, thou art Oliver, and I have spoken unto thee because of thy desires; therefore treasure up these words in thy heart" (D&C 6: 2, 20). To the Prophet's brother, the Lord said, "Behold, I am God; give heed to my word. . . . Behold thou art Hyrum, my son; seek the kingdom of God, and all things shall be added according to that which is just. Build upon my rock, which is my gospel; Deny not the spirit of revelation, nor the spirit of prophecy, for wo unto him that denieth these things; Therefore, treasure up in your heart until the time which is in my wisdom that you shall go forth. Behold, I speak unto all who have good desires, and have thrust in their sickle to reap" (D&C 11:23–27; see also Morm. 9:7–8).

What an extraordinary condescension on the part of Deity to cultivate a personal relationship with His sons and daughters! And yet the scriptures teach that this is not only possible but essential in the Lord's design for humankind. "And seek the face of the Lord always, that in patience ye may possess your souls, and ye shall have eternal life" (D&C 101:38). Seeking the face of the Lord (rather than just His influence) implies a person-to-person (or rather a God-to-person) relationship (see Ex. 33:11; Ether 3:17, 20; 12:39). Beginning with Adam, the Lord sanctioned and directed one-on-one contact with His children: "And thou art after the order of him who was without beginning of days or end of years, from all eternity to all eternity. Behold, thou art one in me, a son of God; and thus may all become my sons. Amen" (Moses 6:67–68).

"Thou art . . ." is one of the most inspiring doctrines of the gospel. Several of the references have shown that this applies not just to the prophets, but to everyone. May we, in all humility and with a prayerful heart, venture to hear, through the inspiration of the Spirit, "Behold, I am God . . . and thou art [your own personal name]. I have a work for thee." May we seek and obtain His inspiration to guide our lives in keeping with His commandments. (Allen)

I Have Learned to Know the Spirit When I See It at Work

In serving as a patriarch, I am particularly sensitive to being " taught from on high." One day a man came for a patriarchal blessing. He explained that he had been seeking an answer to a personal problem he had carried with him for some time. He had prayed about it before coming and felt that the answer would be given through his patriarchal blessing. I had no idea what the answer could be. We prayed together, and I told him that if I was prompted to address it, I would.

As we proceeded with the blessing, no prompting came to his quandary. I felt somewhat disappointed for this brother and closed the blessing. Much to my surprise, this man stood up and with tears in his eyes thanked me for giving him the answer. The Spirit somehow used the occasion and words that I had spoken to reveal to him the answer he was seeking. I suggested that he go home and promptly record the answer as he had received it. From this, I again learned a lesson that it is the Spirit that teaches. This man was similar, in a sense, to Oliver Cowdery. The Lord told Oliver, "Thou hast inquired of me and I did enlighten thy mind. . . . And now, behold, you have received a witness; for . . . I have told you things which no man knoweth" (D&C 6:15, 24).

I don't know if I can fully define the spirit of revelation, but I have learned to know it when I see it or feel it. The Lord told this good man things he didn't even tell me as patriarch. The Lord's words rang in my mind, "You have received a witness. . . . I have told you things which no man knoweth." (Anderson)

LIKENING THE SCRIPTURES TO OUR LIVES

Doctrine and Covenants 9:7–8 If we are to receive spiritual inspiration, we must first put forth intense effort.

Application: The Lord taught Oliver Cowdery the spiritual procedure for inquiring of the Lord. We are endowed with the capacity to reason, ponder, and apply the light of our understanding to challenges. As we do so, investing our time and effort in worthy objectives, the Lord will bless us with the confirmation of the Spirit or direct us away from what is not correct and appropriate. He generally requires study, fasting, and prayer for our greatest growth (see Alma 17:2–3; Matt. 17:20–21).

SUMMARY

We learn through the written and spoken word of God that personal revelation is conditioned on faith and guidance from the Holy Spirit and that the keys to receiving personal revelation are preparation and worthiness. The Lord counsels us, "Draw near unto me and I will draw near unto you; seek me diligently and ye shall find me; ask, and ye shall receive; knock, and it shall be opened unto you. Whatsoever ye ask the Father in my name it shall be given unto you, that is expedient for you" (D&C 88:63–64).

CHAPTER SIX

"I WILL TELL YOU *in* YOUR MIND *and in* YOUR HEART, *by the* HOLY GHOST"

Reading Assignment: Doctrine and Covenants 6; 8; 9; 11.

Additional Reading: Doctrine and Covenants 6:22–23; 8:2–3; 9:8–9; 11:12–14; 42:61; 50:23–24; 85:6; 128:1; 136:32–33.

Sometimes new teachers wonder if they are teaching by the Spirit. How do we know when the Spirit is present? The Spirit manifests itself in different ways. It can cause a burning in our bosoms, eliminate confusion and bring peace to our minds, lead us to do good, fill our souls with joy, and bring us faith and love (see D&C 6:23; 9:7–9; 11:12–13; Gal. 5:22–23). The Spirit also can help teachers know the needs of the students and what to emphasize in the lesson. When you feel these things while teaching, when you see the students' desire to do good, when you feel peace and love and joy in your classroom, please share these feelings with your students. Please help young people identify the Spirit in their lives. That will be a powerful blessing for them. (Patricia P. Pinegar, Liahona, *February 1997, 28)*

THEMES *for* LIVING

1. Recognizing the Communications of the Spirit
2. Concerns and Cautions with Personal Revelation
3. When the Answers Do Not Seem to Come

INTRODUCTION

One of the Lord's greatest promises to His children is to guide them by inspiration through the pathways of mortality: "For behold, again I say unto you that if ye will enter in by the way, and receive the Holy Ghost, it will show unto you all things what ye should do" (2 Ne. 32:5). The Lord does not leave us without an anchor to secure our souls to His abiding principles and doctrines. By pondering with faith and asking in the spirit of hope, we can receive spiritual guidance to transcend the challenges of this probationary state and lead our families along the iron rod toward the love of God that inheres in the gospel of Jesus Christ.

MOMENT OF TRUTH

Great lessons about the Lord's system of spiritual communication with His children can be gleaned from a close reading and pondering of the words in the Doctrine and Covenants. In this regard, Doctrine and Covenants sections 6, 8, and 9 are particularly useful, as the discussion in the previous chapter demonstrated. Section 11 is also helpful for deepening our understanding of personal inspiration and the confirmation of the Spirit. Here is a brief background to that section.

Section 11: Given through the Prophet Joseph Smith for his brother Hyrum in May 1829 at Harmony, Susquehanna County, Pennsylvania, subsequent to the restoration of the Aaronic Priesthood (May 15 of that year) and the baptism of Samuel H. Smith (May 25). Hyrum had arrived in Harmony for a visit and requested that Joseph inquire of the Lord through the Urim and Thummim for guidance. The resulting revelation is now known as section 11. The two brothers were the closest of friends throughout their lives, and the opportunity for the Prophet to seek a spiritual blessing for Hyrum was a moment of solemn tenderness and joy.

Later on in his career, the Prophet Joseph, beset with mounting persecution and difficulties, was to pay this tribute to Hyrum: "There was Brother Hyrum who next took me by the hand—a natural brother. Thought I to myself, Brother Hyrum, what a faithful heart you have got! Oh may the Eternal Jehovah crown eternal blessings upon your head, as a reward for the care you have had for my soul! O how many are the sorrows we have shared together; and again we find ourselves shackled with the unrelenting hand of oppression. Hyrum, thy name shall be written in the book of the law of the Lord, for those who come after thee to look upon, that they may pattern after thy works" (*HC,* 5:107–8).

1. RECOGNIZING THE COMMUNICATIONS OF THE SPIRIT

THEME: Amid the cacophony of sensory overload that constitutes our modern culture, there comes to the penitent and prayerful seeker of truth a blessing of unspeakable power and joy: the penetrating whisperings of the Spirit of the Lord, imparting truth, giving guidance, confirming the "godly walk and conversation" (D&C 20:69) to be emulated by the Saints. How to recognize and heed these divine communications is the key upon which all righteousness depends.

MODERN PROPHETS SPEAK

Joseph Smith:

> A person may profit by noticing the first intimation of the spirit of revelation; for instance, when you feel pure intelligence flowing into you, it may give you sudden strokes of ideas, so that by noticing it, you may find it fulfilled the same day or soon; (i.e) those things that were presented unto your minds by the Spirit of God, will come to pass; and thus by learning the Spirit of God and understanding it, you may grow into the principle of revelation until you become perfect in Christ Jesus. (*TPJS,* 151)

ILLUSTRATIONS FOR OUR TIMES

The Spirit Is the Key

The following excerpt discusses how missionaries teach investigators how to recognize the Spirit. As we are all seeking to gain a deeper, stronger testimony and receive revelation from the Lord, we are in a way investigators and need to learn to recognize the Spirit as well as any convert to the Church does.

> In Galatians 5:22, we read: "But the fruit of the Spirit is love, joy, peace, longsuffering, gentleness, goodness, faith."

> When our investigators feel these things as they read the Book of Mormon, they'll feel the Spirit and know that the book is true. Sometimes our investigators are unfamiliar with the Spirit, and they need a little help identifying where these wonderful feelings come from.

> "How do you feel when you read the Book of Mormon?" you might ask them.

> "Good," they'll answer.

"All good comes from our Heavenly Father," you'll teach. "And those feelings are a witness that the Book of Mormon is true." The greatest tool we have to bring people unto Christ is the Book of Mormon.

Here are some things that our investigators will feel as they read: They'll understand the glorious truths; they'll recognize particular doctrines; they'll know that it's uplifting and inspired. We must not fail to teach our investigators to recognize the witness of the Spirit. . . .

Investigators tend to seek a sign when they are praying about the Book of Mormon. They want lights to go on three times in succession or a visitation from an angel or something like that. We must not look for incredible signs when we're seeking to discover truth, but we must recognize the signs from the Spirit. That's why we, along with our investigators, must understand Galatians 5:22 and recognize these signs. (Ed J. Pinegar, *Especially for Missionaries,* 4 vols. [American Fork, UT: Covenant Communications, 1997], 1:15–16)

LIKENING THE SCRIPTURES TO OUR LIVES

Doctrine and Covenants 6:22–24 God knows each of us personally and is ready to reveal His wisdom to those with an open heart.

Application: Too often we think of the Spirit communicating to us in vague, general feelings of peace or comfort. But the Lord can and does give us individual and specific attention through personal revelation by the Holy Ghost. The Lord told Oliver Cowdery through Joseph Smith of a private spiritual experience that no one could have known about except Oliver. What a testimony of the Lord's intimate knowledge of each of us! Let us learn to approach the Lord in personal prayer, with confidence in His love, compassion, and mercy, and then remain worthy of His guidance and inspiration.

2. CONCERNS AND CAUTIONS WITH PERSONAL REVELATION

THEME: As with all of the Lord's designs, communication through the Spirit "must needs be done in mine own way" (D&C 104:16). We are to seek the will of the Lord always, asking Him in all faith and humility for those things that support and enhance spiritual growth for ourselves, our families, and those over whom we have been given a stewardship. We do not aggrandize ourselves on a quest to seek light that encroaches over the boundaries of what the Lord has commissioned others to do. Nor do we importune the Lord to grant us power and might to bring about our own worldly triumphs. Rather, we seek that which brings light and truth into our lives, that which edifies and lifts, that which purifies and sanctifies—all for the glory of God and the building up of His kingdom.

MODERN PROPHETS SPEAK

Boyd K. Packer:

> All inspiration does not come from God (see D&C 46:7). The evil one has the power to tap into those channels of revelation and send conflicting signals which can mislead and confuse us. There are promptings from evil sources which are so carefully counterfeited as to deceive even the very elect (see Matt. 24:24).

> Nevertheless, we can learn to discern these spirits. Even with every member having the right to revelation, the Church can be maintained as a house of order.

> Revelation comes in an orderly way in the Church. We are entitled to personal revelation. However, unless we are set apart to some presiding office, we will not receive revelations concerning what others should do. . . .

> An unusual spiritual experience should not be regarded as a personal call to direct others. It is my conviction that experiences of a special, sacred nature are individual and should be kept to oneself.

> Few things disturb the channels of revelation quite so effectively as those people who are misled and think themselves to be chosen to instruct others when they are not chosen.

> Others, fearing they also might go astray, then hold back and do not seek the source of divine revelation. Obedience to constituted priesthood authority will protect us from going astray. (*Ensign,* November 1989, 14)

ILLUSTRATIONS FOR OUR TIMES

To Write in the Name of the Lord

Revelation can be received according to our stewardships, callings, and roles in life (see D&C 28:2, 6–7; 43:2–4). Never suppose that we are entitled to usurp or replace those placed in authority over us. It is true that we can sit in council and give feedback and information, but it is imperative to recognize the rights and privileges pertaining to revelation, as exemplified by the following:

Doubts were raised at the conference that was considering publishing the collected revelations when certain brethren criticized Joseph Smith's language. Such criticisms should not have been taken seriously, because in a revelation received during that same conference the Lord had explained that these revelations "were given unto my servants in their weakness, after the manner of their language, that they might come to understanding" (D&C 1:24). Still, the Lord challenged the critics to "appoint him that is the most wise among you" and have him try to duplicate the "least" of the revelations given through the Prophet (D&C 67:6). (Richard O. Cowan, *Answers to Your Questions about the Doctrine and Covenants* [Salt Lake City: Deseret Book, 1996], 79)

Ask, Seek, and Knock

The spirit of revelation constantly guided Joseph Smith as he received revelations in the Doctrine and Covenants. It is interesting to me that the Lord didn't approach Joseph and say, "Sit down and write. I have a revelation for you." It worked the other way. Joseph would make careful preparation and then approach the Lord for the revelation. The Lord has consistently taught the principle of "ask, seek, and knock" in scripture. Passages containing this admonition appear in the Bible, the Book of Mormon, and the Doctrine and Covenants. Elder Boyd K. Packer said, "No message appears in scripture more times, in more ways than 'Ask, and ye shall receive'" (CR, October 1991, 26). I have come to regard this as one of those laws "irrevocably decreed in heaven . . . upon which all blessings are predicated" (D&C 130:20). I believe that the Lord waits for us to come to Him and then rewards us with answers to our prayers. (Anderson)

LIKENING THE SCRIPTURES TO OUR LIVES

Doctrine and Covenants 88:63–65 The Lord has admonished us to ask in faith, with an eye single to His glory, believing that we shall receive.

Application: Our asking in faith should always be directed to those things that are expedient for our good and the good of others (see Moro. 7:33). We must consider the desire of our hearts in approaching the Lord, that we do not ask amiss. If we are directed by the Spirit in our prayers, then we will always desire that the Lord's will be done—in His own way and within His own time frame (see D&C 88:68).

3. WHEN THE ANSWERS DO NOT SEEM TO COME

THEME: Patience and longsuffering are divine qualities that the Lord demonstrates on behalf of His children—dispensation after dispensation. Similarly, we should be patient and longsuffering as we seek answers through our prayers. The answers will come sooner or later: "And therefore will the Lord wait, that he may be gracious unto you, and therefore will he be exalted, that he may have mercy upon you: for the Lord is a God of judgment: blessed are all they that wait for him" (Isa. 30:18).

MODERN PROPHETS SPEAK

Robert D. Hales:

> Sometimes we are drawn into seeking and giving answers that bring recognition or notoriety to "our" thinking and to "our" opinion. Don't look for signs or answers that build you up. Humility and submissiveness to God will always be fundamental in receiving direction from Him.

> Others operate in a spirit of gratitude to the Lord for the gospel and concentrate on correcting their own imperfections. We can develop the ability to discern what spirit is influencing others and ourselves. We should seek and pray for this gift lest we be deceived. (*Ensign,* February 2002, 12)

Thomas S. Monson:

> And so I pray and calmly wait.
> I know not if the blessing sought
> Will come just in the way I thought,
> But leave my prayers with Him alone,
> Whose ways are wiser than my own—
> Assured that He will grant my quest,
> Or send some answer far more blessed.
> (Eliza M. Hickock)

> Well might the younger generation ask, "But what about today? Does he still hear? Does he continue to answer?" To which I promptly reply: "There is no expiration date on the Lord's injunction to pray. As we remember him, he will remember us."

> Most of the time there are no flags waving or bands playing when prayer is answered. His miracles are frequently performed in a quiet and natural manner. (*Ensign,* August 1995, 2)

ILLUSTRATIONS FOR OUR TIMES

Unanswered Prayers

> I think we all have struggled with the problem of "unanswered" prayers. That's a tough situation to be in. We usually don't worry about whether or not our prayers are being answered when all is well. It's when we're in trouble, when we have special

needs, that we seek with some intensity to obtain answers to our prayers. And when those answers don't seem to come, our need seems to increase.

It's natural in that situation to contemplate, "Where are you, Heavenly Father?" "Are you listening?"

We can answer those questions by remembering that God is constant. He operates by pre-established principles, not unwisely or by whim. We should also remember that he has promised to not leave us alone.

So, it seems to me that if we're not getting answers to our prayers the problem is in our understanding or in our faithfulness or in our asking, not in the Lord.

What are some common problems that may be holding us back from receiving answers? One is that we ask *impatiently*. We sometimes expect the Lord to give us immediate answers. But he hasn't promised that—and sometimes it's for our good that he wait. . . . As long as we continue in our prayers we have the promise of an answer. But we've never been promised an answer to questions that we don't ask and we've never been promised an immediate answer.

A second problem is that we don't *listen*. Our senses are constantly bombarded with other information. . . . But we can make things even worse by failing to make a real effort to listen. We utter our prayers, even with feeling and sincerity, and then immediately rise and jump into bed, rise and run to work, rise and converse with a family member about nonrelated concerns. . . .

Again, the difficulty is not with the Lord; it is with us. I believe he will give us answers fairly freely, but if we are not listening or if we are not in tune, we may not *receive* or understand the answer. The result is that we may think the Lord is not even listening, when the real problem is that *we're* not listening.

We can learn to listen by trying to rid ourselves of outside interference—as well as inside interference—and by taking the time just to feel the Spirit.

What else should we consider as we attempt to receive answers to prayer? First, we must not expect the Lord to do all the work for us. . . .

Second, we must be careful not to "ask for that which [we] ought not" (D&C 8:10). . . .

Third, we must be willing to work for our prayers to come to pass. . . . If a person prays for a testimony, he must do his part by studying and living the commandments. Fourth, we must learn how to recognize the answers when they come. . . .

There are many ways prayers may be answered. Joseph Smith often had heavenly visitations. Moses heard a voice from a burning bush. Some people receive dreams. I must confess that I have never seen a vision nor had such a dream, nor have I ever heard an audible voice speak to me from the other side. But I can identify with Enos, who said, "While I was thus struggling in the spirit, behold, the voice of the Lord came into my mind" (Enos 1:10).

This is the way the Lord usually answers my prayers. Perhaps he knows it is the way I'm best equipped to hear him. (Lindsay R. Curtis, *Ensign*, January 1980, 48)

The Wisdom Tooth

For many years that impacted tooth had been dormant—a phantom object barely protruding from the gum. From time to time various dentists had warned that it really should come out. But it had not offered any challenges—no pain, no discomfort. It had just continued its valueless existence as a kind of bothersome condition that one worries about under the surface of daily life. "This looks like it might be getting some decay," said yet one more dentist a year or so ago. No action—until upon the most recent visit the medical authority made it clear that this wisdom tooth was headed for trouble that could have far-reaching implications for health and well-being. Finally, action was taken in the office of the oral surgeon, and within a half an hour the decades-old problem was history. It would have taken the same half an hour decades ago. Procrastination doesn't help.

In a spiritual context, invisible wisdom teeth are very much like that. Sometimes there are spiritual conditions that call for review, correction, rejuvenation. Sometimes there is a history of transgression that calls for action leading to the miracle of forgiveness. Sometimes the old, impacted memories need to be brought forward so that they can be subjected to spiritual correction: "For godly sorrow worketh to repentance" (2 Cor. 7:10). Rather than carrying an impacted burden for decades, the individual might often find that half an hour of concerted and decisive action, based on sincere, prayerful penitence and with the guidance of loving ecclesiastical leaders, can bring about a wondrous effect, leading to peace and solace. That troublesome wisdom tooth decaying below the surface can be gone—forever—opening up the channels of pure communication once more with our Father in Heaven. It is true that some conditions may take longer than others to heal—but action leading to that process of healing can be taken immediately.

The Lord wants to bless us with the inspiration and the guidance of His Holy Spirit. He wants us to be freed of the burdens of sin and transgression so that pure knowledge can flow into our lives unimpeded, allowing us to rise to our potential as "children of the prophets" and "children of the covenant" (3 Ne. 20:25–26). May we all examine our spiritual condition and ensure that any troublesome, impacted sins are removed—sooner rather than later. (Allen)

LIKENING THE SCRIPTURES TO OUR LIVES

Doctrine and Covenants 136:32–33 Let us be humble, and the Lord will send forth His Spirit to enlighten the mind, invigorate the soul, and broaden the understanding.

Application: Sometimes we think we aren't getting an answer because we have a "stupor of thought" rather than affirmation. We must recognize this as a possibility. But sometimes we don't receive answers to our prayers because we haven't done all we should have before approaching the Lord. Study, ponder, balance, measure, assess, evaluate options, be innovative, plan, strategize, decide to the best of your ability—and then pray humbly for a confirmation of the direction of your life. This is the proactive way of seeking the Lord's counsel and guidance. Stay focused on things spiritual: "And seek the face of the Lord always, that in patience ye may possess your souls, and ye shall have eternal life" (D&C 101:38).

ENRICHMENT

Lessons on Spiritual Communication
In order to receive personal revelation, we must prepare our minds to be receptive to the spirit. The Lord cannot teach us or pour revelation out upon us until we are ready. Elder Russell M. Nelson taught me a valuable principle in Kirtland as we visited sites of Doctrine and Covenants revelation. As we stood in the Newell K. Whitney store and the John Johnson home, I pointed out specific questions Joseph asked the Lord which brought on the many revelations. He asked if I understood the underlying principle of revelations coming after Joseph asked. I requested that he please teach me. He said, "The Lord can only teach an enquiring mind." Just as the Lord told Oliver that he would be told in his heart and mind, we must prepare our hearts and minds to be taught. The Lord emphasized this with Oliver when He added this instruction: "You have supposed that I would give it unto you, when you took no thought save it was to ask me. . . . You must study it out in your mind; then you must ask me . . . but you feared, and the time is past" (D&C 9:7–8, 11). From this we learn that preparing our minds and exerting faith are key components to receiving personal revelation. There is no doubt that our state of mind often prevents the Lord from teaching us.

Our leaders have often counseled us that preparation is important when we seek guidance from the Lord. President David O. McKay once related an experience of a Church leader who was so busy with the affairs of his office that the Lord couldn't reach him with an uplifting experience. Referring to that experience, President McKay encouraged others to seek the Lord in "the morning hours, before we are cluttered with the cares of day." He said that these morning hours "are especially conducive to inspiration." Elder Neal A. Maxwell cited this counsel and then said, "Others have felt that solitude and reading the scriptures can create an atmosphere conducive to the Spirit and can be developed. After all, to read the words of Christ already before us is a good thing to do before asking for more" (Neal A. Maxwell, *Wherefore, Ye Must Press Forward* [Salt Lake City: Deseret Book, 1977], 121).

Prophets from past dispensations also labored with their people to prepare their minds and hearts. Speaking of those whose minds were blinded in his day, Paul concluded that the veil was "upon their heart" but prophesied that when their hearts would "turn to the Lord, the vail shall be taken away" (2 Cor. 3:14–16). Ether promised likewise to those in his day. He said that they would receive "great and marvelous things" when they would "rend that veil of unbelief which doth cause . . . hardness of heart, and blindness of mind" (Ether 4:15).

This preparation of the mind was critical to Joseph Smith and Oliver Cowdery before they could see the Savior in the Kirtland Temple. They wrote, "The veil was taken from our minds, and the eyes of our understanding were opened. We saw the Lord standing upon the breastwork of the pulpit, before us" (D&C 110:1–2). As I was re-reading this recently, the light bulb came on as I realized these words to a new depth. The veil was taken from their *minds* in addition to their *eyes*. Perhaps we need to learn better how to lift the veil from our minds so that we can see more. Joseph often felt that the state of the minds of the Saints stood in the way of receiving spiritual blessings. On New Year's Day of 1836, in reflecting on the state of the Church, Joseph Smith wrote that many who were close to him were being led away by the adversary. He concluded, "The powers of darkness seem to . . . cast a gloomy shade over the minds of my brethren and sisters, which prevents them from seeing things as they really are" (*HC*, 2:352). As parents, home and visiting teachers, and leaders, how often do we give counsel that goes unheeded because the minds of our brothers and sisters prevent them from seeing things as they really are? Do we ever receive counsel that goes unheeded for the same reason? (Anderson)

SUMMARY

There is wisdom and joy in learning to recognize the communications of the Spirit. When we humbly seek the will of the Lord always, there are fewer concerns and distractions associated with the sacred process of cultivating and heeding the promptings of the Holy Ghost. Listening with faith and hope is a skill of discipleship. In those instances where answers don't seem to come, we respond with patience and longsuffering and continue waiting on the Lord, who blesses us "in His own due time" (Enos 1:16; 3 Ne. 5:25; Morm. 5:12), according to His wisdom and love. He has stated: "If thou shalt ask, thou shalt receive revelation upon revelation, knowledge upon knowledge, that thou mayest know the mysteries and peaceable things—that which bringeth joy, that which bringeth life eternal" (D&C 42:61).

CHAPTER SEVEN

"THE FIRST PRINCIPLES and ORDINANCES of the GOSPEL"

Reading Assignment: Doctrine and Covenants 18:10–13, 22; 19:15–19, 23; 20:37; 49:13–14; 88:118; 2 Nephi 2:6–9; Alma 32:27; 42:13–24; Articles of Faith 1:3, 4.

True religious faith teaches us that there are certain principles that must be accepted and obeyed. We must have faith in God the Eternal Father and in his Son, Jesus Christ, and his atoning sacrifice. This must be followed by repentance from all sin; then baptism by immersion, after the example of the Savior, by one having authority; and the laying on of hands for the gift of the Holy Ghost. Other things are necessary, including a contrite spirit, a humble heart, obedience to the ordinances and principles of the gospel, and faithfulness to the end. This encompasses the choosing of right over wrong, following good, and abstaining from evil. (Howard W. Hunter, That We Might Have Joy *[Salt Lake City: Deseret Book, 1994], 178)*

THEMES for LIVING

1. Faith in the Lord Jesus Christ
2. Repentance Made Possible by the Atoning Sacrifice of Our Savior Jesus Christ
3. Baptism by Immersion and Taking upon Us the Name of Jesus Christ
4. The Gift of the Holy Ghost by the Laying On of Hands
5. Enduring to the End: The Pathway to Eternal Life

INTRODUCTION

The Lord's plan for ensuring eternal happiness for His children, through the power of the Atonement, is profoundly simple and glorious. It is based on just a few key steps that open up current vistas and eventual realities of immortality and eternal life to all those who embrace covenant truth with broken hearts and contrite spirits and endure to the end. By way of contrast, the age-long quest to substitute complex and convoluted worldly and materialistic philosophies that purportedly lead to happiness and fulfillment have invariably led humankind down detours toward spiritual bankruptcy and malaise. We are the offspring of God and, as such, can achieve true happiness and joy only by following the patterns of thought and action that accord with divine truth. These patterns are embodied in the principles of faith, repentance, baptism, and receiving the gift of the Holy Ghost by the priesthood of God. The Doctrine and Covenants, along with the other scriptures in the canon of holy writ, reveal, explain, confirm, and enforce the vital and indispensable program for incorporating the first principles and ordinances into our lives: "We believe that through the Atonement of Christ, all mankind may be saved, by obedience to the laws and ordinances of the gospel" (A of F 1:3).

MOMENT OF TRUTH

There are really two moments of truth that apply to the doctrines and teachings covered by this chapter. The first is the singularly sacred and profoundly transforming act of the Atonement itself—those hours of agony on the part of the Redeemer in the garden and on the cross whereby, through His own perfect obedience, He became the "author of eternal salvation unto all those that obey him" (Heb. 5:9). He empowered the system of mercy that could enable mankind, likewise through obedience, to choose the way of eternal life. The second moment of truth is the very hour—which must, of necessity, be experienced by every person who seeks to become a disciple of Christ—in which the irreversible personal commitment to rebirth and rejuvenation is made in the depths of one's soul, thus inaugurating the transition toward that mighty change of heart that allows us to become "his sons and his daughters" (Mosiah 5:7). Those two moments of truth—the Atonement of Christ and the spiritual rebirth of His individual children in keeping with the principles of divine truth—conjoin to constitute the miracle of forgiveness and the means of fulfilling the potential of all humankind to be reborn and return home once again to the presence of the Father and Son.

1. FAITH IN THE LORD JESUS CHRIST

THEME: Faith, which must be centered in Christ, is the first principle of the gospel and the power of salvation through the Atonement. Faith is the moving cause of all action in temporal as well as spiritual concerns, the principal agency through which all things are created, and "the first great governing principle which has power, dominion, and authority over all things" (Joseph Smith, *Lectures on Faith* [Salt Lake City: Deseret Book, 1985], Q&A 1:12). "Remember that without faith you can do nothing" (D&C 8:10).

MODERN PROPHETS SPEAK

Ezra Taft Benson:

> Now let me describe to you what faith in Jesus Christ means. Faith in Him is more than mere acknowledgment that He lives. It is more than professing belief. Faith in Jesus Christ consists of complete reliance on Him. As God, He has infinite power, intelligence, and love. There is no human problem beyond His capacity to solve. Because He descended below all things, He knows how to help us rise above our daily difficulties. (*TETB,* 66)

ILLUSTRATIONS FOR OUR TIMES

"I Saw the Faith of That Boy"

> A little black-haired boy, not more than eight or nine years of age, came up to me after our meeting in Basel [Switzerland], and with fear and trembling he said he wanted to shake hands with me, and when he got hold of my hand, he looked up into my eyes with his big black eyes and he said, "Brother Moyle, would you come and administer to my father?"

> When I went to that boy's home, I met a faithful mother, and an older brother. That mother threw her arms around me, and she said, "Brother Moyle, we have fasted and prayed, and especially this youngest son of mine, that he might have the courage that we older ones lacked to ask you to come to our home and bless our father who is so critically ill."

> I tell you when I saw the faith of that boy, and the faith of that mother and of that son, and of the appreciation that they had for the priesthood of God, it touched my heart to the very core. It gave me a sense of humility I would like to keep all the days of my life. The Spirit of the Lord and his power were there present, and we blessed that good father and gave to that family the desires of their heart through the gift and

power of our Heavenly Father. (Henry D. Moyle, in *Exceptional Stories from the Lives of Our Apostles,* comp. Leon R. Hartshorn [Salt Lake City: Deseret Book, 1972], 175)

LIKENING THE SCRIPTURES TO OUR LIVES

Alma 32:27 In the course of our spiritual progression, righteous desires, when acted upon, will lead to faith and, ultimately, spiritual knowledge.

Application: Knowing its centrality to salvation, Alma pleads with us to develop our faith, no matter how small the seed of our desire is. He knew it is the very foundation of righteousness. Let us remember that the foundation of righteousness is faith. We do all things by faith (see Moro. 7:33). Just men and women live by faith (see Hab. 2:4; Rom. 1:16; Gal. 3:11). We are justified by our faith by the Spirit through the grace of our Savior Jesus Christ and His atoning sacrifice (Rom. 3:28; 5:l). Faith is the shield of protection from the fiery darts of the adversary (see Eph. 6:16). Faith is evidenced by our works (see James 2:18). By faith the prophet Lehi received the blessing and the gift of the Holy Ghost. Living by the Spirit comes from faith (see 1 Ne. 10:17). Faith gives us strength (see Alma 2:30; 14:26), and it can accomplish all things. Ultimately, our faith in Christ is the only way by which we can be saved (see D&C 33:12). It's no wonder that Alma and every other prophet of God have so urgently preached the doctrine of faith in Jesus Christ.

2. REPENTANCE MADE POSSIBLE BY THE ATONING SACRIFICE OF OUR SAVIOR JESUS CHRIST

THEME: When we have faith in Christ, we have faith that His Atonement is real and that He can save us from our sins. We have faith to repent. Through repentance, the second principle of the gospel, we are able to experience the "mighty change of heart" spoken of by King Benjamin (Mosiah 5:2–3; Alma 5:13–14), the means by which we can be cleansed of our sins—even our very desire to sin. True repentance prepares us to enter into a covenant of baptism and spiritual obedience to our Father in Heaven, so that He may bless us with His Spirit and bring about our spiritual rebirth.

MODERN PROPHETS SPEAK

Harold B. Lee:

We must repent daily. In order for good to blossom it must be cultivated and exercised by constant practice, and to be truly righteous there is required a daily pruning of the evil growth of our characters by a daily repentance from sin. (*The Teachings of Harold B. Lee*, ed. Clyde J. Williams [Salt Lake City: Bookcraft, 1996], 113)

Gordon B. Hinckley:

Repentance is one of the first principles of the gospel. Forgiveness is a mark of divinity. There is hope for you. Your lives are ahead, and they can be filled with happiness, even though the past may have been marred by sin. This is a work of saving and assisting people with their problems. This is the purpose of the gospel. (*TGBH*, 548)

ILLUSTRATIONS FOR OUR TIMES

Inside Out

Several years ago I sat at the bishop's desk to interview a young man who was preparing for full-time missionary service. He had joined the Church a couple of years before and was the only Latter-day Saint in his family. He had been faithful and dependable during his brief time in the Church. I asked him all the hard questions, and he answered them to my complete satisfaction; he was as pure a person as I had met in a long time.

"Is there anything you want to tell me?" I asked. "Is there anything we ought to talk about?" I had stressed forcefully that he needed to enter the mission field completely worthy and thus be in a position to obtain the influence of the Holy Ghost.

"There is one thing we ought to discuss," he said. "I really want to be prepared for this mission, and so I've made a plan to make sure I am clean. I have done a lot of thinking in the last few weeks and made a list of every sin I have ever committed, at least the ones I can remember."

"What in the world are you going to do with such a list?" I asked.

He said he planned to devote a day to repenting of each sin.

"You know, Bill," I responded, "we do want to get you into the mission field before you are too old to serve."

He replied, "I know, Bishop. I have it worked out so that I'm repenting of the last one the day before I enter the Missionary Training Center."

I complimented him on his keen sense of timing. My heart went out to him in love, because I knew his was a sincere desire to be worthy. "Could I suggest an alternative program?"

He nodded.

"You know, Bill, there's another approach to this matter of worthiness that I would like you to consider. It's just as important to have a pure heart as it is to have clean hands, maybe even more so."

He agreed.

"I mean, have you given much thought to praying about your nature, as well as your actions?"

He wasn't sure what I meant, so we had a delightful discussion. I reminded him that most of the sins of his past had been covered by his baptism only two years earlier. "Oh, yeah," he said. "I forgot about that." Then we talked about sinfulness as well as sin, about desires as well as deeds. (Robert L. Millet, *Alive in Christ: The Miracle of Spiritual Rebirth* [Salt Lake City: Deseret Book, 1997], 111–12)

LIKENING THE SCRIPTURES TO OUR LIVES

Alma 5:31–33 In His infinite mercy, the Lord has prepared a way to rescue us from the despairs of sin; however, this protection in "the arms of His mercy" can only be enjoyed by the truly penitent.

Application: Let us never forget that we must repent or we cannot be saved. In reality, if we do not repent, believe in Christ, and get baptized, we will be damned (see 3 Ne. 11:34). If we repent, He will receive us and put into effect the plan of mercy on our behalf before the judgment bar of the Father (see Alma 42:13–15). This is His plan, His work, and His glory—that we might be made whole—and it is based on our faith in Christ and our repenting and returning to Him (see Moses 1:39). Perfection is not so much living a perfect life as it is repenting perfectly.

3. BAPTISM BY IMMERSION AND TAKING UPON US THE NAME OF JESUS CHRIST

THEME: Building on our faith in Jesus Christ and His Atonement unto repentance, the next logical step in our spiritual progress is baptism. Cleansing, renewal, rebirth as a new individual, liberation from the effects of sin—these are the beautiful and refreshing factors involved in the third principle of the gospel, baptism, by means of which we enter into a covenant with the Lord to become His sons and daughters, taking upon ourselves His sacred name forever, and promising to keep His commandments and endure to the end.

MODERN PROPHETS SPEAK

Spencer W. Kimball:

> Baptism is a covenant with God. All members have been baptized by immersion in water and have received the Holy Ghost by the laying on of hands by properly authorized men who hold the holy priesthood. We all have been received by baptism into The Church of Jesus Christ when we have humbled ourselves before God, have desired to be baptized, have come forth with broken hearts and contrite spirits, and when we have witnessed before the Church that we are truly repentant of our sins and are willing to take upon us the name of Jesus Christ, having a determination to serve him to the end and thus manifest by our works that we have received the Spirit of Christ unto the remission of our sins. (*TSWK,* 112)

ILLUSTRATIONS FOR OUR TIMES

Be Loyal

> On a hot, humid afternoon in May 1895, two missionaries made their way up the rocky, but thickly wooded hills near Smithville, Tennessee. They had been rejected by the townspeople and so had gone to seek converts among the mountain folk, who survived on hilly, low-productive farms. Traveling on foot, without purse or scrip, the elders relied upon the Spirit of the Lord and the hospitality of the people to meet their needs.

> Toward evening the missionaries arrived at the humble cabin home of my grandfather, Harvey Anderson Pinegar, and his young family. . . . In this humble mountain home the missionaries taught Grandfather and his family the true gospel of Jesus Christ.

> Grandfather wrote in his journal,

> "I investigated their doctern and I became convinced that they belonged to the only true church upon the Earth. So on the 14th day of May, 1895. . . . my wife and myself was baptized by Elder Owen M. Sanderson in Sink Creek a few rods above Jones' Mill in the 7th District of DeKalb County, Tennessee, which caused great dissatisfaction with my folks, however I went on doing the will of my Heavenly Father. I knew the Doctern was of God and not of man." . . .

There was much opposition among the people in the area toward the "Mormon religion." Harvey's happiness at becoming a member of The Church of Jesus Christ of Latter-day Saints was not shared by his brother, sisters, parents, and neighbors. Harvey soon discovered that he would be required to face opposition in the community and in his family. He was serving as a constable at the time. Upon learning of his having joined the Church his bondsmen gave up his bonds—one of these men was his own cousin.

Several times Harvey Pinegar's cabin became a place of refuge for the missionaries. The elders would help Grandfather board up the windows and doors as a protection against mobs who threatened to tar and feather the elders.

Four years after Grandfather joined the Church, my father, then a young lad eight years old, accompanied his family and the members of two other families to a baptismal service. Grandfather was to baptize his young daughter and the daughters of a neighboring family on that cold December 3, 1899. As they traveled toward the stream at Reynold's Mill, they were approached by three men on horseback. When the men asked where they were going, Grandfather explained their intentions. The leader threatened to bring a mob upon them if they carried out the baptismal service. Grandfather informed him that he and the 20 people with him would complete their errand regardless of what the man and his associates did. Grandfather and his party continued their journey to Reynold's Mill.

Arriving at the mill they located a secluded spot for the baptism. The hill above the river was covered with trees, scrub oak, and ivy. My father, young John, was perched on a fallen tree that stretched out across a sandbar into the slow-moving stream. Here he could observe every detail of this sacred ordinance. Grandfather waded out into the stream to find the right depth and then returned to the riverbank for prayer. In the quiet of the prayer John heard the sound of a cracking limb. Opening his eyes and glancing quickly up the hill through the trees he saw the men who had stopped them earlier. They had arrived with a mob to carry out their threat. One of them was by a pile of rocks and was ready to pelt the baptismal participants. Suddenly all eyes were opened as a big redbone hound owned by the leader of the mob bounded down to within a few feet of my father. Young John looked fearfully at the hound as it growled menacingly. These men and their associates were determined to stop the baptisms from being performed. My Grandfather Pinegar courageously proceeded with the services.

Convinced now that these Mormon families were unafraid of his threat, the mob leader commanded his dog to attack Grandfather Pinegar. At this moment an amazing thing happened. The dog let out a low growl and his hair bristled like that on an angry hog's back. Suddenly it bared its teeth and turned on its master, leaping at his throat and knocking him to the ground. The rest of the mob fled in fear when they saw the dog turn on its owner. As soon as the astonished leader could free himself from his dog, he left in hurried pursuit of his associates, with the dog yelping close at his heels.

A miracle had occurred! The Pinegar family and their neighbors thanked the Lord for their deliverance, and the baptismal service continued without further interruption. . . .

I am thankful for the loyalty and faith of my grandfather. His fearlessness established a heritage of faith in and love for the Lord. The sacrifices made by him and others of my forebears have made possible the many blessings of freedom and religious liberty that I enjoy today. I want to show my loyalty to my grandfather by also being loyal to the Lord. (Rex D. Pinegar, *New Era*, July 1976, 4)

LIKENING THE SCRIPTURES TO OUR LIVES

Doctrine and Covenants 20:37 Those who, in humility, desire to serve the Lord and take His name upon them and show this desire through repentance will be received into the Church by baptism.

Application: In baptism, or in partaking of the sacrament to renew our baptismal covenants, we are to be humble, come forth with a broken heart and contrite spirit, truly repent, and take upon ourselves the name of Jesus Christ with *determination* to serve Him to the end of our lives. This determination requires more than mere complacency in the gospel; it demands an active faith unto repentance on our part.

4. THE GIFT OF THE HOLY GHOST BY THE LAYING ON OF HANDS

THEME: The fourth principle of the gospel—the bestowal of the gift of the Holy Ghost by the laying on of hands—is the means by which God's supreme endowment of truth and light is granted to those who are moved by faith to repent of their sins and enter into a covenant of obedience to His commandments, thus qualifying themselves to have His Spirit always with them for guidance, comfort, enlightenment, learning, and the joyful confirmation of their testimony of the Savior's Atonement.

MODERN PROPHETS SPEAK

Bruce R. McConkie:

When we are baptized, we receive the gift of the Holy Ghost, which is the right to the constant companionship of this member of the Godhead based on faithfulness. This is the greatest gift possible to receive in mortality.

There is nothing any of us need as much as the guiding and preserving care of the Holy Spirit—the Spirit that is given by the prayer of faith to those who love and serve the Lord.

I testify that if we love the Lord, keep His commandments, and seek His Spirit, we shall be blessed beyond our fondest hopes. (*Friend,* September 1972, 10)

Ezra Taft Benson:

Pray to Heavenly Father to bless you with His Spirit at all times. We often call the Spirit the Holy Ghost. The Holy Ghost is also a gift from Heavenly Father. The Holy Ghost helps you to choose the right. The Holy Ghost will protect you from evil. He whispers to you in a still, small voice to do right. When you do good, you feel good, and that is the Holy Ghost speaking to you. The Holy Ghost is a wonderful companion. He is always there to help you. (*Ensign,* May 1989, 81)

Gordon B. Hinckley:

That knowledge comes from the word of scripture, and that testimony comes by the power of the Holy Ghost. It is a gift, sacred and wonderful, borne by revelation from the third member of the Godhead. I believe in the Holy Ghost as a personage of spirit who occupies a place with the Father and the Son, these three composing the divine Godhead. (*Ensign,* March 1998, 2)

James E. Faust:

The gift of the Holy Ghost, however, in distinction from the Spirit of God, does not come to all men and women. The ministrations of the Holy Ghost are, however, limited without receiving the gift of the Holy Ghost. The Prophet Joseph Smith taught that "there is a difference between the Holy Ghost and the gift of the Holy Ghost" (*TPJS,* 199). Many outside the Church have received revelation from the Holy Ghost, convincing them of the truth of the gospel. Cornelius, as well as many in attendance on the day of Pentecost, received the Holy Ghost before baptism (see Acts 2:1–12; 10:30–44). It is through this power that seekers after truth acquire a testimony of the Book of Mormon and the principles of the gospel.

The gift of the Holy Ghost comes after one repents and becomes worthy. It is received after baptism by the laying on of hands by those who have the authority. On the day of Pentecost, Peter instructed those who had previously been touched spiritually by the Holy Ghost, "Repent, and be baptized every one of you in the name of Jesus Christ for the remission of sins, and ye shall receive the gift of the Holy Ghost" (Acts 2:38). Those possessing the gift of the Holy Ghost can come to a greater light and testimony. The Holy Ghost bears witness of the truth and impresses upon the soul the reality of God the Father and the Son Jesus Christ so deeply that no earthly power or authority can separate him from that knowledge (see 2 Ne. 31:18). (*Ensign*, April 1996, 2)

LIKENING THE SCRIPTURES TO OUR LIVES

Doctrine and Covenants 11:12–13 "And now, verily, verily, I say unto thee, put your trust in that Spirit which leadeth to do good—yea, to do justly, to walk humbly, to judge righteously; and this is my Spirit. Verily, verily, I say unto you, I will impart unto you of my Spirit, which shall enlighten your mind, which shall fill your soul with joy."

Application: The gift of the Holy Ghost is what helps us to continue in the course we set at baptism of living according to gospel principles. As we live worthy of the Holy Ghost, we receive not only enlightenment, but the joy that is God's will that we experience in this life (see 2 Ne. 2:25).

5. ENDURING TO THE END: THE PATHWAY TO ETERNAL LIFE

THEME: The gospel is not a checklist of ordinances to be completed; it is a lifelong journey to be experienced. We can't have just one moment of faith, one moment of repentance, a single day of commitment to baptismal covenants, only one instance of inspiration from the Holy Ghost and then expect salvation. Abiding in devotion to the first principles of the gospel—faith, repentance, baptism, and the gift of the Holy Ghost—is itself a kind of principle of life called "enduring to the end," marking the milestones of spiritual progress along the pathway leading to eternal life.

MODERN PROPHETS SPEAK

Jeffrey R. Holland:

> *Enduring to the End.* This is another "first principle" beyond the four usually listed, taught by the Father himself. Nephi wrote, "I heard a voice from the Father, saying:

Yea, the words of my Beloved are true and faithful. He that endureth to the end, the same shall be saved." Nephi then added his own witness, saying, "And now, my beloved brethren, I know by this that unless a man shall endure to the end, in following the example of the Son of the living God, he cannot be saved" [2 Ne. 31:15–16]. (*Christ and the New Covenant: The Messianic Message of the Book of Mormon* [Salt Lake City: Deseret Book, 1997], 398)

Jeffrey R. Holland:

Often one hears trite, sometimes consciously apologetic references to "enduring to the end" as an addition to the first principles and ordinances of the gospel. Nevertheless, the doctrine of faithful endurance is infinitely serious, and it is here declared to be a basic principle of the gospel by the God and Father of us all. "Enduring to the end" is an integral element in the doctrine of Christ, and without it, it would have been better not to have known him. (*Christ and the New Covenant: The Messianic Message of the Book of Mormon* [Salt Lake City: Deseret Book, 1997], 54)

ILLUSTRATIONS FOR OUR TIMES

Endure to the End

May I relate an experience. Authorization, as many of you know, has been given by the Brethren for Relief Societies, under specified circumstances, to be organized in nursing or residential homes for older sisters. One day I visited such a Relief Society. The members were between seventy-five and ninety years of age. They were ambulatory, bright of mind, and enthusiastic over their society. The lesson was from the Doctrine and Covenants and was followed by testimony bearing. The sisters contributed intelligently to the lesson discussions. Their offerings reflected a knowledge of Church doctrine and familiarity with the gospel, as well as rich life experiences. It was a delightful meeting. Then came the testimony period. Each sister who spoke, one by one, prayed that she would endure to the end. As I contemplated their intelligent understanding of the gospel as demonstrated in the discussion, and as I considered how late in life it was for most of them, I thought, why would they pray that they might endure to the end? Surely they have already proved themselves.

Later, however, in private conversation with some of them, I was made aware that they were not entirely above reproach, that they had a tendency to excuse themselves for failures to comply with the laws of the gospel because of age and circumstances.

These are a few comments made by these sisters as I talked with them:

One sister said, "We have sacrament meeting here at the home, as well as Relief Society, but I never go to sacrament meeting. I am too old to be preached to." I inquired, "Don't you feel a need to partake of the sacrament?" "No," the sister indifferently replied. "I don't think it matters at my age."

Another sister said, "I want to move to a little better home. I have enough money to do so. I have no one on whom to spend my money but myself. My family does not need it, and I am no longer interested in doing things for others that cost money. I don't even pay tithing. I don't think the Lord expects it of one my age."

Still another sister, who was drinking tea as I called, said, "I almost live on tea. When I was a younger woman, you couldn't have hired me to drink a cup of tea, but I don't think it will be held against me now."

Yet another said, as we heard footsteps near the door, "I hope that's not my daughter. She only comes because she fears criticism if she doesn't. She has very little love for me, and I have very little for her."

One more comment: "I seem to be growing weaker every day, suffering as I do with pain. I used to have the elders administer to me, but I don't believe in that anymore."

Attendance at sacrament meeting, partaking of the sacrament, renewing one's covenants, the payment of tithing, observance of the Word of Wisdom, love of family, priesthood administration—all basic laws of the gospel—had been abandoned by one or the other of these sisters with a feeling of justification; yet each had earnestly prayed that she might endure to the end.

Sympathetic as we may be toward these sisters and toward their circumstances, and understanding as we may be of their actions, yet we must recognize that with clear minds they were justifying the nonobservance of God's laws. I am led to ask also, Has the Lord ever set a retirement age for keeping his commandments? (Belle Spafford, "Endure to the End," in *Remarkable Stories from the Lives of Latter-day Saint Women,* comp. Leon R. Hartshorn, 2 vols. [Salt Lake City: Deseret Book, 1973], 1:231)

LIKENING THE SCRIPTURES TO OUR LIVES

Doctrine and Covenants 14:7 "And if you keep my commandments and endure to the end, you shall have eternal life, which gift is the greatest of all the gifts of God."

Application: The gospel is taught in terms of progression; we have never "arrived" until we reach salvation, and even then we are taught that we will continue to progress eternally. True commitment to the gospel implies enduring to the end. We will press forward in Christ with hope, love, and feasting upon the word of God (see 2 Ne. 31:19–20). This will give us power to endure to the end. We will seek the cause of Zion, publish peace, and be lifted up at the last day (see 1 Ne. 13:37).

SUMMARY

The road map to salvation is mercifully simple and straightforward, marked by the steps of faith in the Lord Jesus Christ, repentance made possible by His atoning sacrifice, baptism by immersion and taking upon us His name, receiving the gift of the Holy Ghost by the laying on of hands, and enduring to the end along the pathway to eternal life. The message is pure and undefiled: "Wherefore, redemption cometh in and through the Holy Messiah; for he is full of grace and truth. Behold, he offereth himself a sacrifice for sin, to answer the ends of the law, unto all those who have a broken heart and a contrite spirit; and unto none else can the ends of the law be answered" (2 Ne. 2:6–7). The outcome is certain: "And as many as repent and are baptized in my name, which is Jesus Christ, and endure to the end, the same shall be saved" (D&C 18:13–14).

CHAPTER EIGHT

RESTORATION *of the* PRIESTHOOD *of* GOD

Reading Assignment: Doctrine and Covenants 13; 20:38–67; 27:12–13; 84:6–30; 107:1–20; 110:11–16; Joseph Smith—History 1:66–73; *Our Heritage,* pages 11–14.

Additional Reading: Doctrine and Covenants 107:23, 35; 42:43–44; 43:15–16; 84:111; 107:23, 25, 33–35, 38–39, 58, 68, 71, 87–88, 93–97; 124:91–93, 124, 128.

The priesthood has been restored, with which are connected all the blessings that ever were associated with any people upon the face of the earth; and if we know today so little in regard to the things of God, and the principles associated with eternity, with the heavens and with the angels, it is because we have not improved our privileges as we might, nor lived up to those principles which God has revealed unto us, and because we are not yet prepared for further advancement. (John Taylor, The Gospel Kingdom: Selections from the Writings and Discourses of John Taylor, ed. G. Homer Durham [Salt Lake City: Improvement Era, 1941], 136–37)

THEMES *for* LIVING

1. The Power and Purpose of the Priesthood
2. Blessings That Come through the Restoration of the Aaronic Priesthood
3. Blessings That Come through the Restoration of the Melchizedek Priesthood

INTRODUCTION

The priesthood of God is the divine and vital administering principle by means of which the Creation was accomplished and the plan of salvation made operational for achieving the "immortality and eternal life of man" (Moses 1:39). President Joseph F. Smith defined the priesthood as follows: "As pertaining to man's existence on this earth, priesthood is the power and authority of God delegated to man on earth to act in all things for the salvation of men. It is the power by which the gospel is preached; by which the ordinances of salvation are performed so that they will be binding on earth and in heaven; by which men are sealed up unto eternal life, being assured of the fulness of the Father's kingdom hereafter; and by which in due course the Lord will govern the nations of the earth and all that pertains to them" (Joseph F. Smith, *Gospel Doctrine: Selections from the Sermons and Writings of Joseph F. Smith,* comp. John A. Widtsoe, 5th ed. [Salt Lake City: Deseret Book, 1939], 136). The Doctrine and Covenants is the principal scriptural medium in the latter days for understanding and applying the principles and policies embodied in the priesthood. Few things could be deemed of greater worth to humankind, and few things should inspire more awe, humble devotion, and enduring commitment, than the singular honor of holding and administering the priesthood of God for and in behalf of His sons and daughters.

MOMENT OF TRUTH

Four extraordinary sections of the Doctrine and Covenants in particular—13, 20, 84, and 107—shed light on the nature and operation of the priesthood of God for the salvation of His children. Details concerning the coming forth of these four sections follow.

Section 13: The ordination of Joseph Smith and Oliver Cowdery to the Aaronic Priesthood along the banks of the Susquehanna River, near Harmony, Susquehanna County, Pennsylvania, on May 15, 1829. Joseph Smith explained the background to this revelation as follows:

> We still continued the work of translation, when in the ensuing month (May, 1829), we on a certain day went into the woods to pray and inquire of the Lord respecting baptism for the remission of sins, that we found mentioned in the translation of the plates. While we were thus employed, praying and calling upon the Lord, a messenger from heaven descended in a cloud of light, and having laid his hands upon us, he ordained us, saying: [section 13 quoted]. The messenger who visited us on this occasion, and conferred this Priesthood upon us, said that his name was John, the same that is called John the Baptist in the New Testament, and that he acted

under the direction of Peter, James and John who held the keys of the Priesthood of Melchizedek, which Priesthood he said would in due time be conferred on us, and that I should be called the first Elder of the Church, and he (Oliver Cowdery) the second. It was on the 15th day of May, 1829, that we were ordained under the hand of this messenger and baptized. Immediately on our coming up out of the water after we had been baptized, we experienced great and glorious blessings from our Heavenly Father. No sooner had I baptized Oliver Cowdery, than the Holy Ghost fell upon him, and he stood up and prophesied many things which should shortly come to pass. And again, so soon as I had been baptized by him, I also had the spirit of prophecy, when standing up, I prophesied concerning the rise of this church, and many other things connected with the Church, and this generation of the children of men. We were filled with the Holy Ghost, and rejoiced in the God of our salvation. (*HC,* 1:39–42)

It is interesting that their questions regarding baptism were answered by John the *Baptist.* The same man who baptized the Savior reinstated the authority to baptize in this dispensation.

Authors' Note: Some days after this monumental event, Peter, James, and John, the Lord's apostolic leadership during the meridian of time, also appeared to Joseph and Oliver, as a continuation of the extraordinary process of priesthood restoration, and conferred upon them the Melchizedek Priesthood (see D&C 27:12–13). This latter event calls to mind the words that Peter declared to his peers: "Repent ye therefore, and be converted, that your sins may be blotted out, when the times of refreshing shall come from the presence of the Lord; And he shall send Jesus Christ, which before was preached unto you: Whom the heaven must receive until the times of restitution of all things, which God hath spoken by the mouth of all his holy prophets since the world began" (Acts 3:19–21). In truth, the times of the restitution of all things were unfolding in the latter days at the hands of this same messenger and his companions, called and sent by the Lord to participate in the Restoration of the gospel and priesthood keys.

In 1848, when Oliver Cowdery returned to the Church, he gave a testimony concerning the restoration of the priesthood very similar to that recorded by Joseph Smith: "I was present with Joseph when a holy angel from God came down from heaven and conferred, or restored the Aaronic priesthood, and said at the same time that it should remain upon the earth while the earth stands. I was also present with Joseph when the Melchizedek priesthood was conferred by the holy angels of God— which we then confirmed on each other by the will and commandment of God. This priesthood is also to remain upon the earth until the last remnant of time. This holy priesthood we conferred upon many, and is just as good and valid as if God had conferred it in person" (Reuben Miller Journal, October 21, 1848, 14).

Section 20: Given through the Prophet Joseph Smith in April of 1830 in Fayette, Seneca County, New York, and known as the "Revelation on Church Organization and Government" (see *HC,* 1:64–70). Also referred to as the "Articles and Covenants of the Church of Christ," section 20 served as a kind of constitution for the restored Church. According to archivist Lyndon W. Cook:

> The revelation was at once a formal declaration of belief as well as a written *modus operandi* for administering the affairs of the divine organization [footnote superscript]. Authored by Joseph Smith and Oliver Cowdery, section 20 soon became a standard against which proper conduct and procedure were measured. The writing of this revelation was begun sometime in 1829 but apparently not completed until *after* 6 April 1830. [Footnote:] Section 20 was first presented to the Church membership for sustaining vote on 9 June 1830 at the first conference of the Church in Fayette, New York.
>
> The "Articles and Covenants" were read aloud to the congregation almost as a routine requirement at the early Church conferences. But as Church leaders became more conversant with the revelation, an entire reading became less frequent. The continual reference to the revelation, evidenced throughout Church records during the lifetime of Joseph Smith, served to teach proper Church policy and procedure to leader and layman alike. (*RPJS,* 31)

Section 84: Given through the Prophet Joseph Smith on September 22 and 23, 1832, at the Whitney store in Kirtland, Ohio (see *HC,* 1:286–95). This is the first revelation received after Joseph and Emma and young Julia moved from Hiram on September 12 into their new quarters above the Whitney store. It appears that the Prophet pursued his translation and received most of his revelations in the upper southeast corner room in the Whitney store. In the opening verse, Joseph writes about the elders returning from their missions, which they had accepted at the Amherst conference in January of 1832 (see D&C 75): "A Revelation of Jesus Christ unto his servant Joseph Smith, Jun., and six elders, as they united their hearts and lifted their voices on high" (D&C 84:1).

This is yet another revelation that came as an answer to prayer. The Prophet gave this background: "The Elders during the month of September began to return from their missions to the Eastern States, and present the histories of their several stewardships in the Lord's vineyard; and while together in these seasons of joy, I inquired of the Lord, and received on the 22nd and 23rd of September, the following revelation on Priesthood: [There follows what is now section 84]" (*HC,* 1:286). Verses 1–41 were apparently given on the 22nd and verses 42–120 on the 23rd. (Note the shift from third to first person beginning with verse 42.) This important section contains significant doctrine, promises, prophecy, and direction, including material on the oath and covenant of the priesthood (verses 33–41).

Section 107: Revelation given through the Prophet Joseph Smith at Kirtland, Ohio, dated March 28, 1835 (see *HC,* 2:209–17). At a special conference in Kirtland on February 14–15, 1835, members of the Quorum of Twelve Apostles were chosen by the Three Witnesses to the Book of Mormon under commission of the First Presidency. After this historic organization, the Prophet met from time to time with the newly called Apostles and gave instructions to them. On one such occasion (March 12, 1835), it was decided that the Twelve should "take their first mission through the eastern States to the Atlantic Ocean and hold conferences in the vicinity of the several branches of the Church for the purpose of regulating all things necessary for their welfare" (*HC,* 2:209). Later, on March 28, in the late afternoon, members of the quorum confessed their sins, committed themselves to greater service, and received instruction from Joseph Smith. Knowing that they would soon depart for the East, members of the Quorum requested that the Prophet "inquire of God for us and obtain a written revelation (if consistent) that we may look upon it when we are separated that our hearts may be comforted" (*HC,* 2:210). The resulting instruction (section 107), which apparently combines various interrelated concepts from this period of time, provides important doctrine and policy on the operation of the priesthood.

1. THE POWER AND PURPOSE OF THE PRIESTHOOD

THEME: The priesthood was delegated by God to man for the purpose of saving and exalting individuals and families by providing for them the correct and authorized framework of doctrines, keys, and ordinances pertaining to eternal life.

MODERN PROPHETS SPEAK

Gordon B. Hinckley:

> I want to speak a little about blessing the people, placing our hands upon their heads and blessing them. Brethren, how great is our opportunity, how tremendous our responsibility, to live worthy to be, as it were, a conduit between the powers of heaven and those upon the earth on whose heads we lay our hands. I suppose every man here who holds the Melchizedek Priesthood has had the opportunity to bless. And I suppose that, when called on to do so, he has prayed within his heart that he might be a worthy instrument to bestow a blessing upon the heads of those who come in

faith. Bless the people when you set them apart and under other circumstances, in times of sickness. You fathers bless your children. Lay your hands upon their heads and bless them. You cannot do a greater thing for them. (*TGBH,* 480–81)

Thomas S. Monson:

> George Albert Smith said, "It is your duty first of all to learn what the Lord wants and then by the power and strength of His holy Priesthood to magnify your calling in the presence of your fellows in such a way that the people will be glad to follow you.
>
> How does one magnify a calling? Simply by performing the service that pertains to it.
>
> We have accepted the call; we have been ordained; we bear the priesthood.
>
> President Stephen L Richards spoke often to holders of the priesthood and emphasized his philosophy pertaining to it. He declared: "The Priesthood is usually simply defined as 'the power of God delegated to man.'" He continues: "This definition, I think, is accurate. But for practical purposes I like to define the Priesthood in terms of service and I frequently call it 'the perfect plan of service.'"
>
> You may well ask, "Where does the path of duty lie?" Brethren, I believe with all my heart that two markers define the path: the *Duty to Prepare* and the *Duty to Serve.* (*Ensign,* May 1996, 43)

LIKENING THE SCRIPTURES TO OUR LIVES

Doctrine and Covenants 20:60 The ordination of a priesthood holder is done "by the power of the Holy Ghost, which is in the one who ordains him."

Application: The Lord's Church has always been authorized by the priesthood. His purpose for this is made clear in these verses: to provide the ordinances whereby His children can return to His presence. This truly is a great power God has given us; the power to act in His name, the power of godliness, is not one to be taken lightly. His purpose in bestowing the priesthood and ours in using it is for the salvation of God's children.

2. BLESSINGS THAT COME THROUGH THE RESTORATION OF THE AARONIC PRIESTHOOD

THEME: The Aaronic Priesthood provides the foundation to initiate the admission of the Saints into the Church and kingdom of God by baptism. Thus, those in this office also oversee the regular renewing of these covenant vows in the administration of the sacrament. The Aaronic Priesthood is also responsible for overseeing the temporal welfare of the Church through the guidance of the bishop, the president of the Aaronic Priesthood in his ward.

MODERN PROPHETS SPEAK

Dallin H. Oaks:

What does it mean that the Aaronic Priesthood holds "the key of the ministering of angels" and of the "gospel of repentance and of baptism, and the remission of sins"? The meaning is found in the ordinance of baptism and in the sacrament. Baptism is for the remission of sins, and the sacrament is a renewal of the covenants and blessings of baptism. Both should be preceded by repentance. When we keep the covenants made in these ordinances, we are promised that we will always have His Spirit to be with us. The ministering of angels is one of the manifestations of that Spirit. (*Ensign,* November 1998, 37)

Gordon B. Hinckley:

With the bestowal of the priesthood comes the right to receive marvelous and wonderful blessings. John declared that the Aaronic Priesthood "holds the keys of the ministering of angels" (D&C 13:1). How marvelous a gift, that if we live worthily, we shall have the right to the company of angels. Here is protection, here is guidance, here is direction—all of these from powers beyond our own natural gifts. (*Ensign,* October 1988, 69)

ILLUSTRATIONS FOR OUR TIMES

The Ministering of Angels

When I was approaching my eighteenth birthday and preparing to enter military service near the close of World War II, I was recommended to receive the Melchizedek Priesthood. Mine was the task of telephoning my stake president, Paul C. Child, for an appointment and interview. He was one who loved and understood the holy scriptures. It was his intent that all others should similarly love and understand them.

Knowing from others of his rather detailed and searching interviews, my telephone conversation with him went something like this:

"Hello, President Child. This is Tom Monson. I have been asked by the bishop to seek an interview with you."

"Fine, Brother Monson. When can you visit me?"

Knowing that his sacrament meeting time was six o'clock, and desiring minimum exposure of my scriptural knowledge to his review, I suggested, "How would Sunday at five o'clock be?"

His response: "Oh, Brother Monson, that would not provide us sufficient time to peruse the scriptures. Could you please come at two o'clock, and bring with you your personally marked and referenced set of scriptures."

Sunday finally arrived, and I visited President Child's home on Indiana Avenue. I was greeted warmly, and then the interview began. He said, "Brother Monson, you hold the Aaronic Priesthood. Have you ever had angels minister to you?"

My reply was: "No, President Child."

"Do you know," said he, "that you are entitled to such?"

Again came my response: "No."

Then he instructed, "Brother Monson, repeat from memory the thirteenth section of the Doctrine and Covenants."

I began, "Upon you my fellow servants, in the name of the Messiah I confer the Priesthood of Aaron, which holds the keys of the ministering of angels . . ." (D&C 13:1).

"Stop," President Child directed. Then in a calm, kindly tone he counseled: "Brother Monson, never forget that as a holder of the Aaronic Priesthood, you are entitled to the ministering of angels." It was almost as if an angel were in the room that day. I have never forgotten the interview. I yet feel the spirit of that solemn occasion. I revere the priesthood of Almighty God. I have witnessed its power. I have seen its strength. I have marveled at the miracles it has wrought. (Thomas S. Monson, *Inspiring Experiences That Build Faith: From the Life and Ministry of Thomas S. Monson* [Salt Lake City: Deseret Book, 1994], 192)

LIKENING THE SCRIPTURES TO OUR LIVES

Doctrine and Covenants 84:26–28 The Aaronic Priesthood holds the keys of the preparatory gospel of repentance and baptism. This priesthood was conferred upon John the Baptist while he was yet in his youth so he could "make straight the way of the Lord" and prepare the people for His coming.

Application: To the young men of the Church the Lord has given a magnificent blessing and responsibility. He has seen fit to confer upon them the Aaronic Priesthood and all its accompanying opportunities to serve. It is through the Aaronic Priesthood that people begin their acquaintance with and membership in the gospel. Through the keys of the bishop as judge, people are able to repent and be worthy of baptism. The office of priest is required to baptize. Priests, teachers, and deacons bless, prepare, and pass the sacrament. Such service allows the possibility of membership and progression in the gospel and therefore should not be treated lightly.

3. BLESSINGS THAT COME THROUGH THE RESTORATION OF THE MELCHIZEDEK PRIESTHOOD

THEME: The Melchizedek Priesthood has the authority and responsibility to look after the spiritual welfare of the members of the Church. Through this priesthood were all other ordinances of the gospel given—the conferring of the Holy Ghost, the sealing powers and other temple ordinances, and so on. This higher priesthood of God enables the penitent and obedient to complete their mortal preparations to enter the presence of the Lord (see D&C 84:22).

MODERN PROPHETS SPEAK

Brigham Young:
> The Priesthood of the Son of God, which we have in our midst, is a perfect order and system of government, and this alone can deliver the human family from all the evils which now afflict its members, and insure them happiness and felicity hereafter. (*Discourses of Brigham Young,* sel. John A. Widtsoe [Salt Lake City: Deseret Book, 1954], 130)

Spencer W. Kimball:
> We commemorate the restoration of the Melchizedek Priesthood, called "the Holy Priesthood after the Order of the Son of God" (D&C 107:3), once more this

month. It is an event of supreme importance to man in this dispensation, for the priesthood is the power and authority of God delegated to man on earth to act in all things pertaining to the salvation of men. It is the means whereby the Lord acts through men to save souls. Without this priesthood power, men are lost. Only through this power does man "hold the keys of all the spiritual blessings of the church," enabling him to receive "the mysteries of the kingdom of heaven, to have the heavens opened" unto him (see D&C 107:18–19), enabling him to enter the new and everlasting covenant of marriage and to have his wife and children bound to him in an everlasting tie, enabling him to become a patriarch to his posterity forever, and enabling him to receive a fulness of the blessings of the Lord. (*Ensign,* June 1975, 3)

ILLUSTRATIONS FOR OUR TIMES

The Manifold Blessings of the Priesthood

In the spring of 1866, during what is called the Black Hawk War, our pioneers were struggling to beat back deadly Indian attacks on many settlements in southern Utah. Two of President Heber C. Kimball's sons were called into military service for a three-month expedition against the Indians. Before they left he gave them a priesthood blessing. Apparently concerned that his sons might shed the blood of their Lamanite brothers, he first counseled them about the great promises God has made to this branch of the house of Israel. He then blessed his sons and promised them they would not see a single Indian on their campaign. His sons, full of fight and eager to smell gunpowder, were disappointed at this promise, but the blessing was fulfilled. When they returned three months later, they reported:

"We . . . rode hundreds of miles, following the tracks of different bands of hostile Indians, and were close upon them a great many times. They were attacking settlements all around us, killing the settlers and driving off stock." But the company did not see a single Indian. (Orson F. Whitney, *Life of Heber C. Kimball, an Apostle,* 2nd ed. [Salt Lake City: Stevens and Wallis, 1945], 429)

* * *

In a priesthood blessing a servant of the Lord exercises the priesthood, as moved upon by the Holy Ghost, to call upon the powers of heaven for the benefit of the person being blessed. Such blessings are conferred by holders of the Melchizedek Priesthood, which has the keys of all the spiritual blessings of the Church (see D&C 107:18, 67).

There are many kinds of priesthood blessings. As I give various examples, please remember that priesthood blessings are available for all who need them, but they are only given on request.

Blessings for the healing of the sick are preceded by anointing with oil, as the scriptures direct (see James 5:14–15; Mark 6:13; D&C 24:13–14; 42:43–48; 66:9). Patriarchal blessings are conferred by an ordained patriarch.

Persons desiring guidance in an important decision can receive a priesthood blessing. Persons who need extra spiritual power to overcome a personal challenge can receive a blessing. . . .

Blessings given in circumstances such as I have just described are sometimes called blessings of comfort or counsel. They are usually given by fathers or husbands or other elders in the family. . . . Priesthood blessings are also given in connection with a priesthood ordination or with the setting apart of a man or woman for a calling in the Church. These are probably the most frequent occasions for priesthood blessings. . . .

What is the significance of a priesthood blessing? Think of a young man preparing to leave home to seek his fortune in the world. If his father gave him a compass, he might use this worldly tool to help him find his way. If his father gave him money, he could use this to give him power over worldly things. A priesthood blessing is a conferral of power over spiritual things. Though it cannot be touched or weighed, it is of great significance in helping us overcome obstacles on the path to eternal life. . . . It is a very sacred responsibility for a Melchizedek Priesthood holder to speak for the Lord in giving a priesthood blessing. As the Lord has told us in modern revelation, "My word . . . shall all be fulfilled, whether by mine own voice or by the voice of my servants, it is the same" (D&C 1:38). If a servant of the Lord speaks as he is moved upon by the Holy Ghost, his words are "the will of the Lord, . . . the mind of the Lord, . . . the word of the Lord, . . . [and] the voice of the Lord" (D&C 68:4). . . .

This is the true church of our Savior. I testify of the saving mission of Jesus Christ. We are bearers of his priesthood. God bless us to exercise that priesthood under his direction, for the blessing of his children. (Dallin H. Oaks, *Ensign,* May 1987, 36)

LIKENING THE SCRIPTURES TO OUR LIVES

Doctrine and Covenants 107:5 "All other authorities or offices in the church are appendages to this priesthood."

Application: The Lord has set up this higher priesthood to be a means of governance of His Church. All that we do in the Church is under the direction of the priesthood. We must honor and sustain the priesthood and those called to bear it if we are to progress in the gospel and build the kingdom.

SUMMARY

Through the Restoration of the gospel of Jesus Christ in the latter days, the powers, purposes, and blessings of the priesthood of God have again been made manifest in the world for the redemption and edification of God's children. By divinely commissioned stages, priesthood doctrines, keys, and administrative policies were revealed in an orderly process through the Prophet Joseph Smith and his colleagues as the kingdom of God was once again established in its glory and fulness. Ultimately, all of the keys—including the sealing powers—were restored for the consummation of the "marvelous work and a wonder" (Isa. 29:14) foretold by prophets of old and confirmed by Apostles in the meridian of time (see Acts 3:19–21). The supreme act of God's benevolence, by means of which the priesthood and its operational keys were again delegated to man, laid the foundation for preparing humankind—all those who would choose the paths of righteousness and obedience—for the Second Coming: "Therefore, the keys of this dispensation are committed into your hands; and by this ye may know that the great and dreadful day of the Lord is near, even at the doors" (D&C 110:16).

CHAPTER NINE

"THE ONLY TRUE *and* LIVING CHURCH"

Reading Assignment: Doctrine and Covenants 20:1–36; 68–69,75–79; 21; 27; 115:1–4; *Our Heritage*, pages 14–16.

Additional Reading: Isaiah 29:14; Daniel 2:55; Revelation 14:6–7; Doctrine and Covenants 65:2.

As we sang "We Thank Thee, O God, for a Prophet," I thought of the Prophet Joseph Smith. How grateful we are for his life and his mission. Joseph Smith was a man committed to his Heavenly Father's work. He loved his fellowmen, and he spent his life in serving them. Joseph Smith was the instrument through which the Lord restored the fulness of the everlasting gospel. He was the prophet of the Restoration.

Joseph Smith's greatness consists in one thing—the truthfulness of his declaration that he saw the Father and the Son and that he responded to the reality of that divine revelation. He was directed to reestablish the true and living Church, restored in these modern times as it existed in the day of the Savior's own mortal ministry. The Prophet Joseph Smith was fearless in pursuing this divine mission. (Howard W. Hunter, THWH, 190)

THEMES *for* LIVING

1. Organization of The Church of Jesus Christ of Latter-day Saints
2. Follow the Prophet: A Commandment of God
3. Church Members Are to Meet Together Oft and Partake of the Sacrament
4. Duties of Church Members

INTRODUCTION

In our day, we are honored and privileged to be witnesses of the fulfillment of specific prophecies given through the Lord's servants in former ages who were given inspired views of the restoration of the kingdom of God for the last time prior to the Second Coming. Speaking through Isaiah in the eighth century B.C., the Lord promised: "Therefore, behold, I will proceed to do a marvellous work among this people, even a marvellous work and a wonder: for the wisdom of their wise men shall perish, and the understanding of their prudent men shall be hid" (Isa. 29:14). During the season of Lehi's departure from Jerusalem by way of commandment, the prophet Daniel declared: "And in the days of these kings shall the God of heaven set up a kingdom, which shall never be destroyed: and the kingdom shall not be left to other people, but it shall break in pieces and consume all these kingdoms, and it shall stand for ever" (Dan. 2:44). In the meridian of time, John the Revelator foretold aspects of the same future event: "And I saw another angel fly in the midst of heaven, having the everlasting gospel to preach unto them that dwell on the earth, and to every nation, and kindred, and tongue, and people, Saying with a loud voice, Fear God, and give glory to him; for the hour of his judgment is come: and worship him that made heaven, and earth, and the sea, and the fountains of waters" (Rev. 14:6–7). What Peter called the "times of refreshing" and "the times of restitution of all things" (Acts 3:19, 21) encompassed the same vision of the future design of the Lord, which has unfolded in our day as the Restoration of the gospel of Jesus Christ and the organization of The Church of Jesus Christ of Latter-day Saints. How grateful we should be that the Lord has seen fit to allow us to be active participants and servants in the building up of His kingdom during the dispensation of the fulness of times.

MOMENT OF TRUTH

In particular, four revelatory events of the Restoration—the receiving of sections 20, 21, 27, and 115—shed light on the themes for this chapter. The previous chapter provided the setting for section 20. Following is an outline of the background and setting for the other three important revelations in this series.

Section 21: Given through the Prophet Joseph Smith on Tuesday, April 6, 1830, in the home of Peter Whitmer Sr. at Fayette, Seneca County, New York, on the historic occasion of the organization of the Church (see *HC,* 1:74–79). The six individuals who acted as charter members for the organizing process were Joseph Smith, Oliver Cowdery, Hyrum Smith, David Whitmer, Samuel H. Smith, and Peter Whitmer Jr. The name of the new church was "The Church of Christ."

Section 27: Given through the Prophet Joseph Smith in August and September of 1830 at Harmony, Susquehanna County, Pennsylvania (see *HC,* 1:106–8). The Prophet recorded in his journal:

> Early in the month of August Newel Knight and his wife paid us a visit at my place in Harmony, Pennsylvania; and as neither his wife nor mine had been as yet confirmed, it was proposed that we should confirm them, and partake together of the Sacrament, before he and his wife should leave us. In order to prepare for this I set out to procure some wine for the occasion, but had gone only a short distance when I was met by a heavenly messenger, and received the following revelation, the first four paragraphs of which were written at this time, and the remainder in the September following [section 27]. . . . In obedience to this revelation we prepared some wine of our own make, and held our meeting. . . . We partook of the sacrament, after which we confirmed the two sisters into the Church, and spent the evening in a glorious manner. The Spirit of the Lord was poured out upon us. We praised the God of Israel and rejoiced exceedingly. (*HC,* 1:106, 108)

Section 115: Given through the Prophet Joseph Smith on April 26, 1838, at Far West, Caldwell County, Missouri, concerning the will of God for building up the kingdom and the house of the Lord in that place (see *HC,* 3:23). The revelation designates the proper name for the Church. A letter from Thomas B. Marsh to Wilford Woodruff soon after this date explains the contents of the revelation:

> Since Br. Joseph came to this place, we have been favored with a lengthy revelation in which many important items are shown forth. First that the Church, shall hereafter be called "The Church of Jesus Christ of Latter-day Saints." Second it saith "Let the City Farwest be a holy and a consecrated land unto me, and it shall be called most holy, for the ground upon which thou standest is holy: Therefore, I command you to build a house unto me, for the gathering together of my Saints, that they may worship me." 3d. It also teaches, that the foundation stone must be laid on the 4th of July next [1838], and that a commencement must be made in this following season; and in one year from that time, to continue the work until it is finished. Thus we see that the Lord is more wise than men, for Phelps & Whitmer thought to commence it long before

this, but it was not the Lord's time, therefore, he over threw it, and has appointed his own time. The plan is yet to be shown to the first presidency, and all the Saints, in all the world, are commanded to assist in building the house. (Quoted in *RPJS,* 227)

We see from this and from what we know of history that the Lord indeed has His own time in establishing His Church. Though the temple at Far West has not been completed (only the cornerstones remain), the Lord has not slowed the work of His kingdom.

1. ORGANIZATION OF THE CHURCH OF JESUS CHRIST OF LATTER-DAY SAINTS

THEME: On April 6, 1830, an event of singular importance in the history of the world took place in a humble cabin in the small town of Fayette, Seneca County, New York. On that occasion the Lord's Church was organized in this dispensation as a divine blessing for all who would come with broken hearts and contrite spirits and covenant to be His children, take upon them His name, and serve Him forever in righteousness. The Church is indeed the organized and authorized structure through which the gospel is to be preached unto all the world, the Saints are to be perfected, and salvation is to be administered and secured for all the hosts of creation—both living and dead—who become heirs of immortality and eternal life.

MODERN PROPHETS SPEAK

James E. Talmage:

> But I pray you consider what the real name means—"The Church of Jesus Christ of Latter-day Saints." We can understand, easily, what "Latter-day" means—modern day, this day; but what does the word "Saint" mean? By derivation, by acceptation, and by the best authority in the language, it means directly, used as an adjective, "holy," and when used as a noun "a holy one," and we, therefore, profess to be a body of holy men, holy women. We proclaim ourselves in the name of Jesus Christ to be the holy ones of the last days, a significant proclamation, blasphemous in the extreme if it be not justified. But that name was given us of God. We do not apologize for it, nor do we preach the doctrines of the gospel, committed to the Church to be preached, in any apologetic manner. We preach in simplicity, in humility, but not by way of apology. . . . We have no apology to offer for our name nor for our membership in the Church, nor for our scriptures that have been given by revelation through the prophets of the Lord unto the people. (CR, April 1922, 72)

Ezra Taft Benson:

> It was predicted in scripture that the Lord would restore His Church in these latter days prior to His second coming. Like the former-day Church, His restored Church was to have Apostles, prophets, and current revelation which added new scripture. We declare that this prophecy has come to pass. Through the Prophet Joseph Smith the Lord has established His Church again on earth. (*TETB*, 111)

LIKENING THE SCRIPTURES TO OUR LIVES

Doctrine and Covenants 115:4 The Lord reveals the name of His church: The Church of Jesus Christ of Latter-day Saints.

Application: The Church is The Church of Jesus Christ of Latter-day Saints. It is important to understand that it is so named because it is founded upon the gospel of Jesus Christ. The name of the Church was a significant part of its organization, and a further witness as to the truth of it. We take the Lord's name upon us when we are baptized and confirmed as members of His Church (see 3 Ne. 27:5–14). We become His sons and daughters (see Mosiah 5:7). He gives us joint ownership of His Church, for it is the "Church of *Jesus Christ*" and also the "Church of Jesus Christ of *Latter-day Saints*." Paul put emphasis on this joint tenancy: "And if children, then heirs; heirs of God, and joint-heirs with Christ; if so be that we suffer with him, that we may be also glorified together" (Rom. 8:17). We are responsible for caring for the Church on the earth, and for our activity in and concerning the Church.

2. FOLLOW THE PROPHET: A COMMANDMENT OF GOD

THEME: The guidance system of the kingdom of God is anchored in the divine commission of prophets, seers, and revelators who communicate the Lord's truths under inspiration of the Holy Spirit. Paul taught: "Now therefore ye are no more strangers and foreigners, but fellowcitizens with the saints, and of the household of God; And are built upon the foundation of the apostles and prophets, Jesus Christ himself being the chief corner stone" (Eph. 2:19–20). By following the Lord's designated prophet as if we were in fact following the Lord Himself, we move in pathways of light and knowledge that accord with divine will.

MODERN PROPHETS SPEAK

Joseph B. Wirthlin:

> The Savior has declared that whether we receive the word of God "by [his] own

voice or by the voice of [his] servants, it is the same" (D&C 1:38). If we are to fol-low Christ, we must follow the prophet, the Lord's mouthpiece on earth. (*Finding Peace in Our Lives* [Salt Lake City: Deseret Book, 1995], 234)

L. Tom Perry:

I pray that all the members of the Church will recognize that there is safety when we follow the prophet and strictly heed his voice. (*Living with Enthusiasm* [Salt Lake City: Deseret Book, 1996], 124)

John A. Widtsoe:

But, which prophet is the most important to us? That is the more incisive question.

The most important prophet in any age is the living prophet. The prophets who have gone before have left to us their precious teachings which will be used for the instruction and comfort of mankind. But, it is the living prophet who helps us by his teachings, example, and direction to meet and to solve the problems of today, our day. To follow the living prophet, the interpreter of the past, is the essence of wisdom. The very strength of the Church lies in the doctrine of continuous revela-tion through a living prophet.

In that sense, the living prophet is the greatest prophet. (*Evidences and Reconciliations* [Salt Lake City: Bookcraft, 1960], 352)

ILLUSTRATIONS FOR OUR TIMES

Follow the Prophet

To help you pass the crucial tests which lie ahead, I am going to give you today sev-eral aspects of a grand key which, if you will honor, will crown you with God's glory and bring you out victorious in spite of Satan's fury.

Soon we will be honoring our prophet on his 85th birthday. As a Church we sing the hymn, "We Thank Thee, O God, for a Prophet." Here then is the grand key— Follow the prophet—and here are *fourteen fundamentals in following the prophet,* the President of The Church of Jesus Christ of Latter-day Saints.

First: *The prophet is the only man who speaks for the Lord in everything.* . . .

Second: *The living prophet is more vital to us than the standard works.* . . .

Third: *The living prophet is more important to us than a dead prophet.* . . .

Fourth: *The prophet will never lead the Church astray. . . .*

Fifth: *The prophet is not required to have any particular earthly training or diplomas to speak on any subject or act on any matter at any time. . . .*

Sixth: *The prophet does not have to say "Thus saith the Lord" to give us scripture. . . .*

Seventh: *The prophet tells us what we need to know, not always what we want to know.*

Eighth: *The Prophet is not limited by men's reasoning. . . .*

Ninth: *The prophet can receive revelation on any matter—temporal or spiritual.*

Tenth: *The prophet may well advise on civic matters. . . .*

Eleventh: *The two groups who have the greatest difficulty in following the prophet are the proud who are learned and the proud who are rich. . . .*

Twelfth: *The prophet will not necessarily be popular with the world or the worldly. . . .*

Thirteenth: *The prophet and his counselors make up the First Presidency—the highest quorum in the Church. . . .*

Fourteenth: *The prophet and the presidency—the living prophet and the First Presidency—follow them and be blessed—reject them and suffer. . . .* (Ezra Taft Benson, "Fourteen Fundamentals in Following the Prophet," *BYU Speeches of the Year, 1977–80,* February 26, 1980, 26–30.)

LIKENING THE SCRIPTURES TO OUR LIVES

Doctrine and Covenants 21:4–6 The words of the prophet are to be received as if they came directly from the mouth of the Lord. The Lord will protect and prosper those who hearken to the words of the prophet.

Application: The Lord here furthers the organization of the Church by appointing His prophet. He outlines the responsibility of members of the Church to follow the prophet. The blessings of following the prophet are like unto those of following our Savior (see 3 Ne. 12:3; 28:34–35; D&C 1:38; 84:35–39). We are empowered by our obedience with the blessing of the Spirit: the gates of hell shall not prevail against us; the powers of darkness are dispersed; the heavens shake for our good and the glory of God. Simply follow the prophet.

3. CHURCH MEMBERS ARE TO MEET TOGETHER OFT AND PARTAKE OF THE SACRAMENT

THEME: "Stand in holy places" has been an age-old directive from the Lord (see D&C 45:32; 101:22). Those places might include the temples of the Lord, the homes of the faithful, and the congregations of Saints assembled in stakes, districts, and missions of Zion to worship in the spirit of truth (John 4:23–24). There is security is the gatherings of the Saints. There is opportunity there to enjoy the interactive communion of the Saints as they study the gospel and seek to remember their covenant vows. There is a feeling of joy in bearing testimonies together and sharing praise for the Lord. We should be grateful to the Lord for instituting circles of worship where common values can be celebrated and the sacrament can be administered by the priesthood.

MODERN PROPHETS SPEAK

Gordon B. Hinckley:

Sacrament meeting, partaking of the sacrament each week—what a glorious blessing that is! What a wonderful privilege to go to sacrament meeting and partake of the sacrament, the emblems of the sacrifice of our Lord Jesus Christ and of the great Atonement which was wrought by Him, that makes possible our moving beyond the grave into a glorious future. I hope that all of us attend our sacrament meetings. I hope we recognize it as an opportunity and as a wonderful blessing. (*Liahona,* August 2000, 3)

David O. McKay:

My brethren and sisters, do we always stop to think, on that sacred Sabbath day when we meet together to partake of the sacrament, that we witness, promise, obligate ourselves, in the presence of one another, and in the presence of God, that we will do certain things? Note them.

The first: We are willing to take upon ourselves the name of the Son. In so doing we choose him as our leader and our ideal; and he is the one perfect character in all the world.

The second: That we will always remember him. Not just on Sunday, but on Monday, in our daily acts, in our self-control. When our brother hurts us, we are going to try to master our feelings and not retaliate in the same spirit of anger. When a brother treats us with contempt, we are going to try to return kindness. That's the spirit of the Christ, and that's what we have promised—that we will do our best to achieve these high standards of Christianity, true Christian principles.

The third: We promise to ". . . keep his commandments which he has given . . ."—tithing, fast offerings, the Word of Wisdom, kindness, forgiveness, love. The obligation of a member of the Church of Jesus Christ is great, but it is as glorious as it is great, because obedience to these principles gives life, eternal life. (*Gospel Ideals: Selections from the Discourses of David O. McKay* [Salt Lake City: Improvement Era, 1953], 146–47)

ILLUSTRATIONS FOR OUR TIME

Meet Together Oft

How can a man who refuses to meet often with his fellow worshipers to keep this commandment have a claim upon the guidance and the blessings of the Lord? Yet strange to say, there are those who seemingly have this false understanding. President George Q. Cannon, many years ago, declared:

"The Lord has commanded his people to meet together oft and eat and drink in remembrance of him, of his sufferings and death, and to witness unto the Father that they are willing to keep his commandments which he has given them. . . . Yet there are members of the Church who seem to attach no particular importance to these meetings. They will allow weeks, yes and months, to pass without having the least anxiety or desire to avail themselves of the privilege of partaking of the Lord's Supper. Can there be any wonder at such people being barren, spiritless and indifferent about the work of the Lord: They neglect the means which the Lord has provided for the nourishing of their spiritual natures, and they are in a state of spiritual starvation—a starvation which is as fatal in its effects upon the spirit as the continued refusal to eat food has upon the natural body. No Latter-day Saint who places proper value upon his standing before the Lord will be guilty of this neglect" (*Juvenile Instrocutor,* 28:89).

President Anthon H. Lund, at the general conference of the Church, April 4, 1920, which was eleven months before his death, also said:

"Now, brethren and sisters, we cannot develop in godliness without going to the meetings. We should be present to hear the servants of God and to partake of the sacrament of the Lord, and renew our covenants with him, showing that we are willing to take upon us his name and keep his commandments. It gives us strength to do so; but by staying away from sacrament meetings, we gradually grow careless, and we think that we cannot be edified by attending them. Do not go to meeting just because a good speaker is going to talk, but go to the meeting as the Lord has commanded that on the Sabbath day we should go to the house of prayer and offer our oblations to the Almighty. Do not let us be lacking in this nor in other duties." (Joseph Fielding Smith, *Seek Ye Earnestly* [Salt Lake City: Deseret Book, 1970], 109–10)

LIKENING THE SCRIPTURES TO OUR LIVES

Doctrine and Covenants 20:76–79 The Lord provides specific prayers to be used in blessing the emblems of the sacrament. Those who partake of the sacrament are covenanting to remember always the Savior by keeping His commandments and taking His name upon them. The Lord has promised to send His Spirit to be with all those who make and keep this promise.

Application: Too often we treat the sacrament as commonplace, failing to consider carefully the words and the miracle of these prayers. With sacred reverence and devotion, we partake of the sacrament to renew our covenants, and by keeping the commandments we receive one of the greatest blessings in mortality to help us stay on the strait and narrow path—the blessing of the Holy Spirit.

4. DUTIES OF CHURCH MEMBERS

THEME: "A godly walk and conversation" (D&C 20:69) is the simple formula the Lord designated as the governing lifestyle of His Saints. If we follow in the footsteps of the Savior, then we are pursuing a "godly walk." If our behavior (our thoughts, actions, words, relationships—our "conversation," in the more antique sense of that word) is congruent with the qualities of Christian discipleship, then we are deporting ourselves as Saints, with a hope fixed in Christ and minds and hearts attuned to the guidance of the Spirit through channels of personal inspiration and revelation.

MODERN PROPHETS SPEAK

Joseph Smith:
> After all that has been said, the greatest and most important duty is to preach the Gospel. (*Discourses of the Prophet Joseph Smith,* comp. Alma P. Burton [Salt Lake City: Deseret Book, 1977], 172)

Thomas S. Monson:
> I like that word *duty.* He did not say "rejoice with you in the fulfillment of an *assignment,* in response to a *calling.*" He said, ". . . in the performance of your *duty.*"

The person who is working on his genealogy fits that description of one who is fulfilling his duty. I know the effort, I know the expense, I know the difficulties through which one may go to uncover one name. I know our Heavenly Father is aware of these efforts. And those for whom we perform these sacred ordinances are aware of our efforts. (*Pathways to Perfection* [Salt Lake City: Deseret Book, 1973], 50)

Robert D. Hales:

Strengthening families is our sacred duty as parents, children, extended family members, leaders, teachers, and individual members of the Church. (*Ensign,* May 1999, 32)

Heber J. Grant:

I maintain that it is the absolute duty of each and every member of The Church of Jesus Christ of Latter-day Saints to so order his life that his example will be worthy of the imitation of all men, thus bringing credit and blessings to himself and his posterity and also making friends for the work of the Lord, which should be the loftiest ambition of every Latter-day Saint. (*Ensign,* March 1972, 67)

ILLUSTRATIONS FOR OUR TIMES

The following is an illustration of how our duty as members is not in our meetings alone. Our duty is to live and exemplify the very teachings we proclaim. Our duty is to build the kingdom.

Another Kind of Mission

My nine-year-old son recently presented me with a "teaching moment." We were seated in front of the fireplace enjoying toasted marshmallows and the warmth of the fire. We were also experiencing the deep contentment and joy of each other's association. It was good to be together. In something of a reflective mood he turned to me and said: "Dad, when will I be old enough to go on a mission?"

I was about to answer his question by saying that if he met the proper requirements, he could expect to be called at the age of nineteen or twenty. But then some deeper implications of his question became clear to me. I wanted him to understand those deeper implications.

"Ralph," I said, "does it make you feel good when you do something for someone you love? Take yesterday, for example. Mom told me that you put Marleen [his younger sister], Ray and Randy [his younger brothers] in your wagon and pulled them all the way to the grocery store and back. She said they were laughing and really enjoying what you did for them. Did it make you happy to see them happy?"

"Yes," he said, after a pause, "I suppose it did. Although I hadn't thought about it that way before."

"The Savior, Ralph, loves us, his brothers and sisters, very much. He loves us so much that he gave his life so that we might come back into the celestial kingdom of our Heavenly Father if we live his teachings. He loves us so much that he gave us the principles which he knew would bring us great joy if we learn to practice them. He loves us so much that he organized his church for us.

"Now if we have found joy in living the gospel, and if we love other people who do not understand it, what do you think we should do?"

"That's easy," he said. "We should tell them about it."

"That's right," I replied, "but there are many ways to tell them about it. One way is to serve as a missionary when called by the authorities of the Church. Many people go when they are about nineteen or twenty. Some are older.

"But there is also another kind of mission. Let us put it this way. If one really understands the principles of the gospel, if he finds joy in living them, and finally, if he loves other people, then each day he may find an opportunity to bring some understanding of those principles to others.

"If we look for these opportunities—these 'teaching moments,' as I call them—we can find them in many places. You told me the other day that some students who are members of our church were cheating in an examination in your class at school. This is a tough situation. You don't want to lose the friendship of those students. But perhaps if you thought a prayer about it, you might find just the right chance to bring a new insight about an important teaching of the Savior into the lives of some of those students.

"This is only one example of a 'teaching moment.' If we promise our Heavenly Father to do our best in living principles taught by the Savior, we will find that our Heavenly Father will bless us and help us find many 'teaching moments.'

"This kind of mission, Ralph, is one that lasts all our lives. The Savior cannot be everywhere, and so he wants us who do understand the gospel to help others who do not understand it. You and I and all of us are now on that kind of mission." (Reed H. Bradford, "Another Kind of Mission," in *Powerful Stories from the Lives of Latter-day Saint Men,* comp. Leon R. Hartshorn [Salt Lake City: Deseret Book, 1974], 46)

LIKENING THE SCRIPTURES TO OUR LIVES

Doctrine and Covenants 27:15–18 The Lord counsels us to put on the "whole armor of God" that we may be able to overcome the temptations of the devil and return safely to the realm of our Father and His Son, Jesus Christ (see also Eph. 6:11–18).

Application: The compelling symbolism in this passage is a reminder that the gospel of Jesus Christ is a defense and a security for the Saints. It is also a uniform of valor that equips the individual with the tools of effective missionary work and service. The individual takes upon himself or herself truth, righteousness, the gospel of peace, faith, salvation, the Spirit, and the word of God—all as vital aspects of the "godly walk and conversation" (D&C 20:69) that the children of God are to acquire and demonstrate. Let us remember this counsel in our daily lives and teach it to our families and fellow students in the gospel.

ENRICHMENT

Responsibility and Blessings of the Organization of the Church. The following are a few more thoughts about the Lord's organization of the Church and our responsibility as members of it.

> In naming his Church in our day, the Lord specifically charged the members of The Church of Jesus Christ of Latter-day Saints to "arise and shine forth, that thy light may be a standard for the nations" (D&C 115:4–5). Anciently he charged the Saints on two continents to be a light unto the people of their societies (Matt. 5:14–16; 3 Ne. 12:14–16). Thus, the true followers of Christ, the faithful members of his Church, have always been identified as children of light; charged with the responsibility of letting that light shine. They are to be a "light unto the Gentiles" (D&C 86:11). Ultimately, through their righteousness, these faithful followers of Christ, these children of light, will be celestial Saints and "shine forth as the sun in the kingdom of their Father" (Matt. 13:43). (*DCE,* 81)

* * *

> The Lord promises that the stakes of Zion will serve as a "defense, and for a refuge" to the faithful who gather to these protective canopies of Christ, there to be nurtured in his ways (D&C 115:6). A refuge is a shelter or protection from danger. Those who accept the gospel of Jesus Christ and gather to his stakes are shielded from spiritual danger and build spiritual strength and defenses to thwart attacks by

the adversary. The congregations of the Saints become fortresses for the faithful. It is significant to note the promise that those who faithfully gather to worship and partake of the sacrament will "more fully" keep themselves "unspotted from the world" (D&C 59:9). (*DCE,* 130)

SUMMARY

The kingdom of God is once again restored to the earth. We are blessed to have a living prophet who holds the keys of the priesthood and administers in all matters as the Lord's mouthpiece. We are exhorted to preach the gospel to every nation, kindred, tongue, and people. We are counseled to perform spiritual work for our dead. We are to perfect the Saints and prepare them in every way to perform their duties with valor and devotion. We are to stand in holy places for protection and enlightenment. We are to gather often to partake of the sacrament and renew our covenants. We are to let our light shine that we may be instruments in the hand of the Lord to bring souls unto Him. The Doctrine and Covenants is the book of revelations specifically designated to teach all of these duties and responsibilities in the latter days and help us prepare for the Second Coming. The destiny of the work of God is certain: "The keys of the kingdom of God are committed unto man on the earth, and from thence shall the gospel roll forth unto the ends of the earth, as the stone which is cut out of the mountain without hands shall roll forth, until it has filled the whole earth" (D&C 65:2).

CHAPTER TEN

"THIS MY VOICE *unto* ALL"

Reading Assignment: Doctrine and Covenants 25.

Additional Reading: Doctrine and Covenants 23:1; 25:13–16; 38:39; 61:36–37; 82:1–6; 90:17; 93:49; 98:19–20; 1 Nephi 19:23.

How many times have parents heard a son or daughter complain, 'Let's not read the scriptures. They deal with people of an ancient day and are boring.' When complaints of this nature are voiced, it is likely that the parents have failed to do what Nephi did. Said he: "I did liken all scriptures unto us, that it might be for our profit and learning" (1 Ne. 19:23).

A woman may read section 25 of the Doctrine and Covenants and say, "How wonderful for Emma." But if that same woman substitutes her name for Emma's and her husband's name for Joseph's, the scripture takes on a new world of meaning. And if she takes the time to list the instructions given and the blessings mentioned, the section becomes a personal guide for living. Thus it is with other portions of scripture applied to us and our times (see D&C 25:1–16). (Carlos E. Asay, Family Pecan Trees: Planting a Legacy of Faith at Home *[Salt Lake City: Deseret Book, 1992], 39)*

THEMES *for* LIVING

1. Likening the Scriptures to Our Lives
2. Cultivating Relationships of Support and Encouragement
3. Be Meek and Lowly—Avoid Pride
4. Rejoice and Be of Good Cheer

INTRODUCTION

The scriptures of the Lord provide a magnificent and unique environment for learning, introspection, testimony building, and strengthening covenant commitments. There is no aspect of the human experience—save only direct personal inspiration and revelation—to equal the blessings of basking in the word of the Lord given through His prophets (both past and present), thereby inculcating into one's heart and mind the principles that the Lord would have us follow in pursuit of spiritual enlightenment and ultimate perfection. Even one simple passage of scripture, such as Doctrine and Covenants 25, provides a universe of truth and wisdom to explore in the process of likening the word of God to our own lives and circumstances. From such a beautiful and brief passage, several vital life-themes can be extracted for application in day-to-day experiences. The scriptures lift, elevate, edify, expand, encourage, fortify, and bless. Let us be ever grateful for the word of God.

MOMENT OF TRUTH

Section 25: Revelation given by a prophet-husband to his beloved wife and partner—a tender moment in which the blessings of the Almighty were pronounced upon "an elect lady" (D&C 25:3) and a sacred commission put into place. The revelation was given in July 1830 at Harmony, Susquehanna County, Pennsylvania (see *HC,* 1:103–4). The travails and joys of Joseph and Emma are without parallel in the annals of the history of Church. What couple in Zion carried a heavier burden, shared a more glorious career, endured more tribulation, contributed more to the salvation of others, celebrated more triumphs, or overcame greater barriers? Later, in August of 1842, Joseph was to write concerning Emma:

> With what unspeakable delight, and what transports of joy swelled my bosom, when I took by the hand, on that night, my beloved Emma—she that was my wife, even the wife of my youth, and the choice of my heart. Many were the reverberations of my mind, when I contemplated for a moment the many scenes we had been called

to pass through, the fatigues and the toils, the sorrows and sufferings, and the joys and consolations, from time to time, which had strewed our paths and crowned our board. Oh what a commingling of thought filled my mind for the moment, again she is here, even in the seventh trouble—undaunted, firm, and unwavering—unchangeable, affectionate Emma! (*HC,* 5:107)

Though Emma worked on the hymnal prior to its appearance in 1835, it was not published until then due to the destruction of the printing press in 1832. "The Church hymnal, which appeared about February 1836, contained a preface, apparently written by Phelps, and ninety hymns. Only the words were printed; no music was included. Forty-two of the hymns had appeared earlier in Church periodicals. Thirty-four were authored by Mormons: twenty-six by W. W. Phelps, three by Parley P. Pratt, one by Thomas B. Marsh and Parley P. Pratt, and one each by Eliza R. Snow, Edward Partridge, Philo Dibble, and William C. Gregg" (*RPJS,* 36).

1. LIKENING THE SCRIPTURES TO OUR LIVES

THEME: As we read the scriptures, including personal revelations given principally upon behalf of certain specific individuals (such as section 25), we can apply the words to our own lives as we step into the situation by proxy and enjoy the light and truth made manifest thereby. The Lord said at the conclusion of section 25: "And verily, verily, I say unto you, that this is my voice unto all. Amen" (verse 16). Thus, the directive is given to all sincere readers to apply the wisdom of the scriptural passages to their own individual lives and circumstances. Such is the case in most manifestations of the word of God imparted through His prophets. A frequent phrase used by the Lord in His pronouncements is, "What I say unto one I say unto all" (see D&C 61:18, 36; 82:5; 92:1; 93:49; see also the variations in Mark 13:37; Alma 12:5; D&C 112:14; JS—M 1:46).

MODERN PROPHETS SPEAK

Neal A. Maxwell:

> No wonder God has so carefully revealed Himself and His character in various theophanies, revelations, and scriptures. Not only is it our task to search and ponder all of these instructive insights, but it is also to apply these revelations developmentally and personally. In this process we are to "liken these scriptures," with their illustrative attributes and qualities, "unto ourselves" (1 Ne. 19:23). (*One More Strain of Praise* [Salt Lake City: Deseret Book, 1999], 54–55)

ILLUSTRATIONS FOR OUR TIMES

How to Apply the Word of God to Our Lives

A method to apply the word of God might be stated simply in four steps:

1. Read the scriptures carefully.

2. Ponder them as they relate to you.

3. Write down each scripture reference and the main idea that is there.

4. Write a personal statement on how you're going to live this scripture.

I will . . . I must . . . I shall . . . I can . . . These first-person commitment statements will make the scriptures live in your life.

See, for example, 1 Nephi 3:7: "And it came to pass that I, Nephi, said unto my father: I will go and do the things which the Lord hath commanded, for I know that the Lord giveth no commandments unto the children of men, save he shall prepare a way for them that they may accomplish the thing which he commandeth them."

Here is what you might write: "I will keep the commandments because the Lord will help me by preparing a way." Other ways we might apply that scripture may be: "I will study the scriptures because the Lord has commanded it, and so I know He will help me stay motivated and learn if I try," or "I will observe a fast on Fast Sunday because the Lord will help me be able to fast." These simple statements lead us to apply scripture directly to our lives. This commitment becomes the paramount key for our profit and learning in our lives.

Look how the Prophet Joseph Smith applied James 1:5–6, believing in the word: "If any of you lack wisdom, let him ask of God, that giveth to all men liberally, and upbraideth not; and it shall be given him. But let him ask in faith, nothing wavering. For he that wavereth is like a wave of the sea driven with the wind and tossed."

The Prophet Joseph took the scripture, went to the Sacred Grove in humble prayer, applied the scripture, and received the First Vision. It is a simple, yet powerful, principle. Applying the scriptures makes the scriptures live in our lives. We become empowered by Christ and His word—we live according to His word in our lives. When the word is internalized in our hearts, it becomes our characters, our very beings. The word "heart" means the mind, the soul, the decision-making center of one's being, the source of motives—the will. When the word is in our hearts and we apply it, we live it. We become not only hearers of the word, but doers of the word. When the words are understood and the doctrine is comprehended in the mind or the spirit, then behavior becomes automatic; it is a natural consequence of the word living in one's life. That is why we are Christlike, because we live Christ's words. His words literally empower our lives. (Pinegar)

LIKENING THE SCRIPTURES TO OUR LIVES

Doctrine and Covenants 84:43–46 The word of God is light and truth unto the children of men—"and whatsoever is light is Spirit, even the Spirit of Jesus Christ."

Application: We have our compass or director (see Alma 37:37–47) for life—it is the word of God. When we choose to follow this compass and liken the teachings to our lives, the scriptures will live in our lives. We will live the word of God.

2. CULTIVATING RELATIONSHIPS OF SUPPORT AND ENCOURAGEMENT

THEME: The relationship of devotion and love reflected in the example of Joseph and Emma and their children can radiate in our own families as well, provided we cultivate wise spiritual priorities, practice unselfishness and compassion, maintain a productive balance in the allocation of our time and energies, and keep the commandments of God.

MODERN PROPHETS SPEAK

Howard W. Hunter:

> To reach success in the family, parents must have love and respect for each other. Husbands, the bearers of the priesthood, should hold their wives in the highest esteem before their children, and wives should love and support their husbands. In return, the children will have love for their parents and for each other. The home will then become a hallowed place where the principles of the gospel can be best lived and where the Spirit of the Lord can dwell. To be a successful father or a successful mother is far greater than to rise to leadership or high places in business, government, or worldly affairs. Home may seem commonplace at times with its routine duties, yet its success should be the greatest of all our pursuits in life. (*THWH,* 156)

ILLUSTRATIONS FOR OUR TIMES

Support in Church Callings

> Recently I interviewed an exceptionally stalwart priesthood holder for a temple recommend. I asked him if he sustained his bishop, his stake president, and the president of the Church. Of course his reply to each question was sincere, humble, and strongly affirmative. Then I asked him if he sustained his wife in her calling. He paused to think about it for a minute before answering that he did.

Then he added, "President, this has been very hard for me. In the past I was the one who held important executive positions in the Church, but now our roles are reversed. My wife is an auxiliary president; the phone calls are all for her, she goes to the leadership meetings, she is in the forefront of action. I'm the one now who stays home to take care of the children often while *she's* doing Church work. I'm doing my best to support her, but this is a new experience."

We counseled together about the eternal importance of husbands and wives working together as a team, sustaining and supporting each other in all aspects of their lives, and then concluded the interview. . . .

I contrast that to the excitement a young couple shared with me. When they moved to a new ward, the husband, who had served exceptionally well with our youth, was called to an administrative position to work with adults. I was a little sad when he wasn't still assigned to youth because of the good rapport and respect he engendered with them. But his wife said, "Don't worry, President, my husband *is* still working with the youth—I'm teaching the Laurels."

This young couple had the right idea. They knew that since they were one, they shared, where appropriate, the positions each held. They knew that they needed each other's help to be successful. . . .

President Kimball explained the kind of partnership husbands and wives should have: "When we speak of marriage as a partnership, let us speak of marriage as a *full* partnership. We do not want our LDS women to be *silent* partners or *limited* partners in that eternal assignment! Please be a *contributing* and *full* partner." (Gerald R. Schiefer, *Ensign*, April 1982, 56)

LIKENING THE SCRIPTURES TO OUR LIVES

Alma 29:14 Alma's joy in the success of Ammon and those who went with him to teach the gospel in the land of Nephi is even greater than Alma's joy in his own success.

Application: Find joy in supporting and cheering for others. Charity is the quality we need in order to do this (see Moro. 7:45). As husband and wife, we are to sublimate our lives for one another. We are to support and sustain each other. For those who are single: they have the joy of lifting the spirits of others they serve. For the widows and widowers: they are blessed to carry on the memory of a loved one and cherish the good memories as they look forward to a blessed reunion.

3. BE MEEK AND LOWLY—AVOID PRIDE

THEME: It is in the cultivation of a broken heart and a contrite spirit that the individual finds the channel of spiritual communication with the Father and honors and accepts the atoning sacrifice of the Son. Pride erects a barrier to blessings of the Spirit. Meekness dissolves that barrier and invites an influx of glory and joy that can come solely through covenant valor and submission to the will of God.

MODERN PROPHETS SPEAK

John Taylor:

> We should be strictly honest, one with another, and with all men; let our word always be as good as our bond; avoid all ostentation of pride and vanity; and be meek, lowly, and humble; be full of integrity and honor; and deal justly and righteously with all men; and have the fear and love of God continually before us, and seek for the comforting influence of the Holy Ghost to dwell with us. (*The Gospel Kingdom: Selections from the Writings and Discourses of John Taylor,* ed. G. Homer Durham [Salt Lake City: Improvement Era, 1941], 343)

James E. Faust:

> What makes it possible, under the Master's touch, for them to serve, lift, and bless so that they touch for good the lives of hundreds, even thousands? After a lifetime of dealing in the affairs of men and women, I believe it is the ability to overcome personal ego and pride; both are enemies to the full enjoyment of the Spirit of God and to walking humbly before him. The ego interferes when husbands and wives fail to ask each other for forgiveness. It prevents the enjoyment of the full sweetness of a higher love. The ego often prevents parents and children from fully understanding one another. The ego enlarges our feelings of self-importance and worth. It blinds us to reality. Pride keeps us from confessing our sins and shortcomings to the Lord and working out our repentance. (*Finding Light in a Dark World* [Salt Lake City: Deseret Book, 1995], 45–46)

ILLUSTRATIONS FOR OUR TIMES

Understanding Pride

Pride is at the crux of most all sins. It is the sin that is universal in nature—most all are afflicted to one degree or another from pride. Pride is expressed in arrogance, haughtiness, self-love, vanity and egotism. Pride creates an enmity between God and man. We must all be about overcoming pride. It is directly opposed to the Christlike quality of humility. It was the downfall of the Jaredites and Nephites. Pride can be our downfall as well if we are not careful. It is not only an attitudinal problem but prideful thoughts are so powerful that they lead to sinful behavior, sins of commission and omission. Pride brings with it other sins that are easily expressed such as selfishness, greed, lust, jealousy, power-seeking, envy and a whole host of trailing problems that will tempt us and lead us to sin. This is why the Lord continually counsels us against pride (see Prov. 16:18; D&C 23:1).

President Kimball has counseled us to overcome pride with humility. He said:

> Humility is not pretentious, presumptuous, nor proud. It is not weak, vacillating, nor servile.

> Humble and meek properly suggest virtues, not weaknesses. They suggest a consistent mildness of temper and an absence of wrath and passion. Humility suggests no affectation, no bombastic actions. It is not turgid nor grandiloquent. It is not servile submissiveness. It is not cowed nor frightened. No shadow or the shaking of a leaf terrorizes it.

> How does one get humble? To me, one must constantly be reminded of his dependence. On whom dependent? On the Lord. How remind one's self? By real, constant, worshipful, grateful prayer. . . .

> Humility is teachableness—an ability to realize that all virtues and abilities are not concentrated in one's self. . . .

> Humility is gracious, quiet, serene—not pompous, spectacular, nor histrionic. It is subdued, kindly, and understanding—not crude, blatant, loud, or ugly. Humility is not just a man or a woman but a perfect gentleman and a gentlelady. It never struts nor swaggers. Its faithful, quiet works will be the badge of its own accomplishments. It never sets itself in the center of the stage, leaving all others in supporting roles. Humility is never accusing nor contentious. It is not boastful.

> When one becomes conscious of his great humility, he has already lost it. When one begins boasting of his humility, it has already become pride—the antithesis of humility.

> Humility is repentant and seeks not to justify its follies. It is forgiving others in the realization that there may be errors of the same kind or worse chalked up against itself. . . .

It is not self-abasement—the hiding in the corner, the devaluation of everything one does or thinks or says; but it is the doing of one's best in every case and leaving of one's acts, expressions, and accomplishments to largely speak for themselves. (Spencer W. Kimball, *TSWK,* 233)

LIKENING THE SCRIPTURES TO OUR LIVES

Doctrine and Covenants 90:17 Beware of pride and high-mindedness, which will act as a "snare upon your souls."

Application: The pitfalls of pride are glaringly evident: allegiance to material wealth rather than spiritual wealth, high-mindedness rather than meekness, covetousness rather than seeking eternal life in humility and contrition. Let us stop and listen for the guidance of the Spirit, which will show us the secure pathway around such pitfalls.

4. REJOICE AND BE OF GOOD CHEER

THEME: The Lord has frequently given us the commandment, "Be of good cheer" (see Matt. 9:12; 14:27; Mark 6:50; John 16:33; Acts 23:11; 27:22, 25; Alma 17:31; 3 Ne. 1:13; D&C 61:36; 68:6; 78:18; 112:4; and many other variations). We have so much to rejoice in: the restored gospel, the ordinances of the temple, and the promise of eternal progress, to name a few. The Lord makes clear that He doesn't want His children to be weighed down by cares of the world, but to experience joy. He wants us to cultivate a walk in life based on hope and on a positive, edifying attitude that is anchored in righteousness and obedience.

MODERN PROPHETS SPEAK

Neal A. Maxwell:

> Being of good cheer is the proximate preparation for ultimate joy. Being of good cheer—one day at a time—precedes that point later on when, if we live righteously, we can justifiably say what Jesus said: "Now behold, my joy is full" [3 Ne. 17:20]. (*The Neal A. Maxwell Quote Book,* ed. Cory H. Maxwell [Salt Lake City: Bookcraft, 1997], 39)

ILLUSTRATIONS FOR OUR TIMES

"Be of Good Cheer"

> Recently, while visiting with a wife who had suddenly lost a husband through a tragic death, I was touched by this lovely lady from Washington, Utah, when she said,

"My heart is heavy and sad, but my soul is of good cheer." There was a powerful inward cheer dominating the sorrowful situation. The promise, "for I the Lord am with you," was triumphing over heartache and despair. People of good cheer soften the sorrow of others as well as those that weigh mightily upon themselves.

None of us will escape tragedy and suffering. Each of us will probably react differently. However, if we can recall the Lord's promise, "for I the Lord am with you," we will be able to face our problems with dignity and courage. We will find the strength to be of good cheer instead of becoming resentful, critical, or defeated. We will be able to meet life's unpleasant happenings with clear vision, strength, and power.

One beautiful "good cheer" lady I have loved deeply over the years is very special. For more than thirty-five years her husband has been afflicted with Parkinson's disease.

They have raised six outstanding children. She has cheerfully cooperated in making it possible for him to function well as a father, husband, bishop, high councilor, and successful building contractor. When his mobility has reached discouraging stages of near zero, she has lifted him. Her neighbors, and they are everyone she knows, find her to be the first visitor when there is an unusual need. Her good cheer is endless. She brings peace of mind and comfort to all with whom she associates. The more I watch her, the more I realize good cheer builds contagious enthusiasm. (Marvin J. Ashton, *Ensign,* May 1986, 66)

A Natural Smile

Your level of spirituality is also directly related to how well you fill the Lord's commandments to "Be of good cheer" and "Lift up your heart and rejoice" (D&C 31:3). How many times in the scriptures did the Lord command us to be of good cheer? He didn't say, "Be of good cheer if everything is going well, if you have enough money to pay all your bills, if your biorhythms are up," or whatever. No. For us to be of good cheer is a commandment and not merely a suggestion.

Here is a practical suggestion that has helped me in the past. Take a sheet of paper and write on it a list of the blessings you consider to be important in whatever order they come to your mind. Then place them in order of priority. What is your most precious blessing? Probably somewhere near the top of your list will be the big "Four *F*s"—your faith, family, freedom, and friends.

Note how many blessings you have at the top of the list for which you would hope to have the courage to give up your mortal lives to protect. Then note how far down the list you go before you come to any blessing that you can buy for money. The most precious blessings are without price; they are priceless.

On those days when you don't feel like smiling, take out your list, read it, and then you can smile very naturally. (Joe J. Christensen, *Ensign,* March 1999, 58)

LIKENING THE SCRIPTURES TO OUR LIVES

Doctrine and Covenants 78:18 With the help of the Lord, we will someday be able to claim the blessings and riches of eternity.

Application: In all of our trials and tribulations we can live with hope and trust in the Lord Jesus Christ. He will nurture and bless us. This is why we should be of "good cheer." Be glad, for He is in our midst (see D&C 29:5). A merry heart is good medicine for everybody (see Prov. 17:22). Do all things with a cheerful heart, and the Lord will surely extend His arm toward us (see D&C 123:17).

SUMMARY

From a short but enlightening section of the Doctrine and Covenants (section 25) we derive a treasure trove of wisdom to apply in our daily circumstances. What better counsel can we receive than to liken the scriptures to our own lives, to cultivate relationships of support and encouragement in our families, to be meek and lowly (avoiding pride), and to rejoice and be of good cheer? The Lord has promised: "And now, verily I say unto you, and what I say unto one I say unto all, be of good cheer, little children; for I am in your midst, and I have not forsaken you; And inasmuch as you have humbled yourselves before me, the blessings of the kingdom are yours" (D&C 61:36–37). At the same time, He has warned us with urgency and power: "For of him unto whom much is given much is required; and he who sins against the greater light shall receive the greater condemnation" (D&C 82:3). And again: "What I say unto one I say unto all; pray always lest that wicked one have power in you, and remove you out of your place" (D&C 93:49). Let us therefore choose the better part and follow in the Lord's footsteps with all devotion, that we might have eternal life.

CHAPTER ELEVEN

"THE FIELD IS WHITE ALREADY *to* HARVEST"

Reading Assignment: Doctrine and Covenants 4; 11; 12; 14; 15; 16; 17; 18; 31; 33; 75; *Our Heritage,* page 11.

Additional Reading: Doctrine and Covenants 42:12; 52:8–9; Alma 17:2–3; 26:22.

I think every member of the Church has the capacity to teach the gospel to non-members. I was told the other day of a crippled woman, homebound, who spends her days in a wheelchair, who has been the means of bringing thirty-seven people into the Church. . . . We need an awareness, an everyday awareness of the great power that we have to do this thing. . . .

I think many of us realize that we could do it, but we lack the desire. Let every man single out another, a friend. Let him get on his knees and pray to the Lord to help him bring that man into the Church. I am as satisfied as I am of anything that with that kind of prayerful, conscientious, directed effort, there isn't a man in this Church who could not convert another. . . .

It is an inspiring experience . . . to witness the manner in which the Lord is weaving the tapestry of his grand design in those foreign parts of the earth. He is gathering his children there as elsewhere—"one of a city and two of a family." He is remembering the promises made of old as he works among those who have seen so much of poverty and misery and evil and oppression. He is answering the prayers of those who have gone before, and who struggled to establish a foothold for the gospel in those distant places. . . .

. . . The work is becoming very much enlarged. It does require a commensurate accumulation of men and means. It requires an expansion of mind and energy, ability and perseverance. Let us prepare ourselves more diligently for the great assignment which God has laid upon us to carry this work to the children of the earth wherever we may be permitted to go. (Gordon B. Hinckley, TGBH, 367)

THEMES *for* LIVING

1. Prepare to Serve "With All Your Heart, Might, Mind, and Strength"
2. The Time Is Now: "The Field Is White"
3. "Open Your Mouths and They Shall Be Filled"
4. The Joy of Missionary Service

INTRODUCTION

According to the Lord's blessings upon Abraham and his seed, the privilege and opportunity to convey the message of the gospel to the world was given to this chosen lineage in perpetuity: "And I will make of thee a great nation, and I will bless thee above measure, and make thy name great among all nations, and thou shalt be a blessing unto thy seed after thee, that in their hands they shall bear this ministry and Priesthood unto all nations" (Abr. 2:9). With the dawning of the Restoration in 1820, the era of missionary work under the Abrahamic covenant was once again opened. As the Church and kingdom of God were reestablished upon the earth, including the priesthood of God and all attendant keys and ordinances, a wave of missionary activity was inaugurated that even now flows over the earth uninterrupted, in ever-growing scope and intensity. "The field is white already to harvest" (D&C 4:4) is a pervasive theme in the pages of the Doctrine and Covenants. The call to thrust one's sickle into the harvest milieu with might is repeated over and over. A careful and prayerful study of those sections of the Doctrine and Covenants outlining in detail the Lord's design for missionary service will provide an inspiring and powerful action plan for success in the program of the Lord's harvest.

MOMENT OF TRUTH

References to the importance of missionary work as a commandment of God are pervasive throughout the Doctrine and Covenants. We have already reviewed in chapter 6 the background to section 11, in which the Lord impressed upon Hyrum Smith the vital role of spreading the gospel: "Behold, the field is white already to harvest; therefore, whoso desireth to reap let him thrust in his sickle with his might, and reap while the day lasts, that he may treasure up for his soul everlasting salvation in the kingdom of God. Yea, whosoever will thrust in his sickle and reap, the same is called of God" (D&C 11:4). Similarly, section 17 contains the directive of the Lord: "And ye shall testify that you have seen them [the plates and associated instruments] . . ." (D&C 17:5; see also the background information in chapter 4).

In addition, sections 4, 12, 14, 15, 16, 18, 31, 32, 33, and 75 include significant material related to the covenant responsibility to spread the word of God for the blessing of humankind. All of these sections comprise a kind of book within a book—a guidebook or syllabus for missionary work in these latter days within the larger framework of the Doctrine and Covenants. Following are details about the setting and background for these sections.

Section 4: Given at Harmony, Susquehanna County, Pennsylvania, in February 1829 through the Prophet Joseph Smith to his father, Joseph Smith Sen.

> Joseph Smith Sr. was the first person to believe the story of the Prophet and encourage him to continue faithful to the teachings of the angel. . . . In February, 1829, he came to his son, the youthful prophet, and asked to know by revelation the will of the Lord. This section of the Doctrine and Covenants is the result of that humble inquiry.

> This revelation is very short, only seven verses, but it contains sufficient counsel and instruction for a life-time study. No one has yet mastered it. . . . It is a revelation to each member of the Church, especially to all who hold the Priesthood. Perhaps there is no other revelation in all our scriptures that embodies greater instruction pertaining to the manner of qualification of members of the Church for the service of God, and in such condensed form than this revelation. It is as broad, as high and as deep as eternity. No elder of the Church is qualified to teach in the Church, or carry the message of Salvation to the world, until he has absorbed, in part at least, this heaven-sent instruction. (Joseph Fielding Smith, *CHMR,* 1:33; see also *HC,* 1:28)

Section 12: Given through the Prophet Joseph Smith in May 1829 at Harmony, Susquehanna County, Pennsylvania, to Joseph Knight, Sen. (see *HC,* 1:47–48). Of this sterling brother, who was from Colesville, New York, the Prophet later wrote this entry in his journal:

> *Tuesday, 22* [1842].—I find my feelings . . . towards my friends revived, while I contemplate the virtues and the good qualities and characteristics of the faithful few, which I am now recording in the Book of the Law of the Lord,—of such as have stood by me in every hour of peril, for these fifteen long years past,—say, for instance, my aged and beloved brother, Joseph Knight, Sen., who was among the number of the first to administer to my necessities, while I was laboring in the commencement of the bringing forth of the work of the Lord, and of laying the foundation of the Church of Jesus Christ of Latter-day Saints. For fifteen years he has been faithful and true, and even-handed and exemplary, and virtuous and kind, never deviating to the right hand or the left. Behold he [is a] righteous man, may God Almighty lengthen out the old man's days; and may his trembling, tortured, and broken body be renewed, and in the vigor of health turn upon him, if it be Thy will, consistently, O God; and it shall be said of him, by the sons of Zion, while there is one of them remaining, that this man was a faithful man in Israel; therefore his name shall never be forgotten. (*HC,* 5:124–25)

Sections 14, 15, and 16: Given through the Prophet Joseph Smith in June 1829 in Fayette, Seneca County, New York, to David Whitmer, John Whitmer, and Peter Whitmer, respectively. Again, the theme of "behold, the field is white already to harvest" is emphasized in Doctrine and Covenants 14:3 and reinforced in sections 15 and 16, where it is said that "the thing that will be of the most worth unto you will be to declare repentance unto this people" (15:6 and 16:6). It was during the months of April, May, and June 1829 that much of the Book of Mormon was translated in Harmony, Pennsylvania. These were months of near-penury for the Prophet, who depended on the generosity of the Whitmer family for financial support. David Whitmer traveled the 135 miles from Fayette to Harmony to assist in transferring the Prophet to the Whitmer home to complete the translation. Sections 14, 15, and 16 were received shortly after the arrival of the party in Fayette in the early part of June (see *HC,* 1:48–51).

Section 18: Given through the Prophet Joseph Smith in June 1829 in Fayette, Seneca County, New York, to Oliver Cowdery and David Whitmer as a result of supplication for knowledge concerning the promised restoration of the Melchizedek Priesthood (see *HC,* 1:60–64). The revelation is a declaration of the worth of souls in the eyes of the Lord and a promise of joy for those who labor to bring souls unto Him. The Lord makes clear that the Father has designated the name of Jesus Christ as the only name under which that salvation is possible (verse 23). Oliver and David are to "search out the Twelve" (verse 37) that are to be called to the Quorum of Twelve Apostles. Subsequently, the Three Witnesses of the Book of Mormon did indeed select the Twelve that were called on February 14–15, 1835, as part of the continuing organization of the priesthood structure for the Church.

Section 31: Given through the Prophet Joseph Smith in September 1830 to Thomas B. Marsh at Fayette, Seneca County, New York (according to Manuscript History of the Church; see *HC,* 1:115–17). Thomas Marsh had moved his residence to Palmyra in that same month after learning about the organization of the new Church. He had been baptized by David Whitmer and ordained an elder at the Whitmer home. Section 31 continues the Lord's instructions for him to carry on missionary work: "Lift up your heart and rejoice, for the hour of your mission is come; and your tongue shall be loosed, and you shall declare glad tidings of great joy unto this generation. You shall declare the things which have been revealed to my servant, Joseph Smith, Jun. You shall begin to preach from this time forth, yea, to reap in the field which is white already to be burned" (D&C 31:3–4). Thomas Marsh had a colorful and varied experience in the Church. He was ordained one of the Twelve on April 26, 1835, but was later excommunicated for apostasy on March 17, 1839. He was rebaptized on July 16, 1857, in Florence, Nebraska, and arrived in Utah in September 1857, where his return to the Church was approved by Church leaders on September 6 of that same year. In 1859 he settled in Spanish Fork, Utah. He taught school there and was reordained an elder on March 11, 1859, and then a high priest by November 1861. He received the endowment and was sealed to Hannah Adams in the Endowment House on November 1, 1862. Later he moved to Ogden, Utah, where he died in January 1866 (see *RPJS,* 42–43).

Section 33: Given through the Prophet Joseph Smith in October 1830 at Fayette, Seneca County, New York, to Ezra Thayre and Northrop Sweet, who had sought the will of the Lord concerning their role in the Restoration (see *HC,* 1:126–27). Ezra Thayre had provided employment for Joseph Smith Sr. in New York and was later baptized by Parley P. Pratt in October of 1830. He was ordained an elder and a high priest, participated in missionary work (though with some degree of reluctance), and later became disaffected. Northrop Sweet was also baptized by Parley P. Pratt in October 1830 and was ordained an elder the following June. At first he accepted the revelation but soon fell away from the restored Church (see Susan Easton Black, *Who's Who in the Doctrine and Covenants* [Salt Lake City: Bookcraft, 1997], 310–11, 318–21).

Section 75: Given through the Prophet Joseph Smith on January 25, 1832, at Amherst, Lorain County, Ohio, some fifty miles to the west of Kirtland (see *HC,* 1:242–45). The occasion was a special conference of the Church at which Joseph Smith was sustained and ordained President of the High Priesthood. The elders assembled (including Orson Hyde, Hyrum Smith, Samuel H. Smith, Luke Johnson, and others) received counsel of the Lord in respect to their stewardships as emissaries of the Lord in proclaiming His gospel.

1. PREPARE TO SERVE "WITH ALL YOUR HEART, MIGHT, MIND, AND STRENGTH"

THEME: Service in the vineyard of the Lord requires focused and devoted preparation. The heart is prepared through the "mighty change" that King Benjamin's people experienced (Mosiah 5:2; Alma 5:13), whereby they became sons and daughters of the Lord, having cultivated a broken heart and a contrite spirit. Our minds are prepared through prayerful immersion in the word of God, which aligns us with God's will and imbues us with the vision of contributing to the divine design of bringing about "the immortality and eternal life of man" (Moses 1:39). Might and strength are prepared by constantly exercising our spiritual faculties of faith and hope, whereby we learn to depend on the strength and might of the Lord, in whom alone is centered the power of salvation.

MODERN PROPHETS SPEAK

George Albert Smith:

> One of the very first revelations that was given by our Heavenly Father, as contained in the Doctrine and Covenants, reads as follows: [4:1–2, quoted.]

> Now I do not understand that we are serving God with all our might if we forsake his children, or if we spend so much of our time selfishly building up ourselves, accumulating things of this life, and leaving his children in darkness, when we could bring them into the light. My understanding is that the most important mission that I have in this life is: first, to keep the commandments of God, as they have been taught to me; and next, to teach them to my Father's children who do not understand them. It makes little difference when I go to the other side, whether I have been a man of wealth in this world or not, unless I have used that wealth to bless my fellow men. Though I be a wanderer in this world, and suffer for the necessities of life, if by reason of the knowledge that my Father has given me I devote myself to the instruction of his children, to planting faith in their hearts, to dissipating the

errors that have come to them by tradition, I believe when I go to the other side that I will find a bank account that will be beyond compare with what I would have if I lived for the things of this earth alone. I read a portion of the section 4 and I want to read that last verse again: [4:2–3, quoted.]

It is not necessary for you to be called to go into the mission field in order to proclaim the truth. Begin on the man who lives next door by inspiring confidence in him, by inspiring love in him for you because of your righteousness, and your missionary work has already begun. [4:4–7, quoted.] (CR, October 1916, 50–51)

Ezra Taft Benson:

It is our duty, divinely imposed, to continue urgently and militantly to carry forward our missionary work. We must continue to call missionaries and send them out to preach the gospel, which was never more needed than now, which is the only remedy for the tragic ills that now afflict the world, and which alone can bring peace and brotherly love back amongst the peoples of the earth.

This is not a matter of our own choosing. It is not something that has been devised by man. The Lord has made it clear to us, my brethren, that the responsibility is ours, as holders of the priesthood, to carry this message of the restored gospel to the people of the world. . . .

As Latter-day Saints everywhere, with personal testimonies of these great events, we accept humbly, gratefully, this major responsibility placed upon the Church. We are happy to be engaged in a partnership with our Heavenly Father in the great work of the salvation and exaltation of His children. Willingly we give of our time and the means with which He may bless us to the establishment of His kingdom in the earth. This we know is our first duty and our great opportunity. This spirit has characterized the missionary work of the Church of Jesus Christ in all ages. It has been an outstanding mark of the ushering in of the dispensation of the fulness of times—our time. Wherever faithful Latter-day Saints are to be found, this spirit of unselfish sacrifice for the greatest cause in all the earth exists. In a statement published to the world during the last world war, the First Presidency of the Church declared: "No act of ours or of the Church must interfere with this God-given mandate" (CR April 1942, 91). (*TETB,* 181)

David O McKay:

The essential qualifications of those who were to participate in the bringing about of this marvelous work . . . were not the possession of wealth, not social distinction, not political preferment, not military achievement, not nobility of birth; but a desire to serve God with all your "heart, might, mind and strength"—spiritual qualities that contribute to nobility of soul. (CR, October 1966, 86).

ILLUSTRATIONS FOR OUR TIMES

The Vision of Service

Doctrine and Covenants section 4 is a beacon of spiritual light, unparalleled in its power to illuminate the entire landscape of righteous service in the most economical of terms. Every missionary—indeed, every laborer in the Church—is well advised to commit these words to memory and ponder them frequently as a standard of service in the Lord's kingdom. It is instructive that the Lord puts strong emphasis at the outset on the faculty of sight as it pertains to service in His kingdom: "Therefore, O ye that embark in the service of God, *see* that ye serve him with all your heart, might, mind and strength" (verse 2, emphasis added). The Lord further includes the attribute of focused spiritual vision as a quality essential for service: "with an eye single to the glory of God" (verse 5).

When our daughter Stephanie was serving her mission in Japan a number of years ago, she experienced a particularly poignant confirmation of the need to cultivate spiritual sight, keeping one's eye "single to the glory of God." During one period of her mission, Stephanie and her companion went for a fairly long period of time with little harvest to show for their labors. They went to the Lord to seek a blessing and guidance, that He might soften the hearts of the people around them and lead them to the honest seekers after truth. Being an artist of some merit, our daughter felt inclined at that time to make simple sketches of the images of unknown Japanese people that came into her mind. There was the image of a young man, an older man, a young woman—strangers that were present to her mind's eye. Without thinking much of these sketches at the time, she continued her labors with her companion in all diligence, attempting to invest the qualities called for in section 4: "And faith, hope, charity and love, with an eye single to the glory of God, qualify him for the work" (verse 5).

Then the miracles began to happen. People began to respond. There was an older man who opened up his heart to the promptings of the Spirit. There was a younger man who came to receive with gratitude the message of the gospel. There was a younger woman who responded to the good news delivered by the young sister missionaries. And the Lord brought others as well into their circle of acquaintance, with hearts that recognized and accepted the truth of the Restoration. One day during this time of spiritual abundance, Stephanie came to focus again on her sketches and found, much to her amazement, that those strangers on paper were not strangers at all, but indeed the very images of the Lord's seekers after truth as they were guided, one by one, into the circle of enlightenment. To the Lord there are no strangers, for all are his choice sons and daughters waiting to become "fellowcitizens with the saints, and of the household of God" (Eph. 2:19). By keeping an open vision, Stephanie received a deep spiritual confirmation of how to "see" with the eye of service, how to "view" the coming blessings bestowed by the "Lord of the harvest" (Alma 26:7) upon His faithful laborers. She learned in a special and remarkable way what King Benjamin's ardent listeners also learned: "And we, ourselves, also, through the infinite goodness of God, and the manifestations of his Spirit, have great views of that which is to come; and were it expedient, we could prophesy of all things" (Mosiah 5:3). Thus the blessings of section 4 of the Doctrine and Covenants were fulfilled for our missionary daughter, just as they are each day fulfilled and can evermore be fulfilled for all who desire in faith to serve the Lord. (Allen)

LIKENING THE SCRIPTURES TO OUR LIVES

Doctrine and Covenants 18:19 In order to do anything in the name of the Lord, we must first cultivate faith, hope, and charity.

Application: Let us take an inventory of our spiritual storehouse to ensure that we have an ample supply of what the Lord has deemed vital to our success in missionary work: faith, hope, charity, temperance, trust.

2. THE TIME IS NOW: "THE FIELD IS WHITE"

THEME: Missionary work is a work that demands immediate action. The workers in the Lord's vineyard are not procrastinators, but given over to initiative, valor, and prompt response to the guidance of the Spirit.

MODERN PROPHETS SPEAK

Gordon B. Hinckley:

> I believe . . . with all my heart that the field is white ready to harvest. . . . I think the answer to an increased number of converts does not lie particularly in our methods—effective as those methods are. Rather, I think we are living in the day of the fulfillment of the word of the Lord given through the Prophet Joel, and repeated by Moroni in his first visitation to the Prophet Joseph.

> "And it shall come to pass afterward, that I will pour out my Spirit upon all flesh . . ." (Joel 2:28).

. . . Great and magnificent as is the work of the . . . missionaries who have been set apart, I am convinced that we have a far greater force for teaching the gospel to the world in the membership of the Church—"every man a missionary"—as has been said here so convincingly tonight. "Every man a missionary!" (*TGBH,* 366)

LIKENING THE SCRIPTURES TO OUR LIVES

Doctrine and Covenants 29:7 Each of us is called to help gather the elect into the fold of God. The elect will hear the word of the Lord and open their hearts to the gospel.

Application: So many people are ready. We simply must thrust in our sickle (see D&C 31:5). The elect are waiting and simply don't know where to find the truth (see D&C 123:12). We are the disciples of Jesus Christ in charge of the gathering of Israel—and this is the last time the vineyard will be worked (see Jacob 5:70–77).

3. "OPEN YOUR MOUTHS AND THEY SHALL BE FILLED"

THEME: When the prepared and the humble teach the gospel, the Spirit prompts them to speak the words of life as the Lord would have this message presented: "Therefore, verily I say unto you, lift up your voices unto this people; speak the thoughts that I shall put into your hearts, and you shall not be confounded before men; For it shall be given you in the very hour, yea, in the very moment, what ye shall say" (D&C 100:5–6).

MODERN PROPHETS SPEAK

Henry B. Eyring:
> Your descendants will teach doctrine to each other because you taught it. Doctrine can more than open minds to spiritual things and hearts to the love of God. When that doctrine brings joy and peace, it also has the power to open mouths. (*Ensign,* May 1999, 73)

Boyd K. Packer:
> If you will speak with humility and honest intent, the Lord will not leave you alone. The scriptures promise that. Consider this one:

> "Therefore, verily I say unto you, lift up your voices unto this people; speak the thoughts that I shall [note that it is future tense] put into your hearts, and you shall not be confounded before men;

"For it shall [again note the future tense] be given you in the very hour, yea, in the very moment, what ye shall say.

"But a commandment I give unto you, that ye shall declare whatsoever thing ye declare in my name, in solemnity of heart, in the spirit of meekness, in all things.

"And I give unto you this promise, that inasmuch as ye do this the Holy Ghost shall be shed forth in bearing record unto all things whatsoever ye shall say" (D&C 100:5–8)

The skeptic will say that to bear testimony when you may not know you possess one is to condition yourself; that the response is manufactured. Well, one thing for sure, the skeptic will never know, for he will not meet the requirement of faith, humility, and obedience to qualify him for the visitation of the Spirit.

Can you not see that that is where testimony is hidden, protected perfectly from the insincere, from the intellectual, from the mere experimenter, the arrogant, the faithless, the proud? It will not come to them. (*Ensign,* January 1983, 51)

ILLUSTRATIONS FOR OUR TIMES

Overcoming Fear

I'll never forget when I served as a mission president in the MTC. The last meeting before the missionaries would go out, I would speak about being bold, obedient, full of love, and courageous in opening their mouths. "Do not be afraid. The worth of souls is great. You have a mighty role in the kingdom." Well, some of them were still afraid. I would ask them on their way to their mission to have a finding experience of opening their mouth. One sweet young sister wrote me a letter after she'd been out two weeks, and this is how it went: "Dear President, after your talk Sunday night I was so nervous I didn't know what to do. I knew I'd be leaving Wednesday, and I was going to have to open my mouth. And I thought, *I can't do it, I can't do it.* So, I fasted and I prayed and I left Wednesday on the plane, and to my joy I had a window seat and my companion sat next to me. So I said, 'Oh dear, I won't be able to talk to anybody on the plane,' and so I was relieved. But then, I got into the airport and I sat down, and here was a man sitting across from me. He was old and different looking, and I didn't know what to do. And all I could remember was your voice telling us, 'Open your mouth; it will be filled, I promise you.' Well, I girded up my loins and I opened my mouth and said, 'Hi, where you headed?' From that little beginning began an hour conversation. Pretty soon we became friends. And after a bit I said, 'If you knew there was another book written about Jesus Christ, would you be interested in reading that? The Book of Mormon?'

"He said, 'Oh, I have a Book of Mormon.' I committed him right there to read the book, and then he told me, 'My daughter is taking the discussions, too.'

"And then I said, 'Is it OK if I have the missionaries come by and see you?' He said, 'That will just be fine.' Oh, President, it's so easy to open your mouth. The Lord will fill it. There's nothing to it." I read that letter every time to departing missionaries because it helped them realize that we can all do it. All of us—member missionaries and full-time proselyting missionaries—can open our mouths and they will be filled. (Pinegar)

LIKENING THE SCRIPTURES TO OUR LIVES

Doctrine and Covenants 28:16 As recipients of the everlasting gospel of Jesus Christ, we each have a responsibility to open our mouths and share the glad tidings with those around us.

Application: The Lord will assist us if we will just open our mouths. Start a conversation and turn it into a teaching moment for the gospel. Remember, the Lord will help you (see D&C 100:5–6).

4. THE JOY OF MISSIONARY SERVICE

THEME: The Lord has promised that joy will attend the actions of those who labor with devotion in His missionary service. There are few experiences in life that bring such a rewarding and edifying measure of joy and happiness as being engaged in sharing the light of the gospel with others.

MODERN PROPHETS SPEAK

Ezra Taft Benson:

> You must not allow yourselves to become discouraged. Missionary work brings joy, optimism, and happiness. Don't give Satan an opportunity to discourage you. Here again, work is the answer. The Lord has given us a key by which we can overcome discouragement: "Come unto me, all ye that labour and are heavy laden, and I will give you rest. Take my yoke upon you, and learn of me; for I am meek and lowly in heart; and ye shall find rest unto your souls. For my yoke is easy and my burden is light" (Matt. 11:28–30). (*TETB*, 205–6)

ILLUSTRATIONS FOR OUR TIMES

True Joy

Alma knew the joy of bringing souls to Christ: "I know that which the Lord hath commanded me, and I glory in it. I do not glory of myself, but I glory in that which the Lord hath commanded me; yea, and this is my glory, that perhaps I may be an instrument in the hands of God to bring some soul to repentance; and this is my joy. And behold, when I see many of my brethren truly penitent, and coming to the Lord their God, then is my soul filled with joy; then do I remember what the Lord has done for me, yea, even that he hath heard my prayer; yea, then do I remember his merciful arm which he extended towards me" (Alma 29:9–10).

The sons of Mosiah knew the worth of souls: "Now they were desirous that salvation should be declared to every creature, for they could not bear that any human soul should perish; yea, even the very thoughts that any soul should endure endless torment did cause them to quake and tremble" (Mosiah 28:3). They knew where their joy was to be found, and Alma rejoiced in their success, "But I do not joy in my own success alone, but my joy is more full because of the success of my brethren, who have been up to the land of Nephi" (Alma 29:14).

And missionaries today have that same joy. A new missionary out just one month said in his weekly letter, "Oh, President Pinegar, I've never been so happy. If can I can dress in white once a month (have a baptism) I'll be the happiest man in the entire world." Elders and sisters return from their missions with much joy and satisfaction. Words from the pulpit repeated over and over, "It was the best two years," or "It was the greatest two years," or "It was the happiest time of my life." Why do missionaries say those words? Because this is true joy—helping people partake of the gospel of Jesus Christ. (Pinegar)

LIKENING THE SCRIPTURES TO OUR LIVES

Doctrine and Covenants 18:15–16 As we labor diligently to bring souls unto Christ, we will be preparing for a time when, in the kingdom of God, we can experience unthinkable joy and satisfaction mingling with those who will hear and accept our testimony of the gospel.

Application: Like God, this is our joy and glory: helping people come unto Christ and partake of His infinite Atonement (see Moses 1:39). We do this as parents, as home and visiting teachers, as priesthood bearers, in our Church callings, as disciples of Christ, as friends and neighbors, and as full-time missionaries. Everyone is a priceless child of God; everyone is in the process of becoming. It is our privilege to participate in this great work. This truly becomes our work and glory as we assist our Heavenly Father and Savior in Their work.

SUMMARY

Within the Doctrine and Covenants there is a corpus of interrelated sections that constitute a powerful missionary guidebook. A prayerful pondering of sections 4, 11, 12, 14, 15, 16, 17, 18, 31, 33, and 75 (along with many other similar passages in holy writ) will provide a substantial framework for successful missionary work in keeping with the Lord's principles and guidelines—whether for the extended commission to labor as a full-time missionary or for the day-by-day harvest in which all the Saints are enlisted as part of their obligations under the Abrahamic covenant. As we liken the scriptures to ourselves (see 1 Ne. 19:23), these sections become advice, counsel, and inspiration for our personal lives as we seek to serve. They apply to us just as they applied to Joseph Smith Sr., Hyrum Smith, Joseph Knight, the Whitmer brothers, and many others among the founding laborers of the Restoration. The power of these scriptures comes to bear in our lives as we live them. Truly, the harvest is at hand and God's laborers are called to serve with all of their "heart, might, mind and strength" (D&C 4:2). Let us remember that "the worth of souls is great in the sight of God" (D&C 18:10). Let us cry repentance unto the world and know the joy of bringing our brothers and sisters back into the fold.

CHAPTER TWELVE

"THE GATHERING *of* MY PEOPLE"

Reading Assignment: Doctrine and Covenants 29:1–8; 33:3–7; 37, 38:24–41; 52:2–5, 42–43; 57:1–3; 110:11; Articles of Faith 1:10; *Our Heritage*, pages 16–23, 37–39.

Additional Reading: 1 Nephi 15:12–17; 22:11–12; Doctrine and Covenants 39:15; 95:8; 105:33; 110:9; 123:12.

And so, having presented his doctrine relative to the restoration of the gospel, the gathering of Israel, and the establishment of Zion—all in the latter days—Jesus said: "And then shall that which is written come to pass," at which point he quoted, with minor improvements, the whole fifty-fourth chapter of Isaiah. In poetic language, using figures of speech common in his day, Isaiah proclaimed that Israel—scattered, barren, without seed born under the covenant—would again break forth into singing; that Zion would enlarge her borders, strengthen her stakes, break forth on the right hand and on the left, and build up the ancient and desolate cities; and that the saints of latter days would no longer be ashamed, nor remember the reproach of their scattered days nor the sorrows of their widowhood. (Bruce R. McConkie, The Mortal Messiah: From Bethlehem to Calvary, *4 vols. [Salt Lake City: Deseret Book, 1979–81], 4:363)*

THEMES *for* LIVING

1. The Lord's Design in Gathering Israel
2. The Gathering Today: "Stand in Holy Places"

INTRODUCTION

The concept of the gathering of Israel—pervasive throughout the scriptures—is memorialized in the tenth article of faith: "We believe in the literal gathering of Israel and in the restoration of the Ten Tribes; that Zion (the New Jerusalem) will be built upon the American continent; that Christ will reign personally upon the earth; and, that the earth will be renewed and receive its paradisiacal glory." This key doctrine is celebrated in the magnificent "new song" presented in Doctrine and Covenants 84 as a triumph of the divine design to bring together the covenant peoples of Israel in the latter days:

The Lord hath brought again Zion;

The Lord hath redeemed his people, Israel,

According to the election of grace,

Which was brought to pass by the faith

And covenant of their fathers.

The Lord hath redeemed his people;

And Satan is bound and time is no longer.

The Lord hath gathered all things in one. (D&C 84:99–100)

The process of the ultimate gathering commenced in the early years of the dawning of the Restoration. In the month of December 1830, the Prophet Joseph Smith and Sidney Rigdon received a revelation near Fayette, New York, in which the first commandment concerning a specific gathering in this dispensation is given: "And again, a commandment I give unto the church, that it is expedient in me that they should assemble together at the Ohio [Kirtland]" (D&C 37:3; see *HC,* 1:139). The persecution against the Church in New York had become bitter, and it was the Lord's design to gather the Saints to Ohio for a season of time, where the spirit was more conducive to the unfolding of the infant Church. In fact, the principle of gathering is a key ingredient in the gospel plan itself, for "gathering" is analogous to building strength, enhancing security, increasing protection, the sharing of knowledge and revealed wisdom, the fostering of temple work, and the more efficient nurturing of spiritual development through obedience to the commandments of Christ. The gathering is a divine process that informs the entire structure of Zion: families gather and stay close together for continuous temporal and spiritual growth; ward families gather for the sharing of spiritual gifts and the cultivation of purity and unity; stakes of Zion gather their Saints to rest in safety below the canopy of heavenly protection; and the whole Church gathers its forces in "holy places" to fulfill the functions of the Abrahamic covenant in carrying the blessings of the priesthood throughout the world. Thus, "gathering" is a divine process, and it will continue until the day when the Lord will have finally "gathered all things in one" (D&C 84:100).

MOMENT OF TRUTH

In addition to Doctrine and Covenants section 37, referred to above, there are many other key references to the gathering in the Doctrine and Covenants, including sections 29, 38, 52, and 57. Here is a brief summary of the historical backgrounds of these revelations to provide a framework for the thematic discussion to follow.

Section 29: Given through the Prophet Joseph Smith in September 1830 at Fayette, Seneca County, New York, some days before the convening of the second conference of the Church in the home of Peter Whitmer (see *HC,* 1:111–15). According to the minutes of the conference found in the *Far West Record,* there were six elders present in addition to Joseph Smith: Oliver Cowdery, David Whitmer, John Whitmer, Peter Whitmer, Samuel H. Smith, and Thomas B. Marsh (very likely the same as those referred to as having been present when section 29 was given—see *HC,* 1:111).

Section 38: Given through the Prophet Joseph Smith on Sunday, January 2, 1831, at Fayette, Seneca County, New York, on the occasion of a conference of the Church held at the home of Peter Whitmer Sr. (see *HC,* 1:140–43). Because section 37 had given the commandment for the Saints to assemble in Ohio, the conference was eager to learn more about the matter. The Lord responded: "I tell you these things because of your prayers; wherefore, treasure up wisdom in your bosoms, lest the wickedness of men reveal these things unto you by their wickedness, in a manner which shall speak in your ears with a voice louder than that which shall shake the earth; but if ye are prepared ye shall not fear. And that ye might escape the power of the enemy, and be gathered unto me a righteous people, without spot and blameless—Wherefore, for this cause I gave unto you the commandment that ye should go to the Ohio; and there I will give unto you my law; and there you shall be endowed with power from on high" (D&C 38:30–32).

The commandment to gather in Ohio was a considerable test for the Saints, and not all heeded the word of the Lord with full devotion. Those who did were privileged to participate in the grand unfolding saga of the ongoing restoration of the Lord's Church and kingdom in the latter days. Joseph Smith and Sidney Rigdon left from New York later that same month (January 1831), arriving in Kirtland toward the end of the month. The remainder of the New York Saints who followed the Lord's commandment were resettled in Kirtland by the middle part of May 1831. Thus the first phase of the gathering in this dispensation was accomplished.

Section 52: Given through the Prophet Joseph Smith on June 7, 1831, on the Isaac Morley farm at Kirtland, Geauga County, Ohio (see *HC,* 1:175–79). This revelation was given following the three-day conference convened on June 3, 1831, as directed in Doctrine and Covenants 44. It had been a rather significant conference attended by a large congregation of Saints. Joseph Smith spoke concerning this conference: "It was clearly evident that the Lord gave us power in proportion to the work to be done, and strength according to the race set before us, and grace and help as our needs required. Great harmony prevailed; several were ordained; faith was strengthened; and humility, so necessary for the blessing of God to follow prayer, characterized the Saints" (*HC,* 1:175).

During this conference, the first high priests in this dispensation were ordained. One of the best descriptions of this conference and the high priests' ordination is from Levi Hancock's journal: "The fourth of June came and we all met in a little string of buildings under the hill near Isaac Morley's in Kirtland, Geauga County, Ohio. Then we all went to a schoolhouse on the hill, about one fourth of a mile ascending nearly all the way. The building was built of logs. It was filled with slab benches. Here the elders were seated and the meeting was opened as usual. . . . Joseph put his hands on Harvey Whitlock and ordained him to the High Priesthood. . . . Then he ordained Jacob Scott and some others to the High Priesthood."

Also during the conference, the Prophet experienced two heavenly visions, one of the Father and the Son. The first occurred while the high priests were being ordained. Levi Hancock records that the Prophet, who was speaking, stepped out onto the floor and said: "I now see God, and Jesus Christ at his right hand, let them kill me, I should not feel death as I am now." John Whitmer, the official Church historian and recorder, wrote of this same appearance: "The Spirit of the Lord fell upon Joseph in an unusual manner. . . . After he had prophesied he laid his hands upon Lyman Wight [and ordained him] to the High Priesthood. . . . And the spirit fell upon Lyman, and he prophesied, concerning the coming of Christ. . . . He saw the heavens opened, and the Son of man sitting on the right hand of the Father. Making intercession for his brethren, the Saints. He said that God would work a work in these last days that tongue cannot express, and the mind is not capable to conceive. The glory of the Lord shone around" (*HC,* 1:176).

In terms of the gathering, it is significant that thirty-two elders were called on this occasion to go on missions to Missouri, which the Lord also declared to be a key gathering place (D&C 52:42–44).

Section 57: Given through the Prophet Joseph Smith in July 1831 at Jackson County, Missouri (Independence). This is the revelation that identifies Independence, Missouri, as a central gathering place of Zion: "Hearken, O ye elders of my church, saith the Lord your God, who have assembled yourselves together, according to my commandments, in this land, which is the land of Missouri, which is the land which I have appointed and consecrated for the gathering of the saints. Wherefore, this is the land of promise, and the place for the city of Zion" (D&C 57:1–2).

Historian Lyndon W. Cook gives the following summary of the background to this revelation:

> Obedient to the instructions of section 52, numerous pairs of missionaries started for Independence, Missouri. Joseph Smith with seven others (Martin Harris, Sidney Rigdon, Edward Partridge, William W. Phelps, Joseph Coe, A. Sidney Gilbert, and his wife, Elizabeth) left Kirtland for Missouri on 19 June 1831. . . . After "viewing the county [and] seeking diligently at the hand of God," Joseph Smith received section 57, which designated "the very spot upon which [the Lord] designed to commence the work of gathering," and the upbuilding of an "holy city," even the New Jerusalem. On 2 August 1831, some twelve miles west of Independence, Sidney Rigdon consecrated and dedicated the land for the gathering of the Saints.

> The revelation clarified that, the place which is now called Independence is the center place; and a spot for the temple is lying westward, upon a lot which is not far from the court-house (see verse 3). On 3 August 1831, the Prophet dedicated a spot, for the construction of a temple, which was located approximately one-half mile west of the courthouse (the courthouse mentioned in verse 3 was a brick structure erected 1828–32). Bishop Edward Partridge purchased a tract of land consisting of 63 and 43/166 acres from Jones H. Flournoy on 19 December 1831 for $130. This purchase included the three-acre temple lot dedicated by the Prophet. (*RPJS,* 91)

1. THE LORD'S DESIGN IN GATHERING ISRAEL

THEME: The Lord loves His children with an infinite love. He yearns to bring them together in the interests of their happiness and spiritual and temporal security, "even as a hen gathereth her chickens under her wings, even as many as will hearken to my voice and humble themselves before me, and call upon me in mighty prayer" (D&C 29:2). At times this gathering is framed in specific terms, such as the call to flock to Kirtland ("And again, a commandment I give unto the church, that it is expedient in me that they should assemble together at the Ohio, against the time that my servant Oliver Cowdery shall return unto them" [D&C 37:3]) or the call to assemble in Missouri ("And thus saith the Lord your God, if you will receive wisdom here is wisdom. Behold, the place which is now called Independence is the center place; and a spot for the temple is lying westward, upon a lot which is not far from the courthouse" [D&C 57:3]). At other times the call is to "stand in holy places" (D&C 45:32; 87:8; 101:22) or to labor in one's own land for the building up of stakes and erecting temples to the Most High. Whatever the prophets of the Lord direct, that we should do.

MODERN PROPHETS SPEAK

Bruce R. McConkie:

> Why is the Lord gathering Israel in these last days? It is to fulfil the covenant made with Abraham and renewed with Isaac and Jacob and others. What is that covenant? It is not the gathering of Israel *per se,* but something far more important than the mere assembling of a people in Jerusalem or on Mount Zion or at any designated place. It is not the allocation of Palestine for the seed of Abraham, or the designation of the Americas as the inheritance of Joseph, though each of these arrangements has a bearing on the fulfillment of the covenant. The gathering of Israel, at whatever place Deity specifies, is a necessary condition precedent, something that makes possible the fulfilling of the ancient covenant. What, then, is the covenant itself? (*The Mortal Messiah: From Bethlehem to Calvary,* 4 vols. [Salt Lake City: Deseret Book, 1979–81], 4:337)

ILLUSTRATIONS FOR OUR TIMES

The Gathering—A Design of the Councils of Heaven

It was Sunday, June 11, 1843. The Prophet Joseph Smith was addressing a large assembly of Saints in Nauvoo. He cited the famous passage from Matthew 23:37: "O Jerusalem, Jerusalem, thou that killest the prophets, and stonest them which are sent unto thee, how oft would I have gathered thy children together, even as a hen gathereth her chickens under her wings, and ye would not!" Using that scripture as his text, Joseph Smith told the audience that he felt inspired to speak of the gathering of Israel, stating:

> It was the design of the councils of heaven before the world was that the principles and laws of the priesthood should be predicated upon the gathering of the people in every age of the world. Jesus did everything to gather the people, and they would not be gathered, and He therefore poured out curses upon them. Ordinances instituted in the heavens before the foundations of the world, in the priesthood, for the salvation of men, are not to be altered or changed. All must be saved on the same principles. It is for the same purpose that God gathers together His people in the last days, to build unto the Lord a house to prepare them for the ordinances and endowments, washings and anointings, etc. . . . If a man gets a fulness of the priesthood of God, he has to get it in the same way that Jesus Christ obtained it, and that was by keeping all the commandments and obeying all the ordinances of the house of the Lord. (*HC,* 5:423–24)

Every needful blessing will be provided to those who seek to gather the lost sheep of Israel. Every help and support from heaven will be brought to bear for the faithful and devoted who feel in their hearts the urgency to come home to holy places of Zion (see *TPJS,* 163, 183).

LIKENING THE SCRIPTURES TO OUR LIVES

Doctrine and Covenants 110:11 Under the direction of Jesus Christ, Moses appeared to Joseph Smith and restored the keys of the gathering of Israel.

Application: The Kirtland period was truly a pentecostal time in the Church (see Enrichment section of this chapter). More revelations were given in this area than in any other, including the restoration of vital priesthood keys. The restoration of the keys to the gathering placed a sacred obligation upon the Saints to act in the service of that gathering. We are responsible in a most direct way for the gathering—preaching the gospel to every nation, kindred, tongue, and people—that all might come unto Christ (see D&C 39:11).

2. THE GATHERING TODAY: "STAND IN HOLY PLACES"

THEME: The ancient American prophet Nephi foresaw in grand detail the panorama of the vast gathering process of the latter days: "Wherefore, the Lord God will proceed to make bare his arm in the eyes of all the nations, in bringing about his covenants and his gospel unto those who are of the house of Israel. Wherefore, he will bring them again out of captivity, and they shall be gathered together to the lands of their inheritance; and they shall be brought out of obscurity and out of darkness; and they shall know that the Lord is their Savior and their Redeemer, the Mighty One of Israel" (1 Ne. 22:11–12). This gathering commenced at Kirtland, expanded for a season to Missouri, broadened through the westward diaspora of the Saints "unto the utmost bound of the everlasting hills" (Gen. 49:26) in the Salt Lake Valley, and continues even to this day in the assembling of the faithful to the stakes of Zion and her temples in all regions of the world: "I have kept in store a blessing such as is not known among the children of men, and it shall be poured forth upon their heads. And from thence [Ohio] men shall go forth into all nations" (D&C 39:15). Thus, in our day, the call to "stand in holy places" defines the expanding bounds of Zion as the myriad congregations of the Lord's Saints, established in growing measure in homes of faith and stakes of strength, especially wherever the devoted gather in numbers sufficient to call forth the blessings of building and commissioning temples to the Most High: "Behold, it is my will, that all they who call on my name, and worship me according to mine everlasting gospel, should gather together, and stand in holy places" (D&C 101:22; see also 45:32; 87:8).

MODERN PROPHETS SPEAK

Harold B. Lee:

> Of this glorious day of restoration and gathering, another Nephite prophet said: "the Lord . . . has covenanted with all the house of Israel that 'the time comes that they shall be restored to the true church and fold of God'; and that 'they shall be gathered home to the lands of their inheritance, and shall be established in all their lands of promise'" (2 Ne. 9:1–2).

> Now I call your attention to the facts set forth in these scriptures, that the gathering of Israel consists of joining the true church; of coming to a knowledge of the true God and of his saving truths; and of worshiping him in the congregations of the Saints in all nations and among all peoples. Please note that these revealed words speak of the folds of the Lord; of Israel being gathered to the lands of their inheri-

tance; of Israel being established in all their lands of promise; and of there being congregations of the covenant people of the Lord in every nation, speaking every tongue, and among every people when the Lord comes again. (*Ye Are the Light of the World: Selected Sermons and Writings of Harold B. Lee* [Salt Lake City: Deseret Book, 1974], 141)

ILLUSTRATIONS FOR OUR TIMES

The Practice of Gathering

In the early days of the Church, members demonstrated their loyalty by gathering to a central location, usually the headquarters of the Church, for the purpose of strengthening the Lord's kingdom. Thus, in the 19th century, converts relocated to designated gathering places such as Ohio, Missouri, Illinois, or Utah. During its first four decades in Utah, the Church even sponsored a systematic program that assisted converts from the eastern United States and Europe in relocating to Church headquarters in the Intermountain West. . . .

By the 1890s, however, circumstances began to change. The United States government put greater restrictions on immigration. At the same time, the Latter-day Saint stronghold in the West had grown and solidified. The leaders of the Church began to work toward "an expanded vision . . . of the distant stakes of the tent of Zion" [see Isa. 54:2; D&C 82:14]. . . . By the 1920s, the First Presidency specifically admonished the missionaries to cease preaching emigration; the converts in foreign countries could do more to build the kingdom if they would remain in their own lands. The great movement to gather to a central location had been an important phase in our church's history, the First Presidency said, "but we must realize that times and conditions *change* and that therefore the application of the principles and teachings must *change*."

One of the most instructive statements in helping us understand the concept of gathering for the Church today was made by Elder Bruce R. McConkie. While a member of the First Council of the Seventy, he said in a sermon to the Saints of Mexico and Central America in August 1972: "The place of gathering for the Mexican Saints is in Mexico; the place of gathering for the Guatemalan Saints is in Guatemala; the place of gathering for the Brazilian Saints is in Brazil; and so it goes throughout the length and breadth of the whole earth. . . . Every nation is the gathering place for its own people."

President Spencer W. Kimball gave emphasis to this important concept in 1978: "Now the gathering of Israel consists of joining the true church and . . . coming to the knowledge of the true God. . . . Any person, therefore, who has accepted the restored gospel, and who now seeks to worship the Lord in his own tongue and with the Saints in the nations where he lives, has complied with the law of the gathering of Israel and is heir to all of the blessings promised the Saints in these last days." Any adjustments to the current policy will come through the First Presidency. (Arnold K. Garr, *Ensign,* October 1996, 25)

We Are the Gathering

My family—like so many families in the Church—has experienced a variety of moves and transitions over the years occasioned by professional, educational, and other career developments. In such cases there are typically many options and choices to consider within a framework of prayerful planning. We have made it a point to ponder such transitions in the context of the "gathering" in the larger sense—always asking where the Lord would have us go in the interests of being more productive servants. I recall, for example, the anxious hours of decision making, many years ago, relative to the choice of which graduate school to attend to continue my studies. When good fortune opened up the opportunity to select from among several attractive schools in the East, my wife and I spent time fasting and praying for guidance. Soon the choice was made, based on all the information at hand. We went to the Lord for confirmation, which came in the form of a strong spiritual impression that the decision was correct. Thus we went forward with the plan, not knowing at the time that both of us would be privileged in our new environment to serve in many capacities of leadership that would help to build the kingdom. And so it is with the "gathering." The Lord, in His wisdom, places the Saints where they can contribute to the building up of His kingdom.

Just recently the stake presidency in our area was changed after these three valiant brethren and their families had devoted nine long years of their lives in this phase of service to the Lord. The first counselor (who happened to live in our ward) had developed a family travel agenda with his wife in anticipation of the release. How amazed they were when the Lord, acting through His servant, a visiting general authority, reached out and selected this fine brother as the new stake president. He shared with us in a leadership meeting soon thereafter that even the presiding authority had expressed surprise at the call, citing the long years already invested in that capacity, but confirmed that it was the will of the Lord. Thus the "gathering" retained this most capable leader in his home territory where, by assignment from the visiting general authority, he is to learn why the Lord has placed him in this position of leadership.

It is essential to our salvation that we support and actively participate in the gathering of Israel—whether at home or abroad. Being part of this latter-day gathering is one of the features of the "marvellous work and a wonder" that Isaiah foresaw in his vision of the Restoration (Isa. 29:14).

At a conference of priesthood leaders held on Sunday, September 17, 1837, at the Kirtland Temple, the Prophet Joseph Smith "addressed them on the subject of the gathering of the Saints in the last days, and the duties of the different quorums in relation thereto" (*HC,* 2:513). Concurrently, dated September 18, 1837, the Presiding Bishopric, under the leadership of Bishop Newel K. Whitney, released a "memorial" regarding the gathering of Israel and the building up of Zion. This letter includes a compelling appeal to all the Saints abroad to consecrate their tithes and offerings for the support of the Lord's purposes: "Whatever is glorious, whatever is desirable, whatever pertains to salvation, either temporal or spiritual, our hopes, our expectations, our glory, and our reward, all depend on our building up Zion according to the testimony of the Prophets" (517). Joseph Smith called the gathering "a principle I esteem to be of the greatest importance to those who are looking for salvation in this generation, or in these, that may be called, 'the latter times'" (*TPJS,* 83).

It is well worth the effort to ponder our own attitudes and goals relative to the "gathering," to make sure that we are subsuming our will to the will of the Father, willing in every respect to go where He might direct us (whether near home or in far countries), and to cultivate the same attitude of compliant service fostered by Ruth: "And Ruth said, Intreat me not to leave thee, or to return from following after thee: for whither thou goest, I will go; and where thou lodgest, I will lodge: thy people shall be my people, and thy God my God" (Ruth 1:16). (Allen)

LIKENING THE SCRIPTURES TO OUR LIVES

Doctrine and Covenants 97:21 "For this is Zion—THE PURE IN HEART." Peace and joy will be the reward for those who will humble themselves before the Lord and build the foundation of Zion within their hearts.

Application: As shown here, Zion is not just a physical location; it is wherever the Lord's people—the pure in heart—are gathered and unified. In these latter days we gather together in every country, every village and town. We are the Lord's people. We have a mission to gather all of His children (see 1 Ne. 15:12–17). Every country can and should be a Zion—a place where the pure in heart may dwell and build up the kingdom of God. We must build Zion wherever we are.

ENRICHMENT

The Significance of the Kirtland Period. Consider the enormous spiritual productivity that ensued from the gathering of the Saints in Kirtland, Ohio:

1. The organization period for the Church:
    The following offices and organizations were put in place in Kirtland at the places specified: The First Presidency (Newel K. Whitney store), Quorum of the Twelve Apostles (schoolhouse/printing office), First Quorum of Seventy (schoolhouse/printing office), the first patriarch (John Johnson inn), high priests (Isaac Morley farm), seventies (schoolhouse/ printing office) the first stake (Joseph Smith Jr. home), the high council (Joseph Smith Jr. home), and the first bishop (Newel K. Whitney home).

2. The "schooling" period for the Church:
    The Church was given seventy-seven revelations in the Kirtland area—over half of the Doctrine and Covenants. The School of the Prophets was begun. A significant portion of the Pearl of Great Price was received here. The Book of Abraham was translated here. Joseph Smith's inspired translation of the Bible was given here. The first edition of the Doctrine and Covenants and the second edition of the Book of Mormon were printed in Kirtland, and the Lectures on Faith were given in Kirtland.

3. The "pentecostal" period for the Church:
    Unparalleled spiritual manifestations were granted here. Key manifestations include: Additional visions of the Father and the Son (in the log schoolhouse on the Morley farm Joseph Smith and others had a vision of God during the ordination of high priests; in the Johnson home, Joseph Smith and Sidney Rigdon saw the celestial kingdom [D&C 76:20–21]; in the Kirtland Temple Joseph Smith was visited by Christ [D&C 137:3; 110:2–10; and other multiple accounts]; and in the Whitney store during the School of the Prophets [multiple accounts]). Visitations from past prophets also occurred in Kirtland (Moses—D&C 110:11; Elias—D&C 110:12; Elijah—D&C 110:13–16; Adam—D&C 137:5; Abraham—D&C 137:5; Peter; James; and John the Beloved). Several other manifestations were given in this period as well (angels, visions, prophesying, pillar of fire, gift of tongues, sound of mighty wind, horsemen of Israel).

4. Restoration of significant keys:
    The threefold mission of the Church was clarified and authorized: the gathering of Israel and leading of the ten tribes from the north (proclaim the gospel), dispensation of the gospel of Abraham (perfect the Saints), and the "keys of this dispensation" and

temple work were restored (turn the hearts of the fathers to their children and the children to their fathers to redeem the dead).

5. Kirtland served as Church headquarters longer than anywhere except Salt Lake City (1831–38).

6. Kirtland was the site of the first temple in this dispensation, where key temple ordinances were given.

7. Several key revelations and doctrines were given in Kirtland:
The Word of Wisdom, the three degrees of glory, the law of consecration, the United Order, many significant revelations on priesthood, the Civil War prophecy, and so on. (Anderson)

SUMMARY

From a careful study of the Doctrine and Covenants, we gain valuable and uplifting insight into the Lord's design in gathering Israel—whether in specific designated places of historic refuge and spiritual germination such as Kirtland or Missouri, or, as the gathering proceeds today, in the myriad "holy places" we build in our homes, our congregations, and our assemblies in the stakes and missions of the Church throughout the world, or in the dozens of sacred temples of the Lord in many quarters of the earth. Nephi saw it in vision: "And it shall come to pass that my people, which are of the house of Israel, shall be gathered home unto the lands of their possessions; and my word also shall be gathered in one. And I will show unto them that fight against my word and against my people, who are of the house of Israel, that I am God, and that I covenanted with Abraham that I would remember his seed forever" (2 Ne. 29:14).

The Lord uses the gathering to bless His sons and daughters of the covenant: "Yea the hearts of thousands and tens of thousands shall greatly rejoice in consequence of the blessings which shall be poured out, and the endowment with which my servants have been endowed in this house" (D&C 110:9). It is incumbent upon each of us in this, the last dispensation, to participate with full heart and mind in the gathering of the Lord's people, who may come to learn the truth only through our righteous service: "For there are many yet on the earth among all sects, parties, and denominations, who are blinded by the subtle craftiness of men, whereby they lie in wait to deceive, and who are only kept from the truth because they know not where to find it" (D&C 123:12). Let us show them where to find the truth, that they also may be gathered into the fold: "But behold, they are in the hands of the Lord of the harvest, and they are his; and he will raise them up at the last day" (Alma 26:7).

CHAPTER THIRTEEN

"THIS GENERATION SHALL HAVE MY WORD *through* YOU"

Reading Assignment: Doctrine and Covenants 5:10; 21:4–6; 76:50–112; 84:19–25; 88:15–24; 93:29; 107:23, 33, 35; 124:37–42; 128:16–18; 130:22; Bible Dictionary— "Joseph Smith Translation," page 717; *Our Heritage*, pages 23–25, 41, 58.

Additional Reading: Moses 1:40–41; 2 Nephi 3:11–15.

People are converted in their hearts by the Spirit through Joseph Smith. Our message is different. Says the Doctrine and Covenants: This generation shall receive the Lord's word through Joseph Smith (see D&C 5:10). What does that mean? It means exactly what it says. The message is the gospel of Jesus Christ as restored by Joseph Smith, not the Readers Digest, not Time magazine, nor the Bible alone. It means that we teach and testify to and from the First Vision. It means that we declare the Book of Mormon as the word of God. It means that we declare and testify to the story of Joseph Smith. It means that we teach the restoration of keys, priesthood, sealing power. It means that we teach from the Doctrine and Covenants. It means almost everything we have is different from all other religions, including the so-called Christian churches. (James E. Faust and James P. Bell, In the Strength of the Lord: The Life and Teachings of James E. Faust *[Salt Lake City: Deseret Book, 1999], 279)*

THEMES for LIVING

1. Joseph Smith: Mouthpiece of God in the Fulness of Times
2. Plain and Precious Truths Restored through the Prophet Joseph Smith

INTRODUCTION

In a sequence of remarkable events, beginning with the First Vision in the spring of 1820, the Prophet Joseph Smith participated in and served as a devoted instrument of the Restoration of the gospel of Jesus Christ and His kingdom on earth—the most important developments in the earth's history since the Atonement and Resurrection of the Savior. What the Prophet Joseph accomplished in his short lifetime on behalf of the covenant people of the Lord and of all humankind is chronicled in meticulous detail in the Doctrine and Covenants and contemporaneous *History of the Church*. His service is further memorialized and confirmed through the distillate of divine truth preserved in the ancient and restored scriptures of the Book of Mormon and the Pearl of Great Price—all of this generated through Joseph's divine, prophetic commission. A spiritual witness of the efficacy of his work and the authenticity of his office and calling is an essential pillar in one's testimony of the gospel of Jesus Christ. If the Book of Mormon is verily the word of God—as Moroni challenged us to learn by spiritual means (see Moro. 10:4–5)—then Joseph Smith, the inspired translator, must of necessity be a prophet of God. If the inexorable blossoming of the kingdom of God in the fulness of times is a manifestation of God's hand extending unto the blessing and saving of countless adherents of His gospel plan, then Joseph Smith, through whom the Church was again restored, must of necessity be a prophet of God. There is no compromising the congruence and alignment of prophet and the fruits by which a prophet can be discerned to the spiritual eyes of the honest at heart. "Surely the Lord God will do nothing, but he revealeth his secret unto his servants the prophets" (Amos 3:7) is the Lord's promise to His people that He would never leave them alone to find their way. In every dispensation of time there were prophets to act as the mouthpiece of the Almighty. In our day, that man was Joseph Smith, who taught and restored truth, laying the foundation for the Restoration upon which all the Lord's subsequent prophets have labored to further the cause of righteousness and salvation in the world. His presiding apostolic office has been perpetuated from prophet to prophet even down until this day.

MOMENT OF TRUTH

The footprints of the Prophet Joseph and his extraordinary spiritual and social contributions can be traced across this historical terrain of the Restoration by pondering the relevant mile-markers included in such sections of the Doctrine and Covenants as 76, 84, 88, 93, 107, 124, 128, and 130. The setting and background to sections 84 and 107 were given in chapter 6, and those to section 93 in chapter 2. The setting and background to section 124 will be given in chapter 29, and those to section 128 in chapter 30. In the present chapter we include some historical material for sections 88 and 130—both highly instructive as illustrations of what the Prophet Joseph Smith has contributed to the process of saving souls and exalting the valiant and sanctified.

Section 88: Given through the Prophet Joseph Smith on December 27–28, 1832 (verses 1–126), and January 3, 1833 (verses 127–41), in the translating room at the Whitney store, Kirtland, Geauga County, Ohio (see *HC,* 1:302–12). Ten brethren (Joseph Smith Jr., Joseph Smith Sr., Sidney Rigdon, Orson Hyde, Hyrum Smith, Samuel H. Smith, Newel K. Whitney, Frederick G. Williams, Ezra Thayer, and John Murdock) were present at this conference of high priests. Each offered prayer separately and vocally as well as expressing a determination to keep the commandments. They met until 9:00 P.M. on the first day and then adjourned until 9:00 A.M. on the morning of the second day and, after prayer, "received the residue of the revelation." In the Kirtland Revelation Book it was described as "Given by Joseph the seer and written by F. G. Williams assistan[t] scribe and councellor to s[ai]d Joseph." One of the best known of all revelations, it contains sublime doctrine on many key topics and a variety of new commandments to the Saints, such as solemn assemblies (verse 70), building the Kirtland Temple (verse 119), establishing the School of the Prophets (verse 127), and instituting the ordinance of washing of feet. In addition, it admonishes the Saints in personal duties such as retiring and rising early, cultivating charity, remembering prayer, and ceasing to be idle or finding fault with others (verses 123–26).

That it was a key revelation is evident from the tone and content of the Prophet's personal correspondence and letters to the Brethren in Missouri following this event. Joseph wrote the Church leaders in Missouri on January 14, 1833, and described this revelation as follows:

> I send you the 'olive leaf' which we have plucked from the Tree of Paradise, the
> Lord's message of peace to us. . . . We have the satisfaction of knowing that the Lord
> approves of us, and has accepted us and established His name in Kirtland for the sal-
> vation of the nations; for the Lord will have a place whence His word will go forth,

in these last days, in purity. . . . You will see that the Lord commanded us, in Kirtland, to build a house of God, and establish a school for the Prophets, this is the word of the Lord to us and we must, yea, the Lord helping us, we will obey; as on conditions of our obedience He has promised us great things, yea, even a visit from the heavens to honor us with His own presence. We greatly fear before the Lord lest we should fail of this great honor, which our Master proposes to confer on us; we are seeking for humility and great faith lest we be ashamed in His presence. (*HC,* 1:316–17)

Section 130: Given through the Prophet Joseph Smith on April 2,1843, at Ramus, Hancock County, Illinois (see *HC,* 5:323–25). On this day, at a morning church meeting in Ramus, a small town east of Nauvoo, the Prophet Joseph Smith listened to Orson Hyde preach a sermon in which he said, "It is our privilege to have the Father and Son dwelling in our hearts" (*HC,* 5:323). Afterwards, during a luncheon at the home of the Prophet's sister, Sophronia McCleary, the Prophet told Elder Hyde that he was going to offer some corrections to his sermon. Orson Hyde replied, "They shall be thankfully received." The Prophet then shared with him the important insights contained in Doctrine and Covenants section 130, including, among other topics, key information about the true nature and character of the Father, the Son, and the Holy Ghost: "John 14:23 ['When the Savior shall appear we shall see him as he is. We shall see that he is a man like ourselves']—the appearing of the Father and the Son, in that verse, is a personal appearance; and the idea that the Father and the Son dwell in a man's heart is an old sectarian notion, and is false" (D&C 130:3). Later on that day, at another meeting, the Prophet made public this and many additional items of instruction in Doctrine and Covenants 130 concerning the true nature of God and His laws. It is interesting how kind the Prophet was in his manner of correcting Orson Hyde and how graciously the latter took the correction. Section 130 also contains the celebrated maxim: "Whatever principle of intelligence we attain unto in this life, it will rise with us in the resurrection" (D&C 130:18).

1. JOSEPH SMITH: MOUTHPIECE OF GOD IN THE FULNESS OF TIMES

THEME: What a sacred and awesome responsibility devolved on the young lad Joseph Smith as he walked humbly into the grove near his home in Palmyra, New York, that historic spring morning in 1820 to ask the most important question that could possibly be laid at the feet of the Father. Or, more correctly: what an extraordinary fulfillment this act was of the premortal commission that Joseph surely must have received in the royal courts of heaven as the foundations of the Restoration plan were laid by the Lord and His followers: "And among all these there were many of the noble and great ones; And God saw these souls that they were good, and he stood in the midst of them, and he said: These I will make my rulers; for he stood among those that were spirits, and he saw that they were good" (Abr. 3:22–23). Like Abraham, surely Joseph Smith stood in the midst of these valiant beings and was given a view of his future commission as the prophet of the Restoration, as he later surmised (see *TPJS*, 365). How grateful we should be that he devoted his life to fulfilling the mission he was sent here to complete! How grateful and reverential we should be that he gave his life to seal his testimony as an exemplary prophet of God!

MODERN PROPHETS SPEAK

Joseph Fielding Smith:

> Joseph Smith, Jr., the prophet and seer of these latter days, was called by the Lord Jesus Christ to usher in this final dispensation and to restore for the last time on earth the fulness of his everlasting gospel.

> Joseph Smith is the revealer of the knowledge of Christ and of salvation to the world for this day and generation. To him the Lord said: ". . . this generation shall have my word through you" (D&C 10:5).

> When Moroni came to Joseph Smith nearly 150 years ago, that resurrected personage told young Joseph that his name should be had for good and evil among all nations, kindreds, and tongues, or that it should be both good and evil spoken of among all people.

> Fifteen years later the Lord himself elaborated upon this promise by saying to the Prophet, "The ends of the earth shall inquire after thy name, and fools shall have thee in derision, and hell shall rage against thee;

> "While the pure in heart, and the wise, and the noble, and the virtuous, shall seek counsel, and authority, and blessings constantly from under thy hand" (D&C 122:1–2).

> I for one want to be numbered forever among those who seek counsel and authority and blessings as they have come from this great prophet whom the Lord raised up to commence the restoration of all things in this final, glorious gospel dispensation.

> And I am pleased to testify that as the years pass, people in all nations are increasingly turning to Joseph Smith and the gospel restored through his instrumentality

in order to find peace in this life and gain a hope of eternal life in the world to come. On April 6, 1830, as soon as the Church was organized, the Lord, speaking of Joseph Smith, said to the Church: ". . . thou shalt give heed unto all his words and commandments which he shall give unto you as he receiveth them, walking in all holiness before me;

"For his word ye shall receive, as if from mine own mouth, in all patience and faith.

"For by doing these things the gates of hell shall not prevail against you; yea, and the Lord God will disperse the powers of darkness from before you, and cause the heavens to shake for your good, and his name's glory." (*Ensign,* August 1971, 5)

ILLUSTRATIONS FOR OUR TIMES

John Taylor's Witness of the Prophet Joseph

How indebted we are to the Prophet Joseph! We have received by his hand the Book of Mormon, all but a few sections of the Doctrine and Covenants, the entire Pearl of Great Price, the Articles of Faith, the Joseph Smith Translation of the Bible, the *History of the Church,* and many more plain and precious truths. He gave his life for the Restoration of the gospel and kingdom of God. In the words of John Taylor, as recorded in the Doctrine and Covenants:

> Joseph Smith, the Prophet and Seer of the Lord, has done more, save Jesus only, for the salvation of men in this world, than any other man that ever lived in it. In the short space of twenty years, he has brought forth the Book of Mormon, which he translated by the gift and power of God, and has been the means of publishing it on two continents; has sent the fulness of the everlasting gospel, which it contained, to the four quarters of the earth; has brought forth the revelations and commandments which compose this book of Doctrine and Covenants, and many other wise documents and instructions for the benefit of the children of men; gathered many thousands of the Latter-day Saints, founded a great city, and left a fame and name that cannot be slain. He lived great, and he died great in the eyes of God and his people; and like most of the Lord's anointed in ancient times, has sealed his mission and his works with his own blood; and so has his brother Hyrum. In life they were not divided, and in death they were not separated! (D&C 135:3)

LIKENING THE SCRIPTURES TO OUR LIVES

Moses 1:41 The Lord revealed to Moses that, in the last days, the children of men would disregard the word of the Lord and remove many of the plain and precious truths from the writing of Moses. The Lord also revealed that He would restore these truths through the Prophet Joseph Smith to all those who would believe.

Application: The Prophet Joseph is indeed the man raised up to provide for the world the word of God (see 2 Ne. 3:11). We cannot take it lightly lest we stand in condemnation (see D&C 84:57). Let us bring a renewed commitment to our resolve to study the revelations of God as given to us by the hand of the Prophet Joseph.

2. PLAIN AND PRECIOUS TRUTHS RESTORED THROUGH THE PROPHET JOSEPH SMITH

THEME: Consider what marvelous truths and principles the Lord has seen fit to reveal through the prophet of the Restoration: the authority, operational principles, and ordinances of the holy priesthood of God—including the foundational offices of prophets and apostles (see, for example, D&C 107:23–35); knowledge of the premortal existence and the ultimate venues of glory for mankind (three kingdoms of glory—section 76); the exalting principles and sealing purposes of the temple (including baptism for the dead, the endowment, and eternal marriage—see sections 124, 128, and 132), the expanding archive of the word of God (the Book of Mormon, Pearl of Great Price, Doctrine and Covenants, and the Joseph Smith Translation of the Bible), and the true nature and character of the Godhead, among many others. These transcendent truths give hope and confidence to all earnest and sincere seekers after truth.

MODERN PROPHETS SPEAK

Ezra Taft Benson:

> In the Church we have no fear that any discovery of new truths will ever be in conflict with these standards—with any fundamental basic principle which we advocate in the Gospel. truth is always consistent. This fact gives to us as members of the Church a feeling of great security, a feeling of peace, a feeling of assurance. We know beyond any question that the truths which we advocate, the truths of the gospel restored to the earth through the Prophet Joseph, are in very deed the truths of heaven. These truths will always be consistent with the discovery of any new truths, whether discovered in the laboratory, through research of the scientist, or whether revealed from heaven through prophets of God. Time is always on the side of truth.(CR, April 1958, 60)

ILLUSTRATIONS FOR OUR TIMES

The Greatest Idea I Have Ever Heard

Among university-age students that are members, as well as other members of The Church of Jesus Christ of Latter-day Saints, activity levels and affirmative identity are growing. They are even higher today than they were in the 1960s. I am convinced that one powerful reason is found in the truths that have been restored through the Prophet Joseph Smith.

Another impressive illustration of the power of these Restoration ideas happened a number of years ago when I received an invitation to represent our church in a Religion in Life Conference at one of the universities in the Southwest. Two individuals were invited each year to represent their particular religion. The year I went, they had invited representatives from the Mormons and the Moslems. I suppose they had an alphabetical listing and our church appeared by the nickname. As I remember, the Moslem representative was a doctoral candidate studying at the University of Illinois.

The next three days were very busy. I was involved in making twenty-two presentations to classes, large groups, small groups, and faculty members. One of the presentations was to a philosophy class, which met in the evenings for two hours. It was located in one of the science buildings in an amphitheater-like lecture room with a long laboratory table stretched across the front.

My wife, Barbara, and I and our student host arrived a few minutes before the class was to begin. I had no idea who was teaching the class or what his or her attitude might be toward institutionalized religion. The professor met us outside the door and basically said, "Now when you get in there, I don't want you to take the time telling the students about all the ways your church is like other churches. I want you to take the first hour and a half telling them how your church is different from other Christian churches."

Then he added with a twinkle in his eye, "And I want you to tell them in such a way that you will make Mormons out of all of them!" . . .

He opened the door and ushered us into the classroom where about eighty-five students were seated. I was hurriedly outlining in my mind some of the ideas that make our faith distinctive from traditional Christian faiths. (If you had received that assignment, what would you have included?)

During the next hour and a half, I shared with them some of the great ideas we have received in the doctrine and theology of the Church as restored through the Prophet Joseph Smith, including the nature of God, the nature of man, our relationship to our Father in Heaven and Jesus Christ, the Creation, the problem of evil, continuous revelation, a lay priesthood, and eternal progression.

At the conclusion of thirty minutes of good, searching questions and responses, the class ended. I stood near the exit and was speaking with a few students who wanted to ask additional questions. After a few minutes, the professor approached me and said, pointing to the student host, who was a returned missionary, "That fellow over there said that you believe this." He had written in shorthand some notes on a pad and read through them:

"'As man is God once was, and as God is man may become.' Do you believe that?"

I had purposely *not* used that statement during my remarks to the class because I felt that I could raise more dust with that one than I would be able to settle in one class period. I didn't have any idea whether the professor thought the idea was good, bad, or indifferent. I said that the statement came from Lorenzo Snow in the 1830s and explained that as a result of scripture and latter-day revelation, we know a lot more about what God is like now than what He may have been like before. Then, after circumlocuting around and around the question, I finally said, "Yes, we believe that."

He looked down at his notes and slowly and pensively mumbled through the words again: "'As man is God once was, and as God is man may become.' Hmmmm . . ." Then with genuine enthusiasm, he said, "That is the *greatest* idea I have ever heard!"

He was elated. He made his living teaching ideas, and the greatest idea he had ever heard came through the Prophet Joseph Smith. (Joe J. Christensen, in *The Prophet and His Work: Essays from General Authorities on Joseph Smith and the Restoration* [Salt Lake City: Deseret Book, 1996], 121)

LIKENING THE SCRIPTURES TO OUR LIVES

Doctrine and Covenants 84:19–22 The Melchizedek Priesthood holds the keys of the kingdom and knowledge of God. The ordinances of the Melchizedek Priesthood are requisite for any of us to able to see the face of God and live.

Application: Joseph Smith was privileged to see the face of God, and so can the Lord's righteous children eventually have this same sacred honor and privilege through the gift and power of the Melchizedek Priesthood of God, by means of which the "power of godliness is manifest." Let us strive with all our might, mind, and strength to become worthy of this destiny through obedience to the principles and ordinances of the gospel of Jesus Christ as restored through the Prophet Joseph Smith.

SUMMARY

Through a careful and prayerful study of the Doctrine and Covenants, one can gain a conviction and witness that Joseph Smith was indeed the mouthpiece of God in the dispensation of the fulness of times. The scope and volume of the plain and precious truths restored through the Prophet Joseph are astounding. Great blessings from the Lord await those who exercise their faith and choose to obey the laws of God as revealed in the latter days through modern-day prophets, beginning with Joseph Smith. The eternal truths are now here for us to learn and live. The grace of God is available to us as a free gift through the resurrection and—in terms of spiritual sanctification and salvation—based on our obedience and valor "after all we can do" (see 2 Ne. 25:23). What a debt of gratitude we owe to the Prophet Joseph and his faithful colleagues, who opened up our vision to the plan of happiness and the pathway to eternal life! Let us choose to be obedient. Surely, if we love God, we will honor His word given through the prophets and keep the commandments (see John 14:15).

CHAPTER FOURTEEN

THE LAW *of* CONSECRATION

Reading Assignment: Doctrine and Covenants 42:30–42; 51; 78; 82; 104:11–18; *Our Heritage,* page 26.

We read in the Pearl of Great Price how Enoch was called to cry repentance, and through his diligent labors he gathered together those who were willing to make covenant to serve the Lord. These made covenant to obey the celestial law, or the law of consecration, for this is a celestial law, and the celestial kingdom is governed by it. They were willing to give all that they had, even their lives to the kingdom of God. The result was that they became so righteous that they walked with God, and "he dwelt in the midst of Zion; and it came to pass that Zion was not, for God received it up into his own bosom; and from thence went forth the saying, Zion is fled" (Moses 7:69).

This same law was given in its fulness to the saints in early days and they also were commanded to have all things in common, or, to practice the "United Order" which had been given to Enoch, and to the Nephites after the Savior visited them. But the saints at that time were weak spiritually and failed to keep this commandment. Due to this failure they were caused to suffer persecution and failed to redeem Zion, which they might have done at that time had they strictly followed this law of consecration. (Joseph Fielding Smith, The Way to Perfection *[Salt Lake City: Genealogical Society of Utah, 1949], 274)*

THEMES *for* LIVING

1. "For the Salvation of My People": The Law of Consecration Revealed
2. The Law of Consecration: A Celestial and Eternal Law
3. Ways to Consecrate Our Lives to the Lord Today

INTRODUCTION

The Doctrine and Covenants is the Lord's handbook on key principles of heavenly governance, including the law of consecration. The law of consecration is one of the pillars of a Zion society, which must of necessity operate according to the will of the Lord and reflect among the Saints an enduring commitment to benevolence, brotherly love, orderliness, and obeisance to the Almighty. The Lord has asked His righteous people to consecrate their lives for the building up of the kingdom of God (see JST, Matt. 6:38). When we consecrate our lives, we dedicate and set apart our time, talents, and material goods for the Lord's purposes. Consecration is uniquely related to the depth of our conversion to our Savior Jesus Christ. Through consecration we truly sacrifice all things for the Lord. We begin the process of purification of our own lives and, in turn, we are better able to bless our brothers and sisters that they too might enjoy eternal life—this is truly building up the kingdom of God. Part of this law, as we now live it, requires us to provide for our family and be an instrument in the Lord's hands to bless our family and all those we associate with. Consecration is an attitude as well as an observable act of goodness.

MOMENT OF TRUTH

References to the law of consecration are to be found in several key sections of the Doctrine and Covenants, in particular, sections 42, 51, 78, 82, and 104. A brief background portrait of each of these sections is included below in support of the thematic development to follow.

Section 42: Given through the Prophet Joseph Smith on February 9, 1831 (verses 1–73) and February 23, 1831 (verses 74–93), in the Newel K. Whitney home (now a visitors' center) in Kirtland, Geauga County, Ohio. "Known simply as 'The Law,' or 'The Law of the Church,' section 42 contains instructions relative to the law of consecration and stewardship, the Decalogue, and the law of discipline with regard to members who violate Church rules" (*RPJS*, 60). The Lord had promised the Saints on

January 2, 1831, that He would "give unto you my law" (D&C 38:32), a promise repeated again on February 4, 1831 (D&C 41:3; see *HC,* 1:148–54 for the details). Consequently, twelve elders met on February 9 in prayer, and seven elders met later, on February 23, to inquire of the Lord.

From the beginning of the law's implementation, there were difficulties in living it fully:

> Although the Prophet wrote to Martin Harris on 22 February 1831 that the Saints had "received the laws of the kingdom since we came here and the Disciples in these parts have received them gladly," John Whitmer indicated that there were "some that would not receive the Law." Whitmer explained:

> "The time has not yet come that the law can be fully established, for the disciples live scattered and are not organized, our numbers are small, and the disciples untaught, consequently they understand not the things of the kingdom." (*RPJS,* 60)

Section 51: Given through the Prophet Joseph Smith in May 1831 on the Leman Copley farm in Thompson (now in south Madison), Ohio (see *HC,* 1:173–74). Witnesses observed that while receiving revelation, Joseph had an appearance of whiteness or brightness, especially in his face. Orson Pratt, present when section 51 of the Doctrine and Covenants was revealed, observed that "Joseph was as calm as the morning sun. . . . His face was exceedingly white, and seemed to shine" (*Millennial Star* 32 [August 11, 1874]: 498–99). Philo Dibble witnessed the Prophet enveloped in the vision of the heavens in the Johnson home and wrote that Joseph "seemed to be dressed in an element of glorious white, and his face shone as if it were transparent" (*Juvenile Instructor,* May 15, 1892, 303–4). Brigham Young said, "Those who were acquainted with him knew when the Spirit of revelation was upon him, for his countenance wore an expression peculiar to himself while under that influence. He preached by the Spirit of revelation, and taught in his council by it, and those who were acquainted with him could discover it at once, for at such times there was a peculiar clearness and transparency in his face" (*JD,* 9:89).

The Church was nearing a thousand members and was struggling with basic necessities. In May there were preparations underway to receive two hundred Saints coming in from New York (Lucy Mack Smith, the Colesville Branch, and the "main group" led by Thomas B. Marsh). The Colesville Saints, a group of about fifty, settled on Leman Copley's land. Section 51 is directed toward these Saints. This revelation first introduced the specifics of the law of consecration. Bishop Partridge requested the Prophet to ask the Lord for direction and, as a result, this section was given.

The principles of consecration were implemented in various forms in Ohio and Missouri in the 1830s to provide for the needs of the poor and of a financially struggling Church (see *Kirtland, Ohio; Kirtland Economy*). Many of the Latter-day Saints migrating to Ohio and Missouri lacked the means to support themselves, and the Church had few resources to construct buildings such as the temple or to finance publications. The various implementations of the law of consecration helped to meet these practical needs as well as to teach participants to live a celestial law. . . .

Implementation of consecration was difficult for the early Latter-day Saints and occurred only intermittently. The impoverished Missouri Saints were driven and persecuted by mobs, and repeatedly lost personal possessions, lands, and crops. Church property was often taken or destroyed. . . . Under such circumstances, most members required more for their stewardships than they could contribute to the pool of resources. Others were reluctant to donate their surpluses, and some who left the Church pursued legal means to recover consecrated properties. In the face of such obstacles, the sincere efforts of some faithful Saints to implement the law are all the more remarkable. (Daniel H. Ludlow, ed., *Encyclopedia of Mormonism,* 4 vols. [New York: Macmillan, 1992], 314)

As a footnote to the above, it is instructive that Leman Copley withdrew his land from the law of consecration, while the Colesville Saints, by way of contrast, obediently moved to Missouri. Joseph Knight recalls, "We all went to work and made fence and planted and sowed the fields. About this time we were called upon to consecrate our properties. But Brother Copley would not consecrate his property, therefore, he was cut off from the Church. Then we were commanded to take up our journey to the regions westward to the borders of the Lamanites. And we sold out what we could, but Copley took the advantage of us and we could not get anything for what we had done" (quoted in *BYU Studies* 17.1 [Autumn 1976]: 39).

Section 78: Given through the Prophet Joseph Smith in March 1832 at Hiram, Portage County, Ohio, for the purpose of establishing a storehouse for the poor (see *HC,* 1:255–57) and taking other steps to assure "through my providence, notwithstanding the tribulation which shall descend upon you, that the church may stand independent above all other creatures beneath the celestial world" (D&C 78:10). The revelation calls for an order to be established under strictly regulated conditions: "Wherefore, a commandment I give unto you, to prepare and organize yourselves by a bond or everlasting covenant that cannot be broken" (D&C 78:11). This form of bond, or consecrated order, was at this time applied only to a selected number who were called to live it. The United Firm, more commonly known as the United Order, or by some, the Order of Enoch, operated for about two years in Kirtland, with a branch in Missouri. Up to twelve men were given stewardships and joined in this business venture that was to support them and their families, with surpluses to go into the storehouse to support the printing of revelations and other Church needs. This initiative failed when loan payments could not be made due to the destruction of the Missouri printing operation by a mob, the forced closure of the storehouse in Missouri, and other unforeseen expenses (Daniel H. Ludlow, ed., *Encyclopedia of Mormonism,* 4 vols. [New York: Macmillan, 1992], 314). The brethren included in this order are thought to have been Joseph Smith, Sidney Rigdon, Jesse Gause, Oliver Cowdery, Martin Harris, Sidney Gilbert, Newel K. Whitney, Edward Partridge, William W. Phelps, John Whitmer, Frederick G. Williams, and John Johnson.

Section 82: Given through the Prophet Joseph Smith on April 26, 1832, in Independence, Jackson County, Missouri (see *HC,* 1:267–69). Pursuant to Doctrine and Covenants 78, which instructed Joseph Smith, Sidney Rigdon, and Newel K. Whitney to "sit in council" with the members of the Church in Missouri (D&C 78:9), they left Hiram on April 1, 1832, with Jesse Gause to make the long trip. They were pursued by some of the mobbers even as far as Cincinnati and Louisville via the Ohio River. This certainly was a trial for these men to leave their families. It was only one week after Sidney Rigdon and Joseph had been beaten, tarred and feathered, and threatened by the mobs in both Kirtland and Hiram and the subsequent burial of Joseph's baby boy—whose death resulted from exposure during the tar and feathering—probably the day before they left. Their fear of leaving their families behind can be seen in an except of a letter Joseph wrote to W. W. Phelps:

> [We left] our families in affliction amidst of death [and] upon the mercy of mobs & of brethren who you know sometimes are found to be unstable, unbelieving, unmerciful and, in this trying situation, to keep the commandment of God we took our lives in our hands and traveled through every combination of wickedness to your country for your salvation. (Joseph Smith to William W. Phelps, July 31, 1832, Joseph Smith Collection, Church Archives; spelling and punctuation modernized)

April 26 marked a conference of the Church in Missouri where Joseph was "acknowledged by the High priests in the land of Zion 'Missouri' to be President of the High Priesthood according to commandment and ordination in Ohio" (Donald Q. Cannon and Lyndon W. Cook, eds., *Far West Record: Minutes of the Church of Jesus Christ of Latter-day Saints, 1830–1844* [Salt Lake City: Deseret Book, 1983], 44). On his return to Kirtland, Joseph wrote Emma of his commitment to the work: "I will try to be contented with my lot. . . . God is my friend. In him I shall find comfort. I have given my life into His hands. I am prepared to go at his call. I desire to be with Christ. I count not my life dear to me, only to do his will" (Joseph Smith to Emma

Smith, Greenville, Indiana, June 7, 1834). Thus Joseph was reflecting his alignment with the will of the Lord, who proclaimed in the revelation the now famous words: "I, the Lord, am bound when ye do what I say; but when ye do not what I say, ye have no promise" (D&C 82:10).

Section 104: Given through the Prophet Joseph Smith on April 23, 1834, in Kirtland, Geauga County, Ohio, concerning the United Order (see *HC,* 2:54–60). In the Prophet's journal we learn that he "assembled in Council with Elders Sidney Rigdon, Frederick G. Williams, Newel K. Whitney, John Johnson, and Oliver Cowdery." These men, with the addition of Martin Harris, comprised the members of the United Order, or United Firm, in Kirtland. They were in dire financial straits. Their Missouri operations (printing office and store) had essentially been destroyed by mobs. Within two weeks, Zion's Camp would depart to help displaced Missouri Saints. Joseph had sent elders out to collect money and materials to take to their suffering brothers and sisters. Their debts were apparently staggering. Joseph needed two thousand dollars immediately to pay off debts incurred by the Kirtland Firm. A Church council had met on March 17 to raise this money. Fathers Bosley and Nickerson, Elder McWithey, and Brother Roger Orton were optimistic that they could raise the two thousand by April 1. Orson Hyde was left in New York so that he could bring the money back to Kirtland as soon as it was raised. On March 31, Orson wrote to Joseph that they were not likely to succeed and not to expect the money. Joseph wrote Orson a pleading response on April 7 asking him to solicit other Saints in New York for the money. Joseph indicated that if the money could not be raised, then he could not go with Zion's Camp. Joseph then recorded that he, Bishop Whitney, and Frederick G. Williams "bowed down before the Lord, and prayed that He would furnish the means to deliver the Firm from debt" (*HC,* 2:47).

Still without the money, the members of the Firm met on April 10 and "agreed that the Order should be dissolved, and each one have his stewardship set off to him" (*HC,* 2:49). Thirteen days later Joseph dispatched Zebedee Coltrin on a mission to borrow money from a Church member. Joseph wrote that the above brethren assembled on April 23 and "united in asking the Lord to give Elder Zebedee Coltrin influence over Brother Jacob Myres, to obtain the money which he has gone to borrow for us, or cause him to come to this place and bring it himself" (*HC,* 2:54). Joseph added, "I also received the following [D&C 104]." Doctrine and Covenants section 104 disbands the United Order or Firm that had been established in Kirtland (see D&C 78). The Lord makes clear in the new revelation that the order of Zion must follow a heavenly pattern established as "an everlasting order for the benefit of my church, and for the salvation of men. . . . But it must needs be done in mine own way; and behold this is the way that I, the Lord, have decreed to provide for my saints, that the poor shall be exalted, in that the rich are made low. For the earth is full, and there is enough and to spare; yea, I prepared all things, and have given unto the children of men to be agents unto themselves. Therefore, if any man shall take of the abundance which I have made, and impart not his portion, according to the law of my gospel, unto the poor and the needy, he shall, with the wicked, lift up his eyes in hell, being in torment" (D&C 104:1, 16–18).

1. "FOR THE SALVATION OF MY PEOPLE": THE LAW OF CONSECRATION REVEALED

THEME: In the years immediately after the organization of the Church, the Lord began to reveal the details of a sacred law of financial governance that pertains to a Zion people. He did so, as He stated, "that my covenant people may be gathered in one in that day when I shall come to my temple. And this I do for the salvation of my people" (D&C 42:36). Unity, charity, mutual support, social cohesion, self-sufficiency, spiritual growth, and cultivating an eye single to the glory of God were all factors related to the law of consecration. Even though the founding Saints were not able to live this law to its full extent, the celestial organizing pattern was established in the early stages of the Restoration as an objective toward which to point the Church in preparation for the Second Coming.

MODERN PROPHETS SPEAK

Joseph Fielding Smith:

> This order of consecration, the Lord said, was "to advance the cause, which ye have espoused, to the salvation of man, and to the glory of your Father who is in heaven." How strange it is, that so many members of the Church even in this day harden their hearts against the divine plan, which was to be for man's salvation and the glory of God? We are a long way from being worthy of Zion's redemption, and it will not come to any of those who show a rebellious spirit against that which the Lord has revealed. For, as previously stated, such "is not my disciple, and shall be cast out from among you." The great day of casting out will come when the angels who are appointed "shall gather out of his kingdom all things that offend, and them which do iniquity" (Matt. 13:41). . . .
>
> The saints are instructed that it is essential that they be equal in all things, else there can be no righteousness. What would the celestial kingdom be like, if there were not unity and equality prevailing there? So it should be in the Church on earth. The Lord says: "That you may be equal in the bonds of heavenly things, yea, and earthly things, also, for

the obtaining of heavenly things; for if ye are not equal in earthly things ye cannot be equal in obtaining heavenly things; for if you will that I give unto you a place in the celestial world, you must prepare yourselves by doing the things which I have commanded you and required of you" ([D&C 78:] 6–7). It was because Enoch and his people were united in temporal things as also in heavenly things, that they met with such success that the Lord took them. Had there been inequality, selfishness, bickerings, and accusations against Enoch, as we have accusations and fault-finding against the brethren whom the Lord has appointed in this day, then Enoch's city might have found its fate along with all the rest of the world, in Noah's day. Mormon, in writing of the Nephites and Lamanites for two hundred years after the appearing of the Lord to them, says: "And there were no envyings, nor strifes, nor tumults, nor whoredoms, nor lyings, nor murders, nor any manner of lasciviousness; and surely there could not be a happier people among all the people who had been created by the hand of God" (4 Ne. 1:16). What has been done can be done again; but we may well fear that such a condition will not prevail until the Lord does send his angels to "gather out of his kingdom all things that offend, and them which do iniquity," for it appears we will not reach this condition without this drastic measure being taken. (*CHMR*, 2:74–75)

ILLUSTRATIONS FOR OUR TIMES

After the Visit of the Savior

The results of living the law of consecration in sanctity and devotion are evident from the Book of Mormon: "And it came to pass in the thirty and sixth year, the people were all converted unto the Lord, upon all the face of the land, both Nephites and Lamanites, and there were no contentions and disputations among them, and every man did deal justly one with another. And they had all things common among them; therefore there were not rich and poor, bond and free, but they were all made free, and partakers of the heavenly gift. . . . And it came to pass that there was no contention in the land, because of the love of God which did dwell in the hearts of the people. And there were no envyings, nor strifes, nor tumults, nor whoredoms, nor lyings, nor murders, nor any manner of lasciviousness; and surely there could not be a happier people among all the people who had been created by the hand of God" (4 Ne. 1:2–3, 15–16).

"There Is Enough and to Spare"

In our world today, one of the truths that has been lost is what the Lord revealed in Doctrine and Covenants 104:17: "For the earth is full, and there is enough and to spare." Angry voices claiming overpopulation cry out that we must curb births around the world. In a January 30, 2004, ABC News Special *20/20* report entitled, "Lies, Myths and Downright Stupidity," John Stossel disputed a popularly held belief that the world is too crowded. He said:

We've heard protests about this for decades: News articles warn of "the population bomb," "a tidal wave of humanity," and plead, "No more babies." The world population today is more than 6 billion. It seems like so many people. But who says it's too many? There are lots of problems all over the world caused by too many people, says media mogul Ted Turner. But there's no space problem. Our planet is huge. In fact, we could take the entire world population and move everyone to the state of Texas, and the population density there would still be less than that of New York City. But, you might wonder, won't we run out of resources, like food? Paul Ehrlich, author of *Population Bomb,* warned 65 million Americans would starve in a "Great Die Off" in the 1980s. That didn't happen. The 1973 movie *Soylent Green* predicted food riots would erupt in the year 2022 but it doesn't look like this will happen. Turner says population growth is "a time bomb waiting to happen." If it continues, at the current rate, according to Turner, "Eventually you stand around in a desert with nothing to eat." But that too is a myth. We see the pictures of starving masses in populous places, but the starvation is caused by things like civil war and government corruption that interfere with the distribution of food. The good news is with more people, we also have more smart ideas. Every year we learn how to grow more food on less land. Thanks to improved technology, the United Nations now says the world overproduces food. About 15,000 babies are born every hour. But they are not a burden, they are more brains that might cure cancer, more hands to build things, more voices to bring us beautiful music. (Taken from ABC Web site, http://www.abcnews.go.com/sections/2020/US/myths_040130-3.html)

The Lord has created such a beautiful and bountiful earth. If we will trust in the Lord, we will know that He will provide. The only contingency is that we use our agency and opportunity to spread all the good things the Lord has blessed the earth with to each of His children. (Anderson)

LIKENING THE SCRIPTURES TO OUR LIVES

Doctrine and Covenants 78:3–7 The law of consecration was established as an everlasting order to advance the work of the salvation of God's children and magnify the glory of our Father in Heaven. The Lord has taught that before we can be united in the celestial kingdom, we must first learn to be united within our current sphere of existence.

Application: The Lord has given us compelling motivation to help us prepare for the Second Coming. Are we actively engaged in a committed effort to care for the poor and needy about us? Have we established for ourselves and our families a pattern of living that places spiritual things above earthly things in the order of priority—thus subsuming material gain below an interest in furthering the progress of building up the kingdom of God? Do we truly have an eye single to the glory of God? (see JST, Matt. 6:22; Morm. 8:15; D&C 4:5; 82:19). We aren't doing God's will if we are seeking to get gain over one another. We are serving our own interest and the glory of the world if we have to put others below us, and we can't do that and serve God at the same time (see Matt. 25:40).

2. THE LAW OF CONSECRATION: A CELESTIAL AND ETERNAL LAW

THEME: The law of consecration is a gift to the Saints based on the eternal pattern of governance established by the Lord as the epitome for a Zion people: "And thus I grant unto this people a privilege of organizing themselves according to my laws" (D&C 51:15). The Lord states His objective for inaugurating this organizing principle: "That through my providence, notwithstanding the tribulation which shall descend upon you, that the church may stand independent above all other creatures beneath the celestial world" (D&C 78:14). Being organized under the law of God ensures complete self-sufficiency and organizational integrity for the Saints. To the extent that we are able to live according to the law of consecration, we rise in attainment ever closer to the heavenly goal of being prepared to be received by the Lord into His celestial domain.

MODERN PROPHETS SPEAK

Bruce R. McConkie:

> We have covenanted in the waters of baptism to love and serve him, to keep his commandments, and to put first in our lives the things of his kingdom. In return he has promised us eternal life in his Father's kingdom. We are thus in a position to receive and obey some of the higher laws which prepare us for that eternal life which we so sincerely seek.

> Accordingly, I shall now set forth some of the principles of sacrifice and consecration to which the true saints must conform if they are ever to go where God and Christ are and have an inheritance with the faithful saints of ages past.

> It is written: "He who is not able to abide the law of a celestial kingdom cannot abide a celestial glory" (D&C 88:22). The law of sacrifice is a celestial law; so also is the law of consecration. Thus to gain that celestial reward which we so devoutly desire, we must be *able* to live these two laws.

Sacrifice and consecration are inseparably intertwined. The law of consecration is that we consecrate our time, our talents, and our money and property to the cause of the Church: such are to be available to the extent they are needed to further the Lord's interests on earth.

The law of sacrifice is that we are willing to sacrifice all that we have for the truth's sake—our character and reputation; our honor and applause; our good name among men; our houses, lands, and families: all things, even our very lives if need be.

Joseph Smith said, "A religion that does not require the sacrifice of all things never has power sufficient to produce the faith necessary [to lead] unto life and salvation" (*Lectures on Faith* [Salt Lake City: Deseret Book, 1985], 58).

We are not always called upon to live the whole law of consecration and give all of our time, talents, and means to the building up of the Lord's earthly kingdom. Few of us are called upon to sacrifice much of what we possess, and at the moment there is only an occasional martyr in the cause of revealed religion.

But what the scriptural account means is that to gain celestial salvation we must be *able* to live these laws to the full if we are called upon to do so. Implicit in this is the reality that we must in fact live them to the extent we are called upon so to do. (*Ensign,* May 1975, 50)

ILLUSTRATIONS FOR OUR TIMES

"Swallowed Up in the Will of the Father"

Whenever Church members speak of consecration, it should be done reverently while acknowledging that each of us "come[s] short of the glory of God," some of us far short (Rom. 3:23). Even the conscientious have not arrived, but they sense the shortfall and are genuinely striving. Consolingly, God's grace flows not only to those "who love [Him] and keep all [His] commandments," but likewise to those "that [seek] so to do" (D&C 46:9). . . .

Consider three examples of how honorable people in the Church keep back a portion and thus prevent greater consecration (see Acts 5:1–4).

A sister gives commendable, visible civic service. Yet even with her good image in the community, she remains a comparative stranger to Jesus' holy temples and His holy scriptures, two vital dimensions of discipleship. But she could have Christ's image in her countenance (see Alma 5:14).

An honorable father, dutifully involved in the cares of his family, is less than kind and gentle with individual family members. Though a comparative stranger to Jesus' gentleness and kindness, which we are instructed to emulate, a little more effort by this father would make such a large difference.

Consider the returned missionary, skills polished while serving an honorable mission, striving earnestly for success in his career. Busy, he ends up in a posture of some accommodation with the world. Thus he forgoes building up the kingdom first and instead builds up himself. A small course correction now would make a large, even destinational, difference for him later on.

These deficiencies just illustrated are those of omission. Once the telestial sins are left behind and henceforth avoided, the focus falls ever more on the sins of omission. These omissions signify a lack of qualifying fully for the celestial kingdom. Only greater consecration can correct these omissions, which have consequences just as real as do the sins of commission. Many of us thus have sufficient faith to avoid the major sins of commission, but not enough faith to sacrifice our distracting obsessions or to focus on our omissions. (Neal A. Maxwell, *Ensign,* November 1995, 22)

LIKENING THE SCRIPTURES TO OUR LIVES

JST, Matthew 6:38 As recipients of the everlasting gospel, we must embrace the work of the Lord and the advancement of His kingdom as our top priority. If we do so, the Lord has promised that all our remaining needs and desires will be fulfilled.

Application: As we seek to live the law of consecration, we are focused celestially. The thought uppermost in our minds is: Will what we do bless others, bring them closer to God and Christ, persuade them to do good, and build up the kingdom of God? These are the things a consecrated life can do. This is the effort of someone who is not seeking to get gain, but to bless. This is the work of one who is not only trying to live celestially, but to help others live that way too.

3. WAYS TO CONSECRATE OUR LIVES TO THE LORD TODAY

THEME: We now have the opportunity to participate in noble and edifying aspects of the law of consecration, including our fast offerings program and our welfare services program. In addition, the Lord has given us the law of tithing as a perpetual and eternal program to support the building up of the kingdom of God. Through the threefold mission of the Church, we can contribute our time, talents, and resources to magnify our callings for the good of our families and our fellow citizens in the household of God. We can sublimate any materialistic tendencies in our disposition by engaging in the work of the Lord with our "heart, might, mind, and strength" (D&C 4:2)—for His glory, and for the good of His children.

MODERN PROPHETS SPEAK

Brigham Young:

> We cannot expect to receive real wealth until we receive the riches of eternity, which are eternal. Those riches will not be committed to us, until we shall have filled our measures here, having done all the Lord requires of us, towards perfecting ourselves, and assisting him in the work of the salvation of the human family. Not until Jesus shall present all things to the Father, saying, I have completed the work thou gavest me to do; here are the results of my labors. Then, and not until then, can we possess real riches, true riches, eternal riches. How vain it is in man to allow himself to think that he can make himself happy with the pleasures of this world. There is no lasting pleasure here, unless it is in God. (*JD*, 18:213)

Spencer W. Kimball:

> Saints must keep the covenant of consecration. The Lord has blessed us as a people with a prosperity unequaled in times past. The resources that have been placed in our power are good, and necessary to our work here on the earth. But I am afraid that many of us have been surfeited with flocks and herds and acres and barns and wealth and have begun to worship them as false gods, and they have power over us. Do we have more of these good things than our faith can stand? Many people spend most of their time working in the service of a self-image that includes sufficient money, stocks, bonds, investment portfolios, property, credit cards, furnishings, automobiles, and the like to guarantee carnal security throughout, it is hoped, a long and happy life. Forgotten is the fact that our assignment is to use these many resources in our families and quorums to build up the kingdom of God—to further the missionary effort and the genealogical and temple work; to raise our children up as fruitful servants unto the Lord; to bless others in every way, that they may also be fruitful. Instead, we expend these blessings on our own desires, and as Moroni said, "Ye adorn yourselves with that which hath no life, and yet suffer the hungry, and the needy, and the naked, and the sick and the afflicted to pass by you, and notice them not" (Morm. 8:39). (*TSWK,* 357)

ILLUSTRATIONS FOR OUR TIMES

Living the Law

Here are some ideas to help us understand and live the law of consecration:

1. Set some goals and make some plans to live a consecrated life.

- *Plan for a full-time mission.* Such service provides a time when we have no other distractions and can concentrate on building up the kingdom of God (see D&C 138:56).

- *Remember daily opportunities for consecration.* Family togetherness time, providing for the needs of your family, and even taking the opportunity for wholesome recreation is part of living a consecrated life. Follow what the Spirit leads you to do (see 2 Ne. 32:5, 9). Let us avoid going to the extreme in living this law, missing the beauty of life in so doing.

- *Use wisdom and prudence.* Recognize where and how you can best serve and give. Reevaluate your opportunities every once in a while and recommit. Remember, don't run faster than you have strength (see Mosiah 4:27).

- *Be organized.* Prioritize your life and "organize every needful thing" (see D&C 88:119). As you are more organized in your resources, you will be better able to use them to help and lift others.

2. Follow a pattern of consecration.

- *Go to the temple.* Attend the temple often to serve those who have gone before. This will also refresh your mind concerning your covenants (see D&C 138:53–54).

- *Cultivate a spiritual fast.* Fast and pray on a regular basis to better live a consecrated life—don't just go without food on fast Sunday (see Alma 17:3; Hel. 3:35). Not only can you bless others through fast offerings, but you can sacrifice by fasting and praying for others too.

- *Study the word of God.* Regularly search the scriptures to receive instructions from the Lord (see 2 Ne. 32:3; D&C 84:43–45).

- *Foster a charitable attitude.* Remember to give willingly and not begrudgingly (see Moro. 7:6–11). Look for things to share and not simply to possess.

- *Live unselfishly and with gratitude.* Remember that everything is really the Lord's, for He is the creator of all things (see 2 Ne. 2:14–15).

- *Practice modesty and humility.* Concentrate on your needs more than your wants (see Alma 32:14–15). (Pinegar and Allen)

LIKENING THE SCRIPTURES TO OUR LIVES

Doctrine and Covenants 82:19–20 The Lord has established the order of Zion among His people—which is that every man should seek to help and strengthen his neighbors and do all things with an eye single to the glory of God.

Application: To take time from a busy schedule and ponder the enormous blessings bestowed upon us by the Lord yields food for thought: we are blessed beyond all understanding; thus we need to cultivate an attitude of full devotion to things spiritual, a full commitment to do all this asked of us in the name of building the Church and kingdom of God and serving the needs of our fellow beings, forever and ever.

ENRICHMENT

The following is commentary on consecration is given by Hugh Nibley, a noted scholar in the Church. It is taken from his book *Approaching Zion* (ed. Don E. Norton [Salt Lake City and Provo: Deseret Book and Foundation for Ancient Research and Mormon Studies, 1989]).

> All my life I have shied away from these disturbing and highly unpopular—even offensive—themes [the uses of money]. But I cannot do so any longer, because in my old age I have taken to reading the scriptures and there have had it forced upon my reluctant attention, that from the time of Adam to the present day, Zion has been pitted against Babylon, and the name of the game has always been money—"power and gain" (ix). . . . We never should ask the Lord whether or not we should commit adultery, theft, murder, or fraud. Likewise we should never ask, "Should I seek after riches?" because God furnishes us all room and board on this planet free (even eternal life is a gift of God). We can but accept the gifts (by definition a gift cannot be earned) and share them; and they are available but for the asking. On this point "the Book of Mormon

is fiercely emphatic; . . . no one should ever set his heart on riches." It is Satan who exacts a price, who turns the earth's bounty into commodities, which his disciples in turn convert into power and ruin (xiv). . . .

This law, the consummation of the laws of obedience and sacrifice, is the threshold of the celestial kingdom, the last and hardest requirement made of men in this life. It is much harder to keep than the rules of chastity and sobriety, for those temptations subside with advancing age, while desire for the security and status of wealth only increases and grows through the years (168). . . .

As Brigham Young often repeats, "God has given us the things of this world to see what we will do with them." The test will be whether we will set our hearts on the four things that lead to destruction. Whoever seeks for (1) wealth, (2) power, (3) popularity, and (4) the pleasures of the flesh—anyone who seeks those will be destroyed, says the Book of Mormon (1 Ne. 22:23; 3 Ne. 6:15). Need we point out that those four things compose the whole substance of success in the present-day world. They are the things that money will get you (434–35).

SUMMARY

The law of consecration has been revealed by the Lord "for the salvation of my people" (D&C 42:36). This law is celestial and eternal in nature. The Lord has given us today many opportunities to live aspects of this law for the good of our families and the Saints of God—reserving the full implementation for a time soon at hand. Though we are not yet given the opportunity to *fully* live this sacred law, it is a gift from God and a reason for rejoicing: "And ye cannot bear all things now; nevertheless, be of good cheer, for I will lead you along. The kingdom is yours and the blessings thereof are yours, and the riches of eternity are yours" (D&C 78:18). We are commanded: "For Zion must increase in beauty, and in holiness; her borders must be enlarged; her stakes must be strengthened; yea, verily I say unto you, Zion must arise and put on her beautiful garments" (D&C 82:14). An important part of this holy adornment through the priesthood of God is to live the law of consecration as the Lord commands.

CHAPTER FIFTEEN

"SEEK YE EARNESTLY *the* BEST GIFTS"

Reading Assignment: Doctrine and Covenants 46; Articles of Faith 1:7; 1 Corinthians 12–13; Moroni 10:8–18; *Our Heritage*, pages 42–43, 47–48, 63.

Additional Reading: Doctrine and Covenants 42:14; 50:17–30; 20:77, 79; 76:116; 1 Nephi 10:17; Mosiah 23:14; Moroni 10:4–5.

Spiritual gifts come from God. They are the gifts of God; they originate with him and are special blessings that he bestows upon those who love him and keep his commandments. Because they come by the power of the Holy Ghost, they are also called the gifts of the Spirit. Hence, they are received only by those who are in tune with the Spirit.

These gifts are infinite in number and endless in their manifestations because God himself is infinite and endless, and because the needs of those who receive them are as numerous, varied, and different as there are people in the kingdom. All saints are commanded to seek earnestly the best gifts. Chief among them are the testimony of Jesus, a believing spirit, divine wisdom, heavenly knowledge, faith in the Lord, the working of miracles, prophecy, the beholding of angels and ministering spirits, the discerning of spirits, tongues and their interpretations, the gift of preaching, administrative ability, and the insight to discern and recognize all of the gifts of God, lest there be confusion or deception in the Church (D&C 46; Moro. 10; 1 Cor. 12). (Bruce R. McConkie, A New Witness for the Articles of Faith *[Salt Lake City: Deseret Book, 1985], 270)*

THEMES *for* LIVING

1. Seeking and Receiving the Gifts of the Spirit
2. Teaching and Learning by the Spirit

INTRODUCTION

Central to the gospel of Jesus Christ is the knowledge and practice of how to live by the Spirit. Heavenly Father has made this a pillar of His plan of salvation by bestowing the gift of the Holy Ghost upon those faithful and penitent individuals who pass through the waters of baptism and proceed to the baptism of fire. He has likewise endowed His children with one or more gifts of the Spirit to edify and lift themselves and others up in preparation for their various commissions in the ongoing enterprise to build up the kingdom of God. Seeking the best gifts and cultivating them for the good of others is one of the sacred privileges of membership in the Lord's Church.

MOMENT OF TRUTH

Section 46: Given by the Prophet Joseph Smith on March 8, 1831, at Kirtland, Geauga County, Ohio (see *HC,* 1:163–65). Step by step during the Restoration period, the Lord unfolded to His fledgling Church, through the Prophet, the principles and practices that would bring about the emergence of the kingdom of God from obscurity. A key aspect of spiritual development was the commandment of the Lord to seek and apply spiritual gifts for righteous purposes. Important in this regard is Doctrine and Covenants 46. The young Church was still cultivating a standard pattern for conducting church services at this time, including the issue of whether to admit a general audience or limit the services just to members and earnest seekers of the truth. The Lord makes His will known through this revelation: "But notwithstanding those things which are written, it always has been given to the elders of my church from the beginning, and ever shall be, to conduct all meetings as they are directed and guided by the Holy Spirit. Nevertheless ye are commanded never to cast any one out from your public meetings, which are held before the world" (D&C 46:2–3). The revelation continues, including a wonderful treatment concerning the gifts of the Spirit—why they are bestowed upon mankind, how to seek them, and how they are to be used.

1. SEEKING AND RECEIVING THE GIFTS OF THE SPIRIT

THEME: In section 46 we are commanded of the Lord to "seek earnestly the best gifts" and use them for the benefit of all (see verses 8–9). To assist in this process of discovery and cultivation, the Lord has outlined in various places in the scriptures what these gifts comprise and how they lead to magnificent blessings for humankind (see 1 Cor. 12–13; Moro. 10:8–18; D&C 46). Let us prayerfully learn more about these gifts and how they can be used to strengthen individuals and families.

MODERN PROPHETS SPEAK

Joseph Fielding Smith:

Now, the Lord will give us gifts. He will quicken our minds. He will give us knowledge that will clear up all difficulties and put us in harmony with the commandments that he has given us; he will give us a knowledge that will be so deeply rooted in our souls that it can never be rooted out, if we will just seek for the light and the truth and the understanding that are promised to us and that we can receive if we will only be true and faithful to every covenant and obligation pertaining to the gospel of Jesus Christ. (*Ensign,* June 1972, 2)

Dallin H. Oaks:

Spiritual gifts do not come visibly, automatically, and immediately to all who have received the gift of the Holy Ghost. The Prophet Joseph Smith taught that most such gifts are "not visible to the natural vision, or understanding of man," and that it "require[s] time and circumstances to call these gifts into operation" (*TPJS,* 244, 246).

The scriptures tell us that we should desire and zealously seek spiritual gifts (see D&C 46:8; 1 Cor. 12:31; 1 Cor. 14:1, 11). We are also told that some will receive one gift and some will receive another (see D&C 46:11; 1 Cor. 12; Moro. 10:8–18). In every case, the receipt of spiritual gifts is predicated upon faith, obedience, and personal righteousness (see Bruce R. McConkie, *A New Witness for the Articles of Faith* [Salt Lake City: Deseret Book, 1985], 367).

Spiritual gifts are evidently among the "signs [that] shall follow them that believe" (Mark 16:17; see also McConkie, [*New Witness,*] 366).

We are commanded not to seek for signs to develop our faith (see Matt. 12:39; D&C 63:12), for "faith cometh not by signs" (D&C 63:9). But when we have faith, repent, and are born of water and the Spirit, and when we love and serve God with all our hearts, we are eligible to receive spiritual gifts. We may then, as Paul taught, "covet earnestly [which means fervently desire] the best gifts" (1 Cor. 12:31; see also D&C 46:8).

When we believe and seek spiritual gifts to benefit others "and not for a sign" (D&C 46:9), we are told that signs will follow. "Behold, . . . signs follow those that believe. Yea, signs come by faith, not by the will of men, nor as they please, but by the will of God. Yea, signs come by faith, unto mighty works" (D&C 63:9–11). The Holy Ghost "maketh manifest unto the children of men, according to their faith" (Jarom 1:4). (*Ensign,* September 1986, 68)

ILLUSTRATIONS FOR OUR TIMES

"That All May Be Profited Thereby"

The phrase "that all may be profited thereby" [D&C 46:12] is a very important concept to understand about the gifts of the Spirit. The gifts given to each individual are given not only for the one who receives, but also for those who can benefit when the gift is shared with others.

For example, you may be given the gift of faith and never question the existence of God, our Heavenly Father, and His Son, Jesus Christ. . . . With the gift of faith, you may be given the gift of prophecy or testimony.

In addition, you may be given the gift that others would believe on your words, that they might have eternal life if they continue faithful. Many of you, as missionaries for the Church, have experienced all that I have just outlined. Or you may have brought a friend or neighbor into the Church by the way you have lived your life or through your testimony. . . . There have been times when I have laid hands upon one who was ill and felt their spirit and their faith so strongly that they would be healed that I felt a surge of the power of their faith.

The Prophet Joseph Smith taught that the faith to be healed is one of the greatest gifts an individual can have.

On the other hand, I have seen the faith of parents when fathers and mothers desired their children to be healed. Through great faith, their children have been blessed. . . .

Many of you who have gone to foreign lands have been given the gift to speak with tongues and to translate, or have the interpretation of tongues.

"And all these gifts come from God, for the benefit of the children of God" (D&C 46:26). . . . The gift of tongues is used by missionaries to teach the gospel to the nations of the world. . . . The gift to ponder; looking to God for direction. . . . The gift to hear and respond to the still, small voice. . . . The gift to be calm, which includes the ability to curb anger and to be temperate rather than contentious. . . . The gift to study and to listen. . . . And, perhaps the greatest gift of all, to have charity. There are many gifts. Elder Bruce R. McConkie (1915–85) of the Quorum of the Twelve Apostles wrote, "Spiritual gifts are endless in number and infinite in variety" (*A New Witness for the Articles of Faith* [Salt Lake City: Deseret Book, 1985], 371). (Robert D. Hales, *Ensign,* February 2002, 12)

LIKENING THE SCRIPTURES TO OUR LIVES

Doctrine and Covenants 46:11–26 All children of God are recipients of a gift through the Spirit of God. It is imperative that we discover what our own gifts are and cultivate these gifts that all may be profited thereby.

Application: As noted from the above passage, we can receive gifts of the Spirit for a variety of blessings. All the blessings are blessings of the Spirit. Each of God's children is blessed with a gift of the Spirit. When we gather together, we are touched by the gifts and abilities of others, and all are edified.

2. TEACHING AND LEARNING BY THE SPIRIT

THEME: The Lord's blessing to humankind is the ability to communicate and learn through the Spirit. The foundation for all learning is the word of God as recorded in the holy scriptures and given by the voice of living prophets. The Spirit of the Lord confirms the truth of the word of God and brings peace and light into the lives of those who study the gospel and desire to learn more of the Lord and His ways.

MODERN PROPHETS SPEAK

Ezra Taft Benson:

> Carry the right message, and then teach with the Spirit. The Spirit is the single most important ingredient in this work. Through the Spirit, the individuals and families you teach will know of your love and concern for them and will also know of the truthfulness of your message and will have a desire to follow it. (*Ensign,* May 1987, 48)

ILLUSTRATIONS FOR OUR TIMES

A Four-Point Program for Spiritual Guidance

To me, the best directions about how to get the help of the Holy Ghost, directions that I have tested and know to be true, were given by President Marion G. Romney. I will give you his instructions in his own words. Then together let us see if we can figure out how we can work to prepare for that Sunday School teacher or quorum leader or sacrament meeting speaker to whom we will listen next Sunday.

Here are President Romney's instructions: "If you want to obtain and keep the guidance of the Spirit, you can do so by following this simple four-point program. One, *pray.* Pray diligently. Pray with each other. Pray in public in the proper places. . . . Learn to talk to the Lord; call upon his name in great faith and confidence. Second, *study* and learn the gospel. Third, *live righteously;* repent of your sins by confessing them and forsaking them. Then conform to the teachings of the gospel. Fourth, *give service* in the Church." And then President Romney concludes this way: "If you will do these things, you will get the guidance of the Holy Spirit and you will go through this world successfully, regardless of what the people of the world say or do." . . .

You may not know who your Sunday School teacher or quorum instructor or Relief Society teacher will be next Sunday, so you may not know their names either, but you can do the same thing. You can pray specifically that the Holy Ghost will come to them as they prepare to teach and again as you sit at their feet to listen.

I'm not sure I understand how this works, but I know it works. A few years ago when I was preparing to speak to a large group of students at Brigham Young University, I felt some impressions of something I was supposed to teach them. These impressions came with more than the normal intellectual force. In fact, I felt the power that I have come to know as the teaching of the Holy Spirit. But something else came. As I received the idea for my talk, I felt with it an impression that I was receiving it because of the prayers of one or more of the young people to whom I would be speaking. Now, I am not so egotistical as to think that many of them even knew I was coming. I wouldn't think I was on very many people's minds, but I must have been on someone's mind. Perhaps it wasn't so much that anyone was naming me, but someone must have been pleading to be given some help, to be taught something, to be given some assurance, and I must have been the most available servant, or at least the one who was going to go there next. (Henry B. Eyring, *To Draw Closer to God: A Collection of Discourses* [Salt Lake City: Deseret Book, 1997], 14–16)

LIKENING THE SCRIPTURES TO OUR LIVES

Doctrine and Covenants 42:14 All truth is taught by and through the Spirit. The Lord has promised to send the Spirit to all who prayerfully seek to teach the work of God.

Application: Let us never forget: It is the Spirit that teaches and testifies of the truth. Truth without the testimony of the Spirit is hollow. To qualify for the Spirit becomes all-important in the teaching process (see Mosiah 23:14).

SUMMARY

The Doctrine and Covenants is the Lord's confirming handbook for seeking and receiving the gifts of the Spirit, and also for teaching and learning by the Spirit. The gifts of the Spirit "are given for the benefit of those who love me and keep all my commandments, and him that seeketh so to do; that all may be benefited" (D&C 46:9). Through the Spirit we can add light and truth to our lives and strengthen our families by giving them greater access to the blessings of the Lord: "That which is of God is light; and he that receiveth light, and continueth in God, receiveth more light; and that light groweth brighter and brighter until the perfect day" (D&C 50:24). May we cultivate the best gifts and live in such a way that the Spirit may help us "know the truth of all things" (Moro. 10:5).

CHAPTER SIXTEEN

"THOU SHALT . . . OFFER UP THY SACRAMENTS *upon* MY HOLY DAY"

Reading Assignment: Doctrine and Covenants 59; Bible Dictionary, "Sabbath," pages 764–65.

The injunction from God to "Remember the sabbath day, to keep it holy" (Ex. 20:8) has been in force throughout human history. There is power in keeping the Sabbath day holy. I testify that God lives, that we are his children, that he loves us, and that he gives us commandments so he can bless us as we keep them and thereby have joy. As we keep the Sabbath day holy he will bless us, and we will achieve a quiet power for good as individuals, as families, and as nations, that we cannot obtain in any other way. (John H. Groberg, Ensign, *November 1984, 79)*

THEMES *for* LIVING

1. The Sabbath Day: A Day of Rest and Worship
2. The Sabbath Day: Renewing Our Covenants through the Sacrament
3. Blessings of Keeping the Sabbath Day Holy

INTRODUCTION

The Sabbath is a day of rest. Man's rest implies, in large measure, a respite from work-day involvements; however, the Lord's "rest" is defined as "the fulness of his glory" (D&C 84:24). In that sense, the Sabbath is a special day on which we continue our prayerful quest—our penitent rehearsal—in preparation for entering the Lord's rest when that hour arrives for each of us, individually, to join the ranks of those who are "taken home to that God who gave them life" (Alma 40:11).

The Sabbath is a day on which earthly cares are set aside in deference to the cares of the Spirit, a day on which we can focus our whole might, mind, and soul on the affairs of the kingdom, on communal worship, on the renewing of our covenants by partaking of the sacrament, on scripture study, on paying our tithes and offerings, and on service to our fellow beings. Many of these practices, of course, are done through-out the week as well; however, the Sabbath brings a unique opportunity for a more coordinated alignment with things spiritual. Just as we don our Sunday best for the Sabbath, so do we put on our best spiritual countenance and demeanor on the Lord's day and present ourselves before Him with deeper reverence and gratitude for His blessings and lovingkindness. The Sabbath is a gift from God. Only those distracted by earthly entanglements would consider keeping the Sabbath holy a burden or a trial; the righteous and faithful look forward to it as the gateway to God's glory, a more sure way to step forward toward communion with the Spirit, and a milestone that marks, each week, the passage of yet another unit of mortal experience leading back home.

MOMENT OF TRUTH

Section 59: Given through the Prophet Joseph Smith on August 7, 1831, in Jackson County, Missouri (see *HC,* 1:196–201). As part of the Restoration, the Lord provided spe-cial guidance on keeping the Sabbath day holy. The substance of this revelation is a trib-ute to those who were obedient to the Lord's commandment concerning the gathering to Zion (such as Joseph and Polly Knight), a review of the Ten Commandments, and a treat-ment of the doctrine of the Sabbath. The Colesville Saints (some sixty in number) had been evicted from Leman Copley's land in Thompson, Ohio, and had arrived in Jackson County about two weeks before this revelation was received. Polly Knight, wife of Joseph Knight Sr., lived long enough to reach Zion and then passed away on August 6. She was buried the following day, the date of this revelation, which begins: "Behold, blessed, saith the Lord, are they who have come up unto this land with an eye single to my glory, accord-ing to my commandments. For those that live shall inherit the earth, and those that die shall rest from all their labors, and their works shall follow them; and they shall receive a crown in the mansions of my Father, which I have prepared for them" (D&C 59:1–2).

Concerning the events of August 7, 1831, Joseph Smith relates: "On the 7th, I attended the funeral of Sister Polly Knight, wife of Joseph Knight, Sen. This was the first death in the Church in this land, and I can say, a worthy member sleeps in Jesus till the resurrection" (*HC,* 1:199). The Knight family was loyal to Joseph and his cause even prior to his receiving the golden plates. On the family's journey to Missouri from Kirtland, Polly Knight's health worsened. "Yet," relates her son Newel, "she would not consent to stop traveling; her only, or her greatest desire was to set her feet upon the land of Zion, and to have her body interred in that land. I went on shore and bought lumber to make a coffin in case she should die before we arrived at our place of destination—so fast did she fail. But the Lord gave her the desire of heart, and she lived to stand upon that land" (*HC,* 1:199).

1. THE SABBATH DAY: A DAY OF REST AND WORSHIP

THEME: Honoring the Sabbath is a commandment of God. There are rich blessings in store when we take the time to tune our spirits to the will of God frequently—and especially on the Lord's day. The Sabbath is an antidote to pride—a simple and beautiful way to remind ourselves to be humble, to be grateful, to "look to God and live" (Alma 37:47).

MODERN PROPHETS SPEAK

Spencer W. Kimball:

> The Sabbath is a holy day in which to do worthy and holy things. Abstinence from work and recreation is important but insufficient. The Sabbath calls for constructive thoughts and acts, and if one merely lounges about doing nothing on the Sabbath, he is breaking it. To observe it, one will be on his knees in prayer, preparing lessons, studying the gospel, meditating, visiting the ill and distressed, sleeping, reading wholesome material, and attending all the meetings of that day to which he is expected. [Failure] to do these proper things is a transgression on the omission side. (*The Miracle of Forgiveness* (Salt Lake City: Deseret Book, 1969), 96–97)

Henry B. Eyring:

> But once the meetings are over, what is wrong with schoolwork? Nothing, intrinsically. Schoolwork is a good thing to do—on most days. However, every hour you study secular subjects on the Sabbath is an hour you don't spend in the Lord's service, in the ways he asks us to spend his day.

Although time outside meetings on a Sunday can be well spent with the scriptures, I've felt the love and companionship of the Holy Ghost and of the Savior as often, or perhaps more often, in service to others. Most Sundays during my years as a student at the Harvard Business School, I drove out in a red Volkswagen to visit some branch of the Church in the New England countryside. My 600 classmates would be recovering from a night of parties or having worked until late Saturday; then they'd start homework sometime Sunday. I didn't begin that work until early Monday.

The rewards of those years aren't the fact that I did better academically than most, but more that I remember the warmth of the Master's presence in those cold, old halls and on those wooden folding chairs in Providence, in Worcester, or on Cape Cod.

My desk still holds a pack of slightly faded five-by-seven cards on which I wrote outlines of sermons, never given, which came to me on rides with President Wilbur Cox as we headed home in the Sunday twilight. I've long since discarded the class papers I turned in during those years. (*Ensign,* January 1978, 14)

ILLUSTRATIONS FOR OUR TIMES

A Day of Reverence

The small island kingdom of Tonga lies immediately next to the international dateline, so it is the first country in the world to greet the Sabbath day. It is a small country and, in the counting of the world, a poor country. But years ago a wise Tongan king decreed that the Sabbath would be kept holy in Tonga forever.

Modern civilization has come in many ways to Tonga. If one goes to the capital of Nuku'alofa on a weekday, he finds the usual heavy traffic of trucks and cars and the bustle of thousands of shoppers making their regular purchases from well-stocked stores and markets. One sees people line up to view the latest movies and to rent videos. One can watch modern buses whisk tourists off to catch their jet planes, or observe the speed and clarity of a satellite call to the United States. The streets are crowded and business is good. You might wonder, "What is so different about this town from hundreds of others like it throughout the world?"

But when Sunday dawns on the kingdom of Tonga, a transformation takes place. If one goes downtown, he sees deserted streets—no taxis or buses or crowds of people. All the stores, all the markets, all the movie theaters, all the offices are closed. No planes fly, no ships come in or out, no commerce takes place. No games are played. The people go to church. Tonga is remembering to keep the Sabbath day holy.

It is significant that the first country in the world to greet the holy Sabbath keeps the Sabbath holy.

Has the Lord blessed them? Maybe the world cannot see his blessings, but in the ways that really count, he has blessed them abundantly. He has blessed them with the gospel of Jesus Christ, and a larger percentage of the population there belongs to the Church than in any other country.

Simple, well-kept chapels dot the land. Clean, smiling local missionaries are found everywhere. A beautiful, exceptionally well-attended temple stands in Tonga in fulfillment of promises made years and ages ago. And, as would be expected, their attendance at meetings and faithfulness in tithing are very near the top. Recently the Saints have been blessed with some fairly intense opposition that is having the effect of further sanctifying the true seekers of eternal life.

Does the Lord love and bless those who keep the Sabbath day holy? I testify that he does in eternally meaningful ways. I further testify that when we eventually see things through the proper perspective of eternal truth, we will be amazed at how much we were blessed in important—though often unperceived—ways through keeping the Sabbath holy; and to our sorrow we may sense how many blessings we kept from ourselves by not consistently keeping the Sabbath day holy.

There is a direct correlation between the proper observance of the Sabbath and true reverence for God, which includes obedience to his other commandments.

We can't all live in Tonga, but we can all keep the Sabbath day holy and receive the blessings that come therefrom—and they come to us wherever we live, personally as well as collectively. (John H. Groberg, *Ensign,* November 1984, 79)

LIKENING THE SCRIPTURES TO OUR LIVES

Doctrine and Covenants 59:9–10 The Sabbath was provided as a day of rest from the labors and cares of this world. Furthermore, the Savior commands us to attend our Sabbath services and offer our sacraments to Him that He may cleanse us from sin and iniquity.

Application: By recognizing the Sabbath as the Lord's day, we are remembering Him. As we worship and serve Him by helping others, we can keep His day holy. In this way we keep ourselves unspotted from the world and receive blessings from the Lord.

2. THE SABBATH DAY: RENEWING OUR COVENANTS THROUGH THE SACRAMENT

THEME: The Lord has given us in the sacrament a profoundly sacred and yet simple process of remembering—remembering His atoning sacrifice, remembering our covenant promises, remembering to be obedient, remembering to live worthy of His Spirit.

"And Jesus said unto them, I am the bread of life: he that cometh to me shall never hunger; and he that believeth on me shall never thirst" (John 6:35). To partake of the emblems of remembering is to rise buoyant in the conviction that the Savior loves us and gave His life for us. Let us be grateful for His redeeming sacrifice and obedient to His counsel.

MODERN PROPHETS SPEAK

Gordon B. Hinckley:

> The sacrament and the partaking of these emblems is the very heart of our sabbath worship. It includes a renewal of covenants with God. It carries with it a promise of His Holy Spirit to be with us. It is a blessing without peer to be enjoyed by all and made possible by the authority given to worthy young men. . . .
>
> I am confident the Savior trusts us, and yet he asks that we renew our covenants with him frequently and before one another by partaking of the sacrament, the emblems of his suffering in our behalf. . . .
>
> As we partake of the sacrament we all stand on a level plane before the Lord. Each is accountable for what he does as he renews his covenants with the Lord in that magnificent and beautiful and simple ordinance of the gospel which carries with it such tremendous meaning. I am grateful for this opportunity. . . .
>
> I feel in my heart that if every member of the Church would resolve within himself or herself that they would partake of the sacrament every week, if possible, we would have greater spirituality and we would have fewer defaults, as it were, among our membership. (*TGBH,* 561)

ILLUSTRATIONS FOR OUR TIMES

Remember Him through the Sacrament

"And he took bread, and gave thanks, and brake it, and gave unto them, saying, This is my body which is given for you: this do in remembrance of me" (Luke 22:19). One Sunday morning, as Janalee Gale, a nurse at a large hospital, was planning her patients' care for the day, she heard an announcement over the intercom about church services for patients.

One woman—a Latter-day Saint—told Janalee that she would like to attend the LDS service. Janalee quickly changed the woman's linen and combed her hair. Although the patient was in constant pain, she didn't complain. Some brethren wheeled her bed to the meeting, and Janalee turned her attention to other patients.

Several days later, the woman buzzed for Janalee. When Janalee responded, the patient took her hand and said, "I just wanted to thank you for helping me get to church last Sunday. I haven't been for awhile because I've been so ill. When I partook of the sacrament . . ." She paused, then continued, "I felt God's Spirit, and I just knew that Christ is my Savior." Both women were moved to tears.

"This beautiful woman, as weak as she was, had faith stronger than I ever had," remembered Janalee. "I couldn't help recalling the times when I had only gone to church out of habit, never partaking of the Spirit, though I always partook of the bread and water. Never would I feel that way again." (Visiting Teaching Message, *Ensign,* April 1990, 70)

Making the Sacrament a Sacred Experience

Partaking of the sacrament should be a sacred experience for each of us. Perhaps on occasion we partake of the sacrament without sufficient thought or too hastily to feel its rich and deep significance. President David O. McKay once set an example for others to follow. Elder Paul H. Dunn shared the following experience with a small group of us in the School of the Prophets room in Kirtland, Ohio. He related sitting in a sacrament meeting with other General Authorities in the Salt Lake Temple. The bread was passed to President McKay first and then to others. Everyone waited for President McKay to eat. He just sat for some time observing the bread. He looked at it. He turned it sideways. While contemplating what it represented, tears came to his eyes. Later in the meeting, he announced that he had indeed felt the presence of the Savior. (Anderson)

LIKENING THE SCRIPTURES TO OUR LIVES

Doctrine and Covenants 20:77, 79 Each week when we partake of the bread and water in remembrance of the Atonement of Christ, we are covenanting with the Lord that we will obey His laws and live our lives according to His will. In return, He promises to bless us with his Holy Spirit to guide us safely back to Him.

Application: The blessing of renewing our covenants with the Lord, remembering Him, taking His name upon us, and keeping His commandments as we partake of the sacrament is just this: that we might have His Spirit always to be with us. This gift will bless us in all things and show us all things to do (see 2 Ne. 32:5).

3. BLESSINGS OF KEEPING THE SABBATH DAY HOLY

THEME: The Lord blessed and hallowed the Sabbath day (Ex. 20:11). When we enter into the Sabbath, we enter into a holy time frame—one in which rich blessings lie in store for those who serve the Lord in righteousness and bring Him gifts of devotion and prayerful worship. The blessings of the Sabbath include peace, spirituality, unity with family and friends, enhanced understanding of the plan of salvation, humility, spiritual awakenings, escape from the fetters of earthly constraints and pressures, and the satisfaction of knowing that one is abiding by the will of the Lord.

MODERN PROPHETS SPEAK

Gordon B. Hinckley:

> If you have any doubt about the wisdom, the divinity of observing the Sabbath Day, . . . stay home and gather your family about you, teach them the gospel, enjoy yourselves together on the Sabbath Day, come to your meetings, participate. You will know that the principle of the Sabbath is a true principle which brings with it great blessings. (*TGBH,* 559)

Dallin H. Oaks:

> I am sorry when any Latter-day Saint does not understand the precious blessing that comes to those who keep the commandment to offer up their sacraments upon each Sabbath day. What is there in life—on the lakes or streams, in places of commercial recreation, or at home reading the Sunday paper—that can provide anything comparable to these blessings? No recreational pleasure can equal the cleansing renewal and the spiritual guidance and growth God has promised those who faithfully partake of

the sacrament and honor Him each Sabbath day. I give thanks for the fulfillment of those promises in my life and affirm their availability to all. (*Ensign,* May 2002, 33)

ILLUSTRATIONS FOR OUR TIMES

The Blessing of Keeping the Sabbath Day Holy

Jesus taught, "The sabbath was made for man" (Mark 2:27). What does that mean? It means for a man to have the joy and happiness which the gospel promises, on this day he must sacrifice the world, set aside his employment as possible, and keep the eternal covenant of the Sabbath day. The Lord commanded: "Wherefore the children of Israel [which includes all Latter-day Saints] shall keep the sabbath . . . throughout their generations, for a perpetual covenant. It is a sign between me and the children of Israel for ever" (Ex. 31:16–17).

Of all people on the earth, the Latter-day Saints must lead out in sanctifying this appointed day each week. "Except your righteousness shall exceed the righteousness of the scribes and Pharisees," said the Lord, "ye shall in no case enter into the kingdom of heaven" (Matt. 5:20).

To this very day, "the matter of Sabbath observance remains . . . as one of the great tests which divides the righteous from the worldly and wicked," said Elder Bruce R. McConkie. (*MD,* 658)

The promises of the Lord to those who keep the Sabbath day holy are so wonderfully clear in the scriptures that they leave one asking, "Why would anyone throw away such blessings for the tawdry, temporary pleasures of the world?" Hear again the words of Jehovah as they roll down from Mount Sinai: "Ye shall keep my sabbaths, and reverence my sanctuary: I am the Lord.

"If ye walk in my statutes, and keep my commandments, and do them;

"Then I will give you rain in due season, and the land shall yield her increase. . . .

". . . And ye shall eat your bread to the full, and dwell in your land safely.

"And I will give [you] peace in the land, . . . neither shall the sword go through your land. . . .

"For I will have respect unto you, and make you fruitful, . . . and establish my covenant with you. . . .

"And I will set my tabernacle [that is, my temple] among you. . . .

"And I will walk among you, and will be your God, and ye shall be my people" (Lev. 26:2–12).

I love the Sabbath day! It has blessed my family in countless ways. I bear a testimony born of personal experience that the commandments of the Lord are "true and faithful" (D&C 71:11).

I know you will be happier, enjoy greater peace, and find your lives made glad as you witness the miracles that come to each person and family who make the sacrifice of keeping this eternal covenant. (H. Aldridge Gillespie, *Ensign,* November 2000, 79)

The Home Game

He was a bright young man, pleasant and articulate, with a charming wife and growing family—just the kind of brother you would want to have as one of your ward clerks. When the Spirit whispered a quiet confirmation, I went to visit him with the invitation. He was honored by the calling but somewhat reserved in his response. "Bishop," he said, "I want to be of help. But you know, there is something I need to explain." *Uh-oh,* I thought to myself, preparing to hear a confession. "Ever since I joined the Church a few years ago," he continued, "I have tried to do my duty and attend my meetings, but I have always had seasons tickets to see the Baltimore Colts play on Sundays. That's why you don't see me at the meetings sometimes."

I thought about his situation for a few seconds, then I felt impressed to offer him a special arrangement. The Lord wanted him to be a part of our team. Therefore, he would complete his Church assignment to the best of his ability and we would work around his schedule. When the team was in town with a home game, he would be away, and we would understand. He accepted the assignment, but I could see that he had a struggle going on inside—and that is just as it should be when one is learning.

For the next few months, every time my wife and I drove past Memorial Stadium on the way to our church meetings, I thought of this young man's struggle. One Sunday when there was a home game, I was surprised when this young man showed up at my office. He was energized, with a kind of glow about him and a sparkle in the eyes. "Bishop," he said, "I have decided to give up my season tickets. The gospel is more important. I will always be here on the Sabbath." There was a full measure of joy in his voice—a reminder of what the Lord said about His holy day: "But remember that on this, the Lord's day, thou shalt offer thine oblations and thy sacraments unto the Most High, confessing thy sins unto thy brethren, and before the Lord. And on this day thou shalt do none other thing, only let thy food be prepared with singleness of heart that thy fasting may be perfect, or, in other words, that thy joy may be full" (D&C 59:12–13).

I put my arm around this young man's shoulder and bore witness to the strength and courage of his correct decision, and I thanked the Lord in my heart for the patient way in which the Spirit often works. The words of the Savior came to my mind: "If any man will do his will, he shall know of the doctrine, whether it be of God, or whether I speak of myself" (John 7:17). Then I thought: There is always a home game. It takes place within the heart of every individual as he or she engages in the choices of life, the choices that go to define character and honor and devotion to the cause of building up the kingdom of God. (Allen)

LIKENING THE SCRIPTURES TO OUR LIVES

Doctrine and Covenants 59:9, 13–17 The Lord commands us to attend church and "offer up thy sacraments upon my holy day" (verse 9). Great blessings are promised to those who do.

Application: Here the Lord promises us "the fulness of the earth" when we keep the Sabbath day holy (verse 16). However, for this blessing to be granted, we must reverence the Sabbath not only in our actions, but in our hearts—"with a glad heart and a cheerful countenance" (verse 15). The Lord wants our sincerity in our worship, not just as an outward show of it.

ENRICHMENT

The following was written by Robert J. Matthews, former chairman of the Department of Ancient Scripture at Brigham Young University:

> The Sabbath has several purposes. It is a holy day specified in the scriptures as a day not only of rest but also of worship. The word *sabbath* is derived from the Hebrew *shabbath,* meaning "to break off" or "to desist," and in this can be seen the idea of rest.
>
> But in the best sense, rest does not mean idleness; it signifies rather a change of emphasis. In plain terms, "keeping the Sabbath day holy" means to cease or to rest from the secular labors of the week and to use the specified day in worshipping God and doing good to our fellow beings. It is a day for spiritual works and refreshment as compared to the secular accomplishments of other days.
>
> The various dimensions of the Sabbath are sometimes spoken of separately in the scriptures. For example, one mention of the Sabbath is found in Exodus 16:23 and has to do with instructions for the Israelites to gather a double amount of manna

the day before the Sabbath so that such labor should not be performed on the Sabbath.

However, Exodus 20:8–11 and 31:12–17 deal with a different aspect of the Sabbath and emphasize that the Lord rested on the seventh day after having created the world. This reconfirms the event told in Genesis 2:1–3, reminding us that the Sabbath was inaugurated in the very beginning. No doubt the sacredness of the Sabbath day was known to the true believers from the time of Adam, although the Bible is not very clear on this point. The scriptures appear to establish the Sabbath at the time of Moses, but this is probably due more to an incompleteness of the earlier record than to an absence of teaching at the time of the early patriarchs.

Still another dimension is shown after the exodus from Egypt, wherein the Sabbath is used to commemorate Israel's deliverance from bondage (Deut. 5:12–15).

And in the last days the Lord has explained that another purpose of the Sabbath is "that thou mayest more fully keep thyself unspotted from the world" by keeping it holy in the way he has commanded us (D&C 59:9).

In New Testament times the Sabbath day was called the "Lord's day" (Rev. 1:10) and was observed on the first day of the week (Acts 20:7), honoring the resurrection of Jesus Christ from the tomb. In the present dispensation the Lord called the day of worship "my holy day" in a revelation given to the Prophet Joseph Smith on Sunday, 7 August 1831 (D&C 59:9–10). Since Jesus is Jehovah, the Creator and the God of Israel, these different aspects of the Sabbath all bear witness of the same Lord Jesus Christ but emphasize different features of his ministry.

When the Pharisees criticized the disciples for picking ears of corn on the Sabbath, Jesus explained to the Pharisees that "the Sabbath was made for man, and not man for the Sabbath.

"Wherefore the Sabbath was given unto man for a day of rest; and also that man should glorify God, and not that man should not eat;

"For the Son of Man made the Sabbath day, therefore the Son of Man is Lord also of the Sabbath" (JST, Mark 2:25–27).

Not only does this manifest a practical view of the Sabbath, it also illustrates its multiple nature: (1) the Sabbath is for man's benefit; (2) it is a day of rest; (3) it is a day of worship; and (4) Jesus is the maker of the Sabbath and is the Lord thereof in any age of the world.

Public and private worship. Proper observance of the Sabbath is a sign and even a test that distinguishes the covenant people of the Lord from those who follow the ways of the world (see Ex. 31:13–18; Neh. 13:15–22; Isa. 56:1–8; Isa. 58:13–14; Jer. 17:19–27). In this respect it serves a purpose similar to the Word of Wisdom and tithing, which soon divide the believers from the nonbelievers in their performance.

Sabbath observance entails more than simply staying at home. It also involves public worship. It was and is a day for the believers to meet together for worship and for instruction. The New Testament informs us that Jesus, "as his custom was," frequently went to the synagogue on the Sabbath day (Luke 4:16).

The most extensive revelation in the current dispensation that deals with the Sabbath day is recorded as Doctrine and Covenants section 59. In this communication the Lord emphasizes the public nature of Sabbath worship by indicating that one should "go to the house of prayer" on the Lord's holy day and "pay thy devotions unto the Most High" (D&C 59:9–10).

Which day is the Sabbath? The Sabbath has eternal significance. The Old Testament declares the Sabbath is to be observed as a "perpetual covenant" (see Ex. 31:13–17), which does not necessarily mean that it should be forever on the same day, but rather that the Sabbath is a covenant for eternity—that is, of eternal significance—and is needed by mortals in every generation for their frequent spiritual rejuvenation. The context of the passage seems to make that point clear. It is evident from the Bible that the sacred day was the seventh day of the week during Old Testament times, whereas in the New Testament it was observed on the first day of the week by the church after the resurrection of Jesus Christ from the grave.

Traditionally The Church of Jesus Christ of Latter-day Saints has recognized Sunday as the day of worship, according to the pattern given in Doctrine and Covenants section 59. However, in the Middle East today, some branches of the Church observe the Sabbath on days other than Sunday, consistent with the custom of the countries in which they are located. This is necessary so that meetings can be held at a time when the members of the Church can be present.

Since the Sabbath is for man and not man for the Sabbath, with its purpose not only to be a day of rest for the individual, but also to be a day of spiritual instruction and public worship, it is important that the Sabbath day be observed at a time when the people can attend. The significant fact seems not to be *which* day is observed so much as *how* and *why* the day is observed and that the local group of believers observe the same day each week.

In the Church the matter of Sabbath-day observance can be settled quite effectively from the fact that the twelve successive Presidents of the Church from the Prophet Joseph Smith to President Spencer W. Kimball have all seen fit to observe Sunday as the proper day, and have thus set the pattern. The important factor is that the programs of the Church are under the direction of the holy priesthood and have the approval of the President of the Church—the prophet, seer, and revelator, and the Lord's representative on earth. When rare exceptions to the established day have seemed necessary, as noted above, the proper priesthood authority is able to make the decision. (*Ensign,* January 1978, 14)

SUMMARY

Why did the Lord command us to keep the Sabbath day holy? That we might better become holy ourselves: "Whereby are given unto us exceeding great and precious promises: that by these ye might be partakers of the divine nature, having escaped the corruption that is in the world through lust" (2 Pet. 1:4). The Sabbath offers to us a regular opportunity to "escape the corruption that is in the world." It also gives us the opportunity to renew our covenants through the sacrament and to show ourselves worthy to receive greater spiritual blessings—especially the blessing of having access to the Spirit of the Lord to guide and direct us on the pathway of life.

CHAPTER SEVENTEEN

THE LAW of TITHING and the LAW of the FAST

Reading Assignment: Doctrine and Covenants 59:13–16, 21; 119; 120.

Additional Reading: Gen. 14:18–20; JST, Gen. 14:37–40; Lev. 27:30; Isa. 58:5–12; Mal. 3:8–12; Matt. 6:16–18; 3 Ne. 13:16–18; 24:8–12; Doctrine and Covenants 64:23.

The Lord . . . makes clear that tithing is his law and is required of all his followers. It is our honor and privilege, our safety and promise, our great blessing to live this law of God. To fail to meet this obligation in full is to deny ourselves the promises and to omit a weighty matter. It is a transgression, not an inconsequential oversight.

Yes, it may take great faith to pay tithes when funds are scarce and demands are great. But we remember the promise from the Father to Malachi. We also remember the Lord's promise in our day: "I, the Lord, am bound when ye do what I say; but when ye do not what I say, ye have no promise" (DC 82:10). (Spencer W. Kimball, President Kimball Speaks Out [Salt Lake City: Deseret Book, 1981], 63)

* * *

To do the best things in the worst times, we should also keep the great companion law to tithing, the law of the fast. In keeping this law, we will receive blessings that are unique and different and separate from those associated with the law of tithing. As I understand the twenty-fifth chapter of Matthew, we will be in large measure judged by the manner in which we keep the law of the fast. . . . Keeping the law of the fast allows us to begin to fulfill our obligations to those in need. (James E. Faust, Reach Up for the Light *[Salt Lake City: Deseret Book, 1990], 51–52)*

THEMES *for* LIVING

1. Tithing: A Commandment with Great Blessings
2. Fasting and Fast Offerings: One of Our Holy Oblations to God

INTRODUCTION

The law of tithing is a key ingredient in the Lord's divine plan for bringing about the sanctification of His sons and daughters. Paying tithing with pure intent and sincere gratitude is a confirmation of one's triumph over a self-centered and prideful attitude. It is an act of reaching out to the Lord for the empowerment of divine humility and obedience the Prophet Joseph Smith yearned for the Saints to have: "Help thy servants to say, with thy grace assisting them: Thy will be done, O Lord, and not ours" (D&C 109:44). Paying tithing is an act of direct participation in the all-encompassing design of the Lord to build up the kingdom of God and spread the gospel to the four quarters of the earth, in keeping with the Abrahamic covenant. It is a holy practice consonant with valiant discipleship: "And all the tithe of the land, whether of the seed of the land, *or* of the fruit of the tree, is the Lord's: it is holy unto the Lord" (Lev. 27:30). Likewise, observing the law of the fast and giving fast offerings on behalf of the poor and needy are an involvement in the Lord's plan for teaching and administering charity among the Saints. Both of these laws—tithing and fasting—are principal channels for experiencing joy and buoyant satisfaction in our daily lives. When viewed in this way, rather than as physical and financial burdens, we see how gracious the Lord is in granting us the privilege of participating in such magnificent laws so we can learn how to be more like Him.

MOMENT OF TRUTH

The Doctrine and Covenants contains the word of the Lord in regard to latter-day instruction on the principles of the Lord's economic laws for His Saints—including the law of tithing and the law of the fast. In particular, sections 59, 119, and 120 are important in this regard. The background of section 59 was discussed in chapter 16 in connection with the Sabbath and the sacrament. Information on the other two sections follows.

Section 119: Given through the Prophet Joseph Smith on July 8, 1838, in Far West, Missouri, in response to his inquiry: "O Lord! Show unto thy servant how much thou requirest of the properties of the people for a tithing" (*HC,* 3:44). Lyndon Cook explained the necessity of this revelation:

> On 6 December 1837, seven months prior to the reception of section 119, Edward Partridge, John Corrill, and Isaac Morley were appointed as a committee to adopt a plan whereby revenue could be raised to defray Church expenses. Their report, given the following day, proposed a voluntary tithing program to assist the poor, compensate Church leaders for services while attending to Church business, and pay for other related Church expenses. The donation, which was to be based on assets, not income, considered widows not having assets over $75 exempt, and it provided for a yearly inventory with the Church bishop.
>
> This voluntary contribution initiative apparently was never implemented, but it undoubtedly served as a prelude to section 119. (*RPJS,* 237–38)

Prior to this time, the law of consecration had been the rule of Church contribution. However, as many Saints had difficulty fulfilling this law, the Lord instituted the law of tithing—the giving of one-tenth of all members' interest annually. This the Lord has given us in preparation and until we are again ready to live the law of consecration.

Section 120: Given through the Prophet Joseph Smith on July 8, 1838, at Far West, Missouri, on the same day on which the previous section was received (see *HC,* 3:44). The revelation gives responsibility for disposing of consecrated offerings to a church council comprised of the First Presidency, bishopric, and high council rather than the bishop alone.

> Read the 120th section and you will see how the Lord said it [tithing] should be disbursed at that time. That was in Zion, Jackson county, when they first went there. Of late years, The Church of Jesus Christ of Latter-day Saints, in conference assembled, has voted for the power to handle the funds of the Church and the properties of the Church by the Trustee-in-trust for the Church. You have done that during this conference. We did it years and years ago. We have done it every conference from the time we came into these vales of the mountains. Now let me say that the

authority is given of God to the man that stands at the head of this Church, to preside over the whole Church, and to be like unto Moses [D&C 28:2; 107:91–92]. He is a prophet, and a seer, and a revelator, and everything in the Church is under his direction. The Bishops receive the tithing. The presiding bishopric handle and keep an account of it, but the Trustee-in-trust is voted upon by the people to have the control and direction and to be responsible for all the funds and properties of the Church. We have endorsed that authority during this conference, as we always have done. It is no new thing. (Charles W. Penrose, CR, April 1905, 73)

* * *

Pursuant to these revelations [sections 119 and 120] , and as explained at recent conferences, the Church has a council on the Distribution of Tithes, made up of the First Presidency, the Council of the Twelve, and the Presiding Bishopric. This Council considers the proposed budget of the Church, which is itemized under general headings, and then approves and authorizes such expenditures as it deems proper.

A subcommittee of this Council on the Distribution of Tithes then makes the detailed appropriations from the sums approved and authorized by the Council. This subcommittee is known as the Committee on Expenditures, and is made up of the First Presidency, three members of the Council of the Twelve, and the Presiding Bishopric. A Church Building Committee acts under the direction of the Committee on Expenditures. The Financial Secretary to the First Presidency acts as the secretary of the Committee of Expenditures. (J. Reuben Clark, CR, April 1948, 116–17)

In 1911, the First Presidency clarified the uses for tithing, outlining how members' donations were and would always be used:

The subject of Church revenues may be touched upon perhaps with profit. The Latter-day Saints believe in tithing. It is a principle of their faith. It is an ancient observance reaching back to patriarchal times, as related in the Bible [Gen. 14:20; Lev. 27:30; Mal. 3:8–10; Heb. 7:9]. It was established in the Church in the year 1838. The manner of its payment and disbursement is revealed by Divine authority and has appeared in the Church books ever since that date. It is complied with religiously by the Church Authorities themselves. It is not the property of the president. He does not claim it or collect it. Tithing is received and receipted for by the local bishops and in the respective wards, who are under the supervision of the local presidents of stakes. The whole income is accounted for to the presiding bishopric of the Church and is under their direction. Their office contains complete records of all the tithings paid during each year. Each tithepayer will find in that office his record. The entire receipts and disbursements are there accounted for in the most complete detail. An auditing committee composed of men well known in the community for their independence of character and business integrity, not of the leading Authorities of the Church, chosen by the general conference, thoroughly inspect and report annually upon them. The funds thus received are not the property of the president of the Church or his associates, nor of the Presiding Bishopric, nor of the local bishops. They belong to the Church and are used for Church purposes, including the building and maintenance of temples, meetinghouses, schools, colleges, universities and other structures, the aid of the poor and afflicted, the extension of missions abroad and the help of new colonies at home, and sundry other objects and but a small amount is used for the support of persons devoting their whole time to the service of the Church, and that not out of the tithing, but from the proceeds of investments made with profit. This includes the presidency and other Church leaders. (Joseph F. Smith, Anthon H. Lund, John Henry Smith, CR, April 1911, 130)

We learn from these statements and from section 120 that the Lord has prepared a way to ensure that the funds donated to His Church are properly handled. The Church treats these funds as the sacred sacrifice of faithful Saints. We can trust that our tithes are used as the Lord would have them used.

1. TITHING: A COMMANDMENT WITH GREAT BLESSINGS

THEME: The law of tithing is an opportunity for faithful Saints to understand and experience the process of being edified and blessed through humble and charitable giving. After all, everything in this world belongs to the Lord, and when He blesses us with a measure of temporal increase, the paying of tithing is but an act of returning a portion of that which was borrowed in the first place. Tithing underwrites the building up of the kingdom of God; but even more importantly, it results in the building up of the character and Christlike nature of the Saints within that kingdom.

MODERN PROPHETS SPEAK

Robert D. Hales:

> Paying tithing helps to qualify us to receive the higher ordinances of the priesthood. To qualify for eternal life, a person must receive all the ordinances of the priesthood administered in the house of the Lord. Tithing is one of the basic standards of judgment by which it is determined whether a person is worthy to receive these ordinances. (*Ensign,* December 1986, 14)

James E. Talmage:

> Tithing is the Lord's revenue system, and He requires it of the people, not because He is lacking in gold or silver, but because [we] need to pay it. . . . The prime . . . purpose behind the establishment of the law of the tithe is the development of the soul of the tithe-payer, rather than the providing of revenue. The latter is an all-important purpose, for so far as money is needed for the carrying on of the work of the Church the Lord requires money that is sanctified by the faith of the giver; but blessings beyond estimate . . . are assured unto him who strictly conforms to the law of the tithe because the Lord hath so commanded. (*The Articles of Faith* [Salt Lake City: The Church of Jesus Christ of Latter-day Saints, 1924], 528–29)

ILLUSTRATIONS FOR OUR TIMES

"Would You Deny Me a Blessing?"

I recollect most vividly a circumstance that occurred in the days of my childhood. My mother was a widow, with a large family to provide for. One spring when we opened our potato pits she had her boys get a load of the best potatoes, and she took them to the tithing office; potatoes were scarce that season. I was a little boy at the time, and drove the team. When we drove up to the steps of the tithing office, ready to unload the potatoes, one of the clerks came out and said to my mother, "Widow Smith, it's a shame that you should have to pay tithing." He said a number of other things that I remember well, but they are not necessary for me to repeat here. The . . . name of that tithing clerk was William Thompson, and he chided my mother for paying her tithing, called her anything but wise or prudent; and said there were others who were strong and able to work that were supported from the tithing office. My mother turned upon him and said:

"William, you ought to be ashamed of yourself. Would you deny me a blessing? If I did not pay my tithing, I should expect the Lord to withhold His blessings from me. I pay my tithing, not only because it is a law of God, but because I expect a blessing by doing it. By keeping this and other laws, I expect to prosper and to be able to provide for my family." Though she was a widow, you may turn to the records of the Church from the beginning unto the day of her death, and you will find that she never received a farthing from the Church to help her support herself and her family; but she paid in thousands of dollars in wheat, potatoes, corn, vegetables, meat, etc. The tithes of her sheep and cattle, the tenth pound of her butter, her tenth chicken, the tenth of her eggs, the tenth pig, the tenth calf, the tenth colt—a tenth of everything she raised was paid. Here sits my brother, who can bear testimony to the truth of what I say, as can others who knew her. She prospered because she obeyed the laws of God. She had abundance to sustain her family. We never lacked so much as many others did; for while we found nettle greens most acceptable when we first came to the valley; and while we enjoyed thistle roots, segoes and all that kind of thing, we were no worse off than thousands of others, and not so bad off as many, for we were never without corn-meal and milk or butter, to my knowledge. Then that widow had her name recorded in the book of the law of the Lord. That widow was entitled to the privileges of the house of God. No ordinance of the Gospel could be denied her, for she was obedient to the laws of God, and she would not fail in her duty though discouraged from observing a commandment of God by one who was in an official position. (Joseph F. Smith, quoted in *Best-Loved Stories of the LDS People,* ed. Jack M. Lyon, Linda Ririe Gundry, and Jay A. Parry [Salt Lake City: Deseret Book, 1997], 149–50)

LIKENING THE SCRIPTURES TO OUR LIVES

Doctrine and Covenants 119:3–4 The Lord has provided the law of tithing as a standing law to His people. He has commanded the Saints to pay "one-tenth of all their interest annually" (verse 4).

Application: The law of tithing is simple. We should give one-tenth of our increase. Let us avoid making this a mathematical or complicated process. Let us simply give 10 percent of our increase to the Lord as He has commanded.

2. FASTING AND FAST OFFERINGS: ONE OF OUR HOLY OBLATIONS TO GOD

THEME: To fast with joy and humility is to remember things spiritual and to confirm our willingness to subsume our own desires and needs beneath the will of the Father. To pay our fast offerings with gladness and charity is a step toward true discipleship, because we practice thereby, if only in a modest way, the redeeming walk that belongs to the kingdom of God.

MODERN PROPHETS SPEAK

Howard W. Hunter:

> To discipline ourselves through fasting brings us in tune with God, and fast day provides an occasion to set aside the temporal so that we might enjoy the higher qualities of the spiritual. As we fast on that day we learn and better understand the needs of those who are less fortunate. (*Ensign,* November 1985, 72)

L. Tom Perry:

> The longer I live, the more impressed I am with the Lord's system of caring for the poor and needy. Surely no man would think of such a simple yet profound way of satisfying human needs—to grow spiritually and temporally through periodic fasting and then donating the amount saved from refraining from partaking of those meals to the bishop to be used to administer to the needs of the poor, the ill, the downtrodden, who need help and support to make their way through life. (*Ensign,* May 1986, 31)

Bruce R. McConkie:

> Fasting, with prayer as its companion, is designed to increase spirituality; to foster a spirit of devotion and love of God; to increase faith in the hearts of men, thus assuring divine favor; to encourage humility and contrition of soul; to aid in the acquirement of righteousness; to teach man his nothingness and dependence upon God; and to hasten those who properly comply with the law of fasting along the path to salvation.
>
> Many specific reasons for fasting are found in the scriptures. It is a general obligation imposed by revelation upon church members in good standing (D&C 59:13–14; 88:76; Luke 5:33–35; 2 Cor. 6:5; 11: 27). It is itself a form of the true worship of God (Luke 2:37; Acts 9:9; Alma 45:1; 4 Ne. 12). It is proper to fast for the sick (2 Sam. 12:16); for special blessings (Mosiah 27:22–23); to gain a testimony (Alma 5:46); to gain revelation (Alma 17:3; 3 Ne. 27:1; Ex. 34:28; Deut. 9:9, 18); for the conversion of nonmembers to the truth (Alma 6:6; 17:9); for guidance in the choice of church officers (Acts 13: 3); as an accompaniment of righteous mourning and sorrow (Alma 28:2–6; 30:2; Hel. 9:10); as a means of sanctifying one's soul (Hel. 3: 35); and for guidance along the path leading to salvation (Omni 1:26). Temples are houses of fasting (D&C 88:119; 95:16; 109:8, 16). To be acceptable fasting must conform to the Lord's law and not be done for hypocritical reasons (Matt. 6:16–18; 3 Ne. 13:16–18). (Bruce R. McConkie, *MD,* 276)

ILLUSTRATIONS FOR OUR TIMES

Blessings and Purpose of the Fast

> The regularly constituted fast consists of abstinence from food once each month, from the evening meal of Saturday to the evening meal on the following Sunday; that is, it means missing two meals on the first Sunday of each month. The value of those two meals given as a voluntary donation for the relief of those who are hungry or otherwise in distress constitutes the fast offering. Think what the sincere observance of this

rule would mean spiritually if every man, woman, and child were to observe the fast and contribute the resultant offering, with the sincere desire of blessing the less fortunate brother or sister or sorrowing child! The great Tolstoy, sensing the need of this bond of sympathetic brotherhood in Christ, once wrote that he had no right to eat his crust of bread if his brother had none. Can you not see associated with this simple act the divine principle of service as expressed in the Master's words: "Inasmuch as ye have done it unto one of the least of these my brethren, ye have done it unto me" (Matt. 25:40)? (*Millennial Star* 85 [1923]: 424–25) . . .

If we contribute to the bishop the value of two meals once a month, we are certainly no poorer financially than we would be if we had consumed those meals as we regularly do. There cannot be any loss to our own family in a financial way, and we have given at least a mite towards alleviation of hunger, perhaps distress, in some home that is less fortunate, less blessed than we. There is no loss to us financially, no man is poorer, no man is deprived of one blessing, no child is deprived of anything that he would have had if he refrained from giving that small contribution. Financially then, nobody who gives it is any the poorer. . . .

Physically, we are better off by refraining from eating at least once a month than we are when we eat regularly three meals a day. I am reminded of having read the opinion of one of our leading athletes who in his training watched the effect of eating three regular meals, then of eating two regular meals and finally of eating one meal daily, regularly, and he concludes so far as he is concerned that when he ate three meals a day he had been eating too much, and when so doing found it necessary to fast at regular periods in order to maintain his vitality to the standard possessed when he ate more sparingly. Physiology books will give us the same lesson. So, generally speaking—each individual must take this for his own good—but generally speaking no person is injured in any way by his depriving himself of those two meals on fast day, but, on the contrary he is benefited physically. . . .

There is still another blessing, and here I believe is the most potent factor, the most saving power in this fast-day requirement. What our young people need, what every man and every woman in this world needs in order to keep himself or herself free and unspotted from the sins of the world, is the power of self-mastery. Each individual should studiously practise self-control. It does not come all at once. Nature never makes cash payments as a whole, says William George Jordan. Her payments are always made in small installments. Those who desire to win self-mastery must do it by constant application. About the only definite command, to fast as given in the Law, refers to this principle as an "affliction of the soul." It is associated with spiritual uplift, and therein is one of the greatest blessings that come to those who will fast as God has asked them to.

Some may say, "Well, that isn't much, I cannot see how the refraining from partaking of food once a month regularly is going to give me any self-control." It does, however; it is one of the best lessons that adults as well as children can practise. Appetite is calling; there is a yearning, and the natural tendency is to yield.

Teach the child to master appetite. Teach him, not harshly, but kindly, with the Spirit of the Lord, with the spirit in which the revelation was given, and you will find that in childhood these little lessons in abstinence coming daily to your boy, unconsciously are placing into his little spirit power that may save him from falling in disgrace sometime when he is driven on by the fire of youth to the very verge of the precipice of destruction. Then is the time that he will need mastery of self, and he will have it. Men who have studied this principle suggest that we need to take some such lesson as this not only weekly or monthly, but daily. (David O. McKay, *Gospel Ideals: Selections from the Discourses of David O. McKay* [Salt Lake City: Improvement Era, 1953], 210–13)

LIKENING THE SCRIPTURES TO OUR LIVES

3 Nephi 13:16–18; see also Matthew 6:16–18 The law of the fast is to be carried out with a joyful countenance. The Lord has promised to reward those who participate in a faithful and joyful fast with innumerable blessings.

Application: As with any commandment given, the Lord expects sincere obedience in our fasting. As He answers us when we pray with real intent, so will He bless our fast offered with full sincerity of heart.

ENRICHMENT

The Law of Tithing
President Joseph Fielding Smith observed the following concerning the law of tithing:

The Lord had given to the Church the law of consecration and had called upon the members, principally the official members, to enter into a covenant that could not be broken and to be everlasting in which they were to consecrate their properties and receive stewardships, for this is the law of the celestial kingdom. Many of those who entered into this solemn covenant broke it and by so doing brought upon their heads, and the heads of their brethren and sisters, dire punishment and persecution. This celestial law of necessity was thereupon withdrawn for the time, or until the time of the redemption of Zion. While suffering intensely because of their debts and lack of means to meet their obligations Joseph Smith and Oliver Cowdery, November 29, 1834, in solemn prayer promised the Lord that they would give one tenth of all that the Lord should give unto them, as an offering to be bestowed upon the poor; they also prayed that their children, and children's children after them should obey this law (*HC*, 2:174–75). Now, however, it became necessary for the law to be given to the whole Church so the Prophet prayed for instruction. The answer they received in the revelation [D&C 119].

The people failed in the law of consecration. The Lord commanded them not to fail in this lesser law for the building up of Zion. Unfortunately we cannot boast very loudly of our faithfulness in the observance of this law. We have good reason to believe that the anger of the Lord will be kindled against all those who violate it, as his anger was kindled against those who broke the higher law. We may not receive the punishment in this life, but surely it will come to all who wilfully break it (D&C 64:23–24).

. . . In more recent times the Church has not called upon the members to give all their surplus property to the Church, but it has been the requirement according to the covenant, that they pay the tenth. It is remarkable how many excuses can be made and interpretations given as to what constitutes the tenth, by many members of the Church. It is written, however, that as we measure it shall be measured to us again. If we are stingy with the Lord, he may be stingy with us, or in other words, withhold his blessings. Then again, we have those among us who are hoping for the coming of the law of consecration thinking that in that day they are going to profit by the equalizing of the wealth of other members of the Church. It is definitely true, however, that all those who will not obey the law of tithing, will not be entitled to enter into the covenants of consecration, but when the day comes for the establishing of Zion and the redemption of the earth, such people will find themselves removed.

. . . Tithe-paying is not a principle new to our dispensation. Whenever the Lord has had a people on the earth who were willing to observe his laws, and they were not practicing the law of consecration, they have been called upon to pay tithes and offerings. Abraham gave tithes of all to Melchizedek, keeper of the Lord's storehouse, and king of Salem (Gen. 14:20). Jacob made a covenant very similar to that of Joseph Smith and Oliver Cowdery (Gen. 28:22). This law was given through Moses to Israel. Malachi said the people in his day had robbed the Lord in withholding their tithes and offerings. The Savior commended those who paid an honest tithing, such as the widow and her mite. This law is one binding upon members of the Church. We call it a free-will offering, and so it is, for everything in the Gospel is by free will, but nevertheless it is a law of God which to us is everlasting. (Joseph Fielding Smith, *CHMR,* 3:120)

Fasting with Real Intent

In the following excerpt, Joseph Fielding McConkie and Robert L. Millet explain the necessity of an important element of obedience concerning the law of fasting and all other laws—sincerity.

> The Saints are to fast for the right reasons. That fasting may be at a time of tragedy or sorrow; when we need spiritual guidance or direction; when we seek for a remission of sins; when we are struggling with a particularly difficult problem or challenge in life; or generally when we feel the need to draw near to God. But fasting is an individual matter. Though during the regular monthly fast we come together at church to teach and testify, and we enjoy social relations—all during the time of a fast—yet our fastings and our prayers are private. Fasting is something to be participated in, not something to be observed. A member of the Church need not "look the part" of one who is fasting. In fact, our obedience and our observance of the fast need to be hidden behind a pleasing appearance and a modest manner which would in no way draw attention to that which needs no attention.

> In general, then, our Redeemer calls us to a higher righteousness, to a higher motivation for righteousness, to a higher and more elevated perspective on why we do what we do. In addressing an apparent paradox in the Sermon on the Mount—the command to "let your light so shine before men" (Matthew 5:16) versus the command to "take heed that ye do not your alms before men" (Matthew 6:1)—Dietrich Bonhoeffer wrote: "How is this paradox to be resolved? . . . From whom are we to hide the visibility of our discipleship? . . . *We are to hide it from ourselves. . . . We must be unaware of our own righteousness,* and see it only insofar as we look unto Jesus. . . . The Christian is a light unto the world, not because of any quality of his own, but only because he follows Christ and looks solely to him. . . .

> *"All that the follower of Jesus has to do is to make sure that his obedience, following, and love are entirely, spontaneous and unpremeditated.* If you do good, you must not let your left hand know what your right hand is doing. . . . Christ's virtue, the virtue of discipleship, can only be accomplished so long as you are entirely unconscious of what you are doing. The genuine work of love is always a hidden work. . . .

"Thus hiddenness has its counterpart in manifestation. For there is nothing hidden that shall not be revealed. . . . God will show us the hidden and make it visible. Manifestation is the appointed reward for hiddenness, and the only question is where we shall receive it and who will give it us. If we want publicity in the eyes of men we have our reward. . . . *If the left hand knows what the right hand is doing, if we become conscious of our hidden virtue, we are forging our own reward, instead of that which God had intended to give us in his own good time*" (*An Eye Single to the Glory of God: Reflections on the Cost of Discipleship* [Salt Lake City: Deseret Book, 1991], 176–78; italics added).

How do we do this? What do we do if our motives are not always the purest? "Do we sit back and avoid deeds of service because our desires are not yet sanctified? Do we refrain from home or visiting teaching, for example, because our motivation is presently clouded more by the spirit of inspection than of expectation and covenant? Certainly not. We have duties to perform, work to do in order to bear off the kingdom of God triumphant. And Zion—as well as its municipals, its citizenry—is being established 'in process of time' (Moses 7:21). Simply stated, disciples do not wait to be transformed before they proceed in the work of the ministry. . . . We are never justified in doing the wrong thing or ignoring the work to be done simply because we are not properly motivated. Rather, the Saints are instructed again and again to seek the Spirit, to ask for, live for, and qualify for the gifts and fruits of the Spirit, which characterize the sons and daughters of Jesus Christ (see Gal. 5:22–23; D&C 46). As that Spirit begins to live in us, to remake us, we come to love the things we before hated and to hate the things we before loved. Because the Spirit is his Spirit, the works likewise become his works. . . . Our service thereby is centered in Christ, our eye single to his glory" (Robert L. Millet, *An Eye Single to the Glory of God: Reflections on the Cost of Discipleship* [Salt Lake City, Deseret Book, 1991], 58–60). (Joseph Fielding McConkie and Robert L. Millet, *Doctrinal Commentary on the Book of Mormon*, 4 vols. [Salt Lake City: Bookcraft, 1987–92], 4:85)

SUMMARY

Heavenly Father provides all things for humankind, including the earth and everything therein. He has asked us to give a tenth of our increase and a generous fast offering. We are stewards. This opportunity to pay our tithes and offerings is a key part of our responsibility to build up the kingdom of God here upon the earth. The Lord's method for handling the temporal affairs of His Church is the law of tithing and the paying of fast offerings. It is also the Lord's method for enriching His Saints with the spiritual blessings that attend the cultivation of a charitable and giving nature. By paying an honest tithe, we can help sanctify and purify ourselves and show our devotion to the Lord. Let us never forget that everything is the Lord's. His chosen servants at the head of the Church are blessed with the sacred right and privilege of allocating tithes and offerings for the highest good. We have the Lord's solemn promise concerning obedience to the law of giving by sacrifice: "Behold, now it is called today until the coming of the Son of Man, and verily it is a day of sacrifice, and a day for the tithing of my people; for he that is tithed shall not be burned at his coming" (D&C 64:23).

CHAPTER EIGHTEEN

"ESTABLISH . . . A HOUSE *of* GOD"

Reading Assignment: Doctrine and Covenants 95; 109; 110; *Our Heritage,* pages 33–36.

Additional Reading: Doctrine and Covenants 88:119; 95:3–17; 97:15–16; 101:22; 124:39.

On this hundredth anniversary of the dedication of the [Salt Lake] temple, may we each dedicate ourselves anew to the service of the Lord. Say the word temple. *Say it quietly and reverently. Say it over and over again.* Temple. Temple. Temple. *Add the word* holy. Holy Temple. *Say it as though it were capitalized, no matter where it appears in the sentence.*

Temple. *One other word is equal in importance to a Latter-day Saint.* Home. *Put the words* holy temple *and* home *together, and you have described the house of the Lord!*

May God grant that we may be worthy to enter there and receive the fulness of the blessings of His priesthood. (Boyd K. Packer, Ensign, *May 1993, 18)*

THEMES *for* LIVING

1. The Will of the Lord Is to Provide Temples for His Children
2. Sacrificing for the Temple Brings Infinite Blessings
3. When the Saints Present the Temple before the Lord
4. The Holy Temple: A Place of Visitation and the Restoration of Keys

INTRODUCTION

The prophet Isaiah foresaw our day in terms of the glories of temple work: "And it shall come to pass in the last days, that the mountain of the Lord's house shall be established in the top of the mountains, and shall be exalted above the hills; and all nations shall flow unto it. And many people shall go and say, Come ye, and let us go up to the mountain of the Lord, to the house of the God of Jacob; and he will teach us of his ways, and we will walk in his paths: for out of Zion shall go forth the law, and the word of the Lord from Jerusalem" (Isa. 2:2–3). The fulfillment of this prophecy began in Kirtland, Ohio, where the first of the Lord's temples in the dispensation of the fulness of times came into service on March 27, 1836. That experience was the culmination of a groundswell of extraordinary events comprising the Restoration to that point— from the First Vision to the return of the priesthood, the coming forth of the Book of Mormon, and the organization of the Church. With the Lord's temple once again standing on the ground, the first bastion of the process by means of which the hearts of the fathers and the hearts of the children should be once again melded together became a reality. The Kirtland Temple is a simple though dignified structure; however, the implication of what transpired there rises beyond the modest scope of this edifice to reach astounding heights of importance for the plan of salvation and the emergence of the Church from obscurity into the light of its divine mission.

The pathway of that emergence passed directly through the Kirtland Temple—and through all temples erected to the Lord since that time. Ponder the words of the Savior in this regard: "Therefore, verily I say unto you, that your anointings, and your washings, and your baptisms for the dead, and your solemn assemblies, and your memorials for your sacrifices by the sons of Levi, and for your oracles in your most holy places wherein you receive conversations, and your statutes and judgments, for the beginning of the revelations and foundation of Zion, and for the glory, honor, and endowment of all her municipals, are ordained by the ordinance of my holy house, which my people are always commanded to build unto my holy name" (D&C 124:39)

MOMENT OF TRUTH

The scriptural record of the commission, construction, dedication, and wondrous visitations relating to the Kirtland Temple, the first in this dispensation, is to be found principally in sections 95, 109, and 110 of the Doctrine and Covenants. An overview of the historical context for these three sections follows.

Section 95: Given through the Prophet Joseph Smith on June 1, 1833, at Kirtland, Geauga County, Ohio, in the Newel K. Whitney store, most likely in the translating room (see *HC,* 1:350–52). The Lord had commanded Joseph Smith to erect the Kirtland Temple in the revelation given December 28, 1832 (see D&C 88:119). In the intervening five months, except for acquiring land, a piece of which was eventually used for the temple, no effort had been made to start building the temple. The Church was in dire circumstances, lacking everything needed to build the temple: money, materials, tools, and experienced manpower. No architectural or engineering plans existed. Benjamin F. Johnson wrote that "there was not a scraper and hardly a plow that could be obtained among the Saints" to prepare the ground for the foundation of the temple (Benjamin F. Johnson, *My Life's Review* [Independence, MO: Zion's Printing & Publishing co., 1947], 16).

Joseph Smith was occupied with other tasks of priority. The Lord had just commanded Joseph to "hasten" to complete his translation of the Bible (he was now in the final month—see D&C 93:53). Church leaders were busily engaged in establishing the United Order or Firm and purchasing properties such as the tannery, the Johnson inn, and the Peter French farm to become part of that enterprise. Troubles in Missouri were beginning to escalate. A mob of three hundred had just met in Missouri to move the Mormons out of their "diggins." The Lord had commanded Joseph to build the schoolhouse in Kirtland, and just one month before this he had appointed a committee to raise money for its construction. Contributors were few. No steps had yet been undertaken to start construction on the temple at Independence, Missouri, other than to lay the cornerstones in 1831.

Heber C. Kimball clarified the situation of the Saints as follows:

> The church was in a state of poverty and distress in consequence of which it appeared almost impossible that the commandment (to build the Kirtland temple) could be fulfilled, at the same time our enemies were raging and threatening destruction upon us, and we had to guard ourselves night after night, and for weeks were not permitted to take off our clothes, and were obliged to lay with our fire locks in our arms to preserve brother Joseph's life. (Journal, bk. 94B, p. 19 [2nd numbering], Church Historical Archives)

In this situation, one can easily see why Joseph had not taken more immediate steps to begin construction of the Kirtland Temple. The Lord now got Joseph's attention in Doctrine and Covenants 95 and addressed the building of the Kirtland Temple. Note the message: Verse 1—The Lord reveals His eternal principle: "Whom I love I also chasten." Verse 2—The Lord chastens the Saints for sinning "a very grievous sin" by not starting construction on the Kirtland Temple sooner. Verse 9—The Lord states for the first time that His promise to endow them "with power from on high" will come in the Kirtland Temple. Verse 11—The Lord promises the Saints that He will give them the power to build the temple if they will be obedient to His "commandment" (see verse 3) and begin construction. Verse 14—The Lord promises that He will show three of them "the manner" in which it will be built. Verses 15–17—The Lord specifies the size and purposes of the two main rooms on the first and second floors of the temple.

Joseph Smith's quick repentance following the Lord's chastisement is a lesson to us all. The Saints quickly sprang into action after this revelation was given. Joseph took his counselors, Sidney Rigdon and Frederick G. Williams, and approached the Lord to be shown the pattern of the temple. Fredrick G. Williams described their experience as follows: "We went upon our knees, called on the Lord, and the Building appeared within viewing distance: I being the first to discover it. Then all of us viewed it together. After we had taken a good look at the exterior, the building seemed to come right over us, and the Makeup of this Hall seems to coincide with what I there saw to a minutia" (quoted in Truman O. Angell, Journal, MS, Special Collections, Lee Library, Brigham Young University, 4).

Joseph then called a meeting to discuss constructing the temple. Lucy Mack Smith said:

> In this council, Joseph requested that each of the brethren should give his views with regard to the house; and when they had all got through, he would give his opinion concerning the matter. . . . Some were in favor of building a frame house, but the majority were of a mind to put up another log house. Joseph reminded them that they were not building a house for a man, but for God; 'and shall we, brethren,' said he, 'build a house for our God, of logs? No, I have a better plan than that. I have a plan of the house of the Lord, given by Himself; and you will soon see by this, the difference between our calculations and His idea of things.' He then gave them a full pattern of the house of the Lord at Kirtland, with which the brethren were highly delighted, particularly Hyrum, who was much more animated than if it were designed for himself. (*History of Joseph Smith* [American Fork, UT: Covenant Communications, 2000], 217)

The urgency to respond to this revelation was shown especially by Hyrum Smith. Lucy relates, "[Hyrum] declared that he would strike the first blow towards building it [the house]. . . . Hyrum ran to the house and caught the scythe and was about returning to the place without giving any explanation, but I stopped him and asked him where he was going with the scythe. He said, "We are preparing to build a house for the Lord, and I am determined to be the first at the work." In a few minutes the fence was removed the young wheat cut and the ground in order for the foundation of the wall, and Hyrum commenced digging away the Earth where the stone were to be laid" (Lucy Mack Smith, *History of Joseph Smith, Revised and Enhanced,* ed. Scot Facer Proctor and Maurine Jensen Proctor [Salt Lake City: Bookcraft, 1996], 321).

The vision of the temple, the meeting to discuss temple construction, the digging of the foundation trench, and the hauling of the first load of stone from the quarry to the temple all occurred within five days of the revelation. Joseph Smith recorded the following on June 5, 1833: "George A. Smith hauled the first load of stone for the Temple, and Hyrum Smith and Reynolds Cahoon commenced digging the trench for the walls of the Lord's house, and finished the same with their own hands" (*HC,* 1:353).

Section 109: Given through the Prophet Joseph Smith and offered as the dedicatory prayer on the occasion of the dedication of the Kirtland Temple on March 27, 1836, at Kirtland, Geauga County, Ohio (see *HC,* 2:420–26). Orson Pratt, one of the Twelve Apostles present at the dedication, was the first to acknowledge that the prayer came by revelation. He wrote the heading in the 1876 edition of the Doctrine and Covenants as follows: "The following prayer was given by revelation to Joseph the Seer and repeated in the Kirtland Temple at the time of its dedication March 27, 1836." Brigham Young, who was also present as an Apostle at the dedication, approved this heading. Oliver Cowdery recorded that he, Joseph Smith, Sidney Rigdon, and scribes Warren Parrish and Warren Cowdery assisted in writing the prayer. This prayer is often used, even today, as a pattern for dedications of all types.

The weeks surrounding the dedication of the Kirtland Temple represented the high point in the seven-year Kirtland period and one of the greatest occasions for rejoicing and spiritual outpouring in Church history. It culminated almost three years of sacrifice and labor. Building the temple had presented gigantic challenges to the Saints, who lacked both manpower and money. Eliza R. Snow said, "The Saints were few in number, and most of them very poor; And, had it not been for the assurance that God had spoken, and had commanded that a house should be built to his name, of which he not only revealed the form, but also designated the dimensions, an attempt towards building that Temple, under the then existing circumstances, would have been, by all concerned, pronounced preposterous" (*An Immortal: Selected Writings of Eliza R. Snow* [Salt Lake City: Nicholas G. Morgan Sr. Foundation, 1957], 54). "Miracle" may be the best explanation for the construction of the Kirtland Temple, which was the result of the Saints' unconquerable faith in the Lord. The Church had virtually no financial resources to support construction of such an edifice.

Brigham Young described their severe obstacles as he acknowledged that the Church was "too few in numbers, too weak in faith, and too poor in purse, to attempt such a mighty enterprise. But by means of all these stimulants, a mere handful of men living on air, and a little hominy and milk and often salt or no salt when milk could not be had; the great Prophet Joseph, in the stone quarry, quarrying rock with his own hands; and the few then in the Church, following his example of obedience and diligence wherever most needed; with laborers on the walls, holding the sword in one hand to protect themselves from the mob, while they placed the stone and moved the trowel with the other" (*JD*, 2:31).

On March 27 the long-awaited day of dedication burst upon a city bulging with visitors. Not even a seven-hour dedication service would deter Saints who had labored and sacrificed all they possessed for this heaven-inspired temple. Personal comforts were discarded as they sat on each other's laps and otherwise occupied any possible space. One thousand Saints squeezed together into a space that accommodates barely four hundred today. The Saints gathered in anticipation of a spiritual climax. Joseph Smith estimated that by 7:00 A.M. on the morning of the dedication, more than one thousand persons waited near the temple doors. Between 7:00 and 8:00 A.M. a number of Church leaders and ushers entered the building. At 8:00 A.M. the temple doors opened, and about one thousand people flowed into the main hall. The doors were finally closed when all available seats were occupied. Hundreds could not enter the building, causing some hard feelings, because many of those left outside had sacrificed greatly for the building of the temple. One member, Frazier Eaton, who had paid seven hundred dollars toward the building, apostatized because he was not admitted. To somewhat accommodate the masses of Saints, Joseph Smith directed that a meeting be held in the schoolhouse west of the temple. After the schoolroom was filled to capacity, many still remained outside, so the brethren opened the temple windows to allow those outside to participate in the meeting as much as possible. To accommodate the Saints' desires, the Prophet scheduled a repeat dedication service for the following Thursday. The dedicatory service began at 9:00 A.M. After prayers, songs, a two-and-one-half-hour sermon by Sidney Rigdon, the sustaining of officers, and an intermission of twenty minutes, Joseph stood and read the dedicatory prayer.

The emphasis of this whole section seems to be that the Saints could now be endowed with power from on high in the temple and that the missionaries would be sent with that power to gather Israel out of the world.

Section 110: A record of the visions manifested to the Prophet Joseph Smith and to Oliver Cowdery in the Kirtland Temple at Kirtland, Geauga County, Ohio, on April 3, 1836 (see *HC*, 2:435–36). This section describes four separate visions granted to Joseph Smith and Oliver Cowdery while standing behind their Melchizedek Priesthood pulpit in the Kirtland Temple. Christ, Moses, Elias, and Elijah appeared that day and issued important declarations and bestowed the keys to the threefold mission of the Church. The occasion was a sacrament meeting. About a thousand persons sat in the pew boxes. After the sacrament had been passed to the congregation, curtains were dropped in front of the Melchizedek Priesthood pulpits, thus creating privacy for Joseph and Oliver. Curtains were also dropped in the assembly area, dividing it into four separate compartments. Designated leaders conducted meetings in each compartment concurrently, blessing babies and confirming new members of the Church. The congregation was apparently not aware of the heavenly proceedings taking place in the Melchizedek Priesthood pulpits. Warren Cowdery, Oliver's brother, recorded Joseph Smith's activities preceding the visions in the Prophet's diary as follows:

> Sabbath, April 3d He attended meeting in the Lord's House. . . . In the P.M. he assisted the other Presidents in distributing the elements of the Lord's Supper to the Church receiving them from the Twelve whose privilege it was to officiate in the sacred desk this day. After having performed this service to his brethren, he retired to the pulpit, the vails being dropped, and bowed himself, with O[liver] Cowdery, in solemn but silent prayer to the Most High. After rising from prayer the following vision was opened to both of them. (Quoted in *An American Prophet's Record: The Diaries and Journals of Joseph Smith*, ed. Scott H. Faulring [Salt Lake City: Signature Books, 1987], 157)

Sunday, April 3, 1836, was significant to Christians and Jews the world over. On this particular Sunday, the Christian world celebrated Easter. The Jewish world celebrated Passover. Traditions important to both worlds were fulfilled that day in the Kirtland Temple. For Christians, the Easter symbolism of the crucifixion and resurrection make Christ's words even more significant as He stood before Joseph and Oliver. He testified to them, "I am he who liveth, I am he who was slain" (D&C 110:4). For Jews, as is still the case, faithful Jewish families outside of Jerusalem provided a chair, a place setting, and a cup of wine at their Passover dinner table for Elijah's return. They also dispatched a child to open the door a crack so that Elijah could enter. Jewish tradition has it that Elijah is to return at Passover time; however, Jewish historians are not able to determine when this tradition began. Although not acknowledged by the Jewish world, Elijah's return in 1836 answered prayers offered throughout two millennia of time and more. Aharon Wiener, a noted Hebrew scholar, explains that Jews yet pray daily and weekly for Elijah's return: daily when grace is offered at meals—"May God in his mercy send us the prophet Elijah"; and weekly in benedictions after the public Sabbath reading—"Let us rejoice, O Lord, through your servant, the prophet Elijah . . . may he come soon and rejoice our heart" (Aharon Wiener, *The Prophet Elijah in the Development of Judaism: A Depth-Psychological Study* [London: Routledge & Kegan Paul, 1978, 132–33).

The Savior and Elijah fulfilled two biblical prophecies at least in part that day. The ancient prophet Malachi declared both prophecies—each one of them important to

Christians and Jews alike. The first was: "The Lord, whom ye seek, shall suddenly come to his temple" (Mal. 3:1). President Joseph Fielding Smith wrote concerning its fulfillment, "I think he has already come and fulfilled that, at least very largely, for Christ did . . . 'suddenly come to his temple' on the 3rd day of April, 1836, and minister to Joseph Smith and Oliver Cowdery, and then send other messengers to confer upon them keys of priesthood" (*DS,* 1:194). Malachi's second prophecy was: "I will send you Elijah the prophet before the coming of the great and dreadful day of the Lord: And he shall turn the heart of the fathers to the children, and the heart of the children to their fathers, lest I come and smite the earth with a curse" (Mal. 4:5). Testifying that he had fulfilled Malachi's promise, Elijah told Joseph and Oliver, "Behold, the time has fully come, which was spoken of by the mouth of Malachi—testifying that he [Elijah] should be sent, before the great and dreadful day of the Lord come. . . . Therefore, the keys of this dispensation are committed into your hands" (D&C 110:15–16).

1. THE WILL OF THE LORD IS TO PROVIDE TEMPLES FOR HIS CHILDREN

THEME: We learn from a careful study of the scriptures that the pinnacle of the Lord's design for His children is the holy temple, with its sealing ordinances, its washings and anointings, and its sacred endowments. In the temple we find the culmination of the plan of salvation; there we make covenants to return us to God. The Kirtland Temple, first in the dispensation of the fulness of times, holds a singularly important place in the history of the Restoration. It inaugurated the unfolding of temple work in the latter days and marked the milestone beyond which lay the establishment of many other houses of the Lord in all quarters of the earth—a process that still moves forward at a great pace.

MODERN PROPHETS SPEAK

Gordon B. Hinckley:

> I have spoken literally hundreds of times in temple dedications. I have offered not a few dedicatory prayers in these sacred houses. I have listened to scores of choirs in a great variety of languages sing the Hosanna Anthem, and I have been emotionally touched as these choir members, standing immediately behind me, have broken down under the emotional stress of their sacred experience.
>
> It has been my consuming desire to have a temple wherever needed so that our people, wherever they might be, could, without too great a sacrifice, come to the House

of the Lord for their own ordinances and for the opportunity of doing vicarious work for the dead. . . . The Church is not complete without temples. The doctrine is not fulfilled without these sacred ordinances. People cannot have a fulness of that to which they are entitled as members of this Church without the House of the Lord.

The Lord has blessed us with the means, through the faithful consecrations of the Saints, to do that which we ought to do and must do. This is the greatest era of temple building in all the history of the world. But it is not enough. We must continue to pursue it until we have a dedicated temple within reach of our faithful people everywhere. (*TGBH,* 629)

Bruce R. McConkie:

We expect to see the day when temples will dot the earth, each one a house of the Lord; each one built in the mountains of the Lord; each one a sacred sanctuary to which Israel and the Gentiles shall gather to receive the blessings of Abraham, Isaac, and Jacob. Perhaps they will number in the hundreds, or even in the thousands, before the Lord returns. (*The Millennial Messiah: The Second Coming of the Son of Man* [Salt Lake City: Deseret Book, 1982], 277)

LIKENING THE SCRIPTURES TO OUR LIVES

Doctrine and Covenants 95:11 "Verily I say unto you, it is my will that you should build a house. If you keep my commandments you shall have power to build it."

Application: It is the Lord's will that we not only have temples, but that we work for them and use them. If He will bestow the power for us to build the structures of our temples, it seems that He will also give us power to labor inside our temples. Truly, the Lord gives great power to His Saints through temples.

2. SACRIFICING FOR THE TEMPLE BRINGS INFINITE BLESSINGS

THEME: It is difficult to image today the extraordinary sacrifice of the early Saints in fulfilling the commandment of the Lord to build the Kirtland Temple. From their poverty arose a magnificent venue for heavenly visitation, the bestowal of keys, the presentation of truth, and the inauguration of an era of glory that still continues with even more urgency today. This story, with its remarkable outcomes, is an inspiration to all who are committed to support and uphold the work of temple building today—

in the eleventh hour of the earth's history, just prior to the Second Coming. There is no sacrifice too great, no commitment too encompassing, no charity too intense, no devotion too heartfelt when it comes to answering the Lord's call to help build His kingdom. From such effort flow the blessings of eternity.

MODERN PROPHETS SPEAK

Thomas S. Monson:

Tabernacles and temples are built with more than stone and mortar, wood and glass. Particularly is this true when we speak of the temple described by the Apostle Paul: "Know ye not that ye are the temple of God, and that the Spirit of God dwelleth in you?" [1 Cor. 3:16]. Such temples are built with faith and fasting. They are built with service and sacrifice. They are built with trials and testimonies. (*Ensign,* September 1997, 2)

M. Russell Ballard:

My brothers and sisters, we must not lose the spirit of sacrifice demonstrated by the handcart pioneers. Some of the Lord's choicest blessings await those who practice this eternal principle through extending themselves in service to God and to their fellowmen. The sacrificing spirit and the happiness that come through service to others can bring peace and joy even amid trials. (*Ensign,* May 1992, 75)

ILLUSTRATIONS FOR OUR TIME

Just a Few Pennies a Day

I would like to tell you also of an experience I had down in New Zealand, going into a humble Maori home. Here we had a situation where a mother and father and twelve children were living the gospel as well as anyone I have ever seen in all my life. As they would gather around each evening to have their family devotional scripture readings and have the children participate, there was a time in the evening when the father would put a few pennies in a glass jar sitting upon the mantel. The house was lighted with candles and kerosene lamps. In this humble home this little jar was always there—just a few pennies each day. This was their family temple fund. (Imagine a family of fourteen trying to save a few pennies a day, knowing that they would have to travel thousands of miles, at least to Hawaii, in order to get to the House of the Lord to do what they wanted to do.) Then they would kneel down in prayer, and from the smallest child they would take their turns and ask Heavenly Father that they might enjoy the rich blessing of having their family sealed together in order that they might have the fulness of the gospel come into their home.

I used to sit there and literally break up inside wondering how these wonderful people would ever realize this blessing. A few pennies a day—they just could not possibly get a family of fourteen to the temple on a few pennies a day, and I did not know how they could ever do it. But they prayed in great faith, and they prayed with devotion, and they meant what they said.

If someone had told me at that time that within my lifetime there would be a temple built within sixty miles of this very home, I would have said, "I don't believe it," because I did not have the same faith these people had. I am not sure that they visualized the building of a temple in New Zealand either, but they knew that their family was going to get together and be sealed and receive the rich blessings of the gospel. I want to tell you that the Lord is mindful of these people. He was mindful of their plea, and he poured his blessings out upon this family—and this family was multiplied by many hundreds throughout the length and breadth of New Zealand. It is a wonderful thing to contemplate the great blessings of the Lord to these Polynesian people as he listens to their prayers of faith. (Robert L. Simpson, in *Outstanding Stories by General Authorities,* comp. Leon R. Hartshorn, 3 vols. [Salt Lake City: Deseret Book, 1970–73], 2:201)

LIKENING THE SCRIPTURES TO OUR LIVES

Doctrine and Covenants 109:5 With the help of the Lord, the early Saints were able to construct a marvelous temple.

Application: The Lord blessed the early Saints' sacrifice by manifesting Himself to them. Similarly, He will bless our sacrifice of temple work by manifesting Himself in our individual lives through all the blessings and guidance He gives us. Sacrifice truly brings forth the blessings of heaven.

3. WHEN THE SAINTS PRESENT THE TEMPLE BEFORE THE LORD

THEME: What joy and edification were manifested at the dedication of the Kirtland Temple! The Saints presented before the Lord a most excellent product of their hands, an offering made with toil and sacrifice. He blessed them with a pentecostal experience and a grand measure of glory, to be followed soon thereafter with His presence and that of many of His servants, prophets holding keys essential for the Church to operate and expand. What joy attends the completion and dedication of all of the Lord's temples wherever they are erected! The Lord blesses all the completed work offered to Him, and He continually urges us to move this work forward. Similarly, families can achieve parallel satisfaction in presenting before the Lord their own "holy place" in the form of a righteous family and a sacred home. Whatever work is completed and presented to the Lord in faith is blessed by Him.

MODERN PROPHETS SPEAK

Bruce R. McConkie:

> The inspired erection and proper use of temples is one of the great evidences of the divinity of the Lord's work. . . . Where there are temples, with the spirit of revelation resting upon those who administer therein, there the Lord's people will be found; where these are not, the Church and kingdom and the truth of heaven are not." (*MD,* 781)

Howard W. Hunter:

> Consider the majestic teachings in the great dedicatory prayer of the Kirtland Temple, a prayer the Prophet Joseph Smith said was given to him by revelation. It is a prayer that continues to be answered upon us individually, upon us as families, and upon us as a people because of the priesthood power the Lord has given us to use in His holy temples. . . .

> Has there ever been a people with such stirring and wonderful promises! No wonder the Lord desires that His followers point themselves toward His example and toward His temples. No wonder He has said that in His holy house, "I will manifest myself to my people in mercy" (D&C 110:7). (*Ensign,* October 1994, 2)

ILLUSTRATIONS FOR OUR TIMES

An Historic Solemn Assembly

> The dedication of the Kirtland Temple occurred on Sunday, March 27, 1836. The early hour of 8:00 A.M. had been set as the time for opening the doors; but so intense was the interest and so eager the expectation, that long before the time hundreds had gathered about the doors. Between nine hundred and a thousand people attended the services. The congregation was seated in solemn assembly, each of the organized bodies of Priesthood with its presiding officers being in its appointed place. Singing, scripture reading, and supplication for Divine grace, were followed by brief addresses; after which the authorities of the Church as then constituted were presented to the people for acceptance or rejection, and a rising vote pledged unanimous support in every instance. The authorities of the Priesthood so sustained comprised all pre-

siding officers from the First Presidency down to the presidency of the deacons. The dedicatory prayer was then offered by Joseph Smith, who affirms that the prayer was given to him by revelation.

The question as to whether the House of the Lord was accepted as duly dedicated was put to the quorums of the Priesthood separately and to the congregation as a whole; the vote in the affirmative was unanimous. The Lord's Supper was then administered, and many of the elders bore solemn testimony to the divinity of the Gospel as restored. The prophet's journal continues:

"President Frederick G. Williams arose and testified that while President Rigdon was making his first prayer, an angel entered the window and took his seat between Father Smith and himself, and remained there during the prayer. President David Whitmer also saw angels in the house. President Hyrum Smith made some appropriate remarks congratulating those who had endured so many toils and privations to build the house. President Rigdon then made a few appropriate closing remarks, and a short prayer, at the close of which we sealed the proceedings of the day by shouting 'Hosanna, Hosanna, Hosanna to God and the Lamb,' three times, sealing it each time with 'Amen, Amen, and Amen.'" (James E. Talmage, *The House of the Lord* [Salt Lake City: Deseret Book, 1968], 99)

LIKENING THE SCRIPTURES TO OUR LIVES

Doctrine and Covenants 109:22 "And we ask thee, Holy Father, that thy servants may go forth from this house armed with thy power, and that thy name may be upon them, and thy glory be round about them, and thine angels have charge over them."

Application: The temple empowers us as we receive the temple ordinances. Our offerings in temple work bless us with power from the Lord and protection as we continue in the service of the Lord.

4. THE HOLY TEMPLE: A PLACE OF VISITATION AND THE RESTORATION OF KEYS

THEME: What grandeur is associated with the heavenly events that took place at the Kirtland Temple during its few years of service in the Restoration! That the Lord should have come to His house to honor His people with extraordinary, divine manifestations and bestow upon them truth of immeasurable power is a miracle of singular proportions. Too often we take for granted that these keys were restored, enabling us even to have the ordinances and opportunities we do today. So magnificent and glorious was this restoration. The Church would not be what it is today without the events of the Kirtland Temple. Let us remember in gratitude the circumstances surrounding the presentation of the Lord's gifts brought to this house to His Saints, and the implication of these gifts for salvation and exaltation through the Atonement. "For behold, I have accepted this house, and my name shall be here; and I will manifest myself to my people in mercy in this house" (D&C 110:7).

MODERN PROPHETS SPEAK

John A. Widtsoe:

> Temple work . . . gives a wonderful opportunity for keeping alive our spiritual knowledge and strength. . . . The mighty perspective of eternity is unraveled before us in the holy temples; we see time from its infinite beginning to its endless end; and the drama of eternal life is unfolded before us. Then I see more clearly my place amidst the things of the universe, my place among the purposes of God; I am better able to place myself where I belong, and I am better able to value and to weigh, to separate and to organize the common, ordinary duties of my life so that the little things shall not oppress me or take away my vision of the greater things that God has given us (CR, April 1922, 97–98).

Joseph Fielding Smith:

> My grandfather Hyrum Smith and Reynolds Cahoon commenced the digging of the trench for the foundation of the Kirtland Temple on the fifth day of June 1833. All of the brethren went to work with their might, for they realized the necessity of a sacred house built to the name of the Lord. The most important reason for the building of the Kirtland Temple was that there might be a sacred place dedicated to the name of the Lord to which his ancient servants might come, as the Savior did himself, to restore the covenants and authorities of the Holy Priesthood. It was in that temple that the Savior appeared, and angels were seen by many at the time of the dedication.
>
> First of all came the Savior, who accepted the house, and the temple was filled with the glory of the Lord. It was in that temple that Moses came, committing the keys of the gathering of Israel. Elias, who lived in the days of Abraham, committed the keys of the dispensation of Abraham; and Elijah came, fulfilling the promise of the Lord through Malachi, turning the hearts of the fathers to the children and the children to their fathers. The evidence of this fulfilment is apparent, for from that day the hearts of thousands of children have turned to their dead fathers, and the great

work of research and preparation of the records of the dead has taken hold of the children who are today working in genealogical research, preparing the way for the performance of temple work for the dead. (*AGQ,* 4:191)

ILLUSTRATIONS FOR OUR TIMES

An Unbroken Chain
We do cherish our temple buildings, but the buildings alone do not bless.

Some years ago, Sister Faust and I visited the Kirtland Temple. Our visit there happened on the evening of a perfect day in autumn. We were very inspired by the quiet location, the magnificent architecture, and the majesty of the special qualities of the building, the design of which was given by the Lord. We were impressed by everything about the building. Professor T. E. McDonald, architectural historian at the University of Illinois, describes the Kirtland Temple as follows: "Although there are in the world many temples, cathedrals, and churches of architectural and historical interest, yet of all these there is none more unique architecturally and more interesting historically than the temple which these Latter-day Saints built in the little village of Kirtland."

When I went back to Salt Lake after that visit to the Kirtland Temple, I was still under strong feelings and impressions about the building. I expressed to my brethren sadness that we do not have possession of the historic edifice.

I said to President Spencer W. Kimball, "President, we just need to have that building."

He replied, "Why don't you get it for us."

Elder Boyd K. Packer, however, remarked by way of comfort that, while we do not have the building, which of course is a great loss, we have what is not only important, but necessary. We still have in our custody and charge all of the keys, and the saving principles and ordinances are intact and secure and will operate in all temples. These keys, principles, and ordinances, however, are not physical in nature— they are sacred gifts held by our loving prophet, to be used and delegated as he deems necessary for carrying on the work. (James E. Faust, *Stories from My Life* [Salt Lake City: Deseret Book, 2001], 114–15)

Threefold Mission of the Church Launched
The events described in section 110 make April 3, 1836, one of the greatest days of our dispensation. Priesthood keys were restored that essentially represent the threefold mission

of the Church to proclaim the gospel, perfect the Saints, and redeem the dead. How I wish that all teachers helping their students to discover the power of these visions could teach them while sitting in the Kirtland Temple! As I have sat in that sacred edifice over the years, I have felt the divine power of events occurring in this structure. It would be my hope that teachers could convey to their students the reality of these visions. These mighty prophets did, in fact and in body, return to the Kirtland Temple. Moses, Elias, and Elijah are only three of eight holy angels seen in vision by Joseph Smith there. Joseph also saw other dispensational prophets in vision there, such as Adam, Abraham, Peter, James, and John.

How important are these events to us? They are so important that, had the keys not been given to Joseph and Oliver, we would not have temples today. Without temples and the sealing power to unite us as couples and families, we could never enter into the highest degree of the celestial kingdom. However, in order for this to be meaningful to us, we need to take advantage of opportunities to be sealed and to have our ancestors sealed. This work is vital. It is critical that we work to remove the veil from our minds and open our understanding of the vitality of temple work.

An experience I had will illustrate the reality and importance of these sealing keys. While serving as a family history advisor in the North America Northeast Area, I was assigned to visit the Louisville Kentucky Stake. As I was stressing the importance of temple work, one of the priesthood leaders, William Wolfe, asked if he could relate his experience as to the reality and importance of the sealing keys. Brother Wolfe electrified the priesthood leaders as he related the following:

> At the time of my father's death in 1979, I was not very active in church work and left the task of having his [temple] work done to my daughter. However, by July 1986 I had come to my senses and performed the temple ordinances for my grandfather, William Enoch Wolfe, and sealed my father, H. Russell Wolfe, to him. As I came through the veil and entered the celestial room, the thought came to my head, as clear as if my father had been at my side and talking to me, "IT'S ABOUT TIME, YOU ORNERY PECKER WOOD"—a phrase that I had not heard nor thought of for years. This is what my father would call one of us kids when we went astray. There will never be any doubt that my father was talking to me that day.

From this account we see that not only are the hearts of the children turned to their fathers, but the hearts of the fathers are turned to us as well. They are eagerly awaiting their work to be done and are working hard on the threefold mission of the Church on their side of the veil as well. How important this work, which centers on the temple, is to all of Heavenly Father's children. (Anderson)

LIKENING THE SCRIPTURES TO OUR LIVES

Doctrine and Covenants 110:9 "Yea the hearts of thousands and tens of thousands shall greatly rejoice in consequence of the blessings which shall be poured out, and the endowment with which my servants have been endowed in this house."

Application: The temple emblematizes the greatest blessings available to members of the Church. President Brigham Young reminds us, "We . . . are enjoying a privilege that we have no knowledge of any other people enjoying since the days of Adam, that is, to have a temple completed, wherein all the ordinances of the house of God can be bestowed upon his people. Brethren and Sisters, do you understand this?" (*JD*, 18:314). President Howard W. Hunter likewise emphasized the importance of attending the temple during his service as an Apostle and President of the Church, "May you let the meaning and beauty and peace of the temple come into your everyday life" (*Ensign*, November 1994, 87). We can enjoy the greatest blessings of the gospel by regularly attending the temple.

SUMMARY

We have been reminded in this chapter that it is the will of the Lord to provide temples for His children so that they might ultimately be empowered to enter His presence and partake of eternal life. Sacrificing to build temples unto the Lord yields infinite blessings. Likewise, great joy attends the process of dedicating these holy edifices and presenting them and the work performed therein in humility and gratitude before the Lord. The Kirtland Temple was a place of divine visitation and the restoration of sacred keys. The temples of today continue the process of putting these keys to work in blessing the lives of countless individuals—both living and dead. The temple is place of glory where we learn to see God: "And inasmuch as my people build a house unto me in the name of the Lord, and do not suffer any unclean thing to come into it, that it be not defiled, my glory shall rest upon it; Yea, and my presence shall be there, for I will come into it, and all the pure in heart that shall come into it shall see God" (D&C 97:15–16). This should be our greatest desire: to worthily serve God and return to His presence. It is through our work in temples that this is made possible.

CHAPTER NINETEEN

THE PLAN *of* SALVATION

Reading Assignment:

The Atonement—Moses 4:2; Doctrine and Covenants 19:16–19; 76:22–24, 40–42; 2 Nephi 9; Alma 34; 3 Nephi 27:13–21.

Premortal Life—Job 38:4–7; Doctrine and Covenants 93:21–23, 29; 138:55–56; Abraham 3:22–28.

Mortality—2 Nephi 2:11, 21, 25, 27; Alma 12:24; 42:2–14; Doctrine and Covenants 29:40–43; Abraham 3:24–26; Articles of Faith 1:3.

Life after Death—Alma 40:11–14; 42:11–13, 15; Doctrine and Covenants 76:111; 88:14–16.

The great plan of salvation is a theme which ought to occupy our strict attention, and be regarded as one of heaven's best gifts to mankind. No consideration whatever ought to deter us from showing ourselves approved in the sight of God, according to His divine requirement. Men not unfrequently forget that they are dependent upon heaven for every blessing which they are permitted to enjoy, and that for every opportunity granted them they are to give an account. You know, brethren, that when the Master in the Savior's parable of the stewards called his servants before him he gave them several talents to improve on while he should tarry abroad for a little season, and when he returned he called for an accounting. So it is now. Our Master is absent only for a little season, and at the end of it He will call each to render an account; and where the five talents were bestowed, ten will be required; and he that has made no improvement will be cast out as an unprofitable servant, while the faithful will enjoy everlasting honors. Therefore we earnestly implore the grace of our Father to rest upon you, through Jesus Christ His Son, that you may not faint in the hour of temptation, nor be overcome in the time of persecution. (HC, 2:23–24)

THEMES *for* LIVING

1. The Great Plan of Happiness
2. Premortal Life
3. Mortality
4. Life after Death

INTRODUCTION

The Atonement is central to all aspects of the gospel. It is the empowering crux of the plan of salvation and the pillar of God's design for "the immortality and eternal of man" (Moses 1:39). All members of the Church, even the very young, have these words on the tongue: "We believe that through the Atonement of Christ, all mankind may be saved, by obedience to the laws and ordinances of the Gospel" (A of F 1:3). Because the Son aligned Himself meticulously and graciously to the will of the Father, the Atonement, in all of its glory, unfolded as a magnificent gift to humankind through the Resurrection and an eternal opportunity for the faithful and obedient to gain access once again to the presence of God: "But, behold, my Beloved Son, which was my Beloved and Chosen from the beginning, said unto me—Father, thy will be done, and the glory be thine forever" (Moses 4:2).

The essence of the doctrine of Christ and the plan of salvation was best articulated by the resurrected Master in the famous words:

> Behold I have given unto you my gospel, and this is the gospel which I have given unto you—that I came into the world to do the will of my Father, because my Father sent me. And my Father sent me that I might be lifted up upon the cross; and after that I had been lifted up upon the cross, that I might draw all men unto me, that as I have been lifted up by men even so should men be lifted up by the Father, to stand before me, to be judged of their works, whether they be good or whether they be

evil—And for this cause have I been lifted up; therefore, according to the power of the Father I will draw all men unto me, that they may be judged according to their works. And it shall come to pass, that whoso repenteth and is baptized in my name shall be filled; and if he endureth to the end, behold, him will I hold guiltless before my Father at that day when I shall stand to judge the world. (3 Ne. 27:13–16)

MOMENT OF TRUTH

From choice passages in the Doctrine and Covenants and related scriptures, we gain a lucid understanding of the plan of salvation or the great plan of happiness. The moment of truth that enlivens these passages with transcendent and enduring meaning is the sacred act of the Atonement itself: "For behold, I, God, have suffered these things for all, that they might not suffer if they would repent; But if they would not repent they must suffer even as I; Which suffering caused myself, even God, the greatest of all, to tremble because of pain, and to bleed at every pore, and to suffer both body and spirit—and would that I might not drink the bitter cup, and shrink— Nevertheless, glory be to the Father, and I partook and finished my preparations unto the children of men" (D&C 19:16–19). The implication is that there is, for each individual, a moment of truth of similar profound meaning—that very moment, namely, where each of us accepts, in full faith and devotion, the atoning sacrifice of the Savior as the essence of our existence and the buoyant, redeeming force to lift us, through our obedience, to the pinnacle of our potential as sons and daughters of God.

1. THE GREAT PLAN OF HAPPINESS

THEME: There is no plan among the philosophies and inventions of humankind that will redeem us. There is no strategy in the world that can lift us out of the world to a state of eternal happiness. But in the design of God there is such a plan, a process of redemption and transcendence based on God-given agency and rooted in obedience and alignment with eternal principles. The plan of salvation is the heart and soul of our spiritual instruction in this probationary state and the unifying theme of all of the scriptures. How grateful we should be that the Lord has made known the details and workings of His plan of mercy through the Restoration of the gospel in these latter days.

MODERN PROPHETS SPEAK

L. Aldin Porter:

It is clear that our Heavenly Father had a plan laid out for the accomplishment of His purposes. In the scriptures we read of the many names of the plan: "the great plan of happiness," "the plan of redemption," "the merciful plan of the great Creator," "the plan of salvation," "the plan of justice," and "the great plan of the Eternal God." Each name emphasizes one aspect or another of the plan. But in reality there is only one plan called by many names through which God means to bring to pass the immortality and eternal life of man. (*New Era*, October 2000, 44)

Neal A. Maxwell:

> One has only to ponder what a striking difference the gospel fulness would make for so many mortals who now view themselves and this life so existentially and provincially. How glorious if these individuals were willing to understand that (1) God has a plan of salvation of which this second estate—or mortality—is a key part; (2) "men are that they might have joy"; (3) we are truly accountable for our thoughts, words, and deeds while here; (4) the resurrection is a reality; and (5) a loving Father is seeing us through this mortal schooling as our Schoolmaster.

> Such knowledge and understanding would not put an end to human imperfection but it would put an end to ultimate uncertainty on the pathway to salvation, making possible tremendous shifts in attitudes and behavior for immense numbers of people on this planet. (*But for a Small Moment* [Salt Lake City: Bookcraft, 1986], 62)

ILLUSTRATIONS FOR OUR TIMES

Water from the Sun

East of Lake Louise in Banff National Park lies Yoho National Park, just over the boundary between Alberta and British Columbia. One of the most spectacular sights in Yoho is Takakaw Falls, where a free-flowing stream of water plunges some thousand feet over a cliff and into a magnificent Rocky Mountain canyon. As a young man, I used to drive a tour bus in that area to earn money for college, and both Lake Louise and Takakaw Falls were valued destinations. The former inspired feelings of eternal peace and calm; the latter inspired awe for the dynamic forces of nature. "Takakaw," I was told by my instructors, was a native Indian word implying "water from the sun." According to the legend, the one who first viewed this extraordinary waterfall saw it against a brilliant sky and had the impression that the river was flowing directly out of the sun. The tourists whom I had the privilege of accompanying to this natural wonder would invariably stand transfixed as they viewed this amazing "water from the sun." Moreover, they could imagine in their mind's eye the invisible high-mountain glacier, far above, that served as the source of the stream. And their hearts resonated with the wonders of nature.

John Taylor once used the image of a stream and its fountain to explain the essential nature of the infinite Atonement as central to the plan of salvation. "Why did it need an infinite atonement? For the simple reason that a stream can never rise higher than its fountain; . . . A man, as a man, could arrive at all the dignity that a man was capable of obtaining or receiving; but it needed a God to raise him to the dignity of a God" (*The Mediation and Atonement* [Salt Lake City: Deseret News Company, 1882], 145). The water to which President Taylor had reference was the Son of God—the "fountain of living waters" (Jer. 2:13; 17:13). It was He who was the source of the eternal water that would quench forever the thirst after spiritual vitality: "But whosoever drinketh of the water that I shall give him shall never thirst; but the water that I shall give him shall be in him a well of water springing up into everlasting life" (John 4:14).

Takakaw Falls is accessed only by navigating fairly daunting switchbacks at one point along the road. Because there is little room to turn, a bus is forced to pull forward into one curve, then back up into the next, and so on. The end of the bus would at times hang over the roadway a considerable distance. As the driver, I used to tease my nervous passengers by saying, "If any of you feel uneasy about these switchbacks, just close your eyes—that's what I do." Somehow they knew that I spoke in jest and that caution, skill, and perseverance would carry the day.

The roadway leading to the fountain of living waters is likewise marked by not a few challenges and tribulations. Full access to the breathtaking view afforded by the plan of salvation can be gained only by faith, humility, and obedience to the laws of the journey. One must constantly hold to the iron rod that Lehi beheld in his dream (1 Ne. 8:19–20, 24, 30; 11:25). On the journey toward the living waters (1 Ne. 11:25) and the tree of life, vision must always be clear and open, "with an eye single to the glory of God" (D&C 4:5; 82:19). In this manner, the journey becomes joyful, regardless of the switchbacks, and the outcome is worth it, for the reward that awaits the faithful traveler is to experience the satisfaction of the yearning for salvation, the ultimate attainment of the source of the stream—water from the Son. (Allen)

LIKENING THE SCRIPTURES TO OUR LIVES

Alma 34:9 According to the great plan of our Father in Heaven, there must be an infinite and eternal atonement made or all of Father's children would unavoidably be lost forever.

Application: The core and center of the plan of salvation is that Jesus Christ would come to atone for our sins, that He might draw all humankind to Him (see 3 Ne. 27:13–14). It is also the foundation of the Church (see 3 Ne. 27:8–11). Without the Atonement, we would perish and be subjected to the devil (see 2 Ne. 9:6–10). This is why we should be filled with eternal gratitude for the plan of redemption of our Heavenly Father and the goodness of our Savior to pay the price of our sins, so that we might live again in Their presence (see John 3:16; 2 Ne. 26:24).

2. PREMORTAL LIFE

THEME: "Where have we come from?" is a question that resonates in every heart. The gospel of Jesus Christ answers that question in sufficient detail to enliven our understanding of the eternal relationship we have with our Heavenly Father and suffuse our lives with a grateful knowledge that we are the offspring of Deity and that our home was in His premortal mansions. With insight into such roots, we are more readily persuaded to abide by God's precepts and commandments in order to return to His presence one day.

MODERN PROPHETS SPEAK

Ezra Taft Benson:

> You are choice sons and daughters of God—precious souls sent to this earth at this special time for a special reason. God loves you, each and every one of His children, and His desire and purpose and glory is to have you return to Him pure and undefiled, having proven yourselves worthy of an eternity in His presence. (*TETB*, 560)

Boyd K. Packer:

> To repeat, the few crucial facts we know about our status in premortal life are these: "Man was also in the beginning with God" (D&C 93:29). We lived in the presence of God, our Eternal Father; we are His offspring. Intelligence, or spirit, was organized as spirit bodies before the world was (see Abr. 3:22). Each of us was endowed with agency. Authority was conferred and leaders were chosen (Alma 13:1–4).
>
> From the scriptures we read: "God saw these souls that they were good, and he stood in the midst of them, and he said: These I will make my rulers; for he stood among those that were spirits, and he saw that they were good" (Abr. 3:23).
>
> In the words of the Prophet Joseph Smith: "God Himself, finding he was in the midst of spirits and glory, because he was more intelligent, saw proper to institute laws whereby the rest could have a privilege to advance like himself" (*TPJS*, 354).
>
> We know little more than this of what our condition was then. Nor does it serve any useful purpose to speculate or wrest the scriptures, seeking after mysteries. There is scarcely time to master the plain and precious truths revealed to guide us through mortality. (*Our Father's Plan* [Salt Lake City: Deseret Book, 1984], 16)

Russell M. Nelson:

> You are one of God's noble and great spirits, held in reserve to come to earth at this

time (see D&C 86:8–11). In your premortal life you were appointed to help prepare the world for the great gathering of souls that will precede the Lord's second coming. You are one of a covenant people. You are an heir to the promise that all the earth will be blessed by the seed of Abraham and that God's covenant with Abraham will be fulfilled through his lineage in these latter days (see 1 Ne. 15:18; 3 Ne. 20:25).

As a member of the Church, you have made sacred covenants with the Lord. You have taken upon yourself the name of Christ (see D&C 18:28; 20:29, 37). You have promised to always remember Him and to keep His commandments. In return, He has agreed to grant His Spirit to be with you (see Moro. 4:3; 5:2; D&C 20:77). (*Ensign,* November 1990, 73)

LIKENING THE SCRIPTURES TO OUR LIVES

Doctrine and Covenants 138:55–56 The Lord prepared His servants with lessons and instructions in the premortal world to come forth and labor to bring souls unto Him.

Application: We made covenants premortally to come forward in these days for the salvation of humankind. In fact, we were there "When the morning stars sang together, and all the sons of God shouted for joy" (Job 38:7). We knew then and we know now what we are here to do. So we must accomplish the great work we are sent here to do.

3. MORTALITY

THEME: "What is the purpose of life?" is a question that escapes no mortal. All yearn to understand why it is that we find ourselves where we are in the circumstances of life and mortality. In the gospel of Jesus Christ, we learn that this life is but an interim act of a greater drama that began in the premortal realm and will transition to a successive phase that holds out the promise of enduring glory and joy. But the implications for this brief interlude on earth are awesome and eternal; indeed, our destiny is determined by our thoughts, desires, and acts while here. We have come to receive a body and pass through a probationary state in which our agency allows us to demonstrate allegiance to the King of Heaven and obedience to His laws and commandments. This life is but a brief hour or two as measured by the clock of eternity—but what stakes there are for us in this mortal time! Let us be ever alert and watchful that we move forward with the "godly walk and conversation" (D&C 20:69) required of the Saints of God.

MODERN PROPHETS SPEAK

Joseph Fielding Smith:

> The real purpose of mortality is twofold: first, to obtain tabernacles of flesh and bones; second, to obtain experiences which could only be had in mortality.
> The simple fact is that we came here to partake of the bitter as well as the sweet, to gain knowledge and wisdom through the experiences which mortality affords that would prepare us to go back and advance to eternal perfection.
>
> In mortal life we are in school where we are being trained in all the necessary experiences that will prepare us for eternal life. Therefore some pain, some sorrow, perhaps disappointments are essential in preparing us to go back as sons and daughters of our Eternal Father, as well as the pleasant things in life in our preparation for the blessings of eternal life. Thus we prepare ourselves for the life to come. Here we are in school being trained in all the necessary preparation for the future existence. Therefore, it is essential that we come in contact with some things that are bitter that we may appreciate the sweet and our earthly education may be complete. If we did not have access to these conditions, our mortal training would be defective and lacking in many features which are essential to the exaltation which awaits us if we are faithful and true. (*AGQ,* 5:58)

ILLUSTRATIONS FOR OUR TIMES

Grateful to Be Alive

> Today, if I may, I would like to take just one sentence from President McKay's beautiful dedicatory prayer offered at the London Temple, and may I quote from that one sentence. Speaking to the Lord, he said: "May we express overwhelming gratitude just to be alive."
>
> I have a personal reason this morning for repeating this sentence from President McKay's dedicatory prayer, because today I am truly grateful just to be alive. A few months ago I became critically ill, and I learned then, as I have never learned before, that the line between life and mortality and death and immortality is very thin indeed. It only takes a few seconds—yes, a very few seconds—to change from life and mortality to death and immortality, and I saw how close one can get to the pale of death. I thought I was passing from this life to the other, and I am truly grateful to the Lord that he permitted me to live. I fully realized then that I was not prepared or ready for that passing, and it brought to my mind a few words that I have read in a poem that goes something like this:

"There is no time that we could set for parting.

"Ever our prayer would be [as mine was],

"Not yet, dear Lord, not yet, just another day."

I realized then more than ever before how dependent we are upon God, our Eternal Father, even for the preservation of our lives. When one faces such a change, and we are all going to face it, when we come close to it, many things come to our minds. I wonder if you are ready for that change. I wonder if you are prepared to change from life to death. I believe that we can become prepared and ready, and I concluded then that if the Lord would permit me to live longer, I intended to live better so that I could die better. (Thorpe B. Isaacson, CR, October 1959, 96)

LIKENING THE SCRIPTURES TO OUR LIVES

Doctrine and Covenants 29:43 God has appointed this life to be a time of probation for His children, that He may elevate them to eternal life if they will believe in Him and keep His commandments.

Application: Because God knew that as mortals we will sin and fall short or our potential, He has given us this time to grow, become strong, and to repent and apply the effect of the Atonement. Now is the time to prepare to meet God. The successful journey through this probationary state is the main purpose of mortality. We should do all in our power to become Christlike and worthy to return to our Heavenly Father's presence.

4. LIFE AFTER DEATH

THEME: "Where will we go after death?" is a question that either haunts the mind, or, as the case may be, fills the heart with sweet anticipation and hopeful yearning. Every individual ponders the question and seeks the answer. In the worldly schemes of humankind there is no answer. It is only through the gospel of Jesus Christ that we have sufficient knowledge of things future to satisfy the deep-seated inner quest for a view of our destiny and coming state. And what a panorama of forward-reaching truth is unfolded to us through the scriptures and the words of living prophets! How grateful we should be that the Lord has opened to us a view of the blessings of the future awaiting those who accept His gospel of atoning grace. How mindful should we be to remember our covenant vows in order to look forward, in faith, to a time when we can again be with Him in our eternal home.

MODERN PROPHETS SPEAK

Joseph Fielding Smith:

> These words of Alma [in Alma 40:11–13], as I understand them, do not intend to convey the thought that all spirits go back into the presence of God for an assignment to a place of peace or a place of punishment and before him receive their individual sentence. "Taken home to God" (compare Eccl. 12:7) simply means that their mortal existence has come to an end, and they have returned to the world of spirits, where they are assigned to a place according to their works with the just or with the unjust, there to await the resurrection. "Back to God" is a phrase which finds an equivalent in many other well-known conditions. For instance: a man spends a stated time in some foreign mission field. When he is released and returns to the United States, he may say, "It is wonderful to be back home"; yet his home may be somewhere in Utah or Idaho or some other part of the West. . . .

> *Paradise* is a term which means a place of departed spirits according to the Prophet Joseph Smith. "Hades, the Greek, or Sheol, the Hebrew, these two significations mean a world of spirits" (*TPJS*, 310). Before the resurrection of Christ, the wicked were shut up in darkness and were not visited. In this awful state they suffered the torment of their consciences not knowing what their fate would be, just as Alma has pictured it. . . .

> . . . The Lord does not delight in punishment, however there is the demand of justice which must be met, and therefore the wicked are forced to suffer, and this suffering helps to cleanse them from their sins. Before the visit of our Savior to the spirit world there was a gulf separating the righteous from the wicked, and the wicked were evidently without knowledge as to what fate awaited them (Luke 16:19–31). The Savior after his crucifixion bridged this gulf and the gospel was carried to those who sat in this darkness and through the instruction of those who held the priesthood, these miserable spirits were taught the gospel. They were granted some measure of blessing according to their works on earth and according to their opportunity or lack of it, to hear the gospel when living on the earth, and accept the same in the spirit world. (*AGQ,* 2:86)

ILLUSTRATIONS FOR OUR TIMES

An Inspired View at the Edge of Life

The evening of my health crisis, I knew something very serious had happened to me. Events happened so swiftly—the pain striking with such intensity, my dear Ruby phoning the doctor and our family, and I on my knees leaning over the bathtub for support and some comfort and hoped relief from the pain. I was pleading to my Heavenly Father to spare my life a while longer to give me a little more time to do His work, if it was His will.

While still praying, I began to lose consciousness. The siren of the paramedic truck was the last that I remembered before unconsciousness overtook me, which would last for the next several days.

The terrible pain and commotion of people ceased. I was now in a calm, peaceful setting; all was serene and quiet. I was conscious of two persons in the distance on a hillside, one standing on a higher level than the other. Detailed features were not discernible. The person on the higher level was pointing to something I could not see.

I heard no voices but was conscious of being in a holy presence and atmosphere. During the hours and days that followed, there was impressed again and again upon my mind the eternal mission and exalted position of the Son of Man. I witness to you that He is Jesus the Christ, the Son of God, Savior to all, Redeemer of all mankind, Bestower of infinite love, mercy, and forgiveness, the Light and Life of the world. I knew this truth before—I had never doubted nor wondered. But now I knew, because of the impressions of the Spirit upon my heart and soul, these divine truths in a most unusual way.

I was shown a panoramic view of His earthly ministry: His baptism, His teaching, His healing the sick and lame, the mock trial, His crucifixion, His resurrection and ascension. There followed scenes of His earthly ministry to my mind in impressive detail, confirming scriptural eyewitness accounts. I was being taught, and the eyes of my understanding were opened by the Holy Spirit of God so as to behold many things.

The first scene was of the Savior and His Apostles in the upper chamber on the eve of His betrayal. Following the Passover supper, He instructed and prepared the sacrament of the Lord's Supper for His dearest friends as a remembrance of His coming sacrifice. It was so impressively portrayed to me—the overwhelming love of the Savior for each. I witnessed His thoughtful concern for significant details—the washing of the dusty feet of each Apostle, His breaking and blessing of the loaf of dark bread and blessing of the wine, then His dreadful disclosure that one would betray Him.

He explained Judas's departure and told the others of the events soon to take place.

Then followed the Savior's solemn discourse when He said to the Eleven: "These things I have spoken unto you, that in me ye might have peace. In the world ye shall have tribulation: but be of good cheer; I have overcome the world" (John 16:33).

Our Savior prayed to His Father and acknowledged the Father as the source of His authority and power—even to the extending of eternal life to all who are worthy.

He prayed, "And this is life eternal, that they might know thee the only true God, and Jesus Christ, whom thou hast sent."

Jesus then reverently added:

"I have glorified thee on the earth: I have finished the work which thou gavest me to do.

"And now, O Father, glorify thou me with thine own self with the glory which I had with thee before the world was" (John 17:3–5).

He pled not only for the disciples called out from the world who had been true to their testimony of Him, "but for them also which shall believe on me through their word" (John 17:20).

When they had sung a hymn, Jesus and the Eleven went out to the Mount of Olives. There, in the garden, in some manner beyond our comprehension, the Savior took upon Himself the burden of the sins of mankind from Adam to the end of the world. His agony in the garden, Luke tells us, was so intense "his sweat was as . . . great drops of blood falling . . . to the ground" (Luke 22:44). He suffered an agony and a burden the like of which no human person would be able to bear. In that hour of anguish our Savior overcame all the power of Satan.

The glorified Lord revealed to Joseph Smith this admonition to all mankind:

"Therefore I command you to repent. . . .

"For . . . I, God, . . . suffered . . . for all, that they might not suffer if they would repent; . . .

"Which suffering caused myself, even God, the greatest of all, to tremble because of pain, and to bleed at every pore, . . .

"Wherefore, I command you again to repent, lest I humble you with my almighty power; and that you confess your sins, lest you suffer these punishments" (D&C 19:15–16, 18, 20)

During those days of unconsciousness I was given, by the gift and power of the Holy Ghost, a more perfect knowledge of His mission. I was also given a more complete understanding of what it means to exercise, in His name, the authority to unlock the mysteries of the kingdom of heaven for the salvation of all who are faithful. My soul was taught over and over again the events of the betrayal, the mock trial, the scourging of the flesh of even one of the Godhead. I witnessed His struggling up the hill in His weakened condition carrying the cross and His being stretched upon it as it lay on the ground, that the crude spikes could be driven with a mallet into His hands and wrists and feet to secure His body as it hung on the cross for public display.

Crucifixion—the horrible and painful death which He suffered—was chosen from the beginning. By that excruciating death, He descended below all things, as is recorded, that through His resurrection He would ascend above all things (see D&C 88:6).

Jesus Christ died in the literal sense in which we will all die. His body lay in the tomb. The immortal spirit of Jesus, chosen as the Savior of mankind, went to those myriads of spirits who had departed mortal life with varying degrees of righteousness to God's laws. He taught them the "glorious tidings of redemption from the bondage of death, and of possible salvation, . . . [which was] part of [our] Savior's foreappointed and unique service to the human family" (James E. Talmage, *Jesus the Christ* [Salt Lake City: Deseret Book, 1977], 671).

I cannot begin to convey to you the deep impact that these scenes have confirmed upon my soul. I sense their eternal meaning and realize that "nothing in the entire plan of salvation compares in any way in importance with that most transcendent of all events, the atoning sacrifice of our Lord. It is the most important single thing that has ever occurred in the entire history of created things; it is the rock foundation upon which the gospel and all other things rest," as has been declared (*MD*, 60). (David B. Haight, *A Light unto the World* [Salt Lake City: Deseret Book, 1997] 6–7)

LIKENING THE SCRIPTURES TO OUR LIVES

Doctrine and Covenants 88:14–16 Through the Atonement of Christ, each of us will enjoy the blessing of the resurrection, which is "the redemption of the soul of man."

Application: The resurrection of the body is the gateway to a state of liberation from the ills and infirmities of the mortal realm, as a great emancipation from disease, deformity, and decay. This resurrection is given to all mortals regardless of their performance or purity on earth. Salvation from sin in another matter. We must remember to honor the covenants, that we may stand blameless before God in the resurrected state and hear His words of mercy and confirmation: "Well done, thou good and faithful servant: thou hast been faithful over a few things, I will make thee ruler over many things: enter thou into the joy of thy lord" (Matt. 25:21).

SUMMARY

The great plan of happiness encompasses all stages of life: premortality, mortality, and postmortality. It is all part of the Lord's design for His children: "For he is the same yesterday, today, and forever; and the way is prepared for all men from the foundation of the world, if it so be that they repent and come unto him. For he that diligently seeketh shall find; and the mysteries of God shall be unfolded unto them, by the power of the Holy Ghost, as well in these times as in times of old, and as well in times of old as in times to come; wherefore, the course of the Lord is one eternal round" (1 Ne. 10:18–19).

We learn in the scriptures that "Adam fell that men might be; and men are, that they might have joy" (2 Ne. 2:25). We also learn the indispensable nature and role of the Atonement for empowering that plan for achieving joy (see D&C 19:15–19). Through the Doctrine and Covenants we have marvelous confirmation of these truths in ways that resonate for the latter-day mentality and circumstances. God has spoken again with power and forcefulness in this dispensation of His plan of salvation and redemption—and the urgent need to conform, with thanksgiving and devotion, to His will and His commandments.

CHAPTER TWENTY

THE KINGDOMS *of* GLORY

Reading Assignment: Doctrine and Covenants 76; 131; 132:19–24; 137.

On February 16, 1832, Joseph Smith and Sidney Rigdon beheld a vision of the eternal glories. In the record of this experience they bear testimony of the reality and personality of the Savior: "And now, after the many testimonies which have been given of him, this is the testimony, last of all, which we give of him: That he lives! For we saw him, even on the right hand of God; and we heard the voice bearing record that he is the Only Begotten of the Father—That by him, and through him, and of him, the worlds are and were created, and the inhabitants thereof are begotten sons and daughters of God" [D&C 76:22–24].

They then describe something of the kingdoms of eternity which they saw. Men in the hereafter shall not be arbitrarily assigned to heaven or hell. The Savior had said, "In my Father's house are many mansions," and Paul had written of a "glory of the sun, and another glory of the moon, and another glory of the stars." In the hereafter, according to the Prophet's teaching, there are various kingdoms and degrees of glory; there are various gradations of exaltation. All men shall be resurrected through the atonement of Christ, but they shall be graded in the life to come according to their obedience to the commandments of God. (Gordon B. Hinckley, What of the Mormons? *[Salt Lake City: Deseret Book, 1947], 101–2)*

THEMES *for* LIVING

1. The Vision of the Kingdoms of Glory and the Testimony
of Our Savior Jesus Christ
2. The Vision of Perdition and the Ungodly
3. The Vision of the Telestial Kingdom
4. The Vision of the Terrestrial Kingdom
5. The Vision of the Celestial Kingdom

INTRODUCTION

The voice of the Lord in the latter days has proclaimed the ultimate destiny of humankind—of every individual who has passed through the gates of the Creation, none excepted. He has revealed the all-encompassing vista of the kingdoms and realms prepared as the postmortal domiciles for all the hosts of heaven belonging to this earth, all who await the Day of Judgment and the bestowal of their appointed inheritance of glory or, in the case of the sons of perdition, their irreversible consignment to outer darkness. He has promised His faithful and valiant all knowledge and wisdom: "For by my Spirit will I enlighten them, and by my power will I make known unto them the secrets of my will—yea, even those things which eye has not seen, nor ear heard, nor yet entered into the heart of man" (D&C 76:10; see also Isa. 64:4; 1 Cor. 2:9). A stunning and compelling glimpse into the archive of the Lord's heavenly truth is afforded to those who study the Doctrine and Covenants—in particular, section 76. The vision of the hereafter recorded there is the most comprehensive presentation of the life to come contained anywhere in holy writ. What was given through the Prophet Joseph Smith and his companion, Sidney Rigdon, concerning the pathway beyond death is an unforgettable savoring of things that await us and a strict delineation of the qualifications that apply to the different outcomes of the judgment process. Who can ever look upon life and the plan of salvation the same way after having studied, pondered, and sought spiritual guidance concerning the ideas and concepts contained in this revelation and related passages from latter-day scriptures? How grateful we are, therefore, for this guidebook of truth that clarifies our journey beyond the veil and elevates for our vision the objectives of achieving the highest possible level of glory and exaltation, based on obedience and covenant honor.

MOMENT OF TRUTH

The vision of the postmortal panorama of existence is covered principally in section 76 of the Doctrine and Covenants and then amplified further in sections 131 and 137 (as well as in many other scriptural references). The background and setting for section 131 will be treated in chapter 31, concerning celestial marriage. Details concerning the other two sections follow.

Section 76: Given through the Prophet Joseph Smith on February 16, 1832, at the John Johnson home in Hiram, Portage County, Ohio (see *HC,* 1:245–52). This vision, with its profound impact upon Church doctrine, resulted from the Prophet's diligent inquiries to the Lord while translating the Bible. It has been said that this is not only one of the greatest revelations given to the Prophet but one of the greatest revelations ever given to mortals. This vision is made up of at least six "sub-visions" which were viewed by Joseph and Sidney. Referring to the origin of this revelation, the Prophet observed:

> For while we were doing the work of translation, which the Lord had appointed unto us, we came to the twenty-ninth verse of the fifth chapter of John, which was given unto us as follows—Speaking of the resurrection of the dead, concerning those who shall hear the voice of the Son of Man: And shall come forth; they who have done good in the resurrection of the just; and they who have done evil, in the resurrection of the unjust. Now this caused us to marvel, for it was given unto us of the Spirit. And while we meditated upon these things, the Lord touched the eyes of our understandings and they were opened, and the glory of the Lord shone round about. (D&C 76:15–19)

In his history, the Prophet elaborates about the questions Elder Rigdon and he were contemplating before the vision was given: "Upon my return from the Amherst conference, I resumed the translation of the scriptures. From sundry revelations which have been received, it was apparent that many important points touching the salvation of man, had been taken from the Bible, or lost before it was compiled. It appeared self-evident from what truths were left, that if God rewarded everyone according to the deeds done in the body, the term 'Heaven,' as intended for the Saints' eternal home must include more kingdoms than one. Accordingly, on the 16th of February 1832, while translating St. John's Gospel, myself and Elder Rigdon saw the following vision: [There follows section 76]" (*HC,* 1:245).

Joseph Smith, in verse 11 of a poem describing the vision, gave its scope as follows:

> I, Joseph the prophet, in spirit beheld,
> And the eyes of the inner man truly did see
> Eternity sketch'd in a vision from God.
> Of what was, and now is, and yet is to be.
> (*Times and Seasons* 4, February 1, 1843, 82)

In this vision, not only did Joseph Smith and Sidney Rigdon see the throne of God, but also their understanding was expanded concerning death, the resurrection, the judgment of God, the differing heavens, and the characteristics of those who will inhabit those heavens. Significantly, Joseph said that they "conversed" with the Savior (D&C 76:14). About a dozen men were present in the room while Joseph and Sidney experienced the vision. An eyewitness, Philo Dibble, wrote:

> The vision which is recorded in the Book of Doctrine and Covenants was given at the house of "Father Johnson," in Hiram, Ohio, and during the time that Joseph and Sidney were in the spirit and saw the heavens open there were other men in the room, perhaps twelve, among whom I was one during a part of the time—probably two-thirds of the time—I saw the glory and felt the power, but did not see the vision. Joseph would, at intervals, say: "What do I see?" as one might say while looking out the window and beholding what all in the room could not see. Then he would relate what he had seen or what he was looking at. Then Sidney replied, "I see the same." Presently Sidney would say, "What do I see?" and would repeat what he had seen or was seeing, and Joseph would reply, "I see the same." This manner of conversation was repeated at short intervals to the end of the vision, and during the whole time not a word was spoken by any other person.

> Not a sound nor motion made by anyone but Joseph and Sidney, and it seemed to me that they never moved a joint or limb during the time I was there, which I think was over an hour, and to the end of the vision. Joseph sat firmly and calmly all the time in the midst of a magnificent glory, but Sidney sat limp and pale, apparently as limber as a rag, observing which, Joseph remarked, smilingly, "Sidney is not used to it as I am." (*Juvenile Instructor,* 27:304)

Joseph Smith gave this description: "Nothing could be more pleasing to the Saints upon the order of the kingdom of the Lord, than the light which burst upon the world through the foregoing vision. Every law, every commandment, every promise, every truth, and every point touching the destiny of man, from Genesis to Revelation, where the purity of the scriptures remains unsullied by the folly of men, go to show the perfection of the theory—of different degrees of glory in the future life—and witnesses the fact that that document is a transcript from the records of the eternal world. The sublimity of the ideas; the purity of the language; the scope for action; the continued duration for completion, in order that the heirs of salvation may confess the Lord and bow the knee; the rewards for faithfulness, and the punishments for sins, are so much beyond the narrow-mindedness of men, that every honest man is constrained to exclaim: 'It came from God'" (*HC,* 1:252).

Although many members refer to this vision as being a vision of the three degrees of glory, it is much more. There are six visions within the overall vision:

1. The Savior and the Father—verses 20–24

2. Lucifer rebelling and being thrust down—verses 25–28

3. The sons of perdition and their fate—verses 29–38, 43–49

4. The celestial glory—verses 50–70, 92–96

5. The terrestrial glory—verses 71–80, 91, 97

6. The telestial glory—verses 81–90, 98–106, 109–13

Also, note these two recurring aspects:

The Lord told them to write down the vision while still in the Spirit—verses 28, 49, 80, 113, 114

Affirmation of the vision and testimony of Christ—verses 12, 14, 22–23, 50, 89, 91, 92, 109, 110, 113, 119

Section 137: Given through the Prophet Joseph Smith in the temple at Kirtland, Geauga County, Ohio, on January 21, 1836 (see *HC,* 2:380–81). This revelation and vision came as the First Presidency and other leaders gathered in Joseph Smith's temple office at the west end of the third or attic floor. The third-floor rooms had been finished sufficiently to begin holding meetings there. In another two months, the Kirtland Temple would be dedicated. On this occasion, these leaders instituted the first ordinance in our dispensation performed in a temple. The ordinance was that of anointing with holy oil. Oliver Cowdery said, "[We] were annointed with the same kind of oil and in the man[ner] that were Moses and Aaron, and those who stood before the Lord in ancient days." Then, referring to the vision described in this revelation,

Oliver said, "The heavens were opened to many, and great and marvelous things were shown" (1836 Diary, *BYU Studies* 12.4 [Summer 1972]: 418). As these leaders participated in this ordinance, a glorious vision of the celestial kingdom burst upon them. The first half of this section describes this vision. Joseph saw the celestial kingdom, its gate, its streets, and the Father and the Son sitting on the throne. He identified certain individuals who apparently either had inherited or would inherit the celestial kingdom, such as Adam, Abraham, father and mother Smith, and his brother Alvin, who had died in 1823. Of those, only Joseph's parents were still alive, and his father was in the room with Joseph at the time of the vision. According to President Joseph Fielding Smith, the prophet was seeing "a vision of the future" (Joseph Fielding Smith, *CHMR,* 3:71).

Joseph made particular mention that he could not distinguish whether he was in the body or out of it. The second half of the section (verses 7–10) is the revelation. According to Joseph, the Lord spoke the words of the revelation to him.

1. THE VISION OF THE KINGDOMS OF GLORY AND THE TESTIMONY OF OUR SAVIOR JESUS CHRIST

THEME: It is the will of God to bestow immortality and eternal lives upon as many of His children as will receive and practice that degree of truth expedient for abiding a celestial level of glory. To such is given all that the Father has: "And he that receiveth my Father receiveth my Father's kingdom; therefore all that my Father hath shall be given unto him. And this is according to the oath and covenant which belongeth to the priesthood" (D&C 84:39).

Through the ministry of the Prophet Joseph Smith, the Lord has outlined with clarity the contours of the kingdoms that are reserved for humankind in the hereafter, according to their several levels and qualifications. At the heart of the process of assigning individuals to such levels is the degree of valor, loyalty, and obedience shown to the Redeemer, Jesus Christ. It is the solemn mission of each individual in mortality to exercise faith in Jesus Christ, manifest repentance, experience baptism at the hands of authorized priesthood representatives, receive and savor the gift of the Holy Ghost in all humility and contrition, and endure to the end. Of such is the kingdom of heaven, and their ultimate placement within the courts on high will depend on their degree of spiritual refinement and enlightenment and the quality of their "godly walk and conversation" (D&C 20:69) before the Lord.

MODERN PROPHETS SPEAK

Joseph Smith:

Could you gaze into heaven five minutes, you would know more than you would by reading all that ever was written on the subject.

All men know that they must die. And it is important that we should understand the reasons and causes of our exposure to the vicissitudes of life and of death, and the designs and purposes of God in our coming into the world, our suffering here, and our departure hence. What is the object of our coming into existence, then dying and falling away, to be here no more? It is but reasonable to suppose that God would reveal something in reference to the matter, and it is a subject we ought to study more than any other. We ought to study it day and night, for the world is ignorant in reference to their true condition and relation. If we have any claim on our Heavenly Father for anything, it is for knowledge on this important subject. (*HC,* 6:50).

Brigham Young:

The vision given to Joseph Smith and Sidney Rigdon is the greatest vision I ever knew given to the children of men, incorporating more in a few pages than any other revelation I have any knowledge of. (*JD,* 8:36)

Neal A. Maxwell:

Of the approximately 70 billion individuals who, up to now, have inhabited this planet, probably not more than one percent have really heard the gospel. Today no more than one-tenth of one percent of the world's population are members of the Church. Even so, before the final judgment and resurrection all will have had an adequate opportunity to hear the gospel of Jesus Christ. This underscores the mercy of God and the justice of God (see D&C 1:2). Infant mortality, which rages in so many parts of the world, is also placed in a reassuring doctrinal context (see D&C 137:10). (*But for a Small Moment* [Salt Lake City: Bookcraft, 1986], 115–16)

LIKENING THE SCRIPTURES TO OUR LIVES

Doctrine and Covenants 76:40–42 This is the gospel of Christ: "That he came into the world, even Jesus, to be crucified for the world, and to bear the sins of the world, and to sanctify the world, and to cleanse it from all unrighteousness."

Application: Through the Atonement, our Savior is the center of the plan of happiness. He makes it possible for us to obtain the greatest degree of glory we are prepared to receive. The degree to which we apply the Atonement in our lives is the degree to which we are perfected (see Moro. 10:32) and worthy to return to God.

2. THE VISION OF PERDITION AND THE UNGODLY

THEME: "For it must needs be, that there is an opposition in all things" declared Lehi to his firstborn in the wilderness (2 Ne. 2:11). The most tragic and awful demonstration of this inevitability is the nature and final status of those who know the light intimately and nevertheless declare it darkness—unto their utter doom and destruction. There is little comfort in studying the fate of the sons of perdition, except as it might offer a repugnant foil against which, by contrast, to delight in that which is good and true, elevating and edifying. It is in a framework of utter darkness that the light of the gospel shines with the greatest luminosity.

MODERN PROPHETS SPEAK

Spencer W. Kimball:

> Those who followed Lucifer in his rebellion in the premortal life and those who in mortality sin against the Holy Ghost are sons of perdition. The ex-mortal sons of perdition will be resurrected, as will everyone else; but they will finally suffer the second death, the spiritual death, for "they are cut off again as to things pertaining to righteousness" (Hel. 14:18).

> In the days of the restoration there apparently were those who taught that the devil and his angels and the sons of perdition should sometime be restored. The Prophet Joseph Smith would not countenance the teaching of this doctrine, and sanctioned the decision of the bishop that any who taught it should be barred from communion.

> In the realms of perdition or the kingdom of darkness, where there is no light, Satan and the unembodied spirits of the pre-existence shall dwell together with those of mortality who retrogress to the level of perdition. These have lost the power of regeneration. They have sunk so low as to have lost the inclinations and ability to repent, consequently the gospel plan is useless to them as an agent of growth and development. (*The Miracle of Forgiveness* [Salt Lake City: Bookcraft, 1969], 125)

ILLUSTRATIONS FOR OUR TIMES

Sons of Perdition

Concerning the potential to commit the unpardonable sin and become sons of perdition, Joseph Smith said, "What must a man do to commit the unpardonable sin? He must receive the Holy Ghost, have the heavens opened unto him, and know God, and then sin against Him. . . . He has got to say that the sun does not shine while he sees it; he has got to deny Jesus Christ when the heavens have been opened unto him, and to deny the plan of salvation with his eyes open to the truth of it." Joseph Smith, however, also warned that some apostates of his day had that potential. He said, "This is the case with many apostates" (*TPJS*, 358). B. H. Roberts said that sons of perdition "commit the same act of high treason that Lucifer in the rebellion of heaven did, and hence are worthy of the same punishment with him. Thank God, the number who commit that fearful crime is but few" (*Outlines of Ecclesiastical History: A Text Book*, 6th ed. [Salt Lake City: The Church of Jesus Christ of Latter-Day Saints, 1950], 419).

How does one become a son of perdition? One source cited Doctrine and Covenants 76:31 and said, "The Lord reveals five steps that will lead a covenant member of the church into the awful status of a son of perdition: (1) Know the power of God; (2) partake of God's power; (3) allow himself to be overcome by the power of the devil; (4) deny the truth; and (5) defy God's power" (L. G. Otten and C. Max Caldwell, *Sacred Truths of the Doctrine and Covenants*, 2 vols. [Springville, UT: LEMB, 1983], 2:29).

If we understood the awful state of such beings, it could help us to resist being overcome by the power of Satan. Sterling W. Sill offered this insight, "The Prophet Joseph Smith once said that 'If you could gaze into heaven for five minutes, you would learn more than by reading all of the books that had ever been written on the subject.' But it seems to me that we might also learn a great deal if we could look into hell for five minutes. Many of us are more effectively motivated by pain and loss than we are by a promise of blessings. Too much pleasure can sometimes be very harmful and lead us away from God, whereas pain sometimes puts us back on the track" (*BYU Speeches of the Year*, January 20, 1960, 5).

Although most of us might not be capable of becoming sons of perdition, we should still constantly be on guard. Brigham Young concluded, "It is for us to choose whether we will be sons and daughters, joint heirs with Jesus Christ, or whether we accept an inferior glory; or whether we sin against the Holy Ghost, which cannot be pardoned or forgiven in this world, nor in the world to come; the penalty of which is to suffer the second death" (*JD*, 18:216–17). (Anderson)

LIKENING THE SCRIPTURES TO OUR LIVES

Doctrine and Covenants 76:35–38 Those who deny the Holy Spirit after having received it will not be redeemed from the second death and will be cast into the lake of fire and brimstone.

Application: The denying of the Holy Ghost, once having had a witness of our Savior Jesus Christ, is the most grievous of all sins. Since the gift of the Holy Ghost is the most precious in mortality, so likewise is the denying of it the most condemning sin. We should seek the Spirit and then, above all, be obedient to its promptings.

3. THE VISION OF THE TELESTIAL KINGDOM

THEME: Even the most wicked—short of being sons of perdition—inherit a kingdom of such glory that it "surpasses all understanding" (D&C 76:89). Nevertheless, they are isolated by their chosen natures, and, tragically, "where God and Christ dwell they cannot come, worlds without end" (D&C 76:112). How much more glorious, by contrast, is the destiny of those in the celestial kingdom who are sanctified to live in the presence of God forever. The symbolism of light—stars, moon, and sun—is an apt way for the Lord to explain to His children the different glories that pertain to the telestial, terrestrial, and celestial realms. While we may be awed by the beauty of the stars, they will never offer us the brilliancy and life that the sun does.

MODERN PROPHETS SPEAK

Russell M. Nelson:

> Another unchanging principle, brothers and sisters, is that of your eventual judgment. Each of you will be judged according to your individual works and the desires of your hearts. You will not be required to pay the debt of any other. Your eventual placement in the celestial, terrestrial, or telestial kingdom will not be determined by chance. The Lord has prescribed unchanging requirements for each. You can know what the scriptures teach, and pattern your lives accordingly. (*Ensign,* November 1993, 33)

Neal A. Maxwell:

> God thus takes into merciful account not only our desires and our performance, but also the degrees of difficulty which our varied circumstances impose upon us. No wonder we will not complain at the final judgment, especially since even the teles-

tial kingdom's glory "surpasses all understanding" (D&C 76:89). God delights in blessing us, especially when we realize "joy in that which [we] have desired" (D&C 7:8). (*Ensign,* November 1996, 21)

Bruce R. McConkie:

Most of the adult people who have lived from the day of Adam to the present time will go to the telestial kingdom. The inhabitants of this lowest kingdom of glory will be "as innumerable as the stars in the firmament of heaven, or as the sand upon the seashore." They will be the endless hosts of people of all ages who have lived after the manner of the world; who have been carnal, sensual, and devilish; who have chosen the vain philosophies of the world rather than accept the testimony of Jesus; who have been liars and thieves, sorcerers and adulterers, blasphemers and murderers (D&C 76:81–112; Rev. 22:15). Their number will include "all the proud, yea, and all that do wickedly" (Mal. 4:1), for all such have lived a telestial law. "And they shall be servants of the Most High; but where God and Christ dwell they cannot come, worlds without end" (D&C 76:112). (*MD,* 778)

ILLUSTRATIONS FOR OUR TIMES

The Meaning of Hell

Among those at death who are assigned to hell are the heirs of the telestial kingdom and the sons of perdition. These spirits will remain in hell, or spirit prison, suffering "the wrath of Almighty God" until the millennial reign is over (see D&C 76:106). At that time, they will be resurrected in the last resurrection, the resurrection of the unjust (see D&C 76:16–17, 81–85; John 5:28–29).

Those who inherit the telestial kingdom constitute the filthy of the earth—the sorcerers, the adulterers, the whoremongers, "and whosoever loves and makes a lie" (see D&C 76:103). But through the mercies of God, even these people will be given a degree of glory. They will be "heirs of salvation," capable of being instructed by the Holy Spirit and by ministering angels (see D&C 76:88).

Elder McConkie wrote that even most murderers will come out of hell, or the spirit prison, in the last resurrection to live in telestial glory:

"When the Lord paraphrases the language of Revelation 21:8 in latter-day revelation (D&C 63:17–18 and D&C 76:103–6) he omits murderers from the list of evil persons. Their inclusion here by John, however, coupled with the fact that only those who deny the truth after receiving a perfect knowledge of it shall become sons of perdition, is a clear indication that murderers shall eventually go to the telestial kingdom, unless of course there are some among those destined to be sons of perdition who are also murderers" (*Doctrinal New Testament Commentary,* 3 vols. [Salt Lake City: Bookcraft, 1965–73], 3:584).

Hell, then, is a temporary quarter of the spirit world where the wicked are restrained in order for justice to be served and to give them a chance to repent. The Lord's promise is that all who do repent will receive a kingdom of glory, according to his judgment of their works. Even those who merit no kingdom of glory will be resurrected, for Christ's atonement broke the bands of death for *all* mankind (see 1 Cor. 15:22; 2 Ne. 9:14–16). Following the resurrection, then, that temporary quarter of the spirit world called hell will no longer be necessary. "After all men are resurrected," wrote Elder McConkie, "the [postearthly] spirit world will be without inhabitants" (*MD,* 762). (H. Donl Peterson, *Ensign,* April 1986, 36)

LIKENING THE SCRIPTURES TO OUR LIVES

Doctrine and Covenants 76:109–12 Those who will inhabit the telestial kingdom will be as innumerable as the sands of the sea. They will be servants of God; however, where God and Christ dwell they cannot come.

Application: Remember that we are judged according to our works and restored and resurrected to the glory of the kingdom that we deserve—but to enter the telestial kingdom one must still confess that Jesus is the Christ.

4. THE VISION OF THE TERRESTRIAL KINGDOM

THEME: The glory of the moon is the image that the Lord chooses to characterize the brightness that pertains to this kingdom, by way of contrast with the starlight nature of the telestial and the sunlight nature of the celestial. "These are they who are not valiant in the testimony of Jesus" (D&C 76:79). This implies that these will have testimonies, though they are not faithful to them. They will have the privilege of beholding the presence of the Son, but "not of the fulness of the Father" (verse 77). Though refulgent and blazing, the glory of this kingdom is not equal to that of the celestial. These passages of scripture offer a poignant reminder of the need for constant vigilance on the part of all sincere seekers after truth, that they might find themselves, through obedience to the laws and ordinances of the gospel, on the right hand of the Savior in that Day of Judgment where the great Landlord will assign His mansions to the Saints.

MODERN PROPHETS SPEAK

Bruce R. McConkie:

> To the terrestrial kingdom will go: (1) Accountable persons who die without law (and who, of course, do not accept the gospel in the spirit world under those particular circumstances which would make them heirs of the celestial kingdom); (2) Those who reject the gospel in this life and who reverse their course and accept it in the spirit world; (3) Honorable men of the earth who are blinded by the craftiness of men and who therefore do not accept and live the gospel law; and (4) Members of The Church of Jesus Christ of Latter-day Saints who have testimonies of Christ and the divinity of the great latter-day work and who are not valiant, but who are instead lukewarm in their devotion to the Church and to righteousness (D&C 76:71–80). (*MD*, 784)

ILLUSTRATIONS FOR OUR TIMES

"Will My Dad Go There?"

> I'm sure all of us feel inadequate at times. Because of the nature of our earth-life probation, we experience temptations; and as we succumb to them, we are separated from our Heavenly Father and his Spirit. This is known as *spiritual death*. But Heavenly Father has provided a way for us to overcome spiritual death and return to his presence.
>
> I was reminded of this great blessing one day when I was teaching a Primary lesson on the plan of salvation. A nine-year-old boy in the class was obviously worried about his dad who, at the time, didn't appear to be very interested in spiritual matters. The boy seemed to be pulled between loyalty for his dad and his own desire to adhere to gospel teachings.
>
> He carefully studied the visual aids lying on the table at the front of the classroom. Pointing to the terrestrial kingdom, he asked, "Sister Rigby, do you think my dad will go there?"
>
> My heart was full, and I couldn't bear his pain. "No, I don't think so," I answered.
>
> He pointed to the telestial kingdom: "Do you think he will have to go there?"
>
> "No," I said, pointing to the celestial kingdom. He smiled, obviously relieved. But then his expression changed to doubt.

"But how could that be?" he asked.

I returned his question to him, motioning to the other visual aids on the table. "You tell me," I said.

He studied the wordstrips for a moment—then quickly picked up two of them. One said "Repentance" and the other said "The Atonement of Jesus Christ." Waving them above his head, he exclaimed, "Oh, yeah! Right on!"

His spontaneous expression of gratitude filled my heart with joy for the life of our Savior and for the hope his mission affords us. And it reconfirmed the testimony in my heart. *All of us* do have access to repentance and to the atonement of Jesus Christ. And *all of us* have the capacity to draw near to the Lord and to be blessed by his Spirit. (Joy Webb Rigby, *Ensign,* August 1984, 14)

LIKENING THE SCRIPTURES TO OUR LIVES

Doctrine and Covenants 76:79 The terrestrial kingdom is reserved for those who are not valiant in the testimony of Jesus. They shall not receive "the crown over the kingdom of our God."

Application: Though more brilliant than the stars, the moon is still only a reflection of the brighter light of the sun. It is similar, but not as bright. Likewise, those who enter this kingdom are similar to celestial beings in that they have testimonies. These, however, are not faithful to them. Let us press forward with valor and endure to the end that we might enjoy the blessings of the celestial kingdom and eternal lives (see 2 Ne. 31:20).

5. THE VISION OF THE CELESTIAL KINGDOM

THEME: "And let virtue garnish thy thoughts unceasingly; then shall thy confidence wax strong in the presence of the Lord" (D&C 121:45). This is the purpose for the gospel of Jesus Christ and the plan of salvation—to guide humankind to a level of righteousness that they might feel confidence in the presence of the Lord, having established themselves as valiant in the testimony of Jesus Christ and having put all enemies beneath their feet, not the least of which are pride, worldliness, and (through the grace of the Atonement) death and sin. Such are destined to inherit the celestial kingdom, even the highest degree thereof, to live forever in the house of the Father and the Son.

MODERN PROPHETS SPEAK

Spencer W. Kimball:

> Those who have believed in Christ, who have forsaken the world, who have taken the Holy Spirit for their guide and been willing to lay their all on the altar, those who have kept the commandments of God—they shall go to a celestial kingdom whose glory is as the sun. (*Ensign,* November 1978, 71)

Bruce R. McConkie:

> An inheritance in this glorious kingdom is gained by complete obedience to gospel or celestial law (D&C 88:16–32). By entering the gate of repentance and baptism candidates find themselves on the strait and narrow path leading to the celestial kingdom. By devotion and faithfulness, by enduring to the end in righteousness and obedience, it is then possible to merit a celestial reward (2 Ne. 31:17–21).

> No unclean thing can enter this kingdom, and the plan of salvation is the system whereby men are washed and cleansed, whereby they are "sanctified by the reception of the Holy Ghost," and thus enabled to stand spotless before the Lord (3 Ne. 27:19–21). "The sanctified" are "them of the celestial world" (D&C 88:2). (*MD*, 116)

ILLUSTRATIONS FOR OUR TIMES

A Comforting Doctrine about Salvation

I had an unforgettable experience while serving as a regional representative. I was assigned to attend a stake conference with Elder Bruce R. McConkie in Columbus, Ohio. As we met with members of the stake, I sensed Elder McConkie's concern that many felt inadequate in terms of doctrine and experience, especially recent converts and recently activated members. During the Saturday evening meeting, Elder McConkie reassured them that they should not be concerned. His message to them was: "Please do not feel that you are not good enough or that you don't know enough or that you will somehow be behind others in the next world because you didn't join the Church or become active as soon as you think you should have." He then made this statement: "The only thing that will matter is that, when death catches you, you are on the right road and you are moving forward. Don't worry that you are not progressing as fast as you think others are. The speed at which you are progressing does not matter. It will just matter that you are moving forward and that you are on the right road." Elder McConkie has made similar statements that are indeed comforting. For example, he said:

> As members of the church, if we chart a course leading to eternal life . . . and are going in the right direction . . . and, step by step and phase by phase, are perfecting our souls

by overcoming the world, then it is absolutely guaranteed—there is no question whatever about it—we shall gain eternal life. . . . If we chart a course and follow it to the best of our ability in this life, then when we go out of this life we'll continue in exactly that same course. (BYU Speeches of the Year, September 5, 1976, 400–401)

And, on another occasion:

If we die in the faith, that is the same thing as saying that our calling and election has been made sure and that we will go on to eternal reward hereafter. As far as faithful members of the Church are concerned, they have charted a course leading to eternal life. . . . If they are in line of their duty, if they are doing what they ought to do, although they may not have been perfect in this sphere, their probation is ended. . . . They will not thereafter depart from the path. (Funeral of Elder S. Dilworth Young, July 13, 1981, quoted in *Seminary Teacher Resource Manual for D&C and Church History, 2002–2003* [Salt Lake City: CES, 2002], 227)

President J. Reuben Clark also taught a comforting doctrine in this regard. He said:

I believe that our Heavenly Father wants to save every one of his children. I do not think he intends to shut any of us off because of some slight transgression, some slight failure to observe some rule or regulation. There are the great elementals that we must observe, but he is not going to be captious about the lesser things. I believe that his juridical concept of his dealings with his children could be expressed in this way: I believe that in his justice and mercy he will give us the maximum reward for our acts, give us all that he can give, and in the reverse, I believe that he will impose upon us the minimum penalty which it is possible for him to impose. (CR, October 1953, 84)

Though just one sin can keep us from the celestial kingdom, we must remember that the Lord is forgiving and merciful. He is willing to let us repent. That is the plan. We must only continue, pressing forward to the end, ever improving, ever drawing nearer to God. (Anderson)

LIKENING THE SCRIPTURES TO OUR LIVES

Doctrine and Covenants 76:69–70 The inhabitants of the celestial kingdom are made perfect through the Atonement of Christ. They will receive the "glory of God, the highest of all."

Application: The sun offers us our brightest, most pure light. So is the gospel light given us through the Son. It is through Him that we can be made perfect (see Moro.

10:32) and be brought back to the presence of God. We are to strive with all diligence to become just men and women, righteous in all things, who live and act according to our faith in Jesus Christ (see Rom. 1:17; Heb. 10:38).

ENRICHMENT

Many Members Aren't Prepared to Receive Doctrine and Revelation

According to some of the early journals, the doctrine given by the Lord to Joseph Smith and Sidney Rigdon conflicted with the prevailing notions of heaven and hell that were being taught by ministers of that day. Brigham Young, in referring to this teaching, stated: "When God revealed to Joseph Smith and Sidney Rigdon that there was a place prepared for all, according to the light they had received and the rejection of evil and practice of good, it was a great trial to many, and some apostatized because God was not going to send to everlasting punishment heathens and infants, but had a place of salvation, in due time, for all, and would bless the honest and virtuous and truthful, whether they ever belonged to any Church or not" (*JD,* 16:42).

On another occasion, Brigham Young said:

> After all, my traditions were such, that when the Vision came first to me, it was so directly contrary and opposed to my former education, I said, wait a little; I did not reject it, but I could not understand it. I then could feel what incorrect traditions had done for me. Suppose all that I have ever heard from my priest and parents— the way they taught me to read the Bible—had been true; my understanding would be diametrically opposed to the doctrine revealed in the Vision. I used to think and pray, to read and think, until I knew, and fully understood it for myself, by the visions of the Holy Spirit. (*Deseret News,* Extra, September 14, 1852, 24)

Many early members of the Church couldn't accept the new doctrine of three degrees of glory. As stated above, some even apostatized. Joseph Holbrook, a missionary sent to New York, met with members in Genesee, not far from Palmyra. He described their reluctance to accept section 76. He said, "We . . . held a prayer meeting and found there was a wrong spirit with some of the brethren, the presiding elder even forbidding us to believe in the vision of Joseph Smith and Sidney Rigdon" ("Autobiography of Joseph Holbrook," typescript, Special Collections, Brigham Young University, Provo, Utah, 27). Because of such resistance, Joseph Smith instructed the first missionaries to England not to teach the vision until the Saints were prepared. He told them to "adhere closely to the first principles of the Gospel, and remain silent concerning . . . the vision . . . until such time as the work was fully established, and it should be clearly made manifest by the Spirit to do otherwise" (*HC,* 2:491).

The Lord recognized this need for preparation in a formal revelation. Almost three months before giving section 76, the Lord commanded Joseph Smith and Sidney Rigdon to "call upon the inhabitants of the earth, and bear record, and prepare the way for the commandments and revelations which are to come" (D&C 71:4). The inability to accept new doctrine may have been part of the reason that Joseph and Sidney were commanded that they should "not write" certain of the things they learned (D&C 76:114–15). If what was given was a trial, just think what a trial it would have been if all that Joseph and Sidney saw had been made known. Joseph and Sidney wrote of "great and marvelous . . . works of the Lord, and . . . mysteries of his kingdom which he showed unto us" (verse 114). Joseph Smith agonized over the fact that he couldn't teach more of what he knew. He said, "I could explain a hundred fold more than I ever have of the glories of the kingdoms manifested to me in the vision, were I permitted, and were the people prepared to receive them. The Lord deals with this people as a tender parent with a child, communicating light and intelligence and the knowledge of his ways as they can bear it" (*HC,* 5:402).

Part of the problem probably lay in a lack of humility and faith. Brigham Young explained his experience with this as follows: "I prayed and reflected about it, and so did others. I became satisfied that, when a revelation came to Joseph for the people . . . [I should] do it . . . not waiting for the manifestations of the Spirit . . . but believing that the Prophet knew more than I knew, that the Lord spoke through him, and that He could do as He pleased about speaking to me" (*JD,* 12:105).

Are there truths and doctrines that might be given to us today if only we were prepared to receive them? Do we have the requisite humility and faith? We should probably stop and ponder this for ourselves. Not only are our leaders prevented from teaching us until we are ready, but the Lord is also. As a "tender parent," He can't communicate "light and intelligence" through personal revelation until we are ready and "can bear it." (Anderson)

SUMMARY

The vision of the kingdoms of glory, viewed within the framework of the testimony of the Savior and Redeemer, Jesus Christ, is one of the most compelling and moving vistas bestowed upon latter-day truth seekers through the Restoration of the gospel. The rising hierarchy of kingdoms—beginning with the utter bleakness and spiritual vacuum of outer darkness (the sons of perdition), continuing upward with the star-like glory of the telestial and the moonlike glory of the terrestrial, and culminating with the pinnacle of the iridescent sunlike glory of the celestial—this picture is indelibly impressed upon the soul of all students of spiritual truth. This vision motivates them as they seek to confirm their ascent toward the only possible objective of the gospel plan that accords with reason and human potentiality: attaining the highest degree of the celestial kingdom and the unspeakable blessings of immortality and eternal lives. The Lord wants us to be with Him in the mansions of everlasting glory: "For thus saith the Lord—I, the Lord, am merciful and gracious unto those who fear me, and delight to honor those who serve me in righteousness and in truth unto the end" (D&C 76:5). He wants us to be sanctified and edified to the full extent, even that we become as He is: "Wherefore, as it is written, they are gods, even the sons of God—Wherefore, all things are theirs, whether life or death, or things present, or things to come, all are theirs and they are Christ's, and Christ is God's. And they shall overcome all things" (D&C 76:58–60). May we do all in our power to respond as worthy disciples of Christ.

CHAPTER TWENTY-ONE

"LOOKING FORTH *for the* GREAT DAY *of the* LORD *to* COME"

Reading Assignment: Doctrine and Covenants 29:9–29; 34:5–12; 45:16–75; 88:86–99; 101:22–34; 133.

Additional Reading: Doctrine and Covenants 27:15–18; 43:20–23.

While we know that all is not well in the world, we bring a message to offset what I said about the awful conditions that confront us, a message from the priesthood to the Church: While all is not well in the world, we testify that God is still in heaven, that Christ will defeat anti-Christ, that the millennium will be ushered in, that Satan will be bound, and there will be a new heaven and a new earth, and you are to join with us in helping to build that new world and prepare for the second coming of the Lord. You are the harbingers and builders of a new and better world.

We challenge you to catch the vision of your exalted callings. Accept the obligation, rise to its privileges and blessings. (Hugh B. Brown, Continuing the Quest *[Salt Lake City: Deseret Book, 1961], 14)*

THEMES *for* LIVING

1. The Second Coming: The Lord Will Come with Power and Glory
2. Preparing for the Second Coming
3. The Millennium: A Thousand Years of Joy and Peace

INTRODUCTION

The fundamental commandment of the Lord, in place from the foundation of the earth, is strictly plain: "And seek the face of the Lord always, that in patience ye may possess your souls, and ye shall have eternal life" (D&C 101:38). The face of the Lord will be revealed to all the world upon His Second Coming: "And there shall be silence in heaven for the space of half an hour; and immediately after shall the curtain of heaven be unfolded, as a scroll is unfolded after it is rolled up, and the face of the Lord shall be unveiled; And the saints that are upon the earth, who are alive, shall be quickened and be caught up to meet him" (D&C 88:95–96). To meet the Lord within a framework of honorable and valiant compliance with His gospel principles is the purpose of our existence, leading to a glorious reunion of joy and a sweet welcoming into the millennial era of life under the direct nurture and leadership of the Savior. How important it is to conduct our individual affairs in this temporal probationary mode in such a way that the Second Coming will be a time of rejoicing and eternal peace, rather than a time of eternal regret and bitter shame.

When the great Jehovah extended the arm of love toward the ancient Israelites at the foot of Sinai and beckoned them to prepare to see His face, they pulled back in fear and sought to cover themselves in the shallow mantle of golden-calf worship. In His wrath at this provocation, the Lord denied them His presence and instituted an interim way of life that would serve to prepare them for greater blessings as they matured in their spiritual growth. The lesson from that episode is clear: "Harden not your heart, as in the provocation, and as in the day of temptation in the wilderness" (Ps. 95:8; see also Heb. 3:8, 15). The prophet Jacob reinforced this lesson in his day: "Wherefore we labored diligently among our people, that we might persuade them to come unto Christ, and partake of the goodness of God, that they might enter into his rest, lest by any means he should swear in his wrath they should not enter in, as in the provocation in the days of temptation while the children of Israel were in the wilderness" (Jacob 1:7; see also Alma 12:36). The Doctrine and Covenants serves as a modern-day handbook on how to prepare ourselves and our families to "seek the face of the Lord always" and experience a blissful and supernal reunion at the Second Coming of the Lord Jesus Christ to inaugurate the millennial reign.

MOMENT OF TRUTH

Within the pages of the Doctrine and Covenants we find enlightenment and rich detail concerning the Second Coming. In particular, sections 29, 34, 45, 88, 101, and 133 are helpful in this regard. Details concerning the backdrop of section 29 were provided in chapter 12, and those concerning section 88 in chapter 13. The other key sections are outlined below.

Section 34: Given through the Prophet Joseph Smith to Orson Pratt on November 4, 1830, at Fayette, Seneca County, New York (see *HC,* 1:127–28). Nineteen-year-old Orson had been converted to the Church through the guidance of his brother, Parley P. Pratt, in September of 1830 and traveled the following month some two hundred miles from the eastern part of New York state to visit the Prophet Joseph at Fayette. The revelation was received in the home of Peter Whitmer Sr. Orson is commended for his whole-hearted acceptance of the gospel and commanded "to lift up your voice as with the sound of a trump, both long and loud, and cry repentance unto a crooked and perverse generation, preparing the way of the Lord for his second coming" (D&C 34:6), which is "soon at hand" (verse 7).

Section 45: Given through the Prophet Joseph Smith on March 7, 1831, at the Morley farm in Kirtland, Geauga County, Ohio (see *HC,* 1:158–63). The Prophet recorded in his journal:

> At this age of the Church [early in the year of 1831] many false reports, lies, and foolish stories, were published in the newspapers, and circulated in every direction, to prevent people from investigating the work, or embracing the faith. A great earthquake in China, which destroyed from one to two thousand inhabitants, was burlesqued in some papers, as "'Mormonism' in China." But to the joy of the Saints who had to struggle against every thing that prejudice and wickedness could invent, I received the following. (*HC,* 1:158)

Key points in the revelation include: (1) strong instruction to the Church, especially regarding the Second Coming of Christ, including attending signs and events, instructions on the resurrection and Millennium, and the confirmation that Christ is our Advocate with the Father; (2) instructions to begin the translation of the New Testament, through which important information would be made known (until this time, only the book of Genesis had been translated; the translation of the remainder began immediately on March 8, 1831); (3) the commandment to gather to build the New Jerusalem; and (4) Christ's declaration: "I am Jesus that was crucified. I am the Son of God" (verse 52).

Section 101: Given through the Prophet Joseph Smith on December 16, 1833, at Kirtland, Geauga County, Ohio (*HC*, 1:458–64). The revelation contains an extraordinary passage concerning the Second Coming (verses 22–34). This passage discussing the peace of the Lord's millennial reign is a sharp contrast to the lives of many of the Saints at the time. This was a time of great persecution for the Saints in Jackson County, Missouri. Historian Lyndon W. Cook summarizes the historical background of the section as follows:

> Upon petitioning the Missouri governor for assistance, church leaders were urged by the state attorney-general to seek both redress and protection under the law. This attempt to normalize conditions produced a vehement response from members of the opposition. The intransigence of non-Mormons in Jackson County was immediately made manifest when, on 31 October 1833, citizens demolished houses and whipped several Mormon men. Violence continued, and judges repeatedly refused to issue warrants against the mobsters. On 4 November 1833 a skirmish on the Big Blue River caused the deaths of one Mormon and two Missourians.
>
> As early as 25 November 1833 Hyde and Gould had returned to Kirtland bearing the tragic news of the Missouri mobbings and bloodshed. And on 10 December 1833 the Prophet learned by letter of the Saints' flight from Jackson County by force.
>
> Section 101, received on 16 December 1833, explained the reasons for the Saints' expulsion from Zion. Moreover, it reiterated the command to purchase land in Jackson and adjoining counties and contained a parable which adumbrated the march of Zion's Camp to rescue the homeless Saints. (*RPJS*, 206)

We see in this section both the Lord's justice and His mercy. He chastens them and allows the persecution on the one hand because of the Saints' transgressions. But He also comforts them, giving them hope for a better world and further guidance and instruction.

Section 133: Given through the Prophet Joseph Smith on November 3, 1831, at Hiram, Portage County, Ohio (see *HC*, 1:229–34). "Section 133, of the Doctrine and Covenants was received at the close of the conference of November 1, 1831, and two days after the Preface, or section 1, was given. It was called 'The Appendix' because it was received after the revelation approving the selection of revelations to be published, and has occupied the position near the end of the volume in all editions and out of its chronological order. The tenor of this section is very similar to that of section 1, in fact, is largely a continuation of the same theme" (Joseph Fielding Smith, *CHMR,* 1:263).

The Prophet wrote in his journal:

> It had been decided by the conference that Elder Oliver Cowdery should carry the commandments and revelations to Independence, Missouri, for printing, and that I should arrange and get them in readiness by the time that he left, which was to be by—or, if possible, before—the 15th of the month [November]. At this time there were many things which the Elders desired to know relative to preaching the Gospel to the inhabitants of the earth, and concerning the gathering; and in order to walk by the true light, and be instructed from on high, on the 3rd of November, 1831, I inquired of the Lord and received the following important revelation, which has since been added to the book of Doctrine and Covenants, and called the Appendix: [D&C 133]. (*HC,* 1:229)

Section 133 is a rich source of knowledge and warning concerning the events associated with the Second Coming.

1. THE SECOND COMING: THE LORD WILL COME WITH POWER AND GLORY

THEME: At His First Coming, the Savior was born into humble circumstances and cloaked in modesty: "Who hath believed our report? and to whom is the arm of the Lord revealed? For he shall grow up before him as a tender plant, and as a root out of a dry ground: he hath no form nor comeliness; and when we shall see him, there is no beauty that we should desire him" (Isa. 53:1–2). By contrast, when He returns at His Second Coming, cloaked in the brilliance of His red robes of judgment (D&C 133:48) and surrounded by the consuming glory of His presence, He will instill in all the inhabitants of the world at an instant the awe of His majesty; all will proclaim His Saviorhood—either by constraint or by joyful witnessing.

MODERN PROPHETS SPEAK

James E. Talmage:
> I have heard it said that the predictions relative to the coming of the Christ are to be explained in a figurative way, that he is to dwell in the hearts of men and that is the second advent. Verily, the Christ shall come in person and shall be seen of the righteous and shall stand upon the earth and reign as rightful King and Lord, and shall send forth the law for the government of the world. (CR, October 1916, 76)

Bruce R. McConkie:

> No event has transpired on earth, since the very day of creation itself, which is destined to have such a transcendent and recognizable effect on man, the earth, and all created things as the imminent return of the Son of Man will have. . . .
>
> It is true that no man knoweth the day nor the hour of his return—"no, not the angels of heaven, but my Father only" (Matt. 24:36), as he himself expressed it—but those who treasure up his word will not be deceived as to the time of that glorious day, nor as to the events to precede and to attend it (JS—M 1:37). The righteous will be able to read the signs of the times. To those in darkness he will come suddenly, unexpectedly, "as a thief in the night," but to "the children of light" who "are not of the night, nor of darkness," as Paul expressed it, that day will not overtake them "as a thief." They will recognize the signs as certainly as a woman in travail foreknows the approximate time of her child's birth (1 Thes. 5:1–6). (*MD*, 688)

LIKENING THE SCRIPTURES TO OUR LIVES

Doctrine and Covenants 45:44 At the time of the Second Coming, the Savior will descend in the clouds of heaven, clothed with glory. Those who are prepared and watch for His coming in righteousness will not be cut off.

Application: Let us be continually watchful and reverent in regard to the Second Coming (see D&C 45:36–39) so that we shall be prepared to meet our Savior. Every day is a day to prepare to meet God (see Alma 34:32), for we never know when we might be called home to meet our Savior.

2. PREPARING FOR THE SECOND COMING

THEME: Our commission in life is to prepare to meet the Savior and enter into His rest. The ancient prophet Micah encapsulated the entire process in a single sentence: "He hath shewed thee, O man, what is good; and what doth the LORD require of thee, but to do justly, and to love mercy, and to walk humbly with thy God?" (Micah 6:8). This philosophy of righteous living is reflected again and again in plainness in the Doctrine and Covenants and in the other holy scriptures. It is for us to read and savor the words of life and bring them with clarity before our families, that we might together endure the rapture of the Second Coming with joy and thanksgiving.

MODERN PROPHETS SPEAK

Delbert L. Stapley:

> The scriptural prophecies of the events that are to precede Christ's second coming serve as a guide and a warning to all inhabitants of the earth. Shouldn't we listen to these warnings as we witness the signs being fulfilled?
>
> As John the Baptist was sent prior to Christ's birth to prepare the way for his ministry, so did God send a prophet to usher in this last dispensation of his gospel in preparation for the second coming of our Savior. The Prophet Joseph Smith testified to a doubting world that Jesus is the Christ, the very Son of God. (*Ensign,* November 1975, 47)

ILLUSTRATIONS FOR OUR TIMES

Spiritual Preparedness

> We learn from this revelation that the mission of the Lord's church is to gather the Lord's elect who will hearken to His voice and prepare them for His second coming (see D&C 33:6–18). The Lord explained that such a mission will be accomplished only as the Church takes the message of the gospel to all of Father's children everywhere. That is our missionary responsibility.
>
> As the saints are gathered into the Church through the covenant making process, they begin to build upon the rock of the gospel of Jesus Christ. This process of building is likened unto the parable of the ten virgins. The Lord directed His saints to have their ". . . lamps trimmed and burning, and oil with you that you may be ready at the coming of the Bridegroom" (D&C 33:17).
>
> What is the oil the Lord said we must have to prepare us for His coming? Elder Spencer W. Kimball has explained as follows:
>
> "In the parable, oil can be purchased at the market. In our lives the oil of preparedness is accumulated drop by drop in righteous living. Attendance at sacrament meetings adds oil to our lamps, drop by drop over the years. Fasting, family prayer, home teaching, control of bodily appetites, preaching the gospel, studying the scriptures— each act of dedication and obedience is a drop added to our store. Deeds of kindness, payment of offerings and tithes, chaste thoughts and actions, marriage in the covenant for eternity—these, too, contribute importantly to the oil with which we can at midnight refuel our exhausted lamps . . ." (Spencer W. Kimball, *Faith Precedes the Miracle* [Salt Lake City: Deseret Book, 1972], 255).

We must all realize that oil of spiritual preparedness must be acquired and retained by each individual. One cannot share such spiritual conditions with another. Speaking of this individual preparation, Elder Kimball has taught:

"The foolish asked the others to share their oil, but spiritual preparedness cannot be shared in an instant. The wise had to go, else the bridegroom would have gone unwelcomed. They needed all their oil for themselves; they could not save the foolish. The responsibility was each for himself" (*Faith Precedes the Miracle*, 255–56). (L. G. Otten and C. M. Caldwell, *Sacred Truths of the Doctrine and Covenants*, 2 vols. [Salt Lake City: Deseret Book, 1982], 1:163–64)

LIKENING THE SCRIPTURES TO OUR LIVES

Doctrine and Covenants 88:86 "Abide ye in the liberty wherewith ye are made free; entangle not yourselves in sin, but let your hands be clean, until the Lord comes."

Doctrine and Covenants 101:22 "Stand in holy places."

Doctrine and Covenants 133:5 "Be ye clean that bear the vessels of the Lord."

Application: These famous scriptural formulas for righteousness constitute the perfect counsel to prepare for the Second Coming. We need to live, day by day, in such a way as to remain faithful, loyal, obedient, pure, and honorable before the Lord. If we remain clean and stand in holy places, the day of reckoning will not overtake us unawares.

3. THE MILLENNIUM: A THOUSAND YEARS OF JOY AND PEACE

THEME: What a glorious vision it is to bring before our mind's eye the magnificence of the millennial era, when the Savior Himself will reign among the Saints and work toward the ultimate completion of His sacred commission from the Father. The faithful residue of scattered Israel can look forward in hope toward that day when they shall be gathered once again to Zion from the north countries: "And there shall they fall down and be crowned with glory, even in Zion, by the hands of the servants of the Lord, even the children of Ephraim. And they shall be filled with songs of everlasting joy" (D&C 133:32–33). United under the leadership of the Holy One of Israel, the Saints will press forward in the sacred work of salvation unimpeded by Lucifer and minions until the final hour has come at the end of the thousand years, and the celestialization of the earth is complete.

MODERN PROPHETS SPEAK

Joseph B. Wirthlin:

> A . . . period of perfect peace will come during the Millennium. "Satan shall be bound, that he shall have no place in the hearts of the children of men" (D&C 45:55). As they live the gospel of Jesus Christ, the righteousness of the people will banish Satan from their midst. We look forward to that day of universal peace and justice, when Christ will reign upon the earth. (*Ensign,* May 1991, 36)

Wilford Woodruff:

> When the Savior comes, a thousand years will be devoted to this work of redemption and temples will appear all over this land of Joseph—North and South America—and also in Europe and elsewhere. (*JD,* 19:230)

LIKENING THE SCRIPTURES TO OUR LIVES

Doctrine and Covenants 45:55 During the Millennium, Satan will have no place in the hearts of the children of men.

Application: We, through righteousness, will bind Satan. We have the power now to bind Satan from our lives by choosing righteousness (see Alma 48:11–13, 17) and exercising our faith that we might live by the Spirit.

ENRICHMENT

What Do We Know of When Christ Will Return?

Though some of what Elder McConkie reports here is somewhat outdated (there are now stakes of Zion in Russia, several in Africa, and even a temple in Hong Kong), his point is still relevant. We have much work to do before the Lord can come again. Perhaps instead of trying to figure out exactly when all this will happen, we should turn our focus instead onto how we can prepare ourselves and build the kingdom for His coming.

> We know some things about the second coming. We do not know, for instance, when the Lord is going to return. We know that no one will know the day or the hour of His return but we do know when He will not come and we can be sure of that and He will not come until we have preached the gospel as restored by Joseph Smith in all the world and to every nation. That means that He's not going to come in the immediate future. It will surprise me if He came in our day or perhaps even

in the day of our children because we have not yet laid the foundation and we haven't done the work that is required. We're doing it rapidly. We're doing it at a greater rate and at a higher tempo than has ever been the case in the past but we're scarcely scratching the surface as far as the proselyting work that is required of us is concerned. We haven't been in Red China. We haven't been in India. We've scarcely been in Africa. We haven't yet preached to the masses of men and we've got to do it before the second coming. . . .

When we say that the gospel is going to be preached in all nations before the second coming, we do not mean that we'll get on the radio or that we will send television broadcasts or that we will publish documents and send them into nations. When we say that we're going to preach the gospel, we mean that the elders of Israel are going to go out two by two into the cities and the communities and visit the families and be personal witnesses of the truth of the message that they are taking. It's a matter of face to face. It's a matter of missionaries being there. It's a matter of having a legal administrator in every nation to preach and then to perform the ordinances of salvation, to perform a baptism so it will be binding on earth and sealed everlastingly in the heavens. . . .

We have a promise that before the Lord comes we will make converts in every nation. It's not just proclaiming the word to ears that do not hear. It's a matter of sifting out the listening ears in the congregations of all people and proclaiming the message and causing the believers to come forward, one of a city and two of a family, the lost sheep of Israel scattered in all the earth awaiting the day when they can be friendshipped and fellowshipped and brought into the kingdom. Now when the Lord comes, all revelations tell us that He's going to find in every nation, speaking every tongue among every party and nationality, people who will be kings and priests, who will live and reign with Him on earth a thousand years. We're not only going to preach. We're going to make converts in every nation and in order to be a king and a priest, you have to get the blessings of the House of the Lord as you know.

I'm implicit in what I am saying, that the Church is going to be established in all the earth and that means stakes of Zion in all nations. The Lord is not going to come until we have stakes of Zion in Russia and . . . China and India . . . and everywhere. . . .

There is a divine timetable. . . . The Lord is sending the gospel to one nation and one area and one people after another in His providences, on His timetable. He's preparing one nation and one people after another to receive the gospel and the fact that we have missions in certain nations and areas of the earth is the absolute proof that those nations and those areas are the places where the gospel should go at this time and at this hour. If you're going to South America, for instance, this is a day for South America, similarly for Asia.

The Lord is opening up the areas of the earth and He's letting us go there as fast as we have the strength and the ability and the means to preach to the peoples involved. It really wouldn't do us much good if we could get in Red China at this time. They've got a billion people over there more or less. We could lose all of the missionary force of the Church ten times over in Red China without accomplishing the preaching that has to be done in that nation before the second coming of the Lord.

Now, when we get big enough and strong enough to get in some added nations where our presence is now denied, some natural, political event will occur and the door will be opened and the iron curtain or the bamboo curtain or whatever will fall and we'll get into the nation and the nations because it's the Lord's work and its success is guaranteed and He'll prepare the way before us.

When He comes, He's going to find congregations of Latter-day Saints in every nation worshipping and loving and serving Him and the lost sheep of scattered Israel gathered in their areas. (Elder Bruce R. McConkie, remarks in the June 1982 Mission Presidents' Seminar; transcript in possession of Karl Ricks Anderson)

SUMMARY

Section 133 of the Doctrine and Covenants—known as the Appendix—together with associated passages of scripture in other sections, makes it clear that the Second Coming is near. We need to be watchful and righteous and to prepare every needful thing so as to meet our Savior with joy and thanksgiving. "And unto him that repenteth and sanctifieth himself before the Lord shall be given eternal life" (D&C 133:62). If we accept our Savior Jesus Christ and come unto Him and live the gospel, we shall be blessed. If not, we are damned: "And whoso believeth in me, and is baptized, the same shall be saved; and they are they who shall inherit the kingdom of God. And whoso believeth not in me, and is not baptized, shall be damned" (3 Ne. 11:33–34). The blessings that await the righteous at the Second Coming are unimaginably glorious: "For since the beginning of the world have not men heard nor perceived by the ear, neither hath any eye seen, O God, besides thee, how great things thou hast prepared for him that waiteth for thee" (D&C 133:45). Therefore, let us live day by day in such a way as to merit the Lord's choicest blessings and be able to stand, sanctified and justified, before His bar of judgment on that fateful day: "Wherefore, lift up your hearts and rejoice, and gird up your loins, and take upon you my whole armor, that ye may be able to withstand the evil day, having done all, that ye may be able to stand . . . and be faithful until I come, and ye shall be caught up, that where I am ye shall be also. Amen" (D&C 27:15, 18).

CHAPTER TWENTY-TWO

THE WORD of WISDOM: "A PRINCIPLE with a PROMISE"

Reading Assignment: Doctrine and Covenants 59:15–21; 88:124; 89; *Our Heritage*, pages 25–26.

Additional Reading: Daniel 1:8; 1 Corinthians 3:16–17; 6:19–20; Doctrine and Covenants 49:19–21.

The physical blessings of health and strength that are promised through obedience to the Word of Wisdom are now well-known and well documented. In addition, the spiritual blessings of "wisdom and great treasures of knowledge, even hidden treasures," come to those who keep their bodies free from addictive substances. When we obey the Word of Wisdom, windows of personal revelation are opened to us and our souls are filled with divine light and truth. If we keep our bodies undefiled, the Holy Ghost "shall come upon [us] and . . . dwell in [our] heart[s]" and teach us "the peaceable things of immortal glory" (Joseph B. Wirthlin, Ensign, *November 1995, 75)*

THEMES for LIVING

1. Give Heed to the Lord's Counsel on Health
2. Avoid That Which Harms the Body
3. Do That Which Nurtures the Body
4. Blessings of Keeping the Word of Wisdom

INTRODUCTION

The Lord has given us the resources of the earth for nurture and sustenance during our days of probation: "For, behold, the beasts of the field and the fowls of the air, and that which cometh of the earth, is ordained for the use of man for food and for raiment, and that he might have in abundance" (D&C 49:19). Yet these things are to be used with wisdom. From the earliest times of humanity on the earth, the inspiration of the Spirit has prompted those who listen to walk in pathways of prudence when it comes to health. The prophet Daniel responded with courage in the Babylonian halls of royalty: "But Daniel purposed in his heart that he would not defile himself with the portion of the king's meat, nor with the wine which he drank: therefore he requested of the prince of the eunuchs that he might not defile himself" (Dan. 1:8). In Book of Mormon times, the people learned to depend on the medicinal qualities of certain herbs: "And there were some who died with fevers, which at some seasons of the year were very frequent in the land—but not so much so with fevers, because of the excellent qualities of the many plants and roots which God had prepared to remove the cause of diseases, to which men were subject by the nature of the climate" (Alma 46:40). In the latter days, the Lord has given similar counsel: "And whosoever among you are sick, and have not faith to be healed, but believe, shall be nourished with all tenderness, with herbs and mild food, and that not by the hand of an enemy" (D&C 42:43).

By far the most complete statement from the Lord concerning health is that given in Doctrine and Covenants 89. The promises outlined there for those who follow the Lord's counsel are extraordinary: they shall have health, wisdom, great treasures of knowledge, and protection from the "destroying angel" (D&C 89:18–21). Why would we not pay strict heed to the Lord's advice when so much is at stake?

MOMENT OF TRUTH

Section 89: Given through the Prophet Joseph Smith on February 27, 1833, in the translating room at the Whitney store in Kirtland, Geauga County, Ohio (see *HC,* 1:327–29). Brigham Young gives this background:

> I think I am as well acquainted with the circumstances which led to the giving of the Word of Wisdom as any man in the Church, although I was not present at the time to witness them. The first school of the prophets [according to the instructions given in D&C 88:127, December 27, 1832] was held in a small room situated over the Prophet Joseph's kitchen, in a house which belonged to Bishop Whitney, and which was attached to his store. . . . The brethren came to that place for hundreds

of miles to attend school in a little room probably no larger than eleven by fourteen. When they assembled together in this room after breakfast, the first they did was to light their pipes, and, while smoking, talk about the great things of the kingdom, and spit all over the room, and as soon as the pipe was out of their mouths a large chew of tobacco would then be taken. Often when the Prophet entered the room to give the school instructions he would find himself in a cloud of tobacco smoke. This, and the complaints of his wife at having to clean so filthy a floor, made the Prophet think upon the matter, and he inquired of the Lord relating to the conduct of the Elders in using tobacco, and the revelation known as the Word of Wisdom was the result of his inquiry. (*JD* 12:157)

Some twenty-two brethren were assembled in the School of the Prophets room when this revelation was given, although Zebedee Coltrin, one of those present, explained that it "was received in an adjoining room, in the presence of two or three brethren" (Minutes of the School of the Prophets, 1833, LDS Church Archives, Salt Lake City, Utah). According to a later reminiscence: "The Prophet Joseph Smith was in an adjoining room, in the School where they were assembled, and came in with that Revelation in his hand. Out of the Twenty two members that were there assembled, all used tobacco more or less, except two. Joseph read the Revelation and when they heard it they all laid aside their pipes and use of tobacco, 'and' said brother Coltrin, 'I have never used it since'" (Minutes of St. George School of the Prophets, December 23, 1883, 3). John Hayes, an acquaintance of Zebedee Coltrin, also related the following: "In company of other Elders at the home of Brother Zebedee Coltrin he testified that he was present in the room with the Prophet Joseph when the Prophet received the revelation on the Word of Wisdom and that the face of the Prophet just shone with brilliance" (Statement by John H. Hayes, April 12, 1933, LDS Church Archives).

1. GIVE HEED TO THE LORD'S COUNSEL ON HEALTH

THEME: Who should know better than the omniscient and benevolent Creator to guide us in the prudent use of the earth's resources for our good and well-being? Let us listen in humble gratitude and obey.

MODERN PROPHETS SPEAK

Ezra Taft Benson:
> The Lord foresaw the situation of today when motives for money would cause men to conspire to entice others to take noxious substances into their bodies.

Advertisements which promote beer, wine, liquors, coffee, tobacco, and other harmful substances are examples of what the Lord foresaw. But the most pernicious example of an evil conspiracy in our time is those who induce young people into the use of drugs.

In all love, we give you warning that Satan and his emissaries will strive to entice you to use harmful substances, because they well know if you partake, your spiritual powers will be inhibited and you will be in their evil power. Stay away from those places or people which would influence you to break the commandments of God. Keep the commandments of God and you will have the wisdom to know and discern that which is evil. (*TETB,* 478)

LIKENING THE SCRIPTURES TO OUR LIVES

1 Corinthians 3:16–17 Just like the sacred temples that now dot the earth, our body is the temple of God and cannot be defiled if we desire the Spirit of God to dwell therein.

Application: The blessings of the Spirit cannot be ours if we are not pure and clean (see 1 Cor. 6:19–20). The Spirit is the key to most all things in our lives; therefore, we must faithfully obey the Word of Wisdom—thus qualifying for the blessings of God.

2. AVOID THAT WHICH HARMS THE BODY

THEME: The Lord knows what will harm the bodies He has created. He also knows the power of addiction some of the substances He warns against can have. In presenting this counsel of what to avoid, the Lord liberates us from the physical, mental, financial, and emotional bondage harmful substances can put us in. There are grave physical and spiritual implications when we stray from the Word of Wisdom.

MODERN PROPHETS SPEAK

N. Eldon Tanner:

It is difficult to understand why there are so many people who fight *against* the counsel of the prophet and *for* the preservation of the very things that will bring them misery and even death. As one example, let us consider the Word of Wisdom. Soon after the restoration of the gospel and organization of the Church, the Lord gave a revelation to the Prophet Joseph Smith which we call the Word of Wisdom. It warned that tea, coffee, alcohol, and tobacco, among other things, were not good for man, and should not be used by the Saints. Now this was quite revolutionary at that time, for the use of these things was not considered detrimental to health. For many years after the revelation was given, people thought the Mormons peculiar because they abstained from these seemingly harmless substances. Then scientists began to discover many harmful effects of tobacco, and today we are made increasingly aware of the health hazards caused by the use of tobacco, tea, coffee, and alcohol, with additional warnings about the risks involved for the unborn children of pregnant women. Latter-day Saints should be able to accept the words of the prophets without having to wait for science to prove the validity of their words. We are most fortunate to have a living prophet at the head of the Church to guide us, and all who heed his counsel will be partakers of the promised blessings which will not be enjoyed by those who fail to accept his messages. (*Ensign,* August 1979, 2)

ILLUSTRATIONS FOR OUR TIMES

"Run and Not Be Weary"

The story was taken from the October 1928 *Improvement Era* and is about Creed Haymond, a young Mormon who applied and was accepted at the University of Pennsylvania. He was an athlete known for his speed, and because of the way he acted and participated, he was chosen to be the captain of the track team.

The annual meet of the Intercollegiate Association of Amateur Athletes of America was held at Harvard Stadium at the end of May of 1919. To Cambridge came the greatest college athletes—1,700 in all. In the tryouts, Penn had qualified 17 men. Cornell, their most feared rival that year, had qualified only 10. The Penn team was in position to be crowned the champions. The scores were made on the first five places—five for first, four for second, three for third, two for fourth, and one for fifth. Naturally, the team that qualified the most men had the greatest opportunity to win the meet.

The Penn coach was in high spirits the night before the meet. He made the rounds of his team members before he retired. He came into Creed's room and said, "Creed, if we do our best tomorrow, we will run away with it."

The coach hesitated. "Creed, I'm having the boys take a little sherry wine tonight. I want you to have some, just a little of course."

"I won't do it, Coach."

"But, Creed, I'm not going to get you drunk. I know what you 'Mormons' believe. I'm giving you this as a tonic, just to put you all on your mettle."

"It won't do me any good, Coach; I can't take it."

The coach replied, "Remember, Creed, you're the captain of the team and our best point winner. Fourteen thousand students are looking to you personally to win this meet. If you fail us we'll lose. I ought to know what is good for you."

Creed knew that other coaches felt that a little wine was useful when men have trained muscles and nerves almost to the snapping point. He knew also that what the coach was asking him to do was against all that he had been taught from his early childhood. He looked his coach in the eye and said, "I won't take it."

The coach replied, "You're a funny fellow, Creed. You won't take tea at the training table. You have ideas of your own. Well, I'm going to let you do as you please."

The coach then left the captain of the team in a state of extreme anxiety. Suppose he made a poor showing tomorrow. What could he say to his coach? He was going up against the fastest men in the world. Nothing less than his best would do. His stubbornness might lose the meet for Penn. His teammates were told what to do, and they had responded. They believed in their coach. What right did he have to disobey? There was only one reason. He had been taught all his life to obey the Word of Wisdom.

It was a critical hour in this young man's life. With all the spiritual forces of his nature pressing in on him, he knelt down and earnestly asked the Lord to give him a testimony as to the source of this revelation that he had believed in and obeyed. Then he went to his bed and slept in sound slumber.

The next morning the coach came into his room and asked, "How are you feeling, Creed?"

"Fine," the captain answered cheerfully.

"All of the other fellows are ill. I don't know what's the matter with them," the coach said seriously.

"Maybe it's the tonic you gave them, Coach."

"Maybe so," answered the coach.

Two o'clock found 20,000 spectators in their seats waiting for the meet to begin. As the events got under way, it was plain that something was wrong with the wonderful

Penn team. Event after event, the Penn team performed well below what was expect-ed of them. Some members were even too ill to participate.

The 100- and 220-yard dash were Creed's races. The Penn team desperately need-ed him to win for them. He was up against the five fastest men in American col-leges. As the men took their marks for the 100-yard dash and the pistol was shot, every man sprang forward into the air and touched the earth at a run—that is, all except one—Creed Haymond. The runner using the second lane in the trials—the lane that Creed was running in at this particular event—had kicked a hole for his toe an inch or two behind the spot where Haymond had just chosen for his. They didn't use starting blocks in those days. With the tremendous thrust that Creed gave, the narrow wedge of earth broke through, and he came down on his knee behind the line.

He got up and tried to make up for the poor start. At 60 yards, he was last in the race. Then he seemed to fly past the fifth man, then the fourth, then the third, then the second. Close to the tape, heart bursting with strain, he swept into that climax with whirlwind swiftness and ran past the final man to victory.

Through some mistake in arrangements, the semifinals for the 220 were not com-pleted until almost the close of the meet. With the same bad breaks that had fol-lowed the Penn team all day, Creed Haymond had been placed in the last qualify-ing heat for the 220-yard dash. Then, five minutes after winning it, he was called upon to start the final 220, the last event of the day. One of the other men who had run in an earlier heat rushed up to him. "Tell the starter you demand a rest before running again. You're entitled to it under the rules. I've hardly caught my breath yet and I ran in the heat before yours."

Creed went panting to the starter and begged for more time. The official said he would give him 10 minutes. But the crowd was clamoring for the final race to begin. Regretfully he called the men to their marks. Under ordinary conditions Creed would not have feared this race. He was probably the fastest man in the world at that distance, but yet he had already run three races that afternoon—one the heart-stop-ping 100-yard dash.

The starter ordered the breathless men to their marks, raised his pistol, and with a puff of smoke the race began. This time the Penn captain literally shot from his marks. Soon Creed emerged from the crowd and took the lead. He sprinted all the way up the field, and with a burst of speed and eight yards ahead of the nearest man, he broke the tape, winning the second race—the 220-yard dash.

Penn had lost the meet, but their captain had astounded the fans with his excellent runs.

At the end of that strange day, as Creed Haymond was going to bed, there suddenly came to his memory his question of the night before regarding the divinity of the Word of Wisdom. The procession of that peculiar series of events then passed before his mind—his teammates had taken wine and had failed; his abstinence had brought victories that even amazed himself. The sweet simple assurance of the Spirit came to him: the Word of Wisdom is of God (adapted from *Improvement Era*, October 1928, 1001–7). (L. Tom Perry, *Ensign*, November 1996, 36)

LIKENING THE SCRIPTURES TO OUR LIVES

Doctrine and Covenants 88:124 A balanced, healthy lifestyle of moderation and cultivating respect for others will contribute to physical, mental, and spiritual invigoration.

Application: There are many scriptures and words from our prophets that teach eternal truths having to do with good health and well-being. Work—do your very best. Be clean in body and mind. Think good thoughts and good things about others. Gain adequate rest, which is absolutely imperative to good health and well-being.

3. DO THAT WHICH NURTURES THE BODY

THEME: As with all commands, in the Word of Wisdom the Lord doesn't just tell us what *not* to do, but gives counsel as to what we *should* do. The riches of the earth, given through the grace and blessing of God, offer grand opportunities for humankind to choose that which will have the most beneficial impact on health and well-being.

MODERN PROPHETS SPEAK

Ezra Taft Benson:
> To a great extent we are physically what we eat. Most of us are acquainted with some of the prohibitions, such as no tea, coffee, tobacco, or alcohol. What needs additional emphasis are the positive aspects—the need for vegetables, fruits, and grains, particularly wheat. In most cases, the closer these can be, when eaten, to their natural state—without overrefinement and processing—the healthier we will be. To a significant degree, we are an overfed and undernourished nation digging an early grave with our teeth, and lacking the energy that could be ours because we

overindulge in junk foods. I am grateful to know that on the Brigham Young University campus you can get apples from vending machines, that you have in your student center a fine salad bar, and that you produce an excellent loaf of natural whole-grain bread. Keep it up and keep progressing in that direction. We need a generation of young people who, as Daniel, eat in a more healthy manner than to fare on the "king's meat"—and whose countenances show it (see Dan. 1). (*TETB*, 476–77)

ILLUSTRATIONS FOR OUR TIMES

Promises of the Word of Wisdom

Allow me to share the experience of a faithful member of the Church who occupies a prominent position among the world's microneurosurgeons. This is a position he has obtained, according to his own testimony, with the help of the Lord and through obedience to the Word of Wisdom. He joined the Church at an early age and promised himself to faithfully live the commandments. As the years went by, he had the opportunity of fulfilling two of his great goals—the opportunity to pursue a university education and to marry the woman of his dreams.

During this period of time something happened that totally changed the course of his life. One of his daughters became seriously ill with a brain disease which ultimately took her life. None of the efforts made in her behalf were sufficient to save her. During this frustrating and painful experience, which happened while he was a medical student at the university, he set a new and challenging goal, that of becoming a neurosurgeon. The fact that his daughter had suffered and died through a brain disease awakened in him the desire to study microneurosurgery, schooling that would be long and difficult.

Microneurosurgery requires, among other things, a great deal of physical discipline and dexterity. At this point in his life, while he was pursuing his studies, he discovered the blessings that come through obedience to the Word of Wisdom. He asked the Lord in humility and love that the promises contained in section 89 of the Doctrine and Covenants would be made manifest in him so he could bless the lives of those who would depend on his skill.

During those difficult learning years, he worked untiringly to become the best in his area of specialization. As the years went by, he gained great dexterity in his hands and mastered the art and the skill necessary to work on the human brain. As we can imagine, any physical slip or unsteadiness in his hands could cause damage to his patients, perhaps injuring them for life.

As he studied section 89 of the Doctrine and Covenants, he obtained a strong testimony that when we refrain from taking into our bodies substances that are harmful to it, we are blessed with intelligence and a healthy and strong body. As a doctor, he knew that these promises were there, within his reach, and he had earnestly sought them in his own behalf.

As the time arrived for his proficiency exam, the final exam in his chosen career, he prepared himself with great care in order to perform to his very best and to demonstrate to the examining doctors the skills he had acquired. The day prior to the examination, he noticed some heavy trembling in his normally skillful hands, and in humility he prayed to the Lord, asking Him to make his hands firm and sure as they had always been to this point. The following day, he discovered with great alarm that there were unsure movements in his hands. He went off to a solitary spot and, in deep meditation, he mentally searched for any sin he may have committed that would cause him to experience this problem. But in his search, he found nothing that might be contrary to the Word of Wisdom. Then he thought: "I need these promises to come to me now," and he prayed to our Father in Heaven with all his heart that His guidance and protection would be with him.

The time came to perform brain surgery on his patient, and when the doctor saw his hands through the microscope, he noted with great emotion that his prayer had been heard and that his hands were steadier than they had ever been.

He felt a great surge of gratitude, and his sure and skillful hands flew in their activity, healing the damaged brain of his patient. The blessings and the promises of the Word of Wisdom were with him, and he was able to carry out this difficult surgery in an hour less than the normal expectation. It was a complete success, and he humbly accepted congratulations from the examining physicians. With gratitude in his heart for the success he had achieved, he returned to his home, and there, with his family, he reviewed the promises of the Lord that "all saints who remember to keep and do these sayings, walking in obedience to the commandments, shall receive health in their navel and marrow to their bones;

"And shall find wisdom and great treasures of knowledge, even hidden treasures;

"And shall run and not be weary, and shall walk and not faint" (D&C 89:18–20).

Today as he visits some of the famous clinics and hospitals, and his colleagues have the opportunity of listening to him, he expresses to them and to members of the press: "First, I am a member of The Church of Jesus Christ of Latter-day Saints, and then I am a microneurosurgeon." Not all prominent men achieve the humility to be able to recognize the blessings of the Lord in their lives, which are the result of obedience to the commandments, as this good member of the Church has done. (Eduardo Ayala, *Ensign,* November 1990, 10)

LIKENING THE SCRIPTURES TO OUR LIVES

Doctrine and Covenants 59:18–19 God created the earth and all things thereon for the benefit and use of man. He expects us to use good judgment and moderation when utilizing the vast natural resources He has made available to us.

Application: The Lord has filled the earth with great bounty. He has provided a way for us to care for ourselves. He has helped us see not only what to avoid in life, but what to seek out as well. Gratitude for all the gifts from God should fill our very souls. The blessing of food that gives us strength to carry on is indeed a wonderful blessing. The blessing of health is not to be taken for granted. We show our gratitude by living well and serving the Lord and our fellow beings with the health He blesses us with.

4. BLESSINGS OF KEEPING THE WORD OF WISDOM

THEME: There are important physical and spiritual advantages awaiting those who heed the Lord's Word of Wisdom.

MODERN PROPHETS SPEAK

Joseph B. Wirthlin:

> The Word of Wisdom was revealed to the Prophet Joseph Smith in 1833. This revelation has been scrutinized and ignored, attacked and defended, ridiculed and praised. Meanwhile, faithful Saints have observed it as a token of their obedience to God. For many years, they could obey it only on faith, in much the same spirit that Adam offered sacrifice. An angel asked him, "Why dost thou offer sacrifices unto the Lord? And Adam said unto him: I know not, save the Lord commanded me" (Moses 5:6). Early members of the Church obeyed the Lord's counsel without the benefit of present medical knowledge, which has validated the physical benefits of their obedience. We now know by scientific evidence what the Saints have known by revelation for 158 years.
>
> Imagine the results we would see if the total populace were to live this law of health and never abuse their bodies with alcoholic beverages, tobacco, and other harmful

substances. What magnitude of decline would we see in automobile accidents, illness and premature death, fetal defects, crime, squandered dollars, broken homes, and wasted lives resulting from alcohol and other addictive drugs? How much would lung cancer, heart disease, and other ailments caused by cigarette smoking decrease? The fruits of this commandment bring innumerable blessings.

Members of the Church have obviously been blessed with health and spirituality by being obedient to this commandment. (*Ensign,* November 1991, 15)

ILLUSTRATIONS FOR OUR TIMES

Observing the Word of Wisdom

I regret that we as a people do not observe it more faithfully. But remarkable have been the blessings that have come of its observance to the degree that we have observed it. Newspapers across the nation have recently run reports on a significant California study. It was conducted by Dr. James Enstrom of the UCLA School of Public Medicine. It included a substantial number of active members of the Church—5,231 high priests and 4,613 of their wives. I quote now from a newspaper story:

"Compared to the other groups, the study found the Mormons had an average of 53 percent fewer fatal cancers . . . , 48 percent fewer deaths from heart disease and 53 percent fewer fatal illnesses of all kinds" (*Salt Lake Tribune,* September 12, 1990).

Dr. Enstrom, speaking of the eight-year study, said that he "can predict that a very active, health-conscious 25-year-old *Mormon* male will live 11 years longer than the average American male of the same age" (*Salt Lake Tribune,* September 12, 1990, italics added). . . .

I thank the Lord for a testimony of the Word of Wisdom. I wish we lived it more fully. But even though we do not, the Lord pours out His blessings upon those who try. . . . To me it is marvelous that beyond the promises of a physical nature is the promise of hidden treasures of knowledge concerning things divine and eternal. . . . I remember a report from the American Medical Association to the effect that heavy smokers die seven years before they would if they did not smoke. Seven years of life. That's as long as many persons spend in high school and college. Seven years—time enough to become a doctor, an architect, an engineer, a lawyer. Seven years in which to enjoy the sunrise and the sunset, the hills and the valleys, the lakes and the seas, the love of our children, the friendship of wonderful people we may know. What a statistical promise confirming the word of the Lord that the destroying angel shall pass by those who walk in obedience and will not slay them (see verse 21).

Then there is that other promise—that they shall have "great treasures of knowledge, even hidden treasures" (verse 19). I think of an experience once told me by one of our Sunday School teachers. One Sunday while they were discussing the Word of Wisdom, someone asked what was meant by hidden treasures of knowledge.

The teacher stuttered and stammered and was saved by the bell. He told the class that they would consider the matter the following Sunday.

During the week he pondered the question but felt that he could not come up with an answer. Near the end of the week, he had lunch with a colleague. The man told him that at one time while traveling, he found himself passing a Mormon church building. He concluded to go in to see how the Mormons worshipped.

The man reported that it was a peculiar kind of service—that one after another stood up in the congregation, told of their experiences, expressed their gratitude, and then almost without exception testified that they knew that God lives, that Jesus Christ is His Son, our living Redeemer. The man drove up the highway that afternoon, saying to himself, *Surely these people have knowledge hidden from the world.* Ponder that thought for a moment. (Gordon B. Hinckley, *TGBH,* 702)

LIKENING THE SCRIPTURES TO OUR LIVES

Doctrine and Covenants 89:18–21 Those who obey the Word of Wisdom will be blessed with health, strength, and knowledge. Furthermore, the Lord has promised that the destroying angel shall pass by them and not slay them.

Application: The blessings of keeping the Word of Wisdom are clear and are not just physical in nature. Good health here implies a mental and spiritual clarity and fulfillment as well. We may claim the blessings through obedience. Life will be longer and the quality of life will be better for those who live this law.

SUMMARY

The Lord's beneficial law of health is "given for a principle with promise, adapted to the capacity of the weak and the weakest of all saints, who are or can be called saints"

(D&C 89:3). The principle for harvesting the rich blessings of this Word of Wisdom is the principle of remembering: "And all saints who remember to keep and do these sayings . . ." (D&C 89:18). Let us therefore remember and be physically and spiritually edified.

CHAPTER TWENTY-THREE

"SEEK LEARNING, EVEN *by* STUDY *and* ALSO *by* FAITH"

Reading Assignment: Doctrine and Covenants 6:7; 19:23; 88:76–80, 118, 122–25; 90:15; 93:36–37, 53; 131:6; 136:32–33; 2 Timothy 3:7; 2 Nephi 9:28–29.

We should also seek learning by faith in God, the giver of revelation. I believe that many of the great discoveries and achievements in science and the arts have resulted from a God-given revelation. Seekers who have paid the price in perspiration have been magnified by inspiration. (Dallin H. Oaks, Ensign, *May 1989, 27)*

THEMES *for* LIVING

1. "Organize Yourselves" for Learning: The School of the Prophets as a Model
2. "Seek Learning, Even By Study and Also By Faith"
3. The Temple: Sacred Halls of Learning

INTRODUCTION

The Doctrine and Covenants is a handbook on the process of spiritual learning and edification. The framework of all gospel-related learning is to act according to the operation of the Spirit of the Lord:

> Verily I say unto you, he that is ordained of me and sent forth to preach the word of truth by the Comforter, in the Spirit of truth, doth he preach it by the Spirit of truth or some other way? And if it be by some other way it is not of God. And again, he that receiveth the word of truth, doth he receive it by the Spirit of truth or some other way? If it be some other way it is not of God. Therefore, why is it that ye cannot understand and know, that he that receiveth the word by the Spirit of truth receiveth it as it is preached by the Spirit of truth? Wherefore, he that preacheth and he that receiveth, understand one another, and both are edified and rejoice together. And that which doth not edify is not of God, and is darkness. That which is of God is light; and he that receiveth light, and continueth in God, receiveth more light; and that light groweth brighter and brighter until the perfect day. (D&C 59:17–24)

Within that framework of sacred learning, the Lord has ordained that His Saints are to seek light and wisdom for the purpose of preparing themselves to enter the Lord's service and do their part in building up the kingdom of God. Faith, prayer, humility, diligence, devoted effort, pondering the scriptures, attention to the various disciplines of principled knowledge cultivated by the best minds, approaching learning in an organized and systematic way—all these contribute to the acquisition of learning consistent with the call to service in God's kingdom.

MOMENT OF TRUTH

Various passages from the Doctrine and Covenants shed light on the process of learning ordained of God. In particular, sections 6, 19, 88, 90, 93, 131, and 136 have cogent and illuminating directives from the Lord on this subject. Except for section 90 (described below), the background to these sections is given in other chapters.

Section 90: Given through the Prophet Joseph Smith on March 8, 1833, in Kirtland, Geauga County, Ohio (see *HC,* 1:329–31). This section signaled an important further step in the organization of the First Presidency. Subsequently, the Prophet wrote, concerning a meeting of the School of the Prophets on March 18, 1833:

I laid my hands on Brothers Sidney [Rigdon] and Frederick [G. Williams], and ordained them to take part with me in holding the keys of this last kingdom, and to assist in the Presidency of the High Priesthood, as my Counselors; after which I exhorted the brethren to faithfulness and diligence in keeping the commandments of God, and gave much instruction for the benefit of the Saints, with a promise that the pure in heart should see a heavenly vision; and after remaining a short time in secret prayer, the promise was verified; for many present had the eyes of their understanding opened by the Spirit of God, so as to behold many things. I then blessed the bread and wine, and distributed a portion to each. Many of the brethren saw a heavenly vision of the Savior, and concourses of angels, and many other things, of which each one has a record of what he saw. (*HC,* 1:334–35)

Some of the key points in this section concerning learning include a caution regarding how seriously we accept revelation and how we react to the adversary's influence (verse 5), a general admonition to cultivate learning (verse 15), a humbling admonition against pride (verses 17–18), and the famous commandment concerning searching diligently and honoring one's covenants (verse 24).

1. "ORGANIZE YOURSELVES" FOR LEARNING: THE SCHOOL OF THE PROPHETS AS A MODEL

THEME: An important dimension of the Restoration of the gospel was the establishment of an institutionalized process for systematic learning. The School of the Prophets was the earliest model of such a process and continues to be an inspiration to devoted students of truth even today.

MODERN PROPHETS SPEAK

Gordon B. Hinckley:

In this same period Joseph Smith organized the "School of the Prophets." Through revelation he had been instructed that those who were to go forth to teach the glad tidings of the restoration of the gospel should first prepare themselves "by study and by faith." This did not mean that those engaged in the ministry of the Church should be trained in seminaries for this purpose, choosing the vocation as one might choose the profession of doctor or lawyer. Each man holding the Priesthood—and this was to include every man in the Church who obeyed the principles of the gospel—had the responsibility of learning enough of the work to enable him to expound and defend the doctrine.

Then, too, it had been made clear by the Prophet that education was a concern of religion. Among his unusual teachings in this connection was the principle that "the glory of God is intelligence." Further, "Whatever principle of intelligence we attain unto in this life, it will rise with us in the resurrection." A broad development of the mind, therefore, was a rightful concern of the Church, and for this purpose the School of the Prophets was established. Not only were there classes of a theological nature; a renowned linguist was retained to teach Hebrew. It was a remarkable innovation in adult education on the Ohio frontier, and was the forerunner of the extensive Mormon educational system. (*What of the Mormons?* [Salt Lake City: Deseret Book, 1947], 104)

ILLUSTRATIONS FOR OUR TIMES

A Legacy of Learning

I often sit in, instruct in, and have been instructed in the hallowed School of the Prophets room in Kirtland. As I enter that small room, eleven by fourteen feet in size, from which major educational institutions have emerged, I am overwhelmed by the importance the Lord placed on education. I often reflect on the words of the Lord given in that building: "The glory of God is intelligence, or, in other words, light and truth" (D&C 93:36). I have thought of His subsequent statements: "It is impossible for a man to be saved in ignorance" (D&C 131:6) and "Whatever principle of intelligence we attain unto in this life, it will rise with us in the resurrection. And if a person gains more knowledge and intelligence in this life through his diligence and obedience than another, he will have so much the advantage in the world to come" (D&C 130:18–19). The more Joseph Smith learned, the more he understood the importance of education. Two years before his death, he concluded, "A man is saved no faster than he gets knowledge" (*HC,* 4:588).

I also reflect in amazement that the early Saints not only understood this doctrine, but also under difficult circumstances implemented it. Although the initial emphasis was on doctrine and spiritual instruction, as their schooling progressed, they studied other subjects in Kirtland, such as Hebrew, penmanship, arithmetic, English grammar, and geology. It was not a chore for them to study difficult subjects; in fact, in February of 1836, while studying the Hebrew language, Joseph Smith wrote, "My soul delights in reading the word of the Lord in the original, and I am determined to pursue the study of the languages, until I shall become master of them, if I am permitted to live long enough. At any rate, so long as I do live, I am determined to make this my object; and with the blessing of God, I shall succeed to my satisfaction" (*HC,* 2:396).

James H. Eells, an educated non-Mormon from Elyria, Ohio, made a critical examination of the Saints in Kirtland. He was impressed with the School of the Prophets and wrote a letter of obvious admiration in March 1836:

The Mormons appear to be very eager to acquire education. Men, women and children lately attended school, and they are now employing Mr. [Joshua] Seixas, the Hebrew teacher, to instruct them in Hebrew; and about seventy men in middle life, from twenty to forty years of age, are most eagerly engaged in the study. They pursue their studies alone until twelve o'clock at night, and attend to nothing else. Of course many make rapid progress. I noticed some fine looking and intelligent men among them. Some in dress and deportment have all the appearance of gentlemen. . . . They are by no means, as a class, men of weak minds. . . . The rise and progress . . . shows religious teachers the importance of having sound instruction imparted along with high excitement, that men may have some other evidence on which their faith rests. (James H. Eells to Brother Leavitt, 1 April 1836, quoted in William Mulder and A. Russell Mortensen, eds., *Among the Mormons* [New York: Alfred Knopf, 1958], 88)

The Church has always emphasized learning and progress, as the several Church-founded universities and institutes of higher learning illustrate. But long before any university was established by the Church, generations before anyone graduated from them, the people of the Church sought learning. Whatever our position or condition in life, we can carry that legacy forward and seek learning. (Anderson)

LIKENING THE SCRIPTURES TO OUR LIVES

Doctrine and Covenants 88:121–26 Constructive learning requires an environment that is conducive to the Spirit. Consequently, the Lord has counseled us to "cease from all your light speeches, from all laughter, from all your lustful desires, from all your pride and light-mindedness, and from all your wicked doings."

Application: An important key to learning is the preparation of the hearer. We must be "ready and worthy" to be taught the word of God. An atmosphere of soberness, charity, and love is an important ingredient for the Spirit to teach us the things of God. We are to treat the instruction of the Lord with care and seriousness. Teaching and learning ought to be done in order, with industry, and by the Spirit. We must not resort to idleness and faultfinding in regard to our preparation and instruction. We must focus on the gospel message and maintaining the Spirit. Then, as we call down the powers of heaven through prayer, we can all be edified and learn together by the Spirit of truth (see D&C 50:17–22).

2. "SEEK LEARNING, EVEN BY STUDY AND ALSO BY FAITH"

THEME: Our minds and faculties are gifts from God. He has counseled us through His prophets to learn and progress through faith and study—always with an eye single to the glory of God.

MODERN PROPHETS SPEAK

Brigham Young:

> One of the greatest blessings that can be bestowed upon the children of men is to have true knowledge concerning themselves, concerning the human family and the designs of Heaven concerning them. It is also a great blessing to have wisdom to use this knowledge in a way to produce the greatest good to ourselves and all men. All the power of earthly wealth cannot give this knowledge and this wisdom.
>
> If mankind could know the object God has in their creation, and what they might obtain by doing right and by applying to the source and fountain of wisdom for information, how quickly they would turn away from every ungodly action and custom. . . . Instead of seeking unto the Lord for wisdom, they seek unto the vain philosophy and the deceit and traditions of men, which are after the rudiments of the world and not after Christ. They are led by their own imaginations and by the dictates of their selfish will, which will lead them in the end, to miss the object of their pursuit. Were you to inquire, of the leading men of the world—of kings, rulers, philosophers and wise men—the end or result of their pursuits, they cannot tell you. This I believe; and I think it is quite evident, according to what I have witnessed. (*JD,* 10:208–9, quoted in Roy W. Doxey, comp., *Latter-day Prophets and the Doctrine and Covenants* [Salt Lake City: Deseret Book, 1978], 3:207)

ILLUSTRATIONS FOR OUR TIMES

The Power of Learning

> May I share with you some thoughts on the power of learning and its relation to self-reliance. To the Saints of this dispensation, the Lord gave important instructions to seek balanced learning. The terms in the scriptures are *study* and *faith.* For example, in Doctrine and Covenants 88:118, the Lord invites us: "Seek ye diligently and teach one another words of wisdom; yea, seek ye out of the best books words of wisdom; seek learning, even by study and also by faith." This same invitation is repeated twice more in the Doctrine and Covenants (see D&C 109:7, 14).

To me, the terms *learning by study* and *learning by faith* say that self-reliance comes from both efforts. Everyone involved in the Relief Society literacy effort knows that literacy takes both study *and* faith. We need to cultivate both of them.

Let me give you an example. Suppose you want to know how the human body works. Faith tells us that our bodies were created through an inspired process, that they were made in the image of our Heavenly Parents, that we have a stewardship over them to keep them sacred and healthy during our mortal probation, and that we will reclaim them as perfect after the resurrection. That is the message of faith. That's like one oar on a boat.

But to understand their workings—whether an illness is caused by a chemical imbalance or through a fever, how to set a broken bone properly, or how to replace an improperly functioning valve in the heart by surgery—that requires intense and detailed study. Study is the other oar by which we can seek and obtain knowledge. What happens if you try to paddle a boat using only one oar? You go around and around in circles. If you paddle hard, you go fast. If you paddle slowly, you turn gently. But you still just go around in circles. It's the same with trying to make study replace faith or trying to exercise faith but without study. We can often find ourselves just going around in circles. I think that the Holy Ghost cannot give us some answers until we are actively seeking knowledge.

Think what great progress has been made in medicine by those who use both oars in their training. For example, Elder Russell M. Nelson, a member of the Council of the Twelve Apostles, used both oars in his former profession as a heart surgeon. With the trained skills of his hands, the knowledge stored in his mind from his study and his experience, and the faith in his heart that he would be sustained by the Holy Ghost as he operated, he has performed modern miracles that have spared the lives and prolonged the vigor and energy of so many people, including Presidents of the Church and many General Authorities. If he had relied only on faith, he still would have been a great man, but he would not have been a great surgeon. If he had relied only on study, he might have been a great surgeon, but I think there are many assignments that the Lord would not have entrusted to him. It is the same with us . . . I have been a lifelong learner, and I love the things I learn each day about the glory of the gospel and the wonders of the world we live in. The promise of eternal progression is a thrilling one to me as I look forward to an eternity of learning. Let us trust both study and faith to keep us going straight, instead of around in circles. (Chieko N. Okazaki, *Ensign,* November 1994, 92)

LIKENING THE SCRIPTURES TO OUR LIVES

2 Nephi 9:28–29 Nephi warned us not to allow learning and knowledge to cause us to forget our dependency on the counsel and direction of our omnipotent Father.

Application: In all our learning, let us remember that pure intelligence is truth and light (see D&C 93:36–37)—the knowledge of God. Such knowledge can save. Human learning has merit, but only so long as we remember to hearken to the counsel of God in using that learning for good, according to His will.

3. THE TEMPLE: SACRED HALLS OF LEARNING

THEME: What we learn in the temples of God is the pinnacle of spiritual truth that will lift us, through faith and devotion, ever closer to our heavenly home.

MODERN PROPHETS SPEAK

John A. Widtsoe:

> The temple ordinances encompass the whole plan of salvation, as taught from time to time by the leaders of the Church, and elucidate matters difficult of understanding. There is no warping or twisting in fitting the temple teachings into the great scheme of salvation. The philosophical completeness of the endowment is one of the great arguments for the veracity of the temple ordinances. Moreover, this completeness of survey and expounding of the Gospel plan, makes temple worship one of the most effective methods in refreshing the memory concerning the whole structure of the gospel.

> Another fact has always appealed to me as a strong internal evidence for the truth of temple work. The endowment and the temple work as revealed by the Lord to the Prophet Joseph Smith fall clearly into four distinct parts: The preparatory ordinances; the giving of instruction by lectures and representations; covenants; and, finally, tests of knowledge. I doubt that the Prophet Joseph Smith, unlearned and untrained in logic, could of himself have made the thing so logically complete. (*The Utah Genealogical and Historical Magazine* 12 [April 1921]: 58)

Boyd K. Packer:

> What we gain *from* the temple will depend to a large degree on what we take *to* the temple in the way of humility and reverence and a desire to learn. If we are teachable we will be taught by the Spirit, in the temple. (*The Holy Temple* [Salt Lake City: Bookcraft, 1980], 46)

ILLUSTRATIONS FOR OUR TIMES

Temple Instruction Is Symbolic

Many years ago I taught seminary with President Abel S. Rich. He was the second seminary teacher hired in the Church and was an authority on the gospel, well-versed in the scriptures. He had been a stake president, a mission president, and a community leader. He had taught the Book of Mormon for thirty-six years and had read it many, many times from cover to cover. . . .

We shared an office at the seminary building. As a new teacher I needed careful preparation and would come an hour, sometimes two, before the opening of school to get my lessons in order. He invariably had preceded me there. During that fall he was reading the Book of Mormon again. I had difficulty in preparing my lessons because he would interrupt me. "Listen to this!" he would say, with some excitement in his voice. And then he would read a passage from the Book of Mormon. "Isn't that marvelous!" he would exclaim. "I wonder when they put that in there?"

It was a new book to him and it will be new as many times as any of us can read it, for the scope of it touches the eternities.

The temple ceremony is like that. It constantly is renewing itself in the minds of those who participate. Have you ever wondered why it is that many patrons of the temple can go session after session, week after week, month after month, year after year, and never become bored or tired or resistant? At the end of that time they are quite as anxious to go as they were in their beginning days.

That is a testimony indeed. By that time, you might imagine, they could have the entire endowment memorized. Yes, they could, and I suppose some of them do, particularly those who are temple workers. How, then, could they continue to learn? The answer to that lies in the fact that the teaching in the temple is symbolic. As we grow and mature and learn from all of the experiences in life, the truths demonstrated in the temple in symbolic fashion take on a renewed meaning. The veil is drawn back a little bit more. Our knowledge and vision of the eternities expands. It is always refreshing. . . .

So look toward the temple. Point your children toward the temple. From the days of their infancy, direct their attention to it, and begin their preparation for the day when they may enter the holy temple.

Meantime, be teachable yourself, be reverent. Drink deeply from the teachings—the symbolic, deeply spiritual teachings—available only in the temple. (Boyd K. Packer, *The Holy Temple* [Salt Lake City: Bookcraft, 1980], 46)

LIKENING THE SCRIPTURES TO OUR LIVES

Doctrine and Covenants 97:13–16 The temples of the Lord provide a place to learn, to offer thanksgiving to the Lord, to pray, and to further the ministry. The Lord has promised to visit His temples as long as they are not defiled and remain free from any unclean thing.

Application: The temple is truly the Lord's house. It is a place of empowerment as we are endowed with blessings from on high. The Lord is there, and if we are prepared to learn by being pure in heart, we can be taught concerning our callings and stewardships and in regard to our ministry and to the building up of the kingdom of God. The temple is indeed a house where we may learn of the mysteries of God and about life everlasting.

ENRICHMENT

The Founding of the School of the Prophets

A spiritual schooling of the Church transpired throughout the Kirtland years. The foreshadowing of this schooling began immediately after the arrival of the Prophet in 1831, when revelation after revelation burst forth upon the Saints. Plans for a printing operation to disseminate revelations and teachings were begun in a meeting in 1832. Within two years of the Saints' arrival in Kirtland, on January 22, 1833, the Lord initiated the School of the Prophets. Levi Hancock built a small room for the school upstairs in the Newel K. Whitney store. This became the first of three locations for the school. Joseph and Emma's bedroom was across the hallway from the school. At first, about twenty to twenty-five Church leaders participated in the school, but later hundreds of people participated. Secular as well as doctrinal topics were discussed and taught. In the revelation known as the Olive Leaf (section 88 of the Doctrine and Covenants), the Lord said that the purpose of the School of the Prophets was for "instruction in all things." Later he urged Saints to "study and learn, and become acquainted with all good books, and with languages, tongues, and people" (see D&C 88:127; 90:15). He further challenged them:

Teach ye diligently . . . of things both in heaven and in the earth, and under the earth; things which have been, things which are, things which must shortly come to pass; things which are at home, things which are abroad; the wars and the perplexities of the nations, and the judgments which are on the land; and a knowledge also of countries and of kingdoms—That ye may be prepared in all things . . . to magnify the calling . . . and the mission with which I have commissioned you. . . . Seek ye diligently and teach one another words of wisdom; yea, seek ye out of the best books words of wisdom; seek learning, even by study and also by faith. (D&C 88:78–79, 80, 118)

The School of the Prophets was regarded as a sacred gathering place. When it was in the Whitney store, the Lord himself referred to it as "the House of the Lord," "a sanctuary," a "tabernacle of the Holy Spirit," and "mine house"(D&C 88:134–37). The Prophet said the school would qualify those who attended "as messengers of Jesus Christ" (*HC,* 2:175). When the school was first organized, the members, to gain entrance, gave a sacred salutation, which identified them as worthy to participate. After entering, they received the ordinance of the washing of feet. As written in the Doctrine and Covenants, section 88, the Lord said, "Ye shall not receive any among you into this school save he is clean from the blood of this generation; And he shall be received by the ordinance of the washing of feet" (D&C 88:138–39). The Lord instructed the Prophet Joseph Smith how to perform the ordinance. When the washing of feet was instituted, many gifts of the Spirit were witnessed, as recorded by Lucy Mack Smith, the Prophet's mother:

> Joseph took all the male portion of our family into the school room [School of the Prophets], and administered to them the ordinance of washing of feet; after which the Spirit fell upon them, and they spake in tongues, and prophecied. The brethren gathered together to witness the manifestations of the power of God. At that time I was on the farm a short distance from the place where the meeting was held, and my children being anxious that I should enjoy the meeting, sent a messenger in great haste for me. I went without delay, and shared with the rest, the most glorious out-pouring of the Spirit of God, that had ever before taken place in the Church. (*History of Joseph Smith by His Mother*, ed. Preston Nibley [Salt Lake City: Bookcraft, 1958], 224)

In preparing themselves for the school, students usually fasted during school hours and broke the fast as the school adjourned by partaking of the sacrament together. The minutes of the School of the Prophets indicate that the sacrament was "administered at times when Joseph appointed, after the ancient order; that is, warm bread to break easy was provided, and broken into pieces as large as [a] fist" (*Salt Lake School of the Prophets: Minute Book 1883* [Salt Lake City: Pioneer Press, 1992], 53).

Several names were used interchangeably for the school: "School of the Prophets," "School of the Elders," and "School of Mine Apostles." The sessions of the school were held during the winters, when there was less work to be done on farms and elders were not traveling as much doing missionary work. For four winters these sessions convened. The earliest sessions were held in the Newel K. Whitney store. During the winter of 1834–35, the location of the School of the Prophets was changed when the schoolhouse and printing office building, behind the Kirtland Temple, was completed. The ground floor was used for classes. This session commenced about the first of November 1834 and lasted for about sixteen weeks. A historian, Lyndon W. Cook, gives this overview of the 1834–35 school term: "A school board (also known as the Kirtland School Committee) consisting of Joseph Smith, Sidney Rigdon, Oliver Cowdery, and Frederick G. Williams directed the operation and instruction of the school. Though the purpose of instruction was aimed at better preparing the elders for the ministry, the initial enrollment included nearly 50 adolescents. The resultant overcrowding forced the school board to dismiss the younger students in favor of the elders. The study of penmanship, arithmetic, English grammar, and geography complemented the theological discussions" (*RPJS*, 189). The delivery and publication of the Lectures on Faith was the most significant accomplishment of this school term. It seems that these lectures were completed for publication after they were given to the School of the Prophets. They were included in the first edition of the Doctrine and Covenants under the title "Lectures on Faith." These seven lectures occupied the first seventy-five pages of the early editions of the Doctrine and Covenants.

In 1836 the Kirtland Temple became the third and final location for the school in Kirtland. As many as 150 students met there during the winter of 1836–37. (Portions of above taken from Karl Ricks Anderson, *Joseph Smith's Kirtland* [Salt Lake City: Deseret Book, 1989], 115–19.)

SUMMARY

We are counseled by the Lord to organize ourselves for meaningful learning—learning of the quality and type that will bless us spiritually and further the work of the ministry. He has said through His Prophet, "Seeking learning, even by study and also by faith" (D&C 88:118). Learning of this kind can take place in the "holy places" to which the Lord has advised us to gather in seeking refuge: our homes, the congregations of the Saints, and the temple itself—one of the most sacred of all learning environments. May we humbly follow the promptings of the Spirit as we seek to expand our minds and hearts with useful knowledge and saving truths.

CHAPTER TWENTY-FOUR

"BE NOT DECEIVED, *but* CONTINUE *in* STEADFASTNESS"

Reading Assignment: Doctrine and Covenants 26; 28; 43:1–17; 49; 50; 52:14–19; *Our Heritage,* page 36.

Additional Reading: 2 Nephi 28:20–22; Doctrine and Covenants 6:4–6; 10:26; 84:54; 93:39; 121:37.

> *Our Father provided the sun, the moon, the stars—heavenly galaxies to guide mariners who sail the lanes of the sea. To all who walk the pathways of life, He cautions: Beware the detours, the pitfalls, the traps. Cunningly positioned are those clever pied pipers of sin beckoning here or there. Do not be deceived. Pause to pray. Listen to that still, small voice which speaks to the depths of our souls the Master's gentle invitation: "Come, follow me." We turn from destruction, from death. We find happiness and life everlasting. (Thomas S. Monson,* Ensign, *July 1999, 2)*

THEMES *for* LIVING

1. Learning to Recognize the Deceptions of Satan
2. Avoiding Deception and Remaining Strong and Steadfast in the Gospel

INTRODUCTION

In these days of turmoil and concern about the security of nations and communities in the face of terrorist threats, we are well counseled to pay diligent heed to the ever-present and even more dangerous kinds of incursions designed to undermine our spiritual well-being and that of our families. Knowing of these evil influences, the Lord has given us, through His prophets, a panoply of defensive strategies to protect ourselves and the cause of Zion from destructive forces and evil encroachments. Our very natures, quickened as we are by the Light of Christ, serve as internal compasses to remind us of the right pathway:

> For behold, the Spirit of Christ is given to every man, that he may know good from evil; wherefore, I show unto you the way to judge; for every thing which inviteth to do good, and to persuade to believe in Christ, is sent forth by the power and gift of Christ; wherefore ye may know with a perfect knowledge it is of God. But whatsoever thing persuadeth men to do evil, and believe not in Christ, and deny him, and serve not God, then ye may know with a perfect knowledge it is of the devil; for after this manner doth the devil work, for he persuadeth no man to do good, no, not one; neither do his angels; neither do they who subject themselves unto him. (Moro. 7:16–17)

The Doctrine and Covenants is a veritable handbook of defensive tactics for the latter days. We are warned and forewarned not to take lightly the word of God as a beacon for our lives: "And your minds in times past have been darkened because of unbelief, and because you have treated lightly the things you have received" (D&C 84:54). We are commanded to cultivate a humble, contrite, prayerful, and obedient pattern of life so that the Spirit can guide us through the pitfalls of mortality and help us avoid the detours leading to apostasy and self-deception. By studying carefully the pages of the Doctrine and Covenants, we can fortify ourselves with the armor of God and resist the temptations that surround us on all sides.

MOMENT OF TRUTH

Many passages in the Doctrine and Covenants identify the strategies and patterns of righteous living that will thwart apostate tendencies and secure the Saints to the iron rod of the Lord. In particular, sections 26, 28, 43, 49, and 50 contain valuable insights into the process of discerning deviant spirits and influences and remaining on the strait and narrow path. Following are brief portraits of these sections to acquaint the reader with the circumstances that resulted in the Lord giving specific revelations of warning and counsel. Section 52, also useful in this regard, was treated in more detail in chapter 12.

Section 26: Given through the Prophet Joseph Smith to Oliver Cowdery and John Whitmer in July 1830 at Harmony, Susquehanna County, Pennsylvania (see *HC,* 1:104). John Whitmer was at the time living with Joseph and Emma and assisting in collating and arranging the revelations that had been given to that point. Verse 2 contains the pointed instruction for securing the forward motion of the cause of Zion and preventing deviation from the doctrines and principles of the gospel: "And all things shall be done by common consent in the church, by much prayer and faith, for all things you shall receive by faith. Amen."

Section 28: Given through the Prophet Joseph Smith to Oliver Cowdery in September 1830 at Fayette, Seneca County, New York (see *HC,* 1:109–11). Joseph could no longer depend on the protection of his father-in-law, Isaac Hale, against the rising threat of persecution; he therefore accepted the invitation of Peter Whitmer Sr. to come and live with his family in Fayette, New York. Newel Knight journeyed to Harmony to retrieve Joseph and Emma and bring them back to Fayette, arriving around the first of September 1830. Shortly thereafter, the Prophet learned about Hiram Page's claims to receiving certain revelations by means of a seer stone. Newel Knight described the circumstances in his journal:

> [Hiram Page] had managed to get up some discussions of feeling among the brethren by giving revelations concerning the government of the Church and other matters, which he claimed to have received through the medium of a stone he possessed. . . . Even Oliver Cowdery and the Whitmer family had given heed to them. . . . Joseph was perplexed and scarcely knew how to meet this new exigency. That night I occupied the same room that he did and the greater part of the night was spent in prayer and supplication. After much labor with these brethren they were convinced of their error, and confessed the same, renouncing [Page's] revelations as not being of God. (LDS Church Archives, Salt Lake City, Utah)

Section 28 identifies clearly one of the first principles of remaining on the strait and narrow path and deflecting the deceptions of the adversary: "But, behold, verily, verily, I say unto thee, no one shall be appointed to receive commandments and revelations in this church excepting my servant Joseph Smith, Jun., for he receiveth them even as Moses" (verse 2).

Section 43: Given through the Prophet Joseph Smith in February 1831 at Kirtland, Geauga County, Ohio (see *HC,* 1:154–56). At the time, some members of the Church were concerned about certain individuals laying claim to receiving revelations. For example, a woman by the name of Hubble came to Kirtland, professing to be a prophetess, and persuaded some members of the Church of her authenticity. Joseph Smith inquired of the Lord and received counsel on how to discern and deflect the influence of such false teachers. As in section 28, the Lord again warns: "And this ye shall know assuredly—that there is none other appointed unto you to receive commandments and revelations until he be taken, if he abide in me" (verse 3).

Section 49: Given through the Prophet Joseph Smith to Sidney Rigdon, Parley P. Pratt, and Leman Copley, in March 1831 (some sources indicate May 1831), at Kirtland, Geauga County, Ohio (see *HC,* 1:167–69). Leman Copley had embraced the restored gospel but still remained attached to some of the teachings of the Shakers which were at variance with the truth. The Prophet inquired of the Lord and received further counsel on how to reach out to the Shakers and disabuse them of their errors—among others, the practice of celibacy, abstention from meat, and the profession that the Lord had already returned for His Second Coming in the form of a woman. In contrast, the Lord proclaims true doctrine:

> Wherefore, be not deceived, but continue in steadfastness, looking forth for the heavens to be shaken, and the earth to tremble and to reel to and fro as a drunken man, and for the valleys to be exalted, and for the mountains to be made low, and for the rough places to become smooth—and all this when the angel shall sound his trumpet. But before the great day of the Lord shall come, Jacob shall flourish in the wilderness, and the Lamanites shall blossom as the rose. Zion shall flourish upon the hills and rejoice upon the mountains, and shall be assembled together unto the place which I have appointed. Behold, I say unto you, go forth as I have commanded you; repent of all your sins; ask and ye shall receive; knock and it shall be opened unto you. (D&C 49:23–26)

Unfortunately, the Shakers rejected this word of the Lord when it was presented unto them. Nevertheless, section 49 stands as a warning to all to remain focused on the doctrine of Christ: faith, repentance, baptism, and the gift of the Holy Ghost.

Section 50: Given through the Prophet Joseph Smith in May 1831 at the Isaac Morley farm in Kirtland, Geauga County, Ohio (see *HC,* 1:170–73). There were strange spiritual manifestations being reported among some members of the Church, as described by Parley P. Pratt:

> We fulfilled this mission, as we were commanded, in a settlement of this strange people [the Shakers], near Cleveland, Ohio; but they utterly refused to hear or obey the gospel. After this I paid a visit to the churches round about Kirtland.

As I went forth among the different branches, some very strange spiritual operations were manifested, which were disgusting, rather than edifying. Some persons would seem to swoon away, and make unseemly gestures, and be drawn or disfigured in their countenances. Others would fall into ecstacies, and be drawn into contortions, cramp, fits, etc. Others would seem to have visions and revelations, which were not edifying, and which were not congenial to the doctrine and spirit of the gospel. In short, a false and lying spirit seemed to be creeping into the Church.

All these things were new and strange to me, and had originated in the Church during our absence, and previous to the arrival of President Joseph Smith from New York.

Feeling our weakness and inexperience, and lest we should err in judgment concerning these spiritual phenomena, myself, John Murdock, and several other Elders, went to Joseph Smith, and asked him to inquire of the Lord concerning these spirits or manifestations.

After we had joined in prayer in his translating room, he dictated in our presence the following revelation [section 50]. (*Autobiography of Parley P. Pratt,* ed. Parley P. Pratt Jr. [Salt Lake City: Deseret Book, 1985], 48)

Section 50 gives some of the most glorious counsel in all of holy writ concerning how to learn and teach by the Spirit, that all participants might be edified and enlightened.

1. LEARNING TO RECOGNIZE THE DECEPTIONS OF SATAN

THEME: The leading offense against the onslaught of evil is understanding the deceptions and dissembling tactics of Lucifer—that we might put up an invincible defensive shield in the name of the Lord: "Stand, therefore, having your loins girt about with truth, having on the breastplate of righteousness, and your feet shod with the preparation of the gospel of peace, which I have sent mine angels to commit unto you; Taking the shield of faith wherewith ye shall be able to quench all the fiery darts of the wicked" (D&C 27:16–17). Such strategies will thwart the trickery of Satan. The Doctrine and Covenants makes clear Satan's core mission: "And that wicked one cometh and taketh away light and truth, through disobedience, from the children of men" (D&C 93:39). Against this evil design the Lord counsels us: "Wherefore, be not deceived, but continue in steadfastness" (D&C 49:23). Then, throughout the revelations of the latter days, He provides the keys and principles of righteous endurance.

MODERN PROPHETS SPEAK

Spencer W. Kimball:

> Lucifer in his diabolical scheming deceives the unwary and uses every tool at his command. Seldom does one go to a convention, a club meeting, a party or social gathering without hearing vulgarity, obscenity and suggestive stories.

> Peter again cautioned us:

> "Be sober, be vigilant; because your adversary, the devil, as a roaring lion, walketh about, seeking whom he may devour" (1 Pet. 5:8).

> And the Savior said that the very elect would be deceived by Lucifer if it were possible. He will use his logic to confuse, and his rationalizations to destroy. He will shade meanings, open doors an inch at a time, and lead from purest white through all the shades of gray to the darkest black. (*BYU Speeches of the Year,* January 5, 1965, 5)

ILLUSTRATIONS FOR OUR TIMES

Spiritual Maladies and Failsafe Cures

The devil uses many things to deceive us and lead us away from God. Some of his methods are obvious and easier to avoid, while others are more cunning and complex. Here are just a few, along with suggested antidotes:

Pride. Pride, or believing only in ourselves, totally takes away the relationship with and dependence upon God. It separates us from Him. Through pride, Satan deceives us into believing that we, as individuals or as a people, know more than God and have no need for Him. It is the damning attribute that we should avoid at all costs. The antidote is humility, the antithesis of pride. It is the beginning virtue of exaltation.

Selfishness. The concern for only oneself and little or no concern for others describes selfishness. Satan tempts us to believe that we deserve everything we want and that our wants are more important than those of others. The antidote to this is selfless love. Love is the ultimate concern that brings about righteous service. Love is the righteous motive for all good deeds.

Greed. Greed, or avarice, is an insatiable desire for gain—we always want more, and especially more than others have. This often leads to dishonest practices that aspire to gain more. But when we truly love our fellow beings, we will have only the desire for all to succeed. The love of Christ—or charity, surely—is the antidote to greed. The united order was a way in which people would have all things in common, no one having "more" than his neighbor. It failed because people were greedy and selfish. If we are ever to succeed in consecrating ourselves to the Lord, we must overcome this self-deception that having more than others will bring us happiness.

Lust. Lust is also an insatiable desire commonly associated with sexual relations. This temptation carries many harmful consequences when acted out. Many souls and families are lost because of this transgression. Understanding several doctrines and principles can help us in overcoming lust: the worth of souls, our divine nature, the concept that we are temples of the most High God, charity, and self-mastery, among others. When we don't understand these ideas, we are easily deceived into believing that the consequences of lust don't matter. When these are internalized, we will have the desire to protect and bless another person and never destroy his or her virtue.

Jealousy, Envy, Gossip. These deviant qualities that lead to sin are a result of resentment toward others for their qualities or possessions. We often tear others down to exonerate or raise ourselves in the eyes of others. This usually happens when we are low in our own self-esteem, self-image, self-worth, or self-confidence. Somehow Satan makes us believe that in so doing, we will feel and be better. Love for our fellow beings and an understanding of the divine nature of all people can overcome jealousy, envy, and gossiping. Isn't it interesting, as we apply this exercise of overcoming temptation, how much power love has? We begin to understand Matthew 22:36–40: love does fulfill all the law and the prophets.

Apathy. When we feel indifferent or fail to care about things of importance, we are apathetic. Apathy leads us into many temptations and sins, deceiving us into believing that important things just don't matter. This is a major tool of the devil. Apathy often follows discouragement. If apathy is failing to care, then ultimate caring will overcome apathy. Love is caring. Love is the opposite of apathy.

Ignorance. The lack of knowledge of gospel truths leaves us in a state of ignorance. We cannot be saved in ignorance (see D&C 131:6). If understanding and appreciating true doctrines and principles can change us for the better, so, likewise, the lack of it will change us for the worse. This is why Satan doesn't want us to learn and progress. Where there is no standard, the desires and appetites of the flesh usually rule. On the other hand, gospel knowledge and the word of God can give us life-saving truths that can and will lead us to salvation if we but learn and obey. The word of God has power (see Alma 31:5).

Anger. Anger provokes and tempts us into irrational behavior. We are aroused to wrath and even rage. We behave in a totally un-Christlike manner. From abuse to road rage, anger leaves a trail of victims, causing the sinner to pay for his heinous behavior. We are deceived if we believe that our anger-based actions and reactions are justified. The presence of anger in a person is a character flaw. We can improve our character through prayer (see Hel. 3:35; Moro. 7:48). We can pray for strength to overcome temptation (see 3 Ne. 18:18). We can search the scriptures and receive strength and courage to move forward. When we truly love another person, we will never act out with anger that results in physical or emotional harm.

Hypocrisy. When we attempt to represent ourselves as what we are not by false pretense, we are hypocrites. The Lord condemned hypocrisy as a very grievous sin (see Matt. 6:2–5,16; 7:5; 23). Steeped in hypocrisy, we are fooled into believing that our outward show of goodness is enough. Like anger, hypocrisy is a character flaw. We seek to raise ourselves in the eyes of others. We were born with self-esteem—we are the divine children of God the Father. When we believe this, we value the worth of others as well as ourselves. We will not seek to put others down in an attempt to elevate ourselves. We will seek not to judge (see 3 Ne. 14:1). Instead, we will seek to "become" like Christ and not act out of pretense or deception for social reasons.

Vanity. When we are preoccupied with our appearance and achievements, we suffer from vanity. Self-aggrandizement reeks of pride. We care more about ourselves than our fellow beings. We are deceived in thinking that we appear and are better than others. Love of our fellow beings, recognition of our true worth, and humility will help overcome vanity. There is also a great joy in honestly praising others. You really feel great when you help others feel better.

Surely the list could go on and on. Satan seeks only to lead us away from God (see D&C 93:39) and will try whatever means he can to do so. As Latter-day Saints, we are not immune to the subtlety and deceptions of Satan and so must ever be watchful.

LIKENING THE SCRIPTURES TO OUR LIVES

Doctrine and Covenants 23:1 The Lord counsels us to beware of pride and temptation.

Application: When we are in a prideful state, we are susceptible to the devil and his temptation. We become more worldly, even to the point of becoming obsessed with the things of the world (see 4 Ne. 1:24). We are more easily led away captive by the devil. Let us seek humility, lest we fall into sin.

2. AVOIDING DECEPTION AND REMAINING STRONG AND STEADFAST IN THE GOSPEL

THEME: Through prayer, faith, and vigilance, we can discern among the influences and "spirits" along the pathway of mortality and make wise judgments and choices that will ensure our spiritual well-being.

MODERN PROPHETS SPEAK

Ezra Taft Benson:

> It is not just that the Book of Mormon teaches us truth, though it indeed does that. It is not just that the Book of Mormon bears testimony of Christ, though it indeed does that, too. But there is something more. There is a power in the book which will begin to flow into your lives the moment you begin a serious study of the book. You will find greater power to resist temptation. You will find the power to avoid deception. (*Ensign,* November 1986, 4)

Russell M. Nelson:

> Committed children of the covenant remain steadfast, even in the midst of adversity. We shall "be chastened and tried, even as Abraham, who was commanded to offer up his only son." Yet we are strengthened by this promise of the Lord: "Ye are lawful heirs, according to the flesh, and have been hid from the world with Christ in God." (*Perfection Pending, and Other Favorite Discourses* [Salt Lake City: Deseret Book, 1998], 193)

LIKENING THE SCRIPTURES TO OUR LIVES

Doctrine and Covenants 52:14–20 The Lord reveals a pattern that we can use to avoid being deceived by false teachers and false prophets. A true prophet will obey the ordinances of God and be prayerful, meek, and contrite.

Application: We can avoid being deceived as we live by the Spirit. To have the Spirit, we must pray (see 3 Ne. 19:9; 18:18; Alma 13:28), increase our faith (see 1 Ne. 10:17), be full of love and purify ourselves (see D&C 76:116), keep the commandments (see D&C 20:77, 79), and put off the natural man (see Mosiah 3:19). Let us look through the lens of discernment, watching for the spirit of meekness, contrition, humility, praiseworthiness, wisdom, and the power to edify—these are the fruits of godlike leadership.

ENRICHMENT

Perspectives on the Theme "Be Not Deceived, But Continue in Steadfastness"
The title for this chapter comes from the warning the Lord gave to the Shakers who lived close to Kirtland. They had many mistaken beliefs; among which was that Christ had already appeared in the form of a woman, Ann Lee. Sidney Rigdon, Parley P. Pratt, and Leman Copley, whose parents lived in the Shaker community, were sent to

read this revelation (D&C 49) to the Shakers. Addressing Christ's Second Coming, the Lord said, "Wherefore, be not deceived, but continue in steadfastness looking forth . . . [to] the great day of the Lord" (D&C 49:23–24). Unfortunately, the Shakers rejected the revelation, even to the unanticipated extent that their presiding elder, Ashbel Kitchell, said, "I told him that the piece he had read, bore on its face, the image of its author; that the Christ that dictated that, I was well acquainted with, and had been, from a boy; that I had been much troubled to get rid of his influence, and I wished to have nothing more to do with him; and as for any gift he had authorized them to exercise among us, I would release them & their Christ from any further burden about us, and take all the responsibility on myself" (Pocket Journal, cited in Elisha D. Blakeman, *BYU Studies* 20.1 [Fall 1979]: 97). Kitchell's comment shows the awful extent of their deception. It also shows how far Satan can lead us off the path if we are not careful.

Satan made many attempts to deceive the Saints and overthrow the Church in Kirtland. Within one month of Joseph and Emma's arrival in Kirtland, a woman came and made the first attempt. John Whitmer, who wrote the early history of the Church, said, "There was a woman by the name of Hubble who professed to be a prophetess of the Lord and professed to have many revelations, and knew the Book of Mormon was true, and that she should become a teacher in the Church of Christ. She appeared very sanctimonious and deceived some who were not able to detect her in her hypocrisy: others however had the spirit of discernment, and her follies and abominations were made manifest. The Lord gave revelation [D&C 43] that the Saints might not be deceived" (John Whitmer, Book of John Whitmer, typescript, Archives, Brigham Young University, Provo, Utah, 4–5). According to early accounts, after Joseph exposed her, she returned home.

The Lord's clear direction in this revelation is that His prophet is the only one designated to receive commandments for the Church and that "none else shall be appointed unto this gift except it be through him. . . . This shall be a law unto you, that ye receive not the teachings of any that shall come before you as revelations or commandments" (D&C 43:4–5).

Throughout the Kirtland years, Satan tried and succeeded in overcoming many Saints and leaders. For example, following the dedication of the Kirtland Temple, he unleashed a vicious attack, using the failure of the Kirtland Safety Society Bank. Even prominent members, including five in the original group of the First Presidency and Twelve Apostles, were affected. Frederick G. Williams was released. Luke Johnson, Lyman Johnson, and John Boynton were excommunicated. Parley Pratt, one of the most stalwart, stumbled and alienated himself from the Prophet. John Taylor said that Parley "with many others . . . were passing under a dark cloud" (B. H. Roberts, *The Life of John Taylor* [Salt Lake City: Bookcraft, 1963], 37–38).

The adversary always caused severe persecution from outside of the Church, even from the beginning. However, persecution from within the Church had to be almost harder to bear, especially since the Lord had given so many warnings about it. Perhaps Satan's efforts to deceive those within the Church were his most effective. W. W. Phelps is a strong case in point. He was one of Joseph Smith's closest associates. He witnessed many of Satan's attempts at deception. He witnessed some of the strange spiritual operations that brought on Doctrine and Covenants 50. As Church printer and leader, he was familiar with the Lord's many warnings. He observed and no doubt was saddened by many who turned against the Prophet during the Kirtland years, yet he himself later succumbed to the adversary and caused severe persecution. During the difficult Missouri trials, Phelps turned against the Prophet and served as a state witness against Joseph. As a result of his and others' testimony, the Prophet was imprisoned in Liberty Jail. It took Phelps two years to repent and send the Prophet a heartfelt letter seeking forgiveness. Joseph forgave him immediately, and he returned. However, many others who succumbed never returned. What a lesson to us today! If even Church leaders can fall, we must always be on the alert and condition ourselves not to be deceived, "but continue in steadfastness." (Anderson)

SUMMARY

Consider the key points of our spiritual defense as taught in the Doctrine and Covenants: follow the prophet, study the scriptures, give yourself over to devoted service in the kingdom, exercise faith, participate in the orderly practice of common consent to sustain the leaders, bear witness of the truth, be obedient to the commandments, follow the promptings of the Spirit, purge out iniquity and cultivate purity, teach the fundamentals of the gospel (faith, repentance, baptism, gift of the Holy Ghost), hold to that which edifies and enlightens, "chase darkness from among you" (D&C 50:25), recognize the blessings of God in all things, "grow in grace and in the knowledge of the truth" (D&C 50:40), do not fear, watch and be ready, esteem the gifts and revelations of God as of great worth, avoid pride and eschew unrighteous dominion, and, finally, give heed to those presenters who are meek, contrite, humble, obedient, and productive of worthy outcomes. This extraordinary list of qualities and behaviors is counsel directly from God through His Prophet. The summum bonum of this doctrine is simply a commitment to remember this maxim: "Wherefore, be not deceived, but continue in steadfastness" (D&C 49:23), always retaining in our hearts and minds a conviction that "that which is of God is light; and he that receiveth light, and continueth in God, receiveth more light; and that light groweth brighter and brighter until the perfect day" (D&C 50:24).

CHAPTER TWENTY-FIVE

PRIESTHOOD: "THE POWER *of* GODLINESS"

Reading Assignment: Doctrine and Covenants 84:33–44; 107; 121:34–46; *Our Heritage,* pages 26–27.

Additional Reading: Doctrine and Covenants 20:38–67; 41:9–12; 90:1–6; 102:1–2.

God wants us, His sons, to hold His priesthood and learn to use it properly. He has explained that "no power or influence can or ought to be maintained by virtue of the priesthood, only by persuasion, by long-suffering, by gentleness and meekness, and by love unfeigned; By kindness, and pure knowledge . . ." (D&C 121:41–42). . . .

Just as clean wires, properly connected, are required to carry electrical power, so clean hands and pure hearts are required to carry priesthood power. Filth and grime slow or prevent the flow of electrical power. Unclean thoughts and actions interfere with individual priesthood power. When we are humble, clean, and pure of hand, heart, and mind, nothing righteous is impossible. An ancient saying declares, "If a man lives a pure life, nothing can destroy him." (John H. Groberg, New Era, May 2003, 39)

THEMES *for* LIVING

1. Restoration of the Priesthood and Its Offices
2. The Oath and Covenant of the Priesthood
3. Magnifying and Using the Priesthood through Righteousness

INTRODUCTION

Perhaps one of the greatest elements of the Restoration is the priesthood—the power of God manifest on earth. This gift offers us so much that we perhaps take for granted. But think on this: without the priesthood, the gospel knowledge restored would have been in vain. We would not have the ability or authority to perform the saving ordinances of the gospel, let alone enjoy the countless other blessings, gifts, and revelations we receive through the priesthood.

MOMENT OF TRUTH

Several important sections of the Doctrine and Covenants contain key references to the priesthood—its offices and organization, its functions and duties, and its blessings for humankind—20, 41, 84, 90, 102, 107, and 121. The background for sections 20, 84, and 107 was treated in chapter 8 and that for section 90 in chapter 23. The background for the other sections is given below.

Section 41: Given through the Prophet Joseph Smith on February 4, 1831, at the Newel K. Whitney home in Kirtland, Geauga County, Ohio (see *HC,* 1:146–47). An important organizational step in the Church was taken with the Lord's calling of Edward Partridge as bishop (verse 9). He was to leave his hatter's shop and serve full time in his new capacity.

Section 102: Minutes of the organization of the first high council of the Church in Joseph Smith's home at Kirtland, Geauga County, Ohio, February 17, 1834 (see *HC,* 2:28–31). Although the high council was given many responsibilities, this section deals with only one responsibility—that of acting as a Church court. Joseph organized the council according to revelation (see verses 1–2). The Lord put the high council in place before organizing the Quorum of the Twelve. Since there was only one stake in the Church at that time, the high council served as the highest authority under the First Presidency. The President of the Church also served as stake president. As more stakes were added, Joseph relinquished this lesser office and stake presidents were chosen over each stake. Stake high council courts (or disciplinary councils) still use this section as a model for reviewing cases today.

Section 121: Given by inspiration through the Prophet Joseph Smith in the form of an epistle while he was imprisoned in Liberty Jail, Clay County, Missouri, dated March 20, 1839 (see *HC,* 3:289–300). On October 27, 1838, Governor Lilburn W. Boggs issued an order to Major-General John B. Clark, giving him command of an overwhelming force of militia and instructions to proceed at once against the Mormons. "Their outrages are beyond all description," said the governor. "They must be exterminated or driven from the State" (*HC,* 3:192). Other generals were ordered to take part, under Clark, in the military crusade. The resulting dislocations and persecutions soon led to the imprisonment of the Prophet Joseph Smith and several of his colleagues for a number of months in the squalor of Liberty Jail. While there, the Prophet penned some of the most sublime passages of scripture having to do with the priesthood and its operation, based on principles of righteousness and covenant valor.

The principles of leadership set forth in section 121 resonate across the generations of time as profoundly important statements on the divine operation of the kingdom of God. Elder Neal Maxwell has stated:

> Obviously this supernal spiritual style of leadership as thus set forth could not be sustained for long by anyone who was casual in his commitment or who was not making significant spiritual strides in developing the attributes of Jesus. This leadership style and attitude here made specific to priesthood bearers matched the attributes and qualities of a true Saint noted in precious lines translated by Joseph Smith a decade before: "And becometh a saint . . . and becometh as a child, submissive, meek, humble, patient, full of love, willing to submit to all things which the Lord seeth fit to inflict upon him, even as a child doth submit to his father" (Mosiah 3:19). (Neal A. Maxwell, *But for a Small Moment* [Salt Lake City: Bookcraft, 1986], 11)

1. RESTORATION OF THE PRIESTHOOD AND ITS OFFICES

THEME: The restoration of the priesthood of God to the earth in the spring of 1829 was a moment of grand historical importance, for it inaugurated the era of priesthood leadership in the dispensation of the fulness of times—never again to be interrupted or terminated—and opened up the gateway for countless millions to be blessed through the power and efficacy of sacred ordinances and sealing powers. The Lord's work "to bring to pass the immortality and eternal life of man" (Moses 1:39) was made possible by this divine act of grace and love through which the power and authority to act in God's name on behalf of His children was once again bestowed upon His servants of the latter days.

MODERN PROPHETS SPEAK

Gordon B. Hinckley:

> The priesthood is here. It has been conferred upon us. We act in that authority. We speak as sons of God in the name of Jesus Christ and as holders of this divinely given endowment. We know, for we have seen the power of the priesthood. We have seen the sick healed, the lame made to walk, and the coming of light and knowledge and understanding to those who have been in darkness.
>
> Paul wrote concerning the priesthood: "No man taketh this honour unto himself, but he that is called of God, as was Aaron" (Heb. 5:4). We have not acquired it through purchase or bargain. The Lord has given it to men who are considered worthy to receive it, regardless of station in life, the color of their skin, or the nation in which they live. It is the power and the authority to govern in the affairs of the kingdom of God. It is given only by ordination by the laying on of hands by those in authority to do so. The qualification for eligibility is obedience to the commandments of God. There is no power on the earth like it. Its authority extends beyond life, through the veil of death, to the eternities ahead. It is everlasting in its consequences. (*Faith: The Essence of True Religion* [Salt Lake City: Deseret Book, 1989], 11)

ILLUSTRATIONS FOR OUR TIMES

How the Priesthood Blesses Our Lives on a Daily Basis

The priesthood of God—its nature and blessings, its operations and functions—touches all of us on a regular basis. Following the restoration of the priesthood in the spring of 1829, the Lord unfolded the priesthood organization and protocols line by line, precept by precept, here a little and there a little, as the Saints became capable of learning more and more about this extraordinary power underlying the kingdom of God and how to use it based on righteous principles. The Doctrine and Covenants contains the chronicle of this unfolding of priesthood quorums and offices, including:

- Apostles, elders, priests, teachers, deacons (D&C 20:38–60).

- Bishop (D&C 41:9–10).

- High Priests (heading of D&C 52).

- First Presidency (D&C 81; 90).

- Patriarch (D&C 124:91; *TPJS,* 38–39).

- High council (D&C 102).

- Quorum of the Twelve Apostles (D&C 107:23–24).

- Seventies (D&C 107:25).

- First Quorum of the Seventy (D&C 107:26, 93–97).

As the Church continues to grow, modern revelation through our living prophets has created additional quorums of the Seventy and Area Authority Seventies, as well as many Church auxiliaries to the priesthood. These are all for the building up of the kingdom of God and the establishment of Zion. They all operate under the direction of the priesthood. They all have a similar purpose—to bless lives and help people come unto Christ.

LIKENING THE SCRIPTURES TO OUR LIVES

Doctrine and Covenants 128:20 Joseph Smith recounts many of the marvelous visitations that occurred during the process of the restoration of the priesthood to the earth. Moroni, Michael, Peter, James, and John, among others, had a part in the Restoration process.

Application: The great blessings of the Restoration come streaming from heaven through the messengers of the Lord. We are so blessed to live in the day when the priesthood has been restored with all its keys and powers so that we, the children of God, can be blessed by its power. Gratitude should fill our souls, and we should do all in our power to be worthy to hold it and receive the blessings that flow from it.

2. THE OATH AND COVENANT OF THE PRIESTHOOD

THEME: The priesthood, as placed in the hands of worthy servants of God, is governed on the basis of a sacred partnership between Deity and His sons. When we accept and magnify the priesthood, with full devotion to the cause and in the spirit of humble and charitable service, ever valiant and committed to righteousness, then He will bless us according to His promise to make us heirs of His kingdom.

MODERN PROPHETS SPEAK

Marion G. Romney:

> A covenant is an agreement between two or more parties. An oath is a sworn attestation to the inviolability of the promises in the agreement. In the covenant of the priesthood the parties are the Father—that's the Lord—and the receiver of the priesthood. Each party to the covenant undertakes certain obligations. The receiver undertakes to magnify his calling in the priesthood. The Father, by oath and covenant, promises the receiver that if he does so magnify his priesthood he will be sanctified by the Spirit unto the renewing of his body; that he will become a member of "the church and kingdom, and the elect of God," and receive the "Father's kingdom; therefore," said the Savior, "all that my Father hath shall be given unto him" (D&C 84:33–34, 38). . . .

> These transcendent blessings the Father promises the receiver of the Melchizedek Priesthood by an oath and covenant which he says "he cannot break, neither can it be moved" (D&C 84:40). But these blessings, as has already been indicated, do not come by ordination alone. Ordination to the priesthood is a prerequisite to receiving them, but it does not guarantee them. For a man to actually obtain them he must faithfully discharge the obligation which is placed upon him when he received the priesthood. That is, he must magnify his calling. (*Ensign*, November 1980, 43)

ILLUSTRATIONS FOR OUR TIMES

"All That My Father Hath"

Many years ago as a young boy, I was not infrequently privileged to observe my father's benevolence and charity toward families who were not favored with very much of the world's abundance. During the summer months, he would from time to time invite this or that young man from a needy family in our small prairie town—mostly of LDS extraction—to join us in our regular Saturday fishing expeditions to Waterton National Park in southern Alberta, near where we were raised.

As it happened, the highway to the park passed along the boundaries of a large cattle ranch that was, at the time, owned and operated by the Church as part of the welfare program. I recall with vivid recollection the day when my father, speaking to one of our needy young travel guests (perhaps twelve years of age or so), asked: "See that land over there?"

"Yes," replied the boy, looking through the car window at what seemed like the endless expanse of the magnificent rolling hills and green fields.

"That's your land," said my father.

There was a moment of profound silence as eyes grew large and questions began to rise up in a young soul. "My land?" asked the young lad, with a hint of excitement in his voice.

"Yes," replied my father, sensing that a teaching moment had arrived in all its potency. "The Lord tells us that if a man lives faithful to his priesthood callings, that 'all that my Father hath shall be given unto him' (D&C 84:38). Since that ranch belongs to the Church, I guess it belongs to you as well. It's your land."

There was more prolonged silence as a young lad—someone who had virtually nothing of the world's material goods—processed within his soul for the first time a sense of the vast wealth that the spiritual dominions of the faithful encompass. I remember watching him smile as I became aware that I was smiling too. A valuable lesson had been learned.

In this world of splendor and opulence, of luxurious palaces and empires, there are endless manifestations of temporal wealth to tease and coddle the appetite of seekers of pleasure and power at every turn. Babylon is a brilliant, though empty, shell of fetching beauty that is all too infectious when one's spiritual guard is down. The intoxicating addiction to worldly wealth is a ploy of the evil one, who knows full well that the eternal glory and wealth of God's kingdom transcend the luster of worldly treasures far more than the sun at noonday would outshine a candle. Who is man that he should covet worldly wealth when the Father has offered him a position as joint-heir to all of the endless universe, all of the realms of glory, all of the eternal radiance of heaven, all of the abundance of God's own kingdom and dominion? Who is man that he should trip over his infatuation with earthly treasure and miss out on infinite eternal rewards reserved for the valiant and obedient through the merits, mercy, and grace of the Redeemer (2 Ne. 2:8)?

In the oath and covenant of the priesthood, revealed through the Prophet Joseph Smith in section 84 of the Doctrine and Covenants, the true program of wealth acquisition is outlined with unmistakable clarity:

> For whoso is faithful unto the obtaining these two priesthoods of which I have spoken, and the magnifying their calling, are sanctified by the Spirit unto the renewing of their bodies. They become the sons of Moses and of Aaron and the seed of Abraham, and the church and kingdom, and the elect of God. And also all they who receive this priesthood receive me, saith the Lord; For he that receiveth my servants receiveth me; And he that receiveth me receiveth my Father; And he that receiveth my Father receiveth my Father's kingdom; therefore all that my Father hath shall be given unto him. And this is according to the oath and covenant which belongeth to the priesthood. Therefore, all those who receive the priesthood, receive this oath and covenant of my Father, which he cannot break, neither can it

be moved. . . . And I now give unto you a commandment to beware concerning yourselves, to give diligent heed to the words of eternal life. For you shall live by every word that proceedeth forth from the mouth of God. For the word of the Lord is truth, and whatsoever is truth is light, and whatsoever is light is Spirit, even the Spirit of Jesus Christ. And the Spirit giveth light to every man that cometh into the world; and the Spirit enlighteneth every man through the world, that hearkeneth to the voice of the Spirit. And every one that hearkeneth to the voice of the Spirit cometh unto God, even the Father. And the Father teacheth him of the covenant which he has renewed and confirmed upon you, which is confirmed upon you for your sakes, and not for your sakes only, but for the sake of the whole world. (D&C 84:33–40, 43–48)

The protocol is solemnly clear: Receive the priesthood in full faith. Magnify your calling. Receive the servants of the Lord. Receive the Lord. Receive the Father. Give diligent heed to the words of eternal life and live thereby. Hearken to the voice of the Spirit. Learn of and honor the covenant. Then "all that my Father hath" shall be given unto you. In a celebrated variant of this doctrine, we hear the Savior declare: "But seek ye first the kingdom of God, and his righteousness; and all these things shall be added unto you" (Matthew 6:33; see also 3 Ne. 13:33). (Allen)

LIKENING THE SCRIPTURES TO OUR LIVES

Doctrine and Covenants 84:33–41 The Lord reveals the oath and covenant of the priesthood. Worthy priesthood holders who magnify their calling will be rewarded with rich blessings—even all our Father has.

Application: The oath and covenant of the priesthood carries with it eternal blessings for those who are true and faithful—sanctification, renewal of the body, the blessings of the seed of Abraham and the elect of God, and all that the Father has. It also bears severe punishments for those who take upon them this great covenant and then turn away from it. When one accepts this great opportunity to serve, one must remember that where much is given, much is required.

3. MAGNIFYING AND USING THE PRIESTHOOD THROUGH RIGHTEOUSNESS

THEME: God will not be mocked. The priesthood is sacred; it must be applied for the blessing of humankind according to covenants of spiritual purity and righteousness.

MODERN PROPHETS SPEAK

Ezra Taft Benson:

It is not enough to receive the priesthood and then sit back passively and wait until someone prods us into activity. When we receive the priesthood, we have the obligation of becoming actively and anxiously engaged in promoting righteousness in the earth, because the Lord says: "He that doeth not anything until he is commanded, and receiveth a commandment with doubtful heart, and keepeth it with slothfulness, the same is damned" (D&C 58:29). . . .

If we could only get the vision of the importance of this priesthood, we wouldn't permit the honors of men, activities in various clubs, fraternal orders, and other organizations, to interfere with our performing our duties wholeheartedly as members of the Church and kingdom of God. The greatest power in this world is the power presented in this priesthood. That is the power that brought this earth into existence. No greater honor or blessing can come to man than the authority to act in the name of God. . . .

May we who hold the priesthood of God be unafraid to step forward and provide the righteous leadership which is necessary in our various fields of activity! This is a time for demonstration, my brethren of the priesthood, to let the world know something of the fruits of Mormonism, something of the testimonies which we bear, something of our faith and our determination to live the gospel. (*TETB,* 218)

Bruce R. McConkie:

These concluding words—"many be called, but few chosen" [Matt. 20:16]—stand forth as the warning-climax of the parable, not alone to Peter and the other first laborers, but to all who are called to service in the vineyard of the Lord. Many are called into the earthly kingdom, but few shall gain full salvation in the heavenly kingdom; many are called to serve missions, but few shall reap the reward that might have been theirs; many are called to the holy priesthood—covenanting thereby to love and serve God and their fellowmen with all their hearts, might, mind, and strength—but few shall be chosen for eternal life in the kingdom of Him whose we are. As he who gave the parable anciently has said to us in our day: "There are many who have been ordained among you, whom I have called but few of them are chosen. They who are not chosen have sinned a very grievous sin, in that they are walking in darkness at noon-day. . . . If you keep not my commandments, the love of the Father shall not continue with you, therefore you shall walk in darkness" (D&C 95:5–6, 12; 121:34–40).

Many are called but few are chosen. It is an awesome warning. (*The Mortal Messiah: From Bethlehem to Calvary,* 4 vols. [Salt Lake City: Deseret Book, 1979–81], 3:310)

ILLUSTRATIONS FOR OUR TIMES

Instruments in the Lord's Hands

I shall never forget the occasion . . . when a friend appealed to me, upon learning that the doctor had announced that his daughter, stricken with diphtheria, would die before morning. He asked me to pray for that daughter, and after leaving his office I prayed with all the earnestness of my soul that God would heal that girl. While praying, the inspiration came to me: "The power of the living God is here on the earth. The Priesthood is here. Hurry! Hurry! . . . Go and rebuke the power of the destroyer, and the girl shall live."

The doctor waiting upon that girl, said she would not live till morning; but when morning came he explained that he could not comprehend it, and that he believed the girl was going to get well. He could not refrain from expressing his surprise at the change in the girl's condition over night. The power of the living God rebuked the destroyer. (Heber J. Grant, quoted in *Teachings of the Presidents of the Church: Heber J. Grant* [Salt Lake City: The Church of Jesus Christ of Latter-day Saints, 2002], 101)

LIKENING THE SCRIPTURES TO OUR LIVES

Doctrine and Covenants 84:19–21 The Lord declares that the higher priesthood holds the key to the mysteries of the kingdom of God. The power of godliness is manifested in the administration of the ordinances of this higher priesthood.

Application: The Melchizedek Priesthood allows humankind the privilege of receiving the gospel, understanding the mysteries—the things that bring joy and eternal life (see D&C 42:61)—receive the ordinances (baptism, the reception of the Holy Ghost, and all our temple blessings) that manifest the power of godliness and the keys to the knowledge of God. Realizing this, can we not see the goodness of God in allowing His children the privilege of exercising His power and authority here upon the earth? These verses should inspire reverence for the priesthood and instill in us a commitment never to defile it, and above all, to live worthy to exercise it.

ENRICHMENT

Priesthood: "The Power of Godliness"
In section 84 of the Doctrine and Covenants—one of the Lord's great revelations on

the priesthood—the Lord speaks of both the lesser, or Aaronic, Priesthood and the greater, or Melchizedek, Priesthood. He announces that "the power of godliness" is manifest through the authority and the ordinances of the greater priesthood. In addressing the role of the Melchizedek, or governing, priesthood, He said that it administers the gospel and holds the key of the mysteries of the kingdom, even the key of the knowledge of God (D&C 84:19–21).

The Lord restored both the Aaronic and Melchizedek Priesthoods in 1829, before the Church was founded. After He established the Church, the Lord, over a six-year period, organized priesthood offices, quorums, and councils and bestowed priesthood keys needed for them to function. It was done so completely that even today the same organization exists. How many earthly organizations or bodies have effectively kept the same organizational structure for over 170 years and experienced the same explosive growth as the Church? There have been times where minor changes have been made, but we have always come back to the organization the Lord put into place from 1830 to 1835. In New York, the Lord revealed the offices of Apostle, elder, priest, teacher, and deacon all at one time (see D&C 20:38–60). In Kirtland, the Lord revealed the offices and councils separately.

Within three days of his arrival in Kirtland (February 4, 1831), Joseph Smith called Edward Partridge to be the first bishop of the Church (see D&C 41:9–10). Within five months of his arrival (June 3, 1831), he organized the office of high priest (see section heading to D&C 52). From 1832 to 1833, he organized and ordained the First Presidency (see section headings and text in D&C 81 and 90; note also that the First Presidency is referred to as "three presiding high priests" in D&C 107:22). On February 17, 1834, the first stake and high council were put in place (see D&C 102). Between August and December 1834, both Joseph Smith Sr. and Joseph Young were ordained patriarchs. (It should be noted, however, that the first patriarchal blessings were given by Joseph Smith on 18 December 1833). The Twelve Apostles were next added on February 14, 1835 (see D&C 107:23–24). Multiple quorums of Seventy were put in place beginning on February 28, 1835 (see D&C 107:25–26, 93–97). In addition to the offices, essential keys were needed in order for the priesthood to function. On April 3, 1836, the crowning step in priesthood restoration came as Moses, Elias, and Elijah bestowed the "keys of this dispensation," under which the priesthood would function (see D&C 110:11–16). Each step was directed by the Lord and built on the same structure used two thousand years ago in Christ's original Church.

This authority, direct from God through His prophets, set this young Church apart from all other churches. It was not a new, man-made church but a church with original, divine, eternal authority, restored from the original Church in Jerusalem by Jesus Christ Himself.

(Portions of above were taken from Karl Ricks Anderson, *Joseph Smith's Kirtland* [Salt Lake City: Deseret Book, 1989], 115–19.)

SUMMARY

What a glorious dawn illuminated the earth as the Restoration of the gospel and the priesthood proceeded to endow the Lord's sons and daughters once again with truth, power, and the means for rising upward toward their inborn potential to be like God and return to Him one day. With lovingkindness and grace, the Lord taught His servants the principles upon which the called could also be the chosen: righteousness, persuasion, long-suffering, gentleness, meekness, love unfeigned, kindness, pure knowledge, avoidance of hypocrisy and guile, obedience to the promptings of the Spirit, increased love, faithfulness, charity toward all without and within the household of faith, and inward-garnishing virtue (D&C 121:34–45). The transcendent blessings of magnifying the priesthood in this way are made clear by the Lord: "then shall thy confidence wax strong in the presence of God; and the doctrine of the priesthood shall distil upon thy soul as the dews from heaven. The Holy Ghost shall be thy constant companion, and thy scepter an unchanging scepter of righteousness and truth; and thy dominion shall be an everlasting dominion, and without compulsory means it shall flow unto thee forever and ever" (D&C 121:45–46).

Let us remember to honor the priesthood in gratitude and humility and thus be found worthy of the Lord's approbation, as was Bishop Edward Partridge: "And this because his heart is pure before me, for he is like unto Nathaniel of old, in whom there is no guile" (D&C 41:11; see also John 1:43–51). And let us likewise remember to be grateful to Joseph Smith, who magnified his calling as the prophet of the Restoration, and upon whom God continued to pour revelation after revelation through trying times so that divine truth could be granted to us to help us pass through mortality, with faith and hope, along the pathway toward immortality and eternal lives.

CHAPTER TWENTY-SIX

"GO YE into ALL the WORLD, and PREACH MY GOSPEL"

Reading Assignment: Doctrine and Covenants 112; *Our Heritage*, pages 29–33, 36.

Additional Reading: Doctrine and Covenants 4; 18:15–16; 31:5; 33:8–11; 42:6; 60:2–3; 88:81; 123:11–12; Alma 6:6; 31:34–35; Helaman 6:3; Mormon 9:22; Moroni 6:4.

Our work is to preach the gospel to the world. It is not self-imposed. We are under divine commandment. The Prophet Joseph Smith preached, "After all has been said, the greatest and most important duty is to preach the gospel." All the other programs are extremely important but, of course, we cannot influence people much by those programs until we get them in the Church.

After his resurrection the Lord took his eleven apostles to the top of the Mount of Olives and said: "And ye shall be witnesses unto me both in Jerusalem, and in all Judea, and in Samaria, and unto the uttermost part of the earth" (Acts 1:8).

These were his last words on earth before he ascended to his heavenly home. What is the significance of the phrase "uttermost part of the earth"? He had already covered the area known to the apostles. Was it only the people in Judea? Or those in Samaria? Or the few millions in the Near East? Where were the "uttermost parts of the earth"? Did he include the hundreds of thousands or even millions in Greece,

Italy, around the Mediterranean, the inhabitants of Central Europe? Did he mean the millions in what is now America? Or did he mean all the living people of all the world and those spirits assigned to this world to come in future centuries? Have we underestimated his language or its meaning? How can we be satisfied with 100,000 converts out of 4 billion people in the world who need the gospel?

The Savior said: "All power is given unto me in heaven and in earth. Go ye therefore, and teach all nations, baptizing them in the name of the Father, and of the Son, and of the Holy Ghost" (Matthew 28:18–19). He said "all nations."

Remember, our ally is our God. He is our commander. He made the plans. He gave the commandment. (Spencer W. Kimball, President Kimball Speaks Out *[Salt Lake City: Deseret Book, 1981], 34)*

THEMES *for* LIVING

1. The Beginnings of Sharing the Gospel throughout the World
2. Valiant despite Persecution

INTRODUCTION

The Kirtland years were really the formal beginnings of missionary work. As the Lord commanded the Church to move to Kirtland in January 1831, just nine months after it was established, He declared, "And from thence (Ohio) men shall go forth into all nations" (D&C 39:15). In Kirtland He further commanded, "And ye shall go forth in the power of my Spirit, preaching my gospel, two by two, in my name, lifting up your voices as with the sound of a trump, declaring my word like unto angels of God" (D&C 42:6). The following year He reemphasized His command as He proclaimed, "Behold, I sent you out to testify and warn the people, and it becometh every man who hath been warned to warn his neighbor" (D&C 88:81). From Kirtland, missionary work spread through the United States and Canada, and missionaries were sent for the first time across the ocean to England.

These Saints knew the divine nature of the work, but they had little comprehension of how far and wide the Church would eventually grow. These faithful Saints, most without formal schooling, received command after command to study and learn. We may think of the missionary training centers in Provo, Utah, and other locations as being rather new innovations. However, our first missionary training center was in Kirtland, Ohio. Missionaries studied Latin, Greek, and Hebrew, in addition to English grammar. From the beginning, the Lord wanted His missionaries to learn additional languages and further insight into the gospel and peoples of the world so they could carry the gospel message to the world. In 1833, He commanded them to "study and learn, and become acquainted . . . with languages, tongues, and people" (D&C 90:15). In the same revelation, He revealed, "Every man shall hear the fulness of the gospel in his own tongue, and in his own language, through those who are ordained unto this power" (D&C 90:11). Then in 1834, Joseph Smith expanded their minds with this prophecy, which must have seemed incredible to them: "It is only a little handfull of Priesthood you see here tonight, but this Church will fill North and South America—It will fill the world" (as quoted by Wilford Woodruff, CR, April 6, 1898, 57). When the Saints gathered to Kirtland, little did they realize that the Church would become a worldwide organization. How hard it must have been for them to comprehend fully what the Lord would do with His Church!

Today, we can look back in gratitude and admiration to the foundation those early Saints, guided by the mouthpiece of the Lord, were able to establish as a framework for carrying out the mission to proclaim the gospel of Jesus Christ to the world.

MOMENT OF TRUTH

Various sections of the Doctrine and Covenants describe the circumstances of early missionary labors and the doctrines pertaining thereto. Section 4 (described in chapter 11) is of particular note. In addition, sections 60 and 112 (described below), among others in the reading assignment, contain pertinent truths about this important subject.

Section 60: Given through the Prophet Joseph Smith on August 8, 1831, in Jackson County, Missouri (see *HC,* 1:201–2). Following the dedication of Jackson County, Missouri, as the site of the New Jerusalem, a conference for the Ohio missionaries was convened on August 4, 1831. The missionaries were desirous of knowing how they should proceed with respect to their return to Ohio. Therefore, the Prophet inquired of the Lord and received section 60 in response. The Lord instructs them how to travel, where and by whom voices are to be lifted up in proclaiming the gospel, and the process of going in pairs to preach the gospel along the way. He makes it very clear that the commission to be missionaries requires full devotion and faith: "But with some I am not well pleased, for they will not open their mouths, but they hide the talent which I have given unto them, because of the fear of man. Wo unto such, for mine anger is kindled against them. And it shall come to pass, if they are not more faithful unto me, it shall be taken away, even that which they have" (D&C 60:2–3). Verse 7 provides an especially compelling job description for the valiant emissary of God: "And in this place let them lift up their voice and declare my word with loud voices, without wrath or doubting, lifting up holy hands upon them. For I am able to make you holy, and your sins are forgiven you" (D&C 60:7).

Section 112: Given through the Prophet Joseph Smith to Thomas B. Marsh on July 23, 1837, at Kirtland, Geauga County, Ohio (see *HC,* 2:499–501). The Prophet characterized this revelation as "the word of the Lord unto Thomas B. Marsh, concerning the Twelve Apostles of the Lamb" (*HC,* 2:499). It was given one day before a meeting of the Twelve, which had been called by Thomas B. Marsh, President of the Quorum of Twelve Apostles. It appears from sources that Thomas desired to unify the Quorum and take leadership in directing assignments of the Twelve. Apparently, some members of the Twelve were not faithful. This period in Church history and even in U.S. history was especially difficult. The Kirtland bank had essentially failed. All banks had closed for a period, and almost all had suspended specie payment. A dark spirit seemed to affect the Church. Previously strong members, even of the Twelve, such as Parley Pratt, Orson Pratt, and Orson Hyde openly criticized Joseph Smith. Three of the Twelve (Luke Johnson, Lyman Johnson, and John F. Boynton) were about to be disfellowshipped and would later be excommunicated. Joseph described the situation in 1837 thus:

> Evil surmisings, fault-finding, disunion, dissension, and apostasy followed in quick succession, and it seemed as though all the powers of earth and hell were combining their influence in an especial manner to overthrow the Church at once, and make a final end. . . . Many became disaffected toward me as though I were the sole cause of those very evils I was most strenuously striving against, and which were actually brought upon us by the brethren not giving heed to my counsel. No quorum in the Church was entirely exempt from the influence of those false spirits who are striving against me for the mastery; even some of the Twelve were so far lost to their high and responsible calling, as to begin to take sides, secretly, with the enemy. (*HC,* 2:487–88)

This period was a test for the Church as a whole, though it seems that the Twelve were put through even greater tests than others. John Taylor explained, "Some people have wondered why so many of the Twelve fell away. God tries people according to the position they occupy." He related that Joseph told the Twelve, "You will have all kinds of trials to pass through. And it is quite as necessary for you to be tried as it was for Abraham and other men of God, and (said he) God will feel after you, and He will take hold of you and wrench your very heart strings, and if you cannot stand it you will not be fit for an inheritance in the celestial kingdom of God" (*JD,* 24:197).

We learn from Church history that many of the difficulties some of the Twelve faced were financial. President Joseph Fielding Smith characterized the revelation as follows:

> The day that the British Missionaries preached the first sermons in England, July 23, 1837, the Lord gave a revelation to the Prophet Joseph Smith directed to Thomas B. Marsh as president of the council of the apostles. . . . Some of the apostles had forsaken their responsibility and had turned their attention to schemes of speculation. We have seen that the years preceding the year 1837, were years of wild speculation throughout the United States and Elder Heber C. Kimball pointed out how this boom had struck Kirtland and some of the brethren had borrowed great sums and had gone into business, at the expense of their ministry. Then when the bauble of false prosperity broke they were left financially stranded; then they began to blame the Prophet Joseph Smith. This revelation to Thomas B. Marsh was a warning and a call to him to bring his brethren back into the line of their duty as apostles of Jesus Christ. (*CHMR,* 3:101)

From this section we truly come to understand the wisdom of Jacob: "Think of your brethren like unto yourselves, and be familiar with all and free with your substance, that they may be rich like unto you. But before ye seek for riches, seek ye for the kingdom of God" (Jacob 2:17–18).

Section 112 is not only instruction to a specific quorum president, but also a clear statement of Church government at the highest levels and a penetrating primer on missionary work: "Contend thou, therefore, morning by morning; and day after day let thy warning voice go forth; and when the night cometh let not the inhabitants of the earth slumber, because of thy speech. Let thy habitation be known in Zion, and remove not thy house; for I, the Lord, have a great work for thee to do, in publishing my name among the children of men. Therefore, gird up thy loins for the work. Let thy feet be shod also, for thou art chosen, and thy path lieth among the mountains, and among many nations. And by thy word many high ones shall be brought low, and by thy word many low ones shall be exalted. Thy voice shall be a rebuke unto the transgressor; and at thy rebuke let the tongue of the slanderer cease its perverseness. Be thou humble; and the Lord thy God shall lead thee by the hand, and give thee answer to thy prayers" (D&C 112:5–10). The Lord gives then this general commandment: "Arise and gird up your loins, take up your cross, follow me, and feed my sheep" (D&C 112:14).

1. THE BEGINNINGS OF SHARING THE GOSPEL THROUGHOUT THE WORLD

THEME: Under the doctrines and principles of the Abrahamic covenant, the priesthood of God has the sacred responsibility to carry the gospel to all quarters of the earth: "And I will make of thee a great nation, and I will bless thee above measure, and make thy name great among all nations, and thou shalt be a blessing unto thy seed after thee, that in their hands they shall bear this ministry and Priesthood unto all nations" (Abr. 2:9). Early on in the Restoration, this charter for missionary work was activated by the Lord; consequently, the work of the ministry among nations was begun amid the poverty and weakness of the people, but it was accounted to the glory of God and quickly expanded to a major process of conversion and gathering. From these early proselyting activities we can discern clearly the hand of the Lord in guiding the infant Church to its adolescent and maturing years. In this period we perceive the exemplary missionary accomplishments of the young Church, which stand as a witness to the power of faith and the marvelous work of God in the latter days.

MODERN PROPHETS SPEAK

Gordon B. Hinckley:

> I rejoice at what is occurring in the great missionary efforts of the Church. This work of teaching the gospel to others was the first responsibility laid upon the Prophet Joseph Smith in the opening of this dispensation. It must never be removed from that preeminent position. (*Ensign,* December 1986, 3)

Ezra Taft Benson:

> As we live the commandments of God, we can look forward with joyful anticipation to the second coming of the Lord Jesus Christ and know that through our efforts we are worthy, with our loved ones, to dwell in His presence for all eternity. Surely nothing is too hard to gain this great goal. We cannot let down for a moment. We must prove, every day of our lives, that we are willing to do the will of the Lord— to spread the restored gospel, to bear testimony to the world, to share the gospel with others. (Quoted by Gordon B. Hinckley, *Ensign,* November 1990, 4)

ILLUSTRATIONS FOR OUR TIMES

Not as the World Reasons

At the time section 112 was given to Thomas B. Marsh and the Twelve, it was a time not only of trial but of opportunity and blessing. Joseph noted that it came on the same day that the gospel was first preached in England. To me, one of the great evidences that Joseph was a prophet is in the fact that at the height of persecution from both within and outside the Church, Joseph opened the missionary efforts to the world. It was not a logical thing to do. It would seem that the Prophet needed his strongest and most stalwart leaders and supporters close to him instead of sending them to foreign lands. In spite of human logic, however, he responded to the inspired voice of the Spirit and called two of the stalwart members of the Twelve, Heber C. Kimball and Orson Hyde. On June 4, 1837, in the Kirtland Temple, the Prophet approached Brother Kimball with the following words, "Brother Heber, the Spirit of the Lord has whispered to me: 'Let my servant Heber go to England and proclaim my Gospel, and open the door of salvation to that nation'" (*HC,* 2:490). In addition, Joseph sent the soon-to-be-appointed Apostle Willard Richards and other faithful brethren to establish the Church in England.

The inspiration of that call was overwhelmingly affirmed one year later when three of those missionaries left England in April 1838, leaving twenty-six branches and thirteen hundred new members of the Church. Heber C. Kimball returned to England the next year on another mission, which produced forty-seven hundred converts. Such an influx of converts more than made up for the loss of Kirtland Saints who left the Church. By 1851, in spite of heavy emigration to the United States, there were more than forty-two thousand Saints and six hundred forty-two congregations in England. By 1856, about twenty-four thousand British converts had immigrated to Illinois and then Utah. (Anderson)

LIKENING THE SCRIPTURES TO OUR LIVES

Doctrine and Covenants 123:12 There are many of our brothers and sisters here on earth who are only kept from the truth because they don't know where to find it.

Application: So much confusion fetters the world today. Many good people are led away from truth because of the devil's counterfeits and blatant lies. Let us set our course to find the honest in heart and the elect of God (see D&C 29:7), that they may be taught the gospel of Jesus Christ. As we open our mouths (see D&C 33:8–11) and warn our neighbors (see D&C 88:81), the Spirit will give us the words to say (see D&C 100:5–6).

2. VALIANT DESPITE PERSECUTION

THEME: "For after much tribulation come the blessings. Wherefore the day cometh that ye shall be crowned with much glory; the hour is not yet, but is nigh at hand" (D&C 58:4; see also 103:12). With these words the Lord characterized the nature of the work of His kingdom—and the blessings that await those who labor with valor, despite the challenges and burdens of mortal travail. It is especially in missionary work that sacrifice is called for. The harvest does not come easily, but it is glorious.

MODERN PROPHETS SPEAK

James E. Faust:

> You must know that Lucifer will oppose you, and be prepared for his opposition. Do not be surprised. He wants you to fail. Discouragement is one of the devil's tools. Have courage and go forward. Recognize that the gospel has been preached with some pain and sorrow from the very beginning of time. Do not expect that your experience will be otherwise. (*Ensign,* May 1996, 40)

Wilford Woodruff:

> In my early missions, when preaching in the Southern States—Arkansas, Tennessee, and Kentucky—I have waded swamps and rivers and have walked seventy miles or more without eating. In those days we counted it a blessing to go into a place where there was a Latter-day Saint. I went once 150 miles to see one; and when I got there he had apostatized, and tried to kill me. Then, after travelling seventy-two miles without food, I sat down to eat my meal with a Missouri mobocrat, and he damning and cursing me all the time. . . . In those days we might travel hundreds and hundreds of miles and you could not find a Latter-day Saint. (*JD,* 12:12)

ILLUSTRATIONS FOR OUR TIMES

The Example of the Early Missionaries of the Restoration

The accounts of persecution of the early missionaries of the Church are too numerous even to catalogue here. Their success, despite hardships we can't even comprehend today, is staggering. In the following story, we see how Elder Kimball was afflicted not only with physical hardship and persecution, but with a confrontation by hell itself. His perseverance is inspiring:

> As husbands, fathers, and brothers left homes to share the gospel with others, their families were often left to fend for themselves. However, both missionaries and families shared intense faith that they would be sustained by the Lord, regardless of illness, poverty, and other trials. For example, when Heber C. Kimball and Orson Hyde left for missions to England, Elder Hyde left his wife with a three-week-old baby. Elder Kimball described the agony that he felt at being separated from his own family:
>
> "The idea of being appointed to such an important mission was almost more than I could bear up under. I felt my weakness and was nearly ready to sink under it, but the moment I understood the will of my heavenly Father, I felt a determination to go at all hazards, believing that he would support me by his almighty power, and although my family were dear to me, and I should have to leave them

almost destitute, I felt that the cause of truth, the gospel of Christ, outweighed every other consideration" (Orson F. Whitney, *Life of Heber C. Kimball* [Salt Lake City; Bookcraft, 1945], 104).

Robert B. Thompson, who accompanied Elder Kimball, described his companion's anguish:

"The door being partly open I entered and felt struck with the sight which presented itself to my view. I would have retired, thinking I was intruding, but I felt riveted to the spot. The father [Heber C. Kimball] was pouring out his soul to [God] that he would grant unto him a prosperous voyage across the mighty ocean, and make him useful wherever his lot should be cast, and that he who careth for the sparrows, and feedeth the young ravens when they cry, would supply the wants of his wife and little ones in his absence. He then, like the patriarchs, and by virtue of his office, laid his hands upon their heads individually, leaving a father's blessing upon them, and commending them to the care and protection of God, while he should be engaged preaching the gospel in foreign lands. . . . [H]is emotions were great, and he was obliged to stop at intervals, while the big tears rolled down his cheeks, an index to the feelings which reigned in his bosom. My heart was not stout enough to refrain; in spite of myself I wept and mingled my tears with theirs at the same time. I felt thankful that I had the privilege of contemplating such a scene. I realized that nothing could induce that man to tear himself from so affectionate a family group— from his partner and children who were so dear to him—but a sense of duty and love to God and attachment to his cause" (Orson F. Whitney, *Life of Heber C. Kimball* [Salt Lake City: Kimball Family, 1888], 108–109).

On his mission to England, Heber learned a lesson from this vision: when people are nearest to the Lord, Satan exerts a greater influence on them to keep them from the Lord. The evening before his first baptism in England, legions of evil spirits appeared in the bedroom. Heber reported: "I perspired exceedingly, my clothes becoming as wet as if I had been taken out of the river. I felt excessive pain, and was in the greatest distress for some time. I cannot even look back on the scene without feelings of horror; yet by it I learned the power of the adversary, his enmity against the servants of God, and got some understanding of the invisible world. We distinctly heard those spirits talk and express their wrath and hellish designs against us. However, the Lord delivered us from them, and blessed us exceedingly that day."

Heber later asked Joseph Smith the meaning of this evil onslaught. He wondered if he might have done something wrong to cause it, but the Prophet reassured him. "No, Brother Heber, at that time you were nigh, unto the Lord; there was only a veil between you and Him, but you could not see Him. When I heard of it, it gave me great joy, for I then knew that the work of God had taken root in that land. It was this that caused the devil to make a struggle to kill you." Joseph then related some of his own experiences with the evil one and said, "The nearer a person approaches the Lord, a greater power will be manifested by the adversary to prevent the accomplishment of His purposes."

Meanwhile, Elder Kimball's prayers were answered at home. His daughter, Helen Mar Whitney, said, "In the absence of my father the Lord was true to his promise. My father's prayer, that he had made upon the heads of his wife and little ones whom he had left poor and destitute, was answered. Kind friends came forward to cheer and comfort them, and administer to their wants." (Karl Ricks Anderson, *Joseph Smith's Kirtland* [Salt Lake City: Deseret Book, 1989], 85–87)

LIKENING THE SCRIPTURES TO OUR LIVES

Doctrine and Covenants 101:35 The Lord will bless His servants who are persecuted or lay down their lives for His name.

Application: As in the early days of the Church, the Lord's Saints are often tried and afflicted. While the Lord does not author the afflictions, He often allows them, as the result of others' agency, so that we may be purified and strengthened in our faith. It is part of His refining process. The Lord blesses all those who are persecuted for His sake (see 3 Ne. 12:10–12). It is an honor and blessing to be accounted worthy to be persecuted for the Lord's sake and in the cause of His kingdom. Blessings and joy are waiting in the kingdom of heaven if we but endure it well.

SUMMARY

The passages on missionary work from the Doctrine and Covenants discussed in this chapter originated with the Lord of harvest (see Matt. 9:38; Luke 10:2; Alma 26:6–8). It is He who inspires and commands the missionary army of Israel as they labor in all diligence on His errand. The purpose is to bring souls to the Lord: "Verily, thus saith the Lord: It shall come to pass that every soul who forsaketh his sins and cometh unto me, and calleth on my name, and obeyeth my voice, and keepeth my commandments, shall see my face and know that I am" (D&C 93:1).

    The formula for coming into the presence of our Savior and our Heavenly Father is clear and simple: First, we must repent and forsake our sins and covenant with our Savior to obey His commandments, praying always for the guidance of the Holy Spirit, that we might endure to the end. Second, we must thrust in our sickles and participate with all our "heart, might, mind and strength" (D&C 4:2), gleaning souls for the Lord in joy as laborers in the worldwide missionary harvest under the aegis of the Abrahamic covenant (see D&C 18:14–16). Through such service, our friends, associates, and all those we teach the gospel to can be "numbered among the people of the church of Christ; and . . . remembered and nourished by the good word of God, to keep them in the right way" (Moro. 6:4).

CHAPTER TWENTY-SEVEN

"THEY MUST NEEDS BE CHASTENED *and* TRIED, EVEN *as* ABRAHAM"

Reading Assignment: Doctrine and Covenants 101; 103; 105; *Our Heritage*, pages 27–29, 37–45.

Additional Reading: Acts 14:21–22; 2 Nephi 2:11; Mosiah 24:13–16; Doctrine and Covenants 50:5; 58:2.

Every individual radiates some influence. Our influence should be for good, for the building up of the kingdom of God. We should have no other purpose, only to bring to pass this great work and see it established in the earth as the Lord would have it.

In the early days of the Church the brethren came to the Prophet Joseph Smith asking what the Lord would have them do. The answer given to them was "to bring forth and establish the cause of Zion." That is our work, to establish Zion, to build up the kingdom of God, to preach the gospel to every creature in the world, that not one soul may be overlooked where there is the possibility for us to present unto him the truth. (Joseph Fielding Smith, DS, 1:237)

THEMES *for* LIVING

1. Building Zion: A Divine Decree
2. Rescuing the Saints: Zion's Camp as a Pattern in Heroism
3. Patience in Redeeming Zion

INTRODUCTION

The call to establish Zion in the latter days is a singularly significant aspect of the Restoration. The travail and testament of the early Saints of the Missouri period confirm that sacrifice is always central to the gospel plan. The Lord will have a Zion people who have learned fully the lessons of obedience (see D&C 105:5–6). This is perhaps the greatest lesson we of today can learn by looking back on this period of intense persecution and tribulation. As we look forward, we can take into our lives the principles of covenant valor in planning—through faith and hope—for the eventual establishment of Zion on this, the American continent (A of F 1:10), and the redemption of the Lord's people.

MOMENT OF TRUTH

From sections 101, 103, and 105 we gain especially cogent insights into what the Lord expects of us as laborers in the process of building up the kingdom of God and contributing to the establishment of Zion. The background to section 101—which was received on December 16, 1833, and contained a parable foreshadowing the march of Zion's Camp to rescue the beleaguered Missouri Saints—was given in chapter 21; following are brief summaries of the backgrounds to the other two sections.

Section 103: Given to the Prophet Joseph Smith on February 24, 1834, in his home at Kirtland, Geauga County, Ohio (*HC*, 2:36–39). The arrival in Kirtland of Lyman Wight and Parley P. Pratt on February 22 initiated the request that prompted this revelation and the historic movement that would be called Zion's Camp. The two men had been sent at the direction of a special conference convened in Clay County, Missouri. The minutes of that conference noted: "It was resolved, that Lyman Wight and Parley P. Pratt be sent as special messengers, to represent the situation of the scattered brethren in Missouri, to the Presidency and Church in Kirtland, and ask their advice" (*HC*, 2:1).

Elders Pratt and Wight had made a great sacrifice to come to Kirtland. They had had to leave their families in Missouri without protection from mob violence and persecution. Parley described his desperate journey from Jackson County to Kirtland thus: "I was at this time entirely destitute of proper clothing for the journey; and I had neither horse, saddle, bridle, money nor provisions to take with me; or to leave with my wife, who lay sick and helpless most of the time. Under the circumstances I knew not what to do. Nearly all had been robbed and plundered, and all were poor." A man named Higbee, "moved by the Spirit," gave him a horse and saddle. A. Sidney Gilbert, whose store had been "broken up, and his goods plundered and destroyed by the mob," gave him some material, which some women made into a suit, and Brother Gilbert furnished a coat (Parley P. Pratt, *Autobiography of Parley P. Pratt,* ed. Parley P. Pratt Jr. [Salt Lake City: Deseret Book, 1985], 87–88). Lyman Wight also placed his faith in the Lord. Before he left, it was reported, "his wife lay by the side of a log in the woods, with a child three days old and he had three days' provisions on hand" (Lyman Wight, *Millennial Star* 27 [July 22, 1865]: 455). "Faith and the blessings of God had cleared up our way to accomplish what seemed impossible," Elder Pratt continued. "We were soon ready, and on the first of February we mounted our horses, and started in good cheer to ride one thousand or fifteen hundred miles through a wilderness country. We had not one cent of money in our pockets on starting. We travelled every day, whether through storm or sunshine, mud, rain or snow" (*Autobiography of Parley P. Pratt,* 88). So dire were the circumstances in Missouri that these brethren were willing to leave in such conditions to deliver their message to the Prophet.

The older Missouri settlers had banded together and demanded that the Mormons leave Jackson County. Local authorities had banned the Church's newspaper, ordered that the printing office discontinue operations, and mandated that stores and businesses operated by Mormons close immediately. When the Saints had refused to abide by these directions, violent mobs had begun harassing them and plundering their property in an effort to drive them from Missouri. One mobber boasted that 203 Mormon homes had been burned. Among the buildings destroyed were the home of W. W. Phelps, which housed the printing press; the Gilbert and Whitney store, a dozen homes near the Big Blue River, and Sidney Gilbert's home.

Individuals has also been humiliated and threatened. An angry mob had dragged Bishop Edward Partridge and Charles Allen to the public square and stripped them of their clothes, smeared their bodies with tar containing lime or some other flesh-eating substance, and then dumped feathers on them. Two Mormons had been seized near the banks of the Big Blue River and pummeled with stones and clubs. In the skirmish that had resulted, one person had been killed and four others wounded.
It appears that after Elders Pratt and Wight reported the above to Joseph Smith, he received the revelation and then presented it to a meeting of the high council in Kirtland. The meeting had been called to give "an audience or hearing to Lyman Wight and Parley P. Pratt" (*HC,* 2:39). The Church faced a dilemma. By revelation, the Lord had appointed and consecrated the land of Missouri for the gathering of the Saints. He had given it as a land of promise with Independence as the "center place" (D&C 57:1–3). Yet this didn't now seem possible of fulfillment. With this revelation, the Lord instructed Joseph Smith to form Zion's Camp and go to Missouri to redeem the land of promise.

Section 105: Given through the Prophet Joseph Smith on June 22, 1834, on Fishing River, Clay County, Missouri (*HC,* 2:108–11). This revelation resulted from the thwarted efforts of Zion's Camp. Having already marched for several weeks (the camp left early in May of that year), the small army arrived in Missouri only to find the government uncooperative in reinstating the Missouri Saints to their land. The land of Zion was unobtainable at that time. Historian Lyndon W. Cook explains:

> The Mormon army crossed the Mississippi River in early June, arriving at the Salt River Branch of the Church in Monroe County, Missouri, on 7 June 1834. After a short respite the camp resumed its march on 12 June. Three days later Orson Hyde and Parley P. Pratt returned to the camp from Jefferson City with news that Governor Daniel Dunklin had "refused to fulfill his promise of reinstating" the Mormons on their lands in Jackson County. Dunklin apparently made his earlier promise in good faith; however, in the intervening six months, as Mormon–non-Mormon conditions worsened, he perceived that an armed conflict would inevitably ensue if the Mormons returned to their lands, and "pragmatically withdrew his promise in order to avert a civil war."
>
> Inasmuch as the camp intended only to work in concert with state authorities and under state protection, the governor's refusal insured that Zion's Camp would not enter Jackson County. With its primary objective out of reach, all that remained for the camp was to move into Clay County, where the body of the Church was residing, and discuss possible compromises.
>
> Section 105, received after Zion's Camp had arrived in Clay County, gave reasons why Zion would not be redeemed in 1834 and explained what must be done to effect that redemption. (*RPJS,* 213)

1. BUILDING ZION: A DIVINE DECREE

THEME: It is the Lord's design to redeem His people and ensure their eternal abode in Zion: "Behold, this is the blessing which I have promised after your tribulations, and the tribulations of your brethren—your redemption, and the redemption of your brethren, even their restoration to the land of Zion, to be established, no more to be thrown down" (D&C 103:13). The establishment of Zion—as a physical abode of the righteous—is a fundamental dimension of the Lord's plan to bring about "the immortality and eternal life of man" (Moses 1:39). Nevertheless, Zion is a unique place—her tenants are those alone who have learned to be celestial in nature, as we learn from our predecessors in this dispensation. They could not establish Zion in full because of their transgressions (see D&C 101:1–3). We cannot establish Zion again on the earth until we—as individuals, families, and the Church as a whole—become purified.

MODERN PROPHETS SPEAK

Bruce R. McConkie:

> By a process of chastening the Lord helps prepare his saints for salvation. It is one of his ways of turning erring souls to paths of righteousness. As varying situations require, chastening may include rebukes for misconduct or subjection to trials and afflictions. It may even take the form of chastisement, meaning corporal punishment.

> Men are chastened for their sins (D&C 58:60; 61:8; 64:8; 75:7; 93:50; 97:6; 103:4; 105:6; 1 Ne. 16:25), to bring them to repentance (D&C 1:27; 98:21), because the Lord loves them (D&C 95:1–2; Hela. 15:3; Rev. 3:19). Chastening is designed to try the faith and patience of the saints (Mosiah 23:21), and those who endure it well gain eternal life. (*Doctrinal New Testament Commentary,* 3 vols. [Salt Lake City: Bookcraft, 1965–73], 3:224)

Bruce R. McConkie:

> The foundations of Zion have been laid, but the promised City of Holiness has yet to be built. We have done some of the things destined to be accomplished in this dispensation; we are now engaged in doing the very things reserved for our time; and there are many things ahead to be done by our children and grandchildren and by all those who shall build on the foundation we are now laying. (*Ensign,* May 1977, 115)

LIKENING THE SCRIPTURES TO OUR LIVES

Doctrine and Covenants 101:41 Out of divine love, the Lord will chasten His children who transgress His laws.

Application: Chastening is a part of true and ultimate love. It is the way the Lord assists us in getting back on the strait and narrow path (see D&C 95:1–2). If He did not love us, He would not put forth the effort to help us correct our ways. Through this chastening process, we come to understand and recognize our faults and thus take the first steps to correct them in the strength of the Lord.

2. RESCUING THE SAINTS: ZION'S CAMP AS A PATTERN IN HEROISM

THEME: Zion's Camp—consisting of courageous practitioners of charity on a mission to succor the Missouri Saints at a time of acute need—is a model of service for all Latter-day Saints to learn from. Following is a brief summary of the contributions of Zion's Camp.

> The camp included contingents from Ohio and Michigan and eventually had a strength of 205 men and 25 wagons. The first group left Kirtland on May 1, 1834, and the camp was ultimately disbanded on June 25, near Rush Creek in Missouri (*HC,* 2:64–114).

> Some of their experiences included the following: the discovery of the skeletal remains of a "white Lamanite" named "Zelph"; an outbreak of cholera that afflicted sixty-eight persons and claimed fourteen lives, partly due to the rebellious spirit shown by some members of the camp; and the divine protection afforded the men when the elements preserved them from mobocracy.

> Upon arriving in Missouri, the Lord informed the Prophet Joseph, who was commander-in-chief of the expedition, that in consequence of transgression, the time for Zion's redemption was not yet at hand (D&C 105). Though many were disappointed, and some even looked upon the march as a failure, it had served a providential purpose.

> As Elder Neal A. Maxwell once said, "those who marched in Zion's Camp were not exploring the Missouri countryside but their own possibilities" (CR, October 1976, 16). From this group came many of the men who were chosen to be the Apostles and other leaders of the early Church. (*DCE,* 658)

MODERN PROPHETS SPEAK

Neal A. Maxwell:

> Notice how often the prophets are themselves brought through a crucible of testing, such as Zion's Camp, the 1834 movement of the two hundred souls from Kirtland to Missouri. Of this effort it has been noted that "in some respects the mission appeared to be a failure. . . ." (Hyrum M. Smith and Janne M. Sjodahl, *Doctrine and Covenants Commentary* [Salt Lake City: Deseret Book, 1978], 667). What was really underway, of course, was the development of leaders. The Prophet Joseph said of this adventure, "We know that angels were our companions, for we saw them" (Hyrum M. Smith and Janne M. Sjodahl, *Doctrine and Covenants Commentary* [Salt Lake City: Deseret Book, 1978], 667).

> The roster of the participants included the names of such men as Jedediah M. Grant, Orson Hyde, David W. Patten, Heber C. Kimball, Orson Pratt, Parley P. Pratt,

George A. Smith, Hyrum Smith, Joseph Smith, Nathan Tanner, Wilford Woodruff, and Brigham Young. The lessons learned and the yield for the future can scarcely be calculated by us, but out of this seeming "furnace of affliction" came the refined cadre who, because of their experience, could call the cadence for future treks and who could pass through even sterner tests.

"All these things" gave those men vital experiences that were for their good—and for the later good of those who would follow these tempered leaders. (*All These Things Shall Give Thee Experience* [Salt Lake City: Deseret Book, 1979], 116)

ILLUSTRATIONS FOR OUR TIMES

Courage to Obey

From the experience of Zion's Camp we gain several insights into the courage of these early Saints. One particular aspect of their courage is their willingness to obey. Remember, many were called to the camp, but only a few heeded that call and joined with their Prophet to bring aid to their fellow Saints. Their courageous obedience was not only a credit to them, but a protection:

> Now, why obey? In Deuteronomy it states, "Thou shalt keep therefore his statutes, and his commandments, which I command thee this day." Now, why: *"that it may go well with thee, and with thy children after thee, and that thou mayest prolong thy days upon the earth, which the Lord thy God giveth thee, for ever"* (Deut. 4:40).

> And again in the Doctrine and Covenants, section 98: "And again I say unto you, if ye observe to do whatsoever I command you, I, the Lord, *will turn away all wrath and indignation from you, and the gates of hell shall not prevail against you"* (D&C 98:22).

> Let's just cite one more example where the Lord watched over and protected his Saints in the Church. This is found in the *History of the Church:* There were threats of a mob on June 19, 1834. As the Mormons were making camp, five men rode up and told them that they would "see hell before morning." They stated that an armed force from Richmond, Ray, and Clay counties was to join a Jackson County force at the Fishing River ford, bent on the utter destruction of the camp.

> While these five men were in the camp, cursing and swearing vengeance, signs of an approaching storm were seen. No sooner had these men left the camp than the storm burst forth in all its fury. Hailstones struck, so large that they cut limbs from the trees, and the limbs fell all around the camp while the trees were twisted from their roots by the force of the wind. The earth trembled and quaked, and the streams

became raging torrents, and the mobbers dispersed, seeking shelter that could not be found. One mobber was killed by lightning and another had his hand torn off by a fractious horse, and in fear they dispersed, saying that if that was the way God fought for the "Mormons" they would go about their business.

On the morning of June 21 (just two days later) Colonel Sconce, with two companions, visited the camp to learn what the intentions of the members were. He said: "I see there is an almighty power that protects this people, for I started from Richmond, Ray County, with a company of armed men, having a fixed determination to destroy you, but was kept back by the storm."

The Prophet then related to these men the sufferings of the Saints, and they left the camp offering to use their influence (see *HC,* 2:103–6).

During all this storm the members of the camp were protected from its fury. Why were they protected? Because of their collective *obedience* to the Lord. (Ted E. Brewerton, *Ensign,* May 1981, 68)

LIKENING THE SCRIPTURES TO OUR LIVES

Doctrine and Covenants 103:27–28 The true indicator of a disciple of Jesus Christ is one who is willing to lay down his life in defense of the Savior and His gospel.

Application: We are here to be tested. We should be willing to lay down all for the kingdom. When we refuse to give of ourselves, we lose ourselves in self-absorption. We have been called to be a light to the world and the saviors of humankind—and this we can do in the strength of the Lord (see D&C 103:9–10). If we aren't willing to do this, we are not living up to the covenants we've made and are not worthy to be called in His name.

3. PATIENCE IN REDEEMING ZION

THEME: The redemption of Zion comes through the orderly application of divine power and the operation of the Spirit in the lives of faithful and valiant sons and daughters of God. This process is one of gradual and consistent growth, promoted through the benevolent and chastening hand of God, crowned ultimately with glory through the dawning of the millennial era. We can all be part of the process of establishing Zion and helping the Lord to perform His redeeming acts of mercy, grace, and love—but we are called upon to repent and learn more perfectly our duty as required by the Master.

MODERN PROPHETS SPEAK

Joseph Fielding Smith:

Because the people were not ready, or able, to abide in the laws which had been given them, the blessings were withdrawn, and the Lord said that they must wait for a little season for the redemption of Zion. In the meantime the people were to be chastened until they learn obedience, through the things which they suffer. After much tribulation would come the blessing and Zion would be redeemed, her Temple would be built, and "they who have been scattered shall be gathered." Zion was not to be moved out of her place. There are indications in the revelations that Zion is not to be built up or redeemed, until the indignation of the Lord shall be poured out without measure upon all nations; and "This will be when the cup of their iniquity is full" (D&C 101).

Some members of the Church have been greatly troubled because the Lord said that the Temple in the City Zion was to be built before the passing of this generation (D&C 88:4–5), but have we fully understood what is meant by a generation? The Lord said in His day, "Verily I say unto you, That there be some of them that stand here, which shall not taste of death, till they have seen the kingdom of God come with power." Since then nearly two thousand years have passed, yet this will be literally fulfilled. I have confidence in the words of the Lord, although some questions have been raised regarding Zion. The fact remains that this holy city and its Temple will be built. This will come after tribulation, and after the nations have been punished for their sins. So it seems to be recorded in the Scriptures. There must also come the reclamation of old Jerusalem and the building of a Temple there. This too, must wait, so it would seem, until the earth is cleansed of its wickedness." (*Signs of the Times* [Salt Lake City: Deseret Book, 1952], 166–67)

Neal A. Maxwell:

The modern Church even today is instructed to "wait for a little season" to build up central Zion. Why? So that we "may be prepared . . . and have experience" (D&C 105:9–10). We gain knowledge through particular experiences, but only incrementally, "in that thing" (Alma 32:34). Hence the ongoingness of it all, and perhaps we can be forgiven for wondering, "Is there no other way?" Personal, spiritual symmetry emerges only from the shaping of prolonged obedience. Twigs are bent, not snapped, into shape. (*Ensign,* May 1990, 33)

ENRICHMENT

A Caution in Viewing the Transgressions of the Missouri Saints

If we are not careful, we could become judgmental of the early Saints in Missouri, of whom the Lord said, "They have not learned to be obedient" (D&C 105:3). The Lord also spoke these seemingly condemning words: "They . . . are full of all manner of evil, and do not impart of their substance" (D&C 105:3). He identified the source of their problem by saying to Joseph Smith that "your brethren . . . have been afflicted, and persecuted . . . in consequence of their transgressions" (D&C 101:1–2).

Even some in Kirtland were critical of their brethren. In a letter dated January 14, 1833, leaders in Kirtland wrote the following: "We have the satisfaction of knowing that the Lord approves of us, and has accepted us and established His name in Kirtland . . . If Zion [meaning the stakes in Missouri] will not purify herself, so as to be approved of in all things in His sight, He will seek another people. . . . Seek to purify yourselves . . . lest the Lord's anger be kindled to fierceness. Repent, repent, is the voice of God to Zion" (*HC,* 1:316). In a seeming response to this attitude, the Lord included this in a subsequent revelation: "I, the Lord, am not well pleased with many who are in the church at Kirtland; For they do not forsake their sins, and their wicked ways, the pride of their hearts, and their covetousness, and all their detestable things, and observe the words of wisdom and eternal life which I have given unto them. Verily I say unto you, that I, the Lord, will chasten them and will do whatsoever I list, if they do not repent and observe all things whatsoever I have said unto them" (D&C 98:19–21).

We cannot discount all that happened or everyone who lived in Zion in that time. Sacrifice was a way of life for the Saints in Missouri. Some even gave their lives in the failed attempt to establish Zion. Could we do any better under the same circumstances? The Lord obviously knew when He sent them to Missouri that they would not succeed at that time. The 1830 period was a time to do the groundwork but not the time to complete the building up of Zion. That is yet a future event. Two months before the Lord gave section 105 at Fishing River, Joseph Smith prophesied that the Church would move to the West, saying, "This people will go into the Rocky mountains. . . . They will raise up a posterity there" (as quoted by Wilford Woodruff, CR, April 6, 1898, 57). The Saints were also aware that for millennia it had been prophesied that the Church would be "established in the top of the mountains . . . and all nations shall flow unto it" (Isa. 2:2).

We need to remember that the Lord's criticism of the Missouri Saints, cited above, measured them against the standard of "the law of the celestial kingdom" (D&C 105:4). Few of us could measure up against the celestial law. It is our challenge to learn the principles the Lord intended that we learn, but to do it without being critical of these suffering Saints. Let us leave judgment to the Lord. Many circumstances existed at that time in Missouri over which the early Saints had no control. Success was, for them, very elusive. From them we learn lessons that will help us to perfect our lives and then, one day, establish Zion. (Anderson)

LIKENING THE SCRIPTURES TO OUR LIVES

Mosiah 24:14 The Lord will visit us in our afflictions and help to ease the burdens we may be called upon to carry.

Application: As the Lord gives us strength to bear our burdens, let us always remember our obligations to Him to serve Him in gratitude—bearing solemn witness at all times and in all places to the truthfulness of the gospel—unto the end (see Mosiah 18:9). We cannot become a Zion people overnight. We must be diligent and patient to the end, bearing whatever afflictions and chastisements may be necessary to truly become the Lord's people.

SUMMARY

From the chronicles of Church history and the related pages of the Doctrine and Covenants, we can garner powerful lessons about the implications of the Lord's decree to build up Zion and what it means when we are called upon to give our all—even our lives, if necessary—for the cause of the Church and kingdom of God. From the admirable sacrifices of Zion's Camp, we can learn, moreover, what it means to take up the commission of rescuing one's fellows in moments of dire stress and persecution. These early episodes in the Lord's unfolding saga of the process of establishing Zion through power and the workings of the Spirit teach us that patience and long-suffering are the requisite qualities of a righteous people waiting for the ultimate triumph of good over the forces of evil: "But blessed are they who are faithful and endure, whether in life or in death, for they shall inherit eternal life" (D&C 50:5).

CHAPTER TWENTY-EIGHT

"O GOD, WHERE ART THOU?"

Reading Assignment: Doctrine and Covenants 121:1–33; 122; *Our Heritage*, pages 45–53.

Additional Reading: Doctrine and Covenants 58:2–5; 98:12, 14–15; 101:1–2, 4; 122:7; 136:31. *Savior's Suffering*—Isaiah 53:5–6; Hebrews 2:17–18; Alma 7:11–12; Doctrine and Covenants 19:15–19; 88:6; 122:5–8.

One cannot look at human suffering, regardless of its causes or origins, and not feel pain and compassion. It is easy to understand why one who lacks an eternal perspective might look at horrifying news footage of starving children in Africa or the devastation of a hurricane and shake a fist at the heavens.

"If there is a God," the empathetic observer might wonder, "how could He allow such things to happen?"

The answer isn't easy, but it isn't that complicated, either. God has put His plan into motion. It proceeds through natural laws—which are, in fact, God's laws. And because they are His, He is bound by them, as are we. In this imperfect world, bad things sometimes happen. The earth's rocky underpinnings occasionally slip and slide, and earthquakes result. Certain weather patterns turn into hurricanes, tornadoes, floods, and drought. That is the nature of our existence on this planet. Dealing with adversity is one of the chief ways in which we are tested and tutored.

Sometimes, however, adversity is man-made. That is where the principle of agency again comes into play. Keep in mind that we were so excited about the plan Heavenly Father and Jesus Christ presented that we literally "shouted for joy" (Job 38:7). We loved the concept of mortality and the exciting notion of moral agency. But because we'd never been mortal before, I'm not sure we could fully comprehend the impact of agency on our lives. (M. Russell Ballard, Our Search for Happiness: An Invitation to Understand The Church of Jesus Christ of Latter-day Saints *[Salt Lake City: Deseret Book, 1993], 76)*

THEMES *for* LIVING

1. The Lord Listens to Our Pleas: The Lessons of Liberty Jail
2. The Role of Adversity in Our Lives
3. The Lord's Counsel and Support of Us in Adversity

INTRODUCTION

The promised glory of the Lord comes to the righteous only after the trial of their faith. "My people must be tried in all things, that they may be prepared to receive the glory that I have for them, even the glory of Zion; and he that will not bear chastisement is not worthy of my kingdom" (D&C 136:31). From the perspective of history, we can look back upon the experiences of the early Saints of this dispensation and learn powerful lessons about how to overcome, and even learn from, adversity. Adversity can descend upon us as a result of disobedience. It can also come naturally as part of the mortal experience. In either case, adversity is a strict schoolmaster and a stringent and uncompromising disciplinarian, as discussed extensively in the previous chapter (see D&C 101:1–4).

In the Doctrine and Covenants, we discover principles that govern the process of both transcending adversity and extracting from our tribulations strength, courage, hope, and vitality—all blessings from the Lord. We learn more fully of the severity and depth of our Savior's suffering and can learn, from His example, patience and strength in tribulation. He views our struggles as one who has triumphed over all foes, including temptation, trial, suffering, death, and hell. In this, He is the supreme example for us to follow.

MOMENT OF TRUTH

There are few passages of scripture that provide a more moving and memorable testimony of spiritual courage in the face of adversity than sections 121 and 122. As the Prophet Joseph Smith, falsely accused and cruelly abused by the civil authorities, languished in the squalor and filth of the prison ironically known as Liberty Jail, he experienced an epiphany of spiritual ascendancy as the Lord opened his vision to greater views of the cause of Zion and buoyed his spirits beyond the suffering of life's tribulations. The resulting epistle penned by the Prophet and sent, first of all, to his beloved Emma has become a jewel in the Lord's inventory of scriptural strength and instruction.

Details on the coming forth of section 121 are given in chapter 25. Below is a review of the similar background to section 122.

Section 122: Given through the Prophet Joseph Smith in March 1839 at Liberty Jail in Liberty, Clay County, Missouri (see *HC,* 3:300–301). Verse 6 implies the setting of this section: "If thou art accused with all manner of false accusations; if thine enemies fall upon thee; if they tear thee from the society of thy father and mother and brethren and sisters; and if with a drawn sword thine enemies tear thee from the bosom of thy wife, and of thine offspring, and thine elder son, although but six years of age, shall cling to thy garments, and shall say, My father, my father, why can't you stay with us? O, my father, what are the men going to do with you? and if then he shall be thrust from thee by the sword, and thou be dragged to prison, and thine enemies prowl around thee like wolves for the blood of the lamb . . ." Lyman Wight verifies that this indeed was the state of Joseph and his family upon his imprisonment. He describes the traumatic event in the Prophet's life to which this verse alludes as follows:

> About the hour the prisoners were to have been shot on the public square in Far West, they were exhibited in a wagon in the town, all of them having families there, but myself; and it would have broken the heart of any person possessing an ordinary share of humanity, to have seen the separation. The aged father and mother of Joseph Smith were not permitted to see his face, but to reach their hands through the curtains of the wagon, and thus take leave of him. When passing his own house, he was taken out of the wagon and permitted to go into the house, but not without a strong guard, and not permitted to speak with his family but in the presence of his guard and his eldest son, Joseph, about six or eight years old, hanging to the tail of his coat, crying father, is the mob going to kill you? The guard said to him, "you damned little brat, go back, you will see your father no more." (Cited in *RPJS,* 240)

It is instructive of Joseph's personality and priorities to consider that much of his concern at this point, having been imprisoned for months now, was for his family. Despite his wretched condition, he was tormented by the fact that he could do nothing to help his family or the Church in these times of need. It is also interesting to consider what great treasures of understanding came from this term of trial for the Prophet: the revelations of sections 121 and 122. The strength and power of these revelations may have done more for the Church than anything he could have done at that time.

1. THE LORD LISTENS TO OUR PLEAS: THE LESSONS OF LIBERTY JAIL

THEME: The Lord knows of our sufferings and afflictions. In His mortal experience in the meridian of time, He walked pathways of tribulation more trying and severe than any of us can imagine: "Surely he hath borne our griefs, and carried our sorrows: yet we did esteem him stricken, smitten of God, and afflicted. But he was wounded for our transgressions, he was bruised for our iniquities: the chastisement of our peace was upon him; and with his stripes we are healed" (Isa. 53:4–5). His condescension imparted to Him lessons in understanding and beneficence that resonate with effectual compassion in all that He does as Redeemer and Savior: "Wherefore in all things it behoved him to be made like unto his brethren, that he might be a merciful and faithful high priest in things pertaining to God, to make reconciliation for the sins of the people. For in that he himself hath suffered being tempted, he is able to succour them that are tempted" (Heb. 2:17–18). His mercy was infused with firsthand experience by virtue of His willingness to see, hear, and feel with mortal perspective.

Thanks be to God that we are blessed to have a Lord and Master who listens to our pleas and our supplications with eternal understanding and ever-loving kindness! Just as He heard the importuning voice of the Prophet Joseph in Liberty Jail, so will He, in turn, hear our cries of anguish and pain sent up to Him from the chambers and byways of mortality to which we have been consigned.

MODERN PROPHETS SPEAK

Ezra Taft Benson:

> I often think of the Prophet Joseph—to me the greatest prophet who has ever lived upon the face of the earth, save Jesus only, whom he represented and served. I think of his trials and tribulations. I thought of them as I once stood in Liberty Jail. He was in that filthy jail, surrounded by vile men, not for a period of days or weeks, but months. And finally, when it seemed as though he could stand it no longer, Joseph cried out and asked Heavenly Father why He would not intervene. The answer came

in revelation to the Prophet in these words: "My son, peace be unto thy soul; thine adversity and thine afflictions shall be but a small moment: And then, if thou endure it well, God shall exalt thee on high; thou shalt triumph over all thy foes" (D&C 121:7–8). Later the Lord uttered this significant statement: "Know thou, my son, that all these things shall give thee experience, and shall be for thy good" (D&C 122:7). God help us to be grateful for our blessings and never to be guilty of the sin of ingratitude. "And he who receiveth all things with thankfulness shall be made glorious; and the things of this earth shall be added unto him, even an hundred fold, yea, more" (D&C 78:19). (*New Era,* November 1991, 4)

Neal A. Maxwell:

Separated from them though he was, Joseph was further assured that the people of the Church "shall never be turned against [him] by the testimony of traitors" (D&C 122:3). It is a comfort that this promise is as valid today as when it was given in March of 1839. Such defectors and other detractors caused trouble then (see D&C 122:4) as they do now. Nevertheless such troubles and afflictions, comparatively speaking, will be "but for a small moment" (D&C 122:4; see also 2 Cor. 4:17). (*But for a Small Moment* [Salt Lake City: Bookcraft, 1986], 11)

Marvin J. Ashton:

Even the chains of fear can be broken by those who will humbly seek God's help and strength. It can be done with this strengthening promise in Doctrine and Covenants 122:4: "Because of thy righteousness . . . thy God shall stand by thee forever and ever." (*Be of Good Cheer* [Salt Lake City: Deseret Book, 1987], 68)

ILLUSTRATIONS FOR OUR TIMES

Out of the Darkness, Light

One of the darkest periods in the history of the Church was the winter of 1838–39. The Saints had been persecuted, robbed, and murdered. The Prophet Joseph Smith and his associates had been betrayed and were imprisoned in Liberty Jail.

But emerging from this dark period were the men who led the Church throughout trying experiences as well as amazing growth and development. It was during those dark days that the Lord revealed to the Prophet Joseph Smith, while in the Liberty Jail, a great revelation. Out of the midst of his tribulations, the Prophet Joseph Smith called upon God for comfort.

The answer came as God replied, "My son, peace be unto thy soul; thine adversity and thine afflictions shall be but a small moment;

"And then, if thou endure it well, God shall exalt thee on high" (D&C 121:7–8).

The Liberty Jail experience truly constituted a refiner's fire for those who participated in it, and it gives us a better understanding and appreciation of the greatness of the Prophet Joseph Smith and the early leaders of the Church.

What can we learn from the Liberty Jail experience that will be helpful to us? Certainly two impressive truths are apparent:

First, the importance of faith in the Lord Jesus Christ and loyalty to our leaders and to the Church.

Second, the need for enduring to the end, regardless of how many difficulties we have to surmount.

As we endure to the end, we may need to ask the Lord for comfort, and we, like the Prophet Joseph Smith, may hear, "My son, peace be unto thy soul" (D&C 121:7). (Franklin D. Richards, *Ensign,* May 1981, 50)

LIKENING THE SCRIPTURES TO OUR LIVES

Doctrine and Covenants 121:7–8 This life is but a small moment in our eternal progression. The Lord has promised to exalt us if we will bear our adversities and afflictions with patience.

Application: We learn from the Prophet Joseph's experience that the Lord does hear our pleas for help in adversity (see D&C 121:1–6). But we also learn that adversity is part of our mortal experience. Let us remember that there is opposition in all things (see 2 Ne. 2:11). Adversity is part of this opposition and necessary for our growth and development. It is easy to say, but hard to comprehend and endure in the stress and challenge of the moment. This is the test of mortality. With this eternal perspective, we can endure all things that we might be worthy of the blessings from our Heavenly Father.

2. THE ROLE OF ADVERSITY IN OUR LIVES

THEME: Beyond tribulation beckon the blessings; beyond adversity lies glory. Abraham was privileged to be taught this principle as the Lord instructed him about the plan of salvation, with its roots in the premortal councils of heaven: "And we will prove them herewith, to see if they will do all things whatsoever the Lord their God shall command them; And they who keep their first estate shall be added upon; and they who keep not their first estate shall not have glory in the same kingdom with those who keep their first estate; and they who keep their second estate shall have glory added upon their heads for ever and ever" (Abr. 3:25–26). In our day, the Lord has confirmed His promise to the faithful: "For after much tribulation come the blessings. Wherefore the day cometh that ye shall be crowned with much glory; the hour is not yet, but is nigh at hand" (D&C 58:4). It is an essential aspect of human progression that individuals must learn to transcend adversity without complaint (following the example of Job) and without doubt in the Lord's counsel (following the example of Abraham). For all Latter-day Saints, the example of Joseph Smith is the most recent and compelling instance of a prophetic servant of God who triumphed over suffering and placed all enemies and tribulations beneath him in valiant service to the end.

MODERN PROPHETS SPEAK

James E. Faust:

> Many in today's generation have not fully known nor appreciated the refining blessings of adversity. Many have never been hungry because of want. Yet I am persuaded that there can be a necessary refining process in adversity that increases our understanding, enhances our sensitivity, makes us more Christlike. Lord Byron said, "Adversity is the first path to truth" (*Don Juan,* canto 12, stanza 50). The life of the Savior and the lives of His prophets clearly and simply teach how necessary adversity is to achieve a measure of greatness. (*Liahona,* May 1998)

ILLUSTRATIONS FOR OUR TIMES

Remember to Look beyond Adversity

As we ponder our life, perceiving that it is a blend of hope and joy, challenge and tribulation, let us remember these two things:

1. Adversity is a universal experience.

- *Adversity is a reminder.* Without adversity, we may forget God (see Hel. 12:2–3). No one person has a monopoly on adversity—we are all in this together.

- *Adversity is a powerful teacher.* Learning to overcome adversity is part of life. It will be for our good (see D&C 98:1–3).

- *Adversity can foster growth.* To wish away adversity will only make you weak. The results will be little or no growth.

- *The key is how we respond.* Great souls are those who handle adversity positively, maintain a good attitude, and have a proper perspective on life.

- *Trust can be the result.* Adversity teaches us to trust in the Lord (see Prov. 3:5–6).

- *The Lord chastens whom He loves.* We are chastened in adversity (see 2 Ne. 5:25; Mosiah 23:21) and then blessed as we grow from it (see Mosiah 24:8–15).

2. There are great benefits that can come through adversity.

- *Humility.* Adversity cultivates within us the quality of humility, confirming our relationship and dependence upon God, which is the beginning virtue of exaltation.

- *Self-Worth.* Overcoming adversity brings great personal satisfaction and a sense of self-worth and self-confidence.

- *Strength.* Overcoming adversity brings one an enduring kind of spiritual strength.

- *Gratitude.* Adversity is the teacher that helps us remember the good times and the blessings of God.

- *Spirituality.* From adversity we can become closer to God, knowing that He not only gives us the strength to overcome but provides blessings in the process.

- *Blessings from the Lord.* The Savior continually nurtures us and strengthens us in our adversity and afflictions (see Alma 7:11–12).

"But for a Small Moment"

In our time, few have felt the anguish of frequent separation from hearth and family as acutely as the Prophet Joseph Smith. While on an expedition to New York for the Church in October 1832, he was alone in the boarding house with time to feel the homesickness of being away from his children and from Emma, who was then expecting their fourth child. He wrote to her during this hour:

> After beholding all that I had any desire to behold, I returned to my room to meditate and calm my mind, and behold the thoughts of home, of Emma and Julia [an adopted daughter], rush upon my mind like a flood and I could wish for a moment

to be with them. My breast is filled with all the feelings and tenderness of a parent and a husband and could I be with you I would tell you many things, yet when I reflect upon this great city like Nineveh not discerning their right hand from their left, yea, more than two-hundred-thousand souls, my bowels are filled with compassion toward them and I am determined to lift up my voice in this city and leave the event with God who holdeth all things in his hands and will not suffer an hair of our heads unnoticed to fall to the ground. . . . I feel as though I wanted to say something to you to comfort you in your peculiar trial and present affliction. I hope God will give you strength that you may not faint. I pray God to soften the hearts of those around you to be kind to you and take the burden off your shoulders as much as possible and not afflict you. I feel for you, for I know your state and that others do not, but you must comfort yourself, knowing that God is your friend in heaven and that you have one true and living friend on Earth, your husband. (*The Personal Writings of Joseph Smith,* ed. Dean C. Jessee [Salt Lake City: Deseret Book, 1984], 253, spelling and syntax modernized)

Here he feels his personal tribulation deeply—and that of his wife—but maintains the perspective that it is for a great cause that he suffers. His willingness to do the will of the Lord is what sustained him in his trials and no doubt blesses him more in the eternities than he suffered here.

Later, in March 1839, from his confinement in Liberty Jail, he wrote to his wife:

My dear Emma, I very well know your toils and sympathize with you. If God will spare my life once more to have the privilege of taking care of you, I will ease your care and endeavor to comfort your heart. I want you to take the best care of the family you can, [and] I believe you will do all you can. I was sorry to learn that Frederick was sick, but I trust he is well again and that you are all well. I want you to try to gain time and write to me a long letter and tell me all you can and even if old Major [their dog] is alive yet and what those little prattlers say that cling around your neck. Do you tell them I am in prison that their lives might be saved? (*The Personal Writings of Joseph Smith,* ed. Dean C. Jessee [Salt Lake City: Deseret Book, 1984], 408, spelling and syntax modernized)

Joseph, like many of the founding leaders of the restored Church, placed the will of God and His purposes ahead of personal will and comfort. The suffering occasioned by loss and separation, the anxiety about longed-for relief and supplicated triumph was destined to last "but for a small moment" (D&C 122:4). The Prophet Joseph lived to see only the first fourteen years of the Church's progress. Though wrought with great struggle, it really was only "a small moment" in the history of the cosmos. The reward of Joseph and these other leaders will be eternal lives in the hereafter and the joy of immortality and eternal togetherness with loved ones. Their example is timeless and still reverberates in the hearts of the grateful heirs of their completed ministry.

There have been times of separation in my own life where I have longed to be at the side of my wife but could not be, because of circumstances. At such times, I have been comforted by the example of valor and righteousness of the Prophet Joseph Smith and have been reminded that these periods of challenges are but a moment in the grand scheme of things for those who serve diligently and strive to honor their covenant promises. (Allen)

LIKENING THE SCRIPTURES TO OUR LIVES

Doctrine and Covenants 127:2 Joseph Smith had great faith even in the face of adversity. God promised Joseph that in the end he would triumph over all his enemies.

Application: The attitude we cultivate in dealing with our adversities will result in either our humility and growth or a hardened heart and rebellion (see Alma 62:41). The Prophet Joseph stands as a monument to all of us for what he suffered and endured for the kingdom of God. He did not simply endure it, but endured it well, glorifying God all the while. He was truly able to rejoice in his tribulations because he had the perspective that all would be made right in the eternities and that he was becoming more worthy in the process. This is the outlook we must develop to rejoice in and overcome adversity.

3. THE LORD'S COUNSEL AND SUPPORT OF US IN ADVERSITY

THEME: We are not alone. What the Lord said by way of comfort to Joseph Smith in his deepest hour of tribulation applies likewise to each of us, as we honor our covenants and uphold all principles of righteousness: "Thy days are known, and thy years shall not be numbered less; therefore, fear not what man can do, for God shall be with you forever and ever" (D&C 122:9). Faith in God's redeeming power and hope in His everlasting charity and kindness—these are two of the essential keys for transcending adversity.

MODERN PROPHETS SPEAK

Gordon B. Hinckley:
> If as a people we will build and sustain one another, the Lord will bless us with the strength to weather every storm and continue to move forward through every adversity. (*TGBH,* 7)

Jeffrey R. Holland:

No, it is not without a recognition of life's tempests but fully and directly because of them that I testify of God's love and the Savior's power to calm the storm. Always remember in that biblical story that He was out there on the water also, that He faced the worst of it right along with the newest and youngest and most fearful. Only one who has fought against those ominous waves is justified in telling *us—as well as the sea*—to "be still." Only one who has taken the full brunt of such adversity could ever be justified in telling us in such times to "be of good cheer." Such counsel is not a jaunty pep talk about the power of positive thinking, though positive thinking is much needed in the world. No, Christ knows better than all others that the trials of life can be very deep and we are not shallow people if we struggle with them. But even as the Lord avoids sugary rhetoric, He rebukes faithlessness and He deplores pessimism. He expects us to believe! (*Ensign,* November 1999, 36)

Robert D. Hales:

Our Savior waits for us to come to Him through our scripture study, pondering, and prayer to our Heavenly Father. Great blessings and lessons come from overcoming adversity. As we are strengthened and healed, we can then lift and strengthen others with our faith. May we be instruments in the Lord's hands in blessing the lives of those in pain. I give you my testimony that God lives and that Jesus is the Christ and that He waits for us to come to Him to give us counsel and compassionate caring. (*Ensign,* November 1998, 14)

ILLUSTRATIONS FOR OUR TIMES

"A Wintry Doctrine"

Elder Neal A. Maxwell has often referred to the necessity of affliction and chastisement in life as "a wintry doctrine." He learned this doctrine more deeply firsthand when he was diagnosed with leukemia with a grim prognosis. More intensely, he learned the suffering of the Savior and His role and support in our own private sufferings, as we learn from his biography:

[Those] close to Elder Maxwell soon learned that he felt he had no claim to a special miracle. He would talk about such people as Richard L. Evans, Bruce R. McConkie, A. Theodore Tuttle, Marvin J. Ashton, and other General Authorities who had met death early. They were better men than I am, he would say. He didn't want to give any false hopes, and, as one friend put it, he didn't want "to promote a fan club to demand a miracle."

This attitude explains what looked like pessimism to some in his closest circle. He had worked so long on making himself "willing to submit" to the Lord (Mosiah 3:19, a verse he had quoted often), that some people thought he was actually too resigned, too ready to yield. He had a related tendency that prompted some to lecture him a little. Since boyhood, he was ever the anticipator—impatient, anxious to get on with whatever was to come next. . . . And if it was time to face death, he had no need to argue or, for him, much worse, to shrink from drinking whatever bitter cup was his.

Colleen [his wife] saw things differently, and she didn't hesitate to coach him with the loving directness she had long cultivated. She could see that in his desire to accept what had been allotted to him, he was reluctant to importune the Lord with much pleading. But she pointed out that Jesus' first cry in the Garden of Gethsemane was, "If is be possible, let this cup pass from me." Only after he had made this earnest plea did the Savior finally submit Himself with, "Nevertheless not as I will, but as thou wilt" (Matthew 26:39). With Jesus as our example in all things, she said, it must be permissible to plead. Then of course we submit, as He did. Neal saw her insight and agreed. (Bruce C. Hafen, *A Disciple's Life* [Salt Lake City: Deseret Book, 2002], 14–15).

What followed was an intense regimen of medical treatments and chemotherapy. The leukemia went into remission for a while (about fifteen months), but Elder Maxwell was not through the trial. The disease returned in full force, requiring more chemotherapy and even some experimental treatments. The beloved Apostle was blessed with a second remission from the disease for some years before passing away. His longevity was surely a miracle bestowed by a merciful and understanding Lord. Elder Maxwell described adversity as instructive. Surely at this time He must have felt very close to the Savior, coming to know Him better and coming to be more like Him. His biography continues:

Perhaps the experiences of such people as Neal Maxwell . . . teach us that those who seek apprenticeship with the Master of mankind must emulate his sacrificial experience to the fullest extent of their personal capacity. Then they might taste His empathy and His charity. For only then are they like him enough to feel his love for others *the way he feels it.* . . .

The Savior's love for all mankind is fully bound up in his exquisite pain. "How sore you know not . . . how hard to bear you know not" (D&C 19:15). Perhaps we cannot know his love without knowing his pain. If so, the personal suffering we confront in the sanctification process—"the fellowship of His suffering"—could move the pure love of Christ from a concept in one's head to a substance in one's heart. And once in the heart, charity will circulate all through the body because it is being moved by "a new heart."

In March 2000 when he was in a pondering mood about his illness, with its implications both dreadful and miraculous, Neal had a sacred experience. . . . The soul voice of the Spirit came into his mind to whisper, "I have given you leukemia that you might teach my people with authenticity." The words sank in deeply, confirming his belief that the Lord had authored his tutorial—and his recovery. (Bruce C. Hafen, *A Disciple's Life* [Salt Lake City: Deseret Book, 2002], 562).

LIKENING THE SCRIPTURES TO OUR LIVES

Alma 7:11–12 Alma testifies that Christ has a perfect ability to comfort us in our pain, sorrow, and affliction because He personally experienced the pain and suffering of all the sons and daughters of God.

Application: Lest we forget: the Lord has suffered all things that He might better succor us and bless us in our adversity. We do not have to suffer alone. He is the only one who can fully and intimately understand our trials. We must turn to Him for our healing and our strength to go forward as we face life's challenges and adversities.

SUMMARY

This chapter has taught us important principles for success along the pathways of mortality: First, the Lord listens to our pleas and responds with compassion and understanding as we seek to honor our promises and embrace righteousness; second, by understanding that adversity plays an essential role in our lives, we can learn how to transcend it and overcome our challenges; third, the Lord offers us constant counsel and support to triumph over adversity through the strength of His almighty hand.

Part of the test of life is dealing with opposition (see 2 Ne. 2:11). The Lord seeks to know whether we will obey the commandments in all situations (see Abr. 3:25). We agreed to the plan. We realized that there is no growth without trials, tribulations, adversity, and opposition in all things. Knowing that this is the plan, we need not fear adversity. As the Lord said, " Therefore, be not afraid of your enemies [adversity], for I have decreed in my heart, saith the Lord, that I will prove you in all things, whether you will abide in my covenant, even unto death, that you may be found worthy. For if ye will not abide in my covenant ye are not worthy of me" (D&C 98:14–15).

CHAPTER TWENTY-NINE

BUILDING *the* KINGDOM *of* GOD *in* NAUVOO, ILLINOIS

Reading Assignment: Doctrine and Covenants 124:1–21, 87–90, 97–110; 126; *Our Heritage*, pages 51–52, 55–58, 61–62.

Additional Reading: JST, Matthew 6:38; Jacob 2:18–19; Doctrine and Covenants 6:6; 105:32.

Teach them to sacrifice to build up the kingdom of God. That sacrifice brings the testimony of the Spirit. The Prophet Joseph translated a wonderful promise written by a prophet long ago for our time:

"And blessed are they who shall seek to bring forth my Zion at that day, for they shall have the gift and the power of the Holy Ghost; and if they endure unto the end they shall be lifted up at the last day, and shall be saved in the everlasting kingdom of the Lamb; and whoso shall publish peace, yea, tidings of great joy, how beautiful upon the mountains shall they be" [1 Ne. 3:37].

All can claim that promise. The youngest and the newest member can seek to build up the kingdom of God. Zion is made up of individuals and families. When their faith increases, the kingdom is established more firmly. We can try to help with that every day. Even the smallest act to build faith in another person or in a family qualifies us for the gift and power of the Holy Ghost. The Holy Ghost testifies of truth. Therefore, in our service, our faith increases that Jesus is the Christ, that our Heavenly Father lives and loves us, and that Joseph was Their prophet. You can expect that, every time you go to a home to build faith, as a home teacher or a visiting teacher or a friend. (Henry B. Eyring, Ensign, *November 2003, 89)*

THEMES *for* LIVING

1. The Lord Always Prepares a Place for His Saints: Nauvoo—City of Refuge
2. Missionary Work as a Central Focus in Building Up the Kingdom of God
3. The Consequence of Failing to Endure to the End
4. The Relief Society Organized: "Charity Never Faileth"

INTRODUCTION

Having been displaced from their Missouri environment by rapacious and evil mobbers, the Saints were guided to establish a new frontier on the banks of the Mississippi River in a swampland that they readily transformed into a thriving metropolis. It reflected the glory and industry of the kingdom of God. For the time being, the Lord absolved the Saints of the sacred commission to build a temple in Independence and commanded that Nauvoo be the site of the next house "for the Most High to dwell in" (D&C 124:27). The building up of the new city was a monument to the resilience, faithfulness, and covenant valor of the Saints. Yet, alas, the luster of Nauvoo, the City Beautiful, was relatively short-lived, for conspiring forces soon generated the destructive perturbations that drove the Saints, yet again, from their rightful lands and onward to their western refuge. The magnificent temple was destroyed by fire and tornado after the exodus. What a glorious event it was, on June 27, 2002, when a prophet of God dedicated the rebuilt Nauvoo Temple! It stands as a splendid memorial witness to the enduring cause of Zion and a reminder of the solemn testimony (declared millennia earlier by Daniel) that the kingdom of God would roll forth, as a stone cut from the mountain without hands, to supersede all earthly kingdoms until it eventually filled the entire world (see Dan. 2:35, 44). Thus we see the workings of the Lord in realizing His glorious designs on behalf of the children of the Most High. For us today, the task is to live the commandments and do our duty with righteous resolve, leaving the rest to the Lord: "But seek ye first the kingdom of God, and his righteousness; and all these things shall be added unto you" (Matt. 6:33).

MOMENT OF TRUTH

Section 124: Given through the Prophet Joseph Smith on January 19, 1841, at Nauvoo, Hancock County, Illinois (see *HC,* 4:274–86). Valuable insights into the progress of the restored Church and its doctrines can be gleaned from thoughtful study of this section of the Doctrine and Covenants. Historian Lyndon W. Cook summarized the background to this section as follows:

> After the Prophet was freed from his Missouri imprisonment (16 April 1839), immediate plans were made to locate the Saints at another gathering place. Upon viewing properties in Lee County, Iowa, and Hancock County, Illinois, Church land agents purchased thousands of acres of unimproved land in these two counties, and soon Nauvoo (Commerce) became the headquarters of the Church.

> With the land problem temporarily solved, Joseph Smith turned his attention to balancing accounts for wrongs suffered in Missouri. With others, the Prophet traveled to Washington, D.C., November 1839–March 1840, where he had an audience with President Martin Van Buren, presented Congress with claims against the state of Missouri, and lobbied for redress of Missouri grievances. After achieving little or no success in the East, Joseph Smith returned to Nauvoo, where he began to build up and strengthen the Church. Section 124, the first known revelation since July 1838, was received about four weeks after the governor of Illinois had signed charters for the city of Nauvoo, the University of Nauvoo, the Nauvoo House Association, the Nauvoo Agricultural and Mechanical Association, and the Nauvoo Legion. The revelation had monumental importance to the Prophet and his associates because its fulfillment engaged nearly every waking moment of the Prophet's time until his death. (*RPJS,* 242–43)

Among other things, the revelation commands that a proclamation concerning the restored gospel be sent to heads of state around the world, that a temple be built in Nauvoo to accommodate sacred ordinances (such as baptisms for the dead), that priesthood leaders accept and fulfill specific duties and tasks assigned of the Lord, and that the quorums and councils of the Church operate according to their several rights and obligations as enumerated.

1. THE LORD ALWAYS PREPARES A PLACE FOR HIS SAINTS: NAUVOO—CITY OF REFUGE

THEME: There is consoling hope in the confirming witness that the Lord is in charge of His Church and kingdom. Though the Saints may be scattered by their enemies and from time to time fall victim to their own weaknesses and shortcomings, nevertheless the blessings of the Lord will sustain them and lead them to places of refuge where they may rise up in the majesty of their callings to serve the Lord in gratitude and fulfill His commissions in righteousness and dignity.

MODERN PROPHETS SPEAK

Gordon B. Hinckley:

> So undergirded beneath and fitly framed above, this Church stands as the creation of the Almighty. It is a shelter from the storms of life. It is a refuge of peace for those in distress. It is a house of succor for those in need. It is the conservator of eternal truth and the teacher of the divine will. It is the true and living Church of the Master. (*Ensign,* February 2004, 3)

Gordon B. Hinckley:

> May you look upon the Church as your great and good friend, your refuge when the world appears to be closing around you, your hope when things are dark, your pillar of fire by night and your cloud by day as you thread the pathways of your lives. (*Ensign,* November 1997, 49)

David B. Haight:

> The only sure way to protect ourselves and our families from the onslaught of the teachings of the world is to commit to live the commandments of God, to attend our Church meetings where we can learn and be strengthened in our testimonies and partake of the sacrament to renew our covenants, to prepare ourselves to worthily enter the temple where we may find a refuge from the world and a place of renewal of our capacity to cope with the evils of the world. (*Ensign,* November 1992, 74)

David B. Haight:

> The moment we step into the house of the Lord, the atmosphere changes from the worldly to the heavenly, where respite from the normal activities of life is found, and where peace of mind and spirit is received. It is a refuge from the ills of life and a protection from the temptations that are contrary to our spiritual well-being. We are told that "he who doeth the works of righteousness shall receive his reward, even

peace in this world, and eternal life in the world to come" (D&C 59:23). (*Ensign*, November 1990, 59)

ILLUSTRATIONS FOR OUR TIMES

The Power of God

We would do well to ponder and memorialize those days in our own lives in which we have witnessed the manifestation of God's power. Isaiah stated: "He giveth power to the faint; and to them that have no might he increaseth strength" (Isa. 40:29). Monday, July 22, 1839, was such a day in the lives of the Saints who had fled to the future site of Nauvoo to start once again the process of establishing a beachhead for the gospel and working toward building the kingdom of God. This day was termed by Wilford Woodruff "a day of God's power" (*Church History in the Fulness of Times* [Salt Lake City: The Church of Jesus Christ of Latter-day Saints, 1993], 218). The Saints had responded to Joseph Smith's call to settle in the new gathering place of Nauvoo on the banks of the Mississippi River. Thousands were arriving there, unaware of the dangers posed by the malaria-bearing mosquitoes that flourished in the as-yet-undrained swamplands nearby. That summer, hundreds contracted the disease, including the Prophet, who took many into his own house so that he and Emma could nurse them. Many of the victims at the settlement and in nearby Quincy lay dying. On July 22, the Prophet, moved by the Spirit, rose up from his sickbed and went out to begin administering to the ill in Nauvoo and in Montrose, Iowa, across the river, healing many in a marvelous manifestation of the power of God (see *HC*, 4:3–5). Wilford Woodruff characterized this extraordinary event as the "greatest day for the manifestation of the power of God through the gift of healing since the organization of the Church" (*Leaves from My Journal*, 65, cited in *Church History in the Fulness of Times* [Salt Lake City: The Church of Jesus Christ of Latter-day Saints, 1993], 219).

In one especially poignant incident, a nonmember traveler from the West who had witnessed the miraculous events of the day beckoned the Prophet to come and heal his stricken three-month-old twins. The Prophet was unable to go back the two miles to the bedside of the children, so he took from his pocket a silk bandanna handkerchief and gave it to Wilford Woodruff with the instructions to take it and wipe the faces of the children, promising that they would be healed: "As long as you keep that handkerchief it shall remain a league between you and me" (*HC*, 4:5). Elder Woodruff obeyed, and the twins were healed. Such were the manifestations of divine intervention on behalf of the beleaguered Saints in Nauvoo and vicinity. Such will be His blessings of comfort and refuge to all of us when we invoke His aid on behalf of our families as we strive to keep His commandments and do our part in building up His kingdom. (Allen)

LIKENING THE SCRIPTURES TO OUR LIVES

Doctrine and Covenants 124:53–55 The Lord promises to save those who were slain in Missouri and commands the Saints to build a temple.

Application: It is comforting to see that in their tribulation, the Lord had compassion on the Saints. He delivered them from the evils of the Missouri mob to a place where they would be free of persecution—for a time, at least. Notice that He didn't deliver them from *all* trial and opposition at this time; they still had to work hard to build up Nauvoo and establish the temple. Their real comfort and refuge was in God, but they weren't through with their work. Likewise, we can find solace in our relationship with God, but we can't stop there.

2. MISSIONARY WORK AS A CENTRAL FOCUS IN BUILDING UP THE KINGDOM OF GOD

THEME: Under the Abrahamic covenant, the priesthood has the privilege and honor of carrying the gospel of Jesus Christ to all the world (see Abr. 2:9–10). No distraction can interfere with this holy calling; no tribulation can excuse a delay in publishing peace to the world and gathering in the honest at heart; no challenge or hardship can prevent the Saints from pursuing their commission to bear witness to the restored gospel in all the world. The unspeakable trials of the Missouri period and the awesome and daunting tasks of building up a new city unto God on the banks of the Mississippi short-circuited the operation of the worldwide missionary effort not a whit. It is a testimony to the faith and fiber of the early Saints that they were able to achieve such a magnificent harvest of missionary success despite the adversity and tribulations of those years.

MODERN PROPHETS SPEAK

Spencer W. Kimball:

> Our great need, and our great calling, is to bring to the people of this world the candle of understanding to light their way out of obscurity and darkness and into the joy, peace, and truths of the gospel.

> I believe we must not weary in our well-doing. I believe it is time again to ask ourselves the question, what can I do to help take the gospel to others and to the inhabitants of this world? (*Ensign,* February 1983, 3)

Wilford Woodruff:

> There never was a set of men since God made the world under a stronger responsibility to warn this generation, to lift up our voices long and loud, day and night as far as we have the opportunity and declare the words of God unto this generation. We are required to do this. This is our calling. [This] is our duty. [This] is our business. (*Deseret News Semi-Weekly,* July 6, 1880, 1)

ILLUSTRATIONS FOR OUR TIMES

"Hurrah, Hurrah for Israel!"

> There was one episode depicted on the records that would nearly bring tears to my eyes as my companion and I would listen to it over and over again. It was the account of Brigham Young and Heber C. Kimball leaving their wives, children, and humble homes to journey to Great Britain in response to their mission calls to that faraway land. Heber C. Kimball records the event in these words:

"September 14th, . . . President Brigham Young left his home at Montrose to start on the mission to England. He was so sick that he was unable to go to the Mississippi, a distance of thirty rods, without assistance. After he had crossed the river he rode behind Israel Barlow on his horse to my house, where he continued sick until the 18th. He left his wife sick with a babe only three weeks old, and all of his other children were sick and unable to wait upon each other. Not one soul of them was able to go to the well for a pail of water, and they were without a second suit to their backs, for the mob in Missouri had taken nearly all he had. On the 17th, Sister Mary Ann Young got a boy to carry her up in his wagon to my house, that she might nurse and comfort Brother Brigham to the hour of starting.

"September 18th, Charles Hubbard sent his boy with a wagon and span of horses to my house; our trunks were put into the wagon by some brethren; I went to my bed and shook hands with my wife who was then shaking with a chill, having two children lying sick by her side; I embraced her and my children, and bade them farewell. My only well child was little Heber P., and it was with difficulty he could carry a couple of quarts of water at a time to assist in quenching their thirst.

"It was with difficulty we got into the wagon, and started down the hill about ten rods; it appeared to me as though my very inmost parts would melt within me at leaving my family in such a condition, as it were almost in the arms of death. I felt as though I could not endure it. I asked the teamster to stop, and said to Brother Brigham, 'This is pretty tough, isn't it; let's rise up and give them a cheer.' We arose, and swinging our hats three times over our heads, shouted: 'Hurrah, hurrah for Israel.' Vilate, hearing the noise, arose from her bed and came to the door. She had a smile on her face. Vilate and Mary Ann Young cried out to us: 'Goodbye, God bless you!' We returned the compliment, and then told the driver to go ahead. After this I felt a spirit of joy and gratitude, having had the satisfaction of seeing my wife standing upon her feet, instead of leaving her in bed, knowing well that I should not see them again for two or three years" (quoted in Orson F. Whitney, *Life of Heber C. Kimball, an Apostle,* 3rd ed. [Salt Lake City: Bookcraft, 1967], 265–66).

I have often wondered how these brethren, as valiant as they were, could do what they did. Truly they were willing to make any sacrifice asked of them to build the kingdom of God. They were laying up "treasures in heaven, where neither moth nor rust doth corrupt" (Matt. 6:20).

There is something else about this story, however, that has always intrigued me. As Brigham Young and Heber C. Kimball left on their missions to Great Britain, there appeared to be a lot of support from their brethren to help them on their way. Israel Barlow assisted Brigham Young across the Mississippi River. Later, Charles Hubbard sent his son with a wagon to the Kimball home to assist the two missionaries as they began their long journey.

If we look carefully at this story, we catch a glimpse of the unity that must have existed among the Saints in those early days. As husbands and fathers would leave for missionary service, their departure was made easier because they knew that brothers, sisters, priesthood leaders, and friends would step in to help fill the void created by their absence.

These brethren were able to invest in building the kingdom of God in faraway lands because they knew that others would be investing in building the kingdom at home by helping their loved ones whenever assistance was needed. There was a unique bonding, a special faith in the community of Saints, dedicated to a common goal, a common purpose. If we return to Jacob's counsel to his people, we see the same message communicated as he instructed them to be familiar with all and to share freely of their substance (see Jacob 2:17).

What this testifies to me is that we can tell whether or not we put the kingdom of God first by looking at how we treat our brothers and sisters in the Church. Is there a special bond uniting us? Is there an absence of envy and backbiting? Do we rejoice in the success of a brother or sister as much as in our own? Do we share our substance so that all may be rich like unto us? Ultimately, are we our brothers' and sisters' keepers?

As I travel throughout the Church I marvel at all the positive things that are occurring. Yet I never feel that we, as a people, are living up to our real potential. My sense is that we do not always work together, that we are still too much interested in aspirations for personal honors and success, and show too little interest in the common goal of building the kingdom of God. (L. Tom Perry, *Ensign,* May 1987, 33)

LIKENING THE SCRIPTURES TO OUR LIVES

Doctrine and Covenants 6:6 "Now, as you have asked, behold, I say unto you, keep my commandments, and seek to bring forth and establish the cause of Zion."

Doctrine and Covenants 105:32 "That the kingdoms of this world may be constrained to acknowledge that the kingdom of Zion is in very deed the kingdom of our God and his Christ; therefore, let us become subject unto her laws."

Application: The Lord explains here how vast and strong Zion would become. This must have seemed incredible to the Saints, following all this time of persecution and obscurity. Nevertheless, they heeded this command to build up Zion. We live in a time when the Church is ever expanding. We also have a part in this call to teach the world the gospel. Incredible as it may seem, we can witness and participate in this spread of the kingdom.

3. THE CONSEQUENCE OF FAILING TO ENDURE TO THE END

THEME: The Lord extends great promises to His aspiring servants. Section 124 of the Doctrine and Covenants outlines many of such promises bestowed on various of the early leaders in the priesthood. In some cases, as with John C. Bennett, Lyman Wight, William Law, and Sidney Rigdon, righteousness and enduring faith did not prevail, and these brethren fell short of their potential and became examples of unsteadiness and rebellion. From them, as well as from their valiant peers, we can learn powerful lessons that the Lord's word will be fulfilled—to our eternal glory and edification, or to our eternal sorrow and remorse, based on our own choices and agency.

MODERN PROPHETS SPEAK

Ezra Taft Benson:

Concerning those who will receive the terrestrial, or lesser, kingdom, the Lord said, "These are they who are *not* valiant in the testimony of Jesus; wherefore, they obtain not the crown over the kingdom of our God" (D&C 76:79; italics added). Not to be valiant in one's testimony is a tragedy of eternal consequence. These are members who know this latter-day work is true, but who fail to endure to the end. Some may even hold temple recommends, but do not magnify their callings in the Church. Without valor, they do not take an affirmative stand *for* the kingdom of God. Some seek the praise, adulation, and honors of men; others attempt to conceal their sins; and a few criticize those who preside over them. (*Ensign,* May 1982, 62)

Robert D. Hales:

We are told in the scriptures that it is essential to endure to the end: "Wherefore, if ye shall be obedient to the commandments, and endure to the end, ye shall be saved at the last day. And thus it is" (1 Ne. 22:31). "Be patient in afflictions, for thou shalt have many; but endure them, for, lo, I am with thee, even unto the end of thy days" (D&C 24:8). "Behold, we count them happy which endure" (James 5:11). (*Ensign,* May 1998, 75)

ILLUSTRATIONS FOR OUR TIMES

Courage on Calvary

Examples of faithfully enduring to the end are taught by prophets of all ages as they demonstrate courage while enduring trials and tribulations to carry forth the will of God. Our greatest example comes from the life of our Savior and Redeemer, Jesus Christ. When suffering upon the cross at Calvary, Jesus felt the loneliness of agency when He pled to His Father in Heaven, "Why hast thou forsaken me?" (Matt. 27:46). The Savior of the world was left alone by His Father to experience, of His own free will and choice, an act of agency which allowed Him to complete His mission of the Atonement.

Jesus knew who He was—the Son of God. He knew His purpose—to carry out the will of the Father through the Atonement. His vision was eternal—"to bring to pass the immortality and eternal life of man" (Moses 1:39).

The Lord could have called on legions of angels to take Him down from the cross, but He faithfully endured to the end and completed the very purpose for which He had been sent to earth, thus granting eternal blessings to all who will ever experience mortality.

It is touching to me that when the Father introduced His Son to prophets in dispensations since, He would say, "This is my beloved Son, in whom I am well pleased" (2 Pet. 1:17), or "Behold my Beloved Son, . . . in whom I have glorified my name" (3 Ne. 11:7).

In our dispensation, the Prophet Joseph Smith endured all manner of opposition and hardship to bring to pass the desire of our Heavenly Father—the restoration of The Church of Jesus Christ of Latter-day Saints. Joseph was harassed and hunted by angry mobs. He patiently endured poverty, humiliating charges, and unkind acts. His people were forcibly driven from town to town, from state to state. He was tarred and feathered. He was falsely charged and jailed.

Imprisoned at Liberty, Missouri, and experiencing deep, emotional temporal feelings that his own hardships and the tests and trials of the Saints would never cease, Joseph prayed: "O God, where art thou? . . . Yea, O Lord, how long shall they suffer these wrongs and unlawful oppressions, before thine heart shall be softened toward them, and . . . be moved with compassion toward them?" (D&C 121:1, 3).

Joseph was told, "My son, peace be unto thy soul; thine adversity and thine afflictions shall be but a small moment" (D&C 121:7). Joseph knew that if he were to stop going forward with this great work, his earthly trials would probably ease. But he could not stop, because he knew who he was, he knew for what purpose he was placed on the earth, and he had the desire to do God's will. (Robert D. Hales, *Ensign,* May 1998, 75)

LIKENING THE SCRIPTURES TO OUR LIVES

2 Nephi 31:20 Nephi taught that we must "press forward with a steadfastness in Christ, having a perfect brightness of hope, and a love of God and of all men." Our Father in Heaven has promised that if we will do so, He will bless us with eternal life.

Application: Just entering into gospel covenants is not enough, as is evidenced by many of the brethren listed in this section. They were faithful, to a point. Past diligence and even prominence in the Church cannot save us. It is the work we do now that brings salvation—now and to the end. To endure to the end, we should press forward in Christ with hope and love, feasting upon the word of God. This will give us power to endure, and to endure well. We will seek the cause of Zion, publish peace, and be lifted up at the last day (see 1 Ne. 13:37).

4. THE RELIEF SOCIETY ORGANIZED: "CHARITY NEVER FAILETH"

THEME: On Thursday, March 17, 1842, the Female Relief Society of Nauvoo was founded under the direction of Joseph Smith. Emma Smith was elected president, with Elizabeth Ann Whitney and Sarah M. Cleveland as counselors. The organization had its beginnings in projects for sewing shirts for the men working on the Nauvoo Temple. The Prophet wrote in his journal concerning this inaugural event: "I gave much instruction, read in the New Testament, and book of Doctrine and Covenants, concerning the Elect Lady [Emma], and showed that the elect meant to be elected to a certain work, etc., and that the revelation was then fulfilled by Sister Emma's election to the Presidency of the Society, she having previously been ordained to expound the scriptures" (*HC,* 4:552–53). On March 24, one week later, he wrote:

> I attended by request, the Female Relief Society, whose object is the relief of the poor, the destitute, the widow and the orphan, and for the exercise of all benevolent purposes. Its organization was completed this day. Mrs. Emma Smith takes the presidential chair; Mrs. Elizabeth Ann Whitney and Sarah M. Cleveland are her counselors; Mrs. Elvira Cole is treasurer, and our well-known and talented poetess, Miss Eliza R. Snow, secretary. There was a very numerous attendance at the organization of the society, and also at the subsequent meetings, of some of our most intelligent, humane, philanthropic and respectable ladies; and we are well assured from a knowledge of those pure principles of benevolence that flow spontaneously from their humane and philanthropic bosoms, that with the resources they will have at command, they will fly to the relief of the stranger; they will pour in oil and wine to the wounded heart of the distressed; they will dry up the tears of the orphan and make the widow's heart to rejoice. (*HC,* 4:567)

The Relief Society grew to around thirteen hundred members by the time the Prophet was martyred on June 27, 1844, and has since become the largest women's organization in the world. Alma taught: "And now, he imparteth his word by angels unto men, yea, not only men but women also. Now this is not all: little children do have words given unto them many times, which confound the wise and the learned" (Alma 32:23). Let us all—men, women, and even children—seek earnestly to serve the Lord through inspiration and devotion in all of our callings.

MODERN PROPHETS SPEAK

James E. Faust:
> I revere the influence and accomplishments of Relief Society. It is the greatest women's organization in the world. You are especially privileged to belong to this wonderful organization. My life has been richly blessed because of Relief Society. My great-grandmother was a ward Relief Society president for 33 years. I have been married to both the stake and ward Relief Society president! Both the same woman! Our eldest daughter now serves as ward Relief Society president. One of our daughters-in-law is a stake

Relief Society president. As my dear Ruth faithfully attended Relief Society over the years, our home and family was blessed with more of spirituality and peace. Things seemed to go smoother because of the spiritual enrichment she received. I feel well schooled in the benefits of Relief Society. I learned long ago to sustain the priesthood and not get in the way of Relief Society. (*Ensign,* November 1996, 94)

ILLUSTRATIONS FOR OUR TIMES

The Prophet Joseph's Counsel to the Relief Society

[The Prophet said,] "You will receive instructions through the order of the Priesthood which God has established, through the medium of those appointed to lead, guide and direct the affairs of the Church in this last dispensation: and I now turn the key in your behalf in the name of the Lord, and this Society shall rejoice, and knowledge and intelligence shall flow down from this time henceforth; this is the beginning of better days to the poor and needy, who shall be made to rejoice and pour forth blessings on your heads.

"When you go home, never give a cross or unkind word to your husbands, but let kindness, charity and love crown your works henceforward; don't envy the finery and fleeting show of sinners, for they are in a miserable situation; but as far as you can, have mercy on them, for in a short time God will destroy them, if they will not repent and turn unto him.

"Let your labors be mostly confined to those around you, in the circle of your own acquaintance, as far as knowledge is concerned, it may extend to all the world; but your administering should be confined to the circle of your immediate acquaintance, and more especially to the members of the Relief Society. Those ordained to preside over and lead you, are authorized to appoint the different officers, as the circumstances shall require. . . ."

President Smith then gave instruction respecting the propriety of females administering to the sick by the prayer of faith, the laying on hands, or the anointing with oil; and said it was according to revelation that the sick should be nursed with herbs and mild food, and not by the hand of an enemy. Who are better qualified to administer than our faithful and zealous sisters, whose hearts are full of faith, tenderness, sympathy and compassion. No one. Said he was never placed in similar circumstances before, and never had given the same instruction; and closed his instructions by expressing his heart-felt satisfaction in improving this opportunity.

The Spirit of the Lord was poured out in a very powerful manner, never to be forgotten by those present on this interesting occasion. (*HC,* 4:607)

LIKENING THE SCRIPTURES TO OUR LIVES

Moroni 7:44–46 Moroni defines charity as the greatest of all godly attributes. Charity "suffereth long, and is kind, and envieth not, and is not puffed up, seeketh not her own, is not easily provoked, thinketh no evil, and rejoiceth not in iniquity but rejoiceth in the truth, beareth all things, believeth all things, hopeth all things, endureth all things." If we do not have charity, then we have nothing.

Application: The Relief Society has emphasized this great doctrine: "Charity Never Faileth." It has become their theme and motto for life. It is the foundation of their organization. To have charity is the ultimate quest in becoming like Christ (see Moro. 7:48), taking upon ourselves His divine nature (see 2 Pet. 1:3–12), serving in the kingdom (see D&C 4:6), and becoming even as He is (see 3 Ne. 27:27). Why does charity never fail? Because Christ never fails. We will be blessed by seeking this great attribute and gift in our lives—to be full of charity, the pure love of Christ.

SUMMARY

Heavenly Father and our Savior have provided every needful thing for the eternal salvation for all humankind—because They love us. We have been given prophets, seers, and revelators, a perfectly organized Church with the priesthood of God directing the work here upon the earth, continuous revelation for our edification, temples to receive the ordinances and covenants of eternal life, and all things necessary for our well-being here upon the earth. From Nauvoo to the Salt Lake Valley, and from there to countless places of light and refuge around the world, the work of the Lord moves forward to achieve its destiny of providing the ultimate blessings of immortality and eternal life to all who will accept the gospel of Jesus Christ and live its teachings in faithfulness unto the end.

CHAPTER THIRTY

"THE PRISONERS SHALL GO FREE"

Reading Assignment: Doctrine and Covenants 2; 124:25–55; 127; 128; Joseph Smith—History 1:36–39; *Our Heritage,* pages 58–61.

Additional Reading: 1 Corinthians 15:29; Doctrine and Covenants 138:28–35, 53–60.

We who live in this day are those whom God appointed before birth to be his representatives on earth in this dispensation. We are of the house of Israel. In our hands lie the sacred powers of being saviors on Mount Zion in the latter days.

With regard to temple and family history work, I have one overriding message: This work must hasten. The work waiting to be done is staggering and escapes human comprehension. Last year we performed proxy temple endowments for about five and a half million persons, but during that year about fifty million persons died. This might suggest futility in the work that lies before us, but we cannot think of futility. Surely the Lord will support us if we use our best efforts in carrying out the commandment to do family history research and temple work. The great work of the temples and all that supports it must expand. It is imperative! (Howard W. Hunter, Ensign, *March 1995, 64)*

THEMES *for* LIVING

1. "A Voice of Gladness": The Lord Reveals Temple Ordinances for the Dead
2. A Commission of Joy: To Build the House of the Lord
3. Saviors on Mount Zion: Vicarious Service for the Dead

INTRODUCTION

In the arid desert of worldly schemes for happiness and human-crafted philosophies of prideful and self-serving relativism, there suddenly appears, after millennia of darkness, the majestic glow of divine truth that illuminates the landscape of human possibilities. The dawning of the Restoration brings forth a rekindling of hope and faith that the Father's plan of salvation can indeed offer divine guidance to a spiritually deprived world—extending even beyond the veil to encompass, through atoning grace, all individuals who have ever lived on the earth. With the Restoration of the gospel of Jesus Christ, there is revealed anew the certainty of divine guidance as the anchor for spiritual progress through living prophets, including the coming forth of the plain and precious redeeming truths eclipsed by the threatening clouds of the great Apostasy. No wonder the Prophet Joseph Smith exclaimed, "Brethren, shall we not go on in so great a cause? Go forward and not backward. Courage, brethren; and on, on to the victory! Let your hearts rejoice, and be exceedingly glad. Let the earth break forth into singing. Let the dead speak forth anthems of eternal praise to the King Immanuel, who hath ordained, before the world was, that which would enable us to redeem them out of their prison; for the prisoners shall go free" (D&C 128:22).

MOMENT OF TRUTH

The extraordinary doctrine concerning vicarious work for the dead is referenced in several passages of the Doctrine and Covenants, including sections 2, 124, 127, 128, and 138. The background to section 124 was treated in chapter 29, and that of section 138 will be treated in chapter 39. Below are brief summaries of the other sections.

Section 2: An extract from the words of the angel Moroni, given on the evening of September 21, 1823, to the Prophet Joseph Smith at the home of Joseph Smith Sr. in Manchester, Ontario County, New York (see *HC,* 1:12). Moroni made three appearances to Joseph in the bedroom of the home during the period from evening until morning, instructing him that the Lord had a work for him to do in translating the ancient record comprising an account of the former inhabitants of America. Moroni quotes a number of scriptures, including the third and fourth chapters of Malachi, wherein is contained Malachi's prophecy of the hearts of the children turning to their fathers, or reference to the great temple work to be wrought in this dispensation.

Sections 127 and 128: Given through the Prophet Joseph Smith in the form of two epistles to the Saints at Nauvoo, dated September 1 and September 6, 1842, respectively, concerning baptism for the dead (see *HC,* 5:142–51). Historian Lyndon W. Cook summarizes the circumstances as follows:

> These two letters, written in the hand of William Clayton, were addressed to "all the Saints in Nauvoo" at a time when the Prophet was making few public appearances because of threats of unlawful arrest. Governor Carlin of Illinois, responding to a demand from the governor of Missouri, issued a warrant for Joseph Smith's arrest as an accessory before the fact in an assault with intent to kill Lilburn W. Boggs, ex-governor of Missouri. Having been arrested but temporarily released on 8 August 1842, the Prophet remained "in retirement" to avoid reapprehension. It was not until 5 January 1843 that Joseph Smith was formally discharged from this arrest.
>
> The letters concern themselves with salvation for the dead, a subject of much interest and discussion in 1842. Baptism for the dead was first publicly announced on 15 August 1840 at the funeral of Seymour Brunson. Immediately after the announcement of the new doctrine, Church members began performing proxy baptisms in the Mississippi River and in local streams. While those administering these vicarious ordinances in 1840 were not without authority, the actions were not recorded; consequently the baptisms were later repeated. On 3 October 1841 Joseph Smith declared, "There shall be no more baptisms for the dead, until the ordinances can be attended to in the Lord's House. . . . For thus saith the Lord." Baptisms for the dead in the Nauvoo Temple were first performed on Sunday, 21 November 1841. With few exceptions, endowments and sealings for the dead were first administered in the St. George, Utah, Temple.
>
> On 31 August 1842, while addressing members of the Female Relief Society in Nauvoo, Joseph Smith remarked that "a few things had been manifested to him . . . respecting the baptism for the dead." Although he desired to wait "until he had opportunity to discuss the subject to greater length," the Prophet emphasized that "all persons baptiz'd for the dead must have a Recorder present, that he may be an eye-witness to testify of it." Sections 127 and 128 both give special attention to the matter of having witnesses and recorders for the work of the dead. (*RPJS,* 284)

1. "A VOICE OF GLADNESS": THE LORD REVEALS TEMPLE ORDINANCES FOR THE DEAD

THEME: "How beautiful upon the mountains are the feet of those that bring glad tidings of good things, and that say unto Zion: Behold, thy God reigneth! As the dews of Carmel, so shall the knowledge of God descend upon them!" (D&C 128:19). Thus did the Prophet Joseph Smith express his joy at the unfolding of the principles and doctrines of mercy and grace underlying the work for the dead as it was to be carried out in the temples of the Most High. In a passage of sublime poetic sweep, he continued:

> Let the mountains shout for joy, and all ye valleys cry aloud; and all ye seas and dry lands tell the wonders of your Eternal King! And ye rivers, and brooks, and rills, flow down with gladness. Let the woods and all the trees of the field praise the Lord; and ye solid rocks weep for joy! And let the sun, moon, and the morning stars sing together, and let all the sons of God shout for joy! And let the eternal creations declare his name forever and ever! And again I say, how glorious is the voice we hear from heaven, proclaiming in our ears, glory, and salvation, and honor, and immortality, and eternal life; kingdoms, principalities, and powers! (D&C 128:23)

This is the attitude we ought to have about performing temple work. Among all the doctrines and practices that distinguish the Church of Jesus Christ of Latter-day Saints and set it apart from all other churches of the world, the vast, encompassing work of the temples of God is perhaps the most unique and compelling. Temple work is the glorious evidence that God has extended to every individual who has ever lived upon the earth, and who will ever be born into this mortal experience, the blessings and opportunities of salvation, immortality, and eternal life.

MODERN PROPHETS SPEAK

Joseph Fielding Smith:
> Malachi declared that if the authority held by Elijah was not restored "the whole earth" would be "smitten with a curse." When the great and dreadful day of the Lord comes, if there had not been restored the sealing power by which the ordinances in the House of the Lord could be performed for both the living and the dead, then the work of the Lord in relation to the salvation of man would fail. The great and dreadful day of the Lord is the day when judgments are poured out upon the wicked and the earth is cleansed of its iniquity. It is not to be a dreadful day to the righteous, but it certainly will be to all that do wickedly, for they will be as stubble and will be burned when the Lord comes in his glory, and they shall be left with

"neither root nor branch" (Malachi 4:1). This sealing power, by which family ties are made secure and by which baptism for the dead becomes effective, is absolutely essential and must be exercised, for all those who died without the knowledge of the Gospel and who would have received it if it had been offered them while they were living on the earth before the end of the earth can come. If these keys were not here, then the dreadful day when Christ shall come would be a day of utter confusion, but the Lord, who knows the end from the beginning, revealed this Priesthood so that all who will, whether living or dead, may escape through the ordinances of the Gospel. (*CHMR,* 3:82)

Bruce R. McConkie:

These sealing keys and powers have been exercised by righteous men in all dispensations from Adam to the present time. They "belong always unto the Presidency of the High Priesthood" (D&C 81:2). Indeed, there can be no true Church and kingdom of God on earth unless the keys of the kingdom are held and exercised by its presiding officers. Where the keys of the kingdom are found, there is the true Church; if these keys are not found, there is no divine Church among men. (*Doctrinal New Testament Commentary,* 3 vols. [Salt Lake City: Bookcraft, 1965–73], 1:425)

LIKENING THE SCRIPTURES TO OUR LIVES

Doctrine and Covenants 128:24 We can offer the Lord a worthy offering in righteousness if we will be diligent in preparing a record of all our kindred dead and complete their work in the holy temples.

Application: We were preserved to come forth in these days to build temples, seek after our dead (see D&C 2; 138:53–54), and perform their temple work that they too might partake of the blessings of our Heavenly Father. The record of these life-saving ordinances will be presented to the Lord.

2. A COMMISSION OF JOY: TO BUILD THE HOUSE OF THE LORD

THEME: With the order to build the Nauvoo Temple (see D&C 124:31), the Saints were commissioned to renew the program, begun in Kirtland, to prepare themselves and their dead to receive the endowment of truth and glory attached to the "ordinance of my holy house, which my people are always commanded to build unto my holy name" (D&C 124:39).

MODERN PROPHETS SPEAK

Gordon B. Hinckley:

> No person has all of the gospel until he is able to receive [the ordinances of the temple]. And the responsibility rests with us to see that the facilities are available. I do not know how much longer I am good for, but I hope to end out my days building temples of the Lord, taking the temples to the people so that they can have the marvelous blessings that are to be obtained here. (*TGBH,* 641)

Howard W. Hunter:

> The building of temples has deep significance for ourselves and mankind, and our responsibilities become clear. We must accomplish the priesthood temple ordinance work necessary for our own exaltation; then we must do the necessary work for those who did not have the opportunity to accept the gospel in life. (*THWH,* 230)

ILLUSTRATIONS FOR OUR TIMES

Fragments of Experience

> If a record had been kept of all the facts connected with the building of the Kirtland and Nauvoo Temples, it would tell a curious story of poverty, self-denial, dependence upon God and wants providentially supplied.
>
> No doubt such a record has been kept, but not here on earth. We have not access to it. But many, very many of those who had the privilege of aiding in the work of building those temples have gone to meet that record. Some doubtless will meet it with satisfaction, with joy untold; others with remorse and self-reproach.
>
> Could the Saints of the present day peruse that record, it would put many of them to the blush to think they had done so little in aid of such works. They would see that, though they have enjoyed peace and plenty, they have done almost nothing towards the temples in our day, compared with what the poor Saints did in building those earlier houses of God. . . .
>
> The case of one of those workmen will serve to illustrate the self-sacrificing disposition manifested by many of those who labored upon that building, as well as the way their simple wants were sometimes supplied by the Almighty.
>
> Brother L— arrived in Nauvoo from England, his native country, in March, 1844. He was an excellent mechanic, had held good situations and been in good circum-

stances in the "old country," and his skill as a workman was such as to command ready employment and high wages in any of the large cities of America, had such been his object.

But he had embraced the gospel and received a testimony of its truth, and afterwards the spirit of gathering with the Saints, which enabled him to brook the taunts and ridicule heaped upon him by friends and relatives for his unpopular faith, and resist the pleading of aged parents, who were loath to part with him.

His faith and zeal were such that he had left friends and property and all that he had formerly held dear, and come to America that he might be with the chosen people of God and assist in building up Zion.

He was ambitious to labor upon the temple, and applied for work immediately upon his arrival in Nauvoo. When informed that there was plenty of work but nothing to pay with, he replied that pay was no consideration.

He took hold with a determination, and worked with all the energy with which the young, strong and enthusiastic nature was capable from that time until the work upon the temple ceased, upwards of two years, and during that time only received in cash for his services the small amount of fifty cents.

Many a time he felt the pangs of hunger, and went to his work fasting rather than join with his family in eating the last ration of food in their possession, but the Lord sustained him by His Spirit, gave him joy in his labors and provided a way for more food to be obtained to sustain the lives of himself and family. (*Fragments of Experience* [Salt Lake City: Juvenile Instructor Office, 1882], 84)

LIKENING THE SCRIPTURES TO OUR LIVES

Doctrine and Covenants 124:55 The Lord commands the early Saints to construct a temple to His name as a demonstration of their faithfulness to Him. He promises to bless the Saints with honor, immortality, and eternal life for obedience to this commandment.

Application: The covenants and ordinances of the temple are required for us to attain the highest degree of glory. But in addition to the covenants made therein, temples are manifestations of faith. Whether in terms of money, labor, or time, the sacrifice of Saints in building up the kingdom through temple work will stand as a testament of how willing and obedient they were. The purpose of temples is for the immortality and eternal life of Heavenly Father's children. We should seek to be worthy of and participate in this glorious work.

3. SAVIORS ON MOUNT ZION: VICARIOUS SERVICE FOR THE DEAD

THEME: Temple work affords the faithful and devoted Saints of God the supreme opportunity to partake of redeeming, saving love in doing for their progenitors what they could not do for themselves. In this way, those who come to the temples of the Most High with the records of their dead to participate in vicarious ordinances are a fulfillment of the view of the ancient prophet Obadiah, who declared, in relationship to the unfolding work of the Lord: "And saviours shall come up on mount Zion" (Obad. 1:21; see also D&C 103:9).

MODERN PROPHETS SPEAK

Joseph Smith:
> The doctrine of baptism for the dead is clearly shown in the New Testament; and if the doctrine is not good, then throw the New Testament away; but if it is the word of God, then let the doctrine be acknowledged; and it was the reason why Jesus said unto the Jews, "How oft would I have gathered thy children together, even as a hen gathereth her chickens under her wings, and ye would not!" (see Matt. 23:37)— That they might attend to the ordinances of baptism for the dead as well as other ordinances of the priesthood, and receive revelations from heaven, and be perfected in the things of the kingdom of God—but they would not. This was the case on the day of Pentecost: those blessings were poured out on the disciples on that occasion. God ordained that he would save the dead and would do it by gathering his people together. (*HC,* 5:425)

Orson Pratt:
> We are willing to go the earth over to save the living; we are willing to build temples and administer in ordinances to save the dead; we are willing to enter the eternal worlds and preach to every creature who has not placed himself beyond the reach of mercy. We are willing to labour both in this world and in the next to save men.
>
> Let all rejoice that the great day of the dispensation of the fulness of times has come. Let the living rejoice; let the dead rejoice; let the heavens and the earth rejoice; let all creations shout hosannah! glory to God in the highest! for he hath brought salvation,

and glory, and honour, and immortality, and eternal life to the fallen sons of men. Amen. (*JD*, 7:90–91)

Wilford Woodruff:

We must go forward, not backward. I bear testimony to you, my brethren and sisters, the whole spirit world is watching your labor and your works, and as I said in the beginning, if the veil was taken from off our eyes, we would see the responsibility of our acts, and what would be the result of these things? We would labor diligently and do all we could for the rearing of these temples for the redemption of our dead; we would sanctify ourselves and keep the Word of Wisdom, and unite ourselves together according to the Law of God. There are many things we do as Latter-day Saints that we should abstain from; we should see the importance of our laboring in the flesh to build up the Zion of God. (CR, April 1880, 11)

ILLUSTRATIONS FOR OUR TIMES

Don't Forget Them

I have come to know firsthand that a very powerful and abiding spirit broods over the work of searching through the records for the names and life stories of our kindred dead. For several years a major portion of my prayers and efforts was devoted to the temple and genealogical work of the Church.

There is something about it that we can feel but that we cannot explain—a very moving spirit, urging us ahead, as though some were pleading with us not to lose them and not to forget them.

A few years ago a mother told me her life story. She had been abandoned by her husband and left to raise a little boy. When he was nine years old he contracted a fatal disease. He came to know somehow, in his little boy mind, that he would not live. And for the last two or three weeks of his life he would cling to his mother and say, "Mama, you won't forget me, will you? Mama, please don't forget me. Mama, I won't be forgotten, will I?"

I was deeply moved, for I sensed that in the pleading of this little boy something of the feelings of every one of us is exposed, hoping that somehow we will at least be remembered, hoping that there will be something about us worth remembering. Our forebears surely felt that too. (Boyd K. Packer, *Memorable Stories with a Message* [Salt Lake City: Deseret Book, 2000], 5–6)

"Saviors on Mount Zion"

If any professing Christian objects to the idea of salvation by proxy, the all-important fact that the entire plan of salvation hinges on that principle should be sufficient to sweep away the objection entirely and forever. "The wages of sin is death." "All have sinned and come short of the glory of God." Jesus of Nazareth died instead of sinners. The just was offered for the unjust. The innocent Christ was a substitute for guilty men. The whole doctrine of the atonement rests upon the principle of salvation by proxy. Jesus is called the Captain of our salvation. He is the head of the host of the army of saviors. It was predicted by Obadiah the prophet that, "Saviors shall come up on Mount Zion" in the last days, and "the kingdom shall be the Lord's" (verse 21). And the inspired writer of the epistle to the Hebrews, speaking of those worthies who through faith performed great wonders and prevailed and obtained a witness from God in olden times, declared: "These all having obtained a good report through faith, received not the promise: God having provided some better thing for us, that they without us should not be made perfect" (Heb. 11:39, 40). Thus the work of human redemption is to be carried on until all the people of the earth shall be judged according to the gospel, every soul having had an opportunity of receiving or rejecting it, either in the body or in the spirit state, and of obeying the ordinances thereof, either in person or vicariously, the living acting for the dead. . . .

At the first glance, this doctrine may strike the modern Christian mind as new and dangerous, but the more it is investigated in all its bearings, the clearer its truth is made apparent, and the more glorious it becomes. The thought that those who receive and obey the gospel of Christ in its fulness while in the flesh, can aid in the work of redemption for their ancestors who are in the spirit world, is most delightful to the reverent soul.

It shows the value of those genealogies which Israel, the covenant people of God, were moved upon in olden times to preserve. It stimulates the faithful in Christ to good works that they may become "saviors on Mount Zion." It explains how the nations composed of millions upon millions of souls that never heard the gospel or the name of Christ Jesus, may ultimately be redeemed and made heirs of salvation. It points out the way by which Christ shall eventually obtain the victory over Satan and prove himself "a ransom for all," presenting his perfect work to the Father, not one soul having been lost but the sons of perdition, who sinned unto death and could not be forgiven in this world or in the world to come. (Charles W. Penrose, *Rays of Living Light* [Salt Lake City: Deseret News Press, 1954], 166–67)

LIKENING THE SCRIPTURES TO OUR LIVES

Doctrine and Covenants 128:15 The salvation of our kindred dead is necessary for our salvation. Paul said "that they without us cannot be made perfect—neither can we without our dead be made perfect."

Application: The work for the dead is of a vicarious nature; it is something that they cannot do for themselves. We become saviors on Mount Zion. A savior is not only one who sacrifices, but who sacrifices in doing something for others that they could not do for themselves. As with service of the highest order, it is always of a vicarious nature, just like our beloved Savior's atoning sacrifice for us. Our exaltation and theirs depends upon our willingness to serve.

ENRICHMENT

Baptism for the Dead

Among the thousands of verses of scripture in the standard works of the Church, few are more important to Latter-day Saints than those found in three sections of the Doctrine and Covenants and in a single verse of Paul's writings (D&C 124:28–42; 127:6; 128:11–18; 1 Cor. 15:29). Each of these deals with the topic of baptism for the dead and, by extension, all vicarious ordinance work for our deceased ancestors.

Inasmuch as baptism is a requirement for salvation in the celestial kingdom (D&C 112:28–29; 3 Ne. 11:33; John 3:5), and because there are billions who have passed from this earth without that saving ordinance, God has set in place the means whereby the living may perform this ordinance in behalf of the dead. It is a labor of love performed within the house of Him who authorizes such saving service.

To the question as to whether we intend to perform this labor of love for *all* who have ever lived, the simple answer is "Yes!" "Why, that is impossible," say some. Elder Boyd K. Packer has responded, "Perhaps, but we shall do it anyway." Further: "And once again we certify that we are not discouraged. We ask no relief of the assignment, no excuse from fulfilling it."

He declared: "I say that no point of doctrine sets this church apart from the other claimants as this one does. Save for it, we would, with all of the others, have to accept the clarity with which the New Testament declares baptism to be essential and then admit that most of the human family could never have it.

"But we have the revelations. We have those sacred ordinances" (*Ensign*, November 1975, 99).

It is significant that two revelations were canonized at the April 1976 general conference of the Church. Both dealt with the principle of redemption for the dead (*Ensign*, May 1976, 19, 127–29; D&C 137, 138). The further hastening of this work was emphasized in a revelation received in June 1978, wherein "every faithful, worthy man in the Church" was authorized to receive the priesthood (D&C OD 2). Not only did this affect the living, but it also had great impact on the millions in the spirit world who had been awaiting the full blessings of the priesthood, including those of the temple. This revelation opened the way to doing the redemptive work for every man, woman, and child who had arrived at the age of accountability but died before receiving the saving ordinances of the gospel.

The significance of this work was stressed by one of the Lord's prophets, President Joseph Fielding Smith: "It matters not what else we have been called to do, or what position we may occupy, or how faithfully in other ways we have labored in the Church, none is exempt from this great obligation. It is required of the apostle as well as the humble elder. . . .

"Some may feel that if they pay their tithing, attend their regular meetings and other duties, give of their substance to the poor, perchance spend one, two, or more years preaching in the world, that they are absolved from further duty. But the greatest and grandest duty of all is to labor for the dead." (DS 2:148–49). (*DCE*, 36)

SUMMARY

"A voice of gladness!" (D&C 128:19) is how the Prophet Joseph Smith characterized the manifestation of truth concerning temple ordinances that was bestowed by the Almighty on His latter-day servants. The commission to go forward with the building of the Nauvoo Temple—just as with any subsequent temple in our day—was a joyful assignment from the Lord, allowing His Saints to serve as "saviors on Mount Zion" to provide the vicarious service of salvation for their kindred dead.

The restoration of the power of the priesthood to exercise all of the keys of the kingdom brought about vicarious work for the dead. Surely our Heavenly Father and our beloved Savior love all of Their children. Temple work manifests this great love as we seek out our dead and do work on their behalf. Because of the grace and mercy of the Lord, He has provided a way whereby all the faithful can have immortality and eternal lives as they make and keep sacred covenants. The temple is the crowning experience of spirituality and the place where all the blessings of the Lord regarding exaltation can be received. Let us live worthy of this consummate blessing from the Lord.

CHAPTER THIRTY-ONE

"SEALED . . . *for* TIME *and for* ALL ETERNITY"

Reading Assignment: Doctrine and Covenants 131:1–4; 132:4–33.

Additional Reading: Genesis 2:18, 24; 1 Corinthians 11:11; Alma 37:35.

If you want salvation in the fullest, that is exaltation in the kingdom of God, so that you may become his sons and his daughters, you have got to go into the temple of the Lord and receive these holy ordinances which belong to that house, which cannot be had elsewhere. No man shall receive the fulness of eternity, of exaltation, alone; no woman shall receive that blessing alone; but man and wife, when they receive the sealing power in the temple of the Lord, if they thereafter keep all the commandments, shall pass on to exaltation, and shall continue and become like the Lord. And that is the destiny of men; that is what the Lord desires for his children. (Joseph Fielding Smith, DS, 2:44)

THEMES *for* LIVING

1. Marriage for Time and All Eternity Is Necessary
to Enter the Highest Degree of Glory
2. Prepare Early to Be Married in the Temple
3. Keep the Covenants of Holy Matrimony to Receive the Promised Blessings

INTRODUCTION

From the earliest passages of scripture, we learn sacred verities concerning the ordained marriage relationship: "And the Lord God said, It is not good that the man should be alone; I will make him an help meet for him. . . . Therefore shall a man leave his father and his mother, and shall cleave unto his wife: and they shall be one flesh" (Gen. 2:18, 24). The kingdom of God, at its fundamental level, is made up of families. Celestial marriage, through the priesthood, is the divinely commissioned structure of family governance and perpetuity, so ordained of God in order to maximize the opportunities for eternal blessings to be poured out upon His children at the highest level possible in this life and in the life to come. Celestial marriage is the key to eternal lives. It is divine marriage, endless marriage, eternal marriage. Without this new and everlasting covenant of celestial marriage, individuals cannot enter into the highest degree of glory and perfection promised of God to His chosen faithful. But through the blessings of this new and everlasting covenant, marriage partners, through a process of perfection, can rise in majesty, sealed unto this relationship by the powers of the priesthood, to attain a continuity of lives and be gods in the heavenly realm. What a glorious and transcendent vista this affords to the Saints laboring in this mortal realm to overcome the challenges of life and receive the higher portion at the Lord's hands. The Restoration of the gospel of Jesus Christ has brought to humankind once again the opportunity to enjoy this most sacred and holy of blessings, even the blessing of eternal marriage.

MOMENT OF TRUTH

Section 131: Instructions given by the Prophet Joseph Smith at Ramus, Hancock County, Illinois, east of Nauvoo, on May 16 and 17, 1832 (see *HC,* 5:392–93). From the Prophet's journal we glean the following details of his visit to Ramus:

> *Tuesday, 16.*—At eleven o'clock, with George Miller, William Clayton, Eliza and Lydia Partridge and J. M. Smith, I started for Carthage where we tarried about half-an-hour conversing with different individuals, when we started for Ramus; arrived about half-past three, p.m., and stayed at William G. Perkins for the evening; then went to Benjamin F. Johnson's with William Clayton to sleep. Before retiring, I gave Brother and Sister Johnson some instructions on the priesthood; and putting my hand on the knee of William Clayton, I said: . . .
>
> Your life is hid with Christ in God, and so are many others. Nothing but the unpardonable sin can prevent you from inheriting eternal life for you are sealed up by the

power of the Priesthood unto eternal life, having taken the step necessary for that purpose.

Except a man and his wife enter into an everlasting covenant and be married for eternity, while in this probation, by the power and authority of the Holy Priesthood, they will cease to increase when they die; that is, they will not have any children after the resurrection. But those who are married by the power and authority of the priesthood in this life, and continue without committing the sin against the Holy Ghost, will continue to increase and have children in the celestial glory. The unpardonable sin is to shed innocent blood, or be accessory thereto. All other sins will be visited with judgment in the flesh, and the spirit being delivered to the buffetings of Satan until the day of the Lord Jesus.

The way I know in whom to confide—God tells me in whom I may place confidence. . . .

Wednesday, 17.—Partook of breakfast at Brother Perkins'; after which we took a pleasure ride through Fountain Green.

At ten a.m. preached from 2nd Peter, 1st chapter and showed that knowledge is power; and the man who has the most knowledge has the greatest power. . . .

Salvation means a man's being placed beyond the power of all his enemies.

The more sure word of prophecy means a man's knowing that he is sealed up into eternal life by revelation and the spirit of prophecy, through the power of the holy priesthood. It is impossible for a man to be saved in ignorance. . . .

In the evening went to hear a Methodist preacher lecture. After he got through, offered some corrections as follows: . . .

The 7th verse of 2nd chapter of Genesis ought to read—God breathed into Adam his spirit [i. e. Adam's spirit] or breath of life; but when the word "rauch" applies to Eve, it should be translated lives.

Speaking of eternal duration of matter, I said:

There is no such thing as immaterial matter. All spirit is matter, but is more fine or pure, and can only be discerned by purer eyes. We cannot see it, but when our bodies are purified, we shall see that it is all matter.

The priest seemed pleased with the correction, and stated his intention to visit Nauvoo. (*HC,* 5:392–93)

Section 132: Given through the Prophet Joseph Smith at Nauvoo, Hancock County, Illinois, and recorded on July 12, 1843 (see *HC,* 5:501–7). Daniel Ludlow summarizes the background as follows:

William Clayton, who was Temple Recorder and private clerk of the Prophet at that time, relates the following: On the morning of the 12th of July, 1843, Joseph and Hyrum Smith came into the office in the upper story of the "brick store," on the bank of the Mississippi River. They were talking on the subject of plural marriage. Hyrum said to Joseph, "If you will write the revelation on celestial marriage, I will take and read it to Emma, and I believe I can convince her of its truth, and you will hereafter have peace." Joseph smiled and remarked, "You do not know Emma as well as I do." Hyrum repeated his opinion and further remarked, "The doctrine is so plain, I can convince any reasonable man or woman of its truth, purity or heavenly origin," or words to their effect. Joseph then said, "Well, I will write the revelation and we will see." He then requested me to get paper and prepare to write. Hyrum very urgently requested Joseph to write the revelation by means of the Urim and Thummim, but Joseph, in reply, said he did not need to, for he knew the revelation perfectly from beginning to end.

Joseph and Hyrum then sat down and Joseph commenced to dictate the revelation on celestial marriage, and I wrote it, sentence by sentence, as he dictated. After the whole was written, Joseph asked me to read it through, slowly and carefully, which I did, and he pronounced it correct. He then remarked that there was much more that he could write, on the same subject, but what was written was sufficient for the present (*HR* 6:225–26).

This was not the first mention of the subject among the Saints. Sarah Ann Kimball and many others knew of it in 1842, and Joseph B. Noble heard of it in the fall of 1840. Orson Pratt says that the Prophet Joseph, in the forepart of 1832, while he was living at the house of Father Johnson at Hiram, Ohio, told Church members that he had enquired of the Lord concerning this doctrine, and received the answer that it was true, but that the time to practice it had not come (Discourse by Orson Pratt, Salt Lake City, October 7, 1869). Consequently, the Law of the Church remained as stated in Doctrine and Covenants 42:22, and as it is today, "Thou shalt love thy wife with all thy heart, and shall cleave unto her and none else."

The revelation is divided into two parts. The first, comprising verses 3–33, deals mainly with the principle of celestial marriage, or marriage for time and all eternity; the second, comprising the remaining verses, deals with plural marriage. The doctrine of celestial marriage remains in force; the practice of plural marriage was abandoned by the acceptancy by the Church, in Conference assembled October 6th, 1890, of the Manifesto of President Woodruff. (Hyrum M. Smith and Janne M. Sjodahl, *Doctrine and Covenants Commentary* [Salt Lake City: Deseret Book, 1978], 820–21). (Daniel H. Ludlow, *A Companion to Your Study of the Doctrine and Covenants,* 2 vols. [Salt Lake City: Deseret Book, 1978], 1:659)

1. MARRIAGE FOR TIME AND ALL ETERNITY IS NECESSARY TO ENTER THE HIGHEST DEGREE OF GLORY

THEME: The Lord, in His infinite mercy and kindness, has revealed to His sons and daughters, through prophecy and revelation in the latter days, the great mystery of how to rise to their absolute peak potential and partake, with Him, of the blessings of eternal creation and the generation of lives forever and ever. Such is the sacred substance of the principle and doctrine of eternal marriage, as set forth in sections 131 and 132 of the Doctrine and Covenants and proclaimed and elucidated ever since by the living prophets of God.

MODERN PROPHETS SPEAK

Howard W. Hunter:

> Just as baptism is a commandment of the Lord, so is temple marriage. As baptism is essential to admittance to the Church, so temple marriage is essential to our exaltation in the presence of God. It is part of our destiny. We cannot fulfill our ultimate aims without it. Do not be satisfied with anything less.
>
> You wouldn't accept a worldly form of baptism, would you?
>
> God has his mode of baptism—by immersion by one who holds the authority.
>
> Then would you accept a worldly form of marriage?
>
> He has his mode of marriage also: It is temple marriage. (*THWH,* 131)

Harold B. Lee:

> Brethren, we are not doing our duty as holders of the priesthood when we go beyond the marriageable age and withhold ourselves from an honorable marriage to these

lovely women, who are seeking the fulfillment of a woman's greatest desire to have a husband, a family, and a home. . . .

Please don't misunderstand what we are saying; but, brethren, think more seriously about the obligations of marriage for those who bear the holy priesthood at a time when marriage should be the expectation of every man who understands the responsibility; for remember, brethren, that only those who enter into the new and everlasting covenant of marriage in the temple for time and eternity, only those will have the exaltation in the celestial kingdom. That is what the Lord tells us.

Now, brethren, will you think seriously about that, and take from us our counsel, and don't rush hastily into it. Take time, yes, but don't neglect your responsibility and your obligations as holders of the holy priesthood. (*Ensign,* January 1974, 96)

ILLUSTRATIONS FOR OUR TIME

Why I Did Not Listen to My Friends

I shall always be grateful, to the day of my death, that I did not listen to some of my friends when, as a young man not quite twenty-one years of age, I took the trouble to travel all the way from Utah County to St. George to be married in the St. George Temple. That was before the railroad went south of Utah County, and we had to travel the rest of the way by team. It was a long and difficult trip in those times, over unimproved and uncertain roads, and the journey each way required several days.

Many advised me not to make the effort—not to go all the way down to St. George to be married. They reasoned that I could have the president of the stake or my bishop marry me, and then when the Salt Lake Temple was completed, I could go there with my wife and children and be sealed to her and have our children sealed to us for eternity.

Why did I not listen to them? Because I wanted to be married for time and eternity— because I wanted to start life right. Later I had cause to rejoice greatly because of my determination to be married in the temple at that time rather than to have waited until some later and seemingly more convenient time.

Some years ago the General Board members of the Young Women's Mutual Improvement Association were traveling throughout the stakes of Zion speaking on the subject of marriage. They urged the young people to start their lives together in the right way by being married right, in the temples of the Lord.

I was out in one of the stakes attending a conference, and one of my daughters, who was the representative of the Young Women's General Board at the conference, said:

"I am very grateful to the Lord that I was properly born, born under the covenant, born of parents that had been properly married and sealed in the temple of the Lord."

Tears came into my eyes, because her mother died before the Salt Lake Temple was completed and I was grateful that I had not listened to the remarks of my friends who had tried to persuade me not to go to the St. George Temple to be married. I was very grateful for the inspiration and determination I had to start life right.

Why did it come to me? It came to me because my mother believed in the gospel, taught me the value of it, gave me a desire to get all of the benefits of starting life right and of doing things according to the teachings of the gospel.

I believe that no worthy young Latter-day Saint man or woman should spare any reasonable effort to come to the house of the Lord to begin life together. The marriage vows taken in these hallowed places and the sacred covenants entered into for time and all eternity are proof against many of the temptations of life that tend to break homes and destroy happiness.(Heber J. Grant, *Gospel Standards: Selections from the Sermons and Writings of Heber J. Grant,* comp. G. Homer Durham [Salt Lake City: Improvement Era, 1981], 359)

LIKENING THE SCRIPTURES TO OUR LIVES

Doctrine and Covenants 131:1–4 In order to obtain the highest of the three degrees of glory within the celestial kingdom, we must enter into the new and everlasting covenant of marriage.

Application: Marriage in the holy temple is ordained of God and is required of all those who qualify, through the grace of God and their righteousness, to enter into their exaltation and have the joy of eternal increase. But simply entering into marriage is not enough; it is only the first step. We must maintain the celestial nature of that marriage. If we want to obtain the highest degree of glory, we must aspire to the highest degree of obedience and righteousness with regard to this sacred commission.

2. PREPARE EARLY TO BE MARRIED IN THE TEMPLE

THEME: Temple marriage is an objective to be reached after patient and devoted preparation have elevated and expanded the soul to a state of readiness to receive these noble and choice blessings from God. Isaiah characterized the process of spiritual advancement in these terms: "For precept must be upon precept, precept upon precept; line upon line, line upon line; here a little, and there a little" (Isa. 28:10). Nephi confirmed this doctrine: "For behold, thus saith the Lord God: I will give unto the children of men line upon line, precept upon precept, here a little and there a little; and blessed are those who hearken unto my precepts, and lend an ear unto my counsel, for they shall learn wisdom; for unto him that receiveth I will give more; and from them that shall say, We have enough, from them shall be taken away even that which they have" (2 Ne. 28:30). In modern times, the Lord has reiterated the process of preparing carefully for greater blessings: "For he will give unto the faithful line upon line, precept upon precept; and I will try you and prove you herewith" (D&C 98:12; see also 128:21). Preparing for temple marriage is perhaps the most critically important channel of spiritual development, for it encompasses, quite literally, all of the key aspects of eternal progression. It is a process that takes work and time, and little by little we become more worthy and more prepared to enter into the temple and partake of the blessings there.

MODERN PROPHETS SPEAK

Russell M. Nelson:

> As temples are prepared for our members, our members need to prepare for the temple. . . . To enter the temple is a tremendous blessing. But first we must be worthy. We should not be rushed. We cannot cut corners of preparation and risk the breaking of covenants we were not prepared to make. That would be worse than not making them at all. (*Ensign,* May 2001, 32)

Boyd K. Packer:

> In the Church we continually stress the highest standards of worthiness. The youth of the Church are urged to prepare themselves for temple marriage. In the most reverent terms we talk about temples and what they mean. And across the Church we continually schedule meetings for married couples who have not yet been to the temple. These meetings, under various titles, embrace the theme of preparation for the temple. (*The Holy Temple* [Salt Lake City: Bookcraft, 1980], 29)

Ezra Taft Benson:

> The most important teachings in the home are spiritual. Parents are commanded to prepare their sons and daughters for the ordinances of the gospel: baptism, confirmation, priesthood ordinations, and temple marriage. They are to teach them to respect and honor the Sabbath day, to keep it holy. Most importantly, parents are to instill within their children a desire for eternal life and to earnestly seek that goal above all else. (*Ensign,* July 1992, 2)

N. Eldon Tanner:

> We need to prepare our children for temple marriage. We can do this by having pictures of temples in evidence, by mentioning the blessings of the temple in our prayers, by telling faith-promoting experiences regarding temple work. (*Ensign,* June 1977, 2)

ILLUSTRATIONS FOR OUR TIMES

Prepared in Her Youth

> At a stake conference in Sandy, Utah, a young woman from Brigham Young University spoke on the subject "Why I Want a Temple Marriage." She recalled lessons learned in Junior Sunday School and Primary. "The Lord is so wonderful," she began.

> "He provides us with a marvelous blessing or commandment, such as temple marriage, and then gives direction to prepare us to keep this commandment. From the first time I learned the meaning of the words and could sing the song 'I Am a Child of God,' I have realized that the Lord has provided teachers, experiences, and lessons in our young lives to encourage us to live righteously. We have been taught correct principles by our parents and teachers and have been shown how to live them. The Lord has given us so many opportunities to prepare for temple marriage that it seems that all our living has been guided toward the accomplishment of this great goal."

> As I listened to her, I thought, "Thank God for the Primary. Thank God for the Junior Sunday School. Thank God for his inspiration to the ones who wrote those beautiful songs." Please, parents and teachers, translate that into action.

> The young woman continued:

> "If I could have only one thing in the world, I would choose to have a testimony. I sing now, with great meaning, 'I Know That My Redeemer Lives.' I am grateful for how the Lord has prepared me for temple marriage, first by blessing me with wonderful parents who were married in the temple, and to whom I give credit. I hope I shall succeed in my own life and marriage. Second, I have had great friends who have always shown the same appreciation of the Church that I have and who have always been an influence for good. Third, the Lord has led me to a young man who holds temple marriage as one of his goals, a young man who knows I wouldn't marry him anywhere else, and who also wouldn't marry me anywhere else.

> Then she closed with this challenge: "May we all have and develop a desire to marry in the temple and let this desire work in us so that temple marriage will be a reality

in our lives." (Harold B. Lee, *Ye Are the Light of the World: Selected Sermons and Writings of Harold B. Lee* [Salt Lake City: Deseret Book, 1974], 300–301)

LIKENING THE SCRIPTURES TO OUR LIVES

Alma 37:35 Alma counsels us to learn the importance of keeping the commandments of the Lord.

Application: Our values and standards can be forged in our younger years. This is why it is so important to teach our children the purpose and blessing of temple marriage when they are young. All of the Church auxiliaries emphasize personal worthiness and preparation for temple marriage. The Young Women's theme, the Aaronic Priesthood goals, and the "For the Strength of Youth" pamphlet all admonish the youth to live worthily and prepare for the temple.

3. KEEP THE COVENANTS OF HOLY MATRIMONY TO RECEIVE THE PROMISED BLESSINGS

THEME: Understanding the importance of temple marriage and then preparing for it is marvelous, but it is not the end of our work. We must worthily keep the covenants we make if we are to receive the blessings of the celestial kingdom. All blessings of God relating to eternal marriage are bestowed by covenant, conditioned upon our faithfulness and obedience to the principles pertaining thereto.

MODERN PROPHETS SPEAK

Gordon B. Hinckley:

> The most important decision of life is the decision concerning your companion. Choose prayerfully. And when you are married, be fiercely loyal one to another. Selfishness is the great destroyer of happy family life. I have this one suggestion to offer. If you will make your first concern the comfort, the well-being, and the happiness of your companion, sublimating any personal concern to that loftier goal, you will be happy, and your marriage will go on through eternity. (*TGBH,* 328–29)

Harold B. Lee:

> Keep your marriage covenants in order to grow in love. Those who go to the marriage altar with love in their hearts, we might say to them in truth, if they will be true to the covenants that they take in the temple, fifty years after their marriage they can say to each other: "We must have not known what true love was when we

were married, because we think so much more of each other today!" And so it will be if they will follow the counsel of their leaders and obey the holy, sacred instructions given in the temple ceremony; they will grow more perfectly in love even to a fulness of love in the presence of the Lord Himself. Young people do not know the true sacredness of marriage until they have been taught by the temple ordinance. (*The Teachings of Harold B. Lee,* ed. Clyde J. Williams [Salt Lake City: Bookcraft, 1996], 243)

Harold B. Lee:

It's possible for every church member to live perfectly the law of marriage, celestial marriage, to learn the duty of husband to wife, wife to husband, parents to children. It's possible for us to learn it perfectly. Some folks have the mistaken notion that if somehow, by hook or crook, they can get into the House of the Lord and be married they are assured of exaltation regardless of what they do, and they'll quote the 132 Section, the 26th verse. But that isn't what the Lord means. The Lord does assure an exaltation to those who make mistakes, if they repent. (*BYU Speeches of the Year,* January 5, 1954, 7)

ILLUSTRATIONS FOR OUR TIMES

Keep Your Covenants

The concluding speaker was the President of the Church. What he said was not comforting. He gave a talk that perhaps only the President of the Church could give; and he perhaps could speak in that way only because he was speaking about a relative. He confirmed that this man had been a good man and said that the good things he had done would earn him a reward; but then he said: "The fact is, he did not keep his covenants."

This man, when he was young, had gone to the temple to be married, to be sealed. Some sweet young girl had persuaded him to change his habits and become worthy, so he stopped doing some wrong things, began to pay his tithing and attend church, eventually received a temple recommend; and then the couple went to the temple and were sealed. But after a while, because the temple was a long way away and they did not return, he forgot. He began to slip back into some of his old habits. He forgot to pay his tithing. He ceased being the man he had become.

His relative, the President of the Church, knew all this, so he acknowledged that all the good he had done would earn him rewards, but he said, "The fact is, he did not keep his covenants." There were things he did that he should not have done, for he had covenanted not to do them. Similarly there were things he had covenanted to do that he had not done. So he had covenanted not to do some things and covenanted to do some things, and he had become loose and lazy on those things. He was basically a good man, maybe a good Christian as far as the world would judge it. But he had not kept his covenants, his agreements.

When you young people go to the temple to be married, you will hear about the importance of your marriage being sealed by the Holy Spirit of Promise. "I, the Lord, am bound when ye do what I say." And if you do what He says, He cannot break those promises; you will receive what is promised. But if you do not keep your part of the covenant the promises will not be fulfilled. There cannot be justice in your receiving the reward if you have not earned it. . . .

When we prepare for the temple, we will be asked questions. One question will be about the Word of Wisdom. "Do you keep the Word of Wisdom?" Well, do you or don't you? Quite often when I am interviewing leaders, I will say, "Are you worthy of a temple recommend?" Often they will say, "Well, I feel I am." And I will say, "But are you worthy?" It does not matter how you feel. It matters whether you are worthy. Then the brother will smile and he will say, "I am worthy." "Do you keep your covenants?" "I keep my covenants." That is a commendable thing. . . .

Now, we must keep our covenants. "Are you morally clean?" "Do you pay your tithing?" "Do you sustain the authorities of the Church?" "Well, yes, everybody but Brother Somebody." No, that is not the way it works. Brother Somebody probably needs your sustaining influence more than anyone. Keep your covenants. Keep your covenants.

When you come to the temple and receive your endowment, and kneel at the altar and be sealed, you can live an ordinary life and be an ordinary soul—struggling against temptation, failing and repenting, and failing again and repenting, but always determined to keep your covenants—and that marriage ordinance will be sealed by the Holy Spirit of Promise. Then the day will come when you will receive the benediction: "Well done, thou good and faithful servant: thou hast been faithful over a few things, I will make thee ruler over many things; enter thou into the joy of thy lord" (Matthew 25:21). (Boyd K. Packer, *Memorable Stories and Parables of Boyd K. Packer* [Salt Lake City: Bookcraft, 1997], 50)

LIKENING THE SCRIPTURES TO OUR LIVES

Doctrine and Covenants 132:19–21 Obedience to the commandments of the Lord is essential to obtaining the highest blessings He has in store for us, which is to gain a fulness of power and knowledge and have an eternal increase.

Application: We simply must keep our sacred covenants of holy matrimony. Our exaltation depends upon it. The blessings are beyond our comprehension. Let us be continually mindful of those things that will build up and bless one another in the marriage relationship. We must build up our marriages now, or we will not have them in the eternities. If we do not build a celestial marriage, we cannot attain that kingdom.

ENRICHMENT

Doctrine and Covenants 132:26 reads:

> Verily, verily, I say unto you, if a man marry a wife according to my word, and they are sealed by the Holy Spirit of promise, according to mine appointment, and he or she shall commit any sin or transgression of the new and everlasting covenant whatever, and all manner of blasphemies, and if they commit no murder wherein they shed innocent blood, yet they shall come forth in the first resurrection, and enter into their exaltation; but they shall be destroyed in the flesh, and shall be delivered unto the buffetings of Satan unto the day of redemption, saith the Lord God.

Joseph Fielding Smith gave the following commentary on this verse:

> Verse 26, in Section 132, is the most abused passage in any scripture. The Lord has never promised any soul that he may be taken into exaltation without the spirit of repentance. While repentance is not stated in this passage, yet it is, and must be, implied. It is strange to me that everyone knows about verse 26, but it seems that they have never read or heard of Matthew 12:31–32, where the Lord tells us the same thing in substance as we find in verse 26, Section 132.
>
> It is wrong to take one passage of scripture and isolate it from all other teachings dealing with the same subject. We should bring together all that has been said by authority on the question. . . .
>
> The Lord said by his own mouth: "And he that endureth not unto the end, the same is he that is also hewn down and cast into the fire, from whence they can no more return, because of the justice of the Father. And this is the word which he hath given unto the children of men. And for this cause he fulfilleth the words which he hath given, and he lieth not, but fulfilleth all his words. And no unclean thing can enter into his kingdom; therefore nothing entereth into his rest save it be those who have washed their garments in my blood, because of their faith, and the repentance of all their sins, and their faithfulness unto the end" [3 Ne. 27:17–19].

So we must conclude that those spoken of in verse 26 are those who, having sinned, have fully repented and are willing to pay the price of their sinning, else the blessings of exaltation will not follow. Repentance is absolutely necessary for the forgiveness, and the person having sinned must be cleansed. . . .

Here is something which those who contend that the Lord has granted immunity from their sins to some, if they have received certain sealings by the Holy Spirit of promise, have overlooked in this passage. I will call attention to these two things. If covenants are broken and enormous sins are committed, but not unto death, there are certain punishments to be inflicted. The mere confession is not enough; the sinners are: (1) to *"be destroyed in the flesh"*; (2) to *"be delivered unto the buffetings of Satan unto the day of redemption."*

Who in the world is so foolish as to wish to sin with the hope of forgiveness, if such a penalty is to be inflicted? No one but a fool! To be "destroyed in the flesh" means exactly that. We cannot destroy men in the flesh, because we do not control the lives of men and do not have power to pass sentences upon them which involve capital punishment. In the days when there was a theocracy on the earth, then this decree was enforced [Gen. 9:4–6; Lev. 20:10]. What the Lord will do in lieu of this because we cannot destroy in the flesh, I am unable to say, but it will have to be made up in some other way.

Then to be turned over to the buffetings of Satan unto the day of redemption, which is the resurrection, must be something horrible in its nature. Who wishes to endure such torment? No one but a fool! I have seen their anguish. I have heard their pleadings for relief and their pitiful cries that they cannot endure the torment. This was in this life. Add to that, the torment in the spirit world before the redemption comes—all of this, mark you, coming *after severe and humble repentance!* . . .

No, the Lord has not prepared for favoritism. He has not placed exemption upon some because they have received marriage for time and for all eternity and had it sealed by the "Holy Spirit of promise." He has not given them the privilege of blaspheming his name, of committing any sin whatever, and then coming forth to receive an exaltation. We should all be grateful for the wonderful principle of repentance; we all need it. But we must not lose sight of the fact that the *celestial kingdom is reserved for those who are sanctified and none others.* . . .

When a man and a woman, in all sincerity, enter into a covenant of marriage for time and all eternity (and after they have "overcome by faith," and are "just and true")

[D&C 76:54], *the Holy Ghost—who is the Spirit of promise—bears record of or ratifies that sealing.* In other words, *he seals the promises appertaining to the marriage covenant upon them.*

Now the Lord has said: "But *there is a possibility that man may fall from grace and depart from the living God;* Therefore let the church take heed and pray always, lest they fall into temptation; Yea, and *even let those who* are sanctified take heed also" [D&C 20:31–34].

If one or both of these covenanting persons break that covenant by which they are sealed by the Holy Spirit of promise, then the *Spirit withdraws the seal* and the guilty party, or parties, stand as if there had been no sealing or promise given. *All covenants are sealed based upon faithfulness.*

Should a person endeavor to receive the sealing blessing by fraud, then the blessing is not sealed, notwithstanding the integrity and authority of the person officiating. Instead of a blessing they will receive a cursing, the heaviest of all [D&C 41:1]. Therefore, a person who may deceive the bishop or any other officer, will stand condemned before the Lord, for he cannot be deceived and justice will be meted to all. (Joseph Fielding Smith, *DS,* 2:94–99)

To the Single Adult Sisters of the Church

I also recognize that not all women in the Church will have an opportunity for marriage and motherhood in mortality. But if those of you in this situation are worthy and endure faithfully, you can be assured of all blessings from a kind and loving Heavenly Father—and I emphasize *all blessings.*

I assure you that if you have to wait even until the next life to be blessed with a choice companion, God will surely compensate you. Time is numbered only to man. God has your eternal perspective in mind.

I also recognize that some of our sisters are widowed or divorced. My heart is drawn to you who are in these circumstances. The Brethren pray for you, and we feel a great obligation to see that your needs are met. Trust in the Lord. Be assured He loves you and we love you.

If you are a single parent, make friends with others in similar situations and develop friendships with married couples. Counsel with your priesthood leaders. Let them know of your needs and wants. Single parenthood is understood by the Lord. He knows the special challenges that are yours. You are His daughters. He loves you and will bless and sustain you. This I know. . . .

Now, to *all* the single adult sisters, regardless of your present situation:

Be faithful. Keep the commandments. Establish a deep and abiding relationship with the Lord Jesus Christ. Know that He is there—always there. Reach out to Him. He does answer prayers. He does bring peace. He does give hope. In the words of the Psalmist: "He is my refuge and my fortress: . . . in him will I trust" (Ps. 91:2). Study carefully the life of the Savior. He is our great exemplar. (Ezra Taft Benson, *Ensign,* November 1988, 96)

SUMMARY

Heavenly Father's desire is that we might gain immortality and eternal life (Moses 1:39). Marriage for time and all eternity is necessary in order for us to enter the highest degree of celestial glory in the hereafter; celestial marriage is key to our becoming exalted. This knowledge, along with all other gospel truths, when understood and lived, will bring all the blessings of God into our lives so that we receive "all that [the] Father hath" (D&C 84:38).

The doctrine of celestial marriage and eternal families is the doctrine of the priesthood that brings meaning to life and to our families. Early preparation is essential in order for temple marriage to become a reality as aspiring couples progress in all worthiness and sanctity. This is the covenant and ordinance that brings to bear all the blessings of Heavenly Father and our Savior as an eternal enrichment for our lives. The promised blessings flowing from eternal marriage are necessarily based upon honoring our holy covenant vows in all respects. In faithfulness, we receive the blessings of Abraham, Isaac, and Jacob. If we are true and loyal, our families will be sealed by the Holy Spirit of Promise, and all the blessings of the Father can be ours.

CHAPTER THIRTY-TWO

"TO SEAL *the* TESTIMONY"

Reading Assignment: Doctrine and Covenants 135; *Our Heritage*, pages 62–66.

Additional Reading: Acts 7:54–60, Hebrews 9:15–17; Mosiah 17:7–10; 3 Nephi 10:15; Doctrine and Covenants 98:13; 136:34–39.

Testimony of martyrs carries special weight. Joseph Smith sealed his testimony with his blood. He could have saved his life. . . . He loved life. He loved his wife and family and friends. He wasn't anxious to go over into eternity. He wanted to live a normal and natural life. He either had to give up his testimony—to recant—or he had to give up his life. He wasn't willing to give up his testimony. He said, "Who am I to deny that I have had heavenly manifestations—that the Lord has appeared before me?"

And so he went calmly, knowing that his life would be taken. He said, "I go as a lamb to the slaughter"; and he went up to Carthage, knowing that the mob was gathering there and knowing they had bullets in their guns. He went calmly and passed on. He said, as he passed on, "Lord, forgive them, for they know not what they do"—almost what Stephen had said when he stood in the pit where others had been stoned. . . .

The great testimonies must be sealed by blood, it seems. Jesus sealed his testimony with his blood. Stephen did. Joseph Smith has now sealed his testimony with blood and died as a young man to say unto all the world that the plates from which the Book of Mormon came forth were found on a hill near Palmyra in the state of New York. And thus, through understanding of this book and the Holy Bible, the gospel of Jesus Christ, through administration of his angels, was again restored to the earth. (Spencer W. Kimball, TSWK, 143)

THEMES *for* LIVING

1. The Martyrdom: The Prophet Joseph Seals His Testimony with His Blood
2. The Prophet Joseph's Great Work for the Salvation of All Humankind

INTRODUCTION

The Savior declared: "And whoso layeth down his life in my cause, for my name's sake, shall find it again, even life eternal" (D&C 98:13). This was the solemn pathway ordained for the Prophet Joseph Smith, who willingly followed the example of the Savior in giving up his temporal life on behalf of spiritual victory. Concerning Christ, the Apostle Paul wrote: "And for this cause he is the mediator of the new testament, that by means of death, for the redemption of the transgressions that were under the first testament, they which are called might receive the promise of eternal inheritance. For where a testament is, there must also of necessity be the death of the testator. For a testament is of force after men are dead: otherwise it is of no strength at all while the testator liveth" (Heb. 9:15–17). The efficacy of the Atonement is a reality for all humankind because the grand Testator brought about the redemption through an infinite sacrifice—giving His life that all might live. In that framework of courage and valor, the reputation and extraordinary accomplishments of the Prophet Joseph live on as a witness of the devotion of his mission and the verity of the gospel principles for which he gave his life.

MOMENT OF TRUTH

Section 135: This moving and inspired memorial was written by John Taylor of the Quorum of the Twelve, a personal witness to the martyrdom of Joseph and Hyrum on June 27, 1844, at the hands of a lawless mob (see *HC,* 6:629–31). Willard Richards, the only other man imprisoned with Joseph, Hyrum, and John Taylor on that fateful day, likewise summarized the tragic event as follows:

Two Minutes in Jail

Possibly the following events occupied near three minutes, but I think only about two, and have penned them for the gratification of many friends.

Carthage, June 27, 1844.

A shower of musket balls were thrown up the stairway against the door of the prison in the second story, followed by many rapid footsteps.

While Generals Joseph and Hyrum Smith, Mr. Taylor, and myself, who were in the front chamber, closed the door of our room against the entry at the head of the stairs, and placed ourselves against it, there being no lock on the door, and no catch that was usable.

The door is a common panel, and as soon as we heard the feet at the stairs head, a ball was sent through the door, which passed between us, and showed that our enemies were desperadoes, and we must change our position.

General Joseph Smith, Mr. Taylor and myself sprang back to the front part of the room, and General Hyrum Smith retreated two-thirds across the chamber directly in front of and facing the door.

A ball was sent through the door which hit Hyrum on the side of his nose, when he fell backwards, extended at length, without moving his feet.

From the holes in his vest (the day was warm, and no one had his coat on but myself), pantaloons, drawers, and shirt, it appears evident that a ball must have been thrown from without, through the window, which entered his back on the right side, and passing through, lodged against his watch, which was in his right vest pocket, completely pulverizing the crystal and face, tearing off the hands and mashing the whole body of the watch. At the same instant the ball from the door entered his nose.

As he struck the floor he exclaimed emphatically, "I am a dead man." Joseph looked towards him and responded, "Oh, dear brother Hyrum!" and opening the door two or three inches with his left hand, discharged one barrel of a six shooter (pistol) at random in the entry, from whence a ball grazed Hyrum's breast, and entering his throat passed into his head, while other muskets were aimed at him and some balls hit him.

Joseph continued snapping his revolver round the casing of the door into the space as before, three barrels of which missed fire. While Mr. Taylor with a walking stick stood by his side and knocked down the bayonets and muskets which were constantly discharging through the doorway, while I stood by him, ready to lend any assistance, with another stick, but could not come within striking distance without going directly before the muzzle of the guns.

When the revolver failed, we had no more firearms, and expected an immediate rush of the mob, and the doorway full of muskets, half way in the room, and no hope but instant death from within.

Mr. Taylor rushed into the window, which is some fifteen or twenty feet from the ground. When his body was nearly on a balance, a ball from the door within entered his leg, and a ball from without struck his watch, a patent lever, in his vest pocket near the left breast, and smashed it into "pie," leaving the hands standing at 5 o'clock, 16 minutes, and 26 seconds, the force of which ball threw him back on the floor, and he rolled under the bed which stood by his side, where he lay motionless, the mob from the door continuing to fire upon him, cutting away a piece of flesh from his left hip as large as a man's hand, and were hindered only by my knocking down their muzzles with a stick; while they continued to reach their guns into the room, probably left handed, and aimed their discharge so far round as almost to reach us in the corner of the room to where we retreated and dodged, and then I recommenced the attack with my stick.

Joseph attempted, as the last resort, to leap the same window from whence Mr. Taylor fell, when two balls pierced him from the door, and one entered his right breast from without, and he fell outward, exclaiming, "Oh Lord, my God!" As his feet went out of the window my head went in, the balls whistling all around. He fell on his left side a dead man.

At this instant the cry was raised. "He's leaped the window!" and the mob on the stairs and in the entry ran out.

I withdrew from the window, thinking it of no use to leap out on a hundred bayonets, then around General Joseph Smith's body.

Not satisfied with this I again reached my head out of the window, and watched some seconds to see if there were any signs of life, regardless of my own, determined to see the end of him I loved. Being fully satisfied that he was dead, with a hundred men near the body and more coming round the corner of the jail, and expecting a return to our room, I rushed towards the prison door, at the head of the stairs, and through the entry from whence the firing had proceeded, to learn if the doors into the prison were open.

When near the entry, Mr. Taylor called out, "Take me." I pressed my way until I found all doors unbarred, returning instantly, caught Mr. Taylor under my arm and rushed by the stairs into the dungeon, or inner prison, stretched him on the floor and covered him with a bed in such a manner as not likely to be perceived, expecting an immediate return of the mob.

I said to Mr. Taylor, "This is a hard case to lay you on the floor, but if your wounds are not fatal, I want you to live to tell the story."

I expected to be shot the next moment, and stood before the door awaiting the onset. (*HC,* 6:620)

1. THE MARTYRDOM: THE PROPHET JOSEPH SEALS HIS TESTIMONY WITH HIS BLOOD

THEME: There is tragedy in the treacherous and sordid circumstances that cost Joseph Smith his life at the hands of an evil mob; yet there is triumph in his martyr's witness that the gospel is true and that no hand can stay the advance of the stone, cut from the mountain without hands, that is rolling forth in glory to fill the entire world (see Dan. 2:35, 44–45).

MODERN PROPHETS SPEAK

Joseph Fielding Smith:

June 27, 1844 . . . Joseph Smith and his brother Hyrum laid down their lives as martyrs for the testimony of Jesus. Their voices had been raised with but one desire—the salvation of their fellowmen. Unselfishly they had proclaimed to an unbelieving world, that the heavens had been opened; the Lord had again communed with man and the gospel had been restored. It has been said of them, "They lived men of God. They died pure and holy, sealing their testimony with their blood. No men ever suffered greater persecutions than they; no men were ever less understood by their generation." It has always been this way. Truth has been forced to travel the rocky road, the hard way, and has always found the dragons, Hate and Intolerance, blocking the path. (*The Restoration of All Things* [Salt Lake City: Deseret News Press, 1945], 38)

Spencer W. Kimball:

Men do not give their lives to perpetuate falsehoods. Martyrdom dissipates all questions as to the sincerity of the martyr. Personalities do not survive the ages. They rise like a shooting star, shine brilliantly for a moment and disappear from view, but a martyr for a living cause, like the sun, shines on forever. Great characters, students, businessmen, scientists, followed the youthful prophet to his death. They were not deceived. They lost him in martyrdom but inspired with the divinity of the Cause went forward without hesitancy. Thousands gave lives they could have saved, in Missouri, Illinois, and crossing the plains, and today a great people hailed for their education, practicability, and virtue, stand to bear witness that the martyrdom of Joseph Smith, like that of the martyrs before him, is another of the infallible proofs of the divinity of the gospel of Jesus Christ, restored in its fulness through that humble prophet. (CR, April 1946, 45, 50)

Bruce R. McConkie:

Thousands who have lived in this dispensation shall find place with "the martyrs under the altar that John saw" (D&C 135:7). They shall be classed with those who "loved not their lives unto the death" (Rev. 12:11); they are "the souls of them that were slain for the word of God, and for the testimony which they held" (Rev. 6:9). They shall "rest yet for a little season, until their fellow servants also and their brethren, that should be killed as they were, should be fulfilled" (Rev. 6:11). Martyrdom is not a thing of the past only, but of the present and of the future, for Satan has not yet been bound, and the servants of the Lord will not be silenced in this final age of warning and judgment. There are forces and powers in the world today, which would silence the tongue and shed the blood of every true witness of Christ in the world, if they had the power and the means to do it. There are those who would destroy every prophet of God, if they could. Martyrs of true religion are yet to have their blood shed in Jerusalem. "And their dead bodies shall lie in the street of the great city, which spiritually is called Sodom and Egypt, where also our Lord was crucified" (Rev. 11:1–12). True it is that "the woman," of whom John wrote is and shall be "drunken with the blood of the saints, and with the blood of the martyrs of Jesus" (Rev. 17:6).

True martyrs of religion receive eternal life. "Whoso layeth down his life in my cause, for my name's sake, shall find it again, even life eternal" (D&C 98:13; Mark 8:35; John 12:25; Rev. 2:10). But the mere laying down of one's life standing alone is not gospel martyrdom. Both the righteous and the wicked have and do sacrifice their lives for friends or country without gaining thereby any hope or assurance of exaltation. Those on the other hand who have the truth and who could escape death by denying it are the martyrs who shall receive a martyr's reward—eternal life. When they seal their testimony with their blood, they are honored and their murderers are condemned (D&C 136:39). (*MD*, 470)

ILLUSTRATIONS FOR OUR TIMES

The following story took place on the evening prior to the martyrdom, June 26, 1844. Dan Jones and John Fullmer were released from Carthage the next day. It is apparent here that the Prophet understood that he would soon die for the cause. It is also apparent that he knew that many of his friends had need still to live for it, as is evidenced by his comments to Dan Jones. Brother Jones did go on to preach the gospel in Wales. What was required of him was not his death, but his willingness to give his life to the gospel.

"Are You Afraid to Die?"

During the evening the Patriarch Hyrum Smith read and commented upon extracts from the Book of Mormon, on the imprisonments and deliverance of the servants of God for the Gospel's sake. Joseph bore a powerful testimony to the guards of the divine authenticity of the Book of Mormon, the restoration of the Gospel, the administration of angels, and that the kingdom of God was again established upon the earth, for the sake of which he was then incarcerated in that prison, and not because he had violated any law of God or man.

They retired to rest late. Joseph and Hyrum occupied the only bedstead in the room, while their friends lay side by side on the mattresses on the floor. Dr. Richards sat up writing until his last candle left him in the dark. The report of a gun fired close by caused Joseph to arise, leave the bed, and lay himself on the floor, having Dan Jones on his left, and John S. Fullmer on his right.

Joseph laid out his right arm, and said to John S. Fullmer, "Lay your head on my arm for a pillow Brother John;" and when all were quiet they conversed in a low tone about the prospects of their deliverance. Joseph gave expression to several presentiments that he had to die, and said "I would like to see my family again" and "I would to God that I could preach to the Saints in Nauvoo once more." Fullmer tried to rally his spirits, saying he thought he would often have that privilege, when Joseph thanked him for the remarks and good feelings expressed to him.

Soon after Dr. Richards retired to the bed which Joseph had left, and when all were apparently fast asleep, Joseph whispered to Dan Jones, "Are you afraid to die?" Dan said, "Has that time come, think you? Engaged in such a cause I do not think that death would have many terrors." Joseph replied, "You will yet see Wales, and fulfill the mission appointed you before you die." (Quoted in *Best-Loved Stories of the LDS People,* ed. Jack M. Lyon, Linda Ririe Gundry, and Jay A. Parry [Salt Lake City: Deseret Book, 1997], 73–74)

LIKENING THE SCRIPTURES TO OUR LIVES

Doctrine and Covenants 135:6 Joseph and Hyrum Smith sealed their testimony of this great work with their own blood when they were martyred at the hands of an angry mob. John Taylor exclaims, "They lived for glory; they died for glory; and glory is their eternal reward. From age to age shall their names go down to posterity as gems for the sanctified."

Application: The great example of the Prophet Joseph and his brother Hyrum will ever stand as a witness to the world of the truthfulness of the gospel of Jesus Christ and His kingdom once again established here upon the earth. We will probably not be required to die for the kingdom, but rather to live to build up the kingdom of God—this is our joy and glory. Let us do all we can to bless our brothers and sisters here upon the earth by inviting them to come unto Christ and partake of His goodness, for we care for the welfare of their souls (see Mosiah 28:3; Alma 6:6; D&C 18:10–16; 31:5; 88:81; 123:12).

2. THE PROPHET JOSEPH'S GREAT WORK FOR THE SALVATION OF ALL HUMANKIND

THEME: Joseph Smith was the mighty instrument of the Restoration in the hands of the Lord. What Joseph did—though in parallel with the sacrifice of all the gospel martyrs throughout history—was unique, for it was he of whom the Lord spoke, saying that it was Joesph "unto whom I have committed the keys of my kingdom, and a dispensation of the gospel for the last times; and for the fulness of times, in the which I will gather together in one all things, both which are in heaven, and which are on earth" (D&C 27:13).

MODERN PROPHETS SPEAK

Brigham Young:

> Joseph Smith holds the keys of this last dispensation, and is now engaged behind the veil in the great work of the last days. . . . No man or woman in this dispensation will ever enter into the celestial kingdom of God without the consent of Joseph Smith. I cannot go there without his consent. He holds the keys of that kingdom for the last dispensation. Should not this comfort all people? They will, by and by, be a thousand times more thankful for such a man as Joseph Smith, Junior, than it is possible for them to be for any earthly good whatever. It is his mission to see that all the children of men in this last dispensation are saved, that can be, through the

redemption. You will be thankful, every one of you, that Joseph Smith, Junior was ordained to this great calling before the worlds were. (Quoted in Leon R. Hartshorn, *Joseph Smith, Prophet of the Restoration* [Salt Lake City: Deseret Book, 1970], 116)

Gordon B. Hinckley:

Within the space of that twenty years preceding his death, Joseph Smith set in motion a program for carrying the gospel to the nations of the earth. I marvel at the boldness with which he moved. Even in the infant days of the Church, in times of dark adversity, men were called to leave their homes and families, to cross the sea, to proclaim the restoration of the gospel of Jesus Christ. His mind, his vision encompassed the entire earth.

Seated in this hall [Salt Lake Tabernacle] today are those from North, Central, and South America; from the British Isles and Africa; from the nations of Europe; from the islands and continents of the Pacific; and from the ancient lands of Asia. You who have come from far and near, you are the flowering of the vision of Joseph Smith, the prophet of God. He was indeed a mighty seer, who saw this day and greater days yet to come as the work of the Lord moves over the earth. (CR, April 1977, 96)

Ezra Taft Benson:

The calling and testing of men for assignment of responsibility in the great work of salvation is, no doubt, going on both sides of the veil. The calling of men to sacred office is not confined to earth life only. There is organization, direction, and assignment in pre-earth life and in post-earth life also.

The greatest activity in this world or in the world to come is directly related to the work and mission of Joseph Smith—man of destiny, prophet of God. That work is the salvation and eternal life of man. For that great purpose this earth was created, prophets of God are called, heavenly messengers are sent forth, and on sacred and important occasions even God, the Father of us all, condescends to come to earth and to introduce His beloved Son.

The Prophet Joseph Smith was not only "one of the noble and great ones," but he gave and continues to give attention to important matters here on the earth even today from the realms above. For in the eyes of the Lord, the God of this world under the Father, it is all one great eternal program in which the Prophet Joseph plays an important role, all through the eternal priesthood and authority of God. . . .

Yes, the glorious work of salvation and exaltation goes on over there with the knowledge and, at least to some extent, the direction of the work here on this side of the veil. And in this direction the Prophet Joseph Smith, head of the greatest and last gospel dispensation, occupies a sacred place. (*God, Family, Country: Our Three Great Loyalties* [Salt Lake City: Deseret Book, 1974], 31)

ILLUSTRATIONS FOR OUR TIMES

"It Is True"

> You and I can't hope to describe adequately the contribution of the Prophet Joseph to the cause of the salvation of God's children. But you can gauge what he has done in your life. A few years ago I went with my two young daughters to the Museum of Church History and Art. They wanted to go through the exhibit on Church history. They took with them the little pink sheets printed with questions that the lovely woman at the front desk gave them. While they were writing down the answers to a question about a stone from the Nauvoo temple, I waited for them at the next exhibit. My eyes went to two faces in a glass case, the death masks of Joseph and Hyrum.

> It took the girls a long time to write. And it took me a long time to look away from those two faces. And when I did, I walked back again. All the artifacts, all the pictorial accounts of adventures, and even the tragedy portrayed before me melted away, and I could think only of a boy and then a man to whom the heavens were opened, who spoke with God the Father and his Son, who was taught by the angel Moroni, ordained by John the Baptist and by Peter, James, and John, empowered and taught by Moses, Elijah, and heavenly beings beyond his recounting and my comprehension. And most wonderful of all, as I stood there, I could hear the whispering of the Spirit say to me, "It is true." (Henry B. Eyring, *To Draw Closer to God* [Salt Lake City: Deseret Book, 1997], 36–37)

LIKENING THE SCRIPTURES TO OUR LIVES

Doctrine and Covenants 4:1–7 The Lord has begun a "marvelous work and a wonder" in our time. The missionary field is "white already to harvest" and the Lord stands ready to bless us for laboring with our might to bring souls unto Him.

Application: Section 4 has been called the great anthem scripture of missionary work. It could also be a description of the Prophet Joseph Smith's life—working with all his heart, might, mind, and strength to bring others to Christ. It really has to do with all who seek to do the will of God and serve Him, that they might bless their brothers and sisters and build up the kingdom of God. As Joseph gave his life for the gospel, let us live worthy of his example by giving our all to further the cause. As we serve, we are to do it with all our heart, full of charity and with an eye single to the glory of God. The more we become like Christ (verses 5–6), the better able we are to serve.

SUMMARY

The Prophet Joseph and his beloved brother Hyrum sealed their testimony with their blood as martyrs for the kingdom of God. Through the inspiration of the Lord, John Taylor declared that their martyrdom surely "cost the best blood of the nineteenth century" in bringing forth the truth to a wicked world (see D&C 135:6). Two and a half years after Carthage, the Lord revealed to His Saints, through Brigham Young, the divine perspective on the martyrdom of Joseph and Hyrum:

> Therefore, marvel not at these things, for ye are not yet pure; ye can not yet bear my glory; but ye shall behold it if ye are faithful in keeping all my words that I have given you, from the days of Adam to Abraham, from Abraham to Moses, from Moses to Jesus and his apostles, and from Jesus and his apostles to Joseph Smith, whom I did call upon by mine angels, my ministering servants, and by mine own voice out of the heavens, to bring forth my work; Which foundation he did lay, and was faithful; and I took him to myself. Many have marveled because of his death; but it was needful that he should seal his testimony with his blood, that he might be honored and the wicked might be condemned. (D&C 136:37–39)

CHAPTER THIRTY-THREE

PRESIDENT BRIGHAM YOUNG LEADS *the* SAINTS

Reading Assignment: Doctrine and Covenants 107:22–24; *Our Heritage*, pages 66–71.

Additional Reading: Joshua 1:1–5; 2 Kings 2:8–15; 2 Nephi 5:27; Jacob 1:12, 18–19.

In the early years of his newly established dispensation, the Lord set his divine law of succession, and prophets have followed each other and will continue to follow each other in never-ending, divinely appointed succession, and the secrets of the Lord will be revealed without measure. (Spencer W. Kimball, Ensign, *May 1977, 76)*

THEMES *for* LIVING

1. The Keys of the Kingdom Given to the Twelve Apostles by the Prophet Joseph and Brigham Young Sustained as President
2. The Brief but Glorious Flowering of Temple Work in Nauvoo
3. The Trials and Miracles of the Saints as They Begin the Journey West

INTRODUCTION

Where the scriptures recount the moments of succession in the prophetic office, there emerge inevitably principles and qualities that characterize the spiritual nature of the transition of leadership in the kingdom of God. Following the death of Moses, the mantle of authority fell upon Joshua to lead the Israelites into the promised land. His office was ordained of God: "There shall not any man be able to stand before thee all the days of thy life: as I was with Moses, so I will be with thee: I will not fail thee, nor forsake thee. Be strong and of a good courage" (Josh. 1:5–6). Similarly, when Elisha succeeded Elijah as prophet, the men of Israel testified: "The Spirit of Elijah doth rest on Elisha. And they came to meet him, and bowed themselves to the ground before him" (2 Kgs. 2:15). Upon the death of Lehi, his son Nephi succeeded to the station of leadership and prepared the way for a future transition: "And it came to pass that I, Nephi, did consecrate Jacob and Joseph, that they should be priests and teachers over the land of my people. And it came to pass that we lived after the manner of happiness" (2 Ne. 5:26–27). Upon the passing of Nephi, these two brothers assumed the reins of leadership: "For I, Jacob, and my brother Joseph . . . did magnify our office unto the Lord, taking upon us the responsibility, answering the sins of the people upon our own heads if we did not teach them the word of God with all diligence; wherefore, by laboring with our might their blood might not come upon our garments; otherwise their blood would come upon our garments, and we would not be found spotless at the last day" (Jacob 1:18–19).

From such passages we gain an understanding of the nature of succession in priesthood leadership: the Lord provides the direction, the Holy Spirit illuminates the transition, the new leadership acts with courage and strength, principles of righteousness are cultivated in order for the Saints to live after the manner of happiness, future leaders are trained and prepared in ongoing ways, and the successor leaders act in all diligence to magnify their office. Upon the passing of the Prophet Joseph Smith, the same principles and qualities of succession were to prevail as Brigham Young assumed the mantle of leadership. The Lord had prepared the way by revealing the nature and powers of authority vested in the several quorums and offices of the priesthood, including the First Presidency and the Quorum of the Twelve, the latter being "equal in authority and power" to the former (D&C 107:24) and hence authorized to act in matters of succession upon the death of the President. Because the transition was blessed with the Lord's divine sanction, the Church as a whole sustained the new prophet-leader wholeheartedly, and the kingdom of God, as prophesied, survived the martyrdom and modern diaspora—and all other impediments to its inexorable unfolding and expansion.

MOMENT OF TRUTH

The background for section 107 has been discussed previously in this book. This revelation on the priesthood is what explained the keys of presiding and authorized the Twelve to carry on in the absence of the Prophet, thus outlining the succession of priesthood authority.

President Gordon B. Hinckley recounted this time of transition during the Nauvoo period:

> In 1841, two years after [Joseph Smith] came to Nauvoo, he broke ground for a house of the Lord that should stand as a crowning jewel to the work of God.
>
> It is difficult to believe that in those conditions and under those circumstances a structure of such magnificence was designed to stand on what was then the frontier of America.
>
> I doubt, I seriously doubt, that there was another structure of such design and magnificence in all the state of Illinois.
>
> It was to be dedicated to the work of the Almighty, to accomplish His eternal purposes.
>
> No effort was spared. No sacrifice was too great. Through the next five years men chiseled stone and laid footings and foundation, walls and ornamentation. Hundreds went to the north, there to live for a time to cut lumber, vast quantities of it, and then bind it together to form rafts which were floated down the river to Nauvoo. Beautiful moldings were cut from that lumber. Pennies were gathered to buy nails. Unimaginable sacrifice was made to procure glass. They were building a temple to God, and it had to be the very best of which they were capable.
>
> In the midst of all of this activity, the Prophet and his brother Hyrum were killed in Carthage on the 27th of June 1844.
>
> None of us living today can comprehend what a disastrous blow that was to the Saints. Their leader was gone—he, the man of visions and revelations. He was not only their leader. He was their prophet. Great was their sorrow, terrible their distress.
>
> But Brigham Young, President of the Quorum of the Twelve, picked up the reins. Joseph had placed his authority upon the shoulders of the Apostles. Brigham determined to

finish the temple, and the work went on. By day and by night they pursued their objective, notwithstanding all of the threats hurled against them by lawless mobs. In 1845 they knew they could not stay in the city they had built from the swamplands of the river. They knew they must leave. It became a time of feverish activity: first, to complete the temple, and secondly, to build wagons and gather supplies to move into the wilderness of the West.

Ordinance work was begun before the temple was entirely completed. It went on feverishly until, in the cold of the winter of 1846, the people began to close the doors of their homes and wagons moved slowly down Parley Street to the water's edge, then across the river and up the banks on the Iowa side. . . .

Back to the east they looked for the last time to the city of their dreams and the temple of their God. Then they looked to the west to a destiny they did not know. . . .

Under the prompting of the Spirit, and motivated by the desires of my father, who had served as mission president in that area and who wished to rebuild the temple for the centennial of Nauvoo but was never able to do so, we announced in the April conference of 1999 that we would rebuild that historic edifice.

Excitement filled the air. Men and women came forth with a desire to be helpful. Large contributions of money and skills were offered. Again, no expense was spared. We were to rebuild the house of the Lord as a memorial to the Prophet Joseph and as an offering to our God. On the recent 27th of June, in the afternoon at about the same time Joseph and Hyrum were shot in Carthage 158 years earlier, we held the dedication of the magnificent new structure. It is a place of great beauty. It stands on exactly the same site where the original temple stood. Its outside dimensions are those of the original. It is a fitting and appropriate memorial to the great Prophet of this dispensation, Joseph the Seer.

How grateful I am, how profoundly grateful for what has happened. Today, facing west, on the high bluff overlooking the city of Nauvoo, thence across the Mississippi, and over the plains of Iowa, there stands Joseph's temple, a magnificent house of God. Here in the Salt Lake Valley, facing east to that beautiful temple in Nauvoo, stands Brigham's temple, the Salt Lake Temple. They look toward one another as bookends between which there are volumes that speak of the suffering, the sorrow, the sacrifice, even the deaths of thousands who made the long journey from the Mississippi River to the valley of the Great Salt Lake. (Gordon B. Hinckley, *Ensign,* November 2002, 4)

1. THE KEYS OF THE KINGDOM GIVEN TO THE TWELVE APOSTLES BY THE PROPHET JOSEPH AND BRIGHAM YOUNG SUSTAINED AS PRESIDENT

THEME: The Lord would not organize His Church on the earth only to have it fall into disarray less than fifteen years later. He had a plan laid out from the beginning. He said, "Behold, mine house is a house of order, saith the Lord God, and not a house of confusion" (D&C 132:8). Succession in the kingdom of God is accomplished in an orderly fashion, according to the statutes and regulations of the priesthood and under the guidance of the Holy Spirit.

MODERN PROPHETS SPEAK

James E. Faust:

> Today I speak of keys other than those of metal. The keys I speak of never rust. These are the keys of life and salvation in the kingdom of God. The Prophet Joseph Smith said, "I will give you a key that will never rust, if you will stay with the majority of the Twelve Apostles, and the records of the Church, you will never be led astray." . . .
>
> Prior to the martyrdom, no doubt with a sense of foreboding, the Prophet Joseph prepared for his death. President Joseph Fielding Smith states:
>
> "The Prophet declared that he knew not why, but the Lord commanded him to endow the Twelve with these keys and priesthood, and after it was done, he rejoiced very much, saying in substance, 'Now, if they kill me, you have all the keys and all the ordinances and you can confer them upon others, and the powers of Satan will not be able to tear down the kingdom as fast as you will be able to build it up, and upon your shoulders will the responsibility of leading this people rest.'"
>
> After learning of the deaths of the Prophet Joseph and the Patriarch Hyrum, Wilford Woodruff reports his meeting with Brigham Young, who was then the President of the Quorum of the Twelve Apostles, as follows: "I met Brigham Young in the streets of Boston, he having just returned, opposite to Sister Voce's house. We reached out our hands, but neither of us was able to speak a word. . . . After we had done weeping we began to converse. . . . In the course of the conversation, he [Brigham Young] smote his hand upon his thigh and said, 'Thank God, the keys of the kingdom are here.'" (*Ensign,* November 1994, 72)

Heber C. Kimball:

> Since Brother Joseph stepped behind the vail, Brother Brigham is his lawful successor. I bear testimony of what Brother Joseph said on the stand at Nauvoo, and I presume hundreds here can bear witness of the same. Said he, "These men that are set here behind me on this stand, I have conferred upon them all the power, Priesthood, and authority that God ever conferred upon me." There are hundreds present this day who heard him utter words to that effect more than once. The Twelve had then received their endowments. Brother Joseph gave them the endowments, and keys and power were placed upon them by him, even as they were placed upon him by Peter, James and John, who ordained him. That is true, gentlemen, because they held the Apostleship last, and had the authority to confer it upon him, or any whom the Father had chosen. Brother Joseph called and ordained the twelve Apostles of the last days, and placed that power upon them. (Quoted in Orson F. Whitney, *Life of Heber C. Kimball, an Apostle* [Salt Lake City: Kimball Family, 1888], 458–59)

ILLUSTRATIONS FOR OUR TIMES

Portrait of Brigham Young

At this time of uncertainty immediately following the martyrdom, the biggest question in the Saints' minds was, Who would lead them? Or would they be led? A gathering was held not long after the Prophet's death. Brigham Young addressed the congregation, and many of the faithful there were blessed with a sign as to who the Lord's chosen leader for them would be.

> "For the first time in my life, for the first time in your lives, for the first time in the kingdom of God in the 19th century, without a Prophet at our head, do I step forth to act in my calling in connection with the Quorum of the Twelve, as Apostles of Jesus Christ . . . whom God has called by revelation through the Prophet Joseph. . . . This people have hitherto walked by sight and not by faith . . . you have had a Prophet as the mouth of the Lord to speak to you, but he has sealed his testimony with his blood, and now, for the first time, are you called to walk by faith, not by sight. . . . When I came to this stand I had peculiar feelings and impressions. The faces of the people seem to say, we want a shepherd to guide and lead us through this world. *All that want to draw away a party from the church after them, let them do it if they can, but they will not prosper.* . . . What do the people want? I feel as though I wanted the privilege to weep and mourn for thirty days at least, then rise up, shake myself, and tell the people what the Lord wants of them. . . . I feel compelled this day to step forth in the discharge of those duties God has placed upon me."

Brigham's heart was tender, but his mind was sure. He spoke but briefly in the morning meeting, and about two hours in the afternoon. He spoke with power and compassion, with logic and persuasion:

"You cannot fill the office of a prophet, seer and revelator: God must do that. . . . The Twelve are appointed by the finger of God. Here is Brigham, have his knees ever faltered? Have his lips ever quivered? Here is Heber and the rest of the Twelve, an independent body who have the keys of the priesthood—the keys of the kingdom of God to deliver to all the world: this is true, so help me God."

As Brigham bore this powerful witness, not only his words stirred the people. Many testified that, as they looked upon him, in voice, bearing, and appearance he was transformed; it was as if the Prophet Joseph himself stood again in their midst. Benjamin F. Johnson recorded his experience:

". . . suddenly, as from Heaven, I heard the voice of the Prophet Joseph that thrilled my whole being, and quickly turning around I saw in the transfiguration of Brigham Young, the tall, straight, and portly form of the Prophet Joseph Smith, clothed in a sheen of light, covering him to his feet; and I heard the real and perfect voice of the Prophet, even to the whistle . . caused by the loss of a tooth . . . broken out by the mob at Hiram. This view, or vision, although but for seconds, was to me as vivid and real as the glare of lightning or the voice of thunder from the heavens, and so deeply was I impressed . . . that for years I dared not tell what was given me of the Lord to see. But when in later years I did publicly bear this testimony, I found that others had testified to having seen and heard the same. But to what proportion of the congregation that were present, I could never know. But I do know that this, my testimony, is true."

When Brigham presented it to the people for a vote—did they want Rigdon as their leader or spokesman, or did they desire to "sustain the Twelve as the First Presidency of this people"?—there was not one dissenting hand raised in opposition to the Twelve. In his journal of that evening, Brigham wrote:

"This day is long to be remembered by me. . . . I arose and spoke to the people, my heart was swollen with compassion toward them and by the power of the Holy Ghost, even the spirit of the prophets I was enabled to comfort the hearts of the Saints. . . . The church was of one heart and one mind, they wanted the Twelve to lead the church as Brother Joseph had done in his day." (Susan Evans McCloud, *Brigham Young: A Personal Portrait* [American Fork, UT.: Covenant Communications, 1996], 121–23)

LIKENING THE SCRIPTURES TO OUR LIVES

Doctrine and Covenants 107:27, 30 Every decision made by the governing quorums of the Church is to be made unanimously, with meekness and humility before the Lord.

Application: Unity in the work is vital for the building up of the kingdom of God. As the Brethren must maintain the humility, meekness, faith, virtue, knowledge, charity, and all other attributes listed above in decisions governing the Church, so is personal righteousness required of each of us in our stewardships, that we might in purity enjoy the blessings of the Spirit to guide us in our decisions.

2. THE BRIEF BUT GLORIOUS FLOWERING OF TEMPLE WORK IN NAUVOO

THEME: For a brief but shining moment, the work of the house of God in Nauvoo enjoyed a spiritual efflorescence that proved to be the consummation of the Saints' labor of love in obeying the voice of the Lord to build unto Him a house worthy of all acceptation. So important was this work to these early Saints that they worked tirelessly to finish the temple, even though they would soon have to leave it. So ought our dedication and faith in temple work to be.

MODERN PROPHETS SPEAK

Howard W. Hunter:
> The building of temples has deep significance for ourselves and mankind, and our responsibilities become clear. We must accomplish the priesthood temple ordinance work necessary for our own exaltation; then we must do the necessary work for those who did not have the opportunity to accept the gospel in life. Doing work for others is accomplished in two steps: first, by family history research to ascertain our progenitors; and second, by performing the temple ordinances to give them the same opportunities afforded to the living. (*THWH,* 230)

Gordon B. Hinckley:
> Joseph Smith . . . administered the first ordinances in the upstairs room of his brick store. Brigham Young pushed and pushed, although he knew that the Saints would have to leave Nauvoo, pushed and pushed for the completion of the temple so that all who could receive their ordinances would have opportunity to do so before they left. . . .

Our people cannot partake of all of the blessings of the gospel unless they can receive their own temple ordinances and then make these ordinances available to those of their kindred dead and others. . . .

These unique and wonderful buildings, and the ordinances administered therein, represent the ultimate in our worship. These ordinances become the most profound expressions of our theology. I urge our people everywhere, with all of the persuasiveness of which I am capable, to live worthy to hold a temple recommend, to secure one and regard it as a precious asset, and to make a greater effort to go to the house of the Lord and partake of the spirit and the blessings to be had therein. I am satisfied that every man or woman who goes to the temple in a spirit of sincerity and faith leaves the house of the Lord a better man or woman. (*TGBH,* 638)

ILLUSTRATIONS FOR OUR TIMES

Dedication of the Work on the Nauvoo Temple

The following excerpts indicate just how hard the Saints were willing to work to complete the temple before they left Nauvoo. Once finished, though, they did not stop there. The Saints put just as much energy and enthusiasm, if not more, into the ordinance work once the temple was ready for use:

On February 3, 1846, it was a bitter cold day in Nauvoo, Illinois. That day, President Brigham Young recorded in his diary:

"Notwithstanding that I had announced that we would not attend to the administration of the ordinances, the House of the Lord was thronged all day. . . . I also informed the brethren that I was going to get my wagons started and be off. I walked some distance from the Temple supposing the crowd would disperse, but on returning I found the house filled to overflowing.

"Looking upon the multitude and knowing their anxiety, as they were thirsting and hungering for the word, we continued at work diligently in the House of the Lord."

And so the temple work continued until 1:30 A.M.

The first two names that appear on the fourth company of the Nauvoo Temple register for that very day, February 3, 1846, are John and Jane Akerley, who received their endowments in the Nauvoo Temple that evening. They were humble, new converts to the Church, without wealth or position. Their temple work was their final concern as they were leaving their homes in Nauvoo to come west. It was fortunate that President Young granted the wish of the Saints to receive their temple blessings because John Akerley died at Winter Quarters, Nebraska. He, along with over 4,000 others, never made it to the valleys of the Rocky Mountains. William Clayton's classic Mormon hymn "Come, Come, Ye Saints" captures well their faith: "And should we die before our journey's through, happy day! All is well!" (James E. Faust, *Ensign,* May 1997, 18)

* * *

Sustained by their fellow Saints, President Young and the Twelve moved quickly. They had two main priorities: (1) complete the Nauvoo Temple so the Saints could receive their endowments; and (2) plan the western exodus. By December 1845 the temple was sufficiently completed that ordinance work could begin. All together, nearly 6,000 Saints gratefully participated in endowment services before commencing their western journey. The completion of the temple amid hostile surroundings was regarded by many of the brethren as an answer to earnest prayer. "Many times we [the Twelve] do not go to bed until three o'clock in the morning," observed Elder Heber C. Kimball, "calling on the Father in the name of Jesus, to protect us, until that house shall be built." (Paul H. Peterson, *Ensign,* August 1999, 32)

LIKENING THE SCRIPTURES TO OUR LIVES

Doctrine and Covenants 124:39–41 The Lord commands the building of the temple for the performance of various temple ordinances.

Application: Here the Lord is instructing the Saints to build the Nauvoo Temple. He has always commanded His people to have a temple, not only to have the ordinances completed therein, but to instruct and prepare them for His coming. Let us remember to do all in our power to prepare ourselves to be worthy of receiving our temple blessings—and teach and inspire others to do the same. As we proceed to do the research and vicarious work for our kindred dead and all of Heavenly Father's children, we will be fortified, as were the Saints of the Nauvoo period. We will have the power of God manifest in our lives to sustain us in whatever we face.

3. THE TRIALS AND MIRACLES OF THE SAINTS AS THEY BEGIN THE JOURNEY WEST

THEME: Sacrifice upon sacrifice, endurance upon endurance, faith upon faith—these are the witnesses and triumphs of a people tested by trial and tragedy, refined by affliction and reversal, sustained by faith and hope, sanctified by refulgent light from God, and drawn onward by an irrepressible conviction to do the will of the Lord. "Come, Come, Ye Saints" became their anthem as the oppressed but scarcely defeated Saints of the Restoration left Nauvoo behind them in the shadows and followed their prophet-leader Brigham Young on the quest to establish the "mountain of the Lord's house" (Isa. 2:2)—"far away in the west."

MODERN PROPHETS SPEAK

Joseph B. Wirthlin:

> When President Brigham Young joined the departing pioneers at their campsite in Iowa on 15 February 1846, the Lord revealed to him to begin organizing a modern "Camp of Israel." On the first of March the advance company began its push westward across Iowa. Hardships caused by cold, snow, rain, mud, sickness, hunger, and death challenged the faith of these hardy pioneers. But they were determined to follow their leaders and to do, no matter the cost, what they believed fervently to be the will of God. Their faith was challenged, and for some it faltered in especially difficult times. But it did not fail them. Many were sustained by the assurances they had received in temple ordinances performed in the Nauvoo Temple. (*Ensign,* May 1996, 32)

ILLUSTRATIONS FOR OUR TIMES

In the Midst of Sorrow

The faithful Saints had little time to recover from losing their beloved Prophet and his brother before they had to be hard at work again, building the temple and preparing to head west. For no one could this have been more difficult than for those widowed and orphaned by the martyrdom. We learn the real character of Hyrum's widow, Mary Fielding Smith, as she pressed on in the years following her husband's death:

> Since becoming a member of the Church, Mary Fielding Smith was called to pass through great sorrow and affliction. Now there had come to her this dreadful blow, enough to crush and discourage one of less spirit and fortitude. She soon learned that there was no time to mourn. She had the care of a large family of fatherless children on her hands. Between the time of the martyrdom and the time of the exodus from Nauvoo her life was spent in the depths of wearisome toil. Most of the Saints were poor, for they had been robbed and driven from place to place, and again they were forced from their homes to seek shelter in the more friendly Indian infested wilderness of the arid west. The family of Hyrum Smith remained in Nauvoo until the summer

of 1846. President Brigham Young had made every effort by promise of extended help to Emma Smith, widow of the Prophet, to aid her to make the journey west with the exiled Saints; but all such offers were haughtily refused. Unfortunately there had arisen a feeling of bitterness in the heart of Emma Smith against Brigham Young and the Twelve. No amount of pleading, no amount of persuasion in kindness, could remove it, she stubbornly refused to make the journey with the Saints. Such extended help was not offered to the widow of Hyrum Smith. With her own hands, and the help of her brother, she fought her own battle of preparation to leave Nauvoo. This test was a severe one. She knew that every inducement had been offered to Emma Smith, but instead of feeling that such offers should be made to her, she had placed her faith in God and was fully converted to His work. She knew that the Lord would provide for He is a husband to the widow and a Father to the fatherless. With a brave heart and unsurpassed fortitude she worked and toiled in the midst of all her sorrow, knowing that there was no peace in Nauvoo for those who remained faithful to the truth for which the martyrs died. (Joseph Fielding Smith, *Life of Joseph F. Smith* [Salt Lake City: Deseret Book, 1969], 130)

Though we cannot really know or judge Emma's heart (scarcely anyone remained who had been called to sacrifice as she had), we can take a page from Mary Fielding Smith's book of life, pressing forward in all diligence. She could easily have given in to grief and doubt, yet she pressed on. It was this spiritual fortitude that sustained many in these early treks to the Rocky Mountains.

LIKENING THE SCRIPTURES TO OUR LIVES

Doctrine and Covenants 136:31 "My people must be tried in all things, that they may be prepared to receive the glory that I have for them, even the glory of Zion; and he that will not bear chastisement is not worthy of my kingdom."

Application: The Saints suffered and went through trials of monstrous proportions as they left Nauvoo, which we will discuss more fully in the next chapter. They paid the price emotionally and temporally, but in their trials the Lord supported and sustained them spiritually. We can learn so much from those who have gone before us—above all, we should show gratitude for them as they sought to establish the kingdom of God in the most trying times. This gratitude should motivate us to give our all for the building up of the kingdom of God as well.

SUMMARY

Under inspiration of the Lord, the keys of the kingdom had been given to the Twelve Apostles by the Prophet Joseph. Upon his death, the process of succession placed the mantle of leadership upon Brigham Young. There was a brief but glorious flowering of holy ordinance work in the Nauvoo Temple before the Saints, once again, were constrained to leave their homes and seek refuge, this time in the west. These were days of trial and triumph, misery and miracles, sacrifice and supernal solace. How grateful we should be that these hearty and devoted people laid the foundation for us, as successor Saints, to live "after the manner of happiness"!

CHAPTER THIRTY-FOUR

FAITH *in* EVERY FOOTSTEP

Reading Assignment: Doctrine and Covenants 136; *Our Heritage*, pages 71–77.

Additional Reading: 1 Nephi 2:19–20; 17:13–14; Ether 1:39–42.

After the martyrdom, the Twelve, with Brigham Young at the head, took over the leadership of the Church. The death of Joseph Smith had not stilled persecution. An exodus from Nauvoo was inevitable. Several places of refuge were presented, such as Texas and Vancouver Island, but in accordance with Joseph's prophecy, the then unknown west among the Rocky Mountains was chosen, and the memorable westward migration began.

Brigham Young in all that he did, repeatedly admitted the leadership of Joseph Smith, even in the journey to the Great Salt Lake Valley. For example, this on March 16, 1856: "The Prophet Joseph has been referred to, and his prophecy that this people would leave Nauvoo and be planted in the midst of the Rocky Mountains. We see it fulfilled as it was declared to the people long before we left Nauvoo" (JD, 3:257–58; see also 4:203; 8:356).

That the famous trek from Nauvoo to Salt Lake Valley was a fulfillment of prophecy, does not detract from the glorious achievement of Brigham Young and his fellow pioneers. That he repeatedly admitted it, publicly and privately, and gave the

Prophet proper credit, rather enhances the greatness of the foremost pioneer. President Young's loyalty to the Prophet was always unsullied. To him, the Prophet was the great restorer of the Lord's eternal truth. His own magnificent work in carrying out the prophecy, subduing the desert, and finding peace for his people, made him one of the world's really great men. (John A. Widtsoe, Evidences and Reconciliations *[Salt Lake City: Bookcraft, 1960], 348)*

THEMES *for* LIVING

1. Preparations for the Journey West
2. Divine Counsel for the Journey
3. "This Is the Right Place": Arrival in the Salt Lake Valley

INTRODUCTION

When monumental movements of Israel are about to take place, the Lord, in His mercy and kindness, provides guidelines for the Saints to follow. To the dynamic and valiant young leader Nephi, He said: "And inasmuch as ye shall keep my commandments, ye shall prosper, and shall be led to a land of promise; yea, even a land which I have prepared for you; yea, a land which is choice above all other lands" (1 Ne. 2:20). Furthermore, the Lord added this promise: "And I will also be your light in the wilderness; and I will prepare the way before you, if it so be that ye shall keep my commandments; wherefore, inasmuch as ye shall keep my commandments ye shall be led towards the promised land; and ye shall know that it is by me that ye are led. Yea, and the Lord said also that: After ye have arrived in the promised land, ye shall know that I, the Lord, am God; and that I, the Lord, did deliver you from destruction; yea, that I did bring you out of the land of Jerusalem" (1 Ne. 17:13–14).

Centuries earlier, the Lord had answered the prayers of the brother of Jared: "Go to and gather together thy flocks, both male and female, of every kind; and also of the seed of the earth of every kind; and thy families; and also Jared thy brother and his family; and also thy friends and their families, and the friends of Jared and their families. And when thou hast done this thou shalt go at the head of them down into the valley which is northward. And there will I meet thee, and I will go before thee into a land which is choice above all the lands of the earth" (Ether 1:41–42). In like manner, the Lord had specific counsel for the Saints when they were driven from Nauvoo and awaited the grand exodus to the Salt Lake Valley. Through whom was that counsel given? Through Brigham Young, the authorized successor to the Prophet Joseph. When the Lord speaks for the kingdom, His voice is heard through His chosen representative, for, as the ancient man of wisdom declared: "Where there is no vision, the people perish: but he that keepeth the law, happy is he" (Prov. 29:18).

MOMENT OF TRUTH

Section 136: "The Word and Will of the Lord" (so identified in verse 1), given through Brigham Young at Winter Quarters, Nebraska, on the west bank of the Missouri River, near Council Bluffs, Iowa (see Journal History of the Church, January 14, 1847). The Saints had departed from Nauvoo in 1846 and established themselves in settlements across Iowa and on the west bank of the Missouri in Nebraska. Church leaders were concerned about organizing the people for the westward migration, and thus members of the Twelve convened on January 14, 1847, at Heber C. Kimball's house to consider the matter. It was on that occasion, as well as during the course of the day at other nearby locations, that Brigham Young received and dictated what is now known as section 136, setting forth divine counsel to prepare for and carry out the journey to the Salt Lake Valley.

Orson F. Whitney later explained the circumstances:

> In 1847 the Latter-day Saints, under the leadership of President Brigham Young began to fulfill the prediction of the Prophet Joseph who had declared, two years before his death, that the Saints would "become a mighty people in the midst of the Rocky Mountains." In the book of Doctrine and Covenants there is a revelation entitled "The Word and Will of the Lord," to a people encamped upon the Missouri river, who had left civilization behind, who had been driven from their homes and were making preparation to cross the great plains and mountains and settle in this then empty and desolate land. That "Word and Will of the Lord" commanded the people of The Church of Jesus Christ of Latter-day Saints to organize themselves into companies of hundreds, fifties, and tens preparatory to the long and wearisome ox-team journey to Salt Lake Valley. (CR, October 1916, 54–55)

1. PREPARATIONS FOR THE JOURNEY WEST

THEME: The Latter-day Saint exodus to the valleys of the Mountain West is among the great historical events of American history. Enormous sacrifice attended this mass movement, and were it not for the inspired leadership and meticulous preparation involved, the suffering and adversity would have been much greater than it was. As it turned out, the Saints journeyed under the merciful hand of the Lord and in His strength, much as ancient Israel crossed the wilderness guided by the cloudy pillar during the day and the heralding fire at night (Neh. 9:12).

MODERN PROPHETS SPEAK

Dallin H. Oaks:

> We praise what the pioneers' unselfishness and sacrifice have done for us, but that is not enough. We should also assure that these same qualities are guiding principles for each of us as we have opportunities to sacrifice for our nations, our families, our quorums, our members, and our Church. This is especially important in societies that have exalted personal interest and individual rights to the point where these values seem to erase the principles of individual responsibility and sacrifice.
>
> Other great qualities in our early pioneers were *obedience, unity,* and *cooperation.* We have all thrilled at the example of the Saints who responded to President Brigham Young's call to rescue the stranded handcart companies, or to pull up roots in settled communities and apply their talents and lives to colonizing new areas.
>
> Our people have always been characterized by their loyalty and obedience to the direction of their leaders, by their unity, and by their extraordinary capacity to cooperate in a common venture. We see the modern manifestations of these pioneer qualities in the great contributions our brothers and sisters make in a wide variety of private projects and common efforts that require unity and cooperation. (*Ensign,* November 1997, 72)

Marvin J. Ashton:

> Certainly preparation precedes power, and if we can prepare ourselves, we have no need to fear. The present and the future belong to those who have the power that comes through preparation. (*Ye Are My Friends* [Salt Lake City: Deseret Book, 1972], 19)

ILLUSTRATIONS FOR OUR TIMES

"All Is Well"

> Do you know what William Clayton was doing when he wrote that *Come Come Ye Saints?* It was on the 15th of April between Nauvoo and Winter Quarters, one of the toughest trips that any people ever took. I beg of you to remember that six hundred people lost their lives in those three hundred miles. He had been sick much of the time. Pick up his journal and read the first twenty pages—the little journal of

William Clayton. He had been ill. His wife, Diantha, was still ill—too ill to travel. As you read those twenty pages, you will notice how often he was writing a letter to be sent back to his wife, hoping that she would be well. Then came the glad news that she had given birth to a son, she herself too ill to move. She struggled against the mumps. He himself was sick, but the morning, I love to read this—the morning the word came that he had a son—notice the practicality of it—he said they had been spending the day in a search for, "Henry Terry's horses are missing. They've been hunted all day, but are not found yet. This morning I composed a new song, 'All Is Well'. I feel to thank my heavenly Father for my boy and pray that he will spare and preserve his life and that of his mother, and so order that it be soon that we may be together again." He asked President Brigham Young, "Could they not send back and bring her along?"

President Young said, "You may."

I tried to conjure up last night that as William Clayton talked to Brigham Young about the new song he had just written, whether either one of them could ever have imagined, even in fancy, that a hundred years later 379 voices of the choir would take that same hymn and sing it to 60,000 people in Europe, and yet they did it. . . . That's faith in its fulfillment. (Adam S. Bennion, in Leon R. Hartshorn, *Exceptional Stories from the Lives of Our Apostles* [Salt Lake City: Deseret Book, 1972], 30–31)

LIKENING THE SCRIPTURES TO OUR LIVES

Doctrine and Covenants 136:2 "Let all the people of the Church of Jesus Christ of Latter-day Saints, and those who journey with them, be organized into companies, with a covenant and promise to keep all the commandments and statutes of the Lord our God."

Application: The task of organizing the Saints to move west was enormous. They were instructed to divide into companies. Each company was to care for the needs of the poor, the widows, and the fatherless in equal proportion according to the property possessed by the company (see D&C 136:4–10). However, we see here that the task of keeping them firm in their faith was of greater importance to the Lord. While He gave instruction as to the logistics of the trek, His concern was for the welfare of their souls. Their physical refuge would have been nothing if they had lost their faith. As then, so the Lord pleads with us now to be organized in our faith, so that He can lead and protect us as He did our forebears.

2. DIVINE COUNSEL FOR THE JOURNEY

THEME: From section 136 we gain not only a perspective on the western migration of the Saints, but counsel for the journey of life we are all called to take. Just as the Lord provided a spiritual and temporal framework for the westward journey of the Saints, so does He also provide careful instructions for our daily journey in life, to cultivate a "godly walk and conversation" (D&C 20:69)—practicing holiness, humility, charity, and righteousness in all things. The Lord teaches us to organize ourselves spiritually and to develop the capacity and fortitude to endure our journey.

MODERN PROPHETS SPEAK

Marvin J. Ashton:

> The true test is, how do we measure up when Christlike conduct standards are applied. (*Be of Good Cheer* [Salt Lake City: Deseret Book, 1987], 6)

Howard W. Hunter:

> We must take time to prepare our minds for spiritual things. The development of spiritual capacity does not come with the conferral of authority. There must be desire, effort, and personal preparation. This requires, of course, as you already know, fasting, prayer, searching the scriptures, experience, meditation, and a hungering and thirsting after the righteous life. (*THWH*, 36)

Dallin H. Oaks:

> We seek spirituality through service to our fellowmen; through worship; through feasting on the word of God, in the scriptures and in the teachings of the living prophets. We attain spirituality through making and keeping covenants with the Lord, through conscientiously trying to keep all the commandments of God. Spirituality is not acquired suddenly. It is the consequence of a succession of right choices. It is the harvest of a righteous life.
>
> Through the lens of spirituality we see all the commandments of God as invitations to blessings. Obedience and sacrifice, loyalty and love, fidelity and family, all appear in eternal perspective. (*Pure in Heart* [Salt Lake City: Bookcraft, 1988], 123)

John A. Widtsoe:

> By proper conduct or righteous living, that is by firm adherence to the Gospel requirements in all the acts of life, a man wins for himself spiritual growth, and the blessings that flow from the larger spiritual life. It is the enjoyment of spiritual peace

that yields the greatest happiness of which man is capable. (*Priesthood and Church Government* [Salt Lake City: Deseret Book, 1939], 57)

ILLUSTRATIONS FOR OUR TIMES

Organized by the Spirit

In early 1847 Brigham Young was ill at a place called Winter Quarters. He had been prayeful and his feelings were mixed. He still was deeply grieved at the loss of his closest earthly friend, Joseph Smith, and was burdened heavily with the kingdom and its leadership. . . .

He had a dream in which he saw the Prophet Joseph Smith. Some beautiful passages demonstrate that Brother Brigham wanted to join the Prophet. If you think that wasn't sincere and lasting, you should know that his last words on earth, thirty years later, would be one word three times repeated—"Joseph, Joseph, Joseph."

After this 1847 interchange and the assurance the Prophet there gave him that he must live on, . . . in the account there are seven different ways in which he says, "Tell the people to get and keep the Spirit of the Lord."

There is a marvelous statement about how we know the spirit received is the Spirit of the Lord, for Joseph says at one point, "They can tell the Spirit of the Lord from all other spirits; it will whisper peace and joy to their souls; it will take malice, hatred, strife and all evil from their hearts; and their whole desire will be to do good, bring forth righteousness and build up the kingdom of God." Then the interesting conclusion: "Be sure to tell the people to keep the Spirit of the Lord; and if they will they will find themselves just as they were organized by our Father in Heaven before they came into the world. Our Father in Heaven organized the human family [in premortal councils], but they are all disorganized and in great confusion." (Truman G. Madsen, *The Radiant Life* [Salt Lake City: Bookcraft, 1994], 105–6)

Pioneer Spirit

When Brigham Young led the Saints from Winter Quarters to the valleys of the Rocky Mountains, he did so under the aegis of the "Word and the Will of the Lord" (D&C 136:1). The protective canopy for their journey was a solemn commitment to be obedient and righteous—"with a covenant and promise to keep all the commandments and statutes of the Lord our God" (D&C 136:2). The promise was clear: "I am he who led the children of Israel out of the land of Egypt; and my arm is stretched out in the last days, to save my people Israel" (D&C 136:22). The same canopy of protection continued to be in force after the settlement in Utah and continues still today as the work of building the kingdom of God rolls forth, secured by our covenants of gospel obedience.

I recall as a young boy listening to my father tell of the testimony of obedience expressed by his father, Heber Simeon Allen. Though the migration of the early pioneers ceased, Grandfather Allen could be considered one of the pioneering settlers in southern Alberta and one of many leaders who served in the colonizing spirit of a Brigham Young. He was called in 1902 by President Joseph F. Smith as stake president and served faithfully in that capacity for thirty-four years. During his tenure, he sacrificed greatly of his time and energy to build up the kingdom through developing his own spirituality and assisting so many in their own spiritual journey. So dedicated was he that he journeyed sixty-one times to Utah to attend general conferences, traveling over fifty thousand miles.

A successful merchant and businessman, he always put the Lord first and served with devotion and dedication in all dimensions of his calling. This dedication brought the spiritual and physical protection promised of the Lord in section 136. He had established a successful mercantile store in the town of Cardston, Alberta. In 1905 a devastating fire hit the town center, destroying a hotel and spreading to other nearby buildings, one after the other. Several eyewitnesses were standing on a hill west of Grandfather's store discussing the enveloping flames. Just when the fire was at its worst, one of them remarked (according to Grandfather's journal): "I guess Brother Allen's store is a goner." "No, it isn't," said another eyewitness. "That store is dedicated." The first replied that this remark "went through him like an electric shock." My grandfather's journal continues: "I was not present during the fire, being in Raymond [a town to the east], but I was told later that suddenly the wind switched and blew from the west; the goods carried across the street [from the hotel] were burned but our store was saved.

"Later, an old friend, Jim Anderson, who grew up with me in Hyrum, Utah, told me about the fire which he had witnessed. He said, 'You must be a pretty good man or your store at Cardston would have been burned,' and then he told me the story of the changing wind, the burning of goods across the street, and the saving of our store in quite a remarkable way."

Grandfather Allen endured in that spiritual fortitude of the pioneers and so was blessed as the Lord had promised (D&C 136:22). Because he adhered to the Lord's commands in his journey through life, he was protected and guided. Upon his retirement and release, President Heber J. Grant and other general authorities traveled to Alberta to honor him and recognize his years of service, rooted in his abiding testimony of the restored gospel and his conviction to honor his gospel covenants. (Allen)

LIKENING THE SCRIPTURES TO OUR LIVES

Doctrine and Covenants 136:19–27 The Lord will stretch forth His arm to save His people in these last days, just as He did in ancient times. He expects us to have compassion toward our fellow beings, be wise with the possessions He blesses us with, and be respectful of the possessions of others.

Application: During this trying time, the Lord was not just concerned with the Saints' physical location. He was worried about where their hearts were. He knew the journey would be difficult and that it would be easy for the Saints to falter. So He gave them commandments to strengthen their spirituality, so as to ensure that they would endure. On our journey together in striving to be a Zion people, we at times encounter circumstances that try our patience and challenge our understanding. It was no different with the pioneers. The Lord's counsel to be charitable in all things is to fortify us in our faith as He did them. He wants us to develop our spirituality so that we, too, can endure in faithfulness.

3. "THIS IS THE RIGHT PLACE": ARRIVAL IN THE SALT LAKE VALLEY

THEME: Just as the Lord tested and tried His people throughout the mighty latter-day exodus, He also granted them ultimately the supreme blessing of "arrival"—accomplishing their journey and attaining the refuge they so dreamed about. It was a relatively desolate place, the Salt Lake Valley, but it afforded a protected environment where they could make the desert "blossom as the rose" (Isa. 35:1) and once again build up a temple to the Most High: "And there shall be a tabernacle for a shadow in the daytime from the heat, and for a place of refuge, and for a covert from storm and from rain" (Isa. 4:6; see also 2 Ne. 14:6).

MODERN PROPHETS SPEAK

Gordon B. Hinckley:

> When they came through Emigration Canyon and he looked out over this valley it was not a promising sight. The salty lake was in the west. The canyon streams emptied into it. The soil was hard and baked under the July sun. No plow had ever broken this soil. These people knew nothing of the climate. They knew nothing of its rainfall or snowpack. They knew nothing of when the frost came. They knew nothing whatever about it. Yet here was Brigham Young, 46 years old, leading a pioneer company to this valley which was to be followed by thousands and thousands of others.

He said, "This is the right place."

It took courage, it took faith, it took vision to bring the thousands who resided in Nauvoo, and yet other thousands who were coming from England and Europe.

The first company arrived on Saturday. They worshiped on Sunday. On Monday they climbed Ensign Peak. The canyon streams were diverted onto the dry soil and the ground was plowed. (*TGBH,* 516)

James E. Faust:

> Throughout the world, pioneers in the gospel have left us a priceless heritage. I acknowledge the faithful pioneers in all of the countries of the world who have helped establish the Church in their lands. First-generation members of the Church are indeed pioneers. They are and have been men and women of deep faith and devotion. Some of the great pioneers of the past, who left us a priceless legacy that belongs to the descendants of all pioneers, are those who came into the Salt Lake Valley and settled in Utah and other parts of western America. (*Finding Light in a Dark World* [Salt Lake City: Deseret Book, 1995], 51)

ILLUSTRATIONS FOR OUR TIMES

Continuing in the Faith of Our Heritage

Whether we are the first in our families to join the Church or have ancestors who crossed the plains with Brigham Young, we have a great legacy of faith to live up to. The pioneering generation of the Church began the work that we are to continue today, in that same spirit of obedience and faith. To live up to this heritage, we must come to understand and emulate it. From Stephen L Richards we learn the following:

> To understand the pioneers and their accomplishments, we must examine their motives. Herein we shall find the difference between them and other pioneers and frontiersmen of our country. They came for freedom and peace, as others have done. They came to make homes for themselves, as others have done. They came to worship God and practise their religion to the satisfaction of their consciences, as others have done; but here is one thing they came for which, so far as I know, has no counterpart in any other pioneer movement: They came with the avowed purpose of establishing a society so that they would be able to take back to the civilization from which they had fled, yes, even to their persecutors, the principles of life and conduct which were the source of their own inspiration, cohesion, success, and happiness. . . .

It was ingrained in their very beings that their greatest blessings would come in blessing others. They knew they had a message that was a boon to mankind; they knew they were under obligation to propagate that message among the peoples of the world; and they never for one moment lost sight of that obligation and their endeavor to fulfil it. In the processes of subduing a most stubborn country, with all its discouragements, disappointments, and exactions of time, energy, patience, and courage, they never ceased to give liberally of their hard-earned substance and their limited manpower in carrying abroad the sacred principles which dominated their lives. . . . Thus the pioneers came and went back as no other people have ever done, and their descendants have kept up the process for a century of time.

What was the compelling force which drove them to such superhuman exertion and such widespread sacrifices? Strange as it may seem, it was their literal acceptance of an ancient prophecy revivified by modern revelation:

"And it shall come to pass in the last days, that the mountain of the Lord's house shall be established in the top of the mountains, and shall be exalted above the hills; and all nations shall flow unto it. And many people shall go and say, Come ye, and let us go up to the mountain of the Lord, to the house of the God of Jacob; and he will teach us of his ways, and we will walk in his paths; for out of Zion shall go forth the law, and the word of the Lord from Jerusalem" (Isa. 2:2–3).

Every pioneer believed that prophecy with his whole heart. He saw the vision of its fulfilment in all his labors, trials, and privations. He wanted a home with comfort for his family, of course. He wanted a good society and prosperity, but all these were subordinate to the fulfilment of this prophecy—the establishment of Zion.

We all rejoice in the general high esteem accorded Brigham Young as a master colonizer, statesman, and empire builder. He is fully entitled to this acclaim from his fellow men, but not many outside his own followers have understood the real secret of his success. It is true that he was practical, far-sighted, and adept at organization, but those who know the inner forces behind his accomplishments will tell you that his power was spiritual, rather than temporal. The unity so essential to the cooperative effort of the people was a spiritual unity, arising out of a universal conviction of the sacred nature of the cause they espoused and a common acceptance of the responsibilities it entailed. In all of Brigham Young's work and ministry there was another in spirit always at his side, always supporting him and inspiring him, whose guidance and direction he ever acknowledged. That was his predecessor, Joseph Smith, the earthly founder of the cause he represented, the inspirer of the people, [the one] through whom their destiny had been revealed. Brigham never forgot and never ignored Joseph; neither did the people. They fought with all their strength to carry out the mission he had put upon them. That mission was both temporal and spiritual but predominantly spiritual.

What then did the pioneers bring? They brought industry in a measure that has seldom been equaled. They taught and practised the gospel of work as the foundation for success and happiness. . . .

They brought education and a love for the artistic and beautiful. Not many of them were scholarly. Their opportunities for learning had been very meager, but they had within them an innate yearning for truth, which, after all, is the real basis for education. It was an integral part of their conception of the purpose of life to develop intelligence and acquire knowledge. Intelligence was invested with the highest possible attributes, proclaimed to be the very glory of God. It was but natural, therefore, that education and its cultural, refining influences should receive their ardent support. . . .

They brought with them a high order of loyalty and a great capacity for firm devotion to the cause they espoused. We can scarcely estimate what this meant to the success of their enterprises. In the main they were rugged individuals, free men, many of whose immediate ancestors had fought for liberty; yet they were willing and eager to consecrate themselves and all they had to the cause which brought them here— the cause they loved. . . .

I come now to the greatest thing of all which the pioneers brought with them, and that I characterize as wisdom, wisdom about the important things in life. The really vital and fundamental aspects of our lives and living may be classified under very few headings. I think about four would be sufficient—the body, character, the family, and the social order. If everything were all right with these four items, the world would be in good order, and wisdom about these things is and always has been the greatest need of mankind. The pioneers brought with them this much required wisdom. It was not of their own making. It was given to them before they came here. In fact, it was not of any man's making, for it was the wisdom of the ages bequeathed to them by divine Providence. (Stephen L Richards, *Where Is Wisdom?* [Salt Lake City: Deseret Book, 1955], 224–25)

LIKENING THE SCRIPTURES TO OUR LIVES

Doctrine and Covenants 121:8 "And then, if thou endure it well, God shall exalt thee on high; thou shalt triumph over all thy foes."

Application: At long last the Saints were brought to a place of rest. They had endured their trek well and had escaped persecution. Was their work through, though? No, nor is ours. The kingdom must ever move forward, and we must continue in the heritage we have been left. Then we, too, will have reached our place of rest in the Lord's kingdom. May we, like those who went before, endure our journey well.

ENRICHMENT

Covenants of the Camp of Israel

One of the identifying characteristics of the Lord's people is that they are a covenant-making people. Modern Israel in the wilderness was no exception. They were to journey according to the organizational structure revealed by the Lord while under covenant to keep the commandments and ordinances of the Lord (see D&C 136:2–4). Some of the specific requirements of their covenant were as follows:

1. Be humble—seek the counsel of the Lord (see D&C 136:19).

2. Keep pledges or promises to fellowmen (see D&C 136:20).

3. Do not covet goods or property of others (see D&C 136:20).

4. Keep the Lord's name sacred (see D&C 136:21).

5. Love fellowmen—control feelings (see D&C 136:23).

6. Keep the Word of Wisdom (see D&C 136:24).

7. Use edifying language (see D&C 136:24).

8. Be honest with neighbors (see D&C 136:25–26).

9. Be a wise steward over personal possessions (see D&C 136:27).

10. Praise the Lord in all activities (see D&C 136:28).

11. Seek comfort from the Lord when in sorrow (see D&C 136:29).

12. Fear not enemies—have faith in the Lord (see D&C 136:17, 30).

13. Learn wisdom by seeking the Lord's spirit (see D&C 136:32–33).

Fulfilling these requirements of the covenants with the Lord will strengthen His people and assist them in obtaining mastery over the weaknesses of the flesh. It is not always an easy thing to be obedient and subject the flesh to the will of the Father. It is a trial for mortals to yield to the Lord's will. However, the Lord's people need to face trials in all things. Only by confronting tribulation can they conquer it. Thus, they are then prepared to receive the glory the Lord has prepared for them (see D&C 136:31). . . .

A covenant involves two parties. After describing His expectations of His people, the Lord declared His portion of the covenant in the form of certain promises that would be fulfilled in His own due time. Some of the promises the Lord made to the Camp of Israel were as follows:

1. Necessities of Life

The saints were promised that obedience to the Lord's law would result in their having sufficient of the world's goods to provide for their needs. Wealth was not implied, but adequacy was assured. Food and clothing are essential to the well-being of a child of God (see D&C 136:10–11).

2. Enemies

No mortal man can stop the work of the Lord. He told the saints there was no need to fear their enemies. The saints were promised that the work of the Lord will prevail (see D&C 136:17).

3. Redemption of Zion

Since the beginning of the work of restoration in this dispensation, the Lord has spoken of the building and establishing of Zion. This revelation was directing the saints in a journey that would take them even further from the designated site of the city of Zion. Yet, the Lord reaffirmed His intention and promised the saints He would yet redeem Zion and fulfill His word pertaining to that anticipated work (see D&C 136:18).

4. Glory of God

People who keep their covenants with the Lord are pure in heart. Such people were promised that if they remained pure, they would yet behold the glory of God (see D&C 136:37). . . .

Under these very difficult conditions, the Lord delivered these specific promises to His covenant people while they wandered in the wilderness of discouragement and despair. Such promises loomed large as the basis for hope, both in their present trials, and in their anticipation of future fulfillment. The Lord has said that all of His promises will be fulfilled (see D&C 1:37).

Now in retrospect, we see that the Lord has kept His promises. The saints are prospering; their enemies have not prevailed. We may also be assured that Zion will yet be redeemed and the glory of the Lord will ever be manifest in the lives and labors of His faithful covenant people. (L. G. Otten and C. M. Caldwell, *Sacred Truths of the Doctrine and Covenants,* 2 vol. [Salt Lake City: Deseret Book, 1982–83], 2:385–87)

SUMMARY

Just like the founding Saints, we are blessed to have living prophets to lead us. Brigham Young led the Saints west in the spirit of covenant obedience—and they were blessed according to the promises of God. So today, we can be assured of the blessings of heaven as we make and keep our sacred covenants and continue our journey with faith in every footstep. Let us make careful preparations and be organized for the forward trek. Let us gratefully acknowledge the Lord's divine counsel and apply it in all righteousness to our daily lives. Let us look forward to the hour when we will again cross the threshold to our heavenly home, for we know in our heart that "this is the right place" for us to be. Meanwhile, there is work to do. There are families to strengthen. There are neighbors to serve in charity. There is much by way of duty and covenant obligation to perform in building the kingdom of God. Wherever we serve, there is opportunity to bless lives and transform our society into a Zion society, reflecting the glory and vitality of heaven: "The wilderness and the solitary place shall be glad for them; and the desert shall rejoice, and blossom as the rose" (Isa. 35:1).

CHAPTER THIRTY-FIVE

"A MISSION *of* SAVING"

Reading Assignment: Doctrine and Covenants 4:4–7; 18:10–16; 52:40; 81:5–6; Moroni 7:45–48; *Our Heritage*, pages 77–80.

Additional Reading: Psalms 142:4; Matthew 25:40; Luke 15:1–7; Alma 31:34–35; 3 Nephi 18:31–32; Doctrine and Covenants 108:7.

I believe that if we are to be wise counselors, we must appreciate the true worth of a human soul. You and I know that in the revelation the Lord gave the Prophet Joseph he said: "Remember, the worth of souls is great in the sight of God" (D&C 18:10). And then he gave us a challenge, saying that if we should labor all our days and bring save it be one soul unto him, how great should be our joy. He added that if we should bring many souls unto the kingdom of our Father, how great should then be our joy (see D&C 18:15–16). We have that capacity to save human souls. Remember the injunction of the Lord: "Feed my lambs. . . . Feed my sheep" (John 21:15–16). Let us feed our youth, and feed them the gospel of Jesus Christ. (Thomas S. Monson, Pathways to Perfection [Salt Lake City: Deseret Book, 1973], 89)

THEMES *for* LIVING

1. A Pattern of Rescue: A Prophet Directs the Rescue of the Martin and Willie Handcart Companies
2. Our Rescue: Through the Atonement of Our Savior Jesus Christ
3. Rescuing Others in Need: Our Duty and Joy

INTRODUCTION

In the gospel of Jesus Christ, "rescue" is a synonym for the administration of charity in the lives of others. The Savior's mission is one of absolute charity and redemptive grace. We are therefore counseled, "Remember the worth of souls is great in the sight of God," and are commannded to seek to bring those souls back to the God who so cherishes them (see D&C 18:10–16). The essence of our religion is the continuing process of "rescuing" our families, our brothers and sisters—and even the strangers at our doors—with unconditional love, and of keeping ourselves in tune with the Spirit in order to perceive where help is needed (see James 1:27). The scriptures and the history of the Church provide memorable examples of how to rise to the call of being "rescuers" on the errand of the Lord.

MOMENT OF TRUTH

The divine commission to rescue and save souls is pervasive throughout the scriptures. We have already discussed the background to sections 4 and 18 of the Doctrine and Covenants. Let's consider another example from the Doctrine and Covenants.

Section 81: Given through the Prophet Joseph Smith in March 1832 at Hiram, Portage County, Ohio (see *HC,* 1:257–58). This section was originally intended for the benefit of Jesse Gause, one of the original counselors to Joseph Smith. Jesse Gause and Sidney Rigdon had been called and ordained as counselors to Joseph Smith one week before this revelation was given. Jesse served as a counselor to the Prophet for five months before he apostatized. The call to serve as a counselor in the First Presidency was subsequently transferred to Frederick G. Williams. Sections 81 and 90 laid the groundwork for the eventual full organization of the First Presidency, which occurred on March 18, 1833. Section 81 calls for faithfulness in carrying out one's appointed office, remembering to pray always, proclaiming the gospel, promoting the glory of God, and heeding the celebrated counsel: "Wherefore, be faithful; stand in the office which I have appointed unto you; succor the weak, lift up the hands which hang down, and strengthen the feeble knees" (D&C 81:5). It is instructive that this specific commission to serve, together with the associated promise of "a crown of immortality and eternal life" (verse 6), was taken from Jesse Gause and given to another who was, at the time, more faithful—a reminder that our own opportunities to serve and succor the needy in official capacities are conditioned on our loyalty and righteousness.

1. A PATTERN OF RESCUE: A PROPHET DIRECTS THE RESCUE OF THE MARTIN AND WILLIE HANDCART COMPANIES

THEME: The history of the restored Church is comprised of an endless web of rescues—the temporal and spiritual rescues of individuals, of families, of communities. From the threads of charity spun during the foundation years of the kingdom of God in this dispensation was formed the fabric of service that characterized a people striving to do the will of the Lord and grow into a Zion people. The prophetic office has ever been one of rescue. The duty of the Saints is organized about the concept of rescue, for we are commissioned to help the Savior to save, to reclaim, to nurture, to bring souls back to Him—just as He made His mission one of atoning redemption. In the episode of the Martin and Willie handcart companies, we see the pattern of rescue as it informs the entire history of God's people, for it was by the order of a prophet of God that steps were taken to organize the campaign of rescue and liberation from circumstances of dire want. So it continues even today—for along the highways and byways of human endeavor await infinite opportunities to serve others in a partnership with the Lord to save souls.

MODERN PROPHETS SPEAK

Gordon B. Hinckley:

> In October 1856, Brigham Young called for volunteers to rescue the Martin Handcart Company, which had run into snow and bitter cold in the highlands of Wyoming. When the rescue party met the company, there were not enough wagons to carry the suffering people—so the handcarts had to keep moving. On November 3 they reached the Sweetwater River, which was filled with chunks of floating ice. Because the pioneers were so weak, three eighteen-year-old boys from the relief party, C. Allen Huntington, George W. Grant, and David P. Kimball, carried nearly every member of the handcart company across the freezing river. When Brigham Young heard of the heroic act, he wept like a child. (*Ensign,* July 1984, 3)

Thomas S. Monson:

> Let us for a moment join Captain Edward Martin and the handcart company he led. While we will not feel the pangs of hunger which they felt or experience the bitter cold that penetrated their weary bodies, we will emerge from our visit with a better appreciation of hardship borne, courage demonstrated, and faith fulfilled. We will witness with tear-filled eyes a dramatic answer to the question "Am I my brother's keeper?" . . .

> Our service to others may not be so dramatic, but we can bolster human spirits, clothe cold bodies, feed hungry people, comfort grieving hearts, and lift to new heights precious souls. (*Ensign,* May 1990, 46)

ILLUSTRATIONS FOR OUR TIMES

"Some You Will Find with Their Feet Frozen"

November 30 was a Sunday. The faithful Saints were assembled in the Tabernacle, with President Young presiding. Having been appraised of the imminent arrival of the belated handcart emigrants, he spoke to the congregation:

> "When those persons arrive I do not want to see them put into homes by themselves; I want to have them distributed in the city among the families that have good and comfortable houses; and I wish all the sisters now before me, and all who know how and can, to nurse and wait upon the newcomers and prudently administer medicine and food to them. To speak upon those things is a part of my religion, for it pertains to taking care of the Saints.

> "As soon as this meeting is dismissed I want the brethren and sisters to repair to their homes, where their bishops will call on them to take in some of this company; the bishops will distribute them as the people can receive them.

> "The afternoon meeting will be omitted, for I wish the sisters to go home and prepare to give those who have just arrived a mouthful of something to eat, and to wash them and nurse them up. You know that I would give more for a dish of pudding and milk, or a baked potato and salt, were I in the situation of those persons who have just come in, than I would for all your prayers, though you were to stay here all the afternoon and pray. Prayer is good, but when baked potatoes and pudding and milk are needed, prayer will not supply their place on this occasion; give every duty its proper time and place.

"Some you will find with their feet frozen to their ankles; some are frozen to their knees and some have their hands frosted. . . . We want you to receive them as your own children, and to have the same feeling for them. We are their temporal saviors, for we have saved them from death." (Quoted in Leon R. Hartshorn, *Classic Stories from the Lives of Our Prophets* [Salt Lake City: Deseret Book, 1975], 62)

The Refiner's Fire

From the following story we learn that more was involved in the rescue of these handcart companies than the physical health and safety of the pioneers. More important than temporal salvation was the salvation of their souls, thoroughly refined through the toil and the hardship of their journey.

Some years ago President David O. McKay told of the experiences of some of those in the Martin Handcart Company. Many of these early converts had emigrated from Europe and were too poor to buy oxen or horses and wagons. They were forced by their poverty to pull handcarts containing all of their belongings across the plains by their own brute strength. President McKay related an occurrence that took place some years after the heroic exodus:

"A teacher, conducting a class, said it was unwise even to attempt, even to permit them (the Martin Handcart Company) to come across the plains under such conditions.

"Some sharp criticism of the Church and its leaders was being indulged in for permitting any company of converts to venture across the plains with no more supplies or protection than a handcart caravan afforded.

"An old man in the corner sat silent and listened as long as he could stand it, then he arose and said things that no person who heard him will ever forget. His face was white with emotion, yet he spoke calmly, deliberately, but with great earnestness and sincerity.

"In substance [he] said, 'I ask you to stop this criticism. You are discussing a matter you know nothing about. Cold historic facts mean nothing here, for they give no proper interpretation of the questions involved. Mistake to send the Handcart Company out so late in the season? Yes. But I was in that company and my wife was in it and Sister Nellie Unthank whom you have cited was there, too. We suffered beyond anything you can imagine and many died of exposure and starvation, but did you ever hear a survivor of that company utter a word of criticism? *Not one of that company ever apostatized or left the Church, because everyone of us came through with the absolute knowledge that God lives for we became acquainted with him in our extremities.*

"'I have pulled my handcart when I was so weak and weary from illness and lack of food that I could hardly put one foot ahead of the other. I have looked ahead and seen a patch of sand or hill slope and I have said, I can go only that far and there I must give up, for I cannot pull the load through it.' He continues:

"'I have gone on to that sand and when I reached it, the cart began pushing me. I have looked back many times to see who was pushing my cart, but my eyes saw no one. I knew then that the angels of God were there.

"'Was I sorry that I chose to come by handcart? No. Neither then or any minute of my life since. *The price we paid to become acquainted with God was a privilege to pay,* and I am thankful that I was privileged to come in the Martin Handcart Company' (*Relief Society Magazine,* January 1948, 8)."

Here, then, is a great truth. In the pain, the agony, and the heroic endeavors of life, we pass through a refiner's fire, and the insignificant and the unimportant in our lives can melt away like dross and make our faith bright, intact, and strong. In this way the divine image can be mirrored from the soul. This pain is part of the purging toll exacted of some to become acquainted with God. In the agonies of life, we seem to listen better to the faint godly whisperings of the Divine Shepherd. (James E. Faust, *To Reach Even unto You* [Salt Lake City: Deseret Book, 1980], 97)

LIKENING THE SCRIPTURES TO OUR LIVES

Doctrine and Covenants 52:40 "And remember in all things the poor and the needy, the sick and the afflicted, for he that doeth not these things, the same is not my disciple."

Application: The rescue of the Martin and Willie handcart companies has a parallel in our lives. Our priorities and goals in our lives should all be about serving and helping others. The welfare of others should be in our minds and hearts—this is charity, that which we seek to possess so that we may bless others and be like our Savior Jesus Christ (see Moro. 7:48).

2. OUR RESCUE: THROUGH THE ATONEMENT OF OUR SAVIOR JESUS CHRIST

THEME: In effect, we have been rescued by the Lord and Savior Jesus Christ through His atoning sacrifice (see 2 Ne. 9; D&C 19:16–19). Let us never forget the price paid by the Lord for us to gain immortality and eternal life. It was a vicarious sacrifice and a supreme act of love. Life is full of myriad echoes of that sacrifice in the countless acts of charity performed daily by the sons and daughters of God. The rescue of the Martin and Willie handcart companies, one of the more dramatic and memorable of such acts, was a vicarious act of sacrifice and love as well. Similarly, the very birth into mortality of each individual was an act of sacrifice and love on the part of his or her mother. As we come to understand these smaller, more immediate acts of sacrifice, we come to more fully understand that supreme sacrifice of our Savior Jesus Christ. We have our lives to live worthily and show our gratitude for all things, and more especially for the Atonement of Jesus Christ.

MODERN PROPHETS SPEAK

Gordon B. Hinckley:

> No member of this Church must ever forget the terrible price paid by our Redeemer who gave his life that all men might live—the agony of Gethsemane, the bitter mockery of his trial, the vicious crown of thorns tearing at his flesh, the blood cry of the mob before Pilate, the lonely burden of his heavy walk along the way to Calvary, the terrifying pain as great nails pierced his hands and feet, the fevered torture of his body as he hung that tragic day, the Son of God crying out, "Father, forgive them; for they know not what they do" (Luke 23:34). . . . We cannot forget that. We must never forget it, for here our Savior, our Redeemer, the Son of God, gave himself a vicarious sacrifice for each of us. (*TGBH*, 26–27)

Gordon B. Hinckley:

> The crowning element of our faith is our conviction of our living God, the Father of us all, and of His Beloved Son, the Redeemer of the world. It is because of our Redeemer's life and sacrifice that we are here. It is because of His sacrificial Atonement that we and all of the sons and daughters of God will partake of the salvation of the Lord. "For as in Adam all die, even so in Christ shall all be made alive" (1 Cor. 15:22). It is because of the sacrificial redemption wrought by the Savior of the world that the great plan of the eternal gospel is made available to us under which those who die in the Lord shall not taste of death but shall have the opportunity of going on to a celestial and eternal glory.
>
> In our own helplessness, He becomes our rescuer, saving us from damnation and bringing us to eternal life.
>
> In times of despair, in seasons of loneliness and fear, He is there on the horizon to bring succor and comfort and assurance and faith. He is our King, our Savior, our Deliverer, our Lord and our God. (*Ensign*, November 1991, 52)

LIKENING THE SCRIPTURES TO OUR LIVES

2 Nephi 9:7 Unless the Atonement of the Savior was an infinite atonement, we would be doomed to an endless state of eternal corruption.

Application: The Atonement is the center of the gospel plan in saving humankind. God loved us so much that He gave His Only Begotten Son (see John 3:16). This is the grace of God, which enables and empowers us to be saved, resurrected, and exalted after all we can do (see 2 Ne. 25:23). We would have been subject to the devil, to rise no more, without the Atonement of the Lord Jesus Christ (see 2 Ne. 9:8–10). As the brave young men were to the temporal salvation of the struggling handcart emigrants, so the Savior is to our spiritual salvation. How grateful we are, and how willing to serve one to whom we owe so much!

3. RESCUING OTHERS IN NEED: OUR DUTY AND JOY

THEME: Unconditional love is the hallmark of a Christ-centered character. King Benjamin taught that as we have all been rescued by Christ unconditionally, we have no right to place conditions on our offering of charity and rescue to a struggling soul:

> And also, ye yourselves will succor those that stand in need of your succor; ye will administer of your substance unto him that standeth in need; and ye will not suffer that the beggar putteth up his petition to you in vain, and turn him out to perish. Perhaps thou shalt say: The man has brought upon himself his misery; therefore I will stay my hand, and will not give unto him of my food, nor impart unto him of my substance that he may not suffer, for his punishments are just—But I say unto you, O man, whosoever doeth this the same hath great cause to repent; and except he repenteth of that which he hath done he perisheth forever, and hath no interest in the kingdom of God. For behold, are we not all beggars? Do we not all depend upon the same Being, even God, for all the substance which we have, for both food and raiment, and for gold, and for silver, and for all the riches which we have of every kind? (Mosiah 4:16–19)

Moreover, the Savior taught the following doctrine about our behavior toward the outsider: "Nevertheless, ye shall not cast him out of your synagogues, or your places of worship, for unto such shall ye continue to minister; for ye know not but what they will return and repent, and come unto me with full purpose of heart, and I shall heal them; and ye shall be the means of bringing salvation unto them" (3 Ne. 18:32). It is

God's place to judge; our place is to serve with charity wherever our help is needed. Our role is to rescue the sheep that wander from the flock of the gospel, restoring them to their Savior (see Luke 15:1–7).

MODERN PROPHETS SPEAK

Harold B. Lee:

> There is a classic example of how our Lord would have us minister to those who need our aid. When Peter and John, as recorded in the book of the Acts of the Apostles, approached a man who had never walked and who was at the gates of the temple begging alms, instead of giving him money the Apostle Peter, you will remember, said to him, "Silver and gold have I none; but such as I have give I thee: In the name of Jesus Christ of Nazareth rise up and walk" (Acts 3:6).

> Then followed a significant statement in the record of that incident. Peter took him by the right hand and lifted him up. Remember that it wasn't enough for Peter to command him to walk; he then took him by the hand and lifted him up.

> So must we, in dealing with our faltering Saints, not be merely priesthood holders who criticize, scold, and condemn. We must, like the Apostle Peter, take them by the arm, encourage them, and give them a sense of security and respect for themselves until they can rise above their difficulties and can stand on their own feet. (*The Teachings of Harold B. Lee,* ed. Clyde J. Williams [Salt Lake City: Bookcraft, 1996], 476)

N. Eldon Tanner:

> Every bishop, every stake president, every leader of any organization knows someone who needs attention, and you and we have the responsibility of going to find that lost sheep. If we had knowledge tonight that some young man [or woman] was lost, if anyone knew of someone who was drowning, we wouldn't hesitate one minute to do all in our power to save that individual, to save the one who was lost, the one who was drowning, the one who was in need of our help. These young men [and women] and these older men [and women] who are inactive in the Church, who have strayed away from the Church because of inactivity or for any reason, need our help and need our attention just as much. They need our prayers and our consideration, and nothing will bring us greater joy and happiness than to see one come back into activity.

> By saving one, we might save a family. We might even save a generation. By losing one, we may lose not only the individual but a family and his posterity. The responsibility is

great. Some of us seem to be very happy if we have from 40 to 70 percent attendance. If you have 40 percent attendance, you have 60 percent who are not in attendance. And if you have 70 percent in attendance, there are still 30 percent not attending, and those are the ones who need our attention, and they need it badly. (*Ensign,* June 1971, 59)

ILLUSTRATIONS FOR OUR TIMES

"Strengthen Thy Brethren"

Brother José de Souza Marques was the type of leader who truly understood the principle taught by the Savior: "And if any man among you be strong in the Spirit, let him take with him him that is weak, that he may be edified in all meekness, that he may become strong also" (D&C 84:106).

As a member of the branch presidency in Fortaleza, Brazil, Brother Marques with the other priesthood leaders developed a plan to reactivate those who were less active in his branch. One of those who was less active was a young man by the name of Fernando Araujo. Recently I spoke to Fernando, and he told me of his experience:

"I became involved in surfing competitions on Sunday mornings and stopped going to my Church meetings. One Sunday morning Brother Marques knocked on my door and asked my nonmember mother if he could talk to me. When she told him I was sleeping, he asked permission to wake me. He said to me, 'Fernando, you are late for church!' Not listening to my excuses, he took me to church.

"The next Sunday the same thing happened, so on the third Sunday I decided to leave early to avoid him. As I opened the gate I found him sitting on his car, reading the scriptures. When he saw me he said, 'Good! You are up early. Today we will go and find another young man!' I appealed to my agency, but he said, 'We can talk about that later.'

"After eight Sundays I could not get rid of him, so I decided to sleep at a friend's house. I was at the beach the next morning when I saw a man dressed in a suit and tie walking towards me. When I saw that it was Brother Marques, I ran into the water. All of a sudden, I felt someone's hand on my shoulder. It was Brother Marques, in water up to his chest! He took me by the hand and said, 'You are late! Let's go.' When I argued that I didn't have any clothes to wear, he replied, 'They are in the car.'

"That day as we walked out of the ocean, I was touched by Brother Marques's sincere love and worry for me. He truly understood the Savior's words: 'I will seek that which was lost, and bring again that which was driven away, and will bind up that which was broken, and will strengthen that which was sick' (Ezek. 34:16). Brother Marques didn't just give me a ride to church—the quorum made sure I remained active. They planned activities that made me feel needed and wanted, I received a calling, and the quorum members became my friends."

Following his reactivation, Brother Araujo went on a full-time mission and has served as bishop, stake president, mission president, and regional representative. His widowed mother, three sisters, and several cousins have also entered the waters of baptism.

When speaking about the work of the Aaronic Priesthood quorums in his ward, Brother Araujo, who is once again serving as a bishop, stated:

"Our rescue work is the focus in all three quorums of the Aaronic Priesthood. We have a list of each one of our lost sheep. The quorum presidencies, advisers, and bishopric divide up and go visit them on a regular basis. We visit not only the less-active members, but we also visit the nonmembers in less-active or part-member families.

"Activities are organized to reach each young man. We discuss each young man in our quorum presidency meetings and in our monthly bishopric youth committee meetings. In 2003 we managed to rescue five priests, one teacher, and two deacons, who are now active in their quorums. We have also reactivated some families and have enjoyed the blessing of seeing some nonmembers enter the waters of baptism." (Mervyn B. Arnold, *Ensign,* May 2004, 46)

LIKENING THE SCRIPTURES TO OUR LIVES

Doctrine and Covenants 81:5 We are commissioned by the Lord to lift and strengthen those around us who are in need.

Application: In all our eternal roles and duties within the Church, it all comes down to strengthening others—to love and nurture them, to strengthen their faith, and to give them hope to carry on and endure to the end.

SUMMARY

In the scriptures and the history of the Restoration, we find a dependable pattern concerning the process of "rescuing." We are to follow the guidance of the prophets of God, who see with greater vision and understanding where help may be needed. We are to follow the Spirit in discerning where succor needs to be administered all around us.

As we cultivate qualities of humility, obedience, and gratitude, we can ensure our own rescue along the pathways of life, which are fraught with temptation and challenges on all sides. Once we come to know the saving power of the Atonement, we can aid in the "rescue" of others by sharing the good news of the gospel and bearing witness with courage about the truth of the saving principles thereof. This means missionary work, in showing the strait and narrow way to those who despair of redemptive answers: "For there are many yet on the earth among all sects, parties, and denominations, who are blinded by the subtle craftiness of men, whereby they lie in wait to deceive, and who are only kept from the truth because they know not where to find it" (D&C 123:12). Above all, we are to emulate the Savior, the Master of charity: "But charity is the pure love of Christ, and it endureth forever; and whoso is found possessed of it at the last day, it shall be well with him" (Moro. 7:47).

CHAPTER THIRTY-SIX

"THE DESERT SHALL REJOICE, *and* BLOSSOM *as the* ROSE"

Reading Assignment: *Our Heritage*, pages 81–96.

Additional Reading: 1 Nephi 3:7; Doctrine and Covenants 58:2–4; 64:33–34; 82:10; 93:1; 130:19–21.

Our forefathers gloried in hard work, but at the same time they drew liberally upon their prodigious spiritual reserves. They did not place their trust "in the arm of flesh." They were strong and courageous in the Lord, knowing that He was their defense, their refuge, their salvation. Strengthened by this faith, they relied on their cherished independence, their frugality, and honest toil. And history records that even the climate was tempered for their sakes, and their humble untiring efforts made "the desert to blossom as the rose."

Their faith was renewed by two of Isaiah's remarkable prophecies concerning the last days—the days in which they knew they were living. In the first of these Isaiah announces: "The wilderness and the solitary place shall be glad for them; and the desert shall rejoice, and blossom as the rose" (Isa. 35:1). And again: "For the Lord shall comfort Zion: he will comfort all her waste places; and he will make her wilderness like Eden, and her desert like the garden of the Lord; joy and gladness shall be found therein, thanksgiving, and the voice of melody" (Isa. 51:3).

And while their natural eyes saw only their log cabins and immediate surroundings, they envisioned the day when the words of Micah would be fulfilled: "But in the last days it shall come to pass, that the mountain of the house of the Lord shall be established in the top of the mountains, and it shall be exalted above the hills; and people shall flow unto it. And many nations shall come, and say, Come, and let us go up to the mountain of the Lord, and to the house of the God of Jacob; and he will teach us his ways, and we will walk in his paths: for the law shall go forth of Zion, and the word of the Lord from Jerusalem" (Micah 4:1–2). (Ezra Taft Benson, This Nation Shall Endure *[Salt Lake City: Deseret Book, 1977], 52–53)*

THEMES *for* LIVING

1. The Blessings of a Temple in the Shadows of the Everlasting Hills
2. Obey the Prophet that the Kingdom of the Lord May Flourish
3. Missionaries Sacrifice and Preach throughout the World

INTRODUCTION

The courage and devotion of the Saints and their prophet-leaders in establishing a beachhead of Zion in the wilderness of Deseret is a chronicle of transcendent inspiration concerning the triumphs that come from unparalleled sacrifice and faith. Through such faith and sacrifice, the Saints flourished and became a blessed people. Though it seemed an impossible task to raise up a city, a temple, and a people to the Lord in the midst of such poverty and struggle, the Saints were obedient and persevered. There is no better theme for what transpired in the valleys of the Rocky Mountains after the exodus from Nauvoo and the arrival in the Salt Lake Valley on July 24, 1847, than what Nephi memorialized in his famous pronouncement: "I will go and do the things which the Lord hath commanded, for I know that the Lord giveth no commandments unto the children of men, save he shall prepare a way for them that they may accomplish the thing which he commandeth them" (1 Ne. 3:7).

MOMENT OF TRUTH

The arrival of the Saints in the Salt Lake Valley was certainly a great turning point in the history of the Church. At last they had a place of their own, away from the world and its persecution. But this new setting brought its own set of problems. Now in the middle of the desert, in poverty and seeming desolation, the Saints were to erect a civilization and a temple to God. Another challenge to the Saints was remaining faithful and diligent, rather than resting on their laurels, thinking they had done enough and didn't need to personally do more to build the kingdom. They had to learn to stay faithful in their obedience and sacrifice, without being compelled through further tribulation. We learn from history that they were not "slothful because of the easiness of the way" (Alma 36:44) but were industrious and obedient. They did not slow down their efforts because they had "arrived" in Zion but continued to build it for future generations.

With the dedication of the Salt Lake Temple by Wilford Woodruff on April 6, 1893, a milestone of historical significance was reached that would resound to the glory of God throughout the earth and herald a period of expanded temple building that was never to cease. In our day we are just beginning to see the unfolding of this sacred movement in scope and reach more fully consonant with the growing needs of a worldwide Church, as Saints in all regions of the earth prepare themselves in righteousness to receive God's highest blessings. Through our obedience and sacrifice, we are given the opportunity to serve, learn, and grow in our temple worship and missionary efforts. How grateful we should be that the Lord, in His mercy and love, has opened the way for the Saints to enjoy these eternal blessings on such a broad scale and experience the joy of thrusting in their sickles with their might to participate in the harvest of the gospel in these latter days.

1. THE BLESSINGS OF A TEMPLE IN THE SHADOWS OF THE EVERLASTING HILLS

THEME: With the erection and completion of the Salt Lake Temple—the fourth such holy structure in the West—the Church raised up a monument of strength, courage, and everlasting praise to God for His matchless kindness. This kindness and goodness of God is in turn manifest in such temples through the endowment of truth and sealing blessings bestowed upon the faithful. Throughout the world, the image of the Salt Lake Temple has become an invitation to flock to the gates of salvation and partake of eternal joy in "the mountain of the Lord's house," as envisioned by ancient prophets (see Isa. 2:2–3, Micah 4:1–2).

MODERN PROPHETS SPEAK

Joseph Fielding Smith:

> The spirit of this work, which had rested so abundantly upon the Prophet Joseph Smith, continued with all its power and authority with President Brigham Young. One of the first commandments he received from the Lord, after entering the Salt Lake Valley, was to build a temple to the Lord's name where these ordinances for the salvation of both the

living and the dead could be performed. From that day to this, the spirit of temple building and of temple work has continued unabated with the Church. (*DS,* 2:170)

Ezra Taft Benson:

> Temples are built and dedicated so that, through the priesthood, parents can be sealed to their children and children can be sealed to their parents. These sealing ordinances apply to both the living and the dead. If we fail to be sealed to our progenitors and our posterity, the purpose of this earth, man's exaltation, will be utterly wasted so far as we are concerned. (*TETB,* 248)

Joseph Smith:

> The Church is not fully organized, in its proper order, and cannot be, until the Temple is completed, where places will be provided for the administration of the ordinances of the Priesthood. (*HC,* 4:603)

Howard W. Hunter:

> All of our efforts in proclaiming the gospel, perfecting the Saints, and redeeming the dead lead to the holy temple. This is because the temple ordinances are absolutely crucial; we cannot return to God's presence without them. (*THWH,* 238)

LIKENING THE SCRIPTURES TO OUR LIVES

D&C 110:7–10 The Lord accepts the temple and will manifest Himself to His people therein. The temple will bless the lives of countless people, and its fame will spread throughout the world.

Application: Though these verses discuss the Kirtland Temple, they certainly apply to any temple of God. This is why we build temples—to come closer to God through receiving the ordinances and personal revelation offered in the temple. The importance of partaking of the life-saving and exalting ordinances is evident as the prophets and the early Saints sought with such vigor and determination to erect temples. Our beloved prophet Gordon B. Hinckley has escalated the effort. Now it is up to us to be worthy as well as diligent in moving forth the work of the Lord to redeem the dead.

2. OBEY THE PROPHET THAT THE KINGDOM OF THE LORD MAY FLOURISH

THEME: The Lord has made clear that His word is extended to the Saints through the mouths of His chosen servants: "What I the Lord have spoken, I have spoken, and I excuse not myself; and though the heavens and the earth pass away, my word shall not pass away, but shall all be fulfilled, whether by mine own voice or by the voice of my servants, it is the same" (D&C 1:38). As we follow the counsel of the prophets of God, we become worthy servants to participate in the growth and expansion of His kingdom throughout the earth. Such has ever been the pattern of heaven, in all dispensations of the gospel, including this dispensation of the fulness of times: from the earliest days of the Restoration, to the flourishing of the Church in the valleys of the Rocky Mountains, to the rapid growth of the Church in the current period, we are ever moving forward.

MODERN PROPHETS SPEAK

Brigham Young:

> Every son and daughter of God is expected to obey with a willing heart every word which the Lord has spoken, and which he will in the future speak to us. It is expected that we hearken to the revelations of his will, and adhere to them, cleave to them with all our might; for this is salvation, and any thing short of this clips the salvation and the glory of the Saints. (*Discourses of Brigham Young*, sel. John A. Widtsoe [Salt Lake City: Deseret Book, 1954], 220)

Spencer W. Kimball:

> The way to perfection is through obedience. Therefore, to each person is given a pattern—obedience through suffering, and perfection through obedience. Let each person learn obedience of faith in all things and thus exemplify the attributes of the Master. (*TSWK,* 168)

ILLUSTRATIONS FOR OUR TIMES

"We Will Make the Desert Blossom Like the Rose"

Upon seeing the Salt Lake Valley, some of the Saints were dubious about staying in the desert. They longed for a better climate and comfort. Those who stayed with President Young, following his counsel, were blessed and participated in the fulfillment of prophecy, as we see in the following story.

> When President Young set his foot down here, upon this desert spot, it was in the midst of persuasion, prayers and petitions on the part of some Latter-day Saints who had gone forward and landed upon the coast of California, that beautiful, rich country, semi-tropical, abounding in resources that no inland country could possess, inviting and appealing for settlers at that time, and just such settlers as President Brigham Young could have taken there—honest people, people who were firm in their faith, who were established in the knowledge of truth and righteousness and in

the testimony of Jesus Christ—which is the spirit of prophecy—and in the testimony of Joseph Smith which was a confirmation of the spirit of Christ and His mission—these people pleaded with President Young. "Come with us," they said, "and let us go to the coast. Go where the roses bloom all the year round, where the fragrance of flowers scents the air, from May until May; where beauty reigns; where the elements of wealth are to be found, and only need to be developed. Come with us."

"No," said President Young; "we will remain here, and we will make the desert blossom like the rose. We will fulfill the Scriptures by remaining here." (Joseph F. Smith, quoted in *Best-Loved Stories of the LDS People,* ed. Jack M. Lyon, Linda Ririe Gundry, and Jay A. Parry [Salt Lake City: Deseret Book, 1997], 116–17)

Extending Zion's Boundaries

As the work progressed, however, it became the will of the Lord that Zion, now well established in Salt Lake City, should spread to other areas of the wilderness. This was the case especially with companies who came later than 1847, when the beginnings of a great city were already established. Many of the Saints would have preferred to stay in the valley once they arrived. It would have been much easier to stay where they would be comfortable and where others had already begun the work. But the Church needed to be established in other areas. So, in obedience to the direction of the prophet, many crossed one wilderness to arrive in Salt Lake, only to be sent out to and remain in another wilderness to continue the work of the kingdom.

Although the Salt Lake Valley was the main arrival point for immigrant families coming into the Utah Territory, it was not the end of the journey for many of them. Some weary travelers barely had time to wash up and enjoy a few meals at a real table before they were on the road again to a more distant settlement.

The Saints established hundreds of new communities throughout parts of what are now Idaho, Nevada, California, Oregon, Wyoming, Arizona, and Utah. By the end of the nineteenth century, in fact, some 325 permanent settlements had been founded in Utah alone.

Families volunteered or were called by Church authorities to settle these new communities, a task that required resourcefulness, patience, and the ability to work together. In addition to building homes and establishing farms in remote areas, rugged pioneers of all ages worked together to build fences, canals, roads, telegraph lines, and railroads. They established blacksmith shops, the silk industry, woolen and flour mills, tanneries, and boot and shoe shops. As new communities were born, schools, meetinghouses, cooperative stores, irrigation systems, and theaters sprang up throughout the Great Basin.

Young persons contributed significantly to these ventures. They planted acres of farmland, fed and tended livestock, learned to spin, sewed burial clothing, thinned sugar beets, produced cheese, learned telegraphy, taught school, carried the mail, and drove heavily loaded wagons through sometimes treacherous terrain.

The contributions made by youth to the settling of the West are only beginning to be understood. To read of the mountain of work they accomplished, even at very young ages, is to comprehend that Mormon youth were valuable partners with their parents in building up the promised land. (Susan Arrington Madsen, ed., *Growing Up in Zion: True Stories of Young Pioneers Building the Kingdom* [Salt Lake City: Deseret Book, 1996], 68)

LIKENING THE SCRIPTURES TO OUR LIVES

D&C 64:33–34 We should not be weary in well-doing, for we are helping to build Zion. Through our willingness and obedience, Zion will become great and we will be blessed.

Application: Like the Saints who have gone before us, we cannot slow down, give in, or give up. We must remain faithful, not just while we're seeking a testimony, a blessing, or worthiness, but also once we have received these things. We should become stronger and stronger in our obedience to the commandments of God as given through His prophet so that we can continue in building the "great work."

3. MISSIONARIES SACRIFICE AND PREACH THROUGHOUT THE WORLD

THEME: The mission of the Church has always been the same: to build and operate the holy temples of the Lord on behalf of the living and the dead, to labor without cease in the task of strengthening families and perfecting the Saints, and to carry the gospel message with devotion and perseverance throughout the world. Even with all the Saints had sacrificed already, they did not lose sight of this key aspect and purpose of the Church. Their example of sacrifice to preach the gospel inspires us today to keep alive their legacy of faith and obedience in sacrifice.

MODERN PROPHETS SPEAK

George Albert Smith:

> As I have traveled to and fro in the world bearing this message, my soul has been filled with joy, and my eyes have been dimmed with tears, when I have seen how perfectly

men's lives may be transformed by the gospel of Jesus Christ. I have seen those who were discouraged, those who were in darkness, those who questioned the purpose of their being, and when they have had taught to them the glorious truths of the gospel of Jesus Christ, they have changed, they have learned to be happy, to be contented, to be satisfied, to be enthusiastic in believing and teaching the gospel that was proclaimed by Jesus Christ when he dwelt upon this earth and traveled in Galilee.

Brethren and sisters, the world does not understand that, but it is our mission to assist them to understand it, and it is not with egotism, it is not with arrogance, but with charity for all, with loving tenderness, that his message is sent forth. (*The Teachings of George Albert Smith,* ed. Robert McIntosh and Susan McIntosh [Salt Lake City: Bookcraft, 1996], 140)

ILLUSTRATIONS FOR OUR TIMES

President Benson on Missionary Work

"Go ye into all the world, and preach the gospel to every creature" (Mark 16:15).

I recall very vividly how the spirit of missionary work came into my life. I was about thirteen years of age when my father received a call to go on a mission. It was during an epidemic in the Whitney community. Parents were encouraged to go to sacrament meeting, but the children were to remain home.

Father and Mother went to sacrament meeting in a one-horse buggy. At the close of the meeting, the storekeeper opened the store just long enough for the farmers to get their mail, since the post office was in the store. There were no purchases, but in this way the farmers saved a trip to the post office on Monday.

As Father drove the horse homeward, Mother opened the mail and, to their surprise, there was a letter from Box B—a call to go on a mission. No one asked if one were ready, willing, or able. The bishop was supposed to know, and the bishop was Grandfather George T. Benson, my father's father.

As Father and Mother drove into the yard, they were both crying—something we had never seen in our family. We gathered around the buggy—there were seven of us then—and asked them what was the matter.

They said, "Everything's fine."

"Why are you crying then?" we asked.

"Come into the living room and we'll explain."

We gathered around the old sofa in the living room and Father told us what had happened. Then Mother said, "We're proud to know that Father's considered worthy to go on a mission. We're crying a bit because it means two years of separation. You know, your father and I have never been separated more than two nights at a time since our marriage—and that was when Father has gone into the canyon to get logs, posts, and firewood."

Father went on his mission, leaving Mother at home with seven children. (The eighth was born four months after he arrived in the field.) There came into that home, however, a spirit of missionary work that never left it. It was not without some sacrifice. Father had to sell our old dry farm in order to finance his mission. He had to move a married couple into part of our home to take care of the row crops, and he left his sons and wife the responsibility for the hay land, the pasture land, and a small herd of dairy cows.

Father's letters were indeed a blessing to the family. To us children, they seemed to come from halfway around the world, but they were only from Springfield and Chicago, Illinois, and Cedar Rapids and Marshalltown, Iowa. Yes, there came into our home, as a result of Father's mission, a spirit of missionary work that never left it.

Later the family grew to eleven children, seven sons and four daughters. All seven sons filled missions, some of them two or three missions. Later one daughter and her husband filled a two-year mission in Great Britain. Two sisters, both widows—one the mother of eight and the other the mother of ten—served as missionary companions in Birmingham, England. The last of the daughters and her husband recently served a mission in San Diego, California.

No other church, to my knowledge, places such an emphasis on missionary work as does The Church of Jesus Christ of Latter-day Saints. Every worthy young man is expected to serve a mission. Older couples, after their children are reared and when health and resources permit, may serve missions. But additionally, every member of the Church is expected to be a missionary by example and invitation to others to investigate our message. (Ezra Taft Benson, *Come unto Christ* [Salt Lake City: Deseret Book, 1983], 87)

LIKENING THE SCRIPTURES TO OUR LIVES

Doctrine and Covenants 31:4–5 We must declare the word of the gospel to the world, for the time of harvest is now. Through our diligence in this work, our sins are forgiven and we are made worthy.

Doctrine and Covenants 123:12 There are yet many of our brothers and sisters upon the earth who are seeking for enlightenment from God and are only kept from the truth because they do not know where to find it.

Application: The sacrifice of those who have gone before to declare the word and preach the gospel to every nation, kindred, tongue, and people is legendary, from the primitive Church and the days of Peter and Paul to the Book of Mormon and its myriad of examples of magnificent missionaries. Now it is our time. So many people out there are waiting, yearning to have the truth in their lives. We can do so many simple and easy things—from placing a copy of the Book of Mormon, prayerfully setting a date for someone to accept the missionaries, praying for those who know not God (see Alma 6:6), distributing pass-along cards, and participating in a whole host of activities to befriend those who know not the gospel of Jesus Christ and its Restoration in these latter days. We are to be full-time member-missionaries and let the spirit of missionary work pervade our lives. Where circumstances permit, we should seek out our bishops and suggest putting in our papers to serve full-time missions. We are the ones (see Jacob 5:70–77; D&C 138:56), and this can be our joy and glory (see Alma 29:9–10; 36:24).

SUMMARY

From a careful study of Church history in modern times, we gain new insight into and appreciation for the profound blessings of having a temple in our midst—a temple that has become an ensign to the nations for the expansion of temple work throughout the world. We strengthen our conviction that obedience to the prophet of God results inevitably in the flourishing of His expanding kingdom in the latter days, particularly through the sacrifice of devoted missionaries in every quarter of the earth. From the blossoming of the Church in the desert valleys of Utah to the unfolding of the kingdom of God in glory around the globe, we deepen our grateful realization of the design of the Father to bless and nurture His children as they rise in the majesty of their potential: "For verily I say unto you, blessed is he that keepeth my commandments, whether in life or in death; and he that is faithful in tribulation, the reward of the same is greater in the kingdom of heaven. Ye cannot behold with your natural eyes, for the present time, the design of your God concerning those things which shall come hereafter, and the glory which shall follow after much tribulation" (D&C 58:2–4). Let us ever be mindful of our heritage of obedience and sacrifice, endeavoring to move the work forward so that we can join those great Saints with our Lord hereafter.

CHAPTER THIRTY-SEVEN

"WE THANK THEE, O GOD, *for a* PROPHET"

Reading Assignment: Doctrine and Covenants 21; 43:1–7; Articles of Faith 1:9; *Our Heritage,* page 131.

Additional Reading: Mosiah 8:13–18, 33; Doctrine and Covenants 1:38; 20:21–26; 43:2–3; 68:3–4; 107:91–92.

There has never been a time, when God has had a work in the earth, that he has recognized without a prophet at its head. We sing in our song, "We thank thee, O God, for a prophet To guide us in these latter days" (Hymns, no. 196), for we have living prophets; we don't have to depend on the dead prophets alone. We have the living prophets to guide and direct us. (LeGrand Richards, Ensign, *May 1975, 95)*

THEMES *for* LIVING

1. Our Essential Need for a Living Prophet
2. The Roles and Christlike Love of Our Living Prophet
3. Heed the Words of Our Living Prophet

INTRODUCTION

The Lord has made abundantly clear that our eyes need to be focused at all times and in all diligence upon His appointed prophet as leader and director of the affairs of the kingdom of God upon the earth: "Wherefore, meaning the church, thou shalt give heed unto all his words and commandments which he shall give unto you as he receiveth them, walking in all holiness before me; For his word ye shall receive, as if from mine own mouth, in all patience and faith. For by doing these things the gates of hell shall not prevail against you; yea, and the Lord God will disperse the powers of darkness from before you, and cause the heavens to shake for your good, and his name's glory" (D&C 21:4–6).

We are to receive counsel of the prophet as if it came from the Lord Himself (see D&C 1:38), for the prophet is invested with indispensable gifts and powers of God in grand measure: "Thus God has provided a means that man, through faith, might work mighty miracles; therefore he becometh a great benefit to his fellow beings" (Mosiah 8:18). The living prophet today is verily our Moses, appointed to deliver us from the bondage of sin, the confinement of worldliness and pride, and the shackles of spiritual passivity. What great love the Lord has manifested in granting us the leadership and light of a living prophet to guide us across the often-troubling and ever-challenging landscape of mortal experience and toward our beckoning heavenly home of peace and glory.

MOMENT OF TRUTH

The Doctrine and Covenants is the written distillate of revelatory pronouncements from the latter-day mouthpiece of God. This work of scripture is evidence of the fact that God speaks today, as He did in former dispensations, through a prophet unto the blessing and spiritual renewal of His children everywhere. Many sections of this most remarkable work attest specifically to the divine commission and empowerment of the living prophet of God, including sections 1, 20, 21, 43, 68, and 107. The background for section 1 was given in chapter 1, for sections 20 and 107 in chapter 8, for section 21 in chapter 9, and for section 43 in chapter 24. The background for section 68, which also clarifies various duties of the First Presidency, is as follows.

Section 68: Given through the Prophet Joseph Smith in November 1831 in connection with a conference at Hiram, Portage County, Ohio, at the request of Orson Hyde, Luke S. Johnson, Lyman E. Johnson, and William E. McLellin (see *HC,* 1:227–29). The revelation contains profoundly important doctrinal declarations, such as the fact that inspired discourse spoken by God's priesthood leaders under the influence of the Holy Ghost constitutes scripture (verses 3–6); the commission to do missionary work for the salvation of humankind (verses 7–12); the right of the First Presidency to call, set apart, and ordain bishops (who are to be high priests)—also that literal descendants of Aaron can, by right, and if worthy, be installed in the office of bishop by the First Presidency (verses 13–21); the fact that only the First Presidency of the Church can try bishops or high priests (verses 22–24); the famous injunction to parents to teach the gospel to their children and see that they are baptized when eight years of age (verses 25–28); and a commandment to be industrious and faithful in the service, remembering to keep the Sabbath day holy and always pray "in the season thereof" (verses 29–35). The references to priesthood offices in this section are similar to those contained in D&C 107:64–84.

How did these four individuals who requested of the Prophet Joseph Smith to know the will of the Lord reverence the revelations given on their behalf? Orson Hyde became an Apostle and filled a number of missions for the Church (despite a period of estrangement), eventually dedicating the land of Israel for the return of Jews (October 24, 1841). Luke Samuel Johnson likewise became an Apostle and also filled a number of missions for the Church, but he was excommunicated and remained alienated from the Church for a number of years before being rebaptized. Lyman Eugene Johnson also became an Apostle but was later excommunicated and lost his life by drowning in the Mississippi. William E. McLellin criticized the language in the revelations received through the Prophet; however, when William was challenged to produce the equal of the inspired revelations (D&C 67:6–7), he failed and soon fell away as an apostate. Eventually he joined forces with the Missouri mobbers acting against the Prophet and other Church leaders. Nevertheless, he maintained his testimony of the Book of Mormon until the end.

It is clear that these four individuals received and honored the revelations given to them through the Prophet Joseph Smith in varying degrees and with varying levels of acceptance and valor. How shall we receive and apply the revelations of God in our lives today?

1. OUR ESSENTIAL NEED FOR A LIVING PROPHET

THEME: In ancient times, God's servant Amos crystallized the essence of the prophetic office in memorable terms: "Surely the Lord God will do nothing, but he revealeth his secret unto his servants the prophets" (Amos 3:7). The grand secret of God is the gospel itself—the good news and plan of action and divinely empowered and authorized keys and ordinances leading to "the immortality and eternal life of man" (Moses 1:39). This plan is designed for the blessing of the Saints as fellow citizens in the household of God, who are "built upon the foundation of the apostles and prophets, Jesus Christ himself being the chief corner stone; In whom all the building fitly framed together groweth unto an holy temple in the Lord: In whom ye also are builded together for an habitation of God through the Spirit" (Eph. 2:20–22). What a magnificent blessing it is to have in our midst a living prophet who conveys the stabilizing, inspiring, edifying, and vitalizing word of God to guide and direct us in these latter days.

MODERN PROPHETS SPEAK

Ezra Taft Benson:

> Let me ask, do we need a true prophet of the Lord on the earth today? Did the people in Noah's day need a prophet to warn them spiritually and temporally? Had a man refused to follow Noah, would he have been saved from the flood? Yet the Bible tells us that in the last days in which we live, the wickedness of the people will become comparable to the wickedness of the people in Noah's day when God cleansed the earth by flood. Do you think we need a prophet today to warn us and prepare us for the cleansing that God promised will come, this time by fire?

> Men's hearts are failing them, spiritually and temporally. Is it of interest for you to know that God has revealed many things for your blessing? He has revealed to a modern prophet a law of health, which, if obeyed, promises a man that he can run and not be weary, and walk and not faint. (*Ensign,* January 1973, 57)

ILLUSTRATIONS FOR OUR TIMES

Brigham Young on the Living Oracles of God

> On one occasion, the Church leader asked President Young to help him respond to members who were critical. For some time, prominent members had been conducting meetings at the home of the Prophet Joseph Smith which seemed calculated to undermine the Prophet's influence. When President Smith and President Young entered the house, the speaker was extolling the virtues of scripture as a test of truth but said nothing of the need for a prophet and seer. When the speaker sat down, the Prophet asked his friend to speak. "I felt like a thousand lions," President Young later recalled. Placing each book of scripture on the stand, he declared to the audience that he would not "give the ashes of a rye straw" for the books without the accompanying teachings of "the living oracles of God." He emphasized strongly that without living prophets The Church of Jesus Christ was "no better than" other churches of the world. (Ronald W. Walker, *Ensign,* February 1998, 51)

LIKENING THE SCRIPTURES TO OUR LIVES

D&C 68:3–4 When the prophet, Apostles, and other inspired leaders speak as they are moved upon by the Holy Ghost, their words are scripture and contain the will, mind, and voice of the Lord.

Application: Without a prophet, we would not receive further revelation concerning the mind and will of the Lord. We would eventually be led astray. Think how quickly other people have fallen without a prophet in their lives. Both individuals and civilizations have decayed in less than one generation because they didn't listen to the prophet of God on the earth. Oh, how we need our beloved prophet! When we come to realize that we need a living prophet to guide and direct us and give us the word of the Lord, we will hearken to his words. Our prophet is a seer and revelator—and indeed possesses all keys to administer the kingdom.

2. THE ROLES AND CHRISTLIKE LOVE OF OUR LIVING PROPHET

THEME: The Apostle Paul explained the spiritual essence of love that is bestowed upon God's servants: "And hope maketh not ashamed; because the love of God is shed abroad in our hearts by the Holy Ghost which is given unto us" (Rom. 5:5). Likewise, love is manifested richly in the lives of the living prophets of God today, who reach out to God's children—and to all the world—in the spirit of charity and benevolence. Love can be manifested in multiple voices: warning, encouraging, instructing, calling to repentance, instilling hope—whatever the Lord through His Spirit may direct for the blessing of His children. The prophet is a beacon of hope, an example of perfecting grace at work, an emissary of the Almighty, an anchor in times of uncertainty and shifting values, a compass of leadership, and a friend who acts in all kindness and charity—all of these roles reflecting the honor and dignity of the office established by the Lord to "to move the cause of Zion in mighty power for good" (D&C 21:7).

MODERN PROPHETS SPEAK

Ezra Taft Benson:

> I testify that there has been, and there is now, and there will be legal successors to the Prophet Joseph Smith who hold the keys of the kingdom of God on earth, even the President of The Church of Jesus Christ of Latter-day Saints (see D&C 21:1–7; D&C 107:91–92; D&C 112:15). He receives revelation from God to direct His

kingdom. Associated with him are others who are prophets, seers, and revelators, even those who make up the presiding quorums of the Church, namely the First Presidency and the Quorum of the Twelve Apostles (see D&C 112:30). (*Ensign,* November 1988, 86)

Russell M. Nelson:

> Recently, President Gordon B. Hinckley declared: "Love of God is the root of all virtue, of all goodness, of all strength of character, of all fidelity to do right. Love the Lord your God, and love his Son, and be ever grateful for their love for us. Whenever other love fades, there will be that shining, transcendent, everlasting love of God for each of us and the love of his Son, who gave his life for us."
>
> Brothers and sisters, race, nationality, occupation, or other interests need not stand in the way. All can look to the Lord. All can place him first in their lives. Those who do so and remain faithful will qualify for his sublime promise: "Every soul who forsaketh his sins and cometh unto me, and calleth on my name, and obeyeth my voice, and keepeth my commandments, shall see my face and know that I am" (D&C 93:1). This glorious destiny can be ours. (*Ensign,* May 1996, 32)

ILLUSTRATIONS FOR OUR TIMES

President Hinckley as an Example of Christlike Love

From the following story we see a brief glimpse of the unconditional, Christlike love so characteristic of a prophet of God. Though he hadn't met the people before, so strong was President Hinckley's love for them as children of God that they could all feel it and were drawn to his message.

> From the outset, Elder Hinckley had an affinity for the Asians. He admired the integrity, resourcefulness, and work ethic of these determined people, and he was attracted to their manner, which though somewhat formal was gracious and accommodating. Though the Church was small and struggling, he saw potential in the modest core of members. Kenji Tanaka, who later became the first stake president in Asia, attended a priesthood meeting during Elder Hinckley's first trip to Japan. "Our expectations were so great," he remembered, "and Elder Hinckley's excitement could be seen in his sparkling eyes. His first word to us was *Subarashii!* The atmosphere of that meeting changed from stiff and formal to friendliness and closeness to him, and a warm feeling prevailed. During that meeting he told us, 'Those who gather together here today are holding the most important power, a far greater power than the Prime Minister of Japan, for the Japanese people.' He inspired us, he motivated us to aim high with strong and clear goals. He had a core of energy

that was radiating and full of love." (Sheri L. Dew, *Go Forward with Faith: The Biography of Gordon B. Hinckley* [Salt Lake City: Deseret Book, 1996], 220)

LIKENING THE SCRIPTURES TO OUR LIVES

Doctrine and Covenants 107:91–92 The leader of the Church has many roles—president, seer, revelator, translator, prophet—and has obtained all the gifts of the Spirit.

Application: As one who fills so many roles, the prophet is so important to this Church. He is an example to us of all the gifts of the Spirit, including charity, which gift is the greatest spiritual gift. So close is he to the Lord that he comes not only to see as He does but to love as He does. Because of the prophet's great love of the Lord and His children, he continually works to fill all his roles in seeking after our salvation (see D&C 21:7).

3. HEED THE WORDS OF OUR LIVING PROPHET

THEME: What greater protection can come to individuals and families than to heed the words of the living prophet? Trials and difficulty are inevitable; enveloping shadows are part of life. But the calming voice of the living prophet dispels doubt and neutralizes the raging of evil in the world—if we but listen and obey: "And all they who receive the oracles of God, let them beware how they hold them lest they are accounted as a light thing, and are brought under condemnation thereby, and stumble and fall when the storms descend, and the winds blow, and the rains descend, and beat upon their house" (D&C 90:5).

MODERN PROPHETS SPEAK

James E. Faust:
> I do not believe members of the Church can be in full harmony with the Savior without sustaining his living prophet on the earth, the president of the Church. If we do not sustain the living prophet, whoever he may be, we die spiritually. Ironically, some have died spiritually by exclusively following prophets who have long been dead. Others equivocate in their support of living prophets, trying to lift themselves up by putting down the living prophets, however subtly. (*Reach Up for the Light* [Salt Lake City: Deseret Book, 1990], 111)

L. Tom Perry:
> Today, by sustaining a . . . prophet, we have placed ourselves under solemn covenant to heed his voice. . . .

He is an inspiration to all of us. He is our prophet. We sit at his feet ready to feast on the wisdom of this true and faithful servant-leader. We stand ready to heed his voice because we know he speaks for the Lord. (*Ensign,* November 1994, 17)

Bruce R. McConkie:

The great need in the world today is not for the Lord to send a prophet to reveal his mind and will. He has done that; we have a prophet; we are guided by many men who have the spirit of inspiration. The great need today is for men to have a listening ear and to give heed to the words that fall from the lips of those who wear the prophetic mantle. (*Ensign,* May 1974, 71)

ILLUSTRATIONS FOR OUR TIMES

Obedience to Counsel Rewarded

I had related to me a rather interesting story of a humble man who lives in the state of Arizona; it is as follows: Dr. John A. Widtsoe of the Council of the Twelve had been visiting in the Snowflake Stake and among other counsel he gave to the brethren was this: "Why don't you drill wells that you might bring more of this arid land under cultivation?"

President Flake of the presidency pondered over the counsel given, and he came to the conclusion that a servant of God had spoken and that it would be wise to follow such counsel. Going to a neighboring town he endeavored to secure the services of a well driller. And the driller said, "Yes, I will drill you a well. I assume you want the usual size pipe, six or eight inches."

President Flake said: "No, I want a twelve-inch pipe." The well driller replied: "Man, you are foolish. There isn't enough water in this country to fill a twelve-inch pipe, and furthermore, I wouldn't take your money to drill a well of that size because it would be a waste of money." And so he refused to drill the well.

But, undaunted, President Flake went to another well driller in a neighboring community. He told the man what he wanted. The man said: "Well, it seems foolish, but nevertheless if you want to spend the money, I will drill the hole and put a twelve-inch pipe in it."

A site was selected for the well on a piece of arid land adjacent to Snowflake, Arizona, and drilling operations were commenced. After the men had drilled for a few days, a government man came along, and he said: "Mr. Flake, I think you are foolish in drilling for water here. I am quite sure that you won't find any. It is my judgment had you gone over here a short distance the possibilities are that you might have found a little water."

But again, undaunted and believing implicitly in the counsel of one of God's servants, the drilling continued and after reaching a depth of two hundred feet, a flow of water was struck in sufficient amount to fill the twelve-inch pipe up within sixty feet of the surface. The ground was broken, cultivated, and crops were planted. A pump was placed on the well, and it delivered nine hundred gallons a minute. This year the crops grown on what was arid land two years ago will pay for the drilling of the well and the pumping equipment installed.

President Flake further indicated that the volume of water has been sufficient, not only to take care of this year's crop, but also will be sufficient to irrigate a total of 175 acres.

President Flake followed the counsel of one of Christ's apostles and received the blessing for obedience rendered, which brings us to the conclusion that we should hearken always to the voices of the prophets to the end that the windows of heaven will be open to us—spiritually and temporally. (Joseph L. Wirthlin, CR, October 1947, 126)

LIKENING THE SCRIPTURES TO OUR LIVES

Doctrine and Covenants 21:4–6 The Church is commanded to follow the prophet, receiving his word as the word of Christ. Doing so not only protects us from harm and evil but will also bring blessings from God.

Application: Following the prophet is following Christ (see D&C 84:36). We cannot set aside the words of our living prophet. He speaks for Christ and reveals His words to the people (see Amos 3:7). When we heed his words, we will always sustain him through our faith and prayers and through the confidence we show by being obedient to his counsel (see D&C 107:22). Consequently, we shall be blessed and not perish (see 2 Ne. 26:8).

SUMMARY

To close this chapter on the great need we have for a prophet, let us consider an ancient example. The people of King Noah were separated from the rest of the Nephites and therefore from the main body of the Church. The people had been apart for only one generation, and yet within that time they had fallen away from the ways of God. So a prophet, Abinadi, was sent to them. Abinadi declared before wicked

King Noah and his court the words that these prideful dissenters did not wish to hear: "For behold, did not Moses prophesy unto them concerning the coming of the Messiah, and that God should redeem his people? Yea, and even all the prophets who have prophesied ever since the world began—have they not spoken more or less concerning these things?" (Mosiah 13:33). Abinadi had to reteach them the gospel, and for that they killed him. Let us not repeat the fatal mistake of King Noah by rejecting the word of God, given under inspiration through his chosen servants. Instead, let us gratefully acknowledge our essential need for the guidance of a living prophet, emulate his Christlike example, and heed his words in all devotion as the Lord has directed. In this manner, we can be assured that the blessings of heaven will attend us and our families along the pathway of life.

CHAPTER THIRTY-EIGHT

"IN MINE OWN WAY"

Reading Assignment: Doctrine and Covenants 38:30; 42:30–31, 42; 58:26–28; 104:13–18; *Our Heritage,* pages 108–9, 111–14.

Additional Reading: 2 Thessalonians 3:10–12; Doctrine and Covenants 56:17–20; 58:27; 88:124; 136:8.

Self-sufficiency is the ability to maintain one's self and relates to women and men being agents for themselves. Independence and self-sufficiency are critical keys to spiritual and temporal growth. A situation that threatens one's ability to be self-sufficient also threatens one's confidence, self-esteem, and freedom. As dependence is increased, the freedom to act is decreased.

Church writings often use the terms "self-sufficiency" and "self-reliance" inter-changeably. Teachings pertaining to Welfare Services emphasize and place considerable importance on both individual and family independence. Six principles form the foundation of the infrastructure of the Welfare Program. Three of these principles emphasize responsibility to care for one's own needs: work, self-reliance, and stewardship; the other three focus on responsibility to others: love, service, and consecration (James E. Faust, "Establishing the Church: Welfare Services Missionaries Are an Important Resource," Ensign, November 1982, 91).

President Spencer W. Kimball defined Welfare Services as the "essence of the Gospel . . . the Gospel in action" ("Welfare Services: The Gospel in Action," Ensign, *November 1977, 77). (Daniel H. Ludlow, ed.,* Encyclopedia of Mormonism, *4 vols. [New York: Macmillan, 1992], 1293)*

THEMES *for* LIVING

1. Spiritual and Temporal Self-Reliance
2. Caring for the Poor and Needy
3. The Welfare Program of the Church

INTRODUCTION

The Lord appointed man to "have dominion over all the beasts of the field, and to eat his bread by the sweat of his brow" (Moses 5:1). We are to work to sustain life; the Lord gives us ample opportunity, but it is up to us to be wise stewards. The same principle is reflected in the realm of spiritual need, as Nephi declared: "For we know that it is by grace that we are saved, after all we can do" (2 Ne. 25:23). "After all we can do" is the simple, profound lever for the implementation of the endowment of divine grace unto salvation. We must do *all* we can to strengthen ourselves spiritually, relying only on the Lord and our own testimonies to obtain salvation. Then is His grace applicable to saving us.

Because the Savior is full of grace, we strive to be gracious to our fellows. Because the Savior is full of saving love, we strive to do all in our power to save our fellows and elevate them to a higher level of joy and self-reliance. The Lord's design to care for His children is centered on industry and self-reliance. He has commanded us to "cease to be idle" (D&C 88:124) and has said further: "Thou shalt not be idle; for he that is idle shall not eat the bread nor wear the garments of the laborer" (D&C 42:42). Nevertheless, those who remain wanting after striving with all their heart and might to lift themselves from need are fully embraced by the spirit of service and charity on the part of their companions. In great measure, charitable service also includes reaching out to teach principles of self-reliance and self-sufficiency. Often those who want for life's basics lack principally in the knowledge of how to open doorways of opportunity. As one hand reaches out to feed and nurture, the other points the way and kindles insight into strategies of self-care and self-nurture for individuals and families.

Service to others—in particular, to those who are wanting in material necessities and in the fundamentals of a spiritual life—is anchored in a defining attitude of selflessness and mercy. The key to such service is that it mirrors in essence the all-embracing charity of the Redeemer. We serve because He serves; we give because He gives; we love unconditionally because of His abiding example of love. We are to do all in our power to ameliorate and render inoperative those conditions that cause pain and suffering. As Brigham Young declared at the beginning of the exodus to the West: "Let each company bear an equal proportion, according to the dividend of their property, in taking the poor, the widows, the fatherless, and the families of those who have gone into the army, that the cries of the widow and the fatherless come not up into the ears of the Lord against this people" (D&C 136:8).

We are no less obligated, upon the continuing journey of life, to do our part in sharing our means with those who have less or who want for the basic needs of mortality. Ours is the opportunity to embark on righteous endeavors that will bless lives and lift spirits: "Verily I say, men should be anxiously engaged in a good cause, and do many things of their own free will, and bring to pass much righteousness; For the power is in them, wherein they are agents unto themselves. And inasmuch as men do good they shall in nowise lose their reward" (D&C:27–28).

MOMENT OF TRUTH

Many passages from the Doctrine and Covenants explain the Lord's program of cultivating self-reliance and promoting caring service on behalf of the needy and the poor (see *Reading Assignment* above). Following is background information on just two of the relevant sections that have not been treated to this point.

Section 44: Given through the Prophet Joseph Smith in the latter part of February 1831 at Kirtland, Geauga County, Ohio (see *HC,*1:157). The revelation called for a conference to be held in Ohio. The conference, the fourth held in the newly organized Church and the first in Ohio, was convened on June 3, 1831. It was on the occasion of this conference that Joseph Smith and others were ordained to the high priesthood. Also mentioned in the revelation at this early date in the Church's history was the law of consecration and the commandment to "visit the poor and the needy and administer to their relief" (verse 6).

Section 56: Given through the Prophet Joseph Smith in June 1831 at Kirtland, Geauga County, Ohio (see *HC,* 1:186–88). Calls had been issued to a number of brethren to journey to Missouri, preaching along the way. But commercial interests got in the way of Ezra Thayre's preparations, and since he had been appointed to be the companion of Thomas B. Marsh, the revelation rescinded the commandment and another was appointed to travel in his stead with Brother Marsh. The framework of the revelation is the establishment of spiritual priorities over material ones, and the

Lord issues a stern warning to both the rich who are prideful and selfish and the poor who are covetous, since both fail to remain humble and grateful for the blessings of heaven: "Behold, thus saith the Lord unto my people—you have many things to do and to repent of; for behold, your sins have come up unto me, and are not pardoned, because you seek to counsel in your own ways. And your hearts are not satisfied. And ye obey not the truth, but have pleasure in unrighteousness" (verses 14–15).

1. SPIRITUAL AND TEMPORAL SELF-RELIANCE

THEME: The quality of self-reliance is rooted in the reality of agency—that God created humankind with the inherent blessing of choice, the freedom to apply the principles of self-guidance under the inspiration of the Almighty: "For the power is in them, wherein they are agents unto themselves. And inasmuch as men do good they shall in nowise lose their reward" (D&C 58:28; see D&C 104:17). This agency extends to temporal as well as to spiritual matters, for God's children can prayerfully elect to use their talents, skills, and energy to learn, plan, and act for the improvement of their situation and the unfolding of increased spirituality. Such was a key part of the design of God's plan for the blessing of His children. We are here to learn and prepare ourselves for our future, in this life and in the life to come. Such preparation is what leads us to hope, for "if [we] are prepared, [we] shall not fear" (D&C 38:30).

MODERN PROPHETS SPEAK

Gordon B. Hinckley:
> If I were a bishop or stake president today, what would I do? I think that I would try to put my major efforts on building the spirituality of the people. . . .

> We need to build ourselves spiritually. We live in a world of rush and go, of running here and there and in every direction. We are very busy people. We have so much to do. We need to get off by ourselves once in awhile and think of the spiritual things and build ourselves spiritually. If you have a study at home, lock yourselves in it. If you have a place in the basement where you can be by yourself, go there. Get by yourself and think of things of the Lord, of things of the Spirit. Let gratitude swell up in your hearts. Think of all the Lord has done for you. How blessed you are, how very blessed you are. Think of your duty and your responsibility. Think of your testimony. Think of the things of God. Just meditate and reflect for an hour about yourself and your relationship to your Heavenly Father and your Redeemer. It will do something for you. (*TGBH,* 608–9)

L. Tom Perry:

Independence and self-reliance are critical to our spiritual and temporal growth. Whenever we get into situations which threaten our self-reliance, we will find our freedoms threatened as well. If we increase our dependence on anything or anyone except the Lord, we will find an immediate decrease in our freedom to act. As President Heber J. Grant declared, "Nothing destroys the individuality of a man, a woman, or a child as much as the failure to be self-reliant." (*Ensign,* November 1991, 64)

Dallin H. Oaks:

Each of us should do all that we can, in the spirit of gospel self-reliance, to provide for ourselves and our families in a temporal and a spiritual way. Then, if it is necessary to reach out for help, we know we have first done all that we can. (*Ensign,* May 1997, 22)

David B. Haight:

They (the early saints) had a majestic dream of great things and lofty ideals: of homes and gardens, temples and meetinghouses, schools and universities. It would take work—hard work—and everyone's best efforts to make it happen. They became experienced colonizers and benefactors to our nation and to humanity. Many of us are a product of that early, inspired colonization—its teachings and blessings of the value of hard work coupled with desire and faith for a better way of life. (*A Light unto the World* [Salt Lake City: Deseret Book, 1997], 138)

ILLUSTRATIONS FOR OUR TIMES

The Celestial Nature of Self-Reliance

Many programs have been set up by well-meaning individuals to aid those who are in need. However, many of these programs are designed with the shortsighted objective of "helping people" as opposed to "helping people help themselves." Our efforts must always be directed toward making able-bodied people self-reliant. I clipped the following article from the *Reader's Digest* some time ago and have told it before, but it bears repeating. It reads:

"In our friendly neighbor city of St. Augustine great flocks of sea gulls are starving amid plenty. Fishing is still good, but the gulls don't know how to fish. For generations they have depended on the shrimp fleet to toss them scraps from the nets. Now the fleet has moved. . . .

"The shrimpers had created a Welfare State for the . . . sea gulls. The big birds never bothered to learn how to fish for themselves and they never taught their children to fish. Instead they led their little ones to the shrimp nets.

"Now the sea gulls, the fine free birds that almost symbolize liberty itself, are starving to death because they gave in to the 'something for nothing' lure! They sacrificed their independence for a handout.

"A lot of people are like that, too. They see nothing wrong in picking delectable scraps from the tax nets of the U.S. Government's 'shrimp fleet.' But what will happen when the Government runs out of goods? What about our children of generations to come?

"Let's not be gullible gulls. We . . . must preserve our talents of self-sufficiency, our genius for creating things for ourselves, our sense of thrift and our true love of independence" ("Fable of the Gullible Gull," *Reader's Digest*, October 1950, p. 32). . . .

Governments are not the only guilty parties. We fear many parents in the Church are making "gullible gulls" out of their children with their permissiveness and their doling out of family resources. Parents who place their children on the dole are just as guilty as a government which places its citizens on the dole. In fact, the actions of parents in this area can be more devastating than any government program.

Bishops and other priesthood leaders can be guilty of making "gullible gulls" out of their ward members. Some members become financially or emotionally dependent on their bishops. A dole is a dole whatever its source. All of our Church and family actions should be directed toward making our children and members self-reliant. We can't always control government programs, but we can control our own homes and congregations. If we will teach these principles and live them, we can do much to counter the negative effects which may exist in government programs in any country. We know there are some who for no reason of their own cannot become self-reliant. President Henry D. Moyle had these people in mind when he said:

"This great principle does not deny to the needy nor to the poor the assistance they should have. The wholly incapacitated, the aged, the sickly are cared for with all tenderness, but every able-bodied person is enjoined to do his utmost for himself to avoid dependence, if his own efforts can make such a course possible; to look upon adversity as temporary; to combine his faith in his own ability with honest toil; to rehabilitate himself and his family to a position of independence; in every case to minimize the need for help and to supplement any help given with his own best efforts.

"We believe [that] seldom [do circumstances arise in which] men of rigorous faith, genuine courage, and unfaltering determination, with the love of independence burning in their hearts, and pride in their own accomplishments, cannot surmount the obstacles that lie in their paths.

"We know that through humble, prayerful, industrious, God-fearing lives, a faith can be developed within us by the strength of which we can call down the blessings of a kind and merciful Heavenly Father and literally see our handicaps vanish and our independence and freedom established and maintained" (CR, April 1948, 5).

Self-reliance is not the end, but a means to an end. It is very possible for a person to be completely independent and lack every other desirable attribute. One may become wealthy and never have to ask anyone for anything, but unless there is some spiritual goal attached to this independence, it can canker his soul. (Marion G. Romney, *Ensign,* November 1982, 91)

LIKENING THE SCRIPTURES TO OUR LIVES

Alma 42:26 From the foundations of this world, God has prepared a plan for our happiness and redemption.

Application: Heavenly Father has prepared the way from the foundation of the world to bless His children through the plan of salvation, which is designed to bring about their immortality and eternal life (see Ether 12:22). We should likewise cultivate a spirit of preparation in our families, in our Church callings, and as we serve our fellow beings. Doing so utilizes the great preparation God has invested in us and prepares us to meet Him again (see Alma 34:32). Preparation is the key to spiritual and temporal self-reliance.

2. CARING FOR THE POOR AND NEEDY

THEME: Christ devoted His ministry and spent His precious blood caring for the "poor and needy"—comprising everyone who has ever lived and who will ever live. "Are we not all beggars?" was the haunting question posed by King Benjamin. "Do we not all depend upon the same Being, even God, for all the substance which we have, for both food and raiment, and for gold, and for silver, and for all the riches which we have of every kind?" (Mosiah 4:19). By extension of this indisputable logic, we should, in kind, also structure our lives to care for the poor and needy around us—those with less than the needful measure of material substance and support, and those with dwindling supplies of spiritual strength and vitality.

MODERN PROPHETS SPEAK

Gordon B. Hinckley:

> When we are called before the bar of God to give an accounting of our performance, I think it unlikely that any of us will be commended for wearing out our lives in an effort to find some morsel of history, incomplete in its context, to cast doubt on the integrity of this work. Rather, I believe we will be examined on what we did to build the kingdom, to bring light and understanding of the eternal truths of the gospel to the eyes and minds of all who are willing to listen, to care for the poor and the needy, and to make of the world a better place as a result of our presence. (*TGBH,* 124)

Marion G. Romney:

> In this modern world plagued with counterfeits for the Lord's plan, we must not be misled into supposing that we can discharge our obligations to the poor and the needy by shifting the responsibility to some governmental or other public agency. Only by voluntarily giving out of an abundant love for our neighbors can we develop that charity characterized by Mormon as "the pure love of Christ" (Moro. 7:47). This we must develop if we would obtain eternal life. (*Ensign,* January 1973, 97)

ILLUSTRATIONS FOR OUR TIMES

Counsel from Elder Dallin H. Oaks

> Ancient and modern scriptures are clear in their commands to care for the poor and the needy. Their passages on these subjects are too numerous to permit extensive quotation and too well-known to require it. Several illustrations will suffice.

> Elder Russell M. Nelson has observed that "when the Lord sent prophets to call Israel back from apostasy, in almost every instance, one of the first charges made was that the poor had been neglected." Thus, part of John the Baptist's message of repentance was, "He that hath two coats, let him impart to him that hath none; and he that hath meat, let him do likewise" (Luke 3:11).

> The prophets of the Book of Mormon taught that the care of the poor was the only way we could obtain essential blessings. The prophet/king Benjamin declared that we must impart of our substance to the poor, "such as feeding the hungry, clothing the naked, visiting the sick and administering to their relief" for the sake of "retaining a remission of [our] sins from day to day, that [we] may walk guiltless before God" (Mosiah 4:26).

After teaching the fundamental principles of the gospel (including the Atonement and the necessity for faith, repentance, and prayer), Amulek continued: "And now . . . do not suppose that this is all; for after ye have done all these things, if ye turn away the needy, and the naked, and visit not the sick and afflicted, and impart of your substance, if ye have, to those who stand in need—I say unto you, if ye do not any of these things, behold, your prayer is vain, and availeth you nothing, and ye are as hypocrites who do deny the faith" (Alma 34:28).

In modern times the Lord told his people they "must visit the poor and the needy and administer to their relief" (D&C 44:6), and "he that doeth not these things, the same is not my disciple" (D&C 52:40). The Lord commanded his saints to "learn to impart one to another as the gospel requires" (D&C 88:123). President Marion G. Romney explained the importance of these commandments by relating them to the Savior's statement that when he comes in his glory, he will divide his people "as a shepherd divideth his sheep from the goats" (Matt. 25:32). He said, "The test on which the division [will] be made on that great day [will] be the care given to the poor and the needy" (Marion G. Romney, "Caring for the Poor and Needy," *Ensign,* January 1973, 97).

Notwithstanding the importance of this duty toward the poor, it comes second to another duty. The Lord's plan for the care of the poor and the needy commands and then presupposes that each of us will provide for ourselves and our families, as far as we are able. This includes caring for the members of our own households—parents caring for children, and children caring for parents. Thereafter, we care for the poor members of the Church, and then extend our assistance to others as far as our means permit. We do this first by paying tithing; second, by donating liberally to the fast offering funds; and then by making other contributions of labor and money as our means permit. That is the duty the Lord has put upon each member of his church.

Traditionally, religions have taught men and women to worship a God who commands them to love one another and to serve one another. But today there are a host of pseudoreligions that teach men and women to worship themselves and to celebrate their worship with the sacrament of self-indulgence. True religion preaches responsibilities, teaching us to give. Modern counterfeits preach rights, teaching us to take. True religion produces a citizenry educated to serve; modern counterfeits produce a citizenry educated to demand service. (Dallin H. Oaks, *The Lord's Way* [Salt Lake City: Deseret Book, 1991], 103)

LIKENING THE SCRIPTURES TO OUR LIVES

Doctrine and Covenants 52:40 A true disciple of Christ remembers to care for the poor, the needy, and the sick.

Application: Our very discipleship depends on the quality of unconditional charity. The scriptures are replete with the counsel to care for the poor and needy. Our devotion to God is expressed in our love and service of our fellow beings (see Matt. 25:40; Mosiah 2:16–17). Our prayers are in vain if we forget the poor and needy (see Alma 34:28-29). If we are blessed abundantly in temporal things and forget those in need, we are in danger of losing our very souls (see D&C 56:16).

3. THE WELFARE PROGRAM OF THE CHURCH

THEME: The Church's program to promote and sustain universal self-reliance among its members is a model of principle-based organizational effectiveness that is recognized and admired among policy makers and government leaders around the world. What they don't always recognize so readily is the fact that the welfare program derives its vitality from the fact that it is also a spiritual program, grounded in the spiritual relationship of the Lord with His children. He loves us and aspires to teach us how to rise, through the inspiration of such programs within the Church, toward a higher plane of happiness and fulfillment as agents unto ourselves.

MODERN PROPHETS SPEAK

Boyd K. Packer:

> When the Church welfare program was first announced in 1936, the First Presidency made this statement: "Our primary purpose was to set up, insofar as possible, a system under which the curse of idleness would be done away with, the evils of the dole abolished, and independence, industry, thrift, and self-respect be once more established amongst our people. *The aim of the Church is to help people help themselves.* Work is to be re-enthroned as a ruling principle in the lives of our Church membership" (CR, October 1936, 3). (*Teach Ye Diligently* [Salt Lake City: Deseret Book, 1975], 233–34)

James E. Faust:

> The purpose of the Church's welfare program is to care for the poor and the needy and make the Latter-day Saints, by their obedience to gospel principles, strong and self-reliant. At the center of caring for the poor and the needy in a worldwide church

are a generous contribution to the fast offerings and personal and family preparedness. At the very heart of taking care of our own needs is our own energy and ability, with help to and from our own families.

I should like to discuss five prescriptions which, if followed, will make each of us better able to control our destinies.

First prescription: Practice thrift and frugality. . . .

Second prescription: Seek to be independent. . . .

Third prescription: Be industrious. . . .

Fourth prescription: Become self-reliant. . . .

Fifth prescription: Strive to have a year's supply of food and clothing. . . . (*Reach Up for the Light* [Salt Lake City: Deseret Book, 1990], 70–74)

ILLUSTRATIONS FOR OUR TIMES

A Story of Service Related by President Thomas S. Monson

The welfare program of the Church is divinely organized. As such, it is a success—not only because the Lord oversees it, but because He commands, instructs, and guides those who operate it for Him. The following account illustrates how important this program is to the Lord and how He will inspire and touch others in answer to prayers.

> Every bishop needs a sacred grove to which he can retire to meditate and to pray for guidance. Mine was our old ward chapel. I could not begin to count the occasions when on a dark night at a late hour I would make my way to the stand of that building where I had been blessed, confirmed, ordained, taught, and eventually called to preside. The chapel was dimly lighted by the street light in front; not a sound would be heard, no intruder to disturb. I would kneel and share with Him above my thoughts, my concerns, my problems.
>
> On one occasion, a year of drought, the commodities at the storehouse had not been their usual quality, nor had they been found in abundance. Many products were missing, especially fresh fruit. My prayer that night is sacred to me. I pleaded that the widows in my ward were the finest women I knew in mortality, that their needs were simple and conservative, that they had no resources on which they might rely.

Could not some way be found for them to receive the fruit that they needed for well-balanced meals?

The next morning I received a call from a ward member, the proprietor of a produce business. "Bishop," he said, "I would like to send a semitrailer filled with oranges, grapefruit, and bananas to the bishops' storehouse to be given to those in need. Could you make arrangements?" Could I make arrangements! The storehouse was alerted. Then each bishop was telephoned and the entire shipment distributed. Bishop Jesse M. Drury, that beloved welfare pioneer and storekeeper, said he had never witnessed a day like it before. He described the occasion with one word: "Wonderful!" (Thomas S. Monson, *Inspiring Experiences That Build Faith: From the Life and Ministry of Thomas S. Monson* [Salt Lake City: Deseret Book, 1994], 111)

LIKENING THE SCRIPTURES TO OUR LIVES

Doctrine and Covenants 42:30–31 We are commanded to remember the poor and consecrate what we have to support them, as organized by the bishop and other leaders of the Church. In doing this for them, it is as though we do it for Christ.

Application: Here the Lord gives the beginnings of the welfare system of the Church. The Lord commands us to help one another as if we were helping Him. Such love gives us the opportunity to sacrifice and others the opportunity for security and growth. The great principles taught by the welfare program are charity, personal responsibility, and accountability—self-reliance, the evils of idleness, the ethic and virtue of work, and concern for the temporal and spiritual welfare of others. As expressed so many times, this is truly the gospel in action. When we take personal responsibility for our actions, we grow. When we help and serve others, we grow.

SUMMARY

This chapter has emphasized the principles of spiritual and temporal self-reliance in caring for ourselves, our families, and the poor and needy in our communities as well as in the far quarters of the earth. The welfare program of the Church is a marvelous manifestation of charitable service and temporal/spiritual guidance and instruction. True discipleship requires a lifestyle that encompasses service to the "needy, the sick and the afflicted" (D&C 52:40).

We are accountable to the Lord for the bounties of the earth that He has given. The Lord wants all of His children to be blessed, and the opportunity is there, if we will only learn to properly care for ourselves and others: "And it is my purpose to provide for my saints, for all things are mine. But it must needs be done in mine own way; and behold this is the way that I, the Lord, have decreed to provide for my saints, that the poor shall be exalted, in that the rich are made low. For the earth is full, and there is enough and to spare; yea, I prepared all things, and have given unto the children of men to be agents unto themselves. Therefore, if any man shall take of the abundance which I have made, and impart not his portion, according to the law of my gospel, unto the poor and the needy, he shall, with the wicked, lift up his eyes in hell, being in torment" (D&C 104:16–18).

Such is the plain and uncompromising truth of what the Lord expects of us. "For of him unto whom much is given much is required" (D&C 82:3; see Luke 12:48). The essence of this requirement is an abundance of selfless charity: "See that ye love one another; cease to be covetous; learn to impart one to another as the gospel requires" (D&C 88:123). The Lord expects full devotion in such matters. However, the rewards for rendering charity and service in exceptional ways are magnificent and eternal: "For behold, the Lord shall come, and his recompense shall be with him, and he shall reward every man, and the poor shall rejoice; And their generations shall inherit the earth from generation to generation, forever and ever" (D&C 56:19–20).

CHAPTER THIRTY-NINE

"THE HEARTS *of the* CHILDREN SHALL TURN *to* THEIR FATHERS"

Reading Assignment: Doctrine and Covenants 2; 110:13–16; 138; Joseph Smith—History 1:37–39; *Our Heritage,* pages 98–99, 101–2, 105–7.

Additional Reading: 1 Corinthians 15:29; 1 Peter 4:6.

We are called upon to assist in saving our own families. This is the great duty the Lord has given to us. It is our privilege to go back and trace our ancestors as far as we can and then go to the temple and do the work for all of them. The Lord will judge whether they are worthy or not to receive what we have done. (Joseph Fielding Smith, DS, 2:192)

THEMES *for* LIVING

1. Elijah Restores the Sealing Keys
2. Urgency of Temple Work for the Dead
3. President Joseph F. Smith: The Vision of the Dead
4. Taking the Temples to the People

INTRODUCTION

The kingdom of God is a kingdom of order, power, and transcendent glory, organized by our Father in Heaven unto the blessing of all who belong to this earthly sphere. As such, the Lord, in His mercy, has prepared a plan to extend every opportunity for spiritual growth and salvation to every soul who has ever lived or who will ever live on earth—including those who have departed this life without the opportunity to learn of the gospel of Jesus Christ or embrace its tenets. The activation and administration of this all-encompassing plan can take place only upon the bestowal of divine keys pertaining thereto and the authorization of the sealing ordinances required in order for such ordinances to have efficacy beyond the veil. The Savior said to Peter: "And I will give unto thee the keys of the kingdom of heaven: and whatsoever thou shalt bind on earth shall be bound in heaven: and whatsoever thou shalt loose on earth shall be loosed in heaven" (Matt. 16:19). Peter and his associates clearly understood the breadth and majestic reach of the gospel plan: "For for this cause was the gospel preached also to them that are dead, that they might be judged according to men in the flesh, but live according to God in the spirit" (1 Pet. 4:6).

Joseph Smith learned the necessity of such keys during the angel Moroni's nocturnal visits of September 21, 1823 (see JS—H 1:36–39). To this end, the Lord commissioned the prophet Elijah to administer the keys of the sealing ordinances for all dispensations. Consequently, the sealing keys were bestowed and activated once again on April 3, 1836, in the Kirtland Temple, inaugurating a sublime spiritual movement of temple work that continues in ever-expanding scope even to this day.

MOMENT OF TRUTH

The great work on behalf of those who have passed beyond the mortal veil is encompassed especially by the messages in three sections of the Doctrine and Covenants: 2, 110, and 138. The background to section 2 was covered in chapter 30 and that of section 110 in chapter 18. Here follows information about the coming forth of section 138.

Section 138: Given through President Joseph F. Smith on October 3, 1918, in Salt Lake City, Utah. The revelation, as so many others in the Doctrine and Covenants, came as a result of the prophet studying the scriptures (see verses 1–6). Though the passage he was studying was one he'd read several times already (in verse 6 he says he was impressed by the passage "more than [he] had ever been before"), this time the Spirit touched him with new understanding. What followed was a beautiful vision of life beyond this earthly realm. Historian Lyndon W. Cook has summarized the circumstances in the following way:

Section 138, known as the "Vision of the Redemption of the Dead," was received by Joseph F. Smith six weeks before his death, during his final illness. President Smith alluded to this vision in his opening remarks at the Eighty-Ninth Semiannual Conference of the Church on 4 October 1918. In this short talk he stated,

"I will not, I dare not, attempt to enter upon many things that are resting upon my mind this morning, and I shall postpone until some future time, the Lord being willing, my attempt to tell you some of the things that are in my mind, and that dwell in my heart. I have not lived alone these five months. I have dwelt in the spirit of prayer, of supplication, of faith and of determination; and I have had my communication with the Spirit of the Lord continuously."

The vision was submitted to President Smith's two counselors, the Quorum of the Twelve Apostles, and the Presiding Patriarch of the Church on 31 October 1918 for approval as revelation. Concerning the occasion, James E. Talmage, member of the Quorum of the Twelve, recorded the following:

"Attended meeting of the First Presidency and the Twelve. Today President Smith, who is still confined to his home by illness, sent to the Brethren the account of a vision through which, as he states, were revealed to him important facts relating to the work of the disembodied Savior in the realm of departed spirits, and of the missionary work in progress on the other side of the veil. By united action the Council of the Twelve, with the Counsellors in the First Presidency, and the Presiding Patriarch accepted and enforced the revelation as the Word of the Lord. President Smith's signed statement will be published in the next issue (December) of the Improvement Era, which is the organ of the Priesthood quorum of the Church. . . ."

Section 138 was first published in *The Improvement Era* (December 1918) and is included in the 1981 edition of the Doctrine and Covenants. (*RPJS,* 306)

1. ELIJAH RESTORES THE SEALING KEYS

THEME: The restoration of the sealing keys through the prophet Elijah on April 3, 1836, began a magnificent, all-encompassing work to bind together worthy families of all generations into the glorious and eternal family of our Father in Heaven. That is the responsibility of our dispensation—to spread the gospel blessings to both the living and the dead, and work to prepare for the Second Coming and become worthy of exaltation. "If it were not so, the whole earth would be utterly wasted at his coming" (D&C 2:3).

MODERN PROPHETS SPEAK

David B. Haight:

> Joseph Smith and Oliver Cowdery had received the Melchizedek Priesthood under the hands of Peter, James, and John; however, it was necessary for the prophet Elijah to restore special keys, "in order that all the ordinances may be attended to in righteousness" (*HC,* 4:211). Thus, the sealing powers and ordinances necessary for the dead as well as the living were to be restored. This was accomplished by Elijah's visit to Joseph and Oliver on April 3, 1836, in the Kirtland Temple.
>
> Elijah's mission was to "turn the heart of the fathers to the children, and the heart of the children to their fathers" (Mal. 4:6). The turning of the hearts of the fathers in the spirit world to the children on earth provides for the gathering of ancestral data of their deceased fathers in order that ordinances might be performed in the temples of the Lord. Thus, the living having their hearts turned to their fathers is in accordance with the premortal agreement we made before the earth was formed. (*Ensign,* November 1990, 59)

Russell M. Nelson:

> For centuries faithful Jews have anticipated the return of Elijah at the Passover. Isn't it interesting that the date of 3 April 1836 was one of the few times when Easter Sunday coincided with the beginning of Passover? Elijah did return as had been hoped, at the Passover, on Easter, to restore keys of the sealing power that were uniquely assigned to him to convey. (*Ensign,* December 1989, 13)

Joseph Fielding Smith:

> This sealing power bestowed upon Elijah, is the power which binds husbands and wives, and children to parents for time and eternity. It is the binding power existing in every Gospel ordinance. . . . It was the mission of Elijah to come, and restore it so that the curse of confusion and disorder would not exist in the kingdom of God. (Quoted in James E. Faust, *Ensign,* May 1993, 35)

ILLUSTRATIONS FOR OUR TIMES

Return of Elijah.
Bruce R. McConkie illustrated the importance of the prophet Elijah to all of the house of Israel, both anciently and presently. The contemporaries of Christ yearned for the sealing power to which Elijah held the keys. Elder McConkie explained:

No tradition was more firmly planted in the hearts of Jewish Israel in Jesus' day than the firm belief that Elijah the prophet would come again to prepare the way before the expected Messiah. Both John and Jesus were assumed by some to be this ancient prophet come again. To this day devout Jews set a vacant chair at their table for Elijah when they celebrate the feast of the Passover. In part, at least, this universal belief grew out of Jehovah's promise given by the mouth of Malachi: "Behold, I will send you Elijah the prophet before the coming of the great and dreadful day of the Lord: And he shall turn the heart of the fathers to the children, and the heart of the children to their fathers, lest I come and smite the earth with a curse" (Mal. 4:5–6). (*The Millennial Messiah: The Second Coming of the Son of Man* [Salt Lake City: Deseret Book, 1982], 265)

He continued:

> But praise God, Elijah has come, as has Elias. On the 3rd day of April in 1836, in the Kirtland Temple, both of these ancient worthies appeared to Joseph Smith and Oliver Cowdery. As the holy account attests: "Elias appeared, and committed the dispensation of the gospel of Abraham"—that is to say, he gave them the great commission given of God to Abraham, which pertained to the family unit and its eternal continuance in the realms ahead—"saying that in us and our seed all generations after us should be blessed." Who Elias was when he dwelt in mortality, we do not know. He may have been Abraham himself. But no matter; what is important is that he brought back the eternal covenant, with all its promises, that Jehovah had given to Abraham, Isaac, and Jacob. . . .

> Elijah did come, not to sit in a vacant chair at some Jewish feast of the Passover, but to the Kirtland Temple on April 3, 1836, to Joseph Smith and Oliver Cowdery. (*The Millennial Messiah: The Second Coming of the Son of Man* [Salt Lake City: Deseret Book, 1982], 268, 279)

This branch of the house of Israel still holds the authority of Elijah in such high regard that they wait even today. We who have those keys restored ought not only to rejoice in the blessings of the gospel but also to remember the great responsibility we have in utilizing them. We are the ones who can bind families together through the keys restored, and so we must not fail those of the house of Israel in this responsibility.

LIKENING THE SCRIPTURES TO OUR LIVES

Doctrine and Covenants 138:47–48 The prophet Elijah planted in the hearts of the children the promises made to their fathers in order to awaken the children to an understanding of the importance of performing the temple work for the redemption of their kindred dead.

Application: Elijah's restoration of the sealing keys and the turning of the hearts of the people to their fathers concerning family history work brings to us the responsibility to save our dead. It is fulfillment not only of prophecy (see D&C 2:1–3) but of the Lord's promise to Abraham that all his seed would be blessed with the gospel. His work is paramount to our dispensation. We are responsible and accountable (see D&C 128:15; 138:54).

2. URGENCY OF TEMPLE WORK FOR THE DEAD

THEME: The work of the temples of the Lord beckons all Saints to participate, unabated, as saviors on Mount Zion (see Obad. 1:22) to complete the vicarious service of charity upon which the salvation of their kindred dead depends. The time for this work to be completed is drawing nigh, as evidenced by Elijah's appearance in the Kirtland Temple: "And by this ye may know that the great and dreadful day of the Lord is near, even at the doors" (D&C 110:16). We cannot spare our efforts in completing this great work assigned to us.

MODERN PROPHETS SPEAK

Ezra Taft Benson:

> We have an obligation to do temple work for our kindred dead. This means that we must do the necessary research in order for their names to be sent to the temples. We cannot be exalted without being eternally linked to our ancestors. (*Come unto Christ* [Salt Lake City: Deseret Book, 1983], 105)

Gordon B. Hinckley:

> This vicarious work constitutes an unprecedented labor of love on the part of the living in behalf of the dead. It makes necessary a vast undertaking of genealogical research to find and identify those who have gone before. (*Be Thou an Example* [Salt Lake City: Deseret Book, 1981], 131)

Gordon B. Hinckley:

> The Lord has made it possible for us in these holy houses to receive our own [ordinances]. Then we have the opportunity and responsibility of extending these same blessings to those who have passed on without the privilege. But in the very process there comes into our own lives a refinement of character, together with increased

spirituality. It is interesting to reflect on the fact that although many on the other side may not receive the ordinances done for them here, those who perform these ordinances will be blessed in the very process of doing so. (*TGBH,* 622–23)

Spencer W. Kimball:

The work for the dead is urgent. Recently I have felt impressed to share some thoughts about the work for the dead because I feel the same urgency for it that I do about the missionary work, since they are basically one and the same. . . .

Missionary work is not limited to proclaiming the gospel to every nation, kindred, tongue, and people now living on the earth. Missionary work is also continuing beyond the veil among the millions and even billions of the children of our Heavenly Father who have died either without hearing the gospel or without accepting it while they lived on the earth. Our great part in this aspect of missionary work is to perform on this earth the ordinances required for those who accept the gospel over there. The spirit world is full of spirits who are anxiously awaiting the performance of these earthly ordinances for them. I hope to see us dissolve the artificial boundary line we so often place between missionary work and temple and genealogical work, because it is the same great redemptive work! . . .

There is an urgency to engage more fully in the redeeming of our kindred dead through more frequent temple attendance. All those who possess temple recommends should use them as often as possible to engage in baptisms, endowments, and sealings for the dead. Other members of the Church should concern themselves seriously with preparations to qualify for temple recommends that they, too, might enjoy these eternal blessings and also act as saviors on Mount Zion. There is an ever-increasing burden of temple work to be done by the Saints, and we should rise to meet this challenge. (*TSWK,* 540)

LIKENING THE SCRIPTURES TO OUR LIVES

Doctrine and Covenants 128:15 We cannot take our responsibility to those who have gone before us lightly. Their salvation depends on us, as our salvation depends on them; we cannot be perfected without one another.

Application: The purpose of the work of our Heavenly Father and His Son is to bring to pass the immortality and eternal life of humankind (see Moses 1:39). A great portion of that work concerns those who have gone before without receiving the blessings of the temple—thus requiring vicarious temple work for which we are accountable. However, this work also contributes to refining our own characters, increasing our spirituality, and binding us to our ancestors. Thus, continual temple work is as necessary for us as it is for our dead. If we fail to do this work, "the whole earth would be utterly wasted at his coming" (D&C 2:3).

3. PRESIDENT JOSEPH F. SMITH: THE VISION OF THE DEAD

THEME: The Lord has blessed His Saints, through a modern-day prophet, with precious additional light and understanding concerning the beneficent plan of salvation and how it applies to those departed hosts who wait upon Him in the spirit realm.

MODERN PROPHETS SPEAK

Joseph F. Smith:

> As I wondered, my eyes were opened, and my understanding quickened, and I perceived that the Lord went not in person among the wicked and the disobedient who had rejected the truth, to teach them; but behold, from among the righteous he organized his forces and appointed his messengers, clothed with power and authority, and commissioned them to go forth and carry the light of the gospel to them that were in darkness, even to all the spirits of men. And thus was the gospel preached to the dead. . . . Thus was it made known that our Redeemer spent his time during his sojourn in the world of spirits, instructing and preparing the faithful spirits of the prophets who had testified of him in the flesh, that they might carry the message of redemption unto all the dead unto whom he could not go personally because of their rebellion and transgression, that they through the ministration of his servants might also hear his words. (*Gospel Doctrine: Selections from the Sermons and Writings of Joseph F. Smith,* comp. John A. Widtsoe, 5th ed. [Salt Lake City: Deseret Book, 1939], 473–74)

Bruce R. McConkie:

> To the great joy of those who love the Lord and his holy word and who desire to be guided from on high, two heaven-sent revelations—both long known in the Church to be scripture!—were added to the standard works at the April 1976 general conference.
>
> In solemn session in the holy temple on March 25, 1976, while the Spirit of the Lord attended, the First Presidency and the Twelve voted unanimously to add to the Pearl of Great Price the following:

A vision of the celestial kingdom, given to the Prophet Joseph Smith in the Kirtland Temple on January 21, 1836, which deals with the salvation of those who die without a knowledge of the gospel and also with the salvation of little children; and a vision given to President Joseph F. Smith in Salt Lake City, Utah, on October 3, 1918, showing the visit of the Lord Jesus Christ in the spirit world and setting forth the doctrine of the redemption of the dead [now included as section 138 of the Doctrine and Covenants]. . . .

In the true Church, where there are apostles and prophets to give the mind and will and voice of the Lord to the Church and the world—among the Saints of the Most High, where all of the elders of Israel are the Lord's ministers to feed the flock of God and preach the gospel to all mankind—nothing is better known or more greatly appreciated than the fact that the canon of scripture is not now and never will be full. (*Ensign,* August 1976, 7)

ILLUSTRATIONS FOR OUR TIMES

The Spirit World

I went to see [Jedediah M. Grant] one day last week, and he reached out his hand and shook hands with me; he could not speak, but he shook hands warmly with me. . . . I laid my hands upon him and blessed him, and asked God to strengthen his lungs that he might be easier, and in two or three minutes he raised himself up and talked for about an hour as busily as he could, telling me what he had seen and what he understood, until I was afraid he would weary himself, when I arose and left him.

He said to me, "Brother Heber, I have been into the spirit world two nights in succession, and, of all the dreads that ever came across me, the worst was to have to again return to my body, though I had to do it. But O," says he, "the order and government that were there! When in the spirit world, I saw the order of righteous men and women; beheld them organized in their several grades, and there appeared to be no obstruction to my vision; I could see every man and woman in their grade and order. I looked to see whether there was any disorder there, but there was none; neither could I see any death nor any darkness, disorder or confusion." He said that the people he there saw were organized in family capacities; and when he looked at them he saw grade after grade and all were organized and in perfect harmony. He would mention one item after another and say, "Why, it is just as Brother Brigham says it is; it is just as he told us many a time."

That is a testimony as to the truth of what Brother Brigham teaches us, and I know it is true, from what little light I have.

He saw the righteous gathered together in the spirit world, and there were no wicked spirits among them. He saw his wife; she was the first person that came to him. He saw many that he knew, but did not have conversation with any except his wife, Caroline. She came to him, and he said that she looked beautiful and had their little child, that died on the Plains, in her arms, and said, "Mr. Grant, here is little Margaret; you know that the wolves ate her up, but it did not hurt her; here she is all right."

"To my astonishment," he said, "when I looked at families there was a deficiency in some, there was a lack, for I saw families that would not be permitted to come and dwell together, because they had not honored their calling here."

He asked his wife, Caroline, where Joseph and Hyrum and Father Smith and others were; she replied, "they have gone away ahead, to perform and transact business for us." The same as when Brother Brigham and his brethren left Winter Quarters and came here to search out a home; they came to find a location for their brethren.

He also spoke of the buildings he saw there, remarking that the Lord gave Solomon wisdom and poured gold and silver into his hands that he might display his skill and ability, and said that the temple erected by Solomon was much inferior to the most ordinary buildings he saw in the spirit world.

In regard to gardens, says Brother Grant, "I have seen good gardens on this earth, but I never saw any to compare with those that were there. I saw flowers of numerous kinds, and some with from fifty to a hundred different colored flowers growing upon one stalk." We have many kinds of flowers on the earth, and I suppose those very articles came from heaven, or they would not be here.

After mentioning the things that he had seen, he spoke of how much he disliked to return and resume his body, after having seen the beauty and glory of the spirit world, where the righteous spirits are gathered together.

Some may marvel at my speaking about these things, for many profess to believe that we have no spiritual existence. But do you not believe that my spirit was organized before it came to my body here? And do you not think there can be houses and gardens, fruit trees, and every other good thing there? The spirits of those things were made, as well as our spirits, and it follows that they can exist upon the same principle. . . .

I never had a view of the righteous assembling in the spirit world, but I have had a view of the hosts of hell, and have seen them as plainly as I see you today. The righteous spirits gather together to prepare and qualify themselves for a future day, and evil spirits have no power over them, though they are constantly striving for the mastery. I have seen evil spirits attempt to overcome those holding the Priesthood, and I know how they act. (Heber C. Kimball, quoted in *Best-Loved Stories of the LDS People,* ed. Jack M. Lyon, Linda Ririe Gundry, and Jay A. Parry [Salt Lake City: Deseret Book, 1997], 222)

LIKENING THE SCRIPTURES TO OUR LIVES

Doctrine and Covenants 138:18 22 Joseph F. Smith saw in vision that those worthy Saints who had passed from this life to the next were joyful in the presence of the Savior. He also observed that the Savior did not visit the spirits of the wicked and unrepentant.

Application: The blessings of a righteous life allow us the privilege of being with the Savior in the spirit world. Those who choose to ignore Him or His prophets will not have the privilege of His presence. Surely there is a blessing or consequence associated with all that we do. We must live so as to choose liberty and eternal life with God (see 2 Ne. 2:27).

4. TAKING THE TEMPLES TO THE PEOPLE

THEME: The modern-day program to extend temple blessings into all corners of the kingdom of God is a miraculous undertaking that demonstrates the wisdom of having a living prophet of God as an emissary of the Almighty in bringing about the plan of salvation on behalf of all—both living and deceased.

MODERN PROPHETS SPEAK

Gordon B. Hinckley:

> If temple ordinances are an essential part of the restored gospel, and I testify that they are, then we must provide the means by which they can be accomplished. All of our vast family history endeavor is directed to temple work. There is no other purpose for it. The temple ordinances become the crowning blessings the Church has to offer. (*Ensign,* May 1998, 87)

Dallin H. Oaks:

> Several years ago President Gordon B. Hinckley announced the construction of a large number of new temples, essentially doubling the number of operating temples of the Church from about 50 to about 100 in just a few years. Having additional temples has

always been the direction to go, but until the prophet of the Lord signaled this as a major initiative, no one could have properly urged such a sudden and dramatic increase for the Church and its people. Only the Lord's prophet could signal the Church to double its operating temples in just a few years. (*Ensign,* October 2003, 10)

Howard W. Hunter:

What a glorious thing it is for us to have the privilege of going to the temple for our own blessings. Then after going to the temple for our own blessings, what a glorious privilege to do the work for those who have gone on before us. This aspect of temple work is an unselfish work. Yet whenever we do temple work for other people, there is a blessing that comes back to us. Thus it should be no surprise to us that the Lord does desire that his people be a temple-motivated people. I repeat what I have said before: It would please the Lord for every adult member to be worthy of—and to carry—a current temple recommend, even if proximity to a temple does not allow immediate or frequent use of it. The things that we must do and not do to be worthy of a temple recommend are the very things that ensure we will be happy as individuals and as families.

Let us truly be a temple-attending and a temple-loving people. We should hasten to the temple as frequently, yet prudently, as our personal circumstances allow. We should go not only for our kindred dead but also for the personal blessing of temple worship, for the sanctity and safety that are within those hallowed and consecrated walls. As we attend the temple, we learn more richly and deeply the purpose of life and the significance of the atoning sacrifice of the Lord Jesus Christ. Let us make the temple, with temple worship and temple covenants and temple marriage, our ultimate earthly goal and the supreme mortal experience. . . .

All of our efforts in proclaiming the gospel, perfecting the Saints, and redeeming the dead lead to the holy temple. This is because the temple ordinances are absolutely crucial; we cannot return to God's presence without them. I encourage everyone to worthily attend the temple or to work toward the day when you can enter that holy house to receive your ordinances and covenants. As the prophets have said, the temple is a place of beauty; it is a place of revelation; it is a place of peace. It is the house of the Lord. It is holy unto the Lord. It must be holy and important to us. (*Ensign,* February 1995, 2)

ILLUSTRATIONS FOR OUR TIME

Crowning Blessings

I wish to make an announcement. As I have previously indicated, in recent months we have traveled far out among the membership of the Church. I have been with many who have very little of this world's goods. But they have in their hearts a great burning faith concerning this latter-day work. They love the Church. They love the gospel. They love the Lord and want to do His will. They are paying their tithing, modest as it is. They make tremendous sacrifices to visit the temples. They travel for days at a time in cheap buses and on old boats. They save their money and do without to make it all possible.

They need nearby temples—small, beautiful, serviceable temples.

Accordingly, I take this opportunity to announce to the entire Church a program to construct some 30 smaller temples immediately. They will be in Europe, in Asia, in Australia and Fiji, in Mexico and Central and South America and Africa, as well as in the United States and Canada. They will have all the necessary facilities to provide the ordinances of the Lord's house.

This will be a tremendous undertaking. Nothing even approaching it has ever been tried before. These will be in addition to the 17 buildings now going forward in England; Spain; Ecuador; Bolivia; the Dominican Republic; Brazil; Colombia; Billings, Montana; Houston, Texas; Boston, Massachusetts; White Plains, New York; and Albuquerque, New Mexico; and the smaller temples in Anchorage, Alaska; Monticello, Utah; and Colonia Juárez, Mexico. This will make a total of 47 new temples in addition to the 51 now in operation. I think we had better add 2 more to make it an even 100 by the end of this century, being 2,000 years "since the coming of our Lord and Savior Jesus Christ in the flesh" (D&C 20:1). In this program we are moving on a scale the like of which we have never seen before. . . .

May God bless the faithful Latter-day Saints. May you be prospered as you live the commandments. May all be honest, and even generous, in the payment of tithes and offerings, and may the windows of heaven be opened and blessings be showered down upon us as a people as we walk with boldness and in faith before the Lord to accomplish His eternal work. (Gordon B. Hinckley, *Ensign,* May 1998, 87)

LIKENING THE SCRIPTURES TO OUR LIVES

Doctrine and Covenants 138:53–54 Many choice spirits were reserved for this time to participate in the great work of building temples and performing saving ordinances therein for the dead.

Application: Everything in the gospel and kingdom of God points to the temple as the crowning blessing here upon the earth. Let us do all in our power to make possible the building of the temples by faithfully honoring the payment of our tithes and offerings. We are to continually seek to be worthy of a temple recommend. We should seek to strengthen and inspire others to do likewise. Let us seek out our kindred dead and prepare every needful thing so that their work might be completed in the temple. Let us make a plan to attend the temple regularly.

ENRICHMENT

The Sealing Powers

Elijah the prophet is spoken of in seven different revelations in the Doctrine and Covenants, most of which refer to his special premillennial mission of restoring the promised sealing powers of the priesthood (2:1–3; 27:9; 35:4; 110:13–16; 128:17–18; 138:46–48). In only one section is he mentioned without referring to his special mission (133:55).

The Prophet Joseph described the mission of Elijah as follows: "Elijah was the last Prophet that held the keys of the Priesthood, and who will, before the last dispensation, restore the authority and deliver the keys of the Priesthood, in order that all the ordinances may be attended to in righteousness. It is true that the Savior had authority and power to bestow this blessing; but the sons of Levi were too prejudiced. 'And I will send Elijah the Prophet before the great and terrible day of the Lord,' etc., etc. Why send Elijah? Because he holds the keys of the authority to administer in all the ordinances of the Priesthood; and without the authority is given, the ordinances could not be administered in righteousness." (*TPJS,* 172)

* * *

In a further clarification of Elijah's mission of "turning" the hearts of the fathers and children to one another, the Prophet said: "Now, the word turn here should be translated bind, or seal" (*TPJS,* 330). "Elijah shall reveal the covenants to seal the hearts of the fathers to the children, and the children to the fathers" (*TPJS,* 323).

* * *

Malachi's ancient prophecy (Mal. 4:5–6) which initially foretold of Elijah's special mission is found in each of the other standard works of the Church (D&C 2:1–3; 3 Ne. 25:5–6; JS—H 1:38–39; other passages already cited). The Jewish people still anticipate the arrival of Elijah, and each year during their Paschal service a place is set for the ancient prophet and the door is opened to admit him as the "forerunner" of the promised Messiah. It is of interest to note that on April 3, 1836, the Jewish people celebrated their Paschal service, opening their doors to Elijah's return (*DS*, 2:100–101). On that very day, he did return to the Kirtland Temple, where he bestowed the long-awaited keys of the sealing power (D&C 110:13–16).

Elijah's power from God extends back to his "sealing" the heavens for a period of three years so that no rain or dew fell on the parched earth (1 Kgs. 17:1). His classic showdown with the wicked priests of Baal is another example of his extraordinary faith and power, and one would do well to contemplate Elijah's searing inquiry: "How long halt ye between two opinions? If the Lord be God, follow him: but if Baal, then follow him" (1 Kgs. 18:21).

Elijah was taken to heaven in "a chariot of fire," without tasting death (2 Kgs. 2:1–11). In other words, he became a translated being with temporary power over death. This was necessary in order that he might return to the Mount of Transfiguration and bestow keys of authority on Peter, James, and John, for he had to possess a tangible earthly body for that mission (*DS*, 2:110–11; Matt. 17:3; Luke 9:30). Following the resurrection of Christ—the "first fruits" thereof—Elijah passed through death and was a resurrected being when he appeared to Joseph Smith and Oliver Cowdery in the Kirtland Temple. (Hoyt W. Brewster Jr., *DCE*, 151)

What It Means to "Ponder"

President Joseph F. Smith informed us that this vision came while he was pondering (see D&C 138:1–11). Pondering, or meditating upon the things of God, opens doors to understanding. The mind and spirit are prepared to receive the promptings and guidance that emanates from the Holy Spirit. The importance of pondering and the reward thereof have been taught by President Marion G. Romney as follows:

"As I have read the scriptures I have been challenged by the word *ponder*, so frequently used in the Book of Mormon. The dictionary says that *ponder* means 'to weigh mentally, think deeply about, deliberate, meditate.' Moroni thus used the term as he closed his record:

"'Behold, I would exhort you that when ye shall read these things . . . that ye would remember how merciful the Lord hath been unto the children of men . . . and *ponder* it in your hearts" (Moro. 10:3, italics added).

"Jesus said to the Nephites:

"'I perceive that ye are weak that ye cannot understand all my words. . . .

"'Therefore, go ye unto your homes, and *ponder* upon the things which I have said, and ask of the Father, in my name that ye may understand . . .' (3 Ne. 17:2–3, italics added).

"*Pondering* is, in my feeling, a form of prayer. It has at least been an approach to the Spirit of the Lord on many occasions. Nephi tells us of one such occasion:

"'For it came to pass,' he wrote, 'after I had desired to know the things that my father had seen and believing that the Lord was able to make them known unto me, as I sat *pondering* in mine heart I was caught away in the Spirit of the Lord, yea, into an exceeding high mountain . . .' (1 Ne. 11:1, italics added).

"Then follows Nephi's account of the great vision he was given by the Spirit of the Lord because he believed the words of his prophet father and had such a great desire to know more that he pondered and prayed about them.

"President Joseph F. Smith tells us that 'on the third of October, in the year nineteen hundred and eighteen, I sat in my room *pondering* over the Scriptures. . . .' He had particular reference at this time to Peter's statement that Christ 'went and preached unto the spirits in prison' (1 Pet. 3:19) while his body lay in the grave.

"'As I *pondered* over these things which are written,' President Smith continued, 'the eyes of my understanding were opened and the Spirit of the Lord rested upon me, and I saw the hosts of the dead, both small and great. . . .' He then gives us an account of his great vision concerning missionary work among the spirits of the dead (Joseph F. Smith, *Gospel Doctrine: Selections from the Sermons and Writings of Joseph F. Smith,* comp. John A. Widtsoe, 5th ed. [Salt Lake City: Deseret Book, 1939], italics added)" (CR, April 1973, 117–18). (L. G. Otten and C. M. Caldwell, *Sacred Truths of the Doctrine and Covenants* [Salt Lake City: Deseret Book, 1982–83], 2:394)

SUMMARY

The plan of happiness is for all humankind. When Elijah restored the sealing keys under divine commission in the latter days, he was able to "plant in the hearts of the children the promises made to the fathers" (D&C 2:2) and usher in a magnificent period of temple work on behalf of the living and the dead. We labor on both sides of the veil for the welfare of those who have died. Through the Atonement, all humankind can "be saved by obedience to the laws and ordinances of the gospel" (A of F 1:3). For this reason we preach the gospel and do temple work for those who await our service beyond the valleys of mortality.

Because the coming of the Lord is near, there is urgency attending this vicarious service in the temples of God. The "Vision of the Redemption of the Dead" revealed through President Joseph F. Smith in 1918 sheds substantial light on the scope of activity being carried on behind the veil in anticipation of our completing temple ordinances for our kindred dead, "that they might be judged according to men in the flesh, but live according to God in the spirit" (1 Pet. 4:6). In our day, the work of building temples in all quarters of the earth has been hastened to accommodate the hosts of faithful Saints who are motivated with a deep desire to participate in this divine commission as saviors on Mount Zion.

CHAPTER FORTY

FINDING JOY *in* TEMPLE *and* FAMILY HISTORY WORK

Reading Assignment: Malachi 3:16–18; Doctrine and Covenants 85:9–12; 128:6–9; Moses 6:5–8, 46; Abraham 1:31.

Labor in the temples brings much joy. The temple endowment if properly understood is a great blessing to him who receives it. It becomes an interpreter and protector of life.

The temple endowment may be received by every faithful member of the Church. It may be taken also for the dead. Thereby an opportunity is given to keep the meaning of the endowment fresh in our minds.

Temple service for the dead is wholly unselfish and consequently has a marvelous refining influence upon those who engage in it. To approach a fulness of spiritual joy, the privileges of the temple must be used as often as possible. (John A. Widtsoe, Program of The Church of Jesus Christ of Latter-day Saints *[Salt Lake City: The Church of Jesus Christ of Latter-day Saints, 1937], 109)*

THEMES *for* LIVING
1. Feeling and Following the Spirit of Elijah
2. Approaches to Family History and Temple Work
3. Church Resources to Help You in Family History and Temple Work

INTRODUCTION

From the foundation of the world, it was decreed that the history of humankind—the deeds and works of all individuals—would be memorialized as a chronicle to guide the ultimate judgments of God: "And a book of remembrance was kept . . . and a genealogy was kept of the children of God. And this was the book of the generations of Adam" (Moses 6:5–8). Furthermore: "But the records of the fathers, even the patriarchs, concerning the right of Priesthood, the Lord my God preserved in mine own hands" (Abr. 1:31).

Through latter-day revelation, much additional light has been shed upon the importance of record-keeping as a key priesthood practice in the kingdom of God. We learn that it is a record of the people's works upon the earth—namely, of the ordinances performed and honored in their lives. In other words, it is our genealogy. Failure to keep such records is condemned by the Lord (see 3 Ne. 23:7–13). Similarly, when a record is kept but a person's name is not found on that record as a result of his or her unworthiness, that person is condemned (see D&C 85:9–12). He or she is denied an inheritance with the Lord.

The records of the Church are kept in congruence with the principle of a parallel and simultaneous heavenly monitoring and recording of events that transpire in the temporal sphere. In addition, through the keys of the priesthood, authorized enactments accomplished in the kingdom of God on the earth are likewise of binding efficacy in the heavens. Our works are recorded, and whatever is performed or sanctioned by the priesthood will also be recorded in heaven; this is how we are judged (see D&C 128:8).

This solemn doctrine arouses in the bosom of all persons of contrition and understanding the compelling desire to honor the covenants of God and abide by His precepts in all diligence. The faithful and obedient are thus motivated to cultivate a "godly walk and conversation" (D&C 20:69) in order to please God and to be found worthy, based on the records of remembrance, to take their places at the right hand of the Lord through the power of the Atonement and in keeping with the harmonizing of the laws of justice and mercy.

MOMENT OF TRUTH

Section 128 of the Doctrine and Covenants makes abundantly clear how vital it is to maintain accurate records of priesthood actions. The background to this section was given in chapter 30. Section 85 likewise illuminates the significance of the books of life and remembrance kept to chronicle the works and deeds of humankind. Following is a brief outline of the background to this section.

Section 85: Given through the Prophet Joseph Smith on November 27, 1832, in the Newel K. Whitney store at Kirtland, Geauga County, Ohio (see *HC,* 1:298–99). The introductory statement for this section gives the background: "This section is an extract from a letter of the Prophet to W. W. Phelps, who was living in Independence, Missouri. Much of it is instruction to John Whitmer, the Church Historian. It was given to answer questions about those saints who had moved to Zion, but who had not received their inheritances according to the established order in the Church." This section is evidence of the strict record-keeping procedures that the Prophet was directed to implement to ensure order and continuity within the kingdom of God. Joseph Smith attributed this section to questions asked by the brethren in Missouri: "In answer to letters received from the brethren in Missouri, I wrote as follows: [*HC,*1:297]." It is also interesting to note that his son Joseph III was born shortly before this, on November 6, and that Brigham Young came to Kirtland and met the Prophet for the first time about November 8.

Though the question was regarding inheritances in this life, the Prophet was also concerned with the more important, eternal inheritance of the Saints. His letter to W. W. Phelps ends with this poetic and heartfelt epilogue:

> Now, Brother William, if what I have said is true, how careful men ought to be what they do in the last days, lest they are cut short of their expectations, and they that think they stand should fall, because they keep not the Lord's commandments; whilst you, who do the will of the Lord and keep His commandments, have need to rejoice with unspeakable joy, for such shall be exalted very high, and shall be lifted up in triumph above all the kingdoms of this world; but I must drop this subject at the beginning [of it].
>
> Oh, Lord, when will the time come when Brother William, Thy servant, and myself, shall behold the day that we may stand together and gaze upon eternal wisdom engraven upon the heavens, while the majesty of our God holdeth up the dark curtain until we may read the round of eternity, to the fulness and satisfaction of our immortal souls? Oh, Lord, deliver us in due time from the little, narrow prison, almost as it were, total darkness of paper, pen and ink;—and a crooked, broken, scattered and imperfect language. . . .
>
> Yours in bonds. Amen.
> Joseph Smith, Jun. (*HC,* 1:299)

1. FEELING AND FOLLOWING THE SPIRIT OF ELIJAH

THEME: The Spirit of Elijah is the consummate power of binding unification among fathers and sons, mothers and daughters, the living and the dead—that the family of God can be sealed His according to the covenants, principles, and saving ordinances of the gospel of Jesus Christ. What a glorious doctrine this is, that the Lord in His mercy has prepared a way for the confluence of all the remnants of Israel, in all ages, toward the ultimate sacred precincts of their eternal abode in the presence of the Father and the Son. Such could not occur without the sealing powers and the spiritual motivation associated with the Spirit of Elijah, upon whom this divine commission has been bestowed.

As Byron R. Merrill put it, we are enjoying the Spirit of Elijah in great abundance today:

> If your thoughts turn backward to the lives and deeds of parents, grandparents, and unknown ancestors with feelings of warmth, gratitude, and a desire to know them better and be bound to them by sacred covenants through eternal power, you are awakening to the Spirit of Elijah. If your thoughts turn forward with love to siblings, children, grandchildren, and posterity, and to the covenants and promises which can bind you eternally to them, you are feeling the Spirit of Elijah. If love and gratitude for the one with whom you have knelt at a sacred altar in a holy temple and with whom you have made solemn and eternal covenants overwhelm you, you are experiencing the Spirit of Elijah. And if you do not currently enjoy any such feelings, you need to get on your knees and prayerfully plead for them until they come! (Byron R. Merrill, *Elijah: Yesterday, Today, and Tomorrow* [Salt Lake City: Bookcraft, 1997], 131)

MODERN PROPHETS SPEAK

Howard W. Hunter:

> Furthermore, the dead are anxiously waiting for the Latter-day Saints to search out their names and then go into the temples to officiate in their behalf, that they may be liberated from their prison house in the spirit world. All of us should find joy in this magnificent labor of love. (*Ensign,* February 1995, 4–5)

Joseph Smith:

> The spirit, power, and calling of Elijah is, that ye have power to hold the key of the revelations, ordinances, oracles, powers and endowments of the fulness of the

Melchizedek Priesthood and of the kingdom of God on the earth; and to receive, obtain, and perform all the ordinances belonging to the kingdom of God, even unto the turning of the hearts of the fathers unto the children, and the hearts of the children unto the fathers, even those who are in heaven. . . .

Now comes the point. What is this office and work of Elijah? It is one of the greatest and most important subjects that God has revealed. He should send Elijah to seal the children to the fathers, and the fathers to the children. . . .

I wish you to understand this subject, for it is important; and if you receive it, this is the Spirit of Elijah, that we redeem our dead, and connect ourselves with our fathers which are in heaven, and seal up our dead to come forth in the first resurrection; and here we want the power of Elijah to seal those who dwell on earth to those who dwell in heaven. This is the power of Elijah and the keys of the kingdom of Jehovah. (*TPJS,* 337)

Russell M. Nelson:

This doctrine [referring to D&C 128:15] and its ordinances are laden with love and are intended to perpetuate the sweetest of life's relationships—in families forever. Just as Jesus gave his life vicariously for each of us, we can serve vicariously for our kindred.

For our beloved ancestors, perhaps we cannot do everything, but we can do something. Meanwhile, we may keep ourselves free from the bondage of sin, worthy and able to endure to the end. Then, when our turn comes to pass through the gateway, we can say as did Paul: "The time of my departure is at hand. I have fought a good fight, I have finished my course, I have kept the faith" (2 Tim. 4:6–7). (*The Gateway We Call Death* [Salt Lake City: Deseret Book, 1995], 107)

Russell M. Nelson:

Elijah's return to earth occurred at the first temple built in this dispensation, where he and other heavenly messengers, under direction of the Lord, entrusted special keys of priesthood authority to the restored Church. . . .

With that, natural affection between generations began to be enriched. This restoration was accompanied by what is sometimes called the Spirit of Elijah—a manifestation of the Holy Ghost bearing witness of the divine nature of the family. Hence, people throughout the world, regardless of religious affiliation, are gathering records of deceased relatives at an ever-increasing rate. (*Ensign,* May 1998, 34)

ILLUSTRATIONS FOR OUR TIMES

Decide to Do Something

I testify that the Spirit of Elijah is touching the hearts of many of Father's children throughout the world, causing the work for the dead to accelerate at an unprecedented pace.

But what about you? Have you prayed about your own ancestors' work? Set aside those things that don't really matter in your life. Decide to do something that will have eternal consequences. Perhaps you have been prompted to look for ancestors but feel that you are not a genealogist. Can you see that you don't have to be anymore? It all begins with love and a sincere desire to help those who can't help themselves.

This is a spiritual work, a monumental effort of cooperation on both sides of the veil where help is given in both directions. It begins with love. Anywhere you are in the world, with prayer, faith, determination, diligence, and some sacrifice, you can make a powerful contribution. Begin now. I promise you that the Lord will help you find a way. And it will make you feel wonderful. (Richard G. Scott, *Ensign,* November 1990, 5)

The Spirit of Elijah

For Church members, the growing interest in genealogy and family history, the formation of so many genealogical and historical societies, and the expanding availability of family history sources were all evidence of the outpouring of the Spirit of Elijah. That feeling was enhanced in 1918 when a revelation to President Joseph F. Smith provided the Saints with a significant new insight into the spirit world and how the dead could receive the gospel.

Church members already understood that preaching the gospel to the dead was begun by the Savior Himself during the three days his body lay in the tomb. During that time, the Apostle Peter taught, "he went and preached unto the spirits in prison; which sometime were disobedient, when once the longsuffering of God waited in the days of Noah, while the ark was a preparing" (1 Pet. 3:19–20). Peter also reminded the New Testament Saints that "for this cause was the gospel preached also to them that are dead, that they might be judged according to men in the flesh, but live according to God in the spirit"(1 Pet. 4:6). But Church president Joseph F. Smith wondered how the Savior could have preached to all the dead in so short a time. While he was pondering the question on 3 October 1918, a vision was opened to his mind. He beheld the Savior in the spirit world and saw him organize missionary work among the spirits of the dead:

"I perceived that the Lord went not in person among the wicked and the disobedient who had rejected the truth, to teach them; But behold, from among the righteous, he organized his forces and appointed messengers, clothed with power and authority, and commissioned them to go forth and carry the light of the gospel to them that were in darkness . . . and thus was the gospel preached to the dead" (D&C 138:29–30).

Since then, the Saints have understood that missionary work continues in the spirit world. The responsibility for genealogical research and the opportunity for temple worship connected with it are both virtually unlimited—at least for the time being. Recently temple building has expanded into many nations, spurring genealogical research worldwide. In 1977, President Spencer W. Kimball explained the responsibility of the Saints:

"We do not know how many millions of spirits are involved. We know that many have passed away in wars, pestilence, and various accidents. We know that the spirit world is filled with the spirits of men who are waiting for you and me to get busy. . . . We wonder about our progenitors—grandparents, great-grandparents, great-great-grandparents, etc. What do they think of you and me? We are their offspring. We have the responsibility to do their temple work. . . . We have a grave responsibility that we cannot avoid, and may stand in jeopardy if we fail to do this important work" (Spencer W. Kimball, "The Things of Eternity—Stand We in Jeopardy?" *Ensign,* January 1977, 5).

The coming of Elijah on 3 April 1836 ushered in the distinctive efforts of Latter-day Saints to seek out their ancestors and perform saving ordinances in their behalf. . . . The Genealogical Society of Utah, succeeded by the Family History Department of the Church, has contributed in a most fundamental way to turning the hearts of the children to the fathers. (James B. Allen, Jessie L. Embry, and Kahlile B. Mehr, *BYU Studies* 34.2 [1994])

LIKENING THE SCRIPTURES TO OUR LIVES

Malachi 4:6 Elijah will come to turn the hearts of the fathers to the children and the hearts of the children to the fathers.

Doctrine and Covenants 27:13 The Lord has bestowed the keys of the kingdom on prophets of this dispensation so that all in heaven and earth can be gathered to Him.

Application: The Spirit of Elijah, like the word of God, has power. It causes us to think of our kindred dead with a sense of appreciation and gratitude, thus giving us the desire to do the necessary temple work for them. It turns our hearts to our living family. Recognizing this great power and blessing in our lives reinforces the importance of family, both here and in the hereafter. It is truly the basic unit of the kingdom of God, and we should do all in our power to strengthen it, for Satan seeks to destroy the family.

2. APPROACHES TO FAMILY HISTORY AND TEMPLE WORK

THEME: Day by day, each of us contributes additional lasting memories to our book of life. What we think, ponder, and do becomes part of our eternal record. What we write into our book of remembrance supplements the annals of our temporal development. The milestones of our progress in the Church are recorded on the records of the kingdom of God and are echoed upon the leaves of the book of life in heaven. What a profound concept, to know that we are to be judged out of these books! Let us endeavor to fill the pages of our book of remembrance with accomplishments that will memorialize the goodness, the kindness, the obedience that will characterize those found worthy in the Day of Judgment.

MODERN PROPHETS SPEAK

Richard G. Scott:

> It was hard to get excited about genealogy work, with its many rules and regulations about commas, periods, and capitalization. The new family history service is quite another matter. It deals with loving, caring, feeling ancestors beyond the veil. (*Ensign,* November 1990, 5)

Dallin H. Oaks:

> There are many different things our members can do to help in the redeeming of the dead, in temple and family history work. Some involve callings. Others are personal. All are expressions of devotion and discipleship. All present opportunities for sacrifice and service. . . .
>
> Some of the most important temple and family history work is done at home. I do not refer just to the important work of keeping family genealogies up-to-date and the much-needed verifying that all sealings have been performed. At home we can keep our journals and gather pictures and data for the books of remembrance of our family members. We can gather and record information available through living relatives. We can write family histories and share their great lessons with our children. . . .

In mapping out our personal efforts in temple and family history work, we need to take a view that is not only broad in scope but at least lifetime in duration. (*Ensign,* June 1989, 6)

ILLUSTRATIONS FOR OUR TIMES

Bridges and Eternal Keepsakes

Family history and temple work have a great power, which lies in their scriptural and divine promise that the hearts of the fathers will turn to the children and those of the children will turn to their fathers. . . . Woodrow Wilson stated: "A nation which does not remember what it was yesterday, does not know what it is today, nor what it is trying to do. We are trying to do a futile thing if we do not know where we came from or what we have been about." . . . Well might this be said of families also: A *family* "which does not remember what it was yesterday, does not know what it is today, nor what it is trying to do. We are trying to do a futile thing if we do not know where we came from or what we have been about." . . . Family history builds bridges to activity in the Church. Family history work solidifies converts and strengthens all members of the Church. Family history research and the preparation of names for the temple can be most valuable in the retention of new members. Faith and confidence grow as family members are included in the saving ordinances of the gospel. During a recent stake conference, I met John and Carmen Day, who were recently baptized. They told me that they had already prepared family names and were planning to enter the temple as soon as they could. Is retention a question here? A new member of the Church can be introduced to family history and temple work very quickly by missionaries, friends, neighbors, and priesthood and auxiliary leaders. Participation in temple ordinances is, after all, at the center of our gospel experience.

No official call is required to participate in family history and the accompanying gospel ordinances. (Dennis B. Neuenschwander, *Ensign,* May 1999, 83)

Family History You Can Do

The following excerpt illustrates the urgency of keeping our records. While the article is too lengthy to include in its entirety, we strongly encourage readers to study the whole article for further ideas. The excerpt is just a glimpse of the author's enthusiasm and creativity.

When you think of doing family history, do you think of spending hours squinting at roll after roll of microfilm, poring over dusty volumes in the library, reviewing Aunt Melba's six-inch-thick book of remembrance with her, and endlessly copying charts and group sheets?

Well, brace yourself. Compiling your family history does not necessarily mean spending hours of tedious investigation into faded records. There are many fun and interesting things you can do to advance your family history cause right in your own home, and they are things you would probably want to do anyway. Here are some simple suggestions to get you started: . . .

Write down what you know about your family history. If my great-grandparents had simply spent a day or two writing a narrative of what they knew about their family, it would be a valuable resource for me. I wish they had written down for my generation such important and interesting facts as the names of their grandparents, aunts, uncles, and cousins, the places they lived, where everyone was born, why their parents decided to move from Kentucky to Missouri, and an account of some of the important events in their lives.

We might say, "But everybody knows who my grandparents and cousins are." That may well be what my great-grandparents thought, too, but I'm here to say, as one of their descendants, that we *don't* know. What seemed at the time to be simple, commonly known information is a mystery for us today. It will be a mystery for your descendants, too, unless it is written down now.

Were you fortunate enough to personally know one of your great-grandparents? My Great-Grandpa Harmon was born in 1879 and lived to be one hundred years old. He died when I was twenty-four years old, so I had the wonderful and rare opportunity to be personally acquainted with my great-grandfather, not only during my early childhood but across years of my adult life. I was able to talk with him, see what he was really like, and learn about the things he had done.

In the year 2009, my grandchildren will look to me as their grandpa. But I will see far beyond the short horizon of generations that they can see. I will have personally known and been acquainted with their Great-Great-Great-Grandfather Harmon! In the year 2009, I will still be relatively young, but I will have personal knowledge of six generations of people (extending from my great-grandfather to my own grandchildren), whose lives will have spanned 130 years of my family's history. When I pass on to join my Great-Grandpa Harmon and my other ancestors, that personal knowledge I have of those six generations will be gone with me, unless I write it down now, to preserve it for the generations to come.

Writing all you know about your family history is the first step toward reaching the central goal of family history work: performing temple ordinances for those of your ancestors who have died without that blessing. . . .

Family history research does not have to be a tedious task. There really are fun things that anyone can do right now at home without any particular training.

If you pursue any of these suggestions—or others that you may come up with, now that you've got the idea—you're doing family history. You don't have to plunge into all of these activities at once. Just pick out one and get started. (Chuck Newhouse, *Ensign,* August 1995, 62)

Other ideas Brother Newhouse explored in the article were arranging family pictures, getting copies of birth and marriage certificates, inviting the ward family history consultants to your family home evening, planning a family excursion to the family history center, keeping a journal, planning a family reunion, making a family calendar with pictures and important dates, taping an interview with a relative, and getting copies of family history records already available. The most important message of the article, and the one we really want to drive home, is to get started. Just do something, and you will be participating in this great work.

LIKENING THE SCRIPTURES TO OUR LIVES

Doctrine and Covenants 4:3 Whoever has the desire to do the work of God is called to do it.

Application: The exciting thing about family history and temple work is that we need no official call to serve. Anyone who wants to move this work forward is called to it. All we have to do is cultivate a desire and willingness, and we are extended the call. Granted, there are callings and assignments made in regard to family history and temple work, but you and I stand before the Lord responsible and accountable for this work as individuals, just as we do for proclaiming the gospel and perfecting the Saints: it comes with membership in the kingdom of God. We should set some goals and make some plans to do all in our power to promote the work of the Lord as we build up the kingdom of God.

3. CHURCH RESOURCES TO HELP YOU IN FAMILY HISTORY AND TEMPLE WORK

THEME: The mission of the Church is to invite all to "come unto Christ." This is done by proclaiming the gospel, perfecting the Saints, and redeeming the dead. The full resources of the Church are allocated to this sacred commission. This is what the Church is all about—building up the kingdom of God. When we ponder the importance of valiant service in family history and temple work, we begin to catch the vision of this great work—the work of our dispensation.

MODERN PROPHETS SPEAK

Gordon B. Hinckley:

> Only a handful of our people used the modest family history resources of the Church around the turn of the century. How things have changed! During each of the last five years more than 750,000 researchers have used the main library here in Salt Lake City and the more than 2,200 family history centers scattered across the world. Approximately 40 percent of those using the Family History Library and 60 percent of the patrons using local centers are not members of the Church. We offer a tremendous service to those not of our faith.

> There is nothing else to compare with this treasury of family history. . . . I feel the Lord has designed that it should be so. This is His church which carries His name, and one of its purposes is to make available to the millions beyond the veil of death the full blessings that lead to eternal life. . . .

> I am confident that the Lord will permit us and direct us to go on building these sacred structures [the temples] as we become worthy of them. One important test of that worthiness will lie in doing the research that becomes the foundation for the major work to be carried on in them. (*TGBH*, 211)

LIKENING THE SCRIPTURES TO OUR LIVES

Moses 6:46 A book of remembrance is kept according to the direction of God.

Application: The Latter-day Saints have always been a record-keeping people, and we are to continue that work today. We should thank the Lord for all the blessings of this day and age when we are allowed to serve and be more productive in our efforts. Think of the times when the effort to do a little required so much, and now, in the comfort of our own homes or a temple nearby (compared to the past), we can magnify our efforts. Truly, the Lord has provided the way for us to be obedient to His command to complete family history work (see 1 Ne. 3:7) in the many resources provided through advanced technology and continuing revelation. Now let us go forward and do our part to build up the kingdom of God.

ENRICHMENT

The Power of Elijah

Over the years I have learned that as we better understand eternal perspectives, our family history will occupy more and more of our attention. Wilford Woodruff, one who understood this principle, said: "I wish . . . that the veil was lifted off the face of the Latter-day Saints; I wish we could see and know the things of God as they do who are laboring . . . in the spirit world; for if this were so, this whole people with very few, if any, exceptions, would lose all interest in the riches of the world and . . . their whole desires and labors would be directed to redeem their dead, to perform faithfully the work and mission given us on earth" (*JD*, 21:301–2).

It seems that there are a number of principles of family history work that apply to this lesson, as follows:

1. *Our ancestors are anxiously waiting for us to complete their temple work.* Many ancestors have progressed to the point of waiting for their temple work to be completed. This halting of their progression is apparently as a prison to them. However, the Lord "ordained" that through keys and ordinances given to Joseph Smith, we would be enabled "to redeem [the dead] out of their prison" (D&C 128:22). Brigham Young said, "What do you suppose the fathers would say if they could speak from the dead? Would they not say: 'We have lain here thousands of years in this prison house, bound and fettered in the association of the filthy and corrupt.' If they had the power the very thunders of heaven would resound in our ears" (Matthias F. Cowley, *Wilford Woodruff: History of His Life and Labors* [Salt Lake City: Bookcraft, 1964], 494). President Woodruff declared that he felt "to say little else to the Latter-day Saints" than to expedite temple building. He said, "The dead will be after you; they will seek after you as they have after us in St. George. They called upon us, knowing that we have keys and power to redeem them" (*JD*, 19:230).

2. *Our ancestors rejoice as we find them and complete their temple ordinances.* When we reach the other side, we will realize our ancestors' gratitude toward us for doing the work that they cannot do for themselves. Scriptures tell us that "the dead" will "speak forth anthems of eternal praise" as our vicarious work redeems and frees them (D&C 128:22).

3. *Finding our ancestors and providing ordinances is true selfless service.* President Gordon B. Hinckley said, "I know of no work in all the world more unselfish than what is done in the temples. It is done in behalf of those who are dead, motivated

by the doctrine that the dead cannot help themselves. The work more nearly approaches the spirit of Christ than any other service I can conceive of" (*Church News,* March 17, 1979, 1).

4. *We must be connected through sealing ordinances to our ancestors.* Joseph Smith taught that it is important for us to understand the Spirit of Elijah and be sealed as a family. He compared this to welding links that connect each of us to our ancestors and also to our children (see D&C 128:18). The Prophet challenged us to receive "all the ordinances, baptisms, confirmations, washings, anointings, ordinations and sealing powers . . . in behalf of all [our] progenitors who are dead . . . and herein is the chain that binds the hearts of the fathers to the children, and the children to the fathers, which fulfills the mission of Elijah" (*HC,* 6:184).

5. *Finding our ancestors and ensuring that their temple work is performed is an essential responsibility for each of us.* Joseph Smith taught that we have primary responsibilities for both the living and the dead. In 1837, he said, "The greatest and most important duty is to preach the gospel" (*HC,* 2:478). Then, three months prior to his death in 1844, he taught, "The greatest responsibility in this world that God has laid upon us is to seek after our dead" (*HC,* 6:313). The work of the Lord is fulfilled as we complete our temple and genealogy labors for the living and for our dead. We can understand why this subject was on Joseph Smith's mind "more than most any other that was given to him" (Wilford Woodruff, *The Discourses of Wilford Woodruff,* ed. G. Homer Durham [Salt Lake City: Bookcraft, 1946], 156).

6. *The task of searching out our ancestors and completing their temple work is necessary to our salvation and perfection.* We are not usually direct beneficiaries of our own service to others. However, in serving our ancestors, we facilitate our own salvation. We are taught that "their salvation is necessary and essential to our salvation" (D&C 128:15). Joseph Smith cautioned us as follows: "Those saints who neglect it in behalf of their deceased relatives do it at the peril of their own salvation" (*HC,* 4:426). The scriptures state: "We without them cannot be made perfect" (D&C 128:18).

7. *Our ancestors' salvation and perfection are dependent upon our searching them out and completing their temple work.* The Lord revealed through Joseph Smith that "neither can they without us be made perfect" (D&C 128:18). The Prophet later added the words, "The fathers without the children nor the children without the fathers" (*HC,* 6:252). Wilford Woodruff taught, "You . . . hold the keys of the salvation of your father's house" (Wilford Woodruff, *The Discourses of Wilford Woodruff,* ed. G. Homer Durham [Salt Lake City: Bookcraft, 1969], 158).

8. *We agreed in the premortal existence to serve as "saviors on Mount Zion" to our ancestors.* "In our preexistent state, in the day of the great council, we made a certain agreement with the Almighty. The Lord proposed a plan, conceived by him. We accepted it. . . . We agreed, right then and there, to be not only saviors for ourselves, but measurably, saviors for the whole human family. . . . With the Lord at the head, we become saviors on Mount Zion, all committed to offering salvation to the untold numbers of spirits" (John A. Widtsoe, "The Worth of Souls," *Utah Genealogical and Historical Magazine* 25 [October 1934]: 189–90). Joseph Smith challenged us "to come up as Saviors on Mount Zion." He said we do this "by . . . going forth and receiving all of the ordinances . . . and sealing powers . . . in behalf of all of the progenitors who are dead, and redeem them that they may come forth in the first resurrection and be exalted" (*HC*, 6:184).

9. *The family, including family history work, is the ultimate purpose of the Church.* President Boyd K. Packer said, "The ultimate purpose of every teaching, every activity in the Church is that parents and their children are happy at home, sealed in an eternal marriage, and linked to their generations" (Boyd K. Packer, *Ensign*, May 1994, 19)

Although we all have many responsibilities, it is critical for us to devote some time to family history. Elder Dallin H. Oaks summarized what brings success: "Our effort is not to get everyone to do everything, but to get everyone to do something" (Dallin H. Oaks, *Church News*, March 26, 1988, 9). May we each strive to do something, even just a little, to bring our families together and fulfill our duty to both the living and the dead. (Anderson)

SUMMARY

To feel and follow the Spirit of Elijah is to accomplish a key aspect of the work of a disciple of the Savior. Obedience in this regard may encompass some or all of the various productive approaches to family history and temple work described in this chapter. The Church has allocated a multiplicity of resources to help us in achieving success in this vital undertaking. Enoch encapsulated the decreed *modus operandi*, indicating that this work shall be done "according to the pattern given by the finger of God; and it is given in our own language" (Moses 6:46). We can use the pattern laid down by our prophets, past and present, to move forward in the Spirit of Elijah to compose our books of remembrance and accomplish the work of the temples—all toward the end of realizing the destiny of God's plan to turn the hearts of the fathers to the children and of the children to their fathers—forever.

CHAPTER FORTY-ONE

"EVERY MEMBER *a* MISSIONARY"

Reading Assignment: Doctrine and Covenants 1:4–5, 30; 4; 65; 84:85–88; 88:81; 109:72–74; 123:12; 138:56; *Our Heritage,* pages 116–17, 124–25.

Additional Reading: Luke 22:32; Doctrine and Covenants 1:23; 4; 16:6; 31:5; 33:8–11; 115:4–6; Mormon 9:22; Moroni 6:4–5.

Not all of us can engage in full-time missionary work, where one might have opportunity to explain the gospel and bear testimony of its divinity many times a day. But every member most definitely can *follow President David O. McKay's inspired slogan, "Every member a missionary." He can befriend and fellowship nonmember neighbors, fellow employees, friends and acquaintances, and those with whom he is engaged in community service. By his interest and association, he should strive to bring those nonmembers to the point where they will willingly receive the . . . missionaries. What every member ought to do, by good example and by bearing testimony, is to portray to nonmembers the joys of gospel living and understanding and thus help to bring them to the stage where they will accept more formal teaching.*

The proper motivation for missionary work of any kind, as for all Church service, is, of course, love for fellowmen; but always such work has its by-product effect on one's own life. Thus, as we become instruments in God's hands in changing the lives of others, our own lives cannot help being lifted. One can hardly help another to the top of the hill without climbing there himself. (Spencer W. Kimball, President Kimball Speaks Out *[Salt Lake City: Deseret Book, 1981], 42–43)*

THEMES *for* LIVING

1. The Church Comes Forth out of Obscurity
2. Our Duty: To Take the Gospel to All the World
3. "Every Member a Missionary"
4. Fellowshipping and Nurturing New Converts

INTRODUCTION

What agenda of action will produce the greatest long-term value for the Saints of God? The Lord has answered this question with consummate clarity: "And now, behold, I say unto you, that the thing which will be of the most worth unto you will be to declare repentance unto this people, that you may bring souls unto me, that you may rest with them in the kingdom of my Father" (D&C 16:6). Our preparation for this sacred calling was made long before we came into the mortal sphere: "Even before they were born, they, with many others, received their first lessons in the world of spirits and were prepared to come forth in the due time of the Lord to labor in his vineyard for the salvation of the souls of men" (D&C 138:56).

This work is what we are here for. We are to continually strengthen ourselves and others in the gospel. This, in large part, means missionary work. As we continue our schooling in the art and practice of missionary labors, we find that the heart and soul of our commission is associated with key inner qualities of discipleship: "And faith, hope, charity and love, with an eye single to the glory of God, qualify [us] for the work. Remember faith, virtue, knowledge, temperance, patience, brotherly kindness, godliness, charity, humility, diligence. Ask, and ye shall receive; knock, and it shall be opened unto you. Amen" (D&C 4:5–6).

Building upon such a rock foundation of faith and godliness, we take up the banner of truth with courage and devotion, knowing that we go forth in the strength of the Lord, "even as Nephi of old" (D&C 33:8). We find the courage to follow the Lord's counsel, "Yea, open your mouths and spare not," because we "shall be laden with sheaves upon [our] backs" and, most importantly, because the Lord promises, "For lo, I am with you" in these efforts (D&C 33:9). With the Lord as our companion, how can we fail? We will be true missionaries in every way as we live our lives. We will consistently share our testimony in both word and deed, scarcely able to refrain from sharing the light of the gospel.

Such is the commission, the walk, and the glory of those who embark in the service of the Lord to proclaim the gospel and gather the sheaves of Israel on behalf of the Lord of the harvest (see Alma 26:7). With Ammon we can rejoice, humbly, in the goodness of God to call us into a work of such magnificent joy and service: "Yea, I know that I am nothing; as to my strength I am weak; therefore I will not boast of myself, but I will boast of my God, for in his strength I can do all things" (Alma 26:12). Truly, with the Lord as our partner, we can see great miracles in our lives and the lives we touch through the great work of spreading the gospel.

MOMENT OF TRUTH

The call to missionary service is pervasive throughout the Doctrine and Covenants. Salient passages are contained in sections 1, 4, 65, 88, 109, 115, and 123. The backgrounds for some of these sections have already been treated in considerable detail as follows: section 1 in chapter 1, section 4 in chapter 11, section 88 in chapter 13, section 109 in chapter 18, and section 115 in chapter 9. Following are summaries of the circumstances surrounding sections 65 and 123.

Section 65: Given through the Prophet Joseph Smith in October 1831 at Hiram, Portage County, Ohio (see *HC,* 1:218). This revelation was given on October 30, though the Prophet recorded in his journal, "In the forepart of October, I received the following prayer through revelation" (*HC,* 1:218, October 1831, Hiram, Ohio). Verse 2 is a vivid echoing of the words of Daniel: "The keys of the kingdom of God are committed unto man on the earth, and from thence shall the gospel roll forth unto the ends of the earth, as the stone which is cut out of the mountain without hands shall roll forth, until it has filled the whole earth" (see Dan. 2:34, 45; see also D&C 109:72–73).

Section 123: Given through the Prophet Joseph Smith in March of 1839 at Liberty, Clay County, Missouri (see *HC,* 3:302–3). While he was confined to the squalor of Liberty Jail on false and spurious charges, the Prophet set forth duties of the Saints concerning the actions of their persecutors. Historian Lyndon W. Cook provided these details of the response of the leadership:

> On 4 May 1839, pursuant to the instructions of section 123, Almon W. Babbitt, Erastus Snow, and Robert B. Thompson were appointed "a traveling committee to gather up and obtain all the libelous reports and publications which have been circulated against the Church" as well as "other historical matter connected with said Church, which they can possibly obtain." Referring to this assignment, Erastus Snow wrote:
>
> "[On 4 May 1839] I was appointed by the conference one of three committee to collect the libilous publications of all kinds that had been published against the

saints and to insert and refute them in a church history which should be compiled by us after the conference."

Joseph Smith advised that Erastus Snow and Almon W. Babbitt each travel and preach as their circumstances would permit and "gather in our travels what publications we could and send them to Elder [Robert B.] Thom[p]son who should be writing and compiling the history which should be subject to our inspection." (*RPJS,* 241–42)

1. THE CHURCH COMES FORTH OUT OF OBSCURITY

THEME: The ancient prophet Isaiah saw in vision the emergence of the latter-day kingdom of God in all its glory: "Therefore, behold, I will proceed to do a marvellous work among this people, even a marvellous work and a wonder: for the wisdom of their wise men shall perish, and the understanding of their prudent men shall be hid" (Isa. 29:14). The Restoration came as a dawn of awakening amid the darkness of spiritual hunger in the world—the Lord having spoken again through a living prophet to establish His work for the last time prior to the Second Coming. What a privilege it is to be associated with such a magnificent movement to bless the lives of all humankind and prepare for the coming of the millennial reign!

MODERN PROPHETS SPEAK

Joseph Fielding Smith:

> Incline thine ear, O Lord; look down upon us in mercy; hear us in these our petitions; and grant us the desires of our hearts in righteousness, as we plead with thee for the welfare of Zion and all her interests and concerns. This is thy church; thou hast established it and hast "brought it forth out of obscurity and out of darkness, the only true and living Church upon the face of the whole earth." Wilt thou now cause it to "shine forth fair as the moon, clear as the sun, and terrible as an army with banners," that all men everywhere may know that this is thy work; that it is thy will that they should come unto thy Son and live his laws and gain salvation in thine eternal kingdom.
>
> O may the interests of Zion prevail and triumph in all the earth! May thy kingdom, which is thy church, "go forth, that the kingdom of heaven may come, that thou, O God, mayest be glorified in heaven so on earth, that thine enemies may be subdued; for thine is the honor, power and glory, forever and ever." (Provo Temple Dedicatory Prayer, quoted in *Ensign,* April 1972, 26)

ILLUSTRATIONS FOR OUR TIMES

"Out of Obscurity and . . . Darkness"

When we speak of bringing the Church out of obscurity in our time, we cannot ignore the fact that President Hinckley has been about that task most of his adult life. President Hinckley, hired in 1935 as executive secretary of the newly formed Church Radio, Publicity, and Mission Literature Committee, helped pioneer the public relations program of the Church.

From that point on, filmstrips, pamphlets, brochures, radio documentaries and dramas were all increasingly used to tell the Church's story. When radio was the instrument of both entertainment and information, the Church employed it. *The Fulness of Times,* a series of 39 episodes of Church history, was broadcast over 400 stations and ran for five years. . . .

In addition, the Mormon Tabernacle Choir's Sunday broadcasts have served generations of radio listeners and television viewers. *Music and the Spoken Word* is the longest continuous weekly broadcast in the history of broadcasting. A choir milestone was in July 1998, when the program celebrated its 70th anniversary year.

In a press conference held on March 13, 1995, President Hinckley and his counselors, Thomas S. Monson and James E. Faust, were announced as the new First Presidency of the Church. President Hinckley not only spoke to the press and thus to the world, but he answered questions of the reporters who attended. He did so with such openness and skill that they heralded it as a new era of communication.

A pivotal moment in President Hinckley's administration came at the Harvard Club in New York City when Mike Wallace asked if he would be willing to be interviewed for a piece on *60 Minutes.* President Hinckley was quiet for what seemed like a long time, in fact probably about 15 or 20 seconds, and then he said, "I believe I'll take a chance." President Hinckley appeared on *60 Minutes* on April 7, 1996, and on September 8, 1998, he appeared on the *Larry King Show,* both distributed worldwide.

Throughout 1997, the Public Affairs Department responded to the request of Elder M. Russell Ballard of the Quorum of the Twelve Apostles that we help tell the Church's story to the world during the Church sesquicentennial. It is fair to say that our fondest dreams were exceeded by considerable measure as the events unfolded. The centerpiece was the reenactment of the wagon train, an idea proposed by members and nonmembers alike and then assisted and publicized by the Church. Once articles appeared in the *New York Times* and *Newsweek,* the rest of the media realized that there was a story on the American prairies waiting to be told.

We are now seeing the Church learning to use the new medium of the World Wide Web to proclaim the gospel, answer questions, further family history research, and proclaim the word of the Lord through His servants. Truly the Church has come a long way. (Bruce L. Olsen, *Ensign,* January 2000, 45)

LIKENING THE SCRIPTURES TO OUR LIVES

Doctrine and Covenants 1:30 Those who have received the gospel will have the power to build up the Church and bring it forth from obscurity.

Doctrine and Covenants 65:2 The Lord has committed the keys of His kingdom unto His chosen people on the earth today. The gospel will roll forth until it fills the entire world.

Application: The Lord has spoken. The gospel will roll forth (see Dan. 2:44). We as a people and as a Church are to bring this about. We are preaching the gospel on every continent. The Book of Mormon has been translated into more than 100 languages. There are over 337 missions with some 60,000 missionaries, and the Church has a presence in over 144 nations and countries. The Church is emerging out of obscurity, and we who are blessed with the gospel can continue to assist in the work of building and strengthening Zion. We can do our part as member and full-time missionaries, fortifying ourselves and those we serve.

2. OUR DUTY: TO TAKE THE GOSPEL TO ALL THE WORLD

THEME: Since the earliest days of the Restoration, the focus has always been on spreading the good news of the gospel. The Lord declared His desire: "That the fulness of my gospel might be proclaimed by the weak and the simple unto the ends of the world, and before kings and rulers" (D&C 1:23). The Saints of God, having received the opportunity to obtain the riches of eternity through the Atonement of Jesus Christ, have the responsibility to share the truth with others: "For of him unto whom much is given much is required; and he who sins against the greater light shall receive the greater condemnation" (D&C 82:3).

MODERN PROPHETS SPEAK

Spencer W. Kimball:

> No person who has been converted to the gospel should shirk his responsibility to teach the truth to others. This is our privilege. This is our duty. (*Ensign,* October 1977, 3)

Gordon B. Hinckley:

> Last year there were approximately 300,000 convert baptisms throughout the Church. This is tremendously significant. This is the equivalent of 120 new stakes of 2,500 members each. Think of that: 120 new stakes in a single year! It is wonderful. But it is not enough. I am not being unrealistic when I say that with concerted effort, with recognition of the duty which falls upon each of us as members of the Church, and with sincere prayer to the Lord for help, we could double that number. (*Ensign,* May 1999, 104)

Howard W. Hunter:

> As the walls in Eastern Europe, the Soviet Union, Africa, China, India, South America, and many other parts of the world come tumbling down, the corresponding need for more missionaries to fulfill the divine commission to take the gospel to all the earth will certainly go up! Are we ready to meet that contingency?
>
> To satisfy the new demands being made upon us in this great missionary work of the last days, perhaps some of us (particularly the older generation whose families are raised) need to take stock to determine whether "walls" that we have built in our own minds need to come down.
>
> For example, how about the "comfort wall" that seems to prevent many couples and singles from going on a mission? How about the "financial wall" of debt that interferes with some members' ability to go, or the "grandchildren wall," or the "health wall," or the "lack of self-confidence wall," or the "self-satisfied wall," or the "transgression wall," or the walls of fear, doubt, or complacency? Does anyone really doubt for a minute that with the help of the Lord he or she could bring those walls crashing down?
>
> We have been privileged to be born in these last days, as opposed to some earlier dispensation, to help take the gospel to all the earth. There is no greater calling in this life. If we are content to hide behind self-made walls, we willingly forgo the blessings that are otherwise ours. (*THWH,* 247)

ILLUSTRATIONS FOR OUR TIMES

"I Was Called to Perform a Mission"

On the fifth day of October, 1875, at the Semi-annual Conference of the Church of Jesus Christ of Latter-day Saints, I was called to perform a mission to the United States.

Just why my name was suggested as a candidate for this mission, and presented at conference for approval or rejection by the people, I cannot say. My mind prior to that time had been entirely given up to temporalities. I had never read to exceed a dozen chapters of the Bible in my life, and little more than that from either the Book of Mormon or Doctrine and Covenants, and concerning Church history was entirely ignorant. Had never made but one attempt to address a public audience, large or small, and that effort was no credit to me. Had been engaged in the railroad business for a number of years, and this occupation would have deprived me of meetings and religious services even had my inclinations led in that direction, which I frankly confess they did not. I had become almost an inveterate smoker, and bought cigars by the wholesale, a thousand at a time. Was addicted to the use of language which, if not profane, was at least vulgar and reprehensible. Frequently visited saloons, but was not an habitual drinker. Was not proficient at billiards, but squandered considerable money in acquiring what little knowledge I possessed of the game; and pool frequently cost me more for drinks than my board bill came to. Though these indiscretions were common and frequent, thanks to a mother's sagacious training, they never led to grosser or more alluring ones.

Nature never endowed me with a superabundance of religious sentiment or veneration; my region of spirituality is not high, but below the average. A phrenologist once said to me: "You are too level-headed to ever make a sanctimonious church member." With this list of disqualifications, which serious reflection helped to magnify, is it surprising that I marveled and wondered if the Church were not running short of missionary material?

One of my fellow employees was at the conference; I was not, because I did not care to be. He heard my name called, abruptly left the meeting and ran over to the telegraph office to call and tell me the startling news. This was the first intimation I had received that such a thing was contemplated. At the very moment this intelligence was being flashed over the wires, I was sitting lazily thrown back in an office rocking chair, my feet on the desk, reading a novel and simultaneously sucking an old Dutch pipe, of massive proportions, just to vary the monotony of cigar smoking.

As soon as I had been informed of what had taken place, I threw the novel in the waste basket, the pipe in a corner and started up town to buy a catechism. Have never read a novel nor smoked a pipe from that hour. Sent in my resignation the same day, to take effect at once, in order that I might have time for study and preparation.

Remarkable as it may seem, and has since appeared to me, a thought of disregarding the call, or of refusing to comply with the requirement, never once entered my mind. The question I asked myself a thousand times, and which seemed so all-important, was: "How can I accomplish this mission? How can I, who am so shamefully ignorant and untaught in doctrine, do honor to God and justice to the souls of men, and merit the trust reposed in me by the Priesthood?" (Eli H. Peirce, quoted in *Best-Loved Stories of the LDS People,* ed. Jack M. Lyon, Linda Ririe Gundry, and Jay A. Parry [Salt Lake City: Deseret Book, 1997], 389–90)

"Hal, You Knew"

"Behold, I sent you out to testify and warn the people, and it becometh every man who hath been warned to warn his neighbor" (D&C 88:81).

That command and warning of danger was given to those called as missionaries at the start of the Restoration. But the duty to warn our neighbor falls on all of us who have accepted the covenant of baptism. We are to talk with nonmember friends and relatives about the gospel. Our purpose is to invite them to be taught by the full-time missionaries who are called and set apart to teach. When a person has chosen to accept our invitation to be taught, a "referral" of great promise has been created, one far more likely to enter the waters of baptism and then to remain faithful. . . .

The missionaries will help and encourage us, but whether such moments at the baptismal font and in the temple come more often will depend largely on how we see our charge and what we choose to do about it. The Lord would not use the word "warn" if there is no danger. Yet not many people we know sense it. They have learned to ignore the increasing evidence that society is unraveling and that their lives and family lack the peace they once thought was possible. That willingness to ignore the signs of danger can make it easy for you to think: Why should I speak to anyone about the gospel who seems content? What danger is there to them or to me if I do or say nothing?

Well, the danger may be hard to see, but it is real, both for them and for us. For instance, at some moment in the world to come, everyone you will ever meet will know what you know now. They will know that the only way to live forever in association with our families and in the presence of our Heavenly Father and His Son,

Jesus Christ, was to choose to enter into the gate by baptism at the hands of those with authority from God. They will know that the only way families can be together forever is to accept and keep sacred covenants offered in the temples of God on this earth. And they will know that you knew. And they will remember whether you offered them what someone had offered you.

It's easy to say, "The time isn't right." But there is danger in procrastination. Years ago I worked for a man in California. He hired me, he was kind to me, he seemed to regard me highly. I may have been the only Latter-day Saint he ever knew well. I don't know all the reasons I found to wait for a better moment to talk with him about the gospel. I just remember my feeling of sorrow when I learned, after he had retired and I lived far away, that he and his wife had been killed in a late night drive to their home in Carmel, California. He loved his wife. He loved his children. He had loved his parents. He loved his grandchildren, and he will love their children and will want to be with them forever.

Now, I don't know how the crowds will be handled in the world to come. But I suppose that I will meet him, that he will look into my eyes, and that I will see in them the question: "Hal, you knew. Why didn't you tell me?"

When I think of him, and when I think of that widow I baptized and her family who will now be sealed to her and to each other, I want to do better. I want to increase my power to invite people to be taught. With that desire and with faith that God will help us, we will do better. It isn't hard to see how. (Henry B. Eyring, *Ensign,* November 1998, 33)

LIKENING THE SCRIPTURES TO OUR LIVES

Mormon 9:22 Jesus Christ has commissioned each of His disciples as follows: "Go ye into all the world, and preach the gospel to every creature."

Application: We are the disciples of Jesus Christ. We follow Him and keep His commandments. We have been commanded by our Savior and all the prophets to take the gospel to all the world (see Mark 16:15; Acts 10:42; Alma 17:4; D&C 1:5; 4:1; 50:17; 84: 85–88; 90:11; and many more). This becomes our work (see D&C 138:56; Jacob 5:70–77) and our joy (see D&C 15:6; 18:10–16). Make plans to be a part of this great latter-day work.

3. "EVERY MEMBER A MISSIONARY"

THEME: Without exception, we can all contribute to the growth of the kingdom of God by embarking with faith, devotion, and courage upon the pathway of missionary service. The Lord entrusts us with the work to "make known his wonderful works among the people" (D&C 65:4). Indeed, we covenanted to witness of Christ when we were baptized (see Mosiah 18:9). The degree of our commitment to this covenant principle will, in large measure, determine our worthiness before the Lord of grace and mercy when the hour of accountability arrives.

MODERN PROPHETS SPEAK

Richard G. Scott:

> Don't wait to be asked. I invite each of you to come forth to participate in some way in the glorious and varied opportunities for missionary service and in strengthening and sustaining those who embrace the gospel as new members. . . .

> Why every member a missionary? Because that is what the Lord has asked us to do. Prayerfully consider it. There are those who would forever call you the angel of understanding and compassion that led them to the truth, fortified them in their faith, or helped them learn to serve the Lord. Do it. Talk to your bishop. Let him help you see the possibilities for joy unbounded in some aspect of "every member a missionary." You will find a renewal of life, excitement, and a deep feeling of personal fulfillment from having the courage to accept a call as a missionary. (*Ensign,* November 1997, 35)

ILLUSTRATIONS FOR OUR TIMES

A Conversation with Elder Franklin D. Richards

> *Ensign:* It is probable that 50 percent or more of the Church membership have not tried to interest anyone in the Church in the past year. Why do you think some of our people are reluctant to invite someone else to learn more about the gospel?

> *Elder Richards:* They're afraid of offending, or they lack faith—or both! And you know, that's sad, because the Lord said that the "elect hear my voice and harden not their hearts" (D&C 29:7). The Lord tells us there are many who will not harden their hearts when we invite them to enjoy the great blessings each of us enjoys. Our job, presumably, is not to

bring every nonmember into the Church—just the elect! And how do you know who the elect are? The Lord says the elect will hear his voice—they'll listen and do something about it. But we must remember that even though a person may not be "elect" today, a year from now, due to something that has happened in his life, his whole attitude may have changed and he may have become one of the elect. That's why we should continually, throughout their lives, politely give people many opportunities to hear the Lord's voice.

Can we do anything less? Hasn't the Lord given all of us many opportunities in our own lives? If we've grown to the stature where we're becoming more like him, then we'll want the same for others. It's as simple as that.

And you know, the Lord gets involved in this! What you must do is commit yourself to do the Lord's assignment; take him at his word, then he opens up the way. I've seen it so many times. He opens up the way by putting people in our paths so we can become the connecting link between them and the missionaries. It's that simple, that basic, and that successful!

I was flying to Chicago a few months ago and sat down by a young college student who had been going to Utah State University. I asked him how he liked it, and he said, "I just loved it." I asked him why, and he answered, "Because I enjoyed the people there."

I said, "A good many of them are Mormons, aren't they?"

And he said, "Yes."

And I said, "Did you meet any?"

He said yes, he had many friends who were Mormons. One had given him a Book of Mormon to read. I asked him if he had read it, and he answered no. I asked him if he had heard of our missionary program. He said yes.

Then I asked, "How would you like to know more about the Mormon Church?"

He liked the idea. He gave me his name and address, and I told him I would arrange to have two young missionaries come by and see him. A few months later I got a letter from the missionaries saying that they had baptized him and were teaching his brothers and sisters and parents.

Just a few months later I was in San Francisco. I got on the plane to return home and sat next to a man who was going to Minneapolis. He was disturbed that the flight had been delayed and he would be arriving late. We visited awhile and I asked him what he did. He replied that he was a research scientist. He then asked me what I did, and I replied, "I guess you could best describe me as a Mormon missionary." I asked, "What do you know about the Mormon Church?" He replied that he had a Book of Mormon but had not read it. He asked me some very interesting questions about our genealogical program. I then asked him if he would like to know more about Mormonism. He said he would, and so I got his name and address and sent the referral to the missionaries in San Francisco. In about three weeks I received a letter from the missionaries telling me they were giving him and his family the discussions.

These are just two of many experiences I have had recently, and I'm telling them because if they can happen to me, they can happen to anyone—but only if we make them happen by taking the initiative. I believe the Lord places many of his elect in our paths—puts them near us—but it is up to us to take the opportunity to be the link between them and the truth. (*Ensign*, October 1977, 39)

LIKENING THE SCRIPTURES TO OUR LIVES

Doctrine and Covenants 1:4–5 The Lord calls His chosen disciples to be "the voice of warning" in the last day. His work will not be held back, for He has commanded it to be done.

Application: We are the Lord's disciples, and therefore have the obligation to warn and teach His children about the gospel. Notice that He doesn't say here "full-time missionaries only" are chosen for this work, but *all* disciples. That means each of us. But He also includes a promise—"none shall stay [us]." The Lord's work will go forward because He commands it to do so. He will help us in the work, because when He commands, He provides a way (see 1 Ne. 3:7).

Doctrine and Covenants 88:81 The Lord expects every individual who has received the gospel to share it with those around him or her.

Application: As members of the Church and as disciples of Jesus Christ, we have an obligation to stand as witnesses of Christ at all times (see Mosiah 18:9). We are to open our mouths and share the gospel (see D&C 33:8–11), or we are not approved of the Lord (see D&C 60:2–3). We should pray for all those who know not God (see Alma 6:6), as many do not know where to find the truth (see D&C 123:12). It is our duty to find people willing to hear the gospel message.

4. FELLOWSHIPPING AND NURTURING NEW CONVERTS

THEME: The Church and kingdom of God is the nurturing enterprise for perfecting the Saints and shepherding their spiritual growth and development. All are enlisted in the service of charitable giving and teaching as families are strengthened to achieve their ultimate destiny.

MODERN PROPHETS SPEAK

Gordon B. Hinckley:

> With the ever-increasing number of converts, we must make an increasingly substantial effort to assist them as they find their way. Every one of them needs three things: a friend, a responsibility, and nurturing with the "good word of God" (Moro. 6:4). It is our duty and opportunity to provide these things. (*TGBH,* 539)

Spencer W. Kimball:

> Yesterday while speaking to the Regional Representatives, I called attention to the challenge facing all of us as we fellowship and teach the gospel to cultural and minority groups living among us. When special attention of some kind is not provided for these good people, we lose them. (*Ensign,* November 1980, 45)

M. Russell Ballard:

> Brothers and sisters, my message is urgent because we need to retain in full fellowship many more of the new converts and return to activity many more of the less active. I urge you to increase the spirit of friendship and pure Christian fellowship in your neighborhoods. A new convert or recently activated member should feel the warmth of being wanted and being welcomed into full fellowship of the Church. Members and leaders of the Church should nurture and love them as Jesus would. (*Ensign,* November 1988, 28)

ILLUSTRATIONS FOR OUR TIMES

Keeping Converts

> When leaders from the Charleston South Carolina Stake are asked how they have been so successful in keeping new members active, it's not uncommon to hear the reply, "We're not really doing anything out of the ordinary." And for the most part it's true; Latter-day Saints in this verdant area of the southern United States are simply following the counsel laid out by the leaders of the Church. Yet by consistently

monitoring the progress of each new convert, members here have seen over 80 percent of those baptized in 1997 remain strong in the gospel. . . .

"I credit a lot of our success in retention to the follow-up our ward leaders have been doing with the convert baptism checklist," says stake president Joseph D. Stubbs. "Bishops have a copy of the checklist for every person who is baptized so they'll know *people* instead of knowing numbers."

The convert baptism checklist is one key the Charleston South Carolina Stake has used to integrate new members into their ward families. Liz Sharp, a marriage and family counselor in Mount Pleasant, South Carolina, was introduced to the Church when she was asked to conduct a series of firesides on building successful marriages and raising children. "I started doing more with the Church through my friend Dee Dee over at the Charleston Ward," says Liz. "I sang in the choir. I thought it was awesome they'd let a nonmember sing with them."

Liz was regularly attending the ward in Charleston with her friend and gradually developing a testimony, but her husband, Joe, was not interested in learning about the Church. On 31 December 1995 she was baptized and became a member of the neighboring Mount Pleasant Ward. "I was so impressed," she says. "Half of the Mount Pleasant Ward showed up for my baptism, people I had never met before."

As items on her convert baptism checklist were accomplished, Liz progressed: she was attending the Gospel Principles class, she accepted a calling in the ward, and she was receiving the *Discussions for New Members.*

At first Joe kept his distance during these discussions, but gradually he became involved. After going through a year's worth of missionaries, he met with the mission president. Joe explained that he was sure the Church was true and that he'd be baptized one day, but he needed spiritual confirmation to go along with his intellectual understanding of the gospel.

Joe's confirmation came as he sat talking with the stake patriarch before Liz arrived to receive her patriarchal blessing. Ten days later, on 23 February 1997, he was baptized and his convert baptism checklist joined Liz's in Bishop Hale's notebook. "It's all laid out. The bishop has a little checkoff sheet in there to keep track of how everybody is doing," Joe says, pointing toward the bishop's office. "And it's his goal to get you into the temple step by step." Joe and Liz succeeded in meeting all their goals and went through the Atlanta Georgia Temple on 10 April 1998. . . .

A second key to the Charleston South Carolina Stake's success in convert retention has been the Discussions for New Members. . . . These lessons have helped converts make the transition from being taught by full-time missionaries to receiving visits from home and visiting teachers. Frank Carter, the stake mission president, explains how the process works: "We've asked that the full-time missionaries give the first discussion for new members, but they should have at least the home teachers or the stake missionaries (now ward missionaries) present. The second discussion should be shared between the full-time missionaries and the stake missionaries with the home teachers present for that too. Then the last four discussions are shared between the home teachers and the stake missionaries." . . .

Pete Schlegel, ward mission leader in the Charleston First Ward, emphasizes a third key in helping new members progress in the gospel: giving converts the opportunity to serve. "We get them going on home and visiting teaching right away," he says. "I always give the bishop a gentle reminder in our priesthood executive committee meeting: We don't have a calling for this young lady or young gentleman yet; we need to start thinking about that, get some inspiration, and get them going." . . . Carolyn Kirmes from the Summerville Ward also received strength from her calling. Shortly after her baptism, and as she waited for her husband to show interest in the Church, she was called to teach in the Relief Society: "I got a calling right away and so I felt needed and valuable. That made a big difference with me." . . .

Why are the basics working for the Charleston South Carolina Stake? Stake mission president Frank Carter says that since stake leaders started keeping track of individual converts, ward leaders and ward members have been more diligent in welcoming and nurturing them. The ward members truly care about and feel accountable for the new converts. . . .

Stake president Joseph D. Stubbs explains the simple success formula that has helped new members in the Charleston Stake remain committed after baptism. "They've had good priesthood leaders to nurture them along, they've had good members to help when it was needed, and they've been given opportunities to serve." (Paul VanDenBerghe, *Ensign,* October 1998, 54)

LIKENING THE SCRIPTURES TO OUR LIVES

Moroni 6:4–5 Those received in baptism are recorded as members of the Church "that they might be remembered and nourished" in the gospel. The Church meets together often, praying, fasting, and edifying one another to keep us "in the right way."

Application: The purpose of the Church is not only to bring souls to Christ but to keep them close to Him. The organization of the Church provides the opportunity for us to associate together "to fast and to pray, and to speak one with another concerning the welfare of [our] souls." Such nourishment is needed by all who enter into baptism. It is not enough to get people to join the Church. They must also continue in the faith, and as member-missionaries, it is our duty to strengthen and encourage their progress.

Luke 22:32 The Lord has prayed that our faith won't waver and that when we receive this faith, we will use it to strengthen others.

Doctrine and Covenants 108:7 We are to bolster and strengthen those around us in all our doings and conversations.

Application: As true Saints and disciples of the Lord Jesus Christ, we are to nurture, bless, and love one another—especially new converts (see John 13:34–35; D&C 81:5). As we serve and strengthen each other, it is as if we do it unto our Savior (see Matt. 25:40). This kind of service is part of our commission to perfect the Saints. All of us struggle at times, and each of us can help others through such trying times and transitions.

SUMMARY

It is in these latter days that the Church has come forth out of obscurity to take its place as "the only true and living church upon the face of the whole earth" (D&C 1:30). It is now our duty as members of the Church to take the gospel to all the world, in keeping with the principle of "every member a missionary." Furthermore, we are to labor diligently to fellowship and nurture new converts as they enter the kingdom of God and move forward toward spiritual perfection. Our commission in this regard is clear as we serve in the strength of the Lord: "Behold, I send you out to reprove the world of all their unrighteous deeds, and to teach them of a judgment which is to come. And whoso receiveth you, there I will be also, for I will go before your face. I will be on your right hand and on your left, and my Spirit shall be in your hearts, and mine angels round about you, to bear you up" (D&C 84:87–88).

What a glorious opportunity we have in contributing to the building up of the Lord's kingdom in the dispensation of the fulness of times in preparation for the Day of Judgment: "Arise and shine forth, that thy light may be a standard for the nations; And that the gathering together upon the land of Zion, and upon her stakes, may be for a defense, and for a refuge from the storm, and from wrath when it shall be poured out without mixture upon the whole earth" (D&C 115:5–6). Let us do all in our power to gather all who are in the Church and those who will join together in the holy places of our wards and stakes. Together we may find refuge and be found worthy of the Lord's blessings and protection in full measure.

CHAPTER FORTY-TWO

CONTINUING REVELATION
to LATTER-DAY PROPHETS

Reading Assignment: Doctrine and Covenants 1:38; 68:1–4; 84:109–10; 107:25, 34, 93–98; 132:8; Official Declaration 2 (pages 293–94); *Our Heritage,* pages 117–19, 125–27.

Additional Reading: Proverbs 29:18; Amos 3:7; Matthew 16:18; 1 Nephi 4:18; 16:9; Alma 5:46; Mormon 8:34.

In each age when the Lord has had a people on earth, He has guided them by revelation. Always that revelation has come through a living prophet. While urging the people to "search the scriptures" and profit by the advice He had given anciently, the Lord nevertheless gave current direction for the present day.

This is one of the outstanding elements of the restoration of the Gospel. The principle of prophecy has been restored. But it was not given merely that future events might be foretold, for such is hardly the whole field of prophecy. Probably more important than giving predictions is providing the day-by-day divine guidance which we need.

Conditions vary from time to time, making continuous guidance necessary. It was never the intent of the Lord to leave His people groping in the dark, but to give them light and direction to help them live successfully, and this He has given through His anointed servants. Anciently Amos said appropriately: "Surely the Lord God will do nothing, but he revealeth his secret unto his servants the prophets." (Mark E. Petersen, The Way to Peace *[Salt Lake City: Bookcraft, 1969], 280)*

THEMES *for* LIVING

1. A Revelation: Church Correlation
2. A Revelation: Every Worthy Male Member to Receive the Priesthood
3. A Revelation: Publication of New Editions of the Scriptures
4. A Revelation: Additional Quorums of the Seventy
5. A Revelation: Words from Living Prophets as Inspired by the Holy Ghost

INTRODUCTION

In instructing Peter and the other disciples on the foundation principles of Church governance, the Savior stated: "And I say also unto thee, That thou art Peter, and upon this rock I will build my church; and the gates of hell shall not prevail against it" (Matt. 16:18). The principle of continuing revelation was at the center of this reference, as Paul later explained: "And he gave some, apostles; and some, prophets; and some, evangelists; and some, pastors and teachers; For the perfecting of the saints, for the work of the ministry, for the edifying of the body of Christ" (Eph. 4:11–12). In our day, the heavens have confirmed once again that the Lord's house "is a house of order . . . and not a house of confusion" (D&C 132:8). As such, the Lord has prepared a way for essential, ongoing truth to flow unimpeded through His chosen servants: "Whosoever receiveth my word receiveth me, and whosoever receiveth me, receiveth those, the First Presidency, whom I have sent, whom I have made counselors for my name's sake unto you" (D&C 112:20). This governance is a blessing of strength, stability, and continued revelation to the Church. Under the direction of the First Presidency, the work of the kingdom goes forth—beginning with the Quorum of the Twelve—through the ministry of all the priesthood offices and associated leadership organizations, acting in unity and devotion as an integrated structural enterprise for carrying out the threefold mission of the Church (see D&C 84:109–10).

Today we are witnessing the predicted "times of refreshing" Peter foresaw in the meridian of time (see Acts 3:19–21). All things are being restored during this dispensation of the fulness of times. But the times of refreshing did not end with the mission of the Prophet Joseph Smith; they continue even unto the present day, where the Lord still "refreshes" us on a continual basis with added guidance through His modern-day prophets, seers, and revelators. How grateful we should be for the consummate gift of continuing revelation! How faithful we should be in following the advice of the Lord's anointed. How anxious we should be to share the truths of the gospel to others in our circle of acquaintance, that they, too, might come to know the blessings of the gospel in their lives.

MOMENT OF TRUTH

The principle of continuing revelation is elucidated and clarified in many passages in the Doctrine and Covenants. Of particular relevance are specific passages in sections 1, 21, 28, 43, 68, 84, 107, and 112. The background circumstances pertaining to these sections have been given in previous chapters: section 1 in chapter 1, section 21 in chapter 9, sections 28 and 43 in chapter 24, section 68 in chapter 37, sections 84 and 107 in chapter 8, and section 112 in chapter 26. In addition, Official Declaration 2, dated September 30, 1978, concerning the availability of priesthood blessings for all worthy males, is explained later on in this chapter.

The real moment of truth pertaining to these passages and doctrines is, in particular, the precious moment when any individual, through prayerful and earnest seeking, ultimately crosses the threshold of conviction and inspiration concerning the verity of continuing revelation, knowing that the Lord speaks again through His chosen servants. That spiritual transition is the moment of truth where the individual places himself or herself in the hands of God, saying, in all humility and devotion, "Thy will be done, O Lord, and not ours" (D&C 109:44). Then is that person willing and ready to receive further light, whether it be regarding the Lord's will on Church organization, priesthood blessings, the canon of scripture, leadership in the Church, or any other doctrine He desires to reveal.

1. A REVELATION: CHURCH CORRELATION

THEME: The concept of "precept upon precept; line upon line" (Isa. 28:10) applies, in general, to the Lord's practice of blessing individuals with added measures of truth in keeping with their level of devotion in accepting and following the truth they have already received. In a particular sense, the doctrine of "line upon line" might also be applied to the unfolding of Church governance practices as the Church expands and matures in the process of realizing its divine commission and as circumstances and needs arise. A key example is the principle of "priesthood correlation" as a development in the process of embracing and implementing principles of efficiency, unity, and fundamental simplicity of gospel instruction throughout the Church. This correlation project coordinated not only the curriculum taught Church-wide but also all the efforts of every auxiliary and other program in the Church, bringing unity and focus in the work of the gospel. As the Lord said, "Again, verily I say unto you, I will show unto you wisdom in me concerning all the churches, inasmuch as they are willing to be guided in a right and proper way for their salvation" (D&C 101:63).

MODERN PROPHETS SPEAK

Harold B. Lee:

> All that we do is to be done "with an eye single to the glory of God" [D&C 82:19]. And what was the glory of God? As the Lord explained it to Moses, it was to bring to pass the immortality and eternal life of man. . . . In all our efforts in the . . . correlation program we have kept these observations always in mind. Simply stated, our two sole objectives in correlation were to keep the priesthood functioning as the Lord has clearly defined it, with the auxiliary organizations properly related thereto, and secondly that the parents and the family magnify their callings as the Lord has commanded. And so we see that everything that is done should be done with that one question in mind: does this activity further the interest of the kingdom, are we keeping our eye single to that prime purpose of the Lord's organization—to save souls and to bring to pass the immortality and the eternal life of man? . . .

> Said in a very generalized way, correlation means . . . to place the priesthood of God where the Lord said it was to be—as the center and core of the Church and kingdom of God—and to see that the Latter-day Saint homes also have their place in the divine plan of saving souls. (*Teachings of Presidents of the Church: Harold B. Lee* [Salt Lake City: The Church of Jesus Christ of Latter-day Saints, 2000], 146, 149)

M. Russell Ballard:

> When the Church correlation program was introduced in 1963, Elder Harold B. Lee explained in general conference that emphasis was to be placed on "the responsibilities of the entire priesthood to 'watch over the Church' as commanded in the early revelations—to be concerned with the whole family as a group and as individuals." He also announced that a "ward Home Teaching committee" was to be established in each ward of the Church, and that its members would "constitute the core of those who now will go out to 'watch over the Church'" (Harold B. Lee, "The Correlation Program," *Improvement Era,* June 1963, 504–505). This committee later became known as the ward priesthood executive committee. (*Counseling with*

Our Councils: Learning to Minister Together in the Church and in the Family [Salt Lake City: Deseret Book, 1997], 100–101)

ILLUSTRATIONS FOR OUR TIMES

Meeting the Needs of a Growing Church

In 1961 the First Presidency of the Church launched a great movement that is now known as the Church correlation program. A letter was sent to the General Church Priesthood Committee that stated the following:

"We of the First Presidency have over the years felt the need of a correlation between and among the courses of study put out by the General Priesthood Committee and by the responsible heads of other Committees of the General Authorities for the instruction of the Priesthood of the Church.

"We have also felt the very urgent need of a correlation of studies among the Auxiliaries of the Church. We have noted what seemed to be a tendency toward a fundamental, guiding concept, particularly among certain of the Auxiliary organizations, that there must be every year a new course of study for each of the Auxiliary organizations so moving. We questioned whether the composite of all of them might not tend away from the development of a given line of study or activity having the ultimate and desired objective of building up a knowledge of the gospel, a power to promulgate the same, a promotion of the growth, faith, and stronger testimony of the principles of the Gospel among the members of the Church. . . .

"We think that the contemplated study by the Committee now set up should have the foregoing matters in mind. We feel assured that if the whole Church curricula were viewed from the vantage point of what we might term the total purpose of each and all of these organizations, it would bring about such a collation and limitation of subjects and subject matters elaborated in the various Auxiliary courses as would tend to the building of efficiency in the Auxiliaries themselves in the matter of carrying out the purposes lying behind their creation and function.

"We would therefore commend to you Brethren of the General Priesthood Committee the beginning of an exhaustive, prayerful study and consideration of this entire subject, with the cooperative assistance of the Auxiliaries themselves so that the Church might reap the maximum harvest from the devotion of the faith, intelligence, skill, and knowledge of our various Auxiliary Organizations and Priesthood Committees.

"This is your authority to employ such necessary technical help as you might need to bring this about. We shall await your report.

"Faithfully your brethren,

"David O. McKay
"J. Reuben Clark, Jr.
"Henry D. Moyle

"THE FIRST PRESIDENCY."

(Harold B. Lee, *Stand Ye in Holy Places* [Salt Lake City: Deseret Book, 1974], 295)

LIKENING THE SCRIPTURES TO OUR LIVES

Doctrine and Covenants 101:54 Victory over the adversary can be accomplished if the watchmen whom the Lord has set upon the tower to guard His vineyard are steadfast in their duties.

Application: The correlation effort under the direction of the prophet acts as a way to ensure that all is in order. It is a way for the "watchmen," or leaders, of the Church to make sure that every member is cared for and taught the same doctrine throughout the Church. Such consistency unifies and strengthens the individual members and the Church as a whole, thus protecting and saving the Lord's vineyard "from the hands of the destroyer."

2. A REVELATION: EVERY WORTHY MALE MEMBER TO RECEIVE THE PRIESTHOOD

THEME: We know that the Lord loves and wishes to bless all His children, though sometimes we don't understand how He is doing so. But we do know that in His own time and in His own way, blessings and revelations will come forth. Extending the reach of priesthood blessings to all worthy male members (D&C—OD 2; dated September 30, 1978) is a primary instance in the ongoing process of modern-day, continuing revelation through God's living prophets.

MODERN PROPHETS SPEAK

James E. Faust:

In our lifetime we have been favored with ongoing communication from the heavens, which have been open to the prophets of our time. Major divine pronouncements have included what we now know as section 138 of the Doctrine and Covenants, given in 1918. Surely one of the greatest divine disclosures came in 1978 when the blessings of the priesthood and temple became available to all worthy male members. Line upon line and precept upon precept, new knowledge and direction have been given to the Church. (*Reach Up for the Light* [Salt Lake City: Deseret Book, 1990], 111)

David B. Haight:

I was in the temple when President Spencer W. Kimball received the revelation regarding the priesthood. I was the junior member of the Quorum of the Twelve. I was there. I was there with the outpouring of the Spirit in that room so strong that none of us could speak afterwards. We just left quietly to go back to the office. No one could say anything because of the powerful outpouring of the heavenly spiritual experience. (*Ensign,* May 1996, 22)

Gordon B. Hinckley:

The question of extending the blessings of the priesthood to blacks had been on the minds of many of the Brethren over a period of years. It had repeatedly been brought up by Presidents of the Church. It had become a matter of particular concern to President Spencer W. Kimball.

Over a considerable period of time he had prayed concerning this serious and difficult question. He had spent many hours in that upper room in the temple by himself in prayer and meditation.

On this occasion he raised the question before his Brethren—his Counselors and the Apostles. Following this discussion we joined in prayer in the most sacred of circumstances. President Kimball himself was voice in that prayer. I do not recall the exact words that he spoke. But I do recall my own feelings and the nature of the expressions of my Brethren. There was a hallowed and sanctified atmosphere in the room. For me, it felt as if a conduit opened between the heavenly throne and the kneeling, pleading prophet of God who was joined by his Brethren. The Spirit of God was there. And by the power of the Holy Ghost there came to that prophet an assurance that the thing for which he prayed was right, that the time had come, and that now the wondrous blessings of the priesthood should be extended to worthy men everywhere regardless of lineage.

Every man in that circle, by the power of the Holy Ghost, knew the same thing. (*Ensign,* October 1988, 69)

ILLUSTRATIONS FOR OUR TIMES

Priesthood Blessings for All

There have been times in the earth's history when the gospel and the priesthood have not been available to all, for they have been given to the children of our Heavenly Father only according to his omniscient wisdom and his timetable for our experiences in eternity. . . .

One member's story illustrates how important the priesthood is for each of us and our families and how grateful we might be for the opportunity to receive it. Joseph William ("Billy") Johnson of Cape Coast, Ghana, first received literature about The Church of Jesus Christ of Latter-day Saints in 1964. He knew that the Church doctrines he read in it were true, and he immediately began teaching them to his family, friends, and anyone else who would listen to him. It was not until four years later that he was able to obtain a copy of the Book of Mormon, to carefully read and pray about it, and to receive a witness of its truth. In letters to Salt Lake City, he had asked for more information about the Church and for missionaries to come to Africa to teach and baptize him. President McKay sent him literature and told him it was not yet time for missionaries to come to his country but that he should continue to study and have faith.

For 14 years Billy Johnson devoted himself to teaching the everlasting gospel and meeting with informal groups of believers. While strengthened by many spiritual experiences, he and members of these groups became discouraged when their pleadings for missionaries were not answered quickly.

During a particularly difficult period, Billy returned home one day much discouraged. As he struggled to obtain comfort and counsel from the Lord, he felt impressed to turn on his shortwave radio and find the BBC news broadcast. He was finally able to tune in the BBC at midnight. He recalls:

"I heard the message of President Kimball's prophecy concerning the priesthood, that all worthy males in all of the world could receive the priesthood. I burst into tears of joy, because I knew the priesthood would come to Africa, and if we did the right things, we would all receive the priesthood."

What joy spread through his heart as he heard the BBC news commentator announce the long-awaited revelation!

Of this event, President Gordon B. Hinckley has observed: "I need not tell you of the electric effect that was felt both within the Church and without. There was much weeping, with tears of gratitude not only on the part of those who previously had been denied the priesthood and who became the immediate beneficiaries of this announcement, but also by men and women of the Church across the world who had felt as we had felt concerning this matter. (Richard Neitzel Holzapfel, *Ensign,* October 1997, 44)

LIKENING THE SCRIPTURES TO OUR LIVES

Doctrine and Covenants Official Declaration 2 The Lord declares that all of His worthy children who hearken to His will shall receive every blessing of the gospel.

Application: We see in this declaration renewed evidence that the Lord truly loves all His children; the worth of every soul is great in His sight (see D&C 18:10). The prophets of this dispensation yearned for the blessings of the priesthood and the temple to be given to all of Heavenly Father's children. At last this blessing was granted, after the test of patience and preparation. It was done in the Lord's way. Let us never forget that it is the Lord who leads this Church. It is His will that we follow. His ways, means, thoughts, and timetable are different and higher than ours (Isa. 55:8–9).

3. A REVELATION: PUBLICATION OF NEW EDITIONS OF THE SCRIPTURES

THEME: Searching, pondering, feasting upon the word—all of these are fundamental practices associated with covenant valor. But modern-day improvements in the tools of searching and pondering make this process all the more efficient and effective. Such tools include the new editions of the scriptures, replete with detailed cross-references and helpful indexes, as well as the powerful search mechanisms and archival inventories of the Church's Internet resources. How grateful we should be for the tireless efforts of skilled academicians and technicians, working under the direction of the Lord's prophets, who bring about these extraordinary improvements in gospel teaching and learning.

MODERN PROPHETS SPEAK

Thomas S. Monson:

> History will ultimately record the details, the triumphs, and the struggles of this publishing saga, but for the present, may I simply say that through great personal

effort on the part of many individuals over a long period of time, coupled with modern technology and, especially, divine guidance, the Church now has new editions of the sacred scriptures available for all to use.

Prestigious awards for them have been numerous, both in America and in Great Britain. A citation presented in October of 1982 by the Laymen's National Bible Committee is typical: "Presented to The Church of Jesus Christ of Latter-day Saints in appreciation of outstanding service to the Bible cause through the publication of its own new edition of the King James version, which features interpretive chapter headings, a simplified footnote system, and the linking of references to all other LDS scriptures, thereby greatly enhancing the study of the Bible by its membership."

The efforts and prayers of those who prepared these works, and even the miracles of publishing, are of no value to you, however, unless you begin to search the new editions. Delve into the study aids and the helpful information which supplement the texts and thus enhance your understanding and increase your testimony. (*Ensign,* December 1985, 46)

Boyd K. Packer:

The Latter-day Saint publication of the King James Version of the Bible and the new triple combination, with all their helps, are of monumental importance to all members of the Church. Everything that could be done has been done to help open the scriptures to members so that they might know the gospel of Jesus Christ.

We hope to open a door and introduce to you a library of revelation and inspiration and light. One day, on your own, as an individual, you must enter there and study by yourself. Today we can but set the door ajar.

Now, we hope that you have a great desire to enter into this library alone, and in quiet study and prayer receive the kind of revelation that comes when you earn it, when you're reading the scriptures. (Quoted in Hoyt W. Brewster Jr., *Ensign,* October 1983, 55)

LIKENING THE SCRIPTURES TO OUR LIVES

2 Nephi 28:30 Those who follow the teachings of the scriptures are blessed with further knowledge and revelation, while those who refuse to receive further teachings of the gospel will have the knowledge and insight they had taken away.

Application: We are taught that there is much more light and knowledge that we can receive, but we have to be faithful in what we have received, and willing and striving to gain more. The new edition of the scriptures is one example of the Lord giving more to the faithful. Gospel study was enhanced in a way to be more personalized, allowing individuals to continue to receive further insight and understanding. Let us take advantage of the blessings of the scriptures to increase our own spirituality.

Luke 24:45 The Lord has the power to open our minds to an understanding of the scriptures.

Application: The 1981 edition of the scriptures brings increased light and knowledge to each of us as we seek to understand better the word of God: a topical guide to give additional sources of closely associated topics, footnotes with cross-references to enlighten our understanding (including references to the Prophet Joseph's translation of the Bible), meanings of words, and a whole host of information through the Bible Dictionary to assist us in our learning. Yes, we have all been blessed by this magnificent work to help us live a more Christlike life—now we have the continuing responsibility to search out and feast upon the word of God.

4. A REVELATION: ADDITIONAL QUORUMS OF THE SEVENTY

THEME: The basic commission to the Seventy is laid down with clarity in the Doctrine and Covenants. They are "to preach the gospel, and to be especial witnesses unto the Gentiles and in all the world" (D&C 107:25). However, the full scope and efficacy of this inspired organizational structure is more and more fully discerned and implemented as this interrelating matrix of service quorums expands and takes its place, under the guidance of the First Presidency and the Quorum of the Twelve, as an indispensable leadership unit of the Church.

MODERN PROPHETS SPEAK

Gordon B. Hinckley:

> The Lord made provision at a general level for a First Presidency, a Quorum of the Twelve Apostles, Quorums of Seventy, and the Presiding Bishopric. At a local level the revelations speak of stake presidents and bishops. We have had in between the general and local authorities for a period of time the Regional Representatives, now more recently these Area Authorities. We have determined to present to the conference the names of these Area Authorities to be ordained Seventies. They will then have a

quorum relationship presided over by the Presidents of the Seventy. They will be known as Area Authority Seventies, to serve for a period of years in a voluntary capacity in the area in which they reside. They are called by the First Presidency and will work under the general direction of the Quorum of the Twelve, the Presidents of the Seventy, and the Area Presidencies in that part of the world in which they live. (*TGBH,* 86)

LIKENING THE SCRIPTURES TO OUR LIVES

Doctrine and Covenants 107:34 The Seventy, under the direction of the Quorum of the Twelve, are commissioned of the Lord to build up the Church in every nation and regulate the affairs of the Church throughout the world.

Application: As the Church continues to expand, the need for leadership also increases. We witness the growth of the Church today in the calling of Area Presidencies throughout the earth, in fulfillment of this verse. They, along with the Area Authority Seventy assigned to their area, direct and regulate the affairs of the Church under the direction of the Quorum of the Twelve Apostles. Recently, even a sixth quorum of the Seventy has been added. How blessed we are to have leaders so intimately involved in the workings of the area in which we live! Surely the Lord cares for His people by making sure that our leaders are close by and accessible to us. We should sustain them with all our hearts as we follow the Lord (see 3 Ne. 28:34–35; D&C 84:36; 112:20).

5. A REVELATION: WORDS FROM LIVING PROPHETS AS INSPIRED BY THE HOLY GHOST

THEME: The Church is guided by living prophets who act for the Lord under inspiration of the Holy Ghost. Individuals and families are guided through the promptings of the Holy Ghost in reference to their several spheres of responsibility. Similarly, stake presidents, bishops, and other Church leaders are entitled to inspiration to ensure that all is governed in keeping with the will of the Lord. Thus the kingdom of God moves forward, sustained by the principle of ongoing revelation bestowed by a merciful and loving Father to all who are called to serve and partake of the blessings of the gospel of Jesus Christ.

MODERN PROPHETS SPEAK

John A. Widtsoe:

> The most important prophet in any age for the people of that age, is the living prophet. The prophets who have gone before have left to us their precious teachings

which will be used for the instruction and comfort of mankind. But it is the living prophet who helps us by his teachings, example, and direction to meet and to solve the problems of today, our day. To follow the living prophet, the interpreter of the past, and the foreteller of the future, is the essence of wisdom. The very strength of the Church restored through the instrumentality of Joseph Smith lies in the doctrine of continuing revelation through a living prophet. (*Joseph Smith—Seeker after Truth, Prophet of God* [Salt Lake City: Bookcraft, 1951], 288)

Joseph B. Wirthlin:

Because of our faith in our prophet, Latter-day Saints echo the words of the Apostle Peter: "We have therefore a more sure knowledge of the word of prophecy, to which word of prophecy ye do well that ye take heed, as unto a light which shineth in a dark place, until the day dawn, and the day star arise in your hearts." The light of divine revelation shines forth from a living prophet to brighten a darkened world. (*Ensign,* May 1996, 32)

Ezra Taft Benson:

Speaking to his prophets, the Lord said: "He that receiveth you receiveth me . . ." (Matt. 10:40). Always the words of the living prophet took precedence, for it was God's message to the people at that particular time. Had any man accepted the ancient scripture in the days of Noah but refused to follow the revelation that Noah received and failed to board the ark, he would have been drowned. Always the words of the living prophets are of the most vital concern to the people; and always, if a man would know of Christ and learn his commandments so that he can obey them, he must seek to find his authorized representatives. (*Ensign,* January 1973, 57)

LIKENING THE SCRIPTURES TO OUR LIVES

Doctrine and Covenants 68:3–4 An important reminder: When the prophet, Apostles, and other Church leaders speak as they are moved upon by the Holy Ghost, their words are scripture and contain the will, mind, and voice of the Lord (see chapter 37, theme 1).

Application: We receive the word of God from our leaders—especially from our living prophets. The words of our prophets are a continuation of the open canon of scripture the Church embraces. Their continued revelation is the word of God, spoken as if by the Lord Himself (see D&C 1:38). We are to live by this word of God (see D&C 84:43–46), for it will tell us all things to do (see 2 Ne. 32:3). When we learn to accept the words of the living prophets and seek to understand and apply them to our lives, it will indeed empower us with "the power of God unto salvation."

SUMMARY

We see that modern-day revelation continues to be given by the Lord through His chosen servants in our day, bringing about such significant developments as priesthood correlation, extending the priesthood to all worthy males, publishing improved editions of the scriptures, expanding the scope and activity of the Seventies, and adding to the sacred canon. All of this occurs within the framework laid down as an integral part of the Restoration, whereby the prophet of the Lord holds all the keys and authority of leadership for the Church as a whole. The Lord counsels us to follow the prophet and be willing to receive his revelation: "For his word ye shall receive, as if from mine own mouth, in all patience and faith." He then tells us why: "For by doing these things the gates of hell shall not prevail against you; yea, and the Lord God will disperse the powers of darkness from before you, and cause the heavens to shake for your good, and his name's glory" (D&C 21:5–6; see 28:2–7; 43:2–3).

An ancient proverb summarized this doctrine aptly: "Where there is no vision, the people perish: but he that keepeth the law, happy is he" (Prov. 29:18). May we flourish under the aegis of divine vision; may we achieve happiness through obedience to the word of Lord as given in the scriptures and through modern-day prophets.

CHAPTER FORTY-THREE

"TAKE *upon* YOU MY WHOLE ARMOR"

Reading Assignment: Doctrine and Covenants 27:15–18; 42:21–24; 51:9; 52:16; 59:6; 63:16, 60–62; 76:25–29; 97:8; 121:45–46; 136:21, 24; Romans 13:12; Ephesians 4:29; 6:11–17; 2 Nephi 1:23; Moses 4:3–4.

Additional Reading: Review the pamphlet *For the Strength of Youth.*

The scriptures tell us to take upon us the "whole armor" of God that we "may be able to withstand the evil day." They promise that the "breastplate of righteousness" and "the shield of faith" will "quench all the fiery darts of the wicked" (D&C 27:15–17). I urge you to obey those teachings and lay claim on those blessings. They include the personal spiritual conversion—the "mighty change . . . in our hearts" (Mosiah 5:2)—that helps us become what our Heavenly Father desires us to become. (Dallin H. Oaks, Ensign, *May 2002, 33)*

THEMES *for* LIVING

1. "Put on the Whole Armor of God"
2. Purity: Live the Law of Chastity
3. Integrity: Be Honest in All Things
4. Use Language That Edifies and Reverences God

INTRODUCTION

Though we aspire to embrace and live the gospel of peace, we are obliged to ply our course through the valleys of war. This battle to overcome evil by means of good has been a reality from as early as the premortal sphere: "For we beheld Satan, that old serpent, even the devil, who rebelled against God, and sought to take the kingdom of our God and his Christ—Wherefore, he maketh war with the saints of God, and encompasseth them round about" (D&C 76:28–29). The war continued in mortality. The Lord enlightened Moses as to this reality, confirming that Satan's only goal is to "destroy the agency of man" and rob us of salvation (see Moses 4:3–4).

And so the war rages on. Then as now, the forces are arrayed on either side to achieve the ultimate victory—which victory is destined to belong to the Father and Son, who uphold the principles of righteousness, valor, and spiritual liberty. Along the pathway to that victory advance the heroes of the covenant, who (unlike Laman and Lemuel and their counterparts in all generations) are willing to follow prophetic counsel: "Awake, my sons; put on the armor of righteousness. Shake off the chains with which ye are bound, and come forth out of obscurity, and arise from the dust" (2 Ne. 1:23).

The scriptures frequently evoke such battle imagery as a reminder that we are constantly at war to uphold the standards of truth in the face of evil assaults from every side. The famous passages detailing the elements of the armor of God (Eph. 6:11–17; D&C 27:15–18) resonate in every breast that is receptive to the commission to move forward in the strength of the Lord. Faith, truth, following the Spirit—these are the mighty weapons of spiritual conquest. Virtue, purity, integrity, godlike discourse and deportment—these are the additional armaments that ensure victory.

Ultimately, the qualities of discipleship that will prevail over the forces of evil and gain dominion—including overcoming the internal aberrations of worldly pride and self-centeredness—are *inner* qualities, as the Prophet Joseph Smith taught us from the confines of his squalid cell at Liberty Jail: "Let thy bowels also be full of charity towards all men, and to the household of faith, and let virtue garnish thy thoughts unceasingly; then shall thy confidence wax strong in the presence of God; and the doctrine of the priesthood shall distil upon thy soul as the dews from heaven. The Holy Ghost shall be thy constant companion, and thy scepter an unchanging scepter of righteousness and truth; and thy dominion shall be an everlasting dominion, and without compulsory means it shall flow unto thee forever and ever" (D&C 121:45–46).

MOMENT OF TRUTH

There are many passages in the Doctrine and Covenants that teach the principle of putting on the whole armor of God and upholding the standards of right and truth.

The reader is encouraged to review the context and background for the various reading selections in sections associated with this chapter, as follows: section 29 in chapter 9; sections 42 and 51 in chapter 14; section 52 in chapter 12; section 59 in chapter 16; section 76 in chapter 20; section 121 in chapter 25, and section 136 in chapter 30. The background to two additional sections referred to in the current chapter is given below.

Section 63: Given through the Prophet Joseph Smith late in August 1831 at the Isaac Morley farm in Kirtland, Geauga County, Ohio (see *HC,* 1:206–11). Joseph Smith returned from his trip to Missouri on August 27, 1831, to find that apostasy was on the rise. At the same time, there was intense interest in the concept and land of Zion. Joseph described how he "enquired" of the Lord concerning the situation at hand: "In these infant days of the Church, there was a great anxiety to obtain the word of the Lord upon every subject that in any way concerned our salvation; and as the land of Zion was now the most important temporal object in view, I enquired of the Lord for further information upon the gathering of the Saints, and the purchase of the land, and other matters, and received the following: [D&C 63.]" (see *HC,* 1:207). Included in the revelation are passages calling the Saints to repentance, especially with respect to immorality and taking the name of the Lord in vain. The Lord called for valor in preaching the gospel and devoting one's talents and resources to the building up of the kingdom of God.

Section 97: Given through the Prophet Joseph Smith on June 4, 1833, in the Newel K. Whitney store at Kirtland, Geauga County, Ohio (see *HC,* 1:400–402). This revelation addresses the affairs of the Church in Missouri. Although the situation was unknown to Joseph Smith at the time, the Saints in Missouri were experiencing insurmountable problems. Thirteen days before this revelation was given, a mob destroyed the printing office, along with most of the almost completed Book of Commandments. The mob then ransacked the Church store and partially stripped Bishop Edward Partridge and Charles Allen of their clothes and tarred and feathered them in the public square, surrounded by hundreds. The mob demanded that the Saints leave Jackson County. On July 23, 1833, in order to prevent a general massacre of the Saints, Church leaders were forced to sign a formal agreement to leave Jackson County by January 1, 1834.

Truly, the sacrifice of these Missouri Saints was great. Included in the revelation are the famous words: "Verily I say unto you, all among them who know their hearts are honest, and are broken, and their spirits contrite, and are willing to observe their covenants by sacrifice—yea, every sacrifice which I, the Lord, shall command—they are accepted of me" (D&C 97:8).

It should be noted that Church leaders in Missouri signed the formal agreement to leave Jackson County on the very day that Joseph and his brethren laid the cornerstones for the Kirtland Temple. Considering this coincidence, Brigham Young's statement comes to mind: "We never began to build a temple without the bells of hell beginning to ring. . . . We completed a temple in Kirtland and in Nauvoo; and did not the bells of hell toll all the time we were building them? They did, every week and every day" (*JD,* 8:356). Such is Brigham Young's reminder that the Saints are ever at war to sustain the cause of right and truth.

Also in this revelation is the promise that the Saints will see God in the temple. Elder David B. Haight encouraged members of the Church to expand their vision as to the meaning of seeing God.

> At Kirtland, the Lord revealed to the Prophet Joseph: "And inasmuch as my people build a house unto me in the name of the Lord, and do not suffer any unclean thing to come into it, that it be not defiled, my glory shall rest upon it . . . and my presence shall be there, for I will come into it, and all the pure in heart that shall come into it shall see God" (D&C 97:15–16). It is true that some have actually seen the Savior, but when one consults the dictionary, one learns that there are many other meanings of the word *see,* such as coming to know Him, discerning Him, recognizing Him and His work, perceiving His importance, or coming to understand Him. (David B. Haight, *Ensign,* November 1990, 61)

1. "PUT ON THE WHOLE ARMOR OF GOD"

THEME: Discipleship is not a passive enterprise. The lifestyle associated with the kingdom of God is one of proactive preparation, training, and service. The Saints of God are ever at war, for the evil one and his minions never sleep and never desist in their dark designs to thwart the plan of salvation. The commission of the Saints is to be ever watchful, ever willing to move forward in the strength of the Lord against the forces that threaten the family and contravene the commitment to "live after the manner of happiness" (2 Ne. 5:27).

MODERN PROPHETS SPEAK

Spencer W. Kimball:
> Put on the full armor of God. Attend to your personal and family prayers and family devotions; keep holy the Sabbath; live strictly the Word of Wisdom; attend to all family duties; and above all, keep your life clean and free from all unholy and impure thoughts and actions. Avoid all associations that degrade and lower the high, righteous standards set up for us. Then your life will sail smoothly, and peace and joy will surround you. (*President Kimball Speaks Out* [Salt Lake City: Deseret Book, 1981], 17)

Boyd K. Packer:

> This shield of faith is not manufactured on an assembly line, only handmade in a cottage industry. Therefore our leaders press members to understand that what is most worth doing must be done at home. Some still do not see that too many out-of-home activities, however well intended, leave too little time to make and fit on the shield of faith at home. (*Ensign,* May 1995, 7)

ILLUSTRATIONS FOR OUR TIMES

Wearing the Armor of God

> I should like to give you from the scriptures some examples which show how those who are clothed in such armor, which means keeping all the commandments of God, are able to withstand the adversary, or their enemies. Let me tell you about David (see 1 Sam. 17).

> The Philistines were at war with Israel, and Goliath, the Philistine, was challenging Israel to send a man to fight him, with the understanding that the losers would be slaves of the conquerors.

> We are told that Goliath had a helmet of brass upon his head and was armed with a coat of mail; that he had brass upon his legs and between his shoulders; that the staff of his spear was like a weaver's beam; that his spear's head weighed six hundred shekels of iron; and a shieldbearer went before him.

> On the other hand, when David agreed to meet the Philistine he took only his staff and chose five smooth stones out of the brook and put them in his shepherd's bag.

> When Goliath saw this young man the Israelites had sent to challenge him, he was disdainful and said: "Come to me, and I will give thy flesh unto the fowls of the air, and to the beasts of the field.

> Then said David to the Philistine, "Thou comest to me with a sword, and with a spear, and with a shield: but I come to thee in the name of the Lord of hosts, the God of the armies of Israel, whom thou hast defied.

> "This day will the Lord deliver thee into mine hand; . . . that all the earth may know that there is a God in Israel" (1 Sam. 17:44–46).

> Then David, clothed with the armor of God, took a stone from his bag and, with his sling, shot it into the forehead of Goliath, an unprotected part of his body, and he fell dead.

Now, President Romney has told you tonight what happened to David after he became king because he did not continue to have the whole armor of God. We must put on the whole armor of God, or we will be vulnerable to temptation in those areas where we have weaknesses and where we have failed to give ourselves the protection offered through keeping the commandments. (N. Eldon Tanner, *Ensign,* May 1979, 44)

* * *

Authors' Note: While the excerpt is too lengthy to include here, we strongly recommend that readers explore President Harold B. Lee's explication of the armor of God in his book *Stand Ye in Holy Places* [Salt Lake City: Deseret Book, 1974], beginning on page 330.

LIKENING THE SCRIPTURES TO OUR LIVES

Doctrine and Covenants 27:15–18 The Saints are commanded to put on the full armor of God to be able to withstand the influences of evil. At the Second Coming of the Savior, the faithful Saints will be caught up to be with Him.

Application: The war against evil has gone on since the beginning. At stake are the souls of God's children. Let us prepare ourselves that we might resist evil, with all its temptations and snares. In order to do this, we are commanded to "put on the armor of God." We are to know and understand *truth.* Let us seek *righteousness* and live accordingly. Let us *prepare with the gospel of peace* every needful thing to do. Above all, let us *be good*—thus avoiding and overcoming evil. Let us increase our *faith* with prayer, by studying the word of God, and by cultivating a lifestyle of charity to ward off the temptations of the devil. Yes, let us put on the *helmet of salvation* to keep our minds and thoughts fixed upon our goal of salvation and living forever with our Heavenly Father in the celestial kingdom.

2. PURITY: LIVE THE LAW OF CHASTITY

THEME: Virtue and purity are indispensable attributes of those who labor in the vineyard of the Lord. Alma counseled his son Shiblon to "see that ye bridle all your passions, that ye may be filled with love" (Alma 38:12). The Spirit can abide only in temples of holiness and purity.

MODERN PROPHETS SPEAK

Spencer W. Kimball:

Sin is still sin and always will be. We stand for a life of cleanliness. From childhood through youth and to the grave, we proclaim the wickedness of sexual life of any kind before marriage, and we proclaim that every one in marriage should hold himself or herself to the covenants that were made.

In other words, as we have frequently said, there should be total chastity of men and women before marriage and total fidelity in marriage. (*Ensign,* November 1975, 7)

David O. McKay:

No one can transgress the laws of chastity and find peace. (*Gospel Ideals: Selections from the Discourses of David O. McKay* [Salt Lake City: Improvement Era, 1976], 473).

Ezra Taft Benson:

We covenant to live the law of chastity. The law of chastity is virtue and sexual purity. This law places us under covenant to live this commandment strictly. "Thou shalt love thy wife with all thy heart, and shalt cleave unto her and none else. And he that looketh upon a woman to lust after her shall deny the faith, and shall not have the Spirit; and if he repents not he shall be cast out. Thou shalt not commit adultery; and he that committeth adultery, and repenteth not, shall be cast out [excommunicated]" (D&C 42: 22–24). . . .

A reason for virtue—which includes personal chastity, clean thoughts and practices, and integrity—is that we must have the Spirit and the power of God in our lives to do God's work. Without that power and influence we are no better off than individuals in other organizations. That virtue shines through and will influence others toward a better life and cause nonmembers to inquire of our faith. (*TETB,* 278)

ILLUSTRATIONS FOR OUR TIMES

Splinters of Glass

We have a three-year-old daughter whom we love very dearly. Not long ago I was doing some studying at my desk at home, and she was in the room playing with a glass of water that was on the desk. As she picked up that large glass with her little fingers, I repeatedly warned her that she must be careful or she would drop the glass, which, of course, she finally did. It shattered as it hit the floor, and splinters went in every direction.

Showing the patience of a wise parent, I immediately spanked her, explaining to her that the spanking was the consequence of her insisting on not listening to me by picking up the glass until it dropped and was broken. She shed some tears and gave me a hug, which she usually does when she knows she is in trouble, and the event was quickly forgotten.

Since she often plays in her bare feet, I took her out of the room and made every effort to sweep up all the glass particles. But the thought came to me that perhaps I hadn't gotten all the splinters of glass, and at some future time when she is playing in that room, those little feet might find the splinters which went undetected, and she would have to suffer anew for that which she did.

For a young person to violate the law of chastity or some other commandment and then to later put his or her life in order—such action, I am sure, will mean the forgiveness of an understanding and loving God. Yet as that person progresses in life and reaches a point where he or she enters into a marriage contract and as they have children of their own, it just might be that a splinter of a previous wrongdoing somewhere on the floor of his or her life might prick the conscience. (Loren C. Dunn, CR, October 1969, 13–14)

LIKENING THE SCRIPTURES TO OUR LIVES

Doctrine and Covenants 63:16 Those who commit adultery or lust after a women will deny the faith, not have the Spirit, and be fearful of the Lord.

Application: Our heart represents the center of our soul, the place where decisions are made and our affections are seated. Thoughts precede actions. Lusting is caused by impure thoughts. We are commanded to seek the love of God that we might have pure hearts, pure thoughts, and righteous actions.

3. INTEGRITY: BE HONEST IN ALL THINGS

THEME: Heavenly Father would have a Zion people, unified in charity and service. "I say unto you, be one; and if ye are not one ye are not mine" (D&C 38:27). We cannot be one in an environment of greed, envy, inequality, and dishonesty. All of us are as nothing when measured against the majesty of God (see Mosiah 4:5, 11). Thus, we are to aspire through integrity and honor to serve our fellow beings and practice honesty in all our dealings.

MODERN PROPHETS SPEAK

James E. Faust:

> Honesty is more than not lying. It is truth telling, truth speaking, truth living, and truth loving. (*Ensign,* November 1996, 41)

Gordon B. Hinckley:

> Be strong . . . with the strength of simple honesty. How easy it is to "lie a little, take the advantage of one because of his words, dig a pit for thy neighbor" (2 Ne. 28:8). Nephi so describes the people of his day, as he also describes so many of our day. How easy it is for us to say, "We believe in being honest, true, chaste, benevolent" (A of F 1:13). But how difficult for so many to resist the temptation to lie a little, cheat a little, steal a little, bear false witness in speaking gossipy words about others. Rise above it, brethren. Be strong in the simple virtue of honesty. . . .
>
> Simple honesty is so remarkable a quality. It is of the very essence of integrity. It demands that we be straightforward, unequivocal, in walking the straight and narrow line of what is right and true. It is so easy to cheat. At times it is so enticing to do so. Better a poor grade than a dishonest act. (*TGBH,* 269)

ILLUSTRATIONS FOR OUR TIMES

He Really Passed the Test

> I had a friend, one time, who went to take a test in school, a test for which he had not studied. Of course he had prayed pretty hard about it. He had asked the Lord to help him remember something he had not bothered to learn. There are some things the Lord cannot do. Other things he can, but he will not. And praying will not work in these cases. I know; I have tried it. But as this friend went in to take this test, he found he was sitting right next to the smartest girl in the class. He said, "Well, this must be the answer to my prayer. Here she is. The Lord provided her, right here." But he was a returned missionary. He had been preaching honesty for two years. It is very difficult to go against that which you have been preaching and for which you have had a witness of the Spirit. While he was arguing with himself about what he was going to do on this test, he flunked the test. But as a matter of fact he really passed.
>
> You see, he had passed the Lord's test, and that is the test that we have to pass here upon this earth. Tests are all around us. Fifty years from the day that he took the test he would not remember what his grade was, and it really would not make any difference so long

as it was honest. But if he cheated on the test, he would remember that, for it makes an indelible imprint on the spirit. It also makes it easier the next time we are faced with a temptation where our honesty is in question to go down that "broad road." Lucifer would not dare tempt you with a sin as grievous as robbing a bank with your first experience with dishonesty. That would turn you off. You would not dare do that. So he will start with something small, something little, something that seems insignificant. If you flunk that one, he will see to it that you get a larger one and then a larger one, until it reaches the point where some people can sit down and methodically work out a plan to rob a bank. Oh, they will rationalize some justification for it, such as, "It is insured by the government so nobody is losing anything." Or, "Well, I really have it coming to me; I have not had the breaks that other people have." This called rationalization, which is a form of lying to yourself. But it is lying, nevertheless. As Nephi said: ". . . And thus the devil cheateth their souls, and leadeth them away carefully down to hell" (2 Ne. 28:21). (Hartman Rector Jr., *BYU Speeches of the Year*, January 5, 1971, 7)

LIKENING THE SCRIPTURES TO OUR LIVES

Doctrine and Covenants 42:21 The unrepentant liar will be cast out.

Doctrine and Covenants 51:9 Honesty promotes fairness and unity, which the Lord has commanded and expects from us.

Application: The lack of integrity, as evidenced by dishonesty, is the cause of a multitude of problems. It destroys trust and undermines love, thus causing credibility to suffer and true communication to fail. We must be honest with ourselves, with our fellow beings, and with our God. In this way our relationships can be built and maintained. We are unified and treat each other justly. The alternative is too heavy a price to pay: "Wo unto the liar, for he shall be thrust down to hell" (see 2 Ne. 9:34).

4. USE LANGUAGE THAT EDIFIES AND REVERENCES GOD

THEME: The word is a gift of God. Our ability to use language—both spoken and written—derives from our divine provenance. We honor our Father in Heaven by cultivating language that is worthy of heavenly acceptance. We live up to our potential when we foster thoughts and discourse that invite the Holy Ghost to dwell within us. "Keep yourselves from evil to take the name of the Lord in vain," we are told; "cease to speak evil one of another . . . and let your words tend to edifying one another"

(D&C 136:21, 24). Furthermore: "Let no corrupt communication proceed out of your mouth, but that which is good to the use of edifying, that it may minister grace unto the hearers" (Eph. 4:29).

MODERN PROPHETS SPEAK

Gordon B. Hinckley:

> The man or the boy who must resort to such language immediately says that he is poverty-ridden in his vocabulary. He does not enjoy sufficient richness of expression to be able to speak effectively without swearing or using foul words. (*TGBH,* 494)

Gordon B. Hinckley:

> You can't use that filthy, dirty language that's so common in the high schools and other schools—you can't do it, if you believe you're a child of God, without betraying your birthright. . . .
>
> Cultivate the art of conversation. It is a tremendous asset. For me there is nothing more delightful than to listen in on the conversation of a group of bright and happy young people such as you. Their dialogue is witty. It is scintillating. It sparkles and is punctuated by laughing even when dealing with serious subjects. But, I repeat, it is not necessary in conversation to profane the name of Deity or to use salty and salacious language of any kind. And let me add that there is plenty of humor in the world without resorting to what we speak of as dirty jokes. I challenge each of you to avoid all such. During the coming week as you talk with friends and associates, see if you can do so without speaking any words that you might regret having said. (*TGBH,* 496–97)

George Q. Cannon:

> Do angels take the Lord's name in vain? The idea is so ridiculous that we scarcely like to ask the question. . . . How dare we do that which angels dare not do? Is it possible for us to argue that that which is forbidden in heaven is praiseworthy on earth? . . .
>
> Though we are sure no boy can tell us any advantage that can arise from the abuse of God's holy name, yet we can tell him many evils that arise therefrom. "To begin," Brother Cannon said, "it is unnecessary and consequently foolish; it lessens our respect for holy things and leads us into the society of the wicked; it brings upon us the disrespect of the good who avoid us; it leads us to other sins, for he who is willing to abuse his Creator is not ashamed to defraud his fellow creature; and also by so doing we directly and knowingly break one of the most direct of God's commandments." (*Juvenile Instructor,* September 27, 1873, 156).

ILLUSTRATIONS FOR OUR TIMES

"How Childish"

I once worked with a group of railroad men who seemed to pride themselves on the use of profanity. They tried to make an art of it. I recall handing a written instruction to a switchman. It was his job to take care of the matter as instructed, but he thought it inconvenient that he should have to do so at that time. On reading the order, he flew into a tantrum. He was a fifty-year-old man, but he acted like a spoiled child. He threw his cap on the ground and jumped on it and let forth such a string of expletives as to seem to cause the air to turn blue around him. Every third or fourth word was the name of Deity spoken in vain.

I thought, how childish can a grown man be? The very idea of a man acting and speaking like that was totally repugnant. I could never again give him my full respect. (Gordon B. Hinckley, *Ensign*, November 1987, 46)

"You Are Speaking about My Best Friend"

President Kimball understood that all individuals struggle with challenges. His own life had not been easy. His counsel, "Suffering can make saints of people as they learn patience, long-suffering, and self-mastery," had been learned by experience. Over the years he had suffered from various physical problems, including typhoid, smallpox, throat cancer, heart attacks, and open-heart surgery. Once as he was being wheeled to an operating room, the hospital orderly pushing the gurney bumped the corner of the door and began to swear, taking the Lord's name in vain. President Kimball looked up at him and said quietly, "Don't say that. You are speaking about my best friend." (Heidi S. Swinton, *In the Company of Prophets* [Salt Lake City: Deseret Book, 1993], 86–87)

LIKENING THE SCRIPTURES TO OUR LIVES

Doctrine and Covenants 52:16 To speak words that edify and uplift with meekness and contrition is to be of God.

Application: Our language is a reflection of our character. Profanity has no place in our vocabulary and is a sign of weakness. We should seek to strengthen, uplift, and edify one another (see D&C 108:7; 136:24). Remember that our words can either condemn and destroy or praise and encourage. Let us do the latter.

Doctrine and Covenants 63:61–62 We must be careful in our use of the Lord's name. Many are under condemnation for misusing the name of God.

Application: Names are so important to one's identity. Part of our identity is our membership in the Church, for we have taken upon us the *name* of Christ. We are dishonoring the Lord when we do anything that would tarnish His name, especially taking it in vain.

SUMMARY

We are counseled to "put on the armour of light" (Rom. 13:12). The scriptures are explicit about what such godly armor consists of: truth girded about our loins, righteousness as our breastplate, the gospel of peace about our feet, faith as our shield, salvation as our helmet, and the Spirit and word as our sword. This "armor" is strengthened and put in place by our personal actions of purity, honesty, and honor. As we live lives based in morality and integrity, we are putting on this armor and valiantly fighting in this war of good and evil.

The Lord has called us his "warriors"—those who are to "gather together for the redemption of my people, and throw down the towers of mine enemies, and scatter their watchmen" (D&C 105:16). As always, spiritual enlistment in the armies of God is ultimately a function of inner purity, faithfulness, and a commitment to sacrifice all for the triumphant victory of the Lord's cause: "Verily I say unto you, all among them who know their hearts are honest, and are broken, and their spirits contrite, and are willing to observe their covenants by sacrifice—yea, every sacrifice which I, the Lord, shall command—they are accepted of me" (D&C 97:8).

CHAPTER FORTY-FOUR

BEING GOOD CITIZENS

Reading Assignment: Doctrine and Covenants 58:21–22, 26–28; 98:4–10; 134; Articles of Faith 1:12; *Our Heritage,* pages 133–34.

Additional Reading: Matthew 22:17–22; 1 Timothy 2:1–2.

Edmund Burke once said, "All that is necessary for the triumph of evil is for good men to do nothing." It is not enough that we wring our hands and moan about conditions in America. We must become responsible citizens and carry out our civic duty. We should be "anxiously engaged" in good causes and leave the world a better place for having lived in it (D&C 58:27).

I think the Lord wants us to be good citizens of this country. I believe He wants us to keep our economic and social thinking straight and not be influenced by policies and programs that strike at the very foundation of all that we hold dear in this country.

We have a measuring rod that no other group has. We have the revelations of the Almighty to indicate to us whether a thing is right or wrong. The Lord has spoken. He has placed a responsibility upon us to see that our form of government is preserved and that good men and honest men are elected for public office. His counsel is found in the Doctrine and Covenants (see D&C 98; 101). We are not left to move in the dark. (Ezra Taft Benson, TETB, 676–77)

THEMES *for* LIVING

1. Participate in Community and Governmental Affairs
2. Obey the Laws of the Land
3. Volunteer Service: Blessing Others and Strengthening the Community

INTRODUCTION

In His infinite wisdom, the Lord has ordained and implemented a design for guiding and blessing His children as they find their way—facing daunting choices and challenges on every side—through their mortal probationary experience. As part of this magnificent design, the Lord has from time to time raised up leaders who espouse the principles of liberty and the free exercise of inalienable rights associated with agency and progress. Where such leadership results in the implementation of laws that protect and nurture the freedom of individuals, the people are truly blessed. The twelfth Article of Faith memorialized the Church's position with respect to such matters: "We believe in being subject to kings, presidents, rulers, and magistrates, in obeying, honoring, and sustaining the law." As the Saints honor, worship, and obey Heavenly Father and His Son, they also have the duty to honor and support the laws of the land. The Lord's plan for building up the kingdom of God provides for an orderly and peaceable involvement in good citizenship within communities, states, and countries—for such involvement will contribute to the cultivation of relationships and environments where the work of God can flourish and proceed unimpeded.

The Savior made this doctrine clear when His detractors attempted to lure Him into a devious trap of competing allegiances: "Tell us therefore, What thinkest thou? Is it lawful to give tribute unto Caesar, or not? But Jesus perceived their wickedness, and said, Why tempt ye me, ye hypocrites? Shew me the tribute money. And they brought unto him a penny. And he saith unto them, Whose is this image and superscription? They say unto him, Caesar's. Then saith he unto them, Render therefore unto Caesar the things which are Caesar's; and unto God the things that are God's" (Matt. 22:17–21). The Savior's message is clear. Though the Saints of God are not of the world, they are of necessity in the world. Being citizens of this world, we are therefore enjoined to pursue a course where we can fulfill our obligations to serve our fellow beings, improve our communities, and protect and nurture their families. This means cooperation with earthly governments and striving to support the good causes and good people here on the earth.

MOMENT OF TRUTH

The Doctrine and Covenants contains divine counsel on how to be good citizens and willingly contribute our talents and leadership toward improving the quality of life in our communities and nations. Sections 58, 98, and 134 are especially helpful in this regard. The background concerning the circumstances relating to these sections is provided below.

Section 58: Given through the Prophet Joseph Smith on August 1, 1831, in Jackson County, Missouri (see *HC,* 1:190–95), shortly after the arrival there of members of the Colesville Branch, as well as Sidney Rigdon. The gathering Saints were eager to know the will of the Lord pertaining to their service and mission in their new surroundings; hence the prophet inquired and received this revelation. Among other choice commands given in the revelation was the mandate to be obedient to the laws of the land (D&C 58:21–22). This is the context for the oft-quoted passage: "For behold, it is not meet that I should command in all things; for he that is compelled in all things, the same is a slothful and not a wise servant; wherefore he receiveth no reward. Verily I say, men should be anxiously engaged in a good cause, and do many things of their own free will, and bring to pass much righteousness; For the power is in them, wherein they are agents unto themselves. And inasmuch as men do good they shall in nowise lose their reward" (D&C 58:26–28). In this manner, the Lord placed emphasis not only on adherence to laws but on the principle of taking initiative in serving others in the spirit of good citizenship. Moreover, we also learn the importance of being good examples in our communities when we read that Martin Harris was also commanded to be a good example to the others in consecrating his property for the building up of the kingdom of God (verse 50)—something he willingly did.

Section 98: Given through the Prophet Joseph Smith on August 6, 1833, at Kirtland, Geauga County, Ohio (see *HC,* 1:403–6). Much persecution was being heaped upon the Saints in Missouri at this time—though the scope and intensity of the persecution taking place some nine hundred miles away was unknown to the Prophet except through revelation. The Saints were enjoined to have patience and to wait upon the Lord and were further counseled that "all things wherewith you have been afflicted shall work together for your good" (D&C 98:3). Then the Lord laid down the following remarkable doctrine concerning the constitutional government of the land: "And that law of the land which is constitutional, supporting that principle of freedom in maintaining rights and privileges, belongs to all mankind, and is justifiable before me. Therefore, I, the Lord, justify you, and your brethren of my church, in befriending that law which is the constitutional law of the land" (D&C 98:5–6). This must have been a hard thing for the Saints to hear, given that their persecution was eventually made a matter of law by wicked men. As a people, they had already been forced from their homes and would eventually be expelled from one state to another by state and local government mandates. Yet the Lord told them that the law of the land is good. He did clarify this statement, though, by saying that while the law is good, "when the wicked rule the people mourn" (verse 9), and sometimes wicked laws are enforced.

This seems to be a revelation about perspective. Without perspective, the Lord's message to the beleaguered Saints in this revelation might have been a bitter pill to swallow—because it is one of patience and peace, extending an olive leaf to their abusive and hateful neighbors. It was also an admonition to realize that this was a test for the Saints through which the Lord was proving them to determine whether they would remain faithful: "For if ye will not abide in my covenant ye are not worthy of me. Therefore, renounce war and proclaim peace, and seek diligently to turn the hearts of the children to their fathers, and the hearts of the fathers to the children" (verses 15–16). This view certainly required an eternal perspective.

Section 134: "A declaration of belief regarding governments and laws in general, adopted by unanimous vote at a general assembly of the Church held at Kirtland, Ohio, August 17, 1835" (from the preface to this section; see *HC,* 2:247–49). According to J. Reuben Clark, these "statements regarding human government . . . are wise and as far-reaching as the Articles of Faith themselves. . . . They were given after the mobbings, plunderings, the assassinations of and part of our experiences in Missouri. They were uttered by a people, who, judged by human standards, had every reason to feel that their government had failed, and that they might not hopefully and successfully look thereto for their protection" (CR, April 1935, 90).

This section, prepared by Oliver Cowdery, served to contradict salacious lies by the enemies of the Church that the Saints were adopting principles and institutions that opposed law and order. The background to the inclusion of this material in the canon of latter-day scripture is as follows:

> A general assembly of the Church of Latter-day Saints was held at Kirtland on the 17th of August, 1835, to take into consideration the labors of a committee appointed by a general assembly of the Church on the 24th of September, 1834, for the purpose of arranging the items of the doctrine of Jesus Christ for the government of the Church. The names of the committee were: Joseph Smith, Jun., Sidney Rigdon, Oliver Cowdery, and Frederick G. Williams, who, having finished said book according to the instructions given them, deem it necessary to call a general assembly of

the Church to see whether the book be approved or not by the authorities of the Church: that it may, if approved, become a law and a rule of faith and practice to the Church. . . .

President Oliver Cowdery then read the following article on "Governments and Laws in General," which was accepted and adopted and ordered to be printed in said book, by a unanimous vote: [Beginning of article.] "That our belief with regard to earthly governments and laws in general may not be misinterpreted nor misunderstood, we have thought proper to present, at the close of this volume, our opinion concerning the same. [D&C 134 follows.]" (Joseph Smith, *HC,* 2:243, 247, quoted in Daniel H. Ludlow, *A Companion to Your Study of the Doctrine and Covenants,* 2 vols. [Salt Lake City: Deseret Book, 1978], 1:681–82)

1. PARTICIPATE IN COMMUNITY AND GOVERNMENTAL AFFAIRS

THEME: Covenant-abiding Saints are also law-abiding citizens of the land where they reside. The Lord has counseled us to participate in the enterprise of serving our communities and country as we engage in building the kingdom of God. This combination of consistent and devoted service to God, country, and our fellow beings furthers the work of the ministry and supports the cause of missionary work throughout the world.

MODERN PROPHETS SPEAK

Joseph Smith:

> If . . . we admit that God is the source of all wisdom and understanding, we must admit that by His direct inspiration He has taught man that law is necessary in order to govern and regulate His own immediate interest and welfare; for this reason, that law is beneficial to promote peace and happiness among men. . . . God is the source from whence proceeds all good; and if man is benefited by law, then certainly, law is good; and if law is good, then law, or the principle of it emanated from God; for God is the source of all good; consequently, then, he was the first Author of law, or the principle of it, to mankind [Alma 5:40]. (*HC,* 2:12–13)

Brigham Young:

> All governments are more or less under the control of the Almighty, and, in their forms, have sprung from the laws that he has from time to time given to man. Those laws, in passing from generation to generation, have been more or less adulterated,

and the result has been the various forms of government now in force among the nations; for, as the Prophet says of Israel, "They have transgressed the laws, changed the ordinances, and broken the everlasting covenant" [Isa. 24:5]. (*JD*, 6:342)

David O. McKay:

When a man uses this God-given right to encroach upon the rights of another, he commits a wrong. Liberty becomes license, and the man a transgressor. It is the function of the state to curtail the violator and to protect the violated. (CR, April 1940, 118)

ILLUSTRATIONS FOR OUR TIMES

Beyond Voting: Some Duties of the LDS Citizen

Political life, whether on the level of school board member, "pressure group" leader, or state governor, refines the political skills of reasoning, persuasion, organization, and negotiation. As the active citizen develops these skills, he also takes the greatest possible advantage of his precious gift of free agency. When one leaves the burden of active political participation to others, he loses the opportunity to affect directly many of the decisions that will shape his world. He abdicates a degree of control over his life and his community which he might otherwise have exercised. The Lord has often indicated his opposition to kingships and other autocratic forms of government that take the opportunity and responsibility for decision-making out of the hands of the people. He surely cannot be pleased when those of his children blessed with a democratic form of government refuse to grasp the opportunities it offers for active civic participation and allow their potential for gaining greater understanding and mastery of self-government to atrophy.

Even for those convinced of the need for a commitment to active citizenship, questions of how and when persist. Although family, church, and job responsibilities can make it difficult or impossible for many Saints to achieve constantly high levels of civic participation, there are many opportunities for meaningful participation in one's "own backyard." Significant problems and challenges often can be met by local civic action, which does not require great expenditures of individual time or resources. For example, neighborhood residents have effectively organized to have a new children's playground built nearby, or to drive pornography from their area. The commitment of time and energy to civic projects need not be full-time or statewide to accomplish meaningful results.

Most systems of democratic government are flexible enough to allow citizens to drop in and out of the more active levels of participation as other commitments require. One young LDS wife, for example, served as chairman of the city's conservation commission until her first child was born. At that point she turned over the demanding responsibilities of the chairmanship to another commissioner. She commented recently that when her children are in school and she has a little more free time, she will again become more active in community affairs.

For some Latter-day Saints, participation in the political life of the community, the state, or the nation is a full-time vocation. For most of us, civic affairs are a more occasional concern. The temptation is strong to allow civic participation to become so totally overshadowed by day-to-day concerns that we never get beyond the "faithful voter" level of activity. In such circumstances, it might be wise to remind ourselves that no constitution or set of protective laws is self-executing. Guarantees of political freedom maintain their force only if citizens are willing to exercise that freedom in their own behalf. If men and women of character fail to participate in the political decisions that shape their lives, others with more selfish motives will inevitably rush in to fill the void. (Cheryll Lynn May, *Ensign,* June 1976, 46)

LIKENING THE SCRIPTURES TO OUR LIVES

Doctrine and Covenants 134:1 Governments are instituted of God for the benefit of His children. He holds all people accountable for their actions in relation to the laws—in making, enforcing, and obeying them.

Application: When the Savior comes again to the earth, we will reside under His direct governance in His millennial reign. Until that time, though, we are to be obedient to the government of the land we live in (see D&C 58:22). It is God's will that there be governments to maintain order and safety in the world. Latter-day Saints are not above this law. We will be held accountable for our support of and obedience to the government.

2. OBEY THE LAWS OF THE LAND

THEME: It is becoming of the Saints of God to respect, uphold, and obey the laws of the land and to participate in the orderly process by which such laws are adopted and refined for the purpose of securing to citizens their inalienable rights of liberty and justice.

MODERN PROPHETS SPEAK

First Presidency: Brigham Young, Heber C. Kimball, Willard Richards:

> Sustain the government of the nation wherever you are, and speak well of it, for this
> is right, and the government has a right to expect it of you so long as that government

sustains you in your civil and religious liberty, in those rights which inherently belong to every person born on the earth; and if you are persecuted in your native land, and denied the privilege of worshipping the true God in spirit and in truth, flee to the land of Zion, to America—to the United States, where constitutional rights and freedom are not surpassed by any nation—where God saw fit, in these last days, to renew the dispensation of salvation, by revelations from the heavens, and where all, by the Constitution and laws of the land, when executed in righteousness, are protected in all the civil and religious freedom that man is capable of enjoying on earth; and our national institutions will never fail, unless it be through the wickedness of the people, and the designs of evil men in brief authority; for those rights were ordained of God on this land, for the establishment of the principles of truth on the earth; and our national organization originated in the heavens. (*Millennial Star* 14 [July 17, 1852]: 321–26)

Joseph F. Smith:

We are told here that no man need break the laws of the land who will keep the laws of God. But this is further defined by the passage which I read afterwards—the law of the land, which all have no need to break, is that law which is the constitutional law of the land, and that is as God himself has defined it. And whatsoever is more or less than this cometh of evil. Now, it seems to me that this makes this matter so clear that it is not possible for any man who professes to be a member of the Church of Jesus Christ of Latter-day Saints to make any mistake, or to be in doubt as to the course he should pursue under the command of God in relation to the observance of the laws of the land. . . .

The Lord Almighty requires this people to observe the laws of the land, to be subject to "the powers that be," so far as they abide by the fundamental principles of good government, but he will hold them responsible if they will pass unconstitutional measures and frame unjust and proscriptive laws, as did Nebuchadnezzar and Darius, in relation to the three Hebrew children and Daniel. If lawmakers have a mind to violate their oath, break their covenants and their faith with the people, and depart from the provisions of the constitution, where is the law, human or divine, which binds me, as an individual, to outwardly and openly proclaim my acceptance of their acts? . . .

I wish to enter here my avowal that the people called Latter-day Saints, as has been often repeated from this stand, are the most law-abiding, the most peaceable, long-suffering and patient people that can today be found within the confines of this republic, and perhaps anywhere else upon the face of the earth; and we intend to continue to be law-abiding so far as the constitutional law of the land is concerned;

and we expect to meet the consequences of our obedience to the laws and commandments of God, like men. (*Gospel Doctrine: Selections from the Sermons and Writings of Joseph F. Smith,* comp. John A. Widtsoe, 5th ed. [Salt Lake City: Deseret Book, 1939], 406)

ILLUSTRATIONS FOR OUR TIMES

"Permission Granted"

President Thomas S. Monson related how the German Saints were blessed because they were careful in honoring and sustaining the law. They received further opportunities in the gospel in the following story:

In our meeting chambers, we sat around a large, round table where once again the only beverages were orange juice and water. I simply can't get over the respect they show for our Church standards. Mr. Honecker began by making us feel welcome, saying that he had observed me and our Church activities for many years and that we taught our members to obey and sustain the law of the land and to be good citizens, that we emphasize the family, and that our Church members were ideal citizens of that land.

Chairman Honecker then gave me the floor to present my matters, although the matters which I was to present had previously been submitted to him, which is their custom, so that he and his associates are never taken unawares. I pointed out that the Church had been established in the German Democratic Republic for many, many years prior to World War II. I emphasized that this was one of the most productive areas for our Church missionary activities in all the world at that particular time. I stated that our membership base is barely holding steady and that this concerns us. I expressed appreciation for the cooperation of the government in granting permission to build the Freiberg Temple and then related that at the open house events for our other chapels and in Freiberg, large numbers of people have stood in line to see our buildings and to inquire concerning the Church. I mentioned that in Freiberg, almost 90,000 persons went to the open house; in Leipzig, about 15,000; in Dresden, 30,000; and in Zwickau, 6,000. I indicated that we really needed to seek from him his permission to recommence the work of full-time proselyting missionaries in the German Democratic Republic. I explained that these missionaries from other nations, when they come to his country and return to their homes, are advocates of the people and the ideals of those people with whom they have worked for two years. By way of illustration, I commented that when the Argentine ambassador came to visit the First Presidency, we were able to take him to Brigham Young University, and there he met with about two hundred missionaries who had been in

Argentina whom he could readily observe were great advocates of Argentina and her people. I then indicated that we would like to have permission for young men and women within the German Democratic Republic to receive mission calls to serve elsewhere in the world and that this would be a broadening benefit, both for the people with whom they labored and for the young missionaries themselves.

Mr. Honecker, at the conclusion of my remarks, then began to speak about his goals in government. For about thirty minutes we heard from him that the German Democratic Republic was really only forty years old and that they had made remarkable strides in the reconstruction following the devastation of World War II. For a moment I realized that I had been serving the people of that nation exactly half the entire life of the country—namely, twenty years out of forty. He then went on to point out that the embargo which our country had placed on technological materials had caused them a delay in the advancement of their nation. Obviously he didn't like this. He then indicated that this only stalled their program but that their own ingenuity had come to the fore and that they had been very successful in inventing new computer chips which may revolutionize the entire country.

He then proceeded to acknowledge our requests and said that in the future all of our young people could meet together in youth conferences, using state facilities if necessary, for he trusted our young people and admired them. This was a great compliment. He then reviewed my request for missionaries and simply said, "Permission granted. I will leave the details to my state secretary, Mr. Löffler. You can work them out with him; but permission is granted, both for missionaries from the outside to come here and for missionaries from our country to go elsewhere." This was the purpose of our visit, and success, through the help of the Lord, had been achieved. (Thomas S. Monson, *Faith Rewarded: A Personal Account of Prophetic Promises to the East German Saints* [Salt Lake City: Deseret Book, 1996], 135–36)

LIKENING THE SCRIPTURES TO OUR LIVES

Doctrine and Covenants 98:5–10 Laws that support freedom of all are "justifiable" before God and should be "befriended" by His Saints. God makes us free, and good laws make us free, but when wicked people rule, evil laws may be enacted, causing a loss of freedom and great hardship on the people. For this reason, good and wise individuals should be sought to lead the people.

Application: God approves of the institution of good governments and expects His Saints to honor such goodness. We, as citizens of the country in which we reside, should do all in our power to ensure that the laws of the land are upheld, promote those who have like values and standards, and set examples as law-abiding citizens. We should also become involved in protecting the righteous laws of the land and seeking fairness and redress of the laws when necessary (see D&C 134:11).

Articles of Faith 1:12 "We believe in being subject to kings, presidents, rulers, and magistrates, in obeying, honoring, and sustaining the law."

Application: We are duty-bound to sustain the laws of our land as long as they accord with this principle: that they "secure to each individual the free exercise of conscience, the right and control of property, and the protection of life" (D&C 134:2). As "all governments necessarily require civil officers and magistrates to enforce the laws of the same" (D&C 134:3), Latter-day Saints have the duty to respect such offices and officers. Similarly, these officers should "administer the law in equity and justice should be sought for and upheld by the voice of the people if a republic, or the will of the sovereign" (D&C 134:3). The people should uphold the government where they reside, "while protected in their inherent and inalienable rights by the laws of such governments" (D&C 134:5). If there is something with respect to governance that needs changing, then the people should work within the law to establish something better.

3. VOLUNTEER SERVICE: BLESSING OTHERS AND STRENGTHENING THE COMMUNITY

THEME: Our mortal experience opens up myriad opportunities for charitable and devoted service to others—in our families, our congregations, our communities, and our nation. Rendering service is a blessing for those who are served, as well as those who serve. Mutual benefit derives from the process of edifying and uplifting one another in the spirit of the gospel of Jesus Christ. The Savior is the epitome of how to give with love and unending compassion.

MODERN PROPHETS SPEAK

Gordon B. Hinckley:

> Those who are engaged in this service know that out of it all comes a sweet and satisfying feeling. This sweet blessing of the Spirit becomes literally a medicine to cure many of the ailments of our lives. From such experiences we come to realize that only when we serve others do we truly serve the Lord. (*Faith: The Essence of True Religion* [Salt Lake City: Deseret Book, 1989], 40)

David O. McKay:

> Live in all things outside yourself by love. As you serve others, the children around you, your father, your mother, your associates, ever striving to make yourself and the world better, then will your souls grow in wisdom. Therein you will find the guide to the happy life. (*Pathways to Happiness* [Salt Lake City: Bookcraft, 1957], 161)

Ezra Taft Benson:

> We urge our members to do their civic duty and to assume their responsibilities as individual citizens in seeking solutions to the problems which beset our cities and communities.
>
> With our wide-ranging mission, so far as mankind is concerned, Church members cannot ignore the many practical problems that require solution if our families are to live in an environment conducive to spirituality. Where solutions to these practical problems require cooperative action with those not of our faith, members should not be reticent in doing their part in joining and leading in those efforts where they can make an individual contribution to those causes which are consistent with the standards of the Church. Individual Church members cannot, of course, represent or commit the Church, but should, nevertheless, be "anxiously engaged" in good causes, using the principles of the gospel of Jesus Christ as their constant guide. (*This Nation Shall Endure* [Salt Lake City: Deseret Book, 1977], 78–79)

LIKENING THE SCRIPTURES TO OUR LIVES

Doctrine and Covenants 58:27–28 The Lord has designated each of us to be agents unto ourselves. He has promised blessings to us if we choose to do good of our own free will.

Application: We have the innate responsibility as members of the Church and good citizens to bless our fellow beings. The Lord should not have to specifically command us to do good; such should become our nature that we are ever involved in good causes to improve the lives of those around us and facilitate the work of the Lord. This can be on a volunteer basis or through community- and government-supported programs. The important thing is to be involved in serving others. Make a plan to serve and bless others.

Mosiah 2:17 King Benjamin taught us that when we are serving others we are also serving God.

Application: When we truly understand the doctrine of the gospel of Jesus Christ, we will come to appreciate life-shaping principles such as those reflected in the parable of the good Samaritan, the Golden Rule, and the admonition of the Savior: "Inasmuch as ye have done it unto one of the least of these my brethren, ye have done it unto me" (Matt. 25:40). We will recognize that our service to God and our fellow beings is not restricted to "Church service"; we are to bless *all* humankind through volunteer service.

SUMMARY

The Lord, through His prophets, has counseled us to participate in community and governmental affairs, obey the laws of the land, and use our talents proactively in rendering volunteer service to bless others and strengthen our communities. The Doctrine and Covenants provides for us a standard for governments and our relationship to them. Government has a responsibility to the people it serves. We in turn have a responsibility to obey and seek to enact good laws and elect righteous leaders. The voice of the Lord has made it clear: "be subject to the powers that be, until he reigns whose right it is to reign, and subdues all enemies under his feet" (D&C 58:22).

CHAPTER FORTY-FIVE

"THE FAMILY IS ORDAINED *of* GOD"

Reading Assignment: "The Family: A Proclamation to the World."

Additional Reading: Isaiah 54:13; 1 Nephi 1:1; Mosiah 4:14–15; Doctrine and Covenants 68:25–28; 93:40.

Fathers and mothers are needed who will rise and stand upon their feet to make of their homes sanctuaries in which children will grow in a spirit of obedience, industry, and fidelity to tested standards of conduct. If our society is coming apart at the seams, it is because the tailor and the seamstress in the home are not producing the kind of stitching that will hold under stress. (Gordon B. Hinckley, TGBH, 201)

THEMES *for* LIVING

1. The Family Is Ordained of God and Is Central
to the Plan of Happiness
2. Families Can Be Together Forever
3. The Power to Create Life in Mortality Is Sacred
4. Sacred Duty of Parenthood: To Love and Teach Your Children
5. Principles of Righteousness Form the Basis for
Success in Marriage and Family Life
6. Strengthening Families: Everyone's Responsibility
The Individual, the Church, and Society

INTRODUCTION

David O. McKay stated: "One of our most precious possessions is our families" (CR, April 1964, 5). He further taught, "No other success can compensate for failure in the home. . . . The poorest shack . . . in which love prevails over a united family is of greater value to God and future humanity than [any other riches]. In such a home God can work miracles and will work miracles. . . . Pure hearts in a pure home are always in whispering distance of Heaven" (CR, April 1964, 5, quoting J. E. McCulloch, *Home: The Savior of Civilization* [Washington, D.C.: The Southern Co-operative League, 1924], 42).

In these and similar statements from the Lord's chosen prophets, we have a compass of values and principles to guide our families toward the realization of their spiritual goals. The greatest commission from God to us as His children is to raise up our families in righteousness and truth. A careful study of the word of God in the Doctrine and Covenants and other scriptures, accompanied by diligent heed to the counsel of the living prophets, can provide access to valuable insights and strategies for strengthening our families in the latter days.

MOMENT OF TRUTH

"The Family: A Proclamation to the World," prepared by the First Presidency and Council of the Twelve Apostles of The Church of Jesus Christ of Latter-day Saints, is a glorious statement of divine truth that encapsulates and confirms with uncompromising boldness and beautiful simplicity the central role of the family in God's plan of salvation. This proclamation was read by President Gordon B. Hinckley as part of his message at the General Relief Society Meeting held September 23, 1995, in Salt Lake City, Utah.

The background for this revelation is the all-too-familiar attack on the family by our present society. In the midst of a world whose media mocks the family and whose social norms enforce family failure, how fortunate we are to have a prophet who can guide us through the maze of cultural decay! The proclamation on the family is the standard we uphold as a means of security and defense in the ever-increasing war waged on the family. Concerning the proclamation, Elder Henry B. Eyring has said:

> Three things about the title are worth our careful reflection. First, the subject: the family. Second, the audience, which is the whole world. And third, those proclaiming it are those we sustain as prophets, seers, and revelators. All this means that the family must be of tremendous importance to us, that whatever the proclamation says could help anyone in the world, and that the proclamation fits the Lord's prom-

ise when he said, "Whether by mine own voice or by the voice of my servants, it is the same" (D&C 1:38). . . . [L]et us note that the proclamation's title tells us something about how to prepare for the words that follow. We can expect that God won't just tell us a few interesting things about the family; he will tell us what a family ought to be and why. Further, we know that our Heavenly Father and his Son, Jesus Christ, want us to become like them so that we can dwell with them forever in families. We know that from this simple statement of their intent: "This is my work and my glory—to bring to pass the immortality and eternal life of man" (Moses 1:39). (*Ensign,* February 1998, 10)

1. THE FAMILY IS ORDAINED OF GOD AND IS CENTRAL TO THE PLAN OF HAPPINESS

THEME: During an era where the institution of the family has come under assault from insidious influences on all sides, it is joyfully refreshing to hold to the iron rod of truth concerning the Lord's designs and commandments about the divine nature of the family unit and its relationship to eternal progression.

MODERN PROPHETS SPEAK

Spencer W. Kimball:
> [God] decreed that the basic unit of society should be the home and the family, and we must be warned that the false culture of the day is turning away from this God-ordained plan. (*Ensign,* May 1979, 4)

The First Presidency and the Quorum of the Twelve Apostles (1980):
> We affirm the sanctity of the family as a divine creation and declare that God our Eternal Father will hold parents accountable to rear their children in light and truth, teaching them "to pray, and to walk uprightly before the Lord" (D&C 68:28). We teach that the most sacred of all relationships, those family associations of husbands and wives and parents and children, may be continued eternally when marriage is solemnized under the authority of the holy priesthood exercised in temples dedicated for these divinely authorized purposes. (Proclamation, April 6, 1980, quoted in *Ensign,* May 1980, 52)

Marion G. Romney:
> Now, families are of infinitely more worth than buildings. They are of more worth than the earth itself. The Lord has said that all his creations, including the earth, are calculated to aid in his great work, "to bring to pass the immortality and eternal life

of man" (Moses 1:39). He has further revealed the fact that no man can gain eternal life except as a member of an enduring and stable family. This being so, it is inconceivable that God would not have a plan and specifications for building the family, his most precious and enduring creation. The fact is, he did have such a plan and specifications. Both are set forth in the scriptures.

To understand and follow God's plans and specifications for building families is as essential to the building of stable and enduring families as is understanding and following plans and specifications for material buildings and planets. That God's plans and specifications for the building of families are not understood and followed accounts in large measure for the instability of the family in modern society. (*Ensign,* February 1972, 57)

LIKENING THE SCRIPTURES TO OUR LIVES

Genesis 1:27–28 God created man and woman in His image and commanded them to multiply and replenish the earth.

Application: The whole purpose of our mortal experience is to gain a body and participate in the learning and growing opportunity of being in a family. Not only did God create us in His image, but He organized us in the image of His own family— eternal marriage between a man and a woman who then bear and raise children. This is the divine organization of heaven, the image of what we strive for in this life.

Abraham 2:11 The Lord established the Abrahamic covenant so that all the families of the earth will be blessed with the gospel through the posterity of Abraham.

Application: So important are families to the Lord that He covenanted with an ancient prophet that families could be saved in the gospel. Everything in the gospel plan points to the exaltation of families. We, the seed of Abraham, are to do all in our power to fulfill that covenant and help families be forever. We, like Lehi, seek the welfare and eternal salvation of our family (see 1 Ne. 8:12).

2. FAMILIES CAN BE TOGETHER FOREVER

THEME: The uniting of families forever through the blessings of the sealing covenants is a choice and magnificent framework for the work of the ministry of God and the building up of His kingdom in the latter days.

MODERN PROPHETS SPEAK

Spencer W. Kimball:

Oh, brothers and sisters, *families can be forever!* Do not let the lures of the moment draw you away from them! *Divinity, eternity,* and *family*—they go together, hand in hand, and so must we! (*Ensign,* November 1980, 4)

Gordon B. Hinckley:

In its ultimate expression the holy priesthood carries with it the authority to seal on the earth and have that sealing effective in the heavens. It is unique and wonderful. It is the authority exercised in the temples of God. It concerns both the living and the dead. It is of the very essence of eternity. It is divine power bestowed by the Almighty as a part of His great plan for the immortality and eternal life of man. . . .

I thank him and love him [Joseph Smith] for the sealing power of the holy priesthood that makes possible and certain the continuance of the family through eternity. I have said many times that if nothing else came out of all of the sorrow and travail and pain of the restoration than the sealing power of the holy priesthood to bind together families forever, it would have been worth all that it has cost. (*TGBH,* 475–76)

ILLUSTRATIONS FOR OUR TIMES

"The Most Beautiful Doctrine"

While serving in the Air Force, one of the pilots in my squadron crashed on a training mission and was killed. I was assigned to accompany my fallen comrade on his final journey home to be buried in Brooklyn. I had the honor of standing by his family during the viewing and funeral services and of representing our government in presenting the flag to his grieving widow at the graveside. The funeral service was dark and dismal. No mention was made of his goodness or his accomplishments. His name was never mentioned. At the conclusion of the services, his widow turned to me and asked, "Bob, what is really going to happen to Don?" I was then able to give her the sweet doctrine of the Resurrection and the reality that, if baptized and sealed in the temple for time and all eternity, they could be together eternally. The clergyman standing next to her said, "That is the most beautiful doctrine I have ever heard" (Robert D. Hales, *Ensign,* November 1996, 66)

LIKENING THE SCRIPTURES TO OUR LIVES

Doctrine and Covenants 130:2 The same family sociality we experience here will be our experience in the next life.

Application: Families are eternal if we establish them in the Lord's way. The Lord has provided the sealing ordinances so families can be together forever. It is up to us to live these covenants so we can be saved in the celestial kingdom. We can't have a telestial family in the celestial kingdom.

Doctrine and Covenants 131:2–3 We are to enter into the new and everlasting covenant of marriage in order to obtain the highest degree of glory our Father has in store for us.

Application: We are all part of God's family, and He wants us to return to Him. The only way we can do that is through our families. God wants His family to be saved, as we want ours saved, and so He provided sealing power so we could be saved. The only way men and women can enjoy the blessings of the highest degree within the celestial kingdom, where families can dwell and have eternal increase, is to be sealed for time and all eternity in the temple of our God. This is essential in regard to families being forever.

3. THE POWER TO CREATE LIFE IN MORTALITY IS SACRED

THEME: The divine plan for the spirit children of our Father in Heaven to come to earth to receive mortal tabernacles essential for their ongoing progression involves a sacred partnership with the heavens. The Lord provides the system of life, with its sustaining vitality, and we provide the family relationships within which pure souls can come to earth to be nurtured and cared for in love. The power to call forth new life in this way is a solemn and beautiful commission from God that requires purity, devotion, courage, and a constant commitment to remember the covenants in faith and gratitude.

MODERN PROPHETS SPEAK

Boyd K. Packer:

First, understand that the power of procreation is good. It is the power to create life.

Think of that! The power to generate life given to man! Through its employment a couple can unselfishly bring children into the world. This power becomes a binding tie in marriage. Those who employ this power in complete worthiness have the promise of eternal increase. Those who do not, face the possibility that it will be withdrawn from them.

In marriage a couple can unselfishly express their love to one another. They reap, as a result, a fulfillment and a completeness and a knowledge of their identity as sons and daughters of God. (*That All May Be Edified* [Salt Lake City: Bookcraft, 1982], 190)

Jeffrey R. Holland:

Suffice it to say that of all the titles God has chosen for Himself, *Father* is the one He favors most, and *creation* is His watchword—especially human creation, creation in His image. You and I have been given something of that godliness, *but under the most serious and sacred of restrictions. The only control placed on us is self-control*—self-control born of respect for the divine sacramental power this gift represents.

My beloved friends, especially my young friends, can you see why personal purity is such a serious matter? Can you understand why the First Presidency and Council of the Twelve Apostles would issue a proclamation declaring that "the means by which mortal life is created [is] divinely appointed" and that "the sacred powers of procreation are to be employed only between man and woman, lawfully wedded as husband and wife"? Don't be deceived and don't be destroyed. Unless such powers are controlled and commandments kept, your future may be burned; your world could go up in flames. Penalty may not come on the precise day of transgression, but it comes surely and certainly enough. And unless there is true repentance and obedience to a merciful God, then someday, somewhere, the morally cavalier and unclean will pray like the rich man who wished Lazarus to "dip . . . his finger in water, and cool my tongue; for I am tormented in this flame" [Luke 16:24]. (*Ensign,* November 1998, 75)

LIKENING THE SCRIPTURES TO OUR LIVES

Moses 5:11 Mother Eve understood that because of the transgression of Adam and Eve in the garden, we are blessed with the sacred opportunity to procreate and also with an understanding of good and evil.

Application: The blessing of mortality that came from Adam and Eve provides for us the sacred opportunity to procreate and provide a mortal experience for the spirit children of God the Father. As married couples sealed in the temple, we receive this sacred obligation and blessing, even rejoicing in our children as a posterity ordained and given to us by our Heavenly Father. This is the way the Lord would have it. Any use of the powers of procreation outside of marriage mocks the sacredness of marriage and family as ordained by God from the beginning.

4. SACRED DUTY OF PARENTHOOD: TO LOVE AND TEACH YOUR CHILDREN

THEME: "I have no greater joy than to hear that my children walk in truth" was how John the Beloved articulated the dream of every devoted parent (see 3 Jn. 1:4). The solemn duty to train children to walk in light and truth is among the most significant and important callings in life.

MODERN PROPHETS SPEAK

Brigham Young:

> Repent, and turn unto God, and teach your children the importance of doing the same, and of the sacredness of the ordinances and the laws of God. . . . If you mothers, will live your religion, then in the love and fear of God teach your children constantly and thoroughly in the way of life and salvation, training them up in the way they should go, when they are old they will not depart from it. I promise you this, it is as true as the shining sun, it is an eternal truth. In this duty we fail; we do not bring up our children in the way they should go, or there would be no turning away, wandering here and there from the society of the Saints. We let our children do too much as they have a mind to; if they want this or that their wishes must be gratified. . . . *Teach Children the Gospel*— If we do not take the pains to train our children, to teach and instruct them concerning these revealed truths, the condemnation will be upon us, as parents, or at least in a measure. (*Discourses of Brigham Young,* sel. John A. Widtsoe [Salt Lake City: Deseret Book, 1954], 201, 206–8)

David O. McKay:

> If I were asked to name the world's greatest need, I should say unhesitatingly wise mothers; and the second, exemplary fathers. (Llewelyn McKay, *Home Memories of President David O. McKay* [Salt Lake City, Deseret Book, 1956], 4)

ILLUSTRATIONS FOR OUR TIMES

Teaching Children

> Sometimes it isn't easy as parents to teach our children. Sometimes we make mistakes. Our children may react with opposition to what we are teaching them. As parents,

we should keep our desire to do our best, constantly show our love, and not blame ourselves if our children choose another way.

In our efforts to help our children desire to walk uprightly before the Lord, we can ask ourselves three questions:

One: What do we teach our children? it is essential that we teach them the gospel of Jesus Christ. "I am the way, the truth, and the life: no man cometh unto the Father, but by me" (John 14:6). I believe the scriptures are the main source to help us teach our children to walk uprightly.

We need to help our children gain a sense of their relationship with heavenly father. They can know taht each person is a literal child of God, that each is born with a divine birthright and unlimited potential. when my nephew was four years old, his father took great delight in asking him to repeat his name. rich would ask, "Mark, what is your name?" Mark would stand up tall and answer with a happy grin, "My name is Mark Andrew Broadbent, Child of God." When our children understand that Heavenly father is real and that He loves and cares about each of them, they will want to walk uprightly. . . .

Question two: Where do we teach our children? The best place to teach our children the gospel is in our homes. A mother of eleven children once said to me, "The gospel needs to be in the air of our homes. Our children should almost be able to feel it. We can provide a safe, comfortable environment for them so they can feel free to learn and to develop their own personal testimonies."

We teach our children everywhere we are with them, and i believe we should have fun with them while we are doing it! We have opportunities many times a day to teach them as we walk together, drive in the car, work side by side, kneel in prayer, talk at the dinner table, and even when we change diapers. It didn't take me long to realize soon after our first child, Natalie, was born that changing diapers was not on my list of favorite things to do. To help me survive this recurring ordeal, I sang Primary songs to her to make it nicer for both of us. Soon the routine of changing diapers became second nature and didn't bother me anymore. However, I continued to sing to Natalie and the rest of our children as I performed this duty, because I realized I had an opportunity many times a day to teach my child.

Question three: How do we teach our children? We teach by example. Our children will learn far more by observing us walk uprightly than any other way. Blair's parents showed him, by their example, the importance of prayer. He remembers many times as a child walking down the hall to his parents' bedroom and seeing them kneeling at the side of their bed, holding hands as they prayed to Heavenly Father. . . .

Our children respond best when taught with respect and love. In the eighth chapter of Moroni, the prophet Mormon is deeply concerned about a dissension that has arisen among the members of the Church. He has written a letter giving counsel to his son, Moroni, regarding the matter. But before he addresses this problem, Mormon expresses his devotion to his son:

"My beloved son, Moroni, I rejoice exceedingly that your Lord Jesus Christ hath . . . called you to his ministry, and to his holy work.

"I am mindful of you always in my prayers, continually praying unto God the Father in the name of his Holy Child, Jesus, that he, through . . . grace, will keep you through the endurance of faith on his name to the end" (Moro. 8:2–3).

First, Mormon reaffirmed his love for Moroni, and then he taught him. When our children first know they are loved, they are more likely to listen and be taught.

Our children will be more able to survive the challenges that will come to them when they know and understand that keeping God's commandments can bring them peace and joy in their lives and enable them to walk uprightly. While traveling in the car with her mother and younger sister, five-year-old Clara sensed that her mother was deeply troubled about something. "Mommy, what's the matter? You seem so sad."

Not wanting to go into detail about her concerns, but feeling that she needed to acknowledge to her daughter that she was worried, Clara's mother asked, "Clara, what would you do if you felt sad and frustrated?"

"Well . . . ," responded Clara, and there was a long pause, "you need to take time out and think. Then you need to pray all the time and read the scriptures, especially the Book of Mormon. You need to bless other people. Just think about the good things people do for you and the good things in your life, not the bad." Young Clara is beginning to understand how to walk uprightly before the Lord. . . .

May God bless us as parents to teach our children to walk uprightly before the Lord. (Ruth B. Wright, *Ensign,* May 1994, 84)

LIKENING THE SCRIPTURES TO OUR LIVES

Doctrine and Covenants 68:25–28 Parents are to teach their children the principles of the gospel and prepare them to be baptized at the age of eight years. If the parents fail in this obligation, then the sin is upon the heads of the parents.

Application: We have duties as parents that cannot be delegated. We stand condemned if we fail to teach our children the ways of the Lord. Let us consider our ways carefully and cultivate family environments where nurture, spirituality, and love are the governing principles.

Mosiah 4:14–15 Parents are to provide physically and spiritually for their children. They are to teach their children not to fight with each other or to sin, but to love and serve one another.

Application: We read in the proclamation on the family a reiteration of this idea— that parents are responsible for the upbringing of their children. They are to care for and teach them the ways of the Lord. In so doing, we show them how to avoid sin and contention and bless their lives. As we learn in Isaiah, if we teach them of the Lord, "great shall be the peace of [our] children" (Isa. 54:13).

5. PRINCIPLES OF RIGHTEOUSNESS FORM THE BASIS FOR SUCCESS IN MARRIAGE AND FAMILY LIFE

THEME: We cannot hope to enjoy enduring relationships within the family without a foundation of gospel light and truth, nor spiritual prosperity without the guiding influence of the Holy Ghost, nor a framework of eternal continuity without the covenant blessings received in worthiness in the temples of God. It is only through valor, courage, and obedience to God's commandments that we have the right to call down from heaven the healing and sustaining influence of the Lord in magnifying our office as parents and edifying our increase as faithful sons and daughters of God.

MODERN PROPHETS SPEAK

M. Russell Ballard:

> In 1995 the First Presidency and the Quorum of the Twelve Apostles issued a significant document called the Proclamation on the Family. Only five times in the

history of the Church have the First Presidency and the Quorum of the Twelve Apostles felt it necessary to make a proclamation to the world on any subject, so you can be sure that this eternal organization we call the family is of extraordinary importance in our Heavenly Father's kingdom. Consider once again the words of the document as it pertains to our discussion of Church councils and family councils. (*Counseling with Our Councils: Learning to Minister Together in the Church and in the Family* [Salt Lake City: Deseret Book, 1997], 151)

ILLUSTRATIONS FOR OUR TIMES

The Truth about My Family

A few weeks before school started, I was sitting on the porch with my friends Grace and Ron when the discussion turned to how much Grace disliked her father.

This wasn't a new topic for her.

"He always embarrasses me in public just by being there. It is just so annoying when he always . . ." She went on to talk about her father's failings and how he wasn't living up to her expectations.

Ron decided he would take over the conversation by talking about his family and how he didn't think his mom was home enough and that he didn't like the way she dressed. He didn't think he should have a curfew or that his dad should yell so much.

The whole time I just sat on the porch swing waiting for them to ask me what I didn't like about my family. I couldn't say I didn't love my family. Moving five times in my lifetime had given my brother, sister, and me really tight bonds. We depended on each other and stuck up for one another. Our closeness was something my mother was very proud of.

Then Grace said, "What about your family, Scott?"

I didn't say anything for a minute. I was choosing my words carefully, knowing the things I said would represent what I believe in. When I finally spoke, I felt the Spirit guiding my words. There were no interruptions from either of them as I spoke of how much my family means to me and that I hope to spend eternity with them. I encouraged them to be more patient with their families. I told them to look at the big picture.

I ran inside the house and got my copy of the proclamation on the family by the First Presidency and Quorum of the Twelve Apostles. I read to them the seventh paragraph, focusing mostly on what qualities we should base our family relationships on: "Happiness in family life is most likely to be achieved when founded upon the teachings of the Lord Jesus Christ. Successful marriages and families are established and maintained on principles of faith, prayer, repentance, forgiveness, respect, love, compassion, work, and wholesome recreational activities" (*Ensign,* November 1995).

After reading that, I said, "This is what my family believes. This is what we want to be and are striving for. I know if I can do all that, then I will be able to stand tall on the Judgment Day with my family, knowing we are going to live together forever." (Scott Bean, *New Era,* March 2003, 26)

LIKENING THE SCRIPTURES TO OUR LIVES

3 Nephi 12:5–9 Christ taught the Beatitudes to the Nephite people, explaining that kindness is rewarded with kindness, mercy begets mercy, and so forth.

Application: The entire sermon given on the mount in Jerusalem and at the temple in Bountiful in Book of Mormon times is the celestial law on how to live a Christlike life. It is the blueprint for how to live in our families and how to treat one another. These doctrines and principles of righteousness, when applied, will help us as individuals and especially in our marriage and family. Success in anything that is eternal is always founded upon gospel principles.

6. STRENGTHENING FAMILIES: EVERYONE'S RESPONSIBILITY—THE INDIVIDUAL, THE CHURCH, AND SOCIETY

THEME: Family success is a pervasive duty that depends on the interaction and mutual support of many individuals and institutions. Nevertheless, it falls to the parents (and sometimes to the single parent) to take the lead in building up the family in righteousness and truth.

MODERN PROPHETS SPEAK

Howard W. Hunter:
> In seeking after the welfare of individuals and families, it is important to remember that the basic unit of the Church is the family. However, in focusing on the family we should remember that in the world in which we live families are not restricted to the traditional grouping of father, mother, and children. Families in the Church

today also consist of couples without children, single parents with children, and single individuals living alone or with roommates. Each of these families must receive priesthood watch care. Often those which may need the most careful watch care are those families of the non-traditional structure. Caring and committed home teachers are needed in each home. None should be neglected. . . .

The Church has the responsibility—and the authority—to preserve and protect the family as the foundation of society. The pattern for family life, instituted from before the foundation of the world, provides for children to be born to and nurtured by a father and mother who are husband and wife, lawfully married. Parenthood is a sacred obligation and privilege, with children welcomed as a "heritage of the Lord" (Ps. 127:3).

A worried society now begins to see that the disintegration of the family brings upon the world the calamities foretold by the prophets. The world's councils and deliberations will succeed only when they define the family as the Lord has revealed it to be. "Except the Lord build the house, they labour in vain that build it" (Ps. 127:1). (*THWH,* 144)

ILLUSTRATIONS FOR OUR TIMES

Take Time for Your Children

As we bear this great responsibility of parenthood, may I share with you, in the spirit of trying to be helpful, a few thoughts that parents might use to strengthen their families against worldly temptations and to bring the love, unity, and success that all desire.

1. Start early. "Columnist Sydney Harris was once asked by an anxious parent, 'How can I get my 16-year-old son to mind me?' He answered simply, 'Shrink him down to six months and start over, differently.'

"This may not be encouraging advice to those with problem teenagers, but to those just starting on the adventure of parenthood, it may serve as a reminder that love and training cannot be postponed" (Jon M. Taylor, *Ensign,* October 1972, p. 9).

In a revelation given through the Prophet Joseph Smith, the Lord explained that all children are innocent before God because of the redemption of Christ (see D&C 93:38). He further said, "But I have commanded you to bring up your children in light and truth" (D&C 93:40).

2. Effective communication. Parents should spend a great deal of time listening, not just telling. This listening should be done with an open mind and heart. When children feel they can talk freely about their feelings, problems, and successes, wonderful relationships develop between parents and children.

3. Enthrone love and unity. It is important to make your children aware of your love and feelings. This can be done by a hundred little acts and gestures, such as tucking children into bed at night after listening to their prayers, offering a comforting arm or ear even though he or she may not be hurt very badly. Encourage children to support each other through attendance at ball games and concerts where a family member is participating.

4. Do things together. Vacations and recreational activities, also family work projects, give parents a good opportunity to teach the importance of developing a good work ethic. Doing things together gives a child and parent an opportunity to share their attention in a common objective.

5. Provide opportunities to learn how to be independent and responsible. Teach children how to make their own decisions, even if it involves their failing once in a while. We need to help children come to an understanding such as Lehi taught, "knowing good from evil; to act for themselves and not to be acted upon" (2 Ne. 2:26).

6. Discipline with love. "'Discipline' and 'punishment' are not synonymous. Punishment suggests hurting, paying someone back for a wrong committed. Discipline implies an action directed toward a goal . . . of helping the recipient to improve himself" (William E. Homan, *Reader's Digest,* October 1969, 187–91). Discipline should always be with love.

7. Service. In his great farewell address, King Benjamin taught, "When ye are in the service of your fellow beings ye are only in the service of your God" (Mosiah 2:17). There are few rewards in life that bring greater feelings of satisfaction, joy, and peace than when one gives meaningful service to a fellow being standing in need.

8. The last and most important is to establish a "house of God." The instruction the Lord gave the Prophet Joseph Smith in the 88th section of the Doctrine and Covenants referred to building a temple. Yet this verse of scripture also beautifully describes the type of home we ought to have:

"Organize yourselves; prepare every needful thing; and establish a house, even a house of prayer, a house of fasting, a house of faith, a house of learning, a house of glory, a house of order, a house of God" (D&C 88:119).

It is not easy for children to stay clean and pure in today's world. There are times when it becomes hard for them to tell right from wrong. We need to teach our children, as Alma taught his son Corianton, "Wickedness never was happiness" (Alma 41:10). (Ben B. Banks, *Ensign,* November 1993, 28)

LIKENING THE SCRIPTURES TO OUR LIVES

Doctrine and Covenants 93:40 "But I have commanded you to bring up your children in light and truth."

Application: Primarily, parents have the responsibility to strengthen and support their families. It is divinely commanded that they do so.

Doctrine and Covenants 75:24 It is the responsibility of the members of the Church to assist and support the missionaries who are called to go abroad spreading the gospel, as well as the families these missionaries are removed from for a short season.

Application: Some families have extreme circumstances wherein they may not be able to meet all of their needs. In the earlier days of the Church, fathers were often called away to perform missionary service. Today this is not the case, but situations still arise where a parent may be absent from the family, or some other trying circumstance may arise. In such cases, the Church is to be an asset in supporting these families, both spiritually and financially.

Doctrine and Covenants 108:7 We are to strengthen everyone in all we do.

Application: It is truly our duty to strengthen and nurture everyone (see Moro. 6:4–5; D&C 81:5), and by so doing we strengthen the family unit. When we teach compassion and live with charity in our hearts, we will truly seek to bless and serve one another.

SUMMARY

Through the word of God we learn these unassailable truths: The family is ordained of God and is central to His plan for us. He provided the means of sealing ordinances whereby we can be saved and our families can be together forever. Knowing as we do the sacred nature of the family as part of Heavenly Father's plan for us, we recognize also the sacredness of the power of procreation. We are not to take the charge to guard our virtue lightly, for the responsibility of family life and parenthood is tremendous. We are to teach our children the principles of righteousness, rearing them in the gospel. It is our responsibility to strengthen families in our roles as members of families, the Church, and society as a whole. We each must answer for our part in the destiny of the family. Fortunately, we have the guidance of the Lord through His prophet to help us fulfill our responsibility.

May we gratefully move forward with devotion, humility, and gratitude to magnify our callings as children of the Most High and guardians of the Lord's rising generations. Truly, "no success can compensate for failure in the home" (David O. McKay, CR, April 1964, 5). We must not fail. In the strength of the Lord we shall succeed.

CHAPTER FORTY-SIX

"ZION—THE PURE *in* HEART"

Reading Assignment: Doctrine and Covenants 57:1–3; 64:33–43; 97:8–28; 105:1–12; Moses 7:12–19, 61–63, 68–69; Articles of Faith 1:10; *Our Heritage,* pages 37–38, 145–46.

Additional Reading: 2 Samuel 5:6–7; 1 Kings 8:1; Matthew 5:8; Hebrews 12:22–23; 3 Nephi 12:8; Doctrine and Covenants 45:66–67; 50:28; 82:14; 97:21; 100:15–17; 101:17–18.

This state of affairs stands in marked contrast to the Zion the Lord seeks to establish through his covenant people. Zion can be built up only among those who are the pure in heart, not a people torn by covetousness or greed, but a pure and selfless people. Not a people who are pure in appearance, rather a people who are pure in heart. Zion is to be in the world and not of the world, not dulled by a sense of carnal security, nor paralyzed by materialism. No, Zion is not things of the lower, but of the higher order, things that exalt the mind and sanctify the heart.

Zion is "every man seeking the interest of his neighbor, and doing all things with an eye single to the glory of God" (D&C 82:19). As I understand these matters, Zion can be established only by those who are pure in heart, and who labor for Zion, for "the laborer in Zion shall labor for Zion; for if they labor for money they shall perish" (2 Ne. 26:31). (Spencer W. Kimball, Ensign, *May 1978, 79)*

THEMES *for* LIVING

1. The Many Definitions of Zion
2. Models from the Past: There Have Been Previous Zion Societies
3. We Have Been Commanded to Establish Zion
4. The Prophecies and Blessings of the Future of Zion

INTRODUCTION

The ultimate design of the Lord is plainly manifest through the voice of the His latter-day prophet: "For I will raise up unto myself a pure people, that will serve me in righteousness" (D&C 100:16). The pure people—"the pure in heart" (D&C 97:21)—constitute Zion. This is what we strive for in our families and the Church as a whole. All the principles of the gospel lead us to be a Zion people, the future of which the Lord has secured through His proclaimed word: "For, behold, I say unto you that Zion shall flourish, and the glory of the Lord shall be upon her; And she shall be an ensign unto the people, and there shall come unto her out of every nation under heaven. And the day shall come when the nations of the earth shall tremble because of her, and shall fear because of her terrible ones. The Lord hath spoken it. Amen" (D&C 64:41–43).

This is the ideal we strive for. But as a people we must first cultivate, through faith and sacrifice, the nature and qualities of a Zion people. First we must live the celestial laws revealed to us through the gospel. This is why the commandments are given, and this is also why the Lord sees fit to chasten us at times (see D&C 105:5–6). He wants us to be His, but He must have a pure people. Only those who have overcome sin through the Atonement of the Savior can be citizens of the city of Zion and heirs to the riches of eternity (see D&C 50:28). Similarly, Zion must of necessity be a people unified in the discipleship of the Redeemer, like unto the people of Enoch (see Moses 7:18). We must be one in purpose, prosperity, and faith. What are the implications of being such a people? Centrally, the unspeakable gift of being in the presence of the Lord continually and of being elevated above the plane of mortal existence into the bosom of God, as Enoch and his people. They "walked with God, and he dwelt in the midst of Zion;" ultimately they were translated because of their purity: "God received [them] up into his own bosom; and from thence went forth the saying, ZION IS FLED" (Moses 7:69).

In our day, the Saints of the Restoration—for all their travail and struggles, triumphs and accomplishments—fell short of the commission to be a Zion people. The

Lord explained: "They were slow to hearken unto the voice of the Lord their God" (D&C 101:7). From these Saints we nevertheless learn memorable lessons about the essentials of becoming a Zion people. To us and our kindred falls the ongoing assignment to prepare ourselves with devotion for the transition—line upon line, precept upon precept—toward becoming a Zion people, willing in all respects to take upon ourselves the qualities of purity, unity, and covenant valor that alone can qualify a people as the people of the Lord.

MOMENT OF TRUTH

The principles upon which Zion must be founded are amply illuminated in the pages of the Doctrine and Covenants, especially in sections 45, 50, 57, 64, 82, 97, 100, 101, and 105. The background to sections 64 and 100 is given below. The background for the other sections was provided in earlier chapters, as follows: section 45 in chapter 21; section 50 in chapter 24; section 57 in chapter 12; section 82 in chapter 14; section 97 in chapter 43; section 101 in chapter 21, and section 105 in chapter 27.

Section 64: Given through the Prophet Joseph Smith to the elders of the Church on September 11, 1831, at the Isaac Morley farm in Kirtland, Geauga County, Ohio (see *HC,* 1:211–14).

This section was given one day before the Prophet and his family, along with Sidney Rigdon, moved to Hiram, Portage County, Ohio, to live with the Johnson family. The Prophet was planning to take up once again the process of translating the Bible, which had been interrupted while he was in Missouri. In his journal the Prophet wrote: "The early part of September was spent in making preparations to remove to the town of Hiram, and renew our work on the translation of the Bible. The brethren who were commanded to go up to Zion were earnestly engaged in getting ready to start in the coming October. On the 11th of September I received the following: [D&C 64]" (*HC,*1:211). Section 64 contains the celebrated statement about how the Saints can use their God-given talents and resources to help build Zion (see D&C 64:33–34, 41–43). The revelation was one of many that would outline the necessity, requirements, and destiny of Zion. Karl Ricks Anderson has recorded the following about the circumstances:

> In Kirtland, Joseph Smith not only set a missionary example but also labored to instill a missionary spirit and vision in his followers. At a meeting at the schoolhouse on the hill above the Morley Farm, Wilford Woodruff heard the Prophet make an astounding prophecy:

"On Sunday night the Prophet called on all who held the Priesthood to gather into the little log school house they had there. It was a small house, perhaps 14 feet square. But it held the whole of the Priesthood of the Church of Jesus Christ of Latter-day Saints who were then in the town of Kirtland. . . . When we got together the Prophet called upon the Elders of Israel with him to bear testimony of this work. . . . When they got through the Prophet said, 'Brethren, I have been very much edified and instructed in your testimonies here tonight. But I want to say to you before the Lord, that you know no more concerning the destinies of this Church and kingdom than a babe upon its mother's lap. You don't comprehend it.' I was rather surprised. He said[,] '[I]t is only a little handfull of Priesthood you see here tonight, but this Church will fill North and South America—it will fill the world. . . . This people will go into the Rocky mountains; they will there build temples to the Most High. They will raise up a posterity there.'"

Though Wilford recorded the instruction and prophecy, he did not understand it at the time. Sixty-four years later, however, standing in the Tabernacle in Salt Lake City, he declared: "I want to bear testimony before God, angels and men that mine eyes behold the day, and have beheld for the last fifty years of my life, the fulfillment of that prophecy. I never expected to see the Rocky Mountains when I listened to that man's voice, but I have, and do today."

As the Church fulfills its destiny, one can see the literal fulfillment of that prophecy that the gospel message would fill the Americas and then the world. (Karl Ricks Anderson, *Joseph Smith's Kirtland* [Salt Lake City: Deseret Book, 1989], 73)

Section 100: Given through the Prophet Joseph Smith and Sidney Rigdon on October 12, 1833, at Perrysburg, New York (see *HC,* 1:419–21). On October 5, 1833, Joseph Smith, Sidney Rigdon, and Freeman Nickerson left Kirtland on a one-month mission to Canada. One week later they stopped at Freeman Nickerson's home in Perrysburg, New York. Joseph had a number of concerns at this time. In August, Oliver Cowdery had come to Kirtland to inform Joseph and the Church of the mob actions in Missouri on July 20 to 23. His heart was no doubt burdened for the Saints in Missouri. After Oliver's arrival from Missouri in August, Joseph sent Orson Hyde and John Gould as messengers to the Saints in Missouri. They were dispatched to assure the Saints that the Church knew of their plight and to advise them in their actions. Joseph must have been concerned for the safety of Orson and John. He and Sidney were also apparently concerned about their own families; in fact, Joseph recorded the following in his journal on October 11, 1833: "I feel very well in my mind. The Lord is with us, but I have much anxiety about my family" (*HC,*1:419).

This revelation is an example to us of how close the Lord is when we have concerns that sometimes supersede our current mission. Joseph Smith and Sidney Rigdon had much to be concerned about at this time in addition to their worry about their families and the Missouri Saints. The Church had laid the cornerstones for the Kirtland Temple just two and a half months before, and opposition was forming in Ohio, just as it always does when the Saints begin to build a temple. This revelation brought comfort to Joseph and Sidney as the Lord counseled them to "let your hearts be comforted" (verse 15). It is interesting that the Lord chose this occasion to reveal important kernels of doctrine. When Joseph arrived back in Kirtland on November 4, he wrote, "I . . . found my family well, according to the promise of the Lord in the revelation of October 12th, for which I felt to thank my Heavenly Father" (*HC,*1:422).

In this small section, the Lord reveals the principles of preaching the gospel that should be emphasized: missionaries are to preach what the Lord would have them say, "for it shall be given you in the very hour, yea, in the very moment, what ye shall say" (verse 6). The missionaries are also to observe the commandment to declare the gospel "in solemnity of heart, in the spirit of meekness" (verse 7). Such humility and solemnity in relying on the Lord results in the promise that "inasmuch as ye do this the Holy Ghost shall be shed forth in bearing record unto all things whatsoever ye shall say" (verse 8). Missionary work is a key aspect of building Zion. Section 100 is therefore a study in the process of how Zion can unfold under the direction of our Father in Heaven.

1. THE MANY DEFINITIONS OF ZION

THEME: The term "Zion" evokes a multiplicity of thoughts and feelings in the hearts of the followers of Christ. The term is perhaps the closest thing to a freestanding linguistic emblem or ensign among all the vocabulary words of the gospel. "Zion" draws the mind heavenward toward God, the spirit inward toward a state of worthiness and gratitude, the heart outward in service toward others, and the feet onward toward a "place of refuge, and for a covert from storm and rain" (Isa. 4:6). Zion is a place, an institution, a state of mind, a noble destination, a people, a vision of perfection, an abode of God, an encapsulating summary of everything that is "honest, true, chaste, benevolent, virtuous, . . . lovely, or of good report or praiseworthy" (Articles of Faith 1:13).

Zion has been specifically defined in the scriptures as the pure in heart (D&C 97:21), the Church (D&C 82:14), the city of Enoch (Moses 7:19), ancient Jerusalem (1 Kgs. 8:1), the New Jerusalem (D&C 45:66–67), Mount Zion (D&C 133:18), or any place of exalted and perfected beings (Heb. 12:22–23).

MODERN PROPHETS SPEAK

Spencer W. Kimball:

> *Zion* is a name given by the Lord to his covenant people, who are characterized by purity of heart and faithfulness in caring for the poor, the needy, and the distressed (see D&C 97:21). (*Ensign,* August 1984, 2)

Spencer W. Kimball:

> Zion is "every man seeking the interest of his neighbor, and doing all things with an eye single to the glory of God" (D&C 82:19). As I understand these matters, Zion can be established only by those who are pure in heart, and who labor for Zion, for "the laborer in Zion shall labor for Zion; for if they labor for money they shall perish" (2 Ne. 26:31).

> As important as it is to have this vision in mind, defining and describing Zion will not bring it about. That can only be done through consistent and concerted daily effort by every single member of the Church. No matter what the cost in toil or sacrifice, we must "do it." That is one of my favorite phrases: "Do It." May I suggest three fundamental things we must do if we are to "bring again Zion," three things for which we who labor for Zion must commit ourselves. (*Ensign,* March 1985, 3)

Gordon B. Hinckley:

> Our forebears dreamed of Zion. "Come to Zion," they said. "Even if you have to walk all the way. Come to Zion. Leave Babylon and gather to the mountains of Ephraim." No one can read the words of Brigham Young, John Taylor, or Wilford Woodruff without knowing that they thought of these mountain valleys as a great gathering place for people of one heart and one mind and one faith, a place where the mountain of the Lord's house should be established in the tops of the mountains and where all nations would flow unto it. (*TGBH,* 725–26)

ILLUSTRATIONS FOR OUR TIMES

"Zion . . . Is a Condition"

Lest we forget that the most important part of Zion is up to us, let us consider the following perspective from a scholar of the scriptures:

> Zion as the "pure in heart" is a condition rather than a place. Ordinarily, we think of Zion as a place, such as North and South America, the center place in Jackson County, or the western part of the United States, but as true as these geographical

places are Zion, the most important factor is the condition. Appropriate to the meaning of Zion and its application to what has already been written, President Young said: "We can make Zion, or we can make Babylon, just as we please. We can make just what we please of this place. The people can make Zion: they can make a heaven within themselves. When people gather here, they should come with a determination to make Zion within themselves, with the resolution that 'I will carry myself full of the Spirit of Zion wherever I go; and this is the way in which I will control evil spirits; for I mean that my spirit shall have control over evil,' and do you not see that such a course will make Zion?" (Roy W. Doxey, *The Doctrine and Covenants Speaks* [Salt Lake City: Deseret Book, 1964], 2:220)

LIKENING THE SCRIPTURES TO OUR LIVES

JST, Genesis 7:23 A Zion people dwell together in unity; they are of one heart and have no poor among them.

Application: No matter how we define Zion—as an internal state of being, the setting of the family, or a geographical location—we are to seek to be worthy members of it. We should seek to become the Lord's people, whom He calls Zion, by being righteous, unified, and of one heart, seeking the welfare of all. These are the defining characteristics of the people in Zion, where we want to be.

2. MODELS FROM THE PAST—THERE HAVE BEEN PREVIOUS ZION SOCIETIES

THEME: Zion is not a utopia ever nestled beyond mortal access: it is a reality that has already been manifested at times upon the earth among mortals. This reality existed only among peoples who have risen to such a noble level of covenant righteousness that their exemplary level of peace, unity, and spiritual attainment have evoked upon them the highest blessings of our Father in Heaven.

MODERN PROPHETS SPEAK

Bruce R. McConkie:

> Holy cities, sacred sites, dwelling places set apart—symbols of celestial rest—such are the capital cities of the saints in all ages. Always the Lord has a Zion, a Jerusalem, a City of Holiness, a place from which his word and his law can go forth; a place to which all men can look to receive guidance from on high; a place where apostles and prophets give counsel to their fellowmen; a place where living oracles commune

with the Infinite and speak forth his mind and announce his will. In every age the Lord gathers his people; in every age the saints come together to worship the Father in the name of the Son; in every age there is a capital city, a city of refuge, a City of Holiness, a Zion of God—a sacred site from which he can send forth his word and govern his people. Such is Jerusalem—Old Jerusalem, New Jerusalem, Jerusalem of the ages. (*The Mortal Messiah: From Bethlehem to Calvary,* 4 vols. [Salt Lake City: Deseret Book, 1979–81], 1:84)

Joseph B. Wirthlin:

A society without guile is possible. I cite two examples from the scriptures. The first is the City of Holiness, even Zion, a city in which the inhabitants were pure in heart and dwelt in righteousness. In fact, Zion is the name given by the Lord to his Saints. That city, referred to as the city of Enoch, was taken up into heaven (see Moses 7:18–21). The second example is the society of the Nephites that lasted for about two hundred years after the resurrected Lord visited and taught them. . . .(4 Ne. 1:2, 16–18).

These are examples of the goal of perfection that we should strive for, even though we know that we must perfect our lives grace upon grace and line upon line (see John 1:16, 2 Ne. 28:30). (*Ensign,* May 1988, 80)

Jeffrey R. Holland:

We may not yet be the Zion of which our prophets foretold and toward which the poets and priests of Israel have pointed us, but we long for it and we keep working toward it. I do not know whether a full implementation of such a society can be realized until Christ comes, but I know that when He did come to the Nephites, His majestic teachings and ennobling spirit led to the happiest of all times, a time in which "there were no contentions and disputations among them, and every man did deal justly one with another. And they had all things common among them; therefore there were not rich and poor, bond and free, but they were all made free, and partakers of the heavenly gift" [4 Ne. 1:2–3]. That blessed circumstance was, I suppose, achieved on only one other occasion of which we know—the city of Enoch, where "they were of one heart and one mind, and dwelt in righteousness; and there was no poor among them" [Moses 7:18]. (*Ensign,* May 1996, 29)

ILLUSTRATIONS FOR OUR TIMES

Becoming Zion
Saints in previous dispensations unveiled to our view the possibilities that lie within our reach.

The city of Enoch, for example, became Zion, and God dwelt there with his people (see Moses 7:16). . . . History records only the accomplishments—not the methods—of Enoch and his people. But their example has inspired faithful people through the ages with these two important truths:

1. It is possible to arrive at a condition in which temporal practices foster spiritual salvation. The scriptures report three additional examples of peoples who reached this condition: the people of Melchizedek in Abraham's time (see JST, Gen. 14:26–36), the New Testament Saints following the Savior's earthly ministry (see Acts 2:44–45; 4:32–37), and the Nephites who were visited by the resurrected Christ (see 4 Ne. 1:2–18).

2. Welfare principles lead to the conditions that characterized Zion: "They were of one heart and one mind" (Moses 7:18). "There was no contention among all the people" (4 Ne. 1:13). "They did walk after the commandments which they had received from their Lord and their God" (4 Ne. 1:12). "The love of God . . . did dwell in the hearts of the people" (4 Ne. 1:15). "They had all things common among them" (4 Ne. 1:3). "There was no poor among them" (Moses 7:18).

The message of history is clear and timely in this pre-millennial era. God has revealed basic principles for the welfare and salvation of his children, and these principles have not changed since the days of Enoch. Other civilizations have lived them and have received the promised, glorious rewards. It is expected that we will rise to the same standard in our dispensation. (*Ensign,* May 1986, 97)

LIKENING THE SCRIPTURES TO OUR LIVES

4 Nephi 1:15–16 There was never a happier people upon the face of the earth than these Nephites who were unified in their love of God.

Application: The Nephite nation following the appearance and teachings of our Savior is a great example of a group who became a Zion people. What qualified them for such a title? The same requirements we face: the love of God in our hearts and the lack of envy, strife, and wickedness of any kind. This is the manner of happiness we are promised we can have as we strive to build these Zion-like qualities. We too can be righteous—of one heart that is pure, filled with the love of God, and free from sin—and seek the welfare of our brothers and sisters.

3. WE HAVE BEEN COMMANDED TO ESTABLISH ZION

THEME: Zion is not a dream but rather a destiny; not a wish but a commandment of God. God will have a pure and righteous people. Where such people emerge in the strength of the Lord, nourished by the blessings of the Almighty, there is Zion.

MODERN PROPHETS SPEAK

Gordon B. Hinckley:

> If we are to build that Zion of which the prophets have spoken and of which the Lord has given mighty promise, we must set aside our consuming selfishness. We must rise above our love for comfort and ease, and in the very process of effort and struggle, even in our extremity, we shall become better acquainted with our God. (*TGBH,* 725)

Ezra Taft Benson:

> Only a Zion people can bring in a Zion society. And as the Zion people increase, so we will be able to incorporate more of the principles of Zion until we have a people prepared to receive the Lord. (*TETB,* 123–24)

ILLUSTRATIONS FOR OUR TIMES

"I Miss the City"

> If I go over what happened a hundred times, I still can't make any sense out of it.

> Look, it was this normal weekend night in the city, and Mother was planning my Sabbath. (We are all supposed to call it the "Sabbath," or "Church Day.") The Sabbath, she reminded me, was the next day.

> "Now tomorrow afternoon after church," she was saying, "Brother Matthew wants you to be available for home teaching. Fortunately for you, all your home teaching families are within walking distance from our house. Your father has no end of trouble getting across the city to see his families all in one afternoon."

> I would not have to ask whether our families would let us in the door. Years ago, some of the families would have slammed their door in our faces, and left me with the afternoon free. But since the city church leaders' activation efforts, everyone is super nice now. They are all more than happy to see me and talk the day away!

But I had no intention of going home teaching the next day. Or even going to church, for that matter.

"Oh, Mother, . . ." I began, knowing full well how this conversation would end. Pleading to get one Sabbath free never seemed to work with my parents. "Oh, Mother, . . ." I began again, "you know I have 100 percent attendance at all my meetings, but just this once, just this one Church Day, I want to do something on my own, in place of church. . . ."

"In place of church?" Her eyes widened. I knew that I was pushing a lost cause, but I kept right on babbling. I have a bad habit of that.

"Yes, in place of church! You know how you are always telling us to get out and enjoy God's world, so I want to go out with my friend Sam on the lake tomorrow. He just built a new boat, and the lake is just a little way from the city . . ."

I was going to end my request with something about "communing with God's world right out in nature," but one look at my mother told me that, even with the theological ending, my argument was not going to get a fair hearing.

"Going boating! On the Sabbath day! Now, what was it we were just discussing in our last family home evening?"

I groaned. The last family home evening had been on keeping the Sabbath day holy. They had asked me to prepare the lesson, and evidently I had been especially convincing.

I tried a different tack. "Now, Mother, you don't believe Heavenly Father is going to send me straight to hell just because I miss one church meeting, do you?"

Her face softened just a bit. But only just a bit. "I believe Heavenly Father wants to give you as many blessings as he possibly can. But if you don't keep the commandments, you may miss some important blessings that he wants you to have."

Like being bored, I thought. Well, there's more than one way to skin a cat. I knew through painful experience that outright defiance would get me nowhere. The last time I tried that I wound up with my mother crying all night while I had to listen to my father give me a lecture on a son's responsibility to listen to his parents. No, this controversy had to be handled with stealth and guile.

The next morning I got up bright and early and dressed in my best. Both Mother and Father were pleased; they usually had to drag me out of bed. I put on my most innocent expression and told them that I was going to attend church on the other side of the city, so I might be back a little late. They gave me a big smile and kissed me good-bye. I almost felt guilty.

The rest, of course, was pretty simple. As soon as I got clear of the city and down by the lake, I stashed my good clothes in the bushes, having worn my fishing cutoffs underneath. I had a great day with Sam on the lake, communing with nature.

At sundown I started back to the city. I didn't think I would have any trouble convincing my parents I had been engaged in healthy church activities the entire day. They were so full of goodness that they seldom even suspected anything less in others.

But when I got to the main highway that's supposed to lead right into the city I didn't see any city lights. That's odd, I said to myself. But I just kept running down the road. The road came to an end, and still, no city.

I mean, there was just an empty field. Now, how could the whole city of Enoch just disappear? (Rolf Devries, *New Era,* July 1990, 49)

LIKENING THE SCRIPTURES TO OUR LIVES

Doctrine and Covenants 82:14–15 We are bound by covenant with the Lord to purify ourselves and to strengthen and expand Zion.

Application: As a people aspiring for the conditions of Zion, there are many things we can and should do to establish Zion. We are to enlarge her borders through missionary service, to strengthen her in continual service, and to beautify her by purifying our hearts, seeking to lift and bless others, and living a righteous life. We have covenanted to do these things. Let us honor our covenants.

4. THE PROPHECIES AND BLESSINGS OF THE FUTURE OF ZION

THEME: The dispensation of the fulness of times provides the unique framework for the unfolding of a Zion people and a Zion city in these latter days. It is the will of the Lord that such an establishment be forthcoming, prospered by the grace and beneficence of His loving care, overshadowed by His merciful Spirit, drawn on by His promised blessings, and secured by the inexorable finality of His word. What a glorious destiny is hereby proffered the Saints of God—to be enlisted in such a magnificent work of edification and eternal progression! What a great responsibility to be engaged on the Lord's errand during the final period of the earth's history leading up to the inauguration of the millennial reign.

MODERN PROPHETS SPEAK

Ezra Taft Benson:

> It is easy to despair when we see about us the moorings of society slipping. We must remember, however, that the Lord sent His Saints into the world "to be a light unto the world, and to be the saviors of men" (D&C 103:9). This is a time when "Zion must arise and put on her beautiful garments" (D&C 82:14). The contrast between the Church and the world will be increasingly marked in the future, which contrast, we hope, will cause the Church to be more attractive to those in the world who desire to live according to God's plan for us, His children. (*Ensign,* May 1978, 32)

Joseph Smith:

> The building up of Zion is a cause that has interested the people of God in every age; it is a theme upon which prophets, priests and kings have dwelt with peculiar delight; they have looked forward with joyful anticipation to the day in which we live; and fired with heavenly and joyful anticipations they have sung and written and prophesied of this our day; but they died without the sight; we are the favored people that God has made choice of to bring about the Latter-day glory; it is left for us to see, participate in and help to roll forward the Latter-day glory. (Quoted in *Ensign,* April 1980, 6)

Boyd K. Packer:

> We now move into an uncertain future. But we are not uncertain. Children, bear testimony, build Zion. Then you will find true success, complete happiness. (*Ensign,* November 1980, 20)

LIKENING THE SCRIPTURES TO OUR LIVES

Doctrine and Covenants 64:41–43 Zion shall flourish in the glory of the Lord, being an ensign to the nations, and will become a force of strength in the world.

Application: The Lord has plans for Zion. As we build it, it will grow in strength and influence in the world. The world will recognize Zion for what it is and be drawn to it (see D&C 97:18–21). Truly it will be a safe haven to us, both in its ultimate fulfillment and in our efforts to build Zion in our lives.

Doctrine and Covenants 97:25 Zion will conquer as long as we are obedient to the Lord in all things.

Application: We as a people, even a Zion people, can and will be blessed as we keep the commandments. We will enjoy the Spirit of the Lord. We will be pure in heart, a righteous people, and enjoy happiness. In Zion we can overcome the world.

SUMMARY

The tenth article of faith confirmed the literal nature of the Lord's plan to organize a vast and eternal assembly of Zion in the last days: "We believe in the literal gathering of Israel and in the restoration of the Ten Tribes; that Zion (the New Jerusalem) will be built upon the American continent; that Christ will reign personally upon the earth; and, that the earth will be renewed and receive its paradisiacal glory."

Varied are the specific definitions of "Zion." The inner core of meaning, however, is that Zion is comprised of the pure in heart, the unified, the sanctified of the Lord. There have been, prior to this dispensation, several Zion societies that have attained preeminence as the people of God. The people of Enoch were counted among such, as were the inner group of Saints assembled about the Savior in the meridian of time, and also several generations of Saints following in the wake of the faithful who learned firsthand from the resurrected Savior as He taught them the way of truth and light in ancient America. Such models of Zion are evidence that the commandment of becoming a people of God can indeed be attained through sacrifice, faith, obedience, and the cultivation of a spirit of pristine purity and uncompromising devotion to the Lord.

There are magnificent blessings that await those who journey with faith and enduring devotion toward a Zion society. It is a process of sacrifice and joy, challenge and fulfillment, effort and reward. Though the pathway be marked with reversals and disappointment, nevertheless, the Saints can proceed joyfully under the divine aegis of the Almighty Himself, who has ordained ultimate triumph for those who endure to the end: "Zion shall not be moved out of her place, notwithstanding her children are scattered. They that remain, and are pure in heart, shall return, and come to their inheritances, they and their children, with songs of everlasting joy, to build up the waste places of Zion" (D&C 101:17–18).

Ultimately the new Zion and the former Zion from the days of Enoch (together with the sanctified societies from other generations) shall experience a transcendent celestial reunion—"caught up together with them in the clouds" (see 1 Thes. 4:17). Oh, how we want to be a part of that reunion, the joy of which can scarce be imagined! "Then shalt thou and all thy city meet them there, and we will receive them into our bosom, and they shall see us; and we will fall upon their necks, and they shall fall upon our necks, and we will kiss each other" (Moses 7:63). That is where the Lord will ultimately dwell during His millennial reign (see Moses 7:64).

Let us be humbly grateful that the Lord has revealed to us through His holy prophets the contours and concepts of Zion—this supreme objective of light and glory for the obedient and faithful in the last days. And let us do all in our power to live the gospel and guide ourselves and our families in the pathways of covenant valor until the hour comes when the Lord—through His grace and our worthiness—can receive us as a pure people unto Himself.

MOMENT OF TRUTH INDEX

A Guide to the Background Summaries of Doctrine and Covenants Sections

D&C Section	Discussed in Chapter(s)	D&C Section	Discussed in Chapter(s)	D&C Section	Discussed in Chapter(s)
1	1	44	38	103	27
2	30	45	21	104	14
3	4	46	15	105	27
4	11	49	24	107	8
5	4	50	24	109	18
6	5	51	14	110	18
8	5	52	12	112	26
9	5	56	38	115	9
10	4	57	12	119	17
11	6	58	44	120	17
12	11	59	16	121	25
13	8	60	26	122	28
14	11	63	43	123	41
15	11	64	46	124	29
16	11	65	41	127	30
17	4	68	37	128	30
18	11	75	11	130	13
19	2	76	2 and 20	131	31
20	8	78	14	132	31
21	9	81	35	133	21
25	10	82	14	134	44
26	24	84	8	135	32
27	9	85	40	136	34
28	24	88	13	137	20
29	12	89	22	138	39
31	11	90	23		
33	11	93	2	**Additional Items:**	
34	21	95	18	The Family: A Proclamation to the World—see chapter 45	
37	12	97	43		
38	12	98	44		
41	25	100	46		
42	14	101	21	Official Declaration 2—see chapter 42	
43	24	102	25		

THEMES FOR LIVING INDEX

A Topical Index of Themes and Key Words by Chapter and Subsection

Note: the first number given is the chapter number; the number after the period is the Themes for Living number within that chapter. Example: 1.1 means chapter 1, theme 1.

ABOUT THE AUTHORS

ED J. PINEGAR presently serves part-time on the faculty at the Orem Institute of Religion at Utah Valley State College in Orem, Utah, and is a teacher at the Senior MTC in Provo. He has served as president of the England, London South Mission; president of the Missionary Training Center in Provo, Utah; and member of the Missionary Programs Advisory Committee. He has produced numerous talk tapes, including several volumes of *Especially for Missionaries*. Brother Pinegar is married to Patricia Peterson Pinegar, who formerly served as general president of the Primary for the Church, and they are the parents of eight children, thirty grandchildren, and one great-grandchild.

RICHARD J. ALLEN is a husband, father, teacher, writer, and organizational consultant. He has served on several stake high councils, in several stake presidencies, and as a bishop. Brother Allen has filled many teaching assignments in the Church, including full-time missionary, Gospel Doctrine teacher, and stake institute instructor. He has served as a faculty member at both Brigham Young University and Johns Hopkins University. Richard has authored or coauthored many articles, manuals, and books, and loves to study the scriptures and Church history. He and his wife, Carol Lynn, have four children and live in Orem, Utah.

KARL RICKS ANDERSON has been a leader in various businesses in Ohio and has been working to bring about restoration efforts in Kirtland, Ohio, for over thirty years. He is the author of the insightful *Joseph Smith's Kirtland* and has coauthored a guidebook on Ohio historic sites. He has also published articles in several publications, including the *Encyclopedia of Mormonism,* the *Historical Atlas of Mormonism,* and the *Encyclopedia of Latter-day Saint History.* Brother Anderson has served as stake president, regional representative, and family history area advisor to the North America Northeast Area, and he has served for twenty-eight years as a seminary and institute teacher. He is currently the patriarch of the Kirtland Stake. He and his wife, Joyce, have spent thirty-five years in the Cleveland area. They have seven children and twenty-two grandchildren.